Why Do You Need this New Edition?

Good reasons why you should buy this *new* edition of *Good Reasons with Contemporary Arguments* . . .

1 In clear, accessible language, *Good Reasons with Contemporary Arguments* tells you why people take the time to write arguments—because they want to change attitudes and take action about issues they care about—and helps you find topics for your own writing.

2 Sample arguments in 6 student essays (4 new) and over 80 professional readings (more than half new) show you how people write and support arguments on current issues.

3 Over 150 illustrations show the pervasiveness and persuasiveness of photographs, charts, graphs, tables, and advertisements in arguments.

4 Brand new visual maps in Chapters 8–13 show at a glance how different kinds of argumentative papers are organized—definition, causal, evaluation, narrative, rebuttal, and proposal—the kinds you're likely to be assigned in college.

5 Step-by-step guides to writing arguments at the ends of Chapters 8–13 give you specific help with planning, organizing, and writing different kinds of argumentative projects.

6 Two new *Issues in Focus* sections (five in all) in Part 6 give you a chance to examine two new issues in depth: climate change and the privacy-versus-security questions raised by biometric technologies.

7 Three new chapters give you more help with research writing, including using library databases, evaluating and using sources, avoiding plagiarism, and writing an argumentative research project.

8 New illustrated writing activities, called *Finding Good Reasons* (in Parts 1 and 3), pair images and text to focus on various contemporary arguments— from banning cell phones while driving and surveillance cameras at traffic lights to a country's "right" to use natural resources—and invite you to join the debates surrounding these issues.

9 New color-coded examples in the MLA and APA chapters help you understand the key elements of source citations.

In memory of our teacher and friend, James L. Kinneavy (1920–1999)

Good Reasons
With
Contemporary Arguments

FOURTH EDITION

Lester Faigley
University of Texas at Austin

Jack Selzer
The Pennsylvania State University

Longman

New York San Francisco Boston
London Toronto Sydney Tokyo Singapore Madrid
Mexico City Munich Paris Cape Town Hong Kong Montreal

Executive Editor: Lynn M. Huddon
Development Editor: Carol Hollar-Zwick
Senior Marketing Manager: Sandra McGuire
Supplements Editor: Donna Campion
Production Manager: Eric Jorgensen
Project Coordination, Text Design, and Electronic Page Makeup: Pre-Press PMG
Cover Designer/Manager: Wendy Ann Fredericks
Cover Photos: *clockwise from top left:* Monica Almeida/The New York Times; Nicole
    Bengiveno/The New York Times; Photo Courtesy of The United States Army; and
    Jeff Topping/The New York Times.
Photo Researcher: Julie Tesser
Senior Manufacturing Buyer: Dennis J. Para
Printer and Binder: Quebecor World Taunton
Cover Printer: Phoenix Color Corporation

For permission to use copyrighted material, grateful ackwledgment is made to the
copyright holders on pp. 619–620, which are hereby made part of this copyright page.

Library of Congress Cataloging-in-Publication Data
Faigley, Lester, 1947–
    Good reasons with contemporary arguments / Lester Faigley, Jack Selzer.—4th ed.
       p. cm.
    ISBN-13: 978-0-205-74337-7
    ISBN-10:   0-205-74337-4
  1. English language—Rhetoric. 2. Persuasion (Rhetoric) 3. Report writing. I. Selzer,
Jack. II. Title.
    PE1431.F35 2008
    B08'.042—dc22

                                                        2008004113

This book includes 2009 MLA guidelines.

Longman
is an imprint of

PEARSON

ISBN-13: 978-0-205-74337-7
ISBN-10: 0-205-74337-4

1 2 3 4 5 6 7 8 9 10—QWT—12 11 10 09

www.pearsonhighered.com

Detailed Contents

Alternate Contents: Types of Arguments   *xiv*

Preface   *xx*

Introduction   1

Persuading with Good Reasons   **1**

What Do We Mean by Argument?   2

What Does *Argument* Mean for College Writers?   2

How Can You Argue Responsibly?   3

How Can You Argue Respectfully?   4

PART 1

Reading and Discovering Arguments

Chapter 1: Why Argue?   **9**

Why Do People Write Arguments?   9

   FINDING GOOD REASONS   *10*

Why Do Some Arguments Succeed?   12

What Are the Goals of Arguments?   16

What Are Rhetorical Appeals?   17

Rachel Carson, The Obligation to Endure   19

Chapter 2: Reading Arguments   **22**

Read Critically   22

Read Actively   22

   FINDING GOOD REASONS   *24*

Recognize Fallacies   26

Respond as a Writer   28

Chapter 3: Finding Arguments   **30**

Find Arguments in Everyday Conversations   30

Find a Topic that Interests You   33

Find a Claim by Exploring   37

   FINDING GOOD REASONS   *39*

Find a Claim by Reading   40

Find Good Reasons   44

Find Evidence to Support Good Reasons   50

Chapter 4: Drafting and Revising Arguments 52

State and Evaluate Your Thesis   52
Think about Your Readers   54
    FINDING GOOD REASONS   55
Organize Your Argument   57
Write an Engaging Title and Introduction   58
Write a Strong Conclusion   59
Evaluate Your Draft   60
Respond to the Writing of Others   62
Edit and Proofread Carefully   64

PART 2   Analyzing Arguments

Chapter 5: Analyzing Written Arguments 69

What Is Rhetorical Analysis?   69
Build a Rhetorical Analysis   69
Analyze the Rhetorical Features   70
Analyze the Rhetorical Context   75
Write a Rhetorical Analysis   79
Barbara Jordan, Statement on the Articles of Impeachment   80
*T. Jonathan Jackson (student), An Argument of Reason and Passion:
    Barbara Jordan's "Statement on the Articles of Impeachment"*   84
    STEPS TO WRITING A RHETORICAL ANALYSIS   *87*

Chapter 6: Analyzing Visual Arguments 90

What Is a Visual Argument?   90
Analyze Visual Persuasion   92
Analyze Visual Evidence   93
Build a Visual Analysis   100
Write a Visual Analysis   100
Angela Yamashita (student), Got Roddick?   101
    STEPS TO WRITING A VISUAL ANALYSIS   104

PART 3   Writing Arguments

Chapter 7: Putting Good Reasons into Action 109

Use Different Approaches to Construct an Argument   110
    FINDING GOOD REASONS   *111*

Chapter 8: Definition Arguments   113

Understand How Definition Arguments Work   113

Recognize Kinds of Definitions   114

    FINDING GOOD REASONS   *117*

Build a Definition Argument   118

Scott McCloud, Setting the Record Straight   121

Chris Nguyen (student), Speech Doesn't Have to Be Pretty to Be Protected   129

    STEPS TO WRITING A DEFINITION ARGUMENT   *134*

Chapter 9: Causal Arguments   137

Understand How Causal Arguments Work   137

Find Causes   138

    FINDING GOOD REASONS   *140*

Build a Causal Argument   142

Annie Murphy Paul, The Real Marriage Penalty   144

Emily Raine, Why Should I Be Nice to You? Coffee Shops and the Politics of Good Service   147

    STEPS TO WRITING A CAUSAL ARGUMENT   *153*

Chapter 10: Evaluation Arguments   156

Understand How Evaluation Arguments Work   156

Recognize Kinds of Evaluations   157

    FINDING GOOD REASONS   159

Build an Evaluation Argument   160

Michael Eric Dyson, Gangsta Rap and American Culture   162

Rashaun Giddens (student), Stop Loss or "Loss of Trust"   163

    STEPS TO WRITING AN EVALUATION ARGUMENT   *174*

Chapter 11: Narrative Arguments   177

Understand How Narrative Arguments Work   178

Recognize Kinds of Narrative Arguments   179

    FINDING GOOD REASONS   *180*

Build a Narrative Argument   181

Leslie Marmon Silko, The Border Patrol State   182

Dagoberto Gilb, My Landlady's Yard   187

    STEPS TO WRITING A NARRATIVE ARGUMENT   *190*

Chapter 12: Rebuttal Arguments   192

Understand How Rebuttal Arguments Work   193

    FINDING GOOD REASONS   *195*

Recognize Kinds of Rebuttal Arguments   196

Build a Rebuttal Argument   199

Dan Stein, Crossing the Line 200

Gregory Rodriguez, Illegal Immigrants—They're Money 202

Steps to Writing a Rebuttal Argument *205*

Chapter 13: Proposal Arguments 210

Understand How Proposal Arguments Work 211

Recognize Components of Proposal Arguments 212

Finding Good Reasons *213*

Build a Proposal Argument 214

Thomas Homer-Dixon and S. Julio Friedmann, Coal in a Nice Shade of Green 216

Kim Lee (student), Let's Make It a Real Melting Pot with Presidential Hopes for All 219

Steps to Writing a Proposal Argument 223

PART 4

Designing and Presenting Arguments

Chapter 14: Designing Arguments 229

Think About Your Readers 229

Know When to Use Images and Graphics 230

Compose and Edit Images 231

Create Tables, Charts, and Graphs 234

Design Pages for Print 236

Design Pages for the Web 238

Chapter 15: Presenting Arguments 238

Plan in Advance 238

Design Effective Visuals 240

Focus on Your Delivery 242

PART 5

Researching Arguments

Chapter 16: Planning Research 247

Analyze the Research Task 247

Find a Subject 247

Ask a Research Question 249

Gather Information About the Subject 249

Draft a Working Thesis 252

Chapter 17: Finding Sources 254

Search with Keywords 255

Find Books 256

Find Journal Articles   256
Find Web Sources   259

Chapter 18: Evaluating and Recording Sources   263

Evaluate Print Sources   263
Find Information to Cite Print Sources   264
Evaluate Database Sources   266
Find Information to Cite a Database Source   266
Evaluate Web Sources   267
Find Information to Cite a Web Source   269

Chapter 19: Writing the Research Paper   270

Review Your Goals and Thesis   270
Determine Your Contribution   270
Determine Your Main Points   271
Avoid Plagiarism   271
Quote Sources Without Plagiarizing   273
Summarize and Paraphrase Sources Without Plagiarizing   274
Incorporate Quotations   276
Incorporate Visuals   278

Chapter 20: Documenting Sources in MLA Style   280

Elements of MLA Documentation   280
MLA In-Text Citations   284
MLA Works-Cited List: Books   287
MLA Works-Cited List: Periodicals   291
MLA Works-Cited List: Library Database Sources   293
MLA Works-Cited List: Online Sources   293
MLA Works-Cited List: Other Sources   295
Sample MLA Paper: *Brian Witkowski (student), Need a Cure for Tribe Fever? How About a Dip in the Lake?*   297

Chapter 21: Documenting Sources in APA Style   304

Elements of APA Documentation   304
APA In-Text Citations   307
APA References List: Books   309
APA References List: Periodicals   310
APA References List: Library Database Sources   311
APA References List: Online Sources   311
APA References List: Other Sources   312

PART 6

Contemporary Arguments   313

Chapter 22: Negotiating the Environment   315

American Environmentalism   315

Contemporary Arguments   316

Edward O. Wilson, The Conservation Ethic   318
  Sidebar: Aldo Leopold, From The Land Ethic   320

N. Scott Momaday, The Way to Rainy Mountain   323

Robert Bullard, How Race Affected the Federal Government's Response to Katrina   328

Wendell Berry, Manifesto: Mad Farmer Liberation Front   331

ISSUE IN FOCUS: CLIMATE CHANGE   333

  Al Gore, What Is Global Warming?   335

  Al Gore, Ten Things to Do to Help Stop Global Warming   338

  Christopher C. Horner, Top Ten "Global-Warming" Myths   339

  Glenn McCoy, And Looking at Our Extended Forecast . . . (cartoon)   340

  Philip Jenkins, Burning at the Stake   343

  Alex Williams, Buying into the Green Movement   345

  Chicago Tribune, Fast Clothes vs. Green Clothes (editorial)   349

  Elisabeth Rosenthal, Environmentally Unfriendly Trend: Fast Fashion   350
    Sidebar: How "Green" Is Your T-Shirt?   351

  FROM READING TO WRITING   352

Chapter 23: Confronting Sexual Difference   353

Sexual Difference in American Culture   353

Contemporary Arguments   354

Carmen Vazquez, Appearances   356

Peter J. Gomes, Homophobic? Read Your Bible   362

Ryan T. Anderson, Struggling Alone   365

ISSUE IN FOCUS: SAME-SEX MARRIAGE   368

  Proposed Amendment to the U.S. Constitution   370

  Matt Davies, We're Here to Defend . . . (cartoon)   370

  House of Representatives, The Defense of Marriage Act   371

  Anna Quindlen, Evan's Two Moms   373

Sonya Geis, A New Tactic in Fighting Marriage
Initiatives   374

FROM READING TO WRITING   376

William F. Jasper, Subversion Through Perversion   377

Marc Haeringer, Coming Out in the Line of Fire   380

Emily Martin and Katie Schwartzmann, Bad for Both
Boys and Girls   383

Andrew Sullivan, The End of Gay Culture   384

Alexa Hackbarth, Vanity, Thy Name Is Metrosexual   396

Chapter 24: Globalization: Importing and Exporting America   400

America's Place in the World   400

Contemporary Arguments   401

Henry Payne, The Bad News Is . . . (cartoon)   401

Mae M. Ngai, No Human Being Is Illegal   406

Michelle Malkin, Beware of Illegal Aliens Seeking
Hazmat Licenses   411

Sidebar: Emma Lazarus, The New Colossus   408

Sidebar: Thomas Bailey Aldrich, The Unguarded Gates   410

Helen Epstein, Immigration Maze   413

Wiley Miller, What's the Worst That Can
Happen . . . ? (cartoon)   414

Todd Gitlin, Under the Sign of Mickey Mouse & Co.   415

Urvashi Butalia, Living the Dream   419

Sidebar: National Readership Survey 2006: Women's Attitudes in
India   421

Laura Carlsen, Wal-Mart vs. Pyramids   422

Darla K. Deardorff, In Search of Intercultural
Competence   421

Chapter 25: Science and Ethics   427

The Ethics of Science and Technology   427

Contemporary Arguments   428

Bill Joy, Why the Future Doesn't Need Us   429

Francis Fukuyama, A Tale of Two Dystopias   438

Ralph C. Merkle, Nanotechnology: Designs for the Future   446

Ursula Franklin, Beautiful, Functional, and Frugal   452

Bill Gates, A Robot in Every Home   453

Christine Soares, Attitude Screen   460

ISSUE IN FOCUS: STEM CELL RESEARCH   462

Ron Reagan, Speech at the Democratic National
Convention, July 21, 2004   464

Pat Oliphant, The Ronald Reagan Eulogy Will
Be Delivered . . . (cartoon)   466

Steven Milloy, Ron Reagan Wrong on Stem Cells   466

Richard M. Doerflinger, Don't Clone Ron
Reagan's Agenda   468

FROM READING TO WRITING   470

Chapter 26: Privacy   472

New Challenges to Personal Privacy   472

Contemporary Arguments   474

David Brin, Three Cheers for the Surveillance Society!   475

Ted Koppel, Take My Privacy, Please!   484

John McPherson, It's Part of the Government's
New Emphasis . . . (cartoon)   488

Randall Larsen, Traveler's Card Might Just Pave the
Way for a National ID Card   488

Jennifer Burk, Counselors Walk a Fine Line Weighing
the Rights of Student and College   490

Jeffrey Zaslow, The End of Youthful Indiscretions:
Internet Makes Them Permanent Blots   492

ISSUE IN FOCUS: BIOMETRICS: MEASURING THE BODY
FOR IDENTITY   494

Steven C. Bennett, Privacy Implications of
Biometrics   496

Paul Saffo, A Trail of DNA and Data   502

FBI, Using Technology to Catch Criminals   506

Russ Ryan, Emerging Biometric Technologies   507
Sidebar: Voice Verification for Transactions   510

J. G. Domke, Will Cash and Credit Cards Become
Extinct in the Not-So-Distant Future?   511

FROM READING TO WRITING   513

Chapter 27: Regulating Substances, Regulating Bodies   515

Private Bodies, Public Controls   515

Contemporary Arguments   517

Joseph A. Califano Jr., The Right Drug to Target:
Cutting Marijuana Use   518

Eric Schlosser, Make Peace with Pot   520

ISSUE IN FOCUS: REGULATING TOBACCO   523

Philip Morris, Camel Lights Ad   523

American Legacy Foundation, Antismoking Ad   524

Gary Trudeau, Doonesbury: The Sin Lobby Gins
Up . . . (cartoon)   525

Douglas Bettcher and Chitra Subramaniam, The
Necessity of Global Tobacco Regulations   526
Walter E. Williams, Nazi Tactics   528
FROM READING TO WRITING   530
Malcolm Gladwell, Drugstore Athlete   531
Bill Amend, What's This? (cartoon)   532
Michael Bérubé, Citizenship and Disability   540
Barry Blitt, *New Yorker* Cover   547
Terrence Rafferty, Kate Winslet, Please Save Us!   548
Susan Llewelyn Leach, Those Extra Pounds—Are
They Government's Business?   554
Mim Udovitch, A Secret Society of the Starving   556
Consumer Freedom, Obesity Ads   565
Pippa Wysong, Modified   566
Eric Lewis, The Subtext of All Tattoos (cartoon)   568
Mothers Against Drunk Driving, Like Father, Like Son Ad   570
Susan Kinzie, A Rare Kind of Rush: A Sorority Based
on Islamic Principles   571

Chapter 28: New Media   **574**

Personal Space in Cyberspace   574
Contemporary Arguments   575
Andrew Keen, Is Google's Data Grinder Dangerous?   576
Sidebar: John Perry Barlow, A Declaration of the
Independence of Cyberspace   578

John Seigenthaler, A False Wikipedia "Biography"   579
Walt Handelsman, Information Superhighway (cartoon)   583
Michael Gerson, Where the Avatars Roam   583
Jessica Bennett and Malcolm Beith, Alternate Universe   585
Marcelle S. Fischler, Putting on Lip Gloss, and a Show,
for YouTube Viewers   591
Sidebar: Joe Duffy and Andrew Keen, Can Anyone
Be a Designer?   592

danah boyd, Facebook's "Privacy Trainwreck":
Exposure, Invasion, and Social Convergence   595
Stephen Williams, Getting Off the Couch   604

Appendix: A Guide to Avoiding Plagiarism   607
Glossary   615
Credits   619
Index   622

Alternate Contents:
Types of Arguments

Definition Arguments

Barbara Jordan, Statement on the Articles of Impeachment   80
Scott McCloud, Setting the Record Straight   121
Chris Nguyen, Speech Doesn't Have to Be Pretty to Be
    Protected (student)   129
Leslie Marmon Silko, The Border Patrol State   182
Edward O. Wilson, The Conservation Ethic   318
Al Gore, What Is Global Warming?   335
Elisabeth Rosenthal, Environmentally Unfriendly Trend: Fast Fashion   350
Anna Quindlen, Evan's Two Moms   373
Andrew Sullivan, The End of Gay Culture   384
Alexa Hackbarth, Vanity, Thy Name Is Metrosexual   396
Mae M. Ngai, No Human Being Is Illegal   406
Emma Lazarus, The New Colossus   408
Darla K. Deardorff, In Search of Intercultural Competence   423
Francis Fukuyama, A Tale of Two Dystopias   438
Ursula Franklin, Beautiful, Functional, and Frugal   452
Bill Gates, A Robot in Every Home   453
David Brin, Three Cheers for the Surveillance Society!   475
Malcolm Gladwell, Drugstore Athlete   531
Michael Bérubé, Citizenship and Disability   540
Susan Llewelyn Leach, Those Extra Pounds—Are They
    Government's Business?   554
Mim Udovitch, A Secret Society of the Starving   556
Susan Kinzie, A Rare Kind of Rush: A Sorority Based
    on Islamic Principles   571
Jessica Bennett and Malcolm Beith, Alternate Universe   585
Joe Duffy and Andrew Keen, Can Anyone Be a Designer?   592
danah boyd, Facebook's "Privacy Trainwreck":
    Exposure, Invasion, and Social Convergence   595

Causal Analysis Arguments

Rachel Carson, The Obligation to Endure   19
Annie Murphy Paul, The Real Marriage Penalty   144
Emily Raine, Why Should I Be Nice to You? Coffee Shops
    and the Politics of Good Service   147
Robert Bullard, How Race Affected the Federal
    Government's Response to Katrina   328
Philip Jenkins, Burning at the Stake   343
Carmen Vazquez, Appearances   356
Anna Quindlen, Evan's Two Moms   373

Andrew Sullivan, The End of Gay Culture   384
Alexa Hackbarth, Vanity, Thy Name Is Metrosexual   396
Todd Gitlin, Under the Sign of Mickey Mouse & Co.   415
Bill Joy, Why the Future Doesn't Need Us   429
Francis Fukuyama, A Tale of Two Dystopias   438
Ralph C. Merkle, Nanotechnology: Designs for the Future   446
Steven Milloy, Ron Reagan Wrong on Stem Cells   466
Jeffrey Zaslow, The End of Youthful Indiscretions:
    Internet Makes Them Permanent Blots   492
Walter E. Williams, Nazi Tactics   528
Susan Llewelyn Leach, Those Extra Pounds—Are
    They Government's Business?   554
Mim Udovitch, A Secret Society of the Starving   556

Evaluation Arguments

Angela Yamashita, Got Roddick? (student)   101
Michael Eric Dyson, Gangsta Rap and American Culture   162
Rashaun Giddens, Stop Loss or "Loss of Trust" (student)   163
Leslie Marmon Silko, The Border Patrol State   182
Edward O. Wilson, The Conservation Ethic   318
Chicago Tribune, Fast Clothes vs. Green Clothes   349
Elisabeth Rosenthal, Environmentally Unfriendly
    Trend: Fast Fashion   350
Anna Quindlen, Evan's Two Moms   373
William F. Jasper, Subversion Through Perversion   377
Emily Martin and Katie Schwartzmann, Bad for
    Both Boys and Girls   383
Mae M. Ngai, No Human Being Is Illegal   406
Todd Gitlin, Under the Sign of Mickey Mouse & Co.   415
Urvashi Butalia, Living the Dream   419
Laura Carlsen, Wal-Mart vs. Pyramids   422
Bill Joy, Why the Future Doesn't Need Us   429
Francis Fukuyama, A Tale of Two Dystopias   438
Ralph C. Merkle, Nanotechnology: Designs
    for the Future   446
Bill Gates, A Robot in Every Home   453
Christine Soares, Attitude Screen   460
David Brin, Three Cheers for the Surveillance Society!   475
Jennifer Burk, Counselors Walk a Fine Line Weighing
    the Rights of Student and College   490
Jeffrey Zaslow, The End of Youthful Indiscretions:
    Internet Makes Them Permanent Blots   492
Paul Saffo, A Trail of DNA and Data   502
Steven C. Bennett, Privacy Implications of Biometrics   502
Russ Ryan, Emerging Biometric Technologies   507
J. G. Domke, Will Cash and Credit Cards Become
    Extinct in the Not-So-Distant Future?   511

Joseph A. Califano Jr., The Right Drug to Target:
  Cutting Marijuana Use   518
Eric Schlosser, Make Peace with Pot   520
American Legacy Foundation, Antismoking Ad   524
Walter E. Williams, Nazi Tactics   528
Malcolm Gladwell, Drugstore Athlete   531
Michael Bérubé, Citizenship and Disability   540
Terrence Rafferty, Kate Winslet, Please Save Us!   548
Susan Llewelyn Leach, Those Extra Pounds—Are
  They Government's Business?   554
Mim Udovitch, A Secret Society of the Starving   556
Pippa Wysong, Modified   566
Susan Kinzie, A Rare Kind of Rush: A Sorority Based
  on Islamic Principles   571
Andrew Keen, Is Google's Data Grinder Dangerous?   576
John Seigenthaler, A False Wikipedia "Biography"   579
Michael Gerson, Where the Avatars Roam   583
Jessica Bennett and Malcolm Beith, Alternate Universe   585
danah boyd, Facebook's "Privacy Trainwreck":
  Exposure, Invasion, and Social Convergence   595

Narrative Arguments

Leslie Marmon Silko, The Border Patrol State   182
Dagoberto Gilb, My Landlady's Yard   187
N. Scott Momaday, The Way to Rainy Mountain   323
Ryan T. Anderson, Struggling Alone   365
Marc Haeringer, Coming Out in the Line of Fire   380
Alexa Hackbarth, Vanity, Thy Name Is Metrosexual   396
Emma Lazarus, The New Colossus   408
Thomas Bailey Aldrich, The Unguarded Gates   410
Helen Epstein, Immigration Maze   413
Laura Carlsen, Wal-Mart vs. Pyramids   422
Bill Joy, Why the Future Doesn't Need Us   429
Ron Reagan, Speech at the Democratic National
  Convention, July 27, 2004   464
Ted Koppel, Take My Privacy, Please!   484
Walter E. Williams, Nazi Tactics   528
Michael Bérubé, Citizenship and Disability   540
Mim Udovitch, A Secret Society of the Starving   556
Susan Kinzie, A Rare Kind of Rush: A Sorority Based
  on Islamic Principles   571
John Seigenthaler, A False Wikipedia "Biography"   579
Marcelle S. Fischler, Putting on Lip Gloss,
  and a Show, for YouTube Viewers   591
danah boyd, Facebook's "Privacy Trainwreck":
  Exposure, Invasion, and Social Convergence   595

Rebuttal Arguments

Dan Stein, Crossing the Line   200

Gregory Rodriguez, Illegal Immigrants—They're Money   202

Christopher C. Horner, Top Ten "Global-Warming" Myths   339

Alex Williams, Buying into the Green Movement   345

Peter J. Gomes, Homophobic? Read Your Bible   362

Emily Martin and Katie Schwartzmann, Bad
    for Both Boys and Girls   383

Thomas Bailey Aldrich, The Unguarded Gates   410

Ralph C. Merkle, Nanotechnology: Designs
    for the Future   446

Steven Milloy, Ron Reagan Wrong on Stem Cells   466

Richard M. Doerflinger, Don't Clone Ron Reagan's
    Agenda   468

Eric Schlosser, Make Peace with Pot   520

Proposal Arguments

Rachel Carson, The Obligation to Endure   19

Thomas Homer-Dixon and S. Julio Friedmann,
    Coal in Nice Shade of Green   216

Kim Lee, Let's Make It a Real Melting Pot with
    Presidential Hopes for All (student)   219

Brian Witkowski, Need a Cure for Tribe Fever? How
    About a Dip in the Lake? (student)   297

Edward O. Wilson, The Conservation Ethic   318

Wendell Berry, Manifesto: The Mad Farmer
    Liberation Front   331

Al Gore, What Is Global Warming?   335

Elisabeth Rosenthal, Environmentally Unfriendly
    Trend: Fast Fashion   350

Anna Quindlen, Evan's Two Moms   373

Sonya Geis, A New Tactic in Fighting Marriage
    Initiatives   374

Marc Haeringer, Coming Out in the Line of Fire   380

Michelle Malkin, Beware of Illegal Aliens Seeking
    Hazmat Licenses   411

Helen Epstein, Immigration Maze   413

Francis Fukuyama, A Tale of Two Dystopias   438

Ralph C. Merkle, Nanotechnology: Designs
    for the Future   446

Bill Gates, A Robot in Every Home   453

Ron Reagan, Speech at the Democratic National
    Convention, July 27, 2004   464

Ted Koppel, Take My Privacy, Please!   484

Steven C. Bennett, Privacy Implications of Biometrics   496
Paul Saffo, A Trail of DNA and Data   502
Russ Ryan, Emerging Biometric Technologies   507
Joseph A. Califano Jr., The Right Drug to Target:
    Cutting Marijuana Use   518
Eric Schlosser, Make Peace with Pot   520
Douglas Bettcher and Chitra Subramaniam, The
    Necessity of Global Tobacco Regulations   526
Michael Bérubé, Citizenship and Disability   540
Andrew Keen, Is Google's Data Grinder Dangerous?   576
John Seigenthaler, A False Wikipedia "Biography"   579
Michael Gerson, Where the Avatars Roam   583
Joe Duffy and Andrew Keen, Can Anyone Be a Designer?   592
Stephen Williams, Getting Off the Couch   604

Visual Arguments

Angela Yamashita, Got Roddick? (student)   101
Scott McCloud, Setting the Record Straight   121
Al Gore, Ten Things to Do to Help Stop Global Warming   338
Glenn McCoy, And Looking at Our Extended
    Forecast . . . (cartoon)   340
Matt Davies, We're Here to Defend . . . (cartoon)   370
Henry Payne, The Bad News Is . . . (cartoon)   401
Wiley Miller, What's the Worst That Can Happen . . . ?
    (cartoon)   414
Pat Oliphant, The Ronald Reagan Eulogy Will Be
    Delivered . . . (cartoon)   466
John McPherson, It's Part of the Government's New
    Emphasis . . . (cartoon)   488
FBI, Using Technology to Catch Criminals   506
Philip Morris, Camel Lights Ad   523
American Legacy Foundation, Antismoking Ad   524
Garry Trudeau, Doonesbury: The Sin Lobby Gins
    Up . . . (cartoon)   525
Bill Amend, What's This? (cartoon)   532
Barry Blitt, *New Yorker* Cover   547
Consumer Freedom, Obesity Ads   565
Eric Lewis, The Subtext of All Tattoos . . . (cartoon)   568
Mothers Against Drunk Driving, Like Father, Like Son Ad   570
Walt Handelsman, Information Superhighway (cartoon)   583

Irony and Satire in Arguments

Glenn McCoy, And Looking at Our Extended Forecast . . . (cartoon)   340
Matt Davies, We're Here to Defend . . . (cartoon)   370
Alexa Hackbarth, Vanity, Thy Name Is Metrosexual   396
Henry Payne, The Bad News Is . . . (cartoon)   401
Pat Oliphant, The Ronald Reagan Eulogy Will Be Delivered . . . (cartoon)   466
David Brin, Three Cheers for the Surveillance Society!   475
Ted Koppel, Take My Privacy, Please!   484
John McPherson, It's Part of the Government's
    New Emphasis . . . (cartoon)   488
Philip Morris, Camel Lights Ad   523
Garry Trudeau, Doonesbury: The Sin Lobby Gins Up . . . (cartoon)   525
Bill Amend, What's This? (cartoon)   532
Consumer Freedom, Obesity Ads   565
Eric Lewis, The Subtext of All Tattoos . . . (cartoon)   568
Mothers Against Drunk Driving, Like Father, Like Son Ad   570
John Perry Barlow, A Declaration of the Independence of Cyberspace   578
Walt Handelsman, Information Superhighway (cartoon)   583

Arguments That Cite Sources

Angela Yamashita, Got Roddick? (student)   101
Brian Witkowski, Need a Cure for Tribe Fever? How
    About a Dip in the Lake? (student)   297
Al Gore, What Is Global Warming?   335
Mae M. Ngai, No Human Being Is Illegal   406
Darla K. Deardorff, In Search of Intercultural Competence   423
Bill Joy, Why the Future Doesn't Need Us   429
Douglas Bettcher and Chitra Subramaniam, The Necessity
    of Global Tobacco Regulations   526
Michael Bérubé, Citizenship and Disability   540
danah boyd, Facebook's "Privacy Trainwreck": Exposure, Invasion,
    and Social Convergence   595

We've enjoyed teaching with *Good Reasons with Contemporary Arguments* for many semesters (and several editions now), and this edition has especially benefited from the experiences of many instructors and students across the country. The increasing number of users for each edition further convinces us that a course focusing on argument is an essential part of a college education. College courses frequently require students to analyze the structure of arguments, to identify competing claims, to weigh the evidence offered, to recognize assumptions, to locate contradictions, and to anticipate opposing views. Just as important, students need to be able to read arguments critically and write arguments skillfully to succeed in the workplace and to participate in public life after college. The long-term issues that affect life after college—education, the environment, social justice, and quality of life, to name a few—have many diverse stakeholders and long, complex histories. They cannot be reduced to slogans and sound bites.

A Straightforward Approach to Argument

Good Reasons with Contemporary Arguments begins by considering why people take the time to write arguments in the first place. People write arguments because they want to change attitudes and beliefs about particular issues, and they want things done about problems they identify. We start out by examining exactly why people write arguments and how written arguments can lead to extended discussion and long-term results. We then provide the practical means to find good reasons that support arguments convincingly: *Good Reasons with Contemporary Arguments* presents steps for analyzing written and visual arguments and for writing definition, causal, evaluation, narrative, rebuttal, and proposal arguments. Finally, we conclude by illustrating those kinds of arguments as they have recently (and compellingly) appeared in contemporary media.

A Rhetorical Approach to Finding Good Reasons

You won't find a lot of complicated terminology in *Good Reasons with Contemporary Arguments*. The only technical terms this book uses are the general classical concepts of *pathos, ethos,* and *logos*—sources of good reasons that emerge from the audience's most passionately held values, from the speaker's expertise and credibility, or from reasonable, commonsense thinking. The crux of teaching argument, in our view, is to appreciate its rhetorical nature. A reason becomes a *good reason* when the audience accepts the writer or speaker as credible and accepts the assumptions and evidence on which the argument is based. Our emphasis on audience and aim is consistent throughout the book.

The Oral and Visual Aspects of Argument

Good Reasons with Contemporary Arguments is also distinctive in its attention to the delivery and presentation of arguments—to oral and visual aspects of argument in addition to the written word. We encourage students to formulate arguments in different genres and different media. Commonly used word-processing programs and Web-page editors now allow writers to include pictures, icons, charts, and graphs; these make design an important part of an argument. While the heart of an argument course should be the critical reading and critical writing of prose, we also believe that students should understand and use visual persuasion when appropriate.

Argument as a Social Act

So that students can see how argument is a social act—that is, how arguments develop out of and respond to other arguments—we have grouped the Part 6 reading selections around interesting current issues: the environment, sexual difference, globalization, science and ethics, privacy, the regulation of substances, and new media. Each chapter offers a range of viewpoints so that teachers and students can see how arguers develop their points in response to the perspectives of others, and so that students can develop their own arguments around those points of view. So that students can observe the range of argumentative styles and approaches that we discuss in the book, we include an unusual diversity of opinions and genres (including ads, cartoons, photographs, charts and graphs, and print arguments) as well as a diversity of writers and writing styles. There are arguments that originally appeared on the Internet and others that were published in magazines and newspapers. There are academic arguments with academic citations as well as public discourses that report firsthand observations without notes and references. There are well known citizens included, such as Edward O. Wilson, N. Scott Momaday, Al Gore, Bill Gates, Anna Quindlen, and Ted Koppel, as well as ordinary citizens in the process of making extraordinary cases. And there are many examples of the kinds of arguments that we discuss in detail in Part 3: definitions, evaluations, causal arguments, narratives, refutations, and proposals.

New to This Edition

- **A new chapter on reading arguments and new professional readings in the first half of the book provide ample instruction and practice in critical reading.**

Chapter 2, "Reading Arguments," helps students to become critical readers, to read actively, to recognize fallacies, and to respond to readings as a writer.

Eight engaging new readings have been added throughout Parts 2 and 3 to exemplify how people write and support arguments about current issues such as rap music, the income gap, the service economy, immigration, and clean energy.

■ **New material has been added on using sources to form and support arguments and on incorporating sources into arguments.**

A new section in Chapter 3 encourages students to find arguments to write about in what they read, see, and hear and guides them in formulating a thesis in relation to the positions of others.

A new chapter, Chapter 17, on finding sources, includes valuable advice on using library databases.

A new chapter, Chapter 18, on evaluating and keeping track of sources offers instruction on how to evaluate print, database, and Web sources and what information you need to record to document each source.

A new chapter, Chapter 19, on writing the research paper, helps students think through how to synthesize ideas from outside sources with their own and add to an ongoing argument, and it describes how to quote and summarize sources without plagiarizing.

New readings in Part 6 illustrate a variety of ways of documenting sources appropriately and effectively.

■ **The importance of visuals in argument is emphasized throughout with a new full-color design and many new visuals.**

Chapter 6, "Understanding Visual Arguments," includes a new analysis of an ad that explains many of the nuances of visual persuasion.

New diagrams in each chapter of Part 3, "Writing Arguments," provide visual maps of the structure of each kind of argument.

More visuals—larger, and in color—such as cartoons, advertisements, charts and graphs, and photographs, demonstrate and analyze the pervasiveness and persuasiveness of images in arguments.

■ **A substantially revised selection of arguments in Part 6, "Contemporary Arguments," engages students in issues that are fresh and provocative.**

Over 80 readings in Part 6—more than half new—join 11 readings in Parts 1 through 5 to engage students in the issues of the day: energy and the environment, same-sex marriage, immigration, robotics, stem cell research, the tension between privacy and security, disabilities, eating disorders, the new media, and more.

Two new Issues in Focus (five in all) gather readings, cartoons, and other visuals for in-depth looks at climate change and the privacy-versus-security questions raised by biometric technologies.

- **A greater emphasis on student work encourages students to understand themselves as writers.**

  Six student essays, four new to this edition, provide examples of the kinds of papers students are often asked to write—rhetorical analysis, visual analysis, definition, evaluation, proposal, and a research paper documented in MLA style—and demonstrate how extended written arguments can be developed.

- **A new full-page feature in Parts 1 and 3, "Finding Good Reasons," gets students thinking and writing about the arguments that surround contemporary issues.**

  Each "Finding Good Reasons" feature introduces a contemporary issue, such as the use of natural resources, surveillance technologies and policies, health and obesity, diversity, and community activism, and highlights key points in the arguments surrounding the issue.

  A half-page illustration, such as a cartoon, photograph, or advertisement, brings another angle to the issue.

  Writing prompts encourage students to explore and enter the conversation about the issue.

- **MLA and APA documentation guidelines are updated and redesigned for clarity.**

  MLA and APA guidelines and examples reflect the most recent guidelines.

  Color-coded sample entries help students recognize and organize key elements such as the author, title, publication information, and so on.

Supplements

The **Instructor's Manual** that accompanies this text was revised by John Jones and is designed to be useful for new and experienced instructors alike. The Instructor's Manual briefly discusses the ins and outs of teaching the material in each chapter. Also provided are in-class exercises, homework assignments, discussion questions for each reading selection, and model paper assignments and syllabi. This revised Instructor's Manual will make your work as a teacher a bit easier. Teaching argumentation and composition becomes a process that has genuine—and often surprising—rewards.

    MyCompLab is a Web application that offers comprehensive and integrated resources for every writer. With MyCompLab, students can learn from interactive tutorials and instruction; practice and develop their skills through grammar, writing, and research exercises; share their writing and collaborate with peers; and receive comments on their writing from instructors and tutors. Go to www.mycomplab.com to register for these premier resources and much more.

Acknowledgments

We are much indebted to the work of many outstanding scholars of argument and to our colleagues who teach argument at Texas and at Penn State. In particular, we thank the following reviewers for sharing their expertise: Jacob Agatucci, Central Oregon Community College; Angie Berdahl, Portland Community College; Dan Ferguson, Amarillo College; Christy Friend, University of South Carolina; Jay L. Gordon, Youngstown State University; Glenn Harris, Mott Community College; Kimberly Harrison, Florida International University; Edwina Jordan, Illinois Central College; Crystal McCage, Central Oregon Community College; Michael Rovasio, California State University, East Bay; Harvey Rubinstein, Hudson County Community College; Stephen Thomas, Community College of Denver; Kyle Torke, United States Air Force Academy; and Pavel Zemilansky, James Madison University. We would also like to acknowledge the work of Gerald Graff and Cathy Birkenstein on strategies for developing arguments in response to sources.

We are grateful also to the faculty and students at New Mexico State University, in particular to Stuart C. Brown, who reviewed the Third Edition and, with Kathryn Valentine, helped us gather feedback from teachers and students who used our textbook in their writing classes. We thank those teachers who sent feedback on their classroom experiences: Skye Anicca, Elizabeth Brasher, Justin Chrestman, Kara Dorris, Blase Drexler, Jeff Frawley, Becki Graham, Joe Killiany, Ryan Lang, Lisa Ramirez, D. H. Retzinger, Yeruwelle de Rouen-Barth, Michaela Spampinato, Melanie D. Viramontes, Nick Voges, Stephen Webber; and we also thank the students who commented honestly on our book: Adam Burnett, Jeremy Calder, Jessica Dunlap, Norma Escobedo, Kelly Harrington, Kevin Hill, Valery Candice Lopez, Emily Mechenbier, Alex Mertz, Kasey Moore, Veronica Salazar, Victoria Schuetze, Manoly Souraphol, and Toan Tran.

We are also grateful to the many students we've taught in our own classes, who have given us opportunities to test these materials in class and have taught us a great deal about the nature of argument.

We have benefited greatly from working with three of the best editors in publishing: Lynn Huddon, executive editor; Joseph Opiela, editor-in-chief; and Carol Hollar-Zwick, development editor. Lynn and Joe have given us excellent advice and continuing support. We've worked with Carol closely, and she has been a delightful pro from the beginning, encouraging us to rethink the book, making the process of writing new and interesting, and shaping and refining our ideas throughout. Victoria Davis also worked with us in the revision and made many fine contributions, and Matt and Erin Newcomb made many indispensable suggestions and contributions to Part 6; without them, this revision would not have been possible. Katy Bastille and Nikki Bruno Clapper at Pre-Press Company and Eric Jorgensen at Pearson Longman did splendid work in preparing our book for publication. Finally, we thank our families, who make it all possible.

LESTER FAIGLEY
JACK SELZER

Persuading with Good Reasons

What Do We Mean by *Argument*?

For over thirty years, the debate over legal abortion has raged in the United States. The following scene is a familiar one: Outside an abortion clinic, a crowd of pro-life activists has gathered to try to stop women from entering the clinic. They carry signs that read ABORTION = MURDER and A BABY'S LIFE IS A HUMAN LIFE. Pro-choice organizers have staged a counterdemonstration. Their signs read KEEP YOUR LAWS OFF MY BODY and WOMEN HAVE THE RIGHT TO CONTROL THEIR BODIES. Police keep the two sides apart, but they do not stop the shouts of "Murderer!" from the pro-life side and "If you're anti-abortion, don't have one!" from the pro-choice side.

When you imagine an argument, you might think of two people engaged in a heated exchange, or two groups of people with different views, shouting back and forth at each other like the pro-choice and pro-life demonstrators. Or you might think of district attorneys and defense lawyers debating strenuously in the courthouse. Like oral arguments, written arguments can resemble these oral arguments in being heated and one sided.

Bumper stickers, for example, usually consist of unilateral statements such as "Be Green," "Save the Whales," or "Share the Road." They provide no supporting evidence or reasons for why anyone should do what they say. Many other kinds of writing lack reasoned argument. Writers of instruction manuals do not try to persuade their readers. Authors assume readers want to do whatever the manual tells them to do; otherwise they would not be consulting the manual. Likewise, an article written by a person committed to a particular cause or belief often assumes that everyone should think the same way. These writers can count on certain words and phrases to produce predictable responses.

1

In college courses, in public life, and in professional careers, however, written arguments cannot be reduced to signs or slogans. Writers of effective arguments do not assume that everyone thinks the same way or holds the same beliefs. They attempt to change people's minds by convincing them of the validity of new ideas or the superiority of a particular course of action. Writers of such arguments not only offer evidence and reasons to support their position but also examine the assumptions on which an argument is based, address opposing arguments, and anticipate their readers' objections.

Extended written arguments make more demands on their readers than most other kinds of writing. Like bumper stickers, these arguments often appeal to our emotions. But they typically do much more. They expand our knowledge with the depth of their analysis. They lead us through a complex set of claims by providing networks of logical relationships and appropriate evidence. They build on what has been written previously by providing trails of sources. Finally, they cause us to reflect on what we read, in a process that we will shortly describe as critical reading.

What Does Argument Mean for College Writers?

Writing in college varies considerably from course to course. A lab report for a biology course looks quite different from a paper in your English class, just as a classroom observation in an education course differs from a case study report in an accounting class.

Nevertheless, much of the writing you will do in college will consist of arguments. Some common expectations about arguments in college writing extend across disciplines. For example, you could be assigned to write a proposal for a downtown light-rail system in a number of different classes—civil engineering, urban planning, government, or management. The emphasis of such a proposal would change depending on the course. In all cases, however, the proposal would require a complex argument in which you describe the problem that the light-rail system would improve, make a specific proposal that addresses the problem, explain the benefits of the system, estimate the cost, identify funding sources, assess alternatives to your plan, and anticipate possible opposition. It's a lot to think about, but you will find that arguments place many demands on writers.

Even though the formats may differ across college courses, setting out a specific proposal or claim supported by reasons and evidence is at the heart of most college writing. Some expectations of arguments—such as making a claim in a thesis statement—may be familiar to you, but others—such as the emphasis on finding alternative ways of thinking about a subject and finding facts that might run counter to your conclusions—may be unfamiliar. The table opposite lists the major expectations of arguments in college and what writers do to fulfill them.

WRITTEN ARGUMENTS...	WRITERS ARE EXPECTED TO...
State explicit claims	Make a claim that isn't obvious. The main claim is often called a **thesis.**
Support claims with reasons	Express reasons in a because clause after the claim (We should do something *because* _____).
Base reasons on evidence	Provide evidence for reasons in the form of facts, statistics, testimony from reliable sources, and direct observations.
Consider opposing positions	Help readers understand why there are disagreements about issues by accurately representing differing views.
Analyze with insight	Provide in-depth analysis what they read and view.
Investigate complexity	Explore the complexity of a subject by asking "Have you thought about this?" or "What if you discard the usual way of thinking about a subject and take the opposite point of view?"
Organize information clearly (structure)	Make the major parts evident to readers and to indicate which parts are subordinate to others.
Signal relationships of parts (transitions)	Indicate logical relationships clearly so that readers can follow an argument without getting lost.
Document sources carefully	Provide the sources of information so that readers can consult the same sources the writer used.

How Can You Argue Responsibly?

In Washington, D.C., it is common to see cars with diplomatic license plates parked illegally. Their drivers know they will not be towed or ticketed. People who abuse the diplomatic privilege are announcing, "I'm not playing by the rules."

 When you begin an argument by saying "in my opinion," you are making a similar announcement. First, the phrase is redundant. A reader assumes that if you make a claim in writing, you believe that claim. More important, a claim is rarely *only* your opinion. Most beliefs and assumptions are shared by many people. If a claim truly is only your opinion, it can be easily dismissed. If your position is likely to be held by at least a few other people, however, then a responsible reader must consider your position seriously.

You argue responsibly when you set out the reasons for making a claim and offer facts to support those reasons. You argue responsibly when you allow readers to examine your evidence by documenting the sources you have consulted. Finally, you argue responsibly when you acknowledge that other people may have positions different from yours.

How Can You Argue Respectfully?

Our culture is competitive, and our goal often is to win. Professional athletes, top trial lawyers, or candidates for president of the United States either win big or lose. But most of us live in a world in which our opponents don't go away when the game is over.

Most of us have to deal with people who disagree with us at times but continue to work and live in our communities. The idea of winning in such situations can only be temporary. Soon enough, we will need the support of those who were on the other side of the most recent issue. You can probably think of times when a friendly argument resulted in a better understanding of all peoples' views. And probably you can think of a time when an argument created hard feelings that lasted for years.

Usually, listeners and readers are more willing to consider your argument seriously if you cast yourself as a respectful partner rather than as a competitor. Put forth your arguments in the spirit of mutual support and negotiation—in the interest of finding the *best* way, not "my way." How can you be the person that your reader will want to join rather than resist? Here are a few suggestions for both your written arguments and for discussing controversial issues.

- **Try to think of yourself as engaged not so much in winning over your audience as in courting your audience's cooperation.** Argue vigorously, but not so vigorously that opposing views are vanquished or silenced. Remember that your goal is to invite a response that creates a dialogue.
- **Show that you understand and genuinely respect your listener's or reader's position even if you think the position is ultimately wrong.** Remember to argue against opponents' positions, not against the opponents themselves. Arguing respectfully often means representing an opponent's position in terms that he or she would accept. Look for ground that you already share with your opponent, and search for even more. See yourself as a mediator. Consider that neither you nor the other

person has arrived at a best solution. Then carry on in the hope that dialogue will lead to an even better course of action than the one you now recommend. Expect and assume the best of your listener or reader, and deliver your best.

■ **Cultivate a sense of humor and a distinctive voice.** Many textbooks about argument emphasize using a reasonable voice. But a reasonable voice doesn't have to be a dull one. Humor is a legitimate tool of argument. Although playing an issue strictly for laughs risks not being taken seriously, nothing creates a sense of goodwill quite as much as tasteful humor. A sense of humor can be especially welcome when the stakes are high, the sides have been chosen, and tempers are flaring.

Consider your argument as just one move in a larger process that might end up helping you. Most times we argue because we think we have something to offer. In the process of developing and presenting your views, however, realize that you might learn something in the course of your research or discussion. You might even change your mind. Holding on to that attitude will keep you from becoming too overbearing and dogmatic.

*Read 1st day ',
discuss —
one point
you were
surprised by

one you agree with?

challenge*

*summarize
into a list of
goals?*

Reading and Discovering Arguments

PART 1   Reading and Discovering Arguments

1. Why Argue? 9

Why do people write arguments? 9

FINDING GOOD REASONS 10

Why do some arguments succeed? 12

What are the goals of arguments? 16

What are rhetorical appeals? 17

Rachel Carson, The Obligation to Endure 19

2. Reading Arguments 2 2

Read critically 22

Read actively 22

FINDING GOOD REASONS 24

Recognize fallacies 26

Respond as a writer 28

3. Finding Arguments 3 0

Find arguments in everyday conversations 30

Find a topic that interests you 33

Find a claim by exploring 37

FINDING GOOD REASONS 39

Find a claim by reading 40

Find good reasons 44

Find evidence to support good reasons 50

4. Drafting and Revising Arguments 5 2

State and evaluate your thesis 52

Think about your readers 54

FINDING GOOD REASONS 55

Organize your argument 57

Write an engaging title and introduction 58

Write a strong conclusion 59

Evaluate your draft 60

Respond to the writing of others 62

Edit and proofread carefully 64

1

Why Argue?

Brown pelicans are common along the coasts of the South and California, but they were headed toward extinction by 1970 because the pesticide DDT caused their eggs to be too thin to support developing chicks to maturity. Although DDT was banned in the United States, many countries continue to use it for agricultural spraying and malaria control even though insects and mosquitoes have developed resistance to it. Should there be an international ban on DDT?

In 1958, Rachel Carson received a copy of a letter that her friend Olga Huckens had sent to the *Boston Herald*. The letter described what had happened the previous summer when Duxbury, Massachusetts, a small town just north of Huckens's home in Cape Cod, had been sprayed several times with the pesticide DDT to kill mosquitoes. Despite the spraying, the mosquitoes had come back as hungry as ever, but the songbirds, bees, and other insects had vanished except for a few dead birds that Huckens had found in her yard. Huckens asked Carson if she knew anyone in Washington, D.C. who could help stop the spraying.

Why Do People Write Arguments?

The letter from Olga Huckens struck a nerve with Rachel Carson. Carson was a marine biologist who had worked for the U.S. Fish and Wildlife Service and had written three highly acclaimed books about the sea and wetlands. In 1945 the editors at *Reader's Digest* had asked Carson if she could write something else for them. Carson replied that she wanted to write about experiments using DDT, which was being hyped as the solution for controlling insect pests. As early as 1945, Carson knew that widespread spraying of DDT would harm fish, waterfowl, and other animals. Eventually people could die too. *Reader's Digest* was not interested in Carson's proposed article, so she dropped the idea and went on to write about other things.

Huckens's 1958 letter brought Carson back to the subject of chemical spraying. In the late 1940s and 1950s, pesticides—especially the chlorinated hydrocarbons DDT, aldrin, and dieldrin—were sprayed on a massive scale throughout the

Finding Good Reasons
WHO'S USING UP EARTH'S RESOURCES?

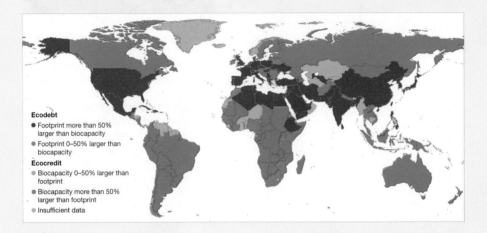

Ecodebt
- Footprint more than 50% larger than biocapacity
- Footprint 0–50% larger than biocapacity

Ecocredit
- Biocapacity 0–50% larger than footprint
- Biocapacity more than 50% larger than footprint
- Insufficient data

In the *Living Planet Report* for 2005, the World Wildlife Federation calculated the ecological footprint for each country on earth. The ecological footprint of a country is determined by its population, the amount of food, timber, and other resources consumed by its average citizen, the area required to produce food, fishing grounds, and the area required to absorb CO_2 emissions minus the amount absorbed by oceans.

Countries fall into four categories: ecological debtor nations (which consume more resources than they can produce), ecological creditor nations (which produce more than they consume), and two categories of ecologically balanced nations, where production and consumption are relatively balanced. In this map you can see that the United States, Mexico, Western Europe, China, India, Pakistan, Japan, and the nations of the Middle East are ecological debtors with footprints more than 50 percent of their biocapacity—what they are able to produce. Nations such as Canada, Russia, Australia, New Zealand, and most nations in South America are ecological creditors, with footprints less than 50 percent of their biocapacity. In its entirety, the *Living Planet Report* makes the argument that nations should live in balance with what their land, rivers, lakes, and seas can support.

Write about it

1. What might be some of the causes of the differences among the ecological footprints of nations?
2. What is likely to happen in the future when some nations have enough resources (such as clean water and food) and others lack them?
3. Does the map succeed as an argument on its own? Does it contain any of the features of written arguments listed on page 3?

United States. Politicians hailed them as a cure for world hunger. In 1957 much of the greater New York City area, including Long Island, was sprayed with DDT to kill gypsy moths. But there were noticeable side effects. Many people complained about the deaths of not only birds, fish, and useful insects but also their own plants, shrubs, and pets. Scientists had written about the dangers of widespread spraying of pesticides, but they had not convinced the public of the hazards or of the urgency for change.

Carson decided that she needed to write a magazine article about the facts of DDT. But when she contacted *Reader's Digest* and other magazines, she found that they still would not consider publishing anything about the subject. Carson then concluded that she should write a short book. She knew that her job was not going to be easy because people in the United States still trusted scientists to solve all problems. Scientists had brought the "green revolution," which greatly increased crop yields through the use of fertilizers and pesticides.

Carson's subject matter was also technical and difficult to communicate to the general public. At that time the public did not think much about air and water pollution, and most people were unaware that pesticides could poison humans as well as insects. Furthermore, Carson was sure to face opposition from the pesticide industry, which had become a multimillion-dollar business. She knew the pesticide industry would do everything it could to stop her from publishing or to discredit her if she did. Still, she wanted to inform people of the dangers of pesticides and argue for limiting their use. Like other writers of arguments, Carson had a **purpose** for writing the book that would become *Silent Spring*.

Silent Spring indeed sounded the alarm about the dangers of pesticides, and the controversy it raised still has not ended. No book has had a greater impact on our thinking about the environment. *Silent Spring* was first published in installments in *The New Yorker* in the summer of 1962, and it created an immediate furor. Chemical companies threatened to sue Carson, and the trade associations that the companies sponsored launched full-scale attacks against the book in pamphlets and magazine articles. The chemical companies treated *Silent Spring* as a public-relations problem. They hired scientists whose only job was to ridicule the book and to dismiss Carson as a "hysterical woman." Some scientists even accused *Silent Spring* of being part of a communist plot to ruin U.S. agriculture.

The public controversy over *Silent Spring* had another effect. It helped to make the book a success shortly after it was published in September 1962. A half-million hardcover copies of *Silent Spring* were sold, and the book stayed on the best-seller list for thirty-one weeks. President John F. Kennedy read *Silent Spring* and met with Carson and other scientists to discuss the pesticide problem. Kennedy requested that the President's Scientific Advisory Committee study the effects of pesticides and write a report. This report found evidence of high levels of pesticides around the world, both in the environment and in the tissues of humans. The report confirmed what Carson had described in *Silent Spring*.

In the words of a news commentator at the time, *Silent Spring* "lit a fire" under the government. Congress held several hearings on the effects of pesticides and other pollutants on the environment. In 1967 the Environmental Defense Fund was formed. It developed the guidelines under which DDT was eventually banned. Three years later, President Richard Nixon became convinced that only an independent agency within the executive branch could operate with enough independence to enforce environmental regulations. Nixon created the Environmental Protection Agency (EPA) in December 1970.

The United States was not the only country to respond to *Silent Spring*. Widely translated, the book inspired legislation on the environment in nearly all industrialized nations. Moreover, it changed the way we think about the environment. Carson pointed out that the nerve gases that were developed for use on America's enemies in World War II were being used as pesticides after the war. She criticized the view that the environment is a battlefield where people make war on natural forces that they believe impede their progress. Instead, she advocated living in coexistence with the environment because people are part of it. She was not totally opposed to pesticides. Her larger goal was to make people more aware that changing one part would affect other parts of the whole. Her message was to try to live in balance with nature. The fact that we still talk so much about the environment is testimony to the lasting power of *Silent Spring*.

Why Do Some Arguments Succeed?

A book titled *Our Synthetic Environment*, which covered much of the same ground as *Silent Spring*, had been published six months earlier. The author, Murray Bookchin, writing under the pen name Lewis Herber, wrote about the pollution of the natural world and its effects on people. Bookchin was as committed to warning people about the hazards of pesticides as Carson, but only a small community of scientists read *Our Synthetic Environment*. Why, then, did Carson succeed in reaching a larger audience?

Carson had far more impact than Bookchin not simply because she was a more talented writer or because she was a scientist while Bookchin was not. Like other writers of successful arguments, she not only knew her purpose for writing *Silent Spring*, but she also thought a great deal about who she was writing for— her **audience.** If she was going to stop the widespread spraying of dangerous pesticides, she knew she would have to connect with the values of a wide audience, an audience that included a large segment of the public as well as other scientists.

The opening chapter of *Silent Spring* begins not by announcing Carson's thesis or listing facts and statistics. Instead, the book starts with a short fable about a small town located amid prosperous farmland, where wildflowers bloom much of the year, trout swim in the streams, and wildlife is abundant. Suddenly, a

TACTICS OF *SILENT SPRING*

Chapter 1 of *Silent Spring* tells a parable of a rural town where the birds, fish, flowers, and plants die and people become sick after a white powder is sprayed on the town. At the beginning of Chapter 2, Rachel Carson begins her argument against the mass aerial spraying of pesticides. Most of her readers were not aware of the dangers of pesticides, but they were well aware of the harmful effects of radiation. Let's look at her tactics:

> The interrelationship of people and the environment provides the basis for Carson's argument.

The history of life on earth has been a history of interaction between living things and their surroundings. To a large extent, the physical form and the habits of earth's vegetation and its animal life have been molded by the environment. Considering the whole span of earthly time, the opposite effect, in which life actually modifies its surroundings, has been relatively slight. Only within the moment of time represented by the present century has one species—man—acquired significant power to alter the nature of his world.

> Carson shifts her language to a metaphor of war against the environment rather than interaction with the natural world.

During the past quarter century this power has not only increased to one of disturbing magnitude but it has changed in character. The most alarming of all man's assaults upon the environment is the contamination of air, earth, rivers, and sea with dangerous and even lethal materials. This pollution is for the most part irrecoverable; the chain of life it initiates not only in the world that must support life but in living tissues is for the most part irreversible. In this now universal contamination of the environment, chemicals are the sinister and little-recognized partners of radiation in changing the very nature of the world—the very nature of its life.

> In 1963 the United States and the Soviet Union signed the first treaty that banned the testing of nuclear weapons above ground, under water, and in space.

> The key move: Carson associates the dangers of chemical pesticides with those of radiation.

Strontium 90, released through nuclear explosions into the air, comes to earth in rain or drifts down as fallout, lodges in the soil, enters into the grass or corn or wheat grown there, and in time takes its abode in the bones of a human being, there to remain until his death. Similarly, chemicals sprayed on croplands or forests or gardens lie long in soil, entering into living organisms, passing from one to another in a chain of poisoning and death. Or they pass mysteriously by underground streams until they emerge and, through the alchemy of air and sunlight, combine into new forms that kill vegetation, sicken cattle, and work unknown harm on those who drink from once-pure wells. As Albert Schweitzer has said, "Man can hardly even recognize the devils of his own creation."

> Albert Schweitzer (1875–1965) was a concert musician, philosopher, and doctor who spent most of his life as a medical missionary in Africa.

strange blight comes on the town, as if an evil spell has been cast upon it. The chickens, sheep, and cattle on the farms grow sick and die. The families of the townspeople and farmers alike develop mysterious illnesses. Most of the birds disappear, and the few that remain can neither sing nor fly. The apple trees bloom, but there are no bees to pollinate the trees, and so they bear no fruit. The wildflowers wither as if they have been burned. Fishermen quit going to the streams because the fish have all died.

But it isn't witchcraft that causes everything to grow sick and die. Carson writes that "the people had done it to themselves." She continues, "I know of no community that has experienced all the misfortunes I describe. Yet every one of these disasters has actually happened somewhere, and many real communities have already suffered a substantial number of them. A grim specter has crept upon us almost unnoticed, and this imagined tragedy may easily become a stark reality." Carson's fable did come true several times after *Silent Spring* was published. In July 1976, a chemical reaction went out of control at a plant near Seveso, Italy, and a cloud of powdery white crystals of almost pure dioxin fell on the town. Children ran out to play in the powder because it looked like snow. Within four days, plants, birds, and animals began dying, and shortly people started getting sick. Most of the people had to go to the hospital, and everyone had to move out of the town. An even worse disaster happened in December 1984, when a storage tank in a pesticide plant exploded near Bhopal, India, showering the town. Two thousand people died quickly, and another 50,000 became sick for the rest of their lives.

If Carson were alive today and writing a book about the dangers of pesticides, she might begin differently. But remember that at the time she was writing, people trusted pesticides and believed that DDT was a miracle solution for all sorts of insect pests. She first had to make people aware that DDT could be harmful to them. In the second chapter of *Silent Spring* (reprinted at the end of this chapter), Carson continued appealing to the emotions of her audience. In 1962 people knew about the dangers of radiation even if they were ignorant about pesticides. They knew that the atomic bombs that had been dropped on Hiroshima and Nagasaki at the end of World War II were still killing Japanese people through the effects of radiation many years later. They feared the fallout from nuclear bombs that were still being tested and stockpiled in the United States and the Soviet Union.

Getting people's attention by exposing the threat of pesticides wasn't enough. There are always people writing about various kinds of threats, and most aren't taken seriously except by those who already believe that the threats exist. Carson wanted to reach people who didn't think that pesticides were a threat but might be persuaded to take this view. To convince these people, she had to explain why pesticides are potentially dangerous, and she had to make readers believe that she could be trusted.

Carson was an expert marine biologist. To write *Silent Spring*, she had to read widely in sciences that she had not studied. She read research about insects, toxic chemicals, cell physiology, biochemistry, plant and soil science, and public health. Then she had to explain complex scientific processes to people who had very little or no background in science. Throughout the book, Carson succeeds in translating scientific facts into language that, to use her words, "most of us" can understand. She establishes her credibility as a scientist by correctly using technical terms such as *necrosis.* At the same time, however she identifies with people who are not scientists and gains their trust by taking their point of view.

Carson's legacy is our awareness of our environment. She reminds us that we share this planet with other creatures and that "we are dealing with life—with living populations and all their pressures and counterpressures, their surges and recessions." She warns us not to dismiss the balance of nature:

> The balance of nature is not the same today as in Pleistocene times, but it is still there: a complex, precise, and highly integrated system of relationships between living things which cannot safely be ignored any more than the law of gravity can be defied with impunity by a man perched on the edge of a cliff. The balance of nature is not a *status quo;* it is fluid, ever shifting, in a constant state of adjustment.

Scientists predict that as many as half the species on Earth will disappear over the next 100 years. Yet other species, including squirrels, rats, coyotes, raccoons, and white-tailed deer, thrive in suburban environments. Should we be concerned about loss of species when there are plenty of animals living nearby?

Since the publication of *Silent Spring*, people around the world have grown much more conscious of the large-scale effects of global warming, acid rain, and the depleted ozone layer in addition to the local effects of pesticides described in Carson's book. The long-term influence of *Silent Spring* helped inspire the nations of today as they attempt to control air and water pollution, to encourage more efficient use of energy and natural resources, and to promote sustainable patterns of consumption.

What Are the Goals of Arguments?

When writing *Silent Spring*, Rachel Carson had two purposes. In the book, she first makes an effective **position** argument against the massive use of synthetic pesticides. This argument alone, however, does not solve the problem of what to do about harmful insects that destroy crops and spread disease. As her second purpose, Carson tackles the more difficult job of offering solutions. In her final chapter, "The Other Road," Carson makes a **proposal** argument for alternatives to the massive use of pesticides.

Carson's two kinds of arguments represent a basic distinction. Some arguments get us to understand something better or to believe something. Others urge us to do something. Most arguments can be characterized as either position arguments or proposal arguments, depending on their purpose.

Position Arguments

In a **position argument,** the writer makes a claim about a controversial issue.

- **The writer first has to define the issue.** Before she could begin arguing against pesticides, Carson had to explain what synthetic pesticides are and how they work. She also had to provide a history of their increasing use after World War II.

- **The writer should take a clear position.** Carson wasted no time setting out her position by describing the threat that high levels of pesticides pose to people worldwide.

- **The writer should make a convincing argument and acknowledge opposing views.** In support of her position, Carson used a variety of strategies, including research studies, quotations from authorities, and her own analyses and observations. She took into account opposing views by acknowledging that harmful insects needed to be controlled and conceded that selective spraying is necessary and desirable.

Proposal Arguments

In a **proposal argument,** the writer proposes a course of action in response to a recognizable problem. The proposal outlines what can be done to improve the situation or to change it altogether.

- **The writer first has to define the problem.** The problem that Carson had to define was complex. The overuse of pesticides was killing helpful insects, plants, and animals and threatening people. In addition, the harmful insects that the pesticides were intended to eliminate were becoming increasingly resistant to the chemicals. More spraying and more frequent spraying produced pesticide-resistant "superbugs." Mass spraying resulted in helping bad bugs such as fire ants by killing off their competition.

- **The writer has to propose a solution or solutions.** Carson does not provide a particular approach to controlling insects, but she does advocate biological solutions. She proposes alternatives to pesticides, such as sterilizing and releasing large numbers of male insects and introducing predators of pest insects. Above all, she urges that we work with nature rather than being at war with it.

- **The solution or solutions must work, and they must be feasible.** Writers should identify the projected consequences of their proposed solution. They should argue that good things will happen, bad things will be avoided, or both. Carson discusses research studies that indicate her solutions would work, and she argues that her alternatives would be less expensive than massive spraying.

Today, we can look at Carson's book with the benefit of hindsight. Not everything that Carson proposed ended up working, but her primary solution—learn to live with nature—has been a powerful one. Mass spraying of pesticides has stopped in the United States, and species that were threatened by the excessive use of pesticides, including falcons, eagles, and brown pelicans, have made remarkable comebacks.

What are Rhetorical Appeals?

When the modern concept of democracy was developed in Greece in the fifth century BCE, the study of rhetoric also began. It's not a coincidence that the teaching of rhetoric was closely tied to the rise of democracy. In the Greek city-states, all citizens had the right to speak and to vote at the popular assembly and in the committees of the assembly that functioned as the criminal courts. Citizens took turns serving as the officials of government. Because the citizens of Athens and other city-states took their responsibilities quite seriously, they highly valued the ability to speak effectively in public. Teachers of rhetoric were held in great esteem.

In the following century, the most important teacher of rhetoric in ancient Greece, Aristotle (384–323 BCE), made the study of rhetoric systematic. He defined **rhetoric** as the art of finding the best available means of persuasion in any situation. Aristotle set out three primary tactics of argument: appeals to the emotions and the deepest-held values of the audience (***pathos***), appeals based on the trustworthiness of the speaker (***ethos***), and appeals to reason (***logos***). Rachel Carson makes these appeals with great skill in *Silent Spring*.

Appeals to Pathos: the Values of the Audience

Appeals to pathos are often associated with emotional appeals, but the term has a broader meaning. Pathos in arguments means connecting with the underlying values, beliefs, and attitudes of readers. Carson appeals to pathos by making us care about nature as well as raising concerns about our own safety. She uses the fate of robins to symbolize her crusade. Robins were the main victims when people sprayed pesticides to battle Dutch elm disease. Robins feed on earthworms, which in turn process fallen elm leaves. The earthworms act as magnifiers of the pesticide, which either kills the robins outright or renders them sterile. Thus, when no robins sang, it was indeed a silent spring.

Appeals to Ethos: the Trustworthiness of the Speaker or Writer

Ethos refers to the credibility of a speaker or writer. We tend to believe people we respect. We also believe people who have our best interests in mind. Readers believe Rachel Carson not just because she is an expert. She convinces us first by establishing that she has people's well-being at heart. She anticipates possible objections and demonstrates that she has thought about opposing positions. She takes time to explain concepts that most people do not understand fully, and she discusses how everyone can benefit if we take a different attitude toward nature. She shows that she has done her homework on the topic. By creating a credible ethos, Carson makes an effective moral argument that humans as a species have a responsibility not to destroy the world they live in.

Appeals to Logos: the Good Reasons or Logic Used to Support an Argument

Logos means persuading by using reasons. It is sometimes referred to as "the argument itself." Logos is the method preferred by Aristotle, scientists, and academic writers in general. Carson offers good reasons to support her main claims. She describes webs of relationships among the earth, plants, animals, and humans, and she explains how changing one part will affect the others. Her point is not that we should never disturb these relationships but that we should be aware of the consequences.

Rachel Carson

The Obligation to Endure

Rachel Carson (1907–1964) was born and raised in Springdale, Pennsylvania, 18 miles up the Allegheny River from Pittsburgh. As she wandered on the family farm, Carson developed the love of nature that she maintained throughout her life. At age 22 she began her career as a marine biologist at Woods Hole, Massachusetts, and she later went to graduate school at Johns Hopkins University in Baltimore. In 1936 she began working in the agency that later became the U.S. Fish and Wildlife Service. Soon she was recognized as a talented writer as well as a meticulous scientist. Carson wrote three highly praised books about the sea and wetlands: Under the Sea Wind *(1941),* The Sea Around Us *(1951), and* The Edge of the Sea *(1954).*

Carson's decision to write Silent Spring *marked a great change in her life. For the first time, she became an environmental activist in addition to being an enthusiastic writer about nature. She had written about the interconnectedness of life in her previous three books, but with* Silent Spring *she had to convince people that hazards lay in what had seemed familiar and harmless. Carson was the first scientist to make a comprehensive argument that links cancer to environmental causes. Earlier in this chapter, we saw how Carson compares pesticides with the dangers of radiation from nuclear weapons. Notice another way that she gets her readers to think differently about pesticides in this selection, which begins Chapter 2 of* Silent Spring.

The history of life on earth has been a history of interaction between living things and their surroundings. To a large extent, the physical form and the habits of the earth's vegetation and its animal life have been molded by the environment. Considering the whole span of earthly time, the opposite effect, in which life actually modifies its surroundings, has been relatively slight. Only within the moment of time represented by the present century has one species—man—acquired significant power to alter the nature of his world.

2   During the past quarter century this power has not only increased to one of disturbing magnitude but it has changed in character. The most alarming of all man's assaults upon the environment is the contamination of air, earth, rivers, and sea with dangerous and even lethal materials. This pollution is for the most part irrecoverable; the chain of evil it initiates not only in the world that must support life but in living tissues is for the most part irreversible. In this now universal contamination of the environment, chemicals are the sinister and little recognized partners of radiation in changing the very nature of the world—the very nature of its life. Strontium 90, released through nuclear explosions into the air, comes to earth in rain or drifts down as fallout, lodges in soil, enters into the grass or corn or wheat grown there, and in time takes up its abode in the bones of a human being, there to remain until his death. Similarly, chemicals sprayed on croplands or forests or gardens lie long in soil,

entering into living organisms, passing from one to another in a chain of poisoning and death. Or they pass mysteriously by underground streams until they emerge and, through the alchemy of air and sunlight, combine into new forms that kill vegetation, sicken cattle, and work unknown harm on those who drink from once-pure wells. As Albert Schweitzer has said, "Man can hardly even recognize the devils of his own creation."

3   It took hundreds of millions of years to produce the life that now inhabits the earth—eons of time in which that developing and evolving and diversifying life reached a state of adjustment and balance with its surroundings. The environment, rigorously shaping and directing the life it supported, contained elements that were hostile as well as supporting. Certain rocks gave out dangerous radiation; even within the light of the sun, from which all life draws its energy, there were short-wave radiations with power to injure. Given time—time not in years but in millennia—life adjusts, and a balance has been reached. For time is the essential ingredient; but in the modern world there is no time.

4   The rapidity of change and the speed with which new situations are created follow the impetuous and heedless pace of man rather than the deliberate pace of nature. Radiation is no longer merely the background radiation of rocks, the bombardment of cosmic rays, the ultraviolet of the sun that have existed before there was any life on earth; radiation is now the unnatural creation of man's tampering with the atom. The chemicals to which life is asked to make its adjustment are no longer merely the calcium and silica and copper and all the rest of the minerals washed out of the rocks and carried in rivers to the sea; they are the synthetic creations of man's inventive mind, brewed in his laboratories, and having no counterparts in nature.

5   To adjust to these chemicals would require time on the scale that is nature's; it would require not merely the years of a man's life but the life of generations. And even this, were it by some miracle possible, would be futile, for the new chemicals come from our laboratories in an endless stream; almost five hundred annually find their way into actual use in the United States alone. The figure is staggering and its implications are not easily grasped—500 new chemicals to which the bodies of men and animals are required somehow to adapt each year, chemicals totally outside the limits of biologic experience.

6   Among them are many that are used in man's war against nature. Since the mid-1940s over 200 basic chemicals have been created for use in killing insects, weeds, rodents, and other organisms described in the modern vernacular as "pests"; and they are sold under several thousand different brand names.

7   These sprays, dusts, and aerosols are now applied almost universally to farms, gardens, forests, and homes—nonselective chemicals that have the power to kill every insect, the "good" and the "bad," to still the song of birds and the leaping of fish in the streams, to coat the leaves with a deadly film, and to linger on in soil—all this though the intended target may be only a few

weeds or insects. Can anyone believe it is possible to lay down such a barrage of poisons on the surface of the earth without making it unfit for all life? They should not be called "insecticides," but "biocides."

8   The whole process of spraying seems caught up in an endless spiral. Since DDT was released for civilian use, a process of escalation has been going on in which ever more toxic materials must be found. This has happened because insects, in a triumphant vindication of Darwin's principle of the survival of the fittest, have evolved super races immune to the particular insecticide used, hence a deadlier one has always to be developed—and then a deadlier one than that. It has happened also because, for reasons to be described later, destructive insects often undergo a "flareback," or resurgence, after spraying, in numbers greater than before. Thus the chemical war is never won, and all life is caught in its violent crossfire.

9   Along with the possibility of the extinction of mankind by nuclear war, the central problem of our age has therefore become the contamination of man's total environment with such substances of incredible potential for harm—substances that accumulate in the tissues of plants and animals and even penetrate the germ cells to shatter or alter the very material of heredity upon which the shape of the future depends.

10   Some would-be architects of our future look toward a time when it will be possible to alter the human germ plasm by design. But we may easily be doing so now by inadvertence, for many chemicals, like radiation, bring about gene mutations. It is ironic to think that man might determine his own future by something so seemingly trivial as the choice of an insect spray.

11   All this has been risked—for what? Future historians may well be amazed by our distorted sense of proportion. How could intelligent beings seek to control a few unwanted species by a method that contaminated the entire environment and brought the threat of disease and death even to their own kind? Yet this is precisely what we have done. We have done it, moreover, for reasons that collapse the moment we examine them. We are told that the enormous and expanding use of pesticides is necessary to maintain farm production. Yet is our real problem not one of *overproduction*? Our farms, despite measures to remove acreages from production and to pay farmers *not* to produce, have yielded such a staggering excess of crops that the American taxpayer in 1962 is paying out more than one billion dollars a year as the total carrying cost of the surplus-food storage program. And is the situation helped when one branch of the Agriculture Department tries to reduce production while another states, as it did in 1958, "It is believed generally that reduction of crop acreages under provisions of the Soil Bank will stimulate interest in use of chemicals to obtain maximum production on the land retained in crops."

12   All this is not to say there is no insect problem and no need of control. I am saying, rather, that control must be geared to realities, not to mythical situations, and that the methods employed must be such that they do not destroy us along with the insects.

2

Reading Arguments

We constantly "read" what is going on around us. But can we tell what these people might be thinking?

Along with learning to write well, thinking critically is one of the most important abilities you will develop in college. You will be asked to think in depth about what you read, as well as what you see in movies, television shows, print advertisements, paintings, photographs, or Web sites. Becoming a better thinker will help you to become a better writer because you will understand subjects in greater complexity and you will be better able to evaluate and to revise what you write.

Critical thinking begins with critical reading. Reading arguments requires you to read critically because you need know more than the writer's main points. Arguments don't fall out of the sky but instead are part of a larger conversation about ideas. Reading one turn in a conversation is not enough to understand why a subject is being discussed at a particular time or to gain a sense of the major points of view. To become aware of how a particular argument fits into the larger conversation, you must explore beyond the text itself.

Read Critically

Critical reading is the four-part process described in the box on the facing page, and you will often need to read an assignment more than once to cover all of the points in the process. First, ask where a piece of writing came from and why it was written. Second, read the text carefully to find the author's central claim or thesis and the major points. Third, decide if you can trust the author. Fourth, read the text again to understand how it works.

Read Actively

If you own what you are reading, read with a pencil in hand. (Avoid pens and highlighters—they don't erase, and often you won't remember why you high-lighted a particular sentence.)

ethos, pathos, logos

QUESTIONS FOR READING ARGUMENTS CRITICALLY

1. Where did the argument come from?

- Who wrote this argument? What do you know about the author?
- Where did the argument first appear? Was it published in a book, newspaper, magazine, or electronic source?
- What else has been written about the topic or issue? Is the topic new, or has it been written about for many years? *ethos*
- What do you expect after reading the title?

2. What does the argument say? *~~good~~ summary*

- What is the topic or issue?
- What is the writer's thesis or overall point?
- What reasons or evidence does the writer offer?
- Who are the intended readers? What does the writer assume the readers know and believe?

3. Can you trust the writer? *ETHOS*

- Does the writer have the necessary knowledge and experience to write about this subject? You may need to do some research to find out more about the author.
- Do you detect a bias in the writer's position? Does the writer seem to favor one side or another?
- Are the facts relevant to the writer's claims? Are the facts correct? Where did the facts come from?
- Does the writer refer to expert opinions or research about this subject? Are these sources reliable?
- Does the writer acknowledge alternative views and unfavorable evidence? Does the writer deal fairly with the views of others?

4. How does the argument work?

- How is the piece of writing organized? How are the major points arranged?
- How does the writer conclude his or her argument? Does the conclusion follow logically from the evidence the writer offers? What impression does the reader take away?
- How would you characterize the writing style? Describe the language that the writer uses.
- How does the writer represent herself or himself?
- Is the page design attractive and correctly formatted? Are photos, tables, and graphics well integrated into the text and clearly labeled?

Finding Good Reasons

HAS THE INTERNET MADE EVERYONE WRITERS?

Before the Internet was invented, readers had to make some effort to respond to writers by writing to them directly, sending a letter to the editor, or even scribbling or spray-painting a response. The Internet has changed the interaction between writers and readers by allowing readers to respond easily to writers and, in turn, turning readers into writers. Look, for example, at Amazon.com. An incredible amount of writing surrounds any best-selling book—often an author's Web site and blog, newspaper reviews, and over a hundred readers' reviews. Or read a political, sports, culture, fashion, or parenting blog and the comments by readers of those blogs. Think about how the Internet has changed the relationship between readers and writers.

To find a blog that interests you, use a blog search engine such as Bloglines (www. bloglines. com), Google Blog Search (blogsearch.google.com), IceRocket (blogs.icerocket.com), or Technorati (www. technorati. com).

Write about it

1. Using a blog search engine or an online newspaper, find a blog by an author, politician, or news columnist. Answer as many of the questions for critical reading on page 23 as you can.

2. Write a summary of the blog entry.

3. What kinds of reasons do blog writers give for their responses to what they read?

4. How are blogs and online book reviews like or unlike traditional book reviews in print?

Annotating what you read

Using annotating strategies will make the effort you put into reading more rewarding.

- **Mark major points and key concepts.** Sometimes major points are indicated by headings, but often you will need to locate them.
- **Connect with your experience.** Think about your own experiences and how they match up or don't match up with what you are reading.
- **Connect passages.** Notice how ideas connect to each other. Draw lines and arrows. If an idea connects to something from a few pages earlier, write a note in the margin with the page number.
- **Ask questions.** Note anything that puzzles you, including words you don't know and need to look up.

The passage below is from Nell Irvin Painter's *Creating Black Americans: African-American History and Its Meanings, 1619 to the Present* (2006). Painter argues that while history and culture connect African Americans to Africa, the identity of African Americans is a New World identity. Painter uses the term *African Diaspora* to refer to the dispersion of African people from their native lands in Africa.

Definition: African Americans are a new people born in the Western Hemisphere

language as indicator

The three centuries separating African Americans from their immigrant ancestors profoundly influenced their identity. A strong case can be made for seeing African Americans as a new, Creole people, that is, as a people born and forged in the Western Hemisphere. Language provides the most obvious indicator: people of African descent in the Diaspora do not speak languages of Africa as their mother tongue. For the most part, they speak *Look up* Portuguese, Spanish, English, and French as a mother tongue, although millions speak Creole languages (such as Haitian Creole and South Carolinian Gullah) that combine African grammars and English vocabulary. As the potent engine of culture, language influences thought, psychology, and education. Language boundaries now divide descendants whose African ancestors may have been family and close neighbors speaking the same language. One descendant in Nashville, Tennessee, may not understand the Portuguese of her distant cousin now living in Bahia, Brazil. Today, with immigrants from Africa forming an increasing proportion of people calling themselves African American, the woman in Nashville might herself be an African immigrant and speak an African language that neither her black neighbors in Tennessee nor her distant cousin in Brazil can understand. Religion, another crucial aspect of culture, distinguishes the different peoples of the African Diaspora. Millions of Africans are Muslims, for instance, while most African

example—different languages divide Af Ams from African ancestor

religion another indicator

example—Af Ams would not agree to be judged by Muslim law

Americans see themselves as Christian. They would hardly agree to place themselves under the Sharia, the legal system inspired by the Koran, which prevails in Northern Nigeria.

Mapping

Drawing a map of a text can help you to identify key points and to understand the relationships among concepts. Below is a map of the passage by Nell Irvin Painter.

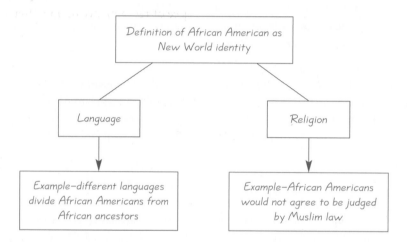

Recognize Fallacies

Just as important as understanding the structure of an argument is recognizing where it goes off track. To be convincing, good reasons rely on evidence that readers will accept as valid. Often this evidence is missing or distorted.

Recognizing where good reasons go off track is one of the most important aspects of critical reading. What passes as political discourse is often filled with claims that lack evidence or substitute emotions for evidence. Such faulty reasoning often contains one or more **logical fallacies**. For example, politicians know that the public is outraged when the price of gasoline goes up, and they try to score political points by accusing oil companies of price gouging. It sounds good to angry voters—and it may well be true—but unless the politician defines what *price gouging* means and provides evidence that oil companies are guilty, the argument has no more validity than children calling each other bad names on the playground.

Following are some of the more common fallacies.

Fallacies of logic

- **Begging the question** *Politicians are inherently dishonest because no honest person would run for public office.* The fallacy of begging the question occurs when the claim is restated and passed off as evidence.

- **Either-or** *Either we eliminate the regulation of businesses or else profits will suffer.* The either-or fallacy suggests that there are only two choices in a complex situation. Rarely, if ever, is this the case. Consider, for example, the case of Enron, which was unregulated but went bankrupt.

- **False analogies** *Japan quit fighting in 1945 when we dropped nuclear bombs on them. We should use nuclear weapons against other countries.* Analogies always depend on the degree of resemblance of one situation to another. In this case, the analogy fails to recognize that circumstances today are very different from those in 1945. Many countries now possess nuclear weapons, and we know their use could harm the entire world.

- **Hasty generalization** *We have been in a drought for three years; that's a sure sign of climate change.* A hasty generalization is a broad claim made on the basis of a few occurrences. Climate cycles occur regularly over spans of a few years. Climate trends, however, must be observed over centuries.

- **Non sequitur** *A university that can raise a billion dollars from alumni should not have to raise tuition.* A non sequitur (a Latin term meaning "it does not follow") ties together two unrelated ideas. In this case, the argument fails to recognize that the money for capital campaigns is often donated for special purposes such as athletic facilities and is not part of a university's general revenue.

- **Oversimplification** *No one would run stop signs if we had a mandatory death penalty for doing it.* This claim may be true, but the argument would be unacceptable to most citizens. More complex, if less definitive, solutions are called for.

- ***Post hoc* fallacy** *The stock market goes down when the AFC wins the Super Bowl in even years.* The *post hoc* fallacy (from the Latin *post hoc, ergo propter hoc,* which means "after this, therefore because of this") assumes that events that follow in time have a causal relationship.

- **Rationalization** *I could have finished my paper on time if my printer had been working.* People frequently come up with excuses and weak explanations for their own and others' behavior. These excuses often avoid actual causes.

- **Slippery slope** *We shouldn't grant citizenship to illegal immigrants now living in the United States because no one will want to obey our laws.* The slippery slope fallacy maintains that one thing inevitably will cause something else to happen.

Fallacies of emotion and language

- **Bandwagon appeals** *It doesn't matter if I copy a paper off the Web because everyone else does.* This argument suggests that everyone is doing it, so why shouldn't you? But on close examination, it may be that everyone really isn't doing it—and in any case, it may not be the right thing to do.

- **Name calling** Name calling is frequent in politics and among competing groups. People level accusations using names such as *radical, tax-and-spend liberal, racist, fascist, right-wing ideologue.* Unless these terms are carefully defined, they are meaningless.

- **Polarization** *Feminists are all man haters.* Like name calling, polarization exaggerates positions and groups by representing them as extreme and divisive.

- **Straw man** *Environmentalists won't be satisfied until not a single human being is allowed to enter a national park.* A straw man argument is a diversionary tactic that sets up another's position in a way that can be easily rejected. In fact, only a small percentage of environmentalists would make an argument even close to this one.

Respond as a Writer

Engage in a dialogue with what you read. Talk back to the author. If you are having trouble understanding a difficult section, read it aloud and listen to the author's voice. Hearing something read will sometimes help you to imagine being in a conversation with the author.

Making notes

As you read, write down your thoughts. Something you read may remind you of something else. Jot that down.

- Imagine that the author is with you. Which of the writer's points would you respond to in person?
- What questions would you like to ask the author? You may need to look up the answers to these questions.
- What ideas might you develop or interpret differently?

Writing a summary

A useful way to distill information from a reading is to summarize it. When you summarize, you state the major ideas of an entire source or part of a source in your own words. Most summaries are much shorter than the original because they include just the main points, not most of the examples and supporting material. The keys to writing a good summary are identifying the main points and then putting those points into your own words. Note that if you use the exact words from a source in your summary, you must enclose those words in quotation marks.

Example summary

Nell Irvin Painter argues that while African Americans draw much of their heritage from Africa, the concept of an African American identity was forged in the New World. She points out that among the many differences between Africans and their descendants outside Africa, the differences of language and religion are crucial to African American identity.

Building on what you read

A reading journal can help you both as a reader and as a writer. In a reading journal, you'll have a record of your thoughts that you can return to later, a space where you can connect ideas from different readings, and a place to test ideas that you can later develop for a writing assignment.

Example reading journal

Painter writes, "Hip-hop's preoccupation with authentic blackness reflects the difficulty of characterizing African Americans as a whole" (343). I agree because there is much more than hip-hop in the larger African American community and hip-hop has become a world youth culture well established in Britain, France, the Caribbean, Africa, Latin America, Asia—indeed, just about everywhere.

But hip-hop culture also helps to confirm her main point that African American identity has been created in the New World. Think about breakdancing, which is a major part of hip-hop culture that developed on sidewalks, playgrounds, and basketball courts. Like jazz and the blues, breakdancing grew up in African American communities in the United States and spread around the world rather than coming from somewhere else.

3

Finding Arguments

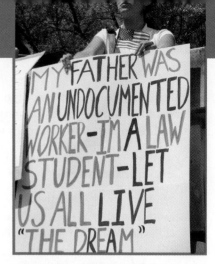

Slogans and bumper stickers are meant to persuade, but technically they are not arguments because they lack reasons. Nevertheless, you can often supply a reason for a claim made on a sign or bumper sticker. What reason might the demonstrator give to support her claim LET US ALL LIVE "THE DREAM"?

Many people think of the term *argument* as a synonym for *debate*. College courses and professional careers, however, require a different kind of argument—one that, most of the time, is cooler in emotion and more elaborate in detail than oral debate. At first glance an argument in writing doesn't seem to have much in common with debate. But the basic elements and ways of reasoning used in written arguments are similar to those we use in everyday conversations.

Find Arguments in Everyday Conversations

Let's look at an example of a conversation. When the pain in his abdomen didn't go away, Jeff knew he had torn something while carrying his friend's heavy speakers up a flight of stairs. He went to the student health center and called his friend Maria when he returned home.

JEFF: I have good news and bad news. The pain is a minor hernia that can be repaired with day surgery. The bad news is that the fee we pay for the health center doesn't cover hospital visits. We should have health coverage.

MARIA: Jeff, you didn't buy the extra insurance. Why should you get it for nothing?

JEFF: Because health coverage is a right.

MARIA: No it's not. Everyone doesn't have health insurance.

JEFF: Well, in some other countries like Canada, Germany, and Britain, they do.

MARIA: Yes, and people who live in those countries pay a bundle in taxes for the government-provided insurance.

JEFF: It's not fair in this country because some people have health insurance and others don't.

MARIA: Jeff, face the facts. You could have bought the extra insurance. Instead you chose to buy a new car.

JEFF: It would be better if the university provided health insurance because students could graduate in four years. I'm going to have to get a second job and drop out for a semester to pay for the surgery.

MARIA: Neat idea, but who's going to pay for it?

JEFF: OK, all students should be required to pay for health insurance as part of their general fee. Most students are healthy, and it wouldn't cost that much more.

In this discussion, Jeff starts out by making a **claim** that students should have health coverage. Maria immediately asks him why students should not have to pay for health insurance. She wants a **reason** to accept his claim.

Distinguishing arguments from other kinds of persuasion

Scholars who study argument maintain that an argument must have a claim and one or more reasons to support that claim. Something less might be persuasive, but it isn't an argument.

A bumper sticker that says NO TOLL ROADS is a claim, but it is not an argument because the statement lacks a reason. Many reasons support an argument against building toll roads.

- We don't need new roads but should build light-rail instead.
- We should raise the gas tax to pay for new roads.
- We should use gas tax revenue only for roads rather than using it for other purposes.

When a claim has a reason attached, then it becomes an argument.

The basics of arguments

A reason is typically offered in a **because clause,** a statement that begins with the word *because* and that provides a supporting reason for the claim. Jeff's first attempt is to argue that students should have health insurance *because* health insurance is a right.

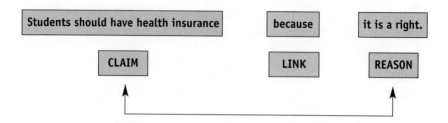

The word *because* signals a link between the reason and the claim. Every argument that is more than a shouting match or a simple assertion has to have one or more reasons. Just having a reason for a claim, however, doesn't mean that the audience will be convinced. When Jeff tells Maria that students have a right to health insurance, Maria replies that students don't have that right. Maria will accept Jeff's claim only if she accepts that his reason supports his claim. Maria challenges Jeff's links and keeps asking "So what?" For her, Jeff's reasons are not good reasons.

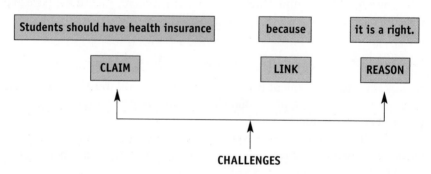

By the end of this short discussion, Jeff has begun to build an argument. He has had to come up with another claim to support his main claim: All students should be required to pay for health insurance as part of their general fee. If he is to convince Maria, he will probably have to provide a series of claims that she will accept as linked to his primary claim. He will also need to find evidence to support these claims.

Benjamin Franklin observed, "So convenient a thing it is to be a rational creature, since it enables us to find or make a reason for every thing one has a mind to do." It is not hard to think of reasons. What *is* difficult is to convince your audience that your reasons are good reasons. In a conversation, you get immediate feedback that tells you whether your listener agrees or disagrees. When you are writing, you usually don't have someone you can question immediately. Consequently, you have to (1) be more specific about what you are claiming, (2) connect with the values you hold in common with your readers, and (3) anticipate what questions and objections your readers might have, if you are going to convince someone who doesn't agree with you or know what you know already.

When you write an argument, imagine a reader like Maria who is going to listen carefully to what you have to say but who is not going to agree with you automatically. Readers like Maria will expect the following.

- A **claim** that is interesting and makes them want to find out more about what you have to say
- At least one **good reason** that makes your claim worth taking seriously
- Some **evidence** that the good reason or reasons are valid
- Some acknowledgment of the **opposing views** and **limitations** of the claim

The remainder of this chapter will guide you through the process of finding a topic, making a claim, finding good reasons and evidence, and anticipating objections to your claim.

Find a Topic That Interests You

When your instructor gives you a writing assignment, look closely at what you are asked to do. Assignments typically contain a great deal of information, and you have to sort through that information. First, circle all the instructions about the length, the due date, the format, the grading criteria, and anything else about the production and conventions of the assignment. This information is important to you, but it doesn't tell you what the paper is supposed to be about.

Reading your assignment

Often your assignment will contain key words such as *analyze, define, evaluate*, or *propose* that will assist you in determining what direction to take. *Analyze* can mean several things. Your instructor might want you to analyze a piece of writing (see Chapter 5), an image (see Chapter 6), or the causes of something (see Chapter 9). *Define* usually means writing a **definition argument,** in which you argue for a definition based on the criteria you set out (see Chapter 8). *Evaluate* indicates an **evaluation argument,** in which you argue that something is good, bad, the best, or the worst in its class according to criteria that you set out (see Chapter 10). An assignment that contains the instructions *Write about an issue using your personal experience* indicates a **narrative argument** (see Chapter 11), while one that says *Take a position in regard to a reading* might lead you to write a **rebuttal argument**

WHAT IS NOT ARGUABLE

Statements of fact. Most facts can be verified by doing research. But even simple facts can sometimes be argued. For example, Mount Everest is usually acknowledged to be the highest mountain in the world at 29,028 feet above sea level. But if the total height of a mountain from base to summit is the measure, then the volcano Mauna Loa in Hawaii is the highest mountain in the world. Although the top of Mauna Loa is 13,667 feet above sea level, the summit is 31,784 above the ocean floor. Thus the "fact" that Mount Everest is the highest mountain on the earth depends on a definition of *highest.* You could argue for this definition.

Claims of personal taste. Your favorite food and your favorite color are examples of personal taste. If you hate fresh tomatoes, no one can convince you that you actually like them. But many claims of personal taste turn out to be value judgments using arguable criteria. For example, if you think that *Alien* is the best science-fiction movie ever made, you can argue that claim using evaluative criteria that other people can consider as good reasons (see Chapter 8). Indeed, you might not even like science fiction and still argue that *Alien* is the best science-fiction movie ever.

Statements of belief or faith. If someone accepts a claim as a matter of religious belief, then for that person, the claim is true and cannot be refuted. Of course, people still make arguments about the existence of God and which religion reflects the will of God. Whenever an audience will not consider an idea, it's possible but very difficult to construct an argument. Many people claim to have evidence that UFOs exist, but most people refuse to acknowledge that evidence as even being possibly factual.

(see Chapter 12). *Propose* means that you should identify a particular problem and explain why your solution is the best one (see Chapter 13).

If you remain unclear about the purpose of the assignment after reading it carefully, talk with your instructor.

Thinking about what interests you

Your assignment may specify the topic you are to write about. If your assignment gives you a wide range of options and you don't know what to write about, look first at the materials for your course: the readings, your lecture notes, and discussion boards. Think about what subjects came up in class discussion.

If you need to look outside class for a topic, think about what interests you. Subjects we argue about often find us. There are enough of them in daily life. We're late for work or class because the traffic is heavy or the bus doesn't run on time. We can't find a place to park when we get to school or work. We have to negotiate through various bureaucracies for almost anything we do—making an appointment to see a doctor, getting a course added or dropped, or correcting a mistake on a bill. Most of the time we grumble and let it go at that. But sometimes we stick with a subject. Neighborhood groups in cities and towns have been especially effective in getting something done by writing about it—for example, stopping a new road from being built, getting better police and fire protection, and getting a vacant lot turned into a park.

Listing and analyzing issues

A good way to get started is to list possible issues to write about. Make a list of questions that can be answered "YES, because . . ." or "NO, because. . . ." (Following are some lists to get you started.) You'll find out that often before you can make a claim, you first have to analyze exactly what is meant by a phrase like *censorship of the Internet*. Does it mean censorship of the World Wide Web or of everything that is transmitted on the Internet, including private email? To be convincing, you'll have to argue that one thing causes another, for good or bad.

Think about issues that affect your campus, your community, the nation, and the world. Which issues interest you? About which issues could you make a contribution to the larger discussion?

Campus

- Should students be required to pay fees for access to computers on campus?
- Should smoking be banned on campus?
- Should varsity athletes get paid for playing sports that bring in revenue?
- Should admissions decisions be based exclusively on academic achievement?
- Should knowledge of a foreign language be required for all degree plans?
- Should your college or university have a computer literacy requirement?
- Should fraternities be banned from campuses if they are caught encouraging alcohol abuse?

Community

- Should people who ride bicycles and motorcycles be required to wear helmets?
- Should high schools be allowed to search students for drugs at any time?

- Should high schools distribute condoms?
- Should bilingual education programs be eliminated?
- Should the public schools be privatized?
- Should bike lanes be built throughout your community to encourage more people to ride bicycles?
- Should more tax dollars be shifted from building highways to funding public transportation?

Nation/World

- Should driving while talking on a cell phone be banned?
- Should capital punishment be abolished?
- Should the Internet be censored?
- Should the government be allowed to monitor all phone calls and all email to combat terrorism?
- Should handguns be outlawed?
- Should beef and poultry be free of growth hormones?
- Should a law be passed requiring that the parents of teenagers who have abortions be informed?
- Should people who are terminally ill be allowed to end their lives?
- Should the United States punish nations with poor human rights records?

Narrowing a list

1. Put a check beside the issues that look most interesting to write about or the ones that mean the most to you.
2. Put a question mark beside the issues that you don't know very much about. If you choose one of these issues, you will probably have to do in-depth research—by talking to people, by using the Internet, or by going to the library.
3. Select the two or three issues that look most promising. For each issue, make another list:
   - Who is most interested in this issue?
   - Whom or what does this issue affect?
   - What are the pros and cons of this issue? Make two columns. At the top of the left one, write "YES, because." At the top of the right one, write "NO, because."
   - What has been written about this issue? How can you find out what has been written?

Finding a topic on the Web

Online subject directories can help you identify the subtopics of a large, general topic. Try the subject index of your library's online catalog. You'll likely find subtopics listed under large topics. Online encyclopedias, such as Britannica.com, also can be helpful in identifying subtopics.

One of the best Web subject directories for finding arguments is Yahoo's Issues and Causes directory. This directory provides subtopics for major issues and provides links to the Web sites of organizations interested in particular issues.

Yahoo! Issues and Causes directory
(dir.yahoo.com/Society_and_Culture/Issues_and_Causes/)

Find a Claim by Exploring

Once you have identified a general topic, the next step is to explore that topic to find a possible claim. You don't have to decide exactly what to write about at this stage. Your goal is to find out how much you already know and what you need to learn more about. Experienced writers use several strategies for exploring a topic.

Freewriting

The goal of **freewriting** is to write as quickly as you can without stopping for a set time—usually five or ten minutes. Set a timer and then write as fast as you can, even if you wander off the topic. Don't stop to correct mistakes. Write the same sentence again if you get stuck momentarily. The constant flow of words will generate ideas, some useful and some not. After you've finished, read what you have written and single out any key ideas.

> *Freewrite on privacy*
>
> *I get so much junk email and junk mail. How did so many people get my email and mail addresses? How is it collected? How does it get passed around? How do I find this out? Friend told me about a question in an interview—they had asked him about personal data but it wasn't about him. A lot of people have the same names. Easy to mix up people. Scary. How could you fix it? Amazon account tracks what I buy. Do they sell that information? What are the laws? Data is sold to the highest bidder. And there are breaches in security where credit card numbers are stolen but people aren't informed.*
>
> *Ideas to Use*
> 1. *The sharing of personal information and mistakes that can result.*
> 2. *The misuse of personal information by corporations.*
> 3. *Breaches in security without people being notified.*

You may want to take one of the ideas you have identified to start another freewrite. After two or three rounds of freewriting, you should begin to identify a claim such as the following.

- There should be federal laws that give people access to the personal information that businesses collect and the opportunity to correct mistakes.
- There should be federal laws that protect the personal data of individuals from being sold to the highest bidder.
- There should be federal laws that make it a crime to conceal breaches of security that expose the personal data of individuals.

Brainstorming

Another method of discovery is to brainstorm. The end result of **brainstorming** is usually a list—sometimes of questions, sometimes of statements. These questions and statements give you ways to develop your topic. A list of questions on secondhand smoke is on page 40.

Finding Good Reasons
ARE TRAFFIC CAMERAS INVADING YOUR PRIVACY?

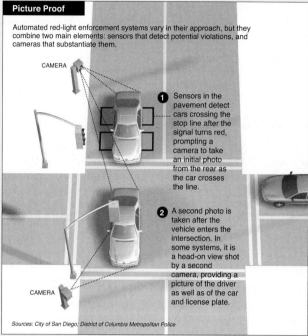

Picture Proof

Automated red-light enforcement systems vary in their approach, but they combine two main elements: sensors that detect potential violations, and cameras that substantiate them.

CAMERA

1 Sensors in the pavement detect cars crossing the stop line after the signal turns red, prompting a camera to take an initial photo from the rear as the car crosses the line.

2 A second photo is taken after the vehicle enters the intersection. In some systems, it is a head-on view shot by a second camera, providing a picture of the driver as well as of the car and license plate.

CAMERA

Sources: City of San Diego; District of Columbia Metropolitan Police

Frank O'Connell/The New York Times

Cameras that photograph the license plates and drivers of vehicles who run red lights are currently in use in 22 U.S. states. Cameras aimed at catching speeders, already common in Europe, are beginning to be installed in U.S. cities as well. Traffic cameras have become money machines for some communities, but they also have provoked intense public opposition and even vandalism—people have spray painted and shot cameras in attempts to disable them.

Write about it

1. How do you feel about using cameras to catch red-light runners? Speeders? People who don't pay parking tickets? Make a list of as many possible topics as you can think of about the use of cameras to scan license plates.

2. Select one of the possible topics. Write it at the top of a sheet of paper, and then write nonstop for five minutes. Don't worry about correctness. If you get stuck, write the same sentence again.

3. When you finish, read what you have written and circle key ideas.

4. Put each key idea on a sticky note. If you think of other ideas, write them on separate sticky notes. Then look at your sticky notes. Put a star on the central idea. Put the ideas that are related next to each other. You now have the beginning of an idea map.

- How much of a risk is secondhand smoke?
- What are the effects of secondhand smoke on children?
- How do the risks of secondhand smoke compare to other kinds of pollution?
- Which states ban all exposure to secondhand smoke? exposure in restaurants? exposure in the workplace?
- Who opposes banning exposure to secondhand smoke?

Answering such questions can lead you to potential claims such as these.

- Smoking should be prohibited in all workplaces, including restaurants and bars, to prevent health risks to nonsmokers.
- Because over half the children under five years of age in the United States live in households with at least one adult smoker, a massive education campaign should target these adults about the harm they are inflicting on their children.

Making an idea map

When you have an ample amount of information about a topic, you need to begin making connections among the facts, data, and ideas you have collected. One method of assembling ideas is an **idea map**, which describes visually how the many aspects of a particular issue relate to each other. Idea maps are useful because you can see everything at once and make connections among the different aspects of an issue—definitions, causes, proposed solutions, and opposing points of view.

A good way to get started is to write down ideas on sticky notes. Then you can move the sticky notes around until you figure out which ideas fit together. Constructing an idea map will help you identify claims and begin to think about reasons that can support those claims.

Find a Claim by Reading

Much college writing draws on and responds to sources—books, articles, reports, and other material written by other people. Every significant issue discussed in today's world has an extensive history of discussion involving many people and various points of view. Before you formulate a claim about a significant issue, you need to become familiar with the conversation that's already happening by reading about it.

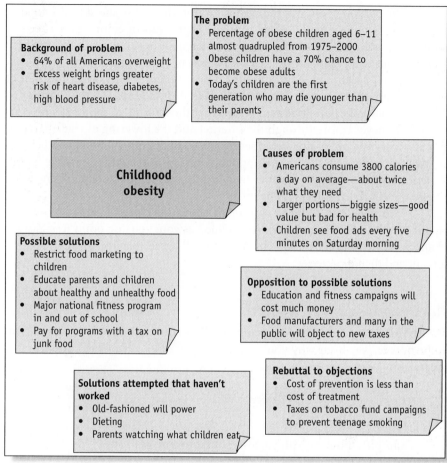

Idea map on childhood obesity

One of the most controversial and talked-about subjects in recent years is the outsourcing of white-collar and manufacturing jobs to low-wage nations. Since 2000 an estimated 400,000 to 500,000 American jobs each year have gone to cheap overseas labor markets. The Internet has made this migration of jobs possible, allowing companies to outsource highly skilled jobs in fields such as software development, data storage, and even examining X-rays and MRI scans along with low-skilled jobs.

You may have read about this or another complex and controversial topic in one of your courses. Just as in a conversation with several people who hold different views, you may agree with some people, disagree with some, and with others agree with some of their ideas up to a point but then disagree.

CNN commentator Lou Dobbs has been sharply critical of outsourcing. In *Exporting America: Why Corporate Greed Is Shipping American Jobs Overseas*

(2006), Dobbs blames large corporations for putting profits ahead of the good of the nation. He accuses both Republicans and Democrats of ignoring the effects of a massive trade deficit and the largest national debt in American history, which Dobbs claims will eventually destroy the American way of life.

Thomas Friedman, columnist for *The New York Times*, takes a different viewpoint on outsourcing in *The World Is Flat: A Brief History of the Twenty-first Century* (2006). By *flat,* Friedman means that the nations of the world are connected like never before through the Internet and the lowering of trade barriers, putting every nation in direct competition with all the others. Friedman believes that outsourcing is not only unstoppable, but also desirable. He argues that Americans need to adapt to the new reality and rethink our system of education, or else we will be left hopelessly behind.

If you decide to write an argument about the issue of outsourcing, you might use either Dobbs's or Friedman's book as your starting point in making a claim. You could begin by using either book to disagree, to agree, or to agree up to a point and then disagree.

No: Disagreeing with a source

It's easy to disagree by simply saying an idea is dumb, but readers expect you to be persuasive about why you disagree and to offer reasons to support your views.

> X claims that _____, but this view is mistaken because _____.

Example claim: Arguing against outsourcing resulting from free-trade policies

> Thomas Friedman claims that the world is "flat," giving a sense of a level playing field for all, but it is absurd to think that the millions of starving children in the world have opportunities similar to those in affluent countries who pay $100 for basketball shoes made by the starving children.

Example claim: Arguing in favor of outsourcing resulting from free-trade policies

> Lou Dobbs is a patriotic American who recognizes the suffering of manufacturing workers in industries like steel and automobiles, but he neglects that the major cause of the loss of manufacturing jobs in the United States and China alike is increased productivity—the 40 hours of labor necessary to produce a car just a few years ago has now been reduced to 15.

Yes: Agreeing with a source with an additional point

Sources should not make your argument for you. With sources that support your position, indicate exactly how they fit into your argument with an additional point.

I agree with _____ and will make the additional point that _____.

Example claim: Arguing against outsourcing resulting from free trade policies

Lou Dobbs's outcry against the outsourcing of American jobs also has a related argument: We are dependent not only on foreign oil, but also on foreign clothing, foreign electronics, foreign tools, foreign toys, foreign cars and trucks—indeed, just about everything—which is quickly eroding the world leadership of the United States.

Example claim: Arguing in favor of outsourcing resulting from free trade policies

Thomas Friedman's claim that the Internet enables everyone to become an entrepreneur is demonstrated by thousands of Americans, including my aunt, who could retire early because she developed an income stream by buying jeans and children's clothes at garage sales and selling them to people around the world on eBay.

Yes, but: Agreeing and disagreeing simultaneously with a source

Incorporating sources is not a matter of simply agreeing or disagreeing with them. Often you will agree with a source up to a point, but you will come to a different conclusion. Or you may agree with the conclusions, but not agree with the reasons put forth.

I agree with _____ up to a point, but I disagree with the conclusion _____ because _____.

Example claim: Qualifying the argument against outsourcing resulting from free-trade policies

Lou Dobbs accurately blames our government for giving multinational corporations tax breaks for exporting jobs rather than regulating the loss of millions of jobs, but the real problem lies in the enormous appetite of Americans for inexpensive consumer products like HD televisions that is supported by borrowing money from overseas to the point that our dollar has plummeted in value.

Example claim: Qualifying the argument in favor of outsourcing resulting from free-trade policies

Thomas Friedman's central claim that the world is being "flattened" by globalization and there is not much we can do to stop it is essentially correct, but he neglects the social costs of globalization around the world, where the banner of free trade has been the justification for devastating the environment, destroying workers' rights and the rights of indigenous peoples, and ignoring laws passed by representative governments.

Find Good Reasons

A good reason works because it includes a valid link to your claim. Your readers are almost like a jury that passes judgment on your good reasons. If they accept them and cannot think of other, more compelling good reasons that oppose your position, you will convince them.

Most good reasons derive from mulling things over "reasonably" or, to use the technical term, from logos. *Logos* refers to the logic of what you communicate; in fact, logos is the root of our modern word *logic*. Good reasons are thus commonly associated with logical appeals. Over the years, rhetoricians have devised questions to help speakers and writers find good reasons to support their arguments.

Use the questions in the box on the next two pages to guide you in thinking about the good reasons you can use to develop your argument. Get in the habit of asking these questions every time you are asked to write an argument. If one question does not seem to work for you at first, try it again on your next assignment. If you ask the questions systematically, you will probably have more good reasons than you need for your arguments.

Can you argue by definition?

Probably the most powerful kind of good reason is an **argument from definition.** You can think of a definition as a simple statement: _____ *is a* _____. You use these statements all the time. When you need a course to fulfill your social-science requirement, you look at the list of courses that are defined as social-science courses. You find out that the anthropology class you want to take is one of them. It's just as

QUESTIONS FOR FINDING GOOD REASONS

Can you argue by definition—from "the nature of the thing"?

- Can you argue that while many (most) people think X is a Y, X is better thought of as a Z?

  Most people do not think of humans as an endangered species, but small farmers have been successful in comparing their way of life to an endangered species and thus have extended the definition of an endangered species to include themselves.

- Can you argue that while X is a Y, X differs from other Ys and might be thought of as a Z?

  Colleges and universities are similar to public schools in having education as their primary mission, but unlike public schools, colleges and universities receive only part of their operating costs from tax revenues and therefore, like a business, must generate much of their own revenue.

Can you argue from value?

- Can you grade a few examples of the kind of thing you are evaluating as good, better, and best (or bad and worse)?

  There have been lots of great actors in detective films, but none compare to Humphrey Bogart.

- Can you list the features you use to determine whether something is good or bad and then show why one is most important?

  Coach Powers taught me a great deal about the skills and strategy of playing tennis, but most of all, she taught me that the game is fun.

Can you compare or contrast?

- Can you think of items, events, or situations that are similar or dissimilar to the one you are writing about?

  We should require a foreign language for all students at our college because our main competitor does not have such a requirement.

- Can you distinguish why your subject is different from one usually thought of as similar?

(continued)

While poor people are often lumped in with the unemployed and those on welfare, the majority of poor people do work in low-paying jobs.

Can you argue from consequence?

- Can you argue that good things will happen or that bad things will be avoided if a certain course of action is followed?

  Eliminating all income tax deductions would save every taxpayer many hours and would create a system of taxation that does not reward people for cheating.

- Can you argue that while there were obvious causes of Y, Y would not have occurred had it not been for X?

  A 17-year-old driver is killed when her car skids across the grass median of an interstate highway and collides with oncoming traffic. Even though a slick road and excessive speed were the immediate causes, the driver would be alive today if the median had had a concrete barrier.

- Can you argue for an alternative cause rather than the one many people assume?

  Politicians take credit for reducing the violent crime rate because of "get-tough" police policies, but in fact, the rate of violent crime is decreasing because more people are working.

Can you counter objections to your position?

- Can you think of the most likely objections to your claim and turn them into your own good reasons?

  High school administrators might object to requiring computer literacy because of cost, but schools can now lease computers and put them on a statewide system at a cost less than they now pay for textbooks.

- Can the reverse, or opposite, of an opposing claim be argued?

  A proposed expressway through a city is supposed to help traffic, but it also could make traffic worse by encouraging more people to drive to the city.

important when _____ *is not a* _____. Suppose you are taking College Algebra, which is a math course taught by the math department, yet it doesn't count for the math requirement. The reason it doesn't count is because College Algebra is not defined as a college-level math class. So you have to enroll next semester in Calculus I.

Many definitions are not nearly as clear-cut as the math requirement. If you want to argue that figure skaters are athletes, you will need to define what an athlete is. You start thinking. An athlete competes in an activity, but that definition alone is too broad, since many competitions do not require physical activity. Thus, an athlete must participate in a competitive physical activity and must train for it. But that definition is still not quite narrow enough, because soldiers also train for competitive physical activity. You decide to add that the activity must be a sport and that it must require special competence and precision. Your **because clause** turns out as follows: *Figure skaters are athletes because true athletes train for and compete in physical sporting competitions that require special competence and precision.*

If you can get your audience to accept your definitions, you've gone a long way toward convincing them of the validity of your claim. That is why the most controversial issues in our culture—abortion, affirmative action, gay rights, pornography, women's rights, privacy rights, gun control, the death penalty—are argued from definition. Is abortion a crime or a medical procedure? Is pornography protected by the First Amendment, or is it a violation of women's rights? Is the death penalty just or cruel and inhuman? You can see from these examples that definitions often rely on deeply held beliefs.

Because people have strong beliefs about controversial issues, they often don't care about the practical consequences. Arguing that it is much cheaper to execute prisoners who have been convicted of first-degree murder than to keep them in prison for life does not convince those who believe that it is morally wrong to kill. (See Chapter 8.)

Can you argue from value?

A special kind of argument from definition, one that often implies consequences, is the **argument from value**. You can support your claim with a because clause (or several of them) that includes a sense of evaluation. Arguments from value follow from claims like _____ *is a good* _____, or _____ *is not a good* _____.

Evaluation arguments usually proceed from the presentation of certain criteria. These criteria come from the definitions of good and bad, of poor and not so poor, that prevail in a given case. A great burger fulfills certain criteria; so does an outstanding movie, an excellent class, or the best laptop in your price range. Sometimes the criteria are straightforward, as in the burger example. A great burger has to have tasty meat—tender and without gristle, fresh, never frozen—a fresh bun that is the right size, and your favorite condiments.

But if you are buying a laptop computer and want to play the latest games along with your school tasks, you need to do some homework. For realistic graphics the best laptop will have a fast chip, preferably a dual core system. It will be equipped with a wireless modem, so you have access to the Internet at wireless hot spots. The battery life should be at least two hours, the hard drive should be large enough for your needs, the construction should be sturdy, and the warranty should cover the computer for at least three years.

The keys for evaluation arguments are finding the appropriate criteria and convincing your readers that those criteria are the right criteria (see Chapter 10).

Can you compare or contrast?

Evaluation arguments can generate comparisons often enough. But even if they don't generate comparisons, your argument might profit if you get in the habit of thinking in comparative terms—in terms of what things are like or unlike the topic you are discussing. **Claims of comparisons** and **claims of contrast** take the form _____ *is like* _____ or _____ *is not like* _____. If you are having trouble coming up with good reasons, think of comparisons that will help your readers agree with you.

A particular kind of comparison is an analogy. An **analogy** is an extended comparison—one that is developed over several sentences or paragraphs for explanatory or persuasive purposes. Analogies take different forms. A historical analogy compares something that is going on now with a similar case in the past. One of the most frequently used historical analogies is a comparison of a current situation in which one country attacks or threatens another with Germany's seizing Czechoslovakia in 1938 and then invading Poland in 1939, which started World War II. The difficulty with this analogy is that circumstances today are not the same as those in 1939, and it is easy to point out how the analogy fails.

Other analogies make literal comparisons. A literal analogy is a comparison between current situations in which you argue that what is true or works in one situation should be true or should work in another. Most advanced nations provide basic health care to all their citizens either free or at minimal charge. All citizens of Canada are covered for basic medical procedures by the same comprehensive health care system, which is free for both rich and poor. (Canadians pay individually for drugs and adult dental care.) Even though citizens of the United States pay the most expensive health care bills on the planet, Canadians are healthier and live longer than their southern neighbors.

The Canadian analogy has failed to convince members of the U.S. Congress to vote for a similar system in the United States. Opponents of adopting the Canadian system in the United States argue that Canadians are often put on long waiting lists for care, and they lack choice of providers. These opponents believe that the best care can be obtained for the lowest cost if health care is treated like any other service and consumers decide what they are willing to pay. Comparisons can always work both ways.

Analogies are especially valuable when you are trying to explain a concept to a willing listener or reader, but analogies are far from foolproof if the reader does not agree with you from the outset. Using an analogy can be risky if the entire argument depends on the reader's accepting it.

Can you argue from consequence?

Another powerful source of good reasons comes from considering the possible consequences of your position: Can you sketch out the good things that will follow from your position? Can you establish that certain bad things will be avoided if your position is adopted? If so, you will have other good reasons to use.

Causal arguments take the basic form of _____ *causes* _____ (or _____ *does not cause* _____). Very often, causal arguments are more complicated, taking the form _____ *causes* _____ *which, in turn, causes* _____ and so on. In Chapter 1 we describe how *Silent Spring* makes powerful arguments from consequence. Rachel Carson's primary claim is that *DDT should not be sprayed on a massive scale because it will poison animals and people.* The key to her argument is the causal chain that explains how animals and people are poisoned. Carson describes how nothing exists alone in nature. When a potato field is sprayed with DDT, some of that poison is absorbed by the skin of the potatoes and some washes into the groundwater, where it contaminates drinking water. Other poisonous residue is absorbed into streams, where it is ingested by insect larvae, which in turn are eaten by fish. Fish are eaten by other fish, which are then eaten by waterfowl and people. At each stage, the poisons become more concentrated. (See Chapter 9.)

Proposal arguments are future-oriented arguments from consequence. In a proposal argument, you cannot stop with naming good reasons; you also have to show that these consequences would follow from the idea or course of action that you are arguing. For example, if you are proposing designated lanes for bicycles on the streets of your city, you must argue that they will encourage more people to ride bicycles to work and school, reducing air pollution and traffic congestion for everyone. (See Chapter 13.)

Can you counter objections to your position?

Another good way to find convincing good reasons is to think about possible objections to your position. If you can imagine how your audience might counter or respond to your argument, you will probably include in your argument precisely the points that will address your readers' particular needs and objections. If you are successful, your readers will be convinced that you are right. You've no doubt had the experience of mentally saying to a writer in the course of your reading, "Yeah, but what about this other idea?"—only to have the writer address precisely this objection.

You can impress your readers if you've thought about why anyone would oppose your position and exactly how that opposition would be expressed. If you are writing a proposal argument for a computer literacy requirement for all high school graduates, you might think about why anyone would object, since computers are becoming increasingly important to our jobs and lives. What will the practical objections be? What about philosophical ones? Why hasn't such a requirement been put in place already? By asking such questions in your own arguments, you are likely to develop robust because clauses.

Sometimes, writers pose rhetorical questions such as "You might say, 'But won't paying for computers for all students make my taxes go up?'" Stating objections explicitly can be effective if you make the objections as those of a reasonable person with an alternative point of view. But if the objections you state are ridiculous ones, then you risk being accused of setting up a **straw man**—that is, making the position opposing your own so simplistic that no one would likely identify with it. (See Chapter 12.)

Find Evidence to Support Good Reasons

Good reasons are essential ingredients of good arguments, but they don't do the job alone. You must support or verify good reasons with evidence. **Evidence** consists of hard data, examples, personal experiences, episodes, or tabulations of episodes (known as statistics) that are seen as relevant to the good reasons you are putting forward. Thus, a writer of arguments puts forward not only claims and good reasons but also evidence that those good reasons are true.

How much supporting evidence should you supply? How much evidence is enough? As is usual in the case of rhetoric, the best answer is, "It depends." If a reader is likely to find one of your good reasons hard to believe, then you should be aggressive in offering support. You should present detailed evidence in a patient and painstaking way. As one presenting an argument, you have a responsibility not just to *state* a case but to *make* a case with evidence. Arguments that are unsuccessful tend to fail not because of a shortage of good reasons; more often, they fail because the reader doesn't agree that there is enough evidence to support the good reason that is being presented.

If your good reason isn't especially controversial, you probably should not belabor it. Think of your own experiences as a reader. How often do you recall saying to yourself, as you read a passage or listened to a speaker, "OK! OK! I get the point! Don't keep piling up all of this evidence for me because I don't want it or need it." However, such a reaction is rare, isn't it? By contrast, how often do you recall muttering under your breath, "How can you say that? What evidence do you have to back it up?" When in doubt, err on the side of offering too much evidence. It's an error that is seldom made and not often criticized.

When a writer doesn't provide satisfactory evidence to support a because clause, readers might feel that there has been a failure in the reasoning process. In fact, in your previous courses in writing and speaking, you may have learned about various fallacies associated with faulty arguments (pages 27–28).

Strictly speaking, there is nothing false about these so-called logical fallacies. The fallacies most often refer to failures in providing evidence; when you don't provide enough good evidence to convince your audience, you might be accused of committing a fallacy in reasoning. You will usually avoid such accusations if the evidence that you cite is both *relevant* and *sufficient*.

Relevance refers to the appropriateness of the evidence to the case at hand. Some kinds of evidence are seen as more relevant than others for particular audiences. On the one hand, in science and industry, personal testimony is seen as having limited relevance, while experimental procedures and controlled observations have far more credibility. Compare someone who defends the use of a particular piece of computer software because "it worked for me" with someone who defends it because "according to a journal article published last month, 84 percent of the users of the software were satisfied or very satisfied with it." On the other hand, in writing to the general public on controversial issues such as gun control, personal experience is often considered more relevant than other kinds of data.

Sufficiency refers to the amount of evidence cited. Sometimes a single piece of evidence or a single instance will carry the day if it is especially compelling in some way—if it represents the situation well or makes a point that isn't particularly controversial. More often, people expect more than one piece of evidence if they are to be convinced of something. Convincing readers that they should approve a statewide computer literacy requirement for all high school graduates will require much more evidence than the story of a single graduate who succeeded with her computer skills. You will likely need statistical evidence for such a broad proposal.

If you anticipate that your audience might not accept your evidence, face the situation squarely. First, think carefully about the argument you are presenting. If you cannot cite adequate evidence for your assertions, perhaps those assertions must be modified or qualified in some way. If you remain convinced of your assertions, then think about doing more research to come up with additional evidence.

4

Drafting and Revising Arguments

People frequently revise things that they own. What objects have you revised?

Writing is not an assembly-line process of finding ideas, writing a draft, and revising, editing, and proofreading the draft, all in that order. While you write and revise you will often think of additional reasons to support your position. Likely you will work through your paper or project in multiple drafts, strengthening your content, organization, and readability in each successive draft.

State and Evaluate Your Thesis

Once you have identified a topic and have a good sense of how to develop it, the next critical step is to write a **working thesis.** Your **thesis** states your main claim. Much writing that you will do in college and later in your career will require an explicit thesis, usually placed near the beginning.

Focusing your thesis

The thesis can make or break your paper. If the thesis is too broad, you cannot do justice to the argument. Who wouldn't wish for fewer traffic accidents, better medical care, more effective schools, or a cleaner environment? Simple solutions for these complex problems are unlikely.

Stating something that is obvious to everyone isn't an arguable thesis. Don't settle for easy answers. When a topic is too broad, a predictable thesis often results. Narrow your focus and concentrate on the areas where you have the most questions. Those are likely the areas where your readers will have the most questions too.

The opposite problem is less common: a thesis that is too narrow. If your thesis simply states a commonly known fact, then it is too narrow. For example, the growth rate of the population in the United States has doubled since 1970 because of increased immigration. The U.S. Census Bureau provides reasonably accurate statistical information, so this claim is not arguable. But the policies that allow increased immigration and the effects of a larger population—more crowding and higher costs of health care, education, and transportation—are arguable.

Not arguable: The population of the United States grew faster in the 1990s than in any previous decade because Congress increased the rate of legal immigration and the government stopped enforcing most laws against illegal immigration in the interior of the country.

Arguable: Allowing a high rate of immigration helps the United States deal with the problems of an increasingly aging society and helps provide funding for millions of Social Security recipients.

Arguable: The increase in the number of visas to foreign workers in technology industries is the major cause of unemployment in those industries.

Evaluating your thesis

Once you have a working thesis, ask these questions:

- Is it arguable?
- Is it specific?
- Is it manageable given your length and time requirements?
- Is it interesting to your intended readers?

Example 1
Sample thesis

> We should take action to resolve the serious traffic problem in our city.

Is it arguable? The thesis is arguable, but it lacks a focus.

Is it specific? The thesis is too broad.

Is it manageable? Transportation is a complex issue. New highways and rail systems are expensive and take many years to build. Furthermore, citizens don't want new roads running through their neighborhoods.

Is it interesting? The topic has the potential to be interesting if the writer can propose a specific solution to a problem that everyone in the city recognizes.

When a thesis is too broad, it needs to be revised to address a specific aspect of an issue. Make the big topic smaller.

Revised thesis

> The existing freight railway that runs through the center of the city should be converted to a passenger railway because this is the cheapest and quickest way to decrease traffic congestion downtown.

Example 2
Sample thesis

> Over 60 percent of Americans play computer games on a regular basis.

Is it arguable? The thesis states a commonly acknowledged fact. It is not arguable.

Is it specific? The thesis is too narrow.

Is it manageable? A known fact is stated in the thesis, so there is little to research. Several surveys report this finding.

Is it interesting? The popularity of video games is well established. Nearly everyone is aware of the trend.

There's nothing original or interesting about stating that Americans love computer games. Think about what is controversial. One debatable topic is how computer games affect children.

Revised thesis

> Computer games are valuable because they improve children's visual attention skills, literacy skills, and computer literacy skills.

Think About Your Readers

Thinking about your readers doesn't mean telling them what they might want to hear. Instead, imagine yourself in a dialogue with your readers. What questions will they likely have? How might you address any potential objections?

Understanding what your readers know—and do not know

Your readers' knowledge of your subject is critical to the success of your argument. If they are not familiar with the background information, they probably won't understand your argument fully. If you know that your readers will be unfamiliar with your subject, you have to supply background information before attempting to convince them of your position. A good tactic is to tie your new information to what your readers already know. Comparisons and analogies can be very helpful in linking old and new information.

Finding Good Reasons
SHOULD DRIVING WHILE TALKING BE BANNED?

In a movement to improve driving safety, four U.S. states and the District of Columbia have passed laws banning the use of handheld cell phones while driving except for emergency workers and people making 911 calls. Several states are considering similar legislation, while others are considering banning cell phones only for drivers aged 18 and younger.

Proponents of the ban point to a National Highway Traffic Safety Administration study, reporting that approximately 25 to 30 percent of motor vehicle crashes—about 1.2 million accidents each year—are caused by driver distraction. Opponents of the ban argue that anything that distracts the driver—eating potato chips, talking with passengers, spilled coffee—can cause an accident. The answer, they say, is driver education.

Write about it

1. Write a thesis arguing in support of a ban on cell phones while driving, against a ban, or in support of a more limited position such as banning cell-phone use for drivers 18 and under.

2. Think about the audience that would likely oppose your position. For example, if you support a ban on talking while driving, think about the likely responses of high school students, salespeople who spend much of their workdays driving from place to place, and workers who receive assignments by phone. What good reasons would convince readers who hold an opposing view?

3. What reasons would people who oppose your position likely offer in response? What counterarguments could you give to answer these objections?

Understanding your readers' attitudes toward you

To get your readers to take you seriously, you must convince them that they can trust you. You need to get them to see you as

- **Concerned:** Readers want you to be committed to your subject. They also expect you to be concerned about them. After all, if you don't care about them, why should they read what you write?
- **Well informed:** Many people ramble on about any subject without knowing anything about it. College writing requires that you do your homework on a subject.
- **Fair:** Many writers look at only one side of an issue. Readers respect objectivity and an unbiased approach.
- **Ethical:** Many writers use only the facts that support their positions and often distort facts and sources. Critical readers often notice what is being left out. Don't try to conceal what doesn't support your position.

Understanding your readers' attitudes toward your subject

People have prior attitudes about controversial issues. You must take these attitudes into consideration as you write or speak. Imagine, for instance, that you are preparing an argument for a guest editorial in your college newspaper. You are advocating that your state government should provide parents with choices between public and private schools. You plan to argue that the tax dollars that now automatically go to public schools should go to private schools if parents so choose. You have evidence that the sophomore-to-senior dropout rate in private schools is less than half the rate in public schools. Furthermore, students from private schools attend college at nearly twice the rate of public-school graduates. You intend to argue that one of the reasons private schools are more successful is that they spend more money on instruction and less on administration. And you believe that school choice speaks to the American desire for personal freedom.

Not everyone on your campus will agree with your position. How might the faculty at your college or university feel about this issue? How about the administrators, the staff, other students, and interested community members who read the student newspaper? What are their attitudes toward public funding of private schools? How are you going to deal with the objection that many students in private schools do better in school because they come from more affluent families?

Even when you write about a much less controversial subject, you must think carefully about your audience's attitudes toward what you have to say or to write. Sometimes your audience may share your attitudes; other times, your audience may be neutral. At still other times, your audience will have attitudes that differ sharply from your own. Anticipate these various attitudes and act accordingly.

If these attitudes are different from yours, you will have to work hard to counter them without insulting your audience.

Organize Your Argument

Asking a series of questions can generate a list of good reasons, but even if you have plenty, you still have to decide which ones to use and in what order to present them. Thinking about your readers' knowledge, attitudes, and values will help you to decide which reasons to present to your audience.

Writing plans often take the form of outlines, either formal outlines or working outlines. A **formal outline** typically begins with the thesis statement, which anchors the entire outline.

Managing the Risks of Nanotechnology While Reaping the Rewards

THESIS: The revolutionary potential of nanotechnology has arrived in an explosion of consumer products, yet our federal government has yet to recognize the potential risks or to fund research to reduce those risks.

I.   Nanotechnology now is in many consumer products.

    A.   The promise of nanotechnology to revolutionize medicine, energy production, and communication is years in the future, but consumer products are here now.

    B.   Nanotechnology is now in clothing, food, sports equipment, medicines, electronics, and cars.

    C.   Experts predict that 15 percent of manufactured products worldwide will contain nanotechnology in 2014.

    D.   The question that hasn't been asked: Is nanotechnology safe?

II.   Americans have little awareness of nanotechnology.

    A.   Companies have stopped mentioning and advertising nanotechnology.

    B.   Companies and the insurance industry paid $250 billion in asbestos claims in the United States alone.

    C.   Companies fear exposure to lawsuits if nanotechnology is found to be toxic.

A **working outline** is a sketch of how you will arrange the major sections.

Managing the Risks of Nanotechnology While Reaping the Rewards

SECTION 1: Begin by defining nanotechnology—manipulating particles between 1 and 100 nanometers (nanometer is a billionth of a meter). Describe the rapid spread of nanotechnology in consumer products including clothing, food, sports equipment, medicines, electronics, and cars. State projection of 15 percent of global manufactured goods containing nanotechnology in 2014.

SECTION 2: Most Americans know nothing about nanotechnology. Companies have stopped advertising that their products contain nanotechnology because of fear of potential lawsuits. Asbestos, once thought safe, now is known to be toxic and has cost companies $250 billion in lawsuits in the United States alone.

SECTION 3: Almost no research has been done on the safety of nanotechnology, only $11 million in federal research. No testing is required for new products because the materials are common, but materials behave differently at nano-scale (example—aluminum normally inert but combustible at nano-scale).

SECTION 4: Nanoparticles are highly mobile and can cross the blood-brain barrier and through the placenta. They are toxic in brains of fish and may collect in lungs.

SECTION 5: Urge that the federal government develop a master plan for identifying and reducing potential risks of nanotechnology and provide sufficient funding to carry out the plan.

Write an Engaging Title and Introduction

Many writers don't think much about titles, but they are very important. A good title makes the reader want to see what you have to say. Be specific as you can in your title, and if possible, suggest your stance.

Get off to a fast start in your introduction. Convince your reader to keep reading. Cut to the chase. Think about how you can get your readers interested. Consider using one of the following.

- State your thesis concisely.
- Provide a hard hitting fact.
- Ask a question.

- Give a vivid description of a problem.
- Discuss a contradiction or paradox.
- Describe a scenario.

Managing the Risks of Nanotechnology While Reaping the Rewards

The revolutionary potential of nanotechnology for medicine, energy production, and communication is now at the research and development stage, but the future has arrived in consumer products. Nanotechnology has given us products we hardly could have imagined just a few years ago: socks that never stink; pants that repel water yet keep you cool; eyeglasses that won't scratch; "smart" foods that add nutrition and reduce cholesterol; DVDs that are incredibly lifelike; bandages that speed healing; tennis balls that last longer; golf balls that fly straighter; pharmaceuticals that selectively deliver drugs; various digital devices like palm pilots, digital cameras, and cell phones that have longer battery lives and more vivid displays; and cars that are lighter, stronger, and more fuel efficient. These miracle products are now possible because scientists have learned how to manipulate nano-scale particles from 1-100 nanometers (a nanometer is a billionth of a meter; a human hair is about 100,000 nanometers in width). Experts estimate that 15 percent of all consumer products will contain nanotechnology by 2014. In the rush to create new consumer products, however, one question has not been asked: Is nanotechnology safe for those who use the products and the workers who are exposed to nanoparticles daily?

Write a Strong Conclusion

Restating your thesis usually isn't the best way to finish a paper. Conclusions that offer only a summary bore readers. The worst endings say something like "in my paper I've said this." Effective conclusions are interesting and provocative, leaving readers with something to think about. Give your readers something to take away besides a straight summary. Try one of these approaches.

- Issue a call to action.
- Discuss the implications.
- Make recommendations.
- Project into the future.
- Tell an anecdote that illustrates a key point.

The potential risks of nanotechnology are reasonably well known. Among the more obvious research questions are the following:

- How hazardous are nanoparticles for workers who have daily exposure?
- What happens to nanoparticles when they are poured down the drain and eventually enter streams, lakes, and oceans?
- How readily do nanoparticles penetrate the skin?
- What happens when nanoparticles enter the brain?
- What effect do airborne nanoparticles have on the lungs?

Nanotechnology promises untold benefits beyond consumer goods in the fields of medicine, energy production, and communication, but these benefits can be realized only if nanotechnology is safe. The federal government is currently spending over $1 billion each year on nanotechnology research, but it spent only $11 million on risk research in 2007. The federal government needs to create a master plan for risk research and to increase spending at least tenfold to ensure sufficient funding to carry out the plan.

When you finish your conclusion, read your introduction again. The main claim in your conclusion should be closely related to the main subject, question, or claim in your introduction. If they do not match, revise the subject, question, or claim in the introduction to match the conclusion. Your thinking evolves and develops as you write, and often your introduction needs some adjusting if you wrote it first.

Evaluate Your Draft

To review and evaluate your draft, pretend you are someone who is either uninformed about your subject or informed but likely to disagree with you. If possible, think of an actual person and imagine yourself as that person.

Read your draft aloud all the way through. When you read aloud, you often hear clunky phrases and catch errors, but just put checks in the margins so you can return to them later. You don't want to get bogged down with the little stuff. What you are after in this stage is an overall sense of how well you accomplished what you set out to do.

Use the questions in the box on the next two pages to evaluate your draft. Note any places where you might make improvements. When you finish, make a list of your goals for the revision. You may have to write another draft before you move to the next stage.

CHECKLIST FOR EVALUATING YOUR DRAFT

Does your paper or project meet the assignment?

- Look again at your assignment, especially at key words such as *define, analyze causes, evaluate,* and *propose.* Does your paper or project do what the assignment requires? If not, how can you change it?

- Look again at the assignment for specific guidelines including length, format, and amount of research. Does your work meet these guidelines?

Can you better focus your thesis and your supporting reasons?

- You may have started out with a large topic and ended up writing about one aspect of it. Can you make your thesis even more precise?

- Can you find the exact location where you link each reason to your thesis?

Are your main points adequately developed?

- Can you explain your reasons in more detail?

- Can you add evidence to better support your main points?

- Do you provide enough background on your topic?

Is your organization effective?

- Is the order of your main points clear? (You may want to make a quick outline of your draft if you have not done so already.)

- Are there any abrupt shifts or gaps?

- Are there sections or paragraphs that should be rearranged?

Are your key terms adequately defined?

- What are your key terms?

- Can you define these terms more precisely?

Do you consider other points of view?

- Where do you acknowledge views besides your own? If you don't acknowledge other views, where can you add them?

- How can you make your discussion of opposing views more acceptable to readers who hold those views?

(continued)

CHECKLIST FOR EVALUATING YOUR DRAFT *(continued)*

Do you represent yourself effectively?

- Forget for the moment that you wrote what you are reading. What is your impression of the writer?

- Is the tone of the writing appropriate for the subject?

Can you improve your title and introduction?

- Can you make your title more specific and indicate your stance?

- Can you think of a way to start faster and to get your readers interested in what you have to say?

Can you improve your conclusion?

- Can you think of an example that sums up your position?

- Can you discuss an implication of your argument that will make your readers think more about the subject?

- If you are writing a proposal, can you end with a call for action?

Can you improve your visual presentation?

- Is the type style easy to read and consistent?

- Would headings and subheadings help to mark the major sections of your argument?

- If you have statistical data, do you use charts?

- Would illustrations, maps, or other graphics help to explain your main points?

Respond to the Writing of Others

Your instructor may ask you to respond to the drafts of your classmates. Responding to other people's writing requires the same careful attention you give to your own draft. To write a helpful response, you should go through the draft more than once.

First reading

Read at your normal rate the first time through without stopping. When you finish you should have a clear sense of what the writer is trying to accomplish. Try writing the following:

- **Main idea and purpose:** Write a sentence that summarizes what you think is the writer's main idea in the draft.
- **Purpose:** Write a sentence that states what you think the writer is trying to accomplish in the draft.

Second reading

In your second reading, you should be most concerned with the content, organization, and completeness of the draft. Make notes in pencil as you read.

You can get one-on-one help in developing your ideas, focusing your topic, and revising your paper or project at your writing center.

- **Introduction:** Does the writer's first paragraph effectively introduce the topic and engage your interest?
- **Thesis:** What exactly is the writer's thesis? Is it clear? Note in the margin where you think the thesis is located.
- **Focus:** Does the writer maintain focus on the thesis? Note any places where the writer seems to wander off to another topic.
- **Organization:** Are the sections and paragraphs arranged effectively? Do any paragraphs seem to be out of place? Can you suggest a better order for the paragraphs?
- **Completeness:** Are there sections or paragraphs that lack key information or adequate development? Where do you want to know more?
- **Sources:** Are outside sources cited accurately? Are quotations used correctly and worked into the fabric of the draft?

Third reading

In your third reading, turn your attention to matters of audience, style, and tone.

- **Audience:** Who are the writer's intended readers? What does the writer assume the audience knows and believes?
- **Style:** Is the writer's style engaging? How would you describe the writer's voice?
- **Tone:** Is the tone appropriate for the writer's purpose and audience? Is the tone consistent throughout the draft? Are there places where another word or phrase might work better?

When you have finished the third reading, write a short paragraph on each bulleted item above. Refer to specific paragraphs in the draft by number. Then end by answering these two questions:

- What does the writer do especially well in the draft?
- What one or two things would most improve the draft in a revision?

Edit and proofread carefully

When you finish revising, you are ready for one final careful reading with the goals of improving your style and eliminating errors.

Edit for style

- **Check connections between sentences and paragraphs.** Notice how your sentences flow within each paragraph and from paragraph to paragraph. If you need to signal the relationship from one sentence or paragraph to the next, use a transitional word or phrase (e.g., *in addition, moreover, similarly, however, nevertheless*).
- **Check your sentences.** Often you will pick up problems with individual sentences by reading aloud. If you notice that a sentence doesn't sound right, think about how you might rephrase it. If a sentence seems too long, consider breaking it into two or more sentences. If you notice a string of short sentences that sound choppy, consider combining them.
- **Eliminate wordiness.** Look for wordy expressions such as *because of the fact that* and *at this point in time*, which can easily be shortened to *because* and *now*. Reduce unnecessary repetition such as *attractive in appearance* or *visible to the eye* to *attractive* and *visible*. Remove unnecessary words like *very, really,* and *totally*. See how many words you can remove without losing the meaning.

■ **Use active verbs.** Make your style more lively by replacing forms of *be* (*is, are, was, were*) or verbs ending in *–ing* with active verbs. Sentences that begin with *There is (are)* and *It is* can often be rewritten with active verbs.

Proofread carefully

In your final pass through your text, eliminate as many errors as you can. To become an effective proofreader, you have to learn to slow down. Some writers find that moving from word to word with a pencil slows them down enough to find errors. Others read backwards to force them to concentrate on each word.

■ **Know what your spelling checker can and can't do.** Spelling checkers are the greatest invention since peanut butter. They turn up many typos and misspellings that are hard to catch. But spelling checkers do not catch wrong words (*to much for too much*), missing endings (*three dog*), and other similar errors.

■ **Check for grammar and punctuation.** Nothing hurts your credibility more than leaving errors in what you write. Many job application letters get tossed in the reject pile because of a single, glaring error. Readers probably shouldn't make such harsh judgments when they find errors, but often they do. Keep a grammar handbook beside your computer, and use it when you are uncertain about what is correct.

Analyzing Arguments

PART 2 Analyzing Arguments

5. Analyzing Written Arguments 69

What is rhetorical analysis? 69

Build a rhetorical analysis 69

Analyze the rhetorical features 70

Analyze the rhetorical context 75

Write a rhetorical analysis 79

Barbara Jordan, Statement on the Articles of Impeachment 80

T. Jonathan Jackson (student), An Argument of Reason and Passion: Barbara Jordan's "Statement on the Articles of Impeachment" 84

STEPS TO WRITING A RHETORICAL ANALYSIS 87

6. Analyzing Visual Arguments 90

What is a visual argument? 90

Analyze visual persuasion 92

Analyze visual evidence 93

Build a visual analysis 96

Write a visual analysis 100

Angela Yamashita (student), Got Roddick? 101

STEPS TO WRITING A VISUAL ANALYSIS 104

5

Analyzing Written Arguments

"Well, it all depends. Where are these huddled masses coming from?"

What makes a cartoon funny? Is it the drawing, the caption, the readers' knowledge of the context, or all three?

What Is Rhetorical Analysis?

To many people, the term *rhetoric* means speech or writing that is highly ornamental or deceptive or manipulative. You might hear someone say, "That politician is just using a bunch of rhetoric" or "The rhetoric of that advertisement is very deceptive." But the term *rhetoric* is also used in a positive or neutral sense to describe human communication; for instance, *Silent Spring* is one of the most influential pieces of environmental rhetoric ever written. As a subject of study, rhetoric is usually associated with effective communication, following Aristotle's classic definition of rhetoric as "the art of finding in any given case the available means of persuasion."

Rhetoric is not just a means of *producing* effective communication but also a way of *understanding* communication. The two aspects mutually support one another: becoming a better writer makes you a better interpreter, and becoming a better interpreter makes you a better writer.

Rhetorical analysis can be defined as an effort to understand how people attempt to influence others through language and more broadly every kind of important symbolic action—not only speeches, articles, and books, but also architecture, movies, television shows, memorials, Web sites, advertisements, photos and other images, dance, and popular songs. It might be helpful to think of rhetorical analysis as the kind of critical reading discussed in Chapter 2. Critical reading—rhetorical analysis, that is—involves studying carefully any kind of persuasive action in order to understand it better and to appreciate the tactics involved.

Build a Rhetorical Analysis

Rhetorical analysis examines how an idea is shaped and presented to an audience in a particular form for a specific purpose. There are many approaches to rhetorical analysis and no one "correct" way to do it. Generally, though, approaches to rhetorical analysis can be placed between two broad extremes—not mutually exclusive categories but extremes at the ends of a continuum.

At one end of the continuum are analyses that concentrate more on texts than on contexts. They typically use rhetorical concepts to analyze the features of texts. Let's call this approach **textual analysis.** At the other extreme are approaches that emphasize **context** over text. These focus on reconstructing the cultural environment, or context, that existed when a particular rhetorical event took place. That reconstruction provides clues about the persuasive tactics and appeals. Those who undertake **contextual analysis**—as we'll call this second approach—regard particular rhetorical acts as parts of larger communicative chains, or "conversations."

Now let's examine these two approaches in detail.

The statue of Castor stands at the entrance of the Piazza del Campidoglio in Rome. A textual analysis focuses on the statue itself. The size and realism of the statue makes it a masterpiece of classical Roman sculpture.

Analyze the Rhetorical Features

Just as expert teachers in every field of endeavor—from baseball to biology—devise vocabularies to facilitate specialized study, rhetoricians too have developed a set of key concepts to describe rhetorical activities. A fundamental concept in rhetoric is audience. But there are many others. Classical rhetoricians in the tradition of Aristotle, Quintilian, and Cicero developed a range of terms around what they called the canons of rhetoric in order to describe some of the actions of communicators: *inventio* (invention—the finding or creation of information for persuasive acts, and the planning of strategies), *dispostio* (arrangement), *elocutio* (style), *memoria* (the recollection of rhetorical resources that one might call upon, as well as the memorization of what has been invented and arranged), and *pronuntiatio* (delivery). These five canons generally describe the actions of any persuader, from preliminary planning to final delivery.

A contextual analysis focuses on the surroundings and history of the statue. According to legend, Castor (left of staircase) and his twin brother Pollux (right of staircase), the mythical sons of Leda, assisted Romans in an early battle. Romans built a large temple in the Forum to honor them. The statues were discovered in the sixteenth century and in 1583 were brought to stand at the top of the Cordonata, a staircase designed by Michelangelo as part of a renovation of the Piazza del Campidoglio commissioned by Pope Paul III Farnese in 1536.

Over the years, as written discourse gained in prestige against oral discourse, four canons (excepting *memoria*) led to the development of concepts and terms useful for rhetorical analysis. Terms like *ethos*, *pathos*, and *logos*, all associated with invention, account for features of texts related to the trustworthiness and credibility of the writer or speaker (ethos), for the persuasive good reasons in an argument that derive from a community's mostly deeply held values (pathos), and for the good reasons that emerge from intellectual reasoning (logos). Fundamental to the classical approach to rhetoric is the concept of *decorum*, or "appropriateness": Everything within a persuasive act can be understood as reflecting a central rhetorical goal that governs consistent choices according to occasion and audience.

An example will make textual rhetorical analysis clearer. If you have not done so already, read "The Border Patrol State" by Leslie Marmon Silko in Chapter 11 (pp. 182–187). In the pages that follow, we use the concepts of classical rhetoric to better understand this essay.

Silko's purpose and argument

What is the purpose of Silko's essay? She wrote the essay well over a decade ago, but you probably find it to be interesting and readable still because it concerns the perennial American issue of civil rights. In this case, Silko takes issue with practices associated with the Border Patrol of the Immigration and Naturalization Service (INS). She feels they are reenacting the long subjugation of native peoples by the white majority. Silko proposes that the power of the Border Patrol be sharply reduced so that the exploitation of her people might be curtailed, and she supports that thesis with an essay that describes and condemns the Border Patrol's tactics.

Essentially Silko's argument comes down to two good reasons: the Border Patrol must be reformed because "the Immigration and Naturalization Service and Border Patrol have implemented policies that interfere with the rights of U.S. citizens to travel freely within our borders" (para. 8), and because efforts to restrict immigration are ineffective and doomed to fail ("It is no use; borders haven't worked, and they won't work," para. 16). Silko's essay amounts to an evaluation of the Border Patrol's activities, an evaluation that finds those activities lacking on ethical and practical grounds.

Silko's use of logos, pathos, and ethos

Logos

When Silko condemns the unethical actions of the Border Patrol early in the essay, she combines ample evidence with other appeals, including our sense of what is legal, constitutional, fair, and honorable. When she explains the futility of trying to stop immigration, she appeals again to her readers' reasonableness: Constructing walls across the border with Mexico is foolish because "border entrepreneurs have already used blowtorches to cut passageways through the fence" (para. 15), because "a mass migration is already under way" (para. 16), and because "The Americas are Indian country, and the 'Indian problem' is not about to go away" (para. 17).

The bulk of "The Border Patrol State" amounts to an argument by example. The single case—Silko's personal experience, as a Native American, with the border police—stands for many such cases. This case study persuades as other case studies and narratives do—by serving as a representative example that stands for the treatment of many Native Americans.

Pathos

The logical appeals in Silko's essay are reinforced by her emotional appeals.

- The Border Patrol is constructing an "Iron Curtain" that is as destructive of human rights as the Iron Curtain that the Soviet Union constructed around Eastern Europe after World War II (para. 15).
- "Proud" and "patriotic" Native Americans are being harassed: "old Bill Pratt used to ride his horse 300 miles overland . . . every summer to work as a fire lookout" (para. 1).
- Border police terrify American citizens in a way that is chillingly reminiscent of "the report of Argentine police and military officers who became addicted to interrogation, torture, and murder" (paras. 3–5).

The essay's most emotional moment may be when Silko describes how the Border Patrol dog, trained to find illegal drugs and other contraband, including human contraband, seems to sympathize with her and those she is championing: "I saw immediately from the expression in her eyes that the dog hated them" (para. 6); "The dog refused to accuse us: She had an innate dignity that did not permit her to serve the murderous impulses of those men" (para. 7). Clearly the good reasons in "The Border Patrol State" appeal in a mutually supportive way to both the reason and the emotions of Silko's audience. She appeals to the whole person.

Ethos

Why do we take Silko's word about the stories she tells? It is because she establishes her *ethos*, or trustworthiness, early in the essay. Silko reminds her readers that she is a respected, published author who has been on a book tour to publicize her novel *Almanac of the Dead* (para. 3). She buttresses her trustworthiness in other ways too:

- She quotes widely, if unobtrusively, from books and reports to establish that she has studied the issues thoroughly. Note how much she displays her knowledge of INS policies in paragraph 9, for instance.
- She tells not only of her own encounters with the border police (experiences that are a source of great credibility), but also of the encounters of others whom she lists, name after careful name, in order that we might trust her account.
- She demonstrates knowledge of history and geography.
- She connects herself to America generally by linking herself to traditional American values such as freedom (para. 1), ethnic pride, tolerance, and even a love of dogs.

This essay, because of its anti-authoritarian strain, might seem to display politically progressive attitudes at times, but overall, Silko comes off as hardworking, honest, educated, even patriotic. And definitely credible.

Silko's arrangement

Silko arranges her essay appropriately as well. In general the essay follows a traditional pattern. She begins with a long concrete introductory story that hooks the reader and leads to her thesis in paragraph 8. Next, in the body of her essay, she supports her thesis by evaluating the unethical nature of INS policies. She cites their violation of constitutional protections, their similarity to tactics used in nations that are notorious for violating the rights of citizens, and their fundamental immorality. She also emphasizes how those policies are racist in nature (paras. 11–13).

After completing her moral evaluation of INS policy, she turns to the practical difficulties of halting immigration in paragraph 14. The North American Free Trade Agreement (NAFTA) permits the free flow of goods, and even drugs are impossible to stop, so how can people be stopped from crossing borders? Efforts to seal borders are "pathetic" in their ineffectiveness (para. 15). These points lay the groundwork for Silko's surprising and stirring conclusions: "The great human migration within the Americas cannot be stopped; human beings are natural forces of the earth, just as rivers and winds are natural forces" (para. 16); "the Americas are Indian country, and the 'Indian problem' is not about to go away" (para. 17). The mythic "return of the Aztlan" is on display in the box cars that go by as the essay closes. In short, this essay unfolds in a conventional way: it has a standard beginning, middle, and end.

Silko's style

What about Silko's style? How is it appropriate to her purposes? Take a look at paragraphs 3 and 4. You will notice that nearly all of the fourteen sentences in these paragraphs are simple in structure. There are only five sentences that use any form of subordination (clauses that begin with *when*, *that*, or *if*). Many of the sentences consist either of one clause or of two clauses joined by simple coordination (connection with conjunctions such as *and* or *but* or a semicolon). Several of the sentences and clauses are unusually short. Furthermore, in these paragraphs Silko never uses metaphors or other sorts of poetic language. Her choice of words is as simple as her sentences. It all reminds you of the daily newspaper, doesn't it? Silko chooses a style similar to one used in newspaper reporting—simple, straightforward, unadorned—because she wants her readers to accept her narrative as credible and trustworthy. Her tone and voice reinforce her ethos.

There is more to say about the rhetorical choices that Silko made in crafting "The Border Patrol State," but this analysis is enough to illustrate our main point. Textual rhetorical analysis employs rhetorical terminology—in this case, terms borrowed from classical rhetoric such as ethos, pathos, logos, arrangement, style, and tone—as a way of helping us to understand how a writer makes choices to achieve certain effects. And textual analysis cooperates with contextual analysis.

Analyze the Rhetorical Context

Communication as conversation

Notice that in the previous discussion the fact that Leslie Marmon Silko's "The Border Patrol State" was originally published in the magazine *The Nation* did not matter too much. Nor did it matter when the essay was published (October 17, 1994), who exactly read it, what their reaction was, or what other people were saying at the time. Textual analysis can proceed as if the item under consideration "speaks for all time," as if it is a museum piece unaffected by time and space. There's nothing wrong with museums, of course; they permit people to observe and appreciate objects in an important way. But museums often fail to reproduce an artwork's original context and cultural meaning. In that sense museums can diminish understanding as much as they contribute to it. Contextual rhetorical analysis is an attempt to understand communications through the lens of their environments, examining the setting or scene out of which any communication emerges.

Similar to textual analysis, contextual analysis may be conducted in any number of ways. But contextual rhetorical analysis always proceeds from a description of the **rhetorical situation** that motivated the event in question. It demands an appreciation of the social circumstances that call rhetorical events into being and that orchestrate the course of those events. It regards communications as anything but self-contained:

- Each communication is considered as a response to other communications and to other social practices.
- Communications, and social practices more generally, are considered to reflect the attitudes and values of the communities that sustain them.
- Analysts seek evidence of how those other communications and social practices are reflected in texts.

Rhetorical analysis from a contextualist perspective understands individual pieces as parts of ongoing conversations.

The challenge is to reconstruct the conversation surrounding a specific piece of writing or speaking. Sometimes it is easy to do so. You may have appropriate background information on the topic, as well as a feel for what is behind what people are writing or saying about it. People who have strong feelings about the environment, stem cell research, same-sex marriage, or any number of other current issues are well informed about the arguments that are converging around those topics.

But other times it takes some research to reconstruct the conversations and social practices related to a particular issue. If the issue is current, you need to see how the debate is conducted in current magazines, newspapers, talk shows, movies and TV shows, Web sites, and so forth. If the issue is from an earlier time, you must do archival research into historical collections of newspapers, magazines, books, letters, and other documentary sources. Archival research usually involves libraries, special research collections, or film and television archives where it is possible to learn quite a bit about context.

An example will clarify how contextual analysis works to open up an argument to analysis. Let's return to a discussion of Silko's "The Border Patrol State" on pages 182–187. It will take a bit of research to reconstruct some of the "conversations" that Silko is participating in, but the result will be an enhanced understanding of the essay as well as an appreciation for how you might do a contextual rhetorical analysis.

Silko's life and works

You can begin by learning more about Silko herself. The essay provides some facts about her (e.g., that she is a Native American writer of note who is from the Southwest). The headnote on page 182 gives additional information (that her writing usually develops out of Native American traditions and tales). You can learn more about Silko using the Internet and your library's Web site. Silko's credibility, her ethos, is established not just by her textual decisions but also by her prior reputation, especially for readers of *The Nation* who would recognize and appreciate her accomplishments.

Perhaps the most relevant information on the Web is about *Almanac of the Dead*, the novel Silko refers to in paragraph 3. The novel, set mainly in Tucson, involves a Native American woman psychic who is in the process of transcribing the lost histories of her dead ancestors into "an almanac of the dead"—a history of her people. This history is written from the point of view of the conquered, not the conqueror. "The Border Patrol State," it seems, is an essay version of *Almanac of the Dead* in that Silko protests what has been lost—and what is still being lost—in the clash between white and Native American cultures. It is a protest against the tactics of the border police. Or is it?

The context of publication

Through a consideration of the conversations swirling around it, contextual analysis actually suggests that "The Border Patrol State" is just as much about immigration policy as it is about the civil rights of Native Americans. The article first appeared in *The Nation*, a respected, politically progressive magazine that has been appearing weekly for decades. Published in New York City, it is a magazine of public opinion that covers theater, film, music, fiction, and other arts; politics and public affairs; and contemporary culture. If you want to know what left-leaning people are thinking about an issue, *The Nation* is a good magazine to consult. You can imagine that Silko's essay therefore reached an audience of sympathetic readers— people who would be receptive to her message. They would be inclined to sympathize with Silko's complaints and to heed her call for a less repressive Border Patrol.

What is more interesting is that Silko's essay appeared on October 17, 1994 in a special issue of *The Nation* devoted to "The Immigration Wars," a phrase prominent on the magazine's cover. Silko's essay was one of several articles that appeared under that banner, an indication that Silko's argument is not just about the violation of the civil rights of Native Americans but also about the larger issue of immigration policy. "The Border Patrol State" appeared after David Cole's "Five Myths about Immigration," Elizabeth Kadetsky's "Bashing Illegals in California," Peter Kwong's "China's Human Traffickers," two editorials about immigration policy, and short columns on immigration by *Nation* regulars Katha Pollitt, Aryeh Neier, and Christopher Hitchens. Together the articles in this issue of *The Nation* mounted a sustained argument in favor of a liberal immigration policy.

The larger conversation

Why did *The Nation* entitle its issue "The Immigration Wars"? Immigration was a huge controversy in October 1994, just before the 1994 elections. When the 1965 Immigration Act was amended in 1990, the already strong flow of immigrants to the United States became a flood. While many previous immigrants came to the United States from Europe, most recent immigrants have come from Asia, Latin America, the Caribbean islands, and Africa. While earlier immigrants typically passed through Ellis Island and past the Statue of Liberty that welcomed them, most recent immigrants in 1994 were coming to Florida, Texas, and California. The arrival of all those new immigrants revived old fears that have been in the air for decades (that they take away jobs from native-born Americans, that they undermine national values by resisting assimilation and clinging to their own cultures, that they reduce standards of living by putting stress on education and social-welfare budgets). Many people countered those fears by pointing out that immigrants create jobs and wealth, enhance the vitality of American culture, become among the proudest of Americans, and contribute to the tax base of their communities. But those counterarguments were undermined when a tide of illegal immigrants—up to 500,000 per year—was arriving at the time Silko was writing.

The Immigration Wars were verbal wars. In the 1994 election, Republicans had united under the banner of a "Contract with America." Some 300 Republican congressional candidates, drawn together by conservative leader Newt Gingrich, agreed to run on a common platform in an ultimately successful effort to gain control of the House of Representatives. The Contract with America offered a number of conservative initiatives, including a reduction in the size of government, a balanced-budget amendment, crime legislation, a reduction in welfare benefits and capital gains taxes, and benefits increases for seniors on Social Security. More to the point here, it also proposed changes in laws in order to curtail immigration, to reduce illegal immigration, and to deny benefits such as health care, social services, and education to illegal residents.

The Contract with America offered support for California's Proposition 187, another important 1994 proposal. This so-called "Save Our State" initiative was designed to "prevent California's estimated 1.7 million undocumented immigrants from partaking of every form of public welfare including non-emergency medical care, pre-natal clinics and public schools," as Kadetsky explained in her essay in *The Nation*. In the words of the proposition itself, "The People of California find and declare as follows: That they have suffered and are suffering economic hardship caused by the presence of illegal aliens in this state. That they have suffered and are suffering personal injury and damage caused by the criminal conduct of illegal aliens. That they have a right to the protection of their government from any person or persons entering this country illegally." The Republican Contract for America and California's Proposition 187 together constituted the nation's leading domestic issue in October 1994. The war of words about the issue was evident in the magazines, books, newspapers, talk shows, barber shops, and hair salons of America—much as it is today.

Silko's political goals

In this context, it is easy to see that Silko's essay is against more than the Border Patrol. It is an argument in favor of relatively unrestricted immigration, especially for Mexicans and Native Americans. Moreover, it is a direct refutation of the Contract for America and Proposition 187. Proposition 187 states "that [the People of California] have suffered and are suffering economic hardship caused by the presence of illegal aliens in this state, that they have suffered and are suffering personal injury and damage caused by the criminal conduct of illegal aliens, [and] that they have a right to the protection of their government from any person or persons entering this country illegally."

Silko turns the claim around. It is the Border Patrol that is behaving illegally. It is the Border Patrol that is creating economic hardship. It is the border police that are inflicting personal injury and damage through criminal conduct. Finally, it is the U.S. government that is acting illegally by ignoring the treaty of Guadalupe Hidalgo, which "recognizes the right of the Tohano O'Odom (Papago) people to move freely across the U.S.-Mexico border without documents," as Silko writes in a footnote. Writing just before the election of 1994 and in the midst of a spirited national debate, Silko had specific political goals in mind. A contextual analysis of "The Border Patrol State" reveals that the essay is, at least in part, an eloquent refutation of the Contract for America and Proposition 187—two items that are not even named explicitly in the essay!

We could do more contextual analysis here. We could cite many more articles, books, reports, and TV broadcasts that can be compared with "The Border Patrol State," including speeches and TV interviews by Pat Buchanan, who ran for the Republican presidential nomination in 1992 and 1996 on an anti-immigration stance. A discussion of the conversation about immigration in 1994 and about specific contribution to that conversation could be extended for a long time—indefinitely, in fact. There is no need to belabor the point, however; our purpose has been simply to illustrate that contextual analysis of a piece of rhetoric can enrich our understanding.

Write a Rhetorical Analysis

Effective rhetorical analysis, as we have seen, can be textual or contextual in nature. But we should emphasize again that these two approaches to rhetorical analysis are not mutually exclusive. Indeed, many if not most analysts operate between these two extremes; they consider the details of the text, but they also attend to the particulars of context. Textual analysis and contextual analysis inevitably complement each other. Getting at what is at stake in "The Border Patrol State" or any other sophisticated argument takes patience and intelligence. Many arguments appeal to the attitudes and beliefs of audiences. Rhetorical analysis, as a way of understanding how people argue, is both enlightening and challenging.

Try to use elements of both kinds of analysis whenever you want to understand a rhetorical event more completely. Rhetoric is "inside" texts, but it is also "outside" them. Specific rhetorical performances are an irreducible mixture of text and context, and so interpretation and analysis of those performances must account for both as well. Remember, however, the limitations of your analysis. Realize that your analysis will always be somewhat partial and incomplete, ready to be deepened, corrected, modified, and extended by the insights of others. Rhetorical analysis can itself be part of an unending conversation—a way of learning and teaching within a community.

Barbara Jordan

Statement on the Articles of Impeachment

Barbara Jordan (1936–1996) grew up in Houston and received a law degree from Boston University in 1959. Working on John F. Kennedy's 1960 presidential campaign stirred an interest in politics, and Jordon became the first African-American woman elected to the Texas State Senate in 1966. In 1972 she was elected to the United States House of Representatives and thus became the first African-American woman from the South ever to serve in Congress. Jordan was appointed to the House Judiciary Committee. Soon she was in the national spotlight when that committee considered articles of impeachment against President Richard Nixon, who had illegally covered up a burglary of Democratic Party headquarters during the 1972 election. When Nixon's criminal acts reached to the Judiciary Committee, Jordan's opening speech on July 24, 1974, set the tone

for the debate and established her reputation as a moral beacon for the nation. Nixon resigned as president on August 9, 1974, when it was evident that he would be impeached.

Thank you, Mr. Chairman.

Mr. Chairman, I join my colleague Mr. Rangel in thanking you for giving the junior members of this committee the glorious opportunity of sharing the pain of this inquiry. Mr. Chairman, you are a strong man, and it has not been easy but we have tried as best we can to give you as much assistance as possible.

2   Earlier today, we heard the beginning of the Preamble to the Constitution of the United States: "We, the people." It's a very eloquent beginning. But when that document was completed on the seventeenth of September in 1787, I was not included in that "We, the people." I felt somehow for many years that George Washington and Alexander Hamilton just left me out by mistake. But through the process of amendment, interpretation, and court decision, I have finally been included in "We, the people."

3   Today I am an inquisitor. An hyperbole would not be fictional and would not overstate the solemnness that I feel right now. My faith in the Constitution is whole; it is complete; it is total. And I am not going to sit here and be an idle spectator to the diminution, the subversion, the destruction, of the Constitution.

4   "Who can so properly be the inquisitors for the nation as the representatives of the nation themselves?" "The subjects of its jurisdiction are those offenses which proceed from the misconduct of public men." And that's what

we're talking about. In other words, [the jurisdiction comes] from the abuse or violation of some public trust.

5   It is wrong, I suggest, it is a misreading of the Constitution for any member here to assert that for a member to vote for an article of impeachment means that that member must be convinced that the President should be removed from office. The Constitution doesn't say that. The powers relating to impeachment are an essential check in the hands of the body of the legislature against and upon the encroachments of the executive. The division between the two branches of the legislature, the House and the Senate, assigning to the one the right to accuse and to the other the right to judge, the framers of this Constitution were very astute. They did not make the accusers and the judgers the same person.

6   We know the nature of impeachment. We've been talking about it awhile now. It is chiefly designed for the President and his high ministers to somehow be called into account. It is designed to "bridle" the executive if he engages in excesses. "It is designed as a method of national inquest into the conduct of public men." The framers confided in the Congress the power if need be, to remove the President in order to strike a delicate balance between a President swollen with power and grown tyrannical, and preservation of the independence of the executive.

7   The nature of impeachment: a narrowly channeled exception to the separation-of-powers maxim. The Federal Convention of 1787 said that. It limited impeachment to high crimes and misdemeanors and discounted and opposed the term *maladministration*. "It is to be used only for great misdemeanors," so it was said in the North Carolina ratification convention. And in the Virginia ratification convention: "We do not trust our liberty to a particular branch. We need one branch to check the other."

8   "No one need be afraid"—the North Carolina ratification convention— "No one need be afraid that officers who commit oppression will pass with immunity." "Prosecutions of impeachments will seldom fail to agitate the passions of the whole community," said Hamilton in the Federalist Papers, number 65. "We divide into parties more or less friendly or inimical to the accused." I do not mean political parties in that sense.

9   The drawing of political lines goes to the motivation behind impeachment; but impeachment must proceed within the confines of the constitutional term "high crime[s] and misdemeanors." Of the impeachment process, it was Woodrow Wilson who said that "Nothing short of the grossest offenses against the plain law of the land will suffice to give them speed and effectiveness. Indignation so great as to overgrow party interest may secure a conviction; but nothing else can."

10   Common sense would be revolted if we engaged upon this process for petty reasons. Congress has a lot to do: Appropriations, Tax Reform, Health Insurance, Campaign Finance Reform, Housing, Environmental Protection, Energy Sufficiency, Mass Transportation. Pettiness cannot be allowed to stand

in the face of such overwhelming problems. So today we are not being petty. We are trying to be big, because the task we have before us is a big one.

11   This morning, in a discussion of the evidence, we were told that the evidence which purports to support the allegations of misuse of the CIA by the President is thin. We're told that that evidence is insufficient. What that recital of the evidence this morning did not include is what the President did know on June the 23rd, 1972.

12   The President did know that it was Republican money, that it was money from the Committee for the Re-Election of the President, which was found in the possession of one of the burglars arrested on June the 17th. What the President did know on the 23rd of June was the prior activities of E. Howard Hunt, which included his participation in the break-in of Daniel Ellsberg's psychiatrist, which included Howard Hunt's participation in the Dita Beard ITT affair, which included Howard Hunt's fabrication of cables designed to discredit the Kennedy Administration.

13   We were further cautioned today that perhaps these proceedings ought to be delayed because certainly there would be new evidence forthcoming from the President of the United States. There has not even been an obfuscated indication that this committee would receive any additional materials from the President. The committee subpoena is outstanding, and if the President wants to supply that material, the committee sits here. The fact is that on yesterday, the American people waited with great anxiety for eight hours, not knowing whether their President would obey an order of the Supreme Court of the United States.

14   At this point, I would like to juxtapose a few of the impeachment criteria with some of the actions the President has engaged in. Impeachment criteria: James Madison, from the Virginia ratification convention. "If the President be connected in any suspicious manner with any person and there be grounds to believe that he will shelter him, he may be impeached."

15   We have heard time and time again that the evidence reflects the payment to defendants' money. The President had knowledge that these funds were being paid and these were funds collected for the 1972 presidential campaign. We know that the President met with Mr. Henry Petersen 27 times to discuss matters related to Watergate, and immediately thereafter met with the very persons who were implicated in the information Mr. Petersen was receiving. The words are: "If the President is connected in any suspicious manner with any person and there be grounds to believe that he will shelter that person, he may be impeached."

16   Justice Story: "Impeachment" is attended—"is intended for occasional and extraordinary cases where a superior power acting for the whole people is put into operation to protect their rights and rescue their liberties from violations." We know about the Huston plan. We know about the break-in of the psychiatrist's office. We know that there was absolute complete direction on September 3rd when the President indicated that a surreptitious entry had

been made in Dr. Fielding's office, after having met with Mr. Ehrlichman and Mr. Young. "Protect their rights." "Rescue their liberties from violation."

17   The Carolina ratification convention impeachment criteria: those are impeachable "who behave amiss or betray their public trust." Beginning shortly after the Watergate break-in and continuing to the present time, the President has engaged in a series of public statements and actions designed to thwart the lawful investigation by government prosecutors. Moreover, the President has made public announcements and assertions bearing on the Watergate case, which the evidence will show he knew to be false. These assertions, false assertions, impeachable, those who misbehave. Those who "behave amiss or betray the public trust."

18   James Madison again at the Constitutional Convention: "A President is impeachable if he attempts to subvert the Constitution." The Constitution charges the President with the task of taking care that the laws be faithfully executed, and yet the President has counseled his aides to commit perjury, willfully disregard the secrecy of grand jury proceedings, conceal surreptitious entry, attempt to compromise a federal judge, while publicly displaying his cooperation with the processes of criminal justice. "A President is impeachable if he attempts to subvert the Constitution."

19   If the impeachment provision in the Constitution of the United States will not reach the offenses charged here, then perhaps that 18th-century Constitution should be abandoned to a 20th-century paper shredder.

20   Has the President committed offenses, and planned, and directed, and acquiesced in a course of conduct which the Constitution will not tolerate? That's the question. We know that. We know the question. We should now forthwith proceed to answer the question. It is reason, and not passion, which must guide our deliberations, guide our debate, and guide our decision.

21   I yield back the balance of my time, Mr. Chairman. ∎

Sample Student Rhetorical Analysis

T. Jonathan Jackson

Dr. Netaji

English 1101

5 December 2008

background

An Argument of Reason and Passion: Barbara Jordan's

"Statement on the Articles of Impeachment"

On March 9, 1974, the U.S. House Judiciary Committee began an impeachment hearing against President Richard Nixon for his role in the cover-up of the Watergate scandal. On July 25, 1974, Congresswoman Barbara Jordan stood before this committee and delivered an 11-minute speech known as "Statement on the Articles of Impeachment." The argument of this speech is that the president should be impeached because his actions threaten both the Constitution and the people of the United States. Jordan states, "It is reason, and not passion, which must guide our deliberation, guide our debate, and guide our decision." Subsequently, she uses a strong logical argument that she supports with appeals to both her credibility and the audience's feelings of patriotism for the Constitution.

The context of Jordan's speech is important for three reasons. First, the charges against Nixon and his impeachment case were controversial because he was a Republican president and the committee was mostly Democratic. The burden was on Jordan to show that the case for impeachment was not a partisan issue. Second, the speech was televised. Jordan was speaking not only to the committee—an audience well informed about the topic and mostly in support of her argument— but also to a television audience that was not as informed and potentially hostile. Finally, although Jordan was already known in Texas politics, she was new to Congress, and she was a low-ranking member of the committee. Consequently, she had to prove her ethos to both the committee and the wider television audience who did not know her.

At the heart of Jordan's argument is her insistence that the Constitution is important because it protects the rights of the American people. Therefore the Constitution itself should be protected. Thus impeachment is the proper punishment for a president or other leaders who upset the balance of power and act against the Constitution. Using evidence from the North Carolina and Virginia Constitutional

Jackson 2

Conventions, she shows that impeachment is used only for "great misdemeanors" and that we need the branches of government to check the powers of each other. Her next task is to show what these misdemeanors are and to show that Nixon has committed them. Here she appeals to logic in that she not only explains each misdemeanor in full and matches the president's actions to each one, but she also cites reputable sources such as James Madison, who wrote the Federalist Papers; the South Carolina Ratification Convention; and Justice Joseph Story, who as a justice under Madison was known for his work explaining the states' powers under the Constitution. In addition, she emphasizes each point by starting with a key quotation by one of these figures, such as James Madison: "A President is impeachable if he attempts to subvert the Constitution." Then she describes the president's actions that illustrate this quotation—in this case, he told his associates to commit perjury, to hide evidence, and to bribe a judge—and stresses the point with the same quotation she used earlier: "A President is impeachable if he attempts to subvert the Constitution." This repetition of the quotation makes the connection both clearer and more memorable to the audience.

Jordan shows that she has an extensive knowledge of the Constitution and of the facts in the impeachment case, which gains her credibility as someone who can speak knowledgeably on the subject. She also shows her credibility as a citizen, as well as an African-American woman who relies on the Constitution and the Constitutional process for protection. She says that when the Constitution was completed, "I was not included in that 'We, the People.' I felt somehow for many years that George Washington and Alexander Hamilton just left me out by mistake. But through the process of amendment, interpretation, and court decision I have finally been included in 'We, the People.'"

Jordan also addresses the concern that the impeachment case is partisan, an allegation that could damage the credibility of the committee. She recognizes that "the drawing of political lines goes to the motivation behind impeachment," but such a large crime should transcend party lines. She backs this assertion by quoting Woodrow Wilson, who said, "Indignation so great as to overthrow party interest may secure a conviction; but nothing else can." Jordan continues, "Thus, party pettiness cannot, and will not, stand in the way of the committee member's jobs as representatives of the nation: We are trying to be *big*, because the task we have before us is a big one."

Jordan claims that passion should not be a part of the impeachment proceedings, but she uses her passion for the Constitution to connect to her audience's emotions and sense of patriotism: "My faith in the Constitution is whole, it is complete, it is total. And I am not going to sit here and be an idle spectator to the diminution, the subversion, the destruction of the Constitution." She stirs her audience's emotions by repeatedly creating the sense that the Constitution is in physical danger of being destroyed. Not only is it in danger of being figuratively destroyed by Nixon's crimes, but also a failure to impeach him could also destroy the document's integrity. She makes this destruction literal when she says, "If the impeachment provisions will not reach the offenses charged here, then perhaps that eighteenth-century Constitution should be abandoned to a twentieth-century paper shredder." This dramatic image encourages the audience to imagine Nixon actually shredding the Constitution as he ordered the shredding of documents that could link him to crimes. In addition, she makes the American people responsible; "we," meaning both the committee and the television audience, might as well be shredding the Constitution to bits if Nixon is not impeached.

Jordan makes a strong case for impeachment by first appealing to logic and then using her passion for the Constitution to connect to her audience's patriotism. Significantly, because this speech was also televised, Jordan also emerged to a national audience as a powerful speaker. Her clear, rhythmic style is both dramatic and easy to follow. Jordan's reputation as a powerful speaker continues to this day, as does the importance of her speeches, such as this one and other keynote addresses she made throughout her career. In particular, this argument for exercising the checks and balances within our government in order to protect the Constitution and the American people from possible tyranny is an argument that resonates with events today.

Works Cited

Jordan, Barbara. "Statement on the Articles of Impeachment." *American Rhetoric: Top 100 Speeches*. American Rhetoric, 25 July 1974. Web. 21 Nov. 2007.

Steps to Writing a Rhetorical Analysis

Step 1 Select an Argument to Analyze

Find an argument to analyze—a speech or sermon, an op-ed in a newspaper, an ad in a magazine designed for a particular audience, or a commentary on a talk show.

Examples

- Editorial pages of newspapers (but not letters to the editor unless you can find a long and detailed letter)
- Opinion features in magazines such as *Time*, *Newsweek*, and *U.S. News & World Report*
- Magazines that take political positions such as *National Review*, *Mother Jones*, *New Republic*, *Nation*, and *Slate*
- Web sites of activist organizations (but not blog or newsgroup postings unless they are long and detailed)

Step 2 Analyze the Context

Who is the author?

Through research in the library or on the Web, learn all you can about the author of the argument.

- How does the argument you are analyzing repeat arguments previously made by the author?
- Does the author borrow arguments and concepts from previous pieces he or she has written?
- What motivated the author to write? What is the author's purpose for writing this argument?

Who is the audience?

Through research, learn all you can about the place where the argument appeared and the audience.

- Who is the anticipated audience?
- How do the occasion and forum for writing affect the argument?
- How would the argument have been written differently if it had appeared elsewhere?
- What motivated the newspaper or magazine (or other venue) to publish it?

What is the larger conversation?

Through research, find out what else was being said about the subject of your selection. Track down any references made in the text you are examining.

- When did the argument appear?
- Why did it get published at that particular moment?
- What other concurrent pieces of "cultural conversation" (e.g., TV shows, other articles, speeches, Web sites) does the item you are analyzing respond to or "answer"?

Step 3 Analyze the Text

Summarize the argument

- What is the main claim?
- What reasons are given in support of the claim?
- How is the argument organized? What are the components, and why are they presented in that order?

What is the medium and genre?

- What is the medium? A newspaper? a scholarly journal? a Web site? or something else?
- What is the genre? An editorial? an essay? a speech? an advertisement? What expectations does the audience have about this genre?

What appeals are used?

- Analyze the ethos. How does the writer represent himself or herself? Does the writer have any credentials as an authority on the topic? Do you trust the writer? Why or why not?
- Analyze the logos. Where do you find facts and evidence in the argument? What kinds of facts and evidence does the writer present? Direct observation? statistics? interviews? surveys? secondhand sources such as published research? quotations from authorities?
- Analyze the pathos. Does the writer attempt to invoke an emotional response? Where do you find appeals to shared values? You are a member of that audience, so what values do you hold in common with the writer? What values do you not hold in common?

How would you characterize the style?

- Is the style formal, informal, satirical, or something else?
- Are any metaphors used?

Step 4 Write a Draft

Introduction

- Describe briefly the argument you are analyzing, including where it was published, how long it is, and who wrote it.
- If the argument is about an issue unfamiliar to your readers, supply the necessary background.

Body

- Analyze the context, following Step 2.
- Analyze the text, following Step 3.

Conclusion

- Do more than simply summarize what you have said. You might, for example, end with an example that typifies the argument.
- You don't have to end by either agreeing or disagreeing with the writer. Your task in this assignment is to analyze the strategies the writer uses.

Step 5 Revise, Edit, Proofread

For detailed instructions, see Chapter 4.
For a checklist to evaluate your draft, see pages 61–62.

6

Analyzing Visual Arguments

The Stata Center is a controversial building at the Massachusetts Institute of Technology. Why do you think MIT wanted a building so different and whimsical on its campus?

What Is a Visual Argument?

We live in a world flooded with images. They pull on us, compete for our attention, push us to do things. But how often do we think about how they work?

Arguments in written language are visual in one sense: we use our eyes to read the words on the page. But without words, can there be a visual argument? Certainly some visual symbols take on conventional meanings. Signs in airports or other public places, for example, are designed to communicate with speakers of many languages.

Some visual symbols even make explicit claims. A one-way street sign says that drivers should travel only in the one direction. But are such signs arguments? In Chapter 3 we point out that scholars of argument do not believe that everything *is* an argument. Most scholars define an argument as a claim supported by one or more reasons. A one-way sign has a claim: all drivers should go in the same direction. But is there a reason? We all know an unstated reason the sign carries: drivers who go the wrong way violate the law and risk a substantial fine (plus they risk a head-on collision with other drivers).

Visual arguments often are powerful because they invite viewers to create claims and links. For example, the artists who decorated medieval cathedrals taught religious lessons. The facade of the Last Judgment on the front pillar of the Duomo in Orvieto, Italy, shown on the next page, depicts Christ as judge damning sinners to hell. The facade makes a powerful visual argument about the consequences that await the unfaithful.

Facade of Last Judgment, Orvieto, Italy. ca. 1310–1330.

Eighteen-year-old mother from Oklahoma, now a California migrant. Photo by Dorothea Lange. March 1937.

Other visual arguments cannot be explained this easily—even ones that are intended to make claims. Beginning in 1935, the U.S. Farm Security Administration hired photographers to document the effects of the Great Depression and the drought years on Americans. One of the photographers, Dorothea Lange, shot a series of photographs of homeless and destitute migrant workers in California. Her photographs have become some of the most familiar images of the United States in the 1930s. Lange had an immediate goal—getting the government to build a resettlement camp for the homeless workers. She wrote to her boss in Washington that her images were "loaded with ammunition."

Lange titled one of her images "Eighteen-year-old mother from Oklahoma, now a California migrant." The young woman and child in the photograph are obviously quite poor if we assume the tent is where they live. Yet the image doesn't seem to be one of suffering. Lange was a portrait photographer before becoming a documentary photographer, and her experience shows. She takes advantage of the highlighting of the woman's hair from the sun contrasted with the dark interior of the tent to draw our eyes to the woman's face. She doesn't appear to be distressed—just bored. Only later do we notice the dirty face of the child and other details. With another caption—perhaps "Young mother on a camping trip left behind while her husband went for a hike"—we might read the photograph to say something else. And even if we take the image as evidence of poverty, Lange's claim is not evident, just as images of homeless people today do not necessarily make arguments.

Analyze Visual Persuasion

For many years the Italian clothing retailer Benetton has run ad campaigns intended to raise public awareness on issues including AIDS, hunger, pollution, and racism. In 2003, Benetton launched a "Food for Life" campaign codeveloped with the United Nations World Food Programme, with photographs by James Mollison. According to Benetton, "Setting the scene is the symbol for the Food for Life campaign: a man with a mutilated arm, whose metal prosthesis is a spoon." The image is memorable, but it does not make a claim that can be put into words easily.

Advertisements often work in complex ways. Benetton advertises for the same reason other companies advertise—to get consumers to buy their products. The question then becomes how the controversial ads influence consumers to purchase Benetton clothing. Perhaps consumers identify with the messages in

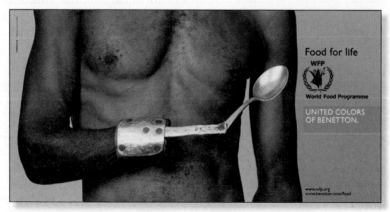

Food for Life. Benetton Ad Campaign. 2003.

Benetton's ads and consequently identify with their clothing. Benetton says on its Web site that its ad campaigns "have succeeded in attracting the attention of the public and in standing out amid the current clutter of images." At the very least the ads give Benetton name recognition. You may have other ideas about why the Benetton ads have been successful, but the point we are making is that explicit claims and reasons are often hard to extract from images.

Analyze Visual Evidence

Photographs

Images and graphics seldom make arguments on their own, but they are frequently used to support arguments. Photographs are commonly used as factual evidence, but as with other kinds of evidence, the significance of images can be contested. In 1936, 21-year-old Arthur Rothstein worked as a photographer for the Resettlement Administration, a federal agency created to help people living in rural poverty. Rothstein sent a photograph of a bleached cow's skull lying on cracked dirt to Roy Stryker, his boss in Washington, D.C. Stryker saw the image as representing the plight of Midwestern plains states in the midst of a severe drought.

But not all people living in plains states found this image—or others like it—representative. A newspaper in Fargo, North Dakota, published one of Rothstein's photographs on the front page under the headline, "It's a fake!" The newspaper accused journalists of making the situation on the plains appear worse than it was and accused Rothstein in particular of using a movable prop to make a cheap point.

Close examination of the set of photographs revealed the skull had been moved about 10 feet, which Rothstein admitted. But he protested that the drought was real enough and there were plenty of cow bones on the ground. Rothstein had followed a long practice among photographers of altering a scene for the purpose of getting a better photograph.

Photographers often manipulated their images in the darkroom, but realistic results required a high skill level. More recently, digital photography

The bleached skull of a steer on the dry, sun-baked earth of the South Dakota Badlands, 1939. Photo by Arthur Rothstein.

has made it relatively easy to alter photographs. You've no doubt seen many of the thousands of altered images that circulate daily—photographs that put heads on different bodies and put people in different places, often within historical images.

The ease of cropping digital photographs reveals an important truth about photography: a photograph represents reality from a particular viewpoint. A high-resolution picture of a crowd can be divided into many smaller images that each say something different about the event. The act of pointing the camera in one direction and not in another shapes how photographic evidence will be interpreted.

Tables, charts, and other graphics

Statistical information is frequently used as evidence in arguments. The problem with giving many statistics in sentence form, however, is that readers shortly lose track of the numbers. Readers require formats such as tables, which allow them to take in an array of numerical data at once. Below is a table on the costs of cancer drugs, which can run up to $100,000 for a few months' treatment.

Charts and graphs present the magnitude and proportion of data with more visual impact than tables. A bar chart showing the number of unredeemed frequent-flyer miles, such as the example opposite, illustrates the problem airlines face in offering free seats to fulfill their mileage redemption obligations much more clearly than a description would.

The Price of Fighting Cancer

The estimated costs of some of a new wave of cancer drugs, which aim at the disease without the side effects of traditional chemotherapy.

CANCER DRUG	MANUFACTURER	APPROVED FOR USE	TYPE OF CANCER TREATED	EST. ANNUAL COST PER PATIENT
Erbitux	ImClone/Bristol-Myers	2004	Colorectal	$ 111,000
Avastin	Genentech	2004	Colorectal	54,000
Herceptin	Genentech	1998	Breast	38,000
Tarceva	Genentech	2004	Lung	35,000

Source: Sanford C. Bernstein & Co.

The New York Times

A table allows a quick comparison of numeric data such as the price of fighting cancer with expensive drugs.

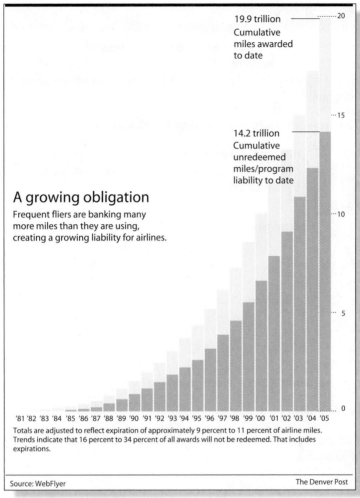

A growing obligation

Frequent fliers are banking many more miles than they are using, creating a growing liability for airlines.

19.9 trillion Cumulative miles awarded to date

14.2 trillion Cumulative unredeemed miles/program liability to date

'81 '82 '83 '84 '85 '86 '87 '88 '89 '90 '91 '92 '93 '94 '95 '96 '97 '98 '99 '00 '01 '02 '03 '04 '05

Totals are adjusted to reflect expiration of approximately 9 percent to 11 percent of airline miles. Trends indicate that 16 percent to 34 percent of all awards will not be redeemed. That includes expirations.

Source: WebFlyer   The Denver Post

Bar charts are useful to represent the magnitude and proportion of data such as the enormous growth of frequent-flyer miles.

Charts can also be misleading. For example, a chart that compares the amounts of calories in competing brands of cereal might list one with 70 calories and another with 80 calories. If the chart begins at zero, the difference looks small. But if the chart starts at 60, the brand with 80 calories appears to have twice the calories of the brand with 70. Furthermore, the chart is worthless if the data is inaccurate or comes from an unreliable source. Creators of charts and graphs have an ethical obligation to present data as fairly and accurately as possible and to provide the sources of the data.

CHECKLIST FOR EVALUATING CHARTS AND GRAPHS

Computer software makes it simple to create charts and graphs. This software, how-ever, does not help you decide which kind of chart or graph is best to use or tell you the purpose of including a chart or graph. Ask these questions when you are analyzing charts and graphs.

- **Is the type of chart appropriate for the information presented?**

 Bar and column charts make comparisons in particular categories. If two or more charts are compared, the scales should be consistent.

 Line graphs plot variables on a vertical and a horizontal axis. They are useful for showing proportional trends over time.

 Pie charts show the proportion of parts in terms of the whole. Segments must add up to 100 percent of the whole.

- **Does the chart have a clear purpose?**

- **Does the title indicate the purpose?**

- **What do the units represent** (dollars, people, voters, percentages, and so on)?

- **What is the source of the data?**

- **Is there any distortion of information?** A bar chart can exaggerate small differences if intervals are manipulated (for example, 42 can look twice as large as 41 if the numbering begins at 40).

Build a Visual Analysis

It's one thing to construct a visual argument yourself; it's another thing to analyze visual arguments that are made by someone else. Fortunately, analyzing arguments made up of images and graphics is largely a matter of following the same strategies for rhetorical analysis that are outlined in Chapter 5—except that you must analyze

Ad for Hofstra University, 1989.

images instead of (or in addition to) words. To put it another way, when you analyze a visual argument, think about the image itself as well as its relationship to other images (and discourses). The arguments implied by visual images, like the arguments made through text alone, are carried both by the context and by the image.

Analyzing context

A critical analysis of a visual image, like the analyses of written arguments that we discussed in the previous chapter, must include a consideration of context. Consider, for example, the above advertisement for Hofstra University. The context for the ad is not difficult to uncover through a bit of research. The ad appeared in 1989 and 1990 when Hofstra, located on Long Island 25 miles from New York City, was celebrating its fiftieth anniversary and hoping to use the occasion to enhance its esteem. At the time, Hofstra enjoyed a good reputation for its professional programs, particularly in education and business (which one-third of the 7500 students were majoring in). However, it was not as highly regarded in the core science and humanities disciplines that are often associated with institutional prestige. In addition, Hofstra was quite well known in the New York metropolitan area—half its students were commuting to school rather than living in dormitories—but it was not attracting many students from outside the region, and its campus life was consequently regarded as mediocre. Its student body was generally well prepared, hardworking, and capable, but its most outstanding applicants were too often choosing other universities.

Feeling that its performance was exceeding its reputation and that it was capable of attracting a more diverse and talented student body, Hofstra conceived of a national ad campaign designed to change the opinions of prospective students and their parents, as well as the general public. It placed the ads—the ad reproduced here is one of a series—in several magazines and newspapers in order to persuade people that Hofstra was an outstanding university not just in the professions but in all fields, and that the opportunities available to its students were varied and valuable.

Analyzing visual and textual elements

Ads make arguments, and the message of the Hofstra ad is something like this: "Hofstra is a prestigious, high-quality institution that brings out the best in students because of its facilities, its academic reputation, its student body, and the strength of its faculty and academic programs." The text of the Hofstra ad expresses that argument specifically: "The best" and "we teach success" are prominently displayed; the size of the print visually reinforces the message; and the fine print supports the main thesis by mentioning Hofstra's facilities (the large library with "a collection [of volumes] larger than that of 95% of American universities," the "television facility . . . with broadcast quality production capability"); its reputation (its ranking in *Barron's Guide to the Most Prestigious Colleges* and its "professionally accredited programs"); and its faculty and students. As we emphasized in the previous chapter, the ad works by offering good reasons and supporting arguments that are based on logical reasoning and evidence, as well as appeals to our most fervently held values. By placing the ad in prestigious publications, Hofstra enhanced its credibility even further.

In this chapter, however, we are emphasizing visuals in arguments. What kind of argument is made and supported by the image of the young girl with the flute? The photo of the girl is black and white, so that it can be printed easily and inexpensively in newspapers and magazines. But the black and white format also contributes a sense of reality and truthfulness, in the manner of black and white photos or documentary films. (Color images, on the other hand, can imply flashiness or commercialism.) Even in black and white, the image is quite arresting. In the context of an ad for Hofstra, the image is particularly intriguing. The girl is young—does she seem about ten or twelve years of age?—and her readiness for distinguished performance suggests that she is a prodigy, a genius—in other words, the kind of person that Hofstra attracts and sustains. The ad implies that you might encounter her on the Hofstra campus sometime: if she is not a student at Hofstra now, she soon will be. Come to Hofstra, and you too can acquire the traits associated with excellence and success.

The girl is dressed up for some kind of musical performance, and the details of her costume imply that the performance is of a high order: it is not just any costume, but one associated with professional performances of the most rarefied kind, a concert that calls for only the best musicians. The delicacy and refinement of the girl are implied by the posture of her fingers, the highly polished flute that she holds with an upright carriage, and the meticulousness of her tie, shirt, and coat. The girl's expression suggests that she is serious, sober, disciplined, but comfortable—the kind of student (and faculty member) that Hofstra features. (The layout and consistent print style used in the ad reinforce that impression: by offering a balanced and harmonious placement of elements and by sticking to the same type style throughout, the ad stands for the values of balance, harmony, consistency, and order.) The girl is modest and unpretentious in expression, yet she looks directly at the viewer with supreme self-confidence. Her age suggests innocence, yet her face proclaims ambition; her age and the quasi-masculine costume (note that she wears neither a ring nor earrings) give her a sexual innocence that is in keeping with the contemplative life. Come to Hofstra, the image proclaims, and you will meet people who are sober and graceful, self-disciplined and confident, ambitious without being arrogant. The ad is supporting its thesis with good reasons implied by its central image—good reasons that we identified with logos and pathos in the previous chapter.

Speaking of pathos, what do you make of the fact that the girl is Asian? On one hand, the Asian girl's demeanor reinforces cultural stereotypes. Delicate, small, sober, controlled, even humorless, she embodies characteristics that recall other Asian-American icons (particularly women), especially icons of success through discipline and hard work. On the other hand, the girl speaks to the Asian community. It is as if she is on the verge of saying, "Come and join me at Hofstra, where you too can reach the highest achievement. And read the copy below me to learn more about what Hofstra has to offer." In this way the girl participates in Hofstra's ambition to attract highly qualified, highly motivated, and high-performing minority students—as well as any other high-performing student, regardless of ethnicity or gender, who values hard work, academic distinction, and the postponement of sensual gratification in return for long-term success.

If she is Asian, the girl is also thoroughly American. She appears not to be an international student but an American of immigrant stock. Her costume, her controlled black hair, and her unmarked face and fingers identify her as achieving the American dream of material success, physical health and well being, and class advancement. If her parents or grandparents came to New York or California as immigrants, they (and she) are now naturalized—100 percent American, completely successful. The social class element to the image is unmistakable: the entire ad speaks of Hofstra's ambition to be among the best, to achieve an elite status. When the ad appeared in 1989, Hofstra was attracting few of the nation's elite students. The girl signals a change. She displays the university's aspiration to become among the nation's elite—those who enjoy material success as well as the leisure, education, and sophistication to appreciate the finest music. That ambition is reinforced by the university's emblem in the lower right-hand corner of the ad. It resembles a coat of arms and is associated with royalty. Hofstra may be a community that is strong in the professions, but it also values the arts.

No doubt there are other aspects of the image that work to articulate and to support the complex argument of the ad. There is more to be said about this ad, and you may disagree with some of the points we have offered. But consider this: By 2007, almost 20 years after the ad was run, college guides were reporting that Hofstra's enrollment had climbed above 8000. Its admissions were more selective, its student body was more diverse and less regional in character, its graduation rate had improved, its sports teams had achieved national visibility, and its minority student population had grown. Many factors contributed to the university's advancement, but it seems likely that this ad was one such factor.

Write a Visual Analysis

Like rhetorical analysis, effective visual analysis takes into account the context of the image as well as its visual elements and any surrounding text. When you analyze a visual image, look carefully at its details and thoroughly consider its context. What visual elements grab your attention first, and how do other details reinforce that impression—what is most important and less important? How do color and style influence impressions? How does the image direct the viewer's eyes and reinforce what is important? What is the relationship between the image and any text that might accompany it? Consider the shapes, colors, and details of the image, as well as how the elements of the image connect with different arguments and audiences.

Consider also what you know or can learn about the context of an image and the design and text that surround it. Try to determine why and when it was created, who created it, where it appeared, and the target audience. Think about how the context of its creation and publication affected its intended audience. What elements have you seen before? Which elements remind you of other visuals?

Sample Student Visual Analysis

Angela Yamashita
Dr. Sanchez
English 15
13 October 2008

Got Roddick?

Andy Roddick is one of the hottest up-and-coming athletes of today. In 2003 he became the youngest American to finish ranked number one in the ATP rankings, and he's known not only for his excellent playing skills but also for his good looks and easygoing attitude. Ex-boyfriend to popular singer Mandy Moore, Roddick has been thrown into the spotlight and is now a teenage crush. It was his picture that stopped me while leafing through *Seventeen* and made me take a longer look. Roddick stands staring at the viewer, racquet over his shoulder, leaning against the net on the court. More prominent than his white pants, white tennis shirt, and white towel draped around his neck is the white milk mustache above his upper lip. The ad reads, "Now serving. I'm into power. So I drink milk. It packs 9 essential nutrients into every glass. Which comes in handy whether

"Got Milk?" ad featuring Andy Roddick

you're an athlete or an energetic fan." At the bottom of the page is the ad slogan (also in white) "Got Milk?"

The "Got Milk?" campaign has been going on since 1993. Its numerous ads try to convince adults to drink more milk. Everyone from rock groups to actors to athletes have participated in this campaign. In today's caffeine-obsessed society of coffee and soda drinkers, America's Dairy Farmers and Milk Processors (the association that sponsors the "Got Milk?" campaign) felt the need to reverse the decline in milk consumption by advertising milk in a new way. The catchy "Got Milk?" proved to be highly successful, and the campaign has been mimicked by many others, including "Got cookies?" "Got fish?" "Got sports?" and even "Got Jesus?" (Philpot). The Andy Roddick ad is typical of the "Got Milk?" series, urging people young and old to drink milk to remain healthy and strong. The Roddick ad primarily uses the appeals ethos and pathos to persuade its audience. (The one gesture toward logos in the ad is the fact that milk has nine nutrients.)

America's Dairy Farmers and Milk Processors uses celebrity endorsements to establish the ethos of their ads. The "Got Milk?" campaign has enlisted a range of celebrities popular with young audiences from Amy Grant to Austin Powers, Britney Spears to Brett Favre, T-Mac (Tracy McGrady) to Bernie Mac. Andy Roddick, the dominant young male player in American tennis, fits squarely in this lineup. Admired by a strong following of young adults (girls for his looks, boys for his athletic ability), Roddick is an ideal spokesman for establishing that milk is a healthy drink. Implicit in the ad is that milk will help you become a better athlete and better looking too.

The ad conveys pathos not simply through Roddick's good looks. His pose is casual, almost slouching, yet his face is serious, one that suggests that he means business not only about playing tennis but also about his drink of choice. The words "I'm into power" don't mess around. They imply that you too can be more powerful by drinking milk. "Now serving" is also in your face, making a play on the word *serving* both as a tennis and a drink term.

The effectiveness of the "Got Milk?" campaign is demonstrated in gallons of milk sold. The campaign began in California in 1993 at a time when milk sales were rapidly eroding. A San Francisco ad agency developed the milk mustache idea, which is credited for stopping the

Yamashita 3

downward trend in milk consumption in California. In 1995 the campaign went national. By 2000 national sales of milk remained consistent in contrast to annual declines in the early 1990s (Stamler). "Got Milk?" gave milk a brand identity that it previously had lacked, allowing it to compete with the well-established identities of Pepsi and Coca-Cola. Milk now has new challengers with more and more people going out to Starbucks and other breakfast bars. Nonetheless, the original formula of using celebrities like Andy Roddick who appeal to younger audiences continues to work. Milk isn't likely to go away soon as a popular beverage.

Yamashita 4

Works Cited

"Got Milk?" Advertisement. Milk Processor Education Program, 2007. Web. 3 Oct. 2008.

Philpot, Robert. "Copycats Mimic 'Got Milk' Ads." *Milwaukee Journal Sentinel* 12 May 2002, final ed.: D3. *LexisNexis Academic*. Web. 6 Oct. 2008.

Stamler, Bernard. "Got Sticking Power?" *New York Times* 30 July 2001, late ed.: C11. *LexisNexis Academic*. Web. 6 Oct. 2008.

Steps to Writing a Visual Analysis

Step 1 Select an Example of Visual Persuasion to Analyze

Many visual objects and images intend to persuade. Of course, all forms of advertising fall into the category of persuasion.

Examples

- Car ads: What draws you to look at and read some ads and skip others? How can you tell whether or not you are the intended audience for a particular ad?
- Maps: What is represented on a map? What is most prominent? What is left out? Maps most often do not make explicit claims, but they are persuasive nonetheless.
- Popular consumer products such as iPods, cell phones, or computers: Why did the iPod become the hottest-selling MP3 player? What makes it or any other popular product stand out?
- Public buildings or parks in your city or town: What messages do they convey?
- Images on an online real estate site: Why are particular pictures of a house displayed? What arguments do those images make?
- Cartoons: What about a cartoon makes it funny—the image, the caption, or the historical context?

Step 2 Analyze the Context

What is the context?

- Why was this image or object created?
- What was the purpose?
- Where did it come from?

Who is the audience?

- What can you infer about the intended audience?
- What did the designer(s) assume the audience knew or believed?

Who is the designer?

- Do you know the identity of the author?
- What else has the designer done?

Step 3 Analyze the Image

What is the subject?

- Can you describe the content?
- How is the image or object arranged?

What is the medium? the genre?

- What is the medium? A printed photograph? an oil painting? an outdoor sign? a building?
- What is the genre? An advertisement? a monument? a portrait? a cartoon? What expectations does the audience have about this genre?

Are words connected to the image or object?

- Is there a caption attached to the image, or are there words in the image?
- Are there words on the building or object?

What appeals are used?

- Are there appeals to ethos—the character of what is represented?
- Are there appeals to logos—the documentation of facts?
- Are there appeals to pathos—the values of the audience? Are there elements that can be considered as symbolic?

How would you characterize the style?

- Is the style formal, informal, comic, or something else?
- Are any visual metaphors used?

Step 4 Write a Draft

- Introduce the image or object and provide the background.

- Make a claim about the image or object you are analyzing. For example, the "Got Milk?" ad featuring Andy Roddick relies on the appeals of ethos and pathos.
- Support your claim with close analysis of the image or object. Describe key features.

Step 5 Revise, Edit, Proofread

- For detailed instructions, see Chapter 4.
- For a checklist to use to evaluate your draft, see pages 61–62.

PART 3

Writing Arguments

PART 3 — Writing Arguments

7. Putting Good Reasons into Action 109

Use different approaches to construct an argument 110

FINDING GOOD REASONS 111

8. Definition Arguments 113

Understand how definition arguments work 113

Recognize kinds of definitions 114

FINDING GOOD REASONS 117

Build a definition argument 118

Scott McCloud, Setting the Record Straight 121

Chris Nguyen (student), Speech Doesn't Have to Be Pretty to Be Protected 129

STEPS TO WRITING A DEFINITION ARGUMENT 134

9. Causal Arguments 137

Understand how causal arguments work 137

Find causes 138

FINDING GOOD REASONS 140

Build a causal argument 142

Annie Murphy Paul, The Real Marriage Penalty 144

Emily Raine, Why Should I Be Nice to You? Coffee Shops and the Politics of Good Service 147

STEPS TO WRITING A CAUSAL ARGUMENT 153

10. Evaluation Arguments 156

Understand how evaluation arguments work 156

Recognize kinds of evaluations 157

FINDING GOOD REASONS 159

Build an evaluation argument 160

Michael Eric Dyson, Gangsta Rap and American Culture 162

Rashaun Giddens (student), Stop Loss or "Loss of Trust" 169

STEPS TO WRITING AN EVALUATION ARGUMENT 174

11. Narrative Arguments 177

Understand how narrative arguments work 178

Recognize kinds of narrative arguments 179

FINDING GOOD REASONS 180

Build a narrative argument 181

Leslie Marmon Silko, The Border Patrol State 182

Dagoberto Gilb, My Landlady's Yard 187

STEPS TO WRITING A NARRATIVE ARGUMENT 190

12. Rebuttal Arguments 192

Understand how rebuttal arguments work 193

FINDING GOOD REASONS 195

Recognize kinds of rebuttal arguments 196

Build a rebuttal argument 199

Dan Stein, Crossing the Line 200

Gregory Rodriguez, Illegal Immigrants—They're Money 202

STEPS TO WRITING A REBUTTAL ARGUMENT 205

13. Proposal Arguments 209

Understand how proposal arguments work 210

Recognize components of proposal arguments 211

FINDING GOOD REASONS 212

Build a proposal argument 213

Thomas Homer-Dixon and S. Julio Friedmann, Coal in a Nice Shade of Green 215

Kim Lee (student), Let's Make It a Real Melting Pot with Presidential Hopes for All 218

STEPS TO WRITING A PROPOSAL ARGUMENT 222

7

Putting Good Reasons into Action

For decades police used breathalyzers to combat drunk driving, but alcohol-related traffic deaths recently began to rise after a period of decline. Law enforcement officials now want alcohol detection devices in every vehicle, like seat belts. Do you think these devices should be required?

Imagine that you bought a new car in June and you are taking some of your friends to your favorite lake over the Fourth of July weekend. You have a great time until, as you are heading home, a drunk driver—a repeat offender—swerves into your lane and totals your new car. You and your friends are lucky not to be hurt, but you're outraged because you believe that repeat offenders should be prevented from driving, even if that means putting them in jail. You also remember going to another state that had sobriety checkpoints on holiday weekends. If such a checkpoint had been at the lake, you might still be driving your new car. You live in a town that encourages citizens to contribute to the local newspaper, and you think you could get a guest editorial published. The question is, how do you want to write the editorial?

- You could tell your story about how a repeat drunk driver endangered the lives of you and your friends.
- You could define driving while intoxicated (DWI) as a more legally culpable crime.
- You could compare the treatment of drunk drivers in your state with the treatment of drunk drivers in another state.
- You could cite statistics that alcohol-related accidents killed 17,941 people in 2006, an increase from 2005.
- You could evaluate the present drunk-driving laws as insufficiently just or less than totally successful.
- You could propose taking vehicles away from repeat drunk drivers and forcing them to serve mandatory sentences.
- You could argue that your community should have sobriety checkpoints at times when drunk drivers are likely to be on the road.
- You could do several of the above.

You're not going to have much space in the newspaper, so you decide to argue for sobriety checkpoints. You know that they are controversial. One of your friends who was in the car with you said that the checkpoints are unconstitutional because they involve search without cause. However, after doing some research to find out whether checkpoints are defined as legal or illegal, you learn that on June 14, 1990, the U.S. Supreme Court upheld the constitutionality of using checkpoints as a deterrent and enforcement tool against drunk drivers.

But you still want to know whether most people would agree with your friend that sobriety checkpoints are an invasion of privacy. You find opinion polls and surveys going back to the 1980s that show that 70 to 80 percent of those polled support sobriety checkpoints. You also realize that you can argue by analogy that security checkpoints for alcohol are similar in many ways to airport security checkpoints that protect passengers. You decide you will finish by making an argument from consequence. If people who go to the lake with plans to drink know in advance that there will be checkpoints, they will find a designated driver or some other means of safe transportation, and everyone else will also be a safer.

The point of this example is that people very rarely set out to define something in an argument for the sake of definition, to compare for the sake of comparison, or to adopt any of the other ways of structuring an argument. Instead, they have a purpose in mind, and they use the kinds of arguments that are discussed in Chapters 8-13—most often in combination—as means to an end. Most arguments use multiple approaches and multiple sources of good reasons. Proposal arguments in particular often analyze a present situation with definition, causal, and evaluative arguments before advancing a course of future action to address that situation. The advantage of thinking explicitly about the structure of arguments is that you often find other ways to argue. Sometimes you just need a way to get started writing about complex issues.

Use Different Approaches to Construct An Argument

An even greater advantage of thinking explicitly about specific kinds of arguments is that they can often give you a sequence for constructing arguments. Take affirmative action policies for granting admission to college as an example. No issue has been more controversial on college campuses during the last ten years.

Definition

What exactly does *affirmative action* mean? It is a policy that attempts to address the reality of contemporary social inequality based on past injustice. But injustice

Finding Good Reasons

WHAT DO WE MEAN BY DIVERSITY?

Colleges and universities talk a great deal about diversity nowadays, but what exactly do they mean by diversity? If diversity is connected with people, do they mean diversity of races and ethnicities? Is it diversity of nations and cultures represented among the students? Should the numbers of students of different races, ethnicities, or family income levels be roughly equal to the population of the state where the school is located? Is a campus diverse if about 60 percent of the students are women and 40 percent men, as many campuses now are? Or if diversity is connected with ideas, what makes for a diverse intellectual experience on a college campus?

Write about it

1. Formulate your own definition of what diversity means on a college campus (see Chapter 8).

2. Evaluate diversity on your campus according to your definition. Is your campus good or bad in its diversity (see Chapter 10)?

3. What are the effects of having a diverse campus, however you define diversity (see Chapter 9)? What happens if a campus isn't diverse?

4. If you consider diversity desirable, write a proposal that would increase diversity on your campus, whether it's interacting with people of different backgrounds or encountering a variety of ideas (see Chapter 13). Or if you think too much emphasis is being placed on diversity, write a rebuttal argument against proponents of diversity (see Chapter 12).

to whom and by whom? Do all members of minorities, all women, and all people with disabilities have equal claims for redress of past injustices? If not, how do you distinguish among them? And what exactly does affirmative action entail? Should all students who are admitted by affirmative action criteria automatically receive scholarships? Clearly, you need to define affirmative action first before proposing any changes in the policy.

Cause and effect

Since affirmative action policies have been around for a few years, you might next investigate how well they have worked. If you view affirmative action as a cause, then what have been its effects? You might find, for example, that the percentage of African Americans graduating from college dropped from 1991 to 2001 in many states. Furthermore, affirmative action policies have created a backlash attitude among many whites who believe, rightly or wrongly, that they are victims of reverse racism. But you might find that enrollment of minorities at your university has increased substantially since affirmative action policies were instituted. And you might come across a book by the then-presidents of Princeton and Harvard, William G. Bowen and Derek Bok, entitled *The Shape of the River: Long-Term Consequences of Considering Race in College and University Admissions*, which examines the effects of affirmative action policies at 28 of the nation's most select universities. They found that African-American graduates of elite schools were more likely than their white counterparts to earn graduate degrees and to take on civic responsibilities after graduation.

Evaluation

With a definition established and evidence collected, you can move to evaluation. Is affirmative action fair? Is the goal of achieving diversity through affirmative action admissions policies a worthy one because white people enjoyed preferential treatment until the last few decades? Or are affirmative action admissions policies bad because they continue the historically bad practice of giving preference to people of certain races and because they cast the people they are trying to help into the role of victims?

Proposal

When you have provided a definition with evidence and have made an evaluation, you have the groundwork for making a recommendation in the form of a proposal. A proposal argues what should be done in the future or what should not be done. It also outlines the good or bad consequences that will follow.

8

Definition Arguments

Is graffiti vandalism? Or is it art?

The continuing controversies about what art is, free speech, pornography, and hate crimes (to name just a few) illustrate why definitions often matter more than we might think. People argue about definitions because of the consequences of something being defined in a certain way. The controversies about certain subjects also illustrate three important principles that operate when definitions are used in arguments.

First, people make definitions that benefit their interests. Early in life you learned the importance of defining actions as "accidents." Windows can be broken through carelessness, especially when you are tossing a ball against the side of the house, but if it's an accident, well, accidents just happen (and don't require punishment).

Second, most of the time when you are arguing about a definition, your audience will either have a different definition in mind or be unsure of the definition. Your mother or father probably didn't think breaking the window was an accident, so you had to convince Mom or Dad that you were really being careful, and the ball just slipped out of your hand. It's your job to get them to accept your definition.

Third, if you can get your audience to accept your definition, then usually you succeed. For this reason, definition arguments are the most powerful arguments.

Understand How Definition Arguments Work

Definition arguments set out criteria and then argue that whatever is being defined meets or does not meet those criteria.

> **Something is (is not) a _____ because it has (does not have) features A, B, and C (or more).**

113

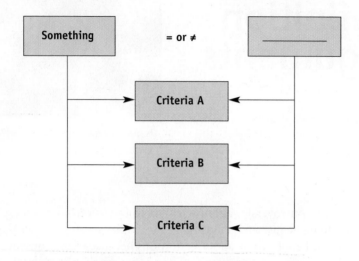

Graffiti is art because it is a means of self expression, it shows an understanding of design principles, and it stimulates both the senses and the mind.

Recognize Kinds of Definitions

Rarely do you get far into an argument without having to define something. Imagine that you are writing an argument about the decades-old and largely ineffective "war on drugs" in the United States. We all know that the war on drugs is being waged against drugs that are illegal, like cocaine and marijuana, and not against the legal drugs produced by the multibillion-dollar drug industry. Our society classifies drugs into two categories: "good" drugs, which are legal, and "bad" drugs, which are illegal.

How exactly does our society arrive at these definitions? Drugs would be relatively easy to define as good or bad if the difference could be defined at the molecular level. Bad drugs would contain certain molecules that define them as bad. The history of drug use in the United States, however, tells us that it is not so simple. In the twentieth century alcohol was on the list of illegal drugs for over a decade, while opium was considered a good drug and was distributed in many patent medicines by pharmaceutical companies. Similarly, LSD and MDMA (methylenedioxymethamphetamine, known better by its street name *ecstasy*) were developed by the pharmaceutical industry but later made illegal. In a few states marijuana is now legal for medicinal use.

If drugs cannot be classified as good or bad by their molecular structure, then perhaps society classifies them by their effects. It might be reasonable to assume that addictive drugs are illegal, but that's not the case. Nicotine is highly addictive and is a legal drug, as are many prescription medicines. Drugs taken for the purpose of pleasure are not necessarily illegal (think of alcohol and Viagra), nor are drugs that alter consciousness or change personality (such as Prozac).

How a drug is defined as legal or illegal apparently is determined by example. The nationwide effort to stop Americans from drinking alcohol during the first decades of the twentieth century led to the passage of the Eighteenth Amendment and the ban on sales of alcohol from 1920 to 1933, known as Prohibition. Those who argued for Prohibition used examples of drunkenness, especially among the poor, to show how alcohol broke up families and left mothers and children penniless in the street. Those who opposed Prohibition initially pointed to the consumption of beer and wine in many cultural traditions. Later they raised examples of the bad effects of Prohibition—the rise of organized crime, the increase in alcohol abuse, and the general disregard for laws.

When you make a definition argument, it's important to think about what kind of definition you will use. Descriptions of three types follow.

Formal definitions

Formal definitions typically categorize an item into the next-higher classification and provide criteria that distinguish the item from other items within that classification. Most dictionary definitions are formal definitions. For example, fish are cold-blooded aquatic vertebrates that have jaws, fins, and scales and are distinguished from other cold-blooded aquatic vertebrates (such as sea snakes) by the presence of gills. If you can construct a formal definition with specific criteria that your audience will accept, then likely you will have a strong argument. The key is to get your audience to agree to your criteria.

Operational definitions

Many concepts cannot be easily defined by formal definitions. Researchers in the natural and social sciences must construct **operational definitions** that they use for their research. For example, researchers who study binge drinking among college students define a binge as five or more drinks in one sitting for a man, and four or more drinks for a woman. Some people think this standard is too low and should be raised to six to eight drinks to distinguish true problem drinkers from the general college population. No matter what the number, researchers must argue that the particular definition is one that suits the concept.

Definitions from example

Many human qualities such as honesty, courage, creativity, deceit, and love must be defined by examples that the audience accepts as representative of the concept. Few would not call the firefighters who entered the World Trade Center on September 11, 2001, courageous. Most people would describe someone with a diagnosis of terminal cancer who refuses to feel self-pity as courageous. But what about a student who declines to go to a concert with her friends so she can study for an exam? Her behavior might be admirable, but most people would hesitate to call it courageous. The key to arguing a **definition from example** is that the examples must strike the audience as typical of the concept, even if the situation is unusual.

When Avenue Café's lease expired, the owners of the building refused to renew the restaurant's lease so they could tear down the building to make room for a hotel complex. The restaurant's owners appealed to the city for historic landmark status and received a generous settlement for relocating. What defines a building as a historic landmark?

Finding Good Reasons
WHAT IS PARODY?

The Adbusters Media Foundation, a Canadian media activist group, takes on specific advertising campaigns with clever spoofs of well-known ads. At the top of the Adbusters sabotage list have been alcohol and cigarette ads, among them the above parody of Absolut Vodka ads. (The caption quotes William Shakespeare: "Drink provokes the desire but takes away the performance.")

Because ads are in the public domain, their copyright status is questionable, and Adbusters has pushed that line. In 1992 Absolut threatened to sue Adbusters, but Absolut quickly backed down when the company recognized that the suit would lead to a public debate about protecting advertisers who sell dangerous products. Had the suit gone forward, the legal definition of parody—a work that comments upon or criticizes a prior work—would likely have been key to the Adbusters defense.

Write about it

1. Which of the following criteria do you think must be present for a work to be considered a parody? Are there any criteria you might change or add?

   - the work criticizes a previous work
   - the work copies the same structure, details, or style of the previous work
   - the connections to the previous work are clear to the audience
   - the work is humorous
   - the title is a play on the previous work
   - the work is presented in either a print, visual, or musical medium

2. Does the "Absolut Impotence" ad meet the criteria above? Would you define it as a parody? Why or why not?

Build a Definition Argument

Because definition arguments are the most powerful arguments, they are often at the center of the most important debates in American history. The major arguments of the civil rights movement were definition arguments, none more eloquent than Martin Luther King Jr.'s "Letter from Birmingham Jail." From 1957 until his assassination in April 1968, King served as president of the Southern Christian Leadership Conference, an organization of primarily African-American clergymen dedicated to bringing about social change. King, who was a Baptist minister, tried to put into practice Mahatma Gandhi's principles of nonviolence in demonstrations, sit-ins, and marches throughout the South. During Holy Week in 1963, King led demonstrations and a boycott of downtown merchants in Birmingham, Alabama, to end racial segregation at lunch counters and discriminatory hiring practices.

On Wednesday, April 10, the city obtained an injunction directing the demonstrations to cease until their legality could be argued in court. After meditation, King decided, against the advice of his associates, to defy the court order and proceed with the march planned for Good Friday morning. On Friday morning, April 12, King and 50 followers were arrested. King was held in solitary confinement until the end of the weekend. He was allowed neither to see his attorneys nor to call his wife. On the day of his arrest, King read in the newspaper a statement objecting to the demonstrations signed by eight white Birmingham clergymen of Protestant, Catholic, and Jewish faiths, urging that the protests stop and that grievances be settled in the courts.

On Saturday morning, King started writing an eloquent response that addresses the criticisms of the white clergymen, who are one primary audience of his response. But King intended his response to the ministers for widespread publication, and he clearly had in mind a larger readership. The clergymen gave him the occasion to address moderate white leaders in the South as well as religious and educated people across the nation and supporters of the civil rights movement. King begins "Letter from Birmingham Jail" by addressing the ministers as "My Dear Fellow Clergymen," adopting a conciliatory and tactful tone from the outset but at the same time offering strong arguments for the

Martin Luther King, Jr.

necessity of acting now rather than waiting for change. A critical part of King's argument is justifying disobedience of certain laws. The eight white clergymen asked that laws be obeyed until they were changed.

King argues that there are two kinds of laws: just and unjust. He maintains that people have a moral responsibility to obey just laws and, by the same logic, "a moral responsibility to disobey unjust laws." The cornerstone of his argument is the ability to distinguish just and unjust laws on clear moral and legal criteria. Otherwise people could selectively disobey any law they choose.

Here's how King makes the distinction:

> A just law is a man-made code that squares with the moral law or the law of God. An unjust law is a code that is out of harmony with the moral law. To put it in the terms of St. Thomas Aquinas: An unjust law is a human law that is not rooted in eternal law and natural law. Any law that uplifts human personality is just. Any law that degrades human personality is unjust. All segregation statutes are unjust because segregation distorts the soul and damages the personality. It gives the segregator a false sense of superiority and the segregated a false sense of inferiority. Segregation, to use the terminology of the Jewish philosopher Martin Buber, substitutes an "I-it" relationship and ends up relegating persons to the status of things. Hence segregation is not only politically, economically and sociologically unsound, it is morally wrong and sinful.

King's analysis of just and unjust laws is a classic definitional argument. According to King, a just law possesses the criteria of being consistent with moral law and uplifting human personality. Just as important, King sets out the criteria of an unjust law, which has the criteria of being out of harmony with moral law and damaging to human personality. The criteria are set out in because clauses: _____ *is a* _____ *because it has these criteria.* The criteria provide the link shown in Figure 8.1. The negative argument can be made in the same way, as shown in Figure 8.2.

An extended definition argument like King's is a two-step process. First you have to determine the criteria. Then you have to argue that what you are defining possesses these criteria. If you want to argue that housing prisoners in unheated and non-air-conditioned tents is cruel and unusual punishment, then you have to make exposing prisoners to hot and cold extremes one of the criteria of cruel and unusual punishment. The keys to a definitional argument are getting your audience to accept your criteria and getting your audience to accept that the case in point meets those criteria. King's primary audience was the eight white clergymen; therefore, he used religious criteria and cited theologians as his authorities. His second criterion, that just laws uplift the human personality, was a less familiar concept than the idea of moral law. King therefore offered a more detailed explanation.

But King also knew that not all of his potential readers would put quite so much stock in religious authorities. Therefore, in his letter he follows the religious criteria with two other criteria that appeal to definitions of democracy. First, King

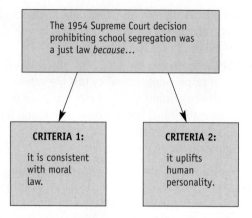

Figure 8.1

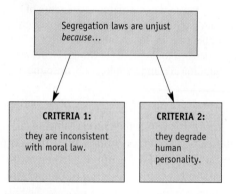

Figure 8.2

argues that "An unjust law is a code that a numerical or power majority group compels a minority group to obey but does not make binding on itself." Just laws, according to King, are ones that everyone should follow. Second, King points out that many African Americans were denied the right to vote in Alabama, and consequently the Alabama legislature that passed the segregation laws was not elected democratically. In all, King sets out four major criteria for defining just and unjust laws (see Figure 8.3).

King's "Letter from Birmingham Jail" draws much of its rhetorical power from its reliance on a variety of arguments that are suited for different readers. An atheist could reject the notion of laws made by God but could still be convinced by the criteria that segregation laws are undemocratic and therefore unjust. To make definitional arguments work, often you must put much effort into identifying and explaining your criteria. You must convince your readers that your criteria are the best ones for what you are defining and that they apply to the case you are arguing.

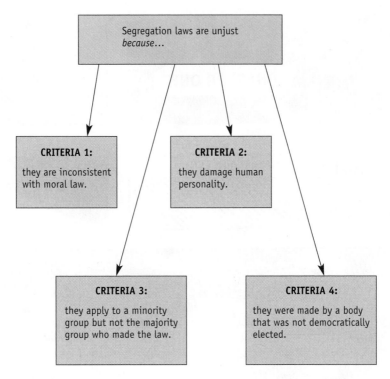

Figure 8.3

Scott McCloud

Setting the Record Straight

Scott McCloud is the pseudonym of Scott Willard McLeod, who was born in Boston in 1960 and graduated from Syracuse University in 1982. After a short stint in the production department at DC Comics, he quickly became a highly regarded writer and illustrator of comics. His works include Reinventing Comics: How Imagination and Technology Are Revolutionizing an Art Form *(2000),* Making Comics: Storytelling Secrets of Comics, Manga and Graphic Novels *(2006), and* Understanding Comics: The Invisible Art *(1993), from which this selection is taken.*

Understanding Comics is a brilliant explanation of how comics combine words and pictures to achieve effects that neither words nor pictures can do alone. At the beginning of the book, McCloud finds it necessary to define what comics are and are not before he can begin to analyze the magic of comics. Notice how he has to refine his criteria several times before he has an adequate definition. ∎

Understanding Comics Copyright © 1993, 1994 by Scott McCloud. Published by Kitchen Sink Press. Reprinted by permission of HarperCollins Publishers Inc.

THE ARTFORM--THE *MEDIUM*--KNOWN AS COMICS IS A *VESSEL* WHICH CAN HOLD ANY *NUMBER* OF *IDEAS* AND *IMAGES*.

THE *"CONTENT"* OF THOSE IMAGES AND IDEAS IS, OF COURSE, UP TO *CREATORS*, AND WE ALL HAVE DIFFERENT *TASTES*.

GLUG
GLUG

PTUI!!!

GAAK
WHEEEEZ
KAF! KAF!
GLUGH-GGH...

ahem

THE *TRICK* IS TO NEVER MISTAKE THE *MESSAGE*--

--FOR THE *MESSENGER*.

COMICS

AT ONE TIME OR ANOTHER VIRTUALLY *ALL* THE GREAT MEDIA HAVE RECEIVED *CRITICAL EXAMINATION*, IN AND OF *THEMSELVES*.

WRITTEN WORD · MUSIC · VIDEO

THEATRE · VISUAL ART · FILM

BUT FOR *COMICS*, THIS ATTENTION HAS BEEN *RARE*. *

LET'S SEE IF WE CAN HELP *RECTIFY* THE SITUATION.

* EISNER'S OWN *COMICS AND SEQUENTIAL ART* BEING A HAPPY EXCEPTION.

*JUXTAPOSED = ADJACENT, SIDE-BY-SIDE.
GREAT ART SCHOOL WORD.

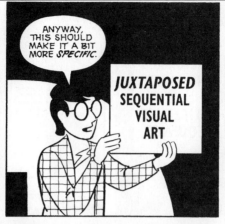

Sample Student Definition Argument

Chris Nguyen
Professor Conley
GOV 322
24 March 2009

Speech Doesn't Have to Be Pretty to Be Protected

Last month six students on our campus were ejected from a university auditorium for wearing T-shirts with WAR CRIMINAL on the front. Was the university justified in removing our fellow students who were not disruptive in any other way?

The First Amendment to the Constitution of the United States of America guarantees the right to freedom of expression. This important right is one of the foundations of our democracy. Yet many Americans do not understand what the right to free speech really means. Free speech is your right to say what you think—within limits. It is not the right to cause mayhem, to threaten violence, or to incite others to violence. Authority figures also need to understand the limits on free speech. Generally, courts have found that, in order for the restriction of free speech to be justified, the speech must incite imminent lawless action (such as a riot), and it must take place on public property. Even in public high schools, where the government has an obligation to protect minors, "imminent lawless action" must be threatened before speech can be repressed.

Clearly, it's not always easy to tell when restriction of free speech is justified. Consider these recent controversies over free speech:

- A student at Warren Hills Regional High School in New Jersey was suspended for wearing a T-shirt that featured the word *redneck* ("Federal Court").
- Jeff and Nicole Rank attended an official visit by President Bush at the West Virginia capitol and were charged with trespassing when they refused to remove T-shirts that read "Love America, Hate Bush" (Bundy).
- Six students were removed from a university auditorium and charged with trespassing during a speech by former U.S. Secretary of State Henry Kissinger for wearing T-shirts that referred to the speaker as a "war criminal."

In the first two cases, it has been established that authorities did not have the right to curtail the speech of the people involved: A federal appeals court decided the first case in favor of the student, and the prosecutor in the second case dropped the charges, admitting that no law had been broken. If we examine the similarities and differences among these three cases, it becomes clear that in the third case, which happened on our own campus last month, the administration's ejection of the students was unconstitutional.

These are the factors the three cases have in common:

1. In each case, the wearers of the shirts did not express themselves in any way other than by wearing the shirts. They did not speak, shout, hold up banners or signs, or call attention to themselves.
2. None of the events where the shirts were worn were disrupted by the shirts. Any disruption that occurred was due to the removal of the wearers by authority figures.
3. None of the T-shirts featured obscene language or imagery.
4. All took place in government-funded venues: a public school, a state capitol, and a state-funded university.

These similarities are important because they show how, in each case, the T-shirt wearers acted within their constitutionally protected right to free expression.

The first two factors above show how each of these cases fails to meet the standard of "imminent lawless action," set in the 1969 case of *Brandenburg v. Ohio*. In that case, the Supreme Court ruled that in order to ban forms of expression, the government had to prove the expression was "directed to and likely to incite imminent lawless action." If the act of expression did not seem likely to cause a riot, for example, it could not be restricted. Simply making people angry or uncomfortable is not justification for censorship.

In the first case, at Warren Hills High School, the only person who objected to the T-shirt was a vice principal, who claimed the term *redneck* was offensive to minority students and violated the school's racial harassment policy ("Federal Court"). The U.S. Court of Appeals for the Third Circuit, however, ruled that the school failed to prove "that the shirt might genuinely threaten disruption or, indeed, that it violated any of the particular provisions of the harassment policy." This decision followed the precedent of another landmark case, *Tinker v. Des Moines*, in which the Supreme Court ruled that, even in public schools, the government must provide evidence that the speech would cause "(a.) a substantial disruption of the school environment, or (b.) an invasion of the rights of others" (Haynes).

In the second case, the government never even made a claim that the T-shirts worn by Jeff and Nicole Rank were inciting lawlessness. The only people who were upset by the Ranks' T-shirts were two Secret Service officers, who ordered the couple to remove the shirts. When they refused, the officers ordered Charleston city police to arrest them, which the police did. The Ranks were charged with trespassing ("Secret Service"). The irony of arresting U.S. citizens for standing peacefully on public, state-owned property was even clear to the prosecutor, who dropped the charges (Bundy).

Moreover, none of the cases met the test for "vulgar or obscene" language. Vulgar and obscene language can be regulated, to some extent, without violating the First Amendment. In 1986, the Supreme Court ruled in the case of *Bethel v. Fraser* that public school officials could prohibit vulgar speech at a school assembly. The court said that "[T]he undoubted freedom to advocate unpopular and controversial views in schools and classrooms must be balanced against the society's countervailing interest in teaching students the boundaries of socially appropriate behavior." The vice principal in the Warren Hills case was the only one who thought *redneck* was offensive, and the fact that the word is used constantly on television and other media shows that it is not considered obscene by society at large.

The Ranks' arrest is a better comparison to the situation at our school, because their shirts were clearly singled out for their political content, not for vulgarity. They carried a message that might have been offensive to some of the president's supporters who were present, but under no circumstances could the content of the shirts be considered obscene. The same is true of the shirts that got my fellow students kicked out of a public event. Calling someone a war criminal is a serious accusation, but it is not obscene.

Finally, public versus private venue is an important factor in the protection of free speech. The Constitution guarantees that the state will not infringe the right to free expression. Private entities are free to do so, however. For example, protestors can be thrown out of a private meeting of club members. Even a shopping mall owner can deny entry to protesters or even to people without shoes. Of course, anyone with private property also has to consider the economic impact of limiting speech. Recently a shopping mall owner had police arrest a man wearing a "Give Peace a Chance" T-shirt ("Man Arrested") that he had just bought in the mall. Not surprisingly, the mall owner received a great deal of bad publicity about this decision. Concerned citizens who felt this action by the mall owner went too far wrote letters to newspapers publicizing the act. They even wrote letters to the police who arrested the man ("Big Support"). The trespassing charges against the man were dropped. This incident illustrates how free speech is negotiated in the marketplace.

In the Ranks' case, the trespassing charges against them were dropped because they were on the statehouse grounds. How can a citizen trespass on public property? In the same vein, how can students be trespassing on their own campus? The six people arrested at our school were students, whose tuition and fees helped pay for the building they were in. What's more, the event was advertised in flyers and newspaper ads as "free and open to the public." How can anyone be charged with trespassing at a public event?

The Warren Hills case was decided in favor of the student, even though the expression took place in a public school. As *Bethel v. Fraser* shows, courts generally rule that schools can take special steps to protect minors: vulgar or obscene speech can be censored, and school-sponsored forms of expression, like newspapers, can be censored. But these actions are justified because the students are minors. Presumably, they need more guidance as they learn about the boundaries of socially acceptable behavior. But most college students are legally adults, so it does not make sense to say our school was "teaching students the boundaries of socially appropriate behavior" by throwing them out of a public event because of their shirts. It is not the job of a college administration to teach manners.

Our school administrators violated the Constitutional rights of six students last month. They forcibly removed them from a public event in a public building. The students were not causing a commotion in any way before their arrests; there was no indication whatsoever that "imminent lawless action" might be provoked by their T-shirts. Because the students in this case were clearly exercising their Constitutional right to free speech, the university administration should immediately drop the trespassing charges against the students. Evidence from prior cases indicates the charges will not stand up in court in any case, so

Nguyen 5

the legal battle will be a waste of money for the college. Furthermore, as an institution of learning that supposedly safeguards the free exchange of ideas, the college should offer a sincere apology to the arrested students. The administrators would send an important message to all students by doing this: Your right to free speech is respected at this school.

Nguyen 6

Works Cited

Bethel School Dist. v. Fraser. 478 US 675. Supreme Court of the US. 1986. *Supreme Court Collection*. Legal Information Inst., Cornell U Law School, n.d. Web. 7 Mar. 2009.

"Big Support for 'Peace' T-shirt Arrestees." *The Smoking Gun*. Turner Entertainment Digital Network, 25 Mar. 2003. Web. 10 Mar. 2009.

Brandenburg v. Ohio. 395 US 444. Supreme Court of the US. 1969. *Supreme Court Collection*. Legal Information Inst., Cornell U Law School, n.d. Web. 7 Mar. 2009.

Bundy, Jennifer. "Trespass Charges Dropped Against Bush Protesters." *CommonDreams.org Newscenter*. CommonDreams.org, 15 July 2004. Web. 18 Mar. 2009.

"Federal Court Says NJ School Can't Ban Redneck T-shirt." *Center for Individual Rights*. Center for Individual Rights, 6 Nov. 2003. Web. 11 Mar. 2009.

Haynes, Charles C. "T-shirt Rebellion in the Land of the Free." *First Amendment*. First Amendment Center, 14 Mar. 2004. Web. 18 Mar. 2009.

"Man Arrested for 'Peace' T-shirt." *CNN.com*. Cable News Network, 4 Mar. 2003. Web. 15 Mar. 2009.

"Secret Service and White House Charged with Violating Free Speech Rights in ACLU Lawsuit." *ACLU*. American Civil Liberties Union, 14 Sept. 2004. Web. 19 Mar. 2009.

Steps to Writing a Definition Argument

Step 1 Make a Claim

Make a definitional claim on a controversial issue that focuses on a key term.

Template

■ _____ is (or is not) a _____ because it has (or does not have) features A, B, and C (or more).

Examples

■ Hate speech (or pornography, literature, films, and so on) is (or is not) free speech protected by the First Amendment because it has (or does not have) these features.

■ Hunting (or using animals for cosmetics testing, keeping animals in zoos, wearing furs, and so on) is (or is not) cruelty to animals because it has (or does not have) these features.

■ A pharmacist who denies a patient birth control (or the morning-after pill) based on his or her religious beliefs is (or is not) in violation of the Hippocratic oath. *because*

■ Displaying pinup calendars (or jokes, innuendo, rap lyrics, and so on) is (or is not) an example of sexual harassment. *because*

Step 2 Think About What's at Stake

■ Does nearly everyone agree with you? If so, then your claim probably isn't interesting or important. If you can think of people who disagree, then something is at stake.

■ Who argues the opposite of your claim?

■ Why or how do they benefit from a different definition?

Step 3 List the Criteria

- Which criteria are necessary for _____ to be a _____?
- Which are not necessary?
- Which are the most important?
- Does your case in point meet all the criteria?

Step 4 Analyze Your Potential Readers

- Who are your readers?
- How does the definitional claim you are making affect them?
- How familiar are they with the issue, concept, or controversy that you're writing about?
- What are they likely to know and not know?
- Which criteria are they most likely to accept with little explanation, and which will they disagree with?
- Which criteria will you have to argue for?

Step 5 Write a Draft

Introduction

- Set out the issue, concept, or controversy.
- Explain why the definition is important.
- Give the background that your intended readers need.

Body

- Set out your criteria and argue for the appropriateness of the criteria.
- Determine whether the criteria apply to the case in point.
- Anticipate where readers might question either your criteria or how they apply to your subject.
- Address opposing viewpoints by acknowledging how their definitions differ and by showing why your definition is better.

Conclusion

■ Do more than simply summarize. You can, for example, go into more detail about what is at stake or the implications of your definition.

Step 6 Revise, Edit, Proofread

■ For detailed instructions, see Chapter 4.
■ For a checklist to use to evaluate your draft, see pages 61–62.

9

Causal Arguments

Why is the number of women studying computer science shrinking at a time when the number of women studying science and engineering is increasing?

Why did the driver who passed you on a blind curve risk his life to get one car ahead at the next traffic light? Why is it hard to recognize people you know when you run into them unexpectedly in an unfamiliar setting? Why does your mother or father spend an extra hour, plus the extra gas, driving to a supermarket across town just to save a few pennies on one or two items on sale?

Life is full of big and little mysteries, and people spend a lot of time speculating about the causes. Most of the time, however, they don't take the time to analyze in depth what causes a trend, event, or phenomenon. But in college and in the workplace, you likely will have to write causal arguments that require in-depth analysis. In a professional career you will have to make many detailed causal analyses: Why did a retail business fail when it seemed to have an ideal location? What causes cost overruns in the development of a new product? What causes people in some circumstances to prefer public transportation over driving?

Understand How Causal Arguments Work

Causal arguments take three basic forms.

1. One cause leads to one or more effects.

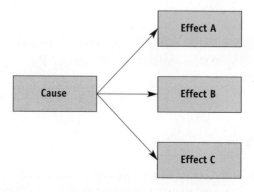

The invention of the telegraph led to the commodities market, the establishment of standard time zones, and news reporting as we know it today.

2. One effect has several causes.

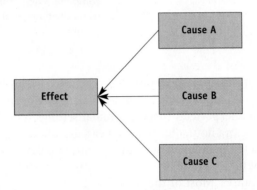

Hurricanes are becoming more financially destructive to the United States because of the greater intensity of recent storms, an increase in the commercial and residential development of coastal areas, and a reluctance to enforce certain construction standards in coastal residential areas.

3. Something causes something else to happen, which in turn causes something else to happen.

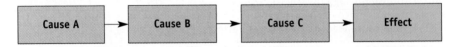

Making the HPV vaccination mandatory for adolescent girls will make unprotected sex seem safer, leading to greater promiscuity, and resulting in more teenage pregnancies.

Find Causes

The causal claim is at the center of a causal argument. Therefore, to get started on a causal argument, you need to propose one or more causes. The big problem with causal arguments is that any topic worth writing about is likely to be complex, making identifying causes difficult. The philosopher John Stuart Mill recognized this problem long ago and devised four methods for finding causes:

- **The Common Factor Method.** When the cause-and-effect relationship occurs more than once, look for something in common in the events and circumstances of each effect; any common factor could be the cause. Scientists have used this method to explain how seemingly different phenomena are associated. There were a variety of explanations of fire until, in the 1700s, Joseph Priestley in England and Antoine Lavoisier in France discovered that oxygen was a separate element and that burning was caused by oxidation.

- **The Single Difference Method.** This method works only when there are at least two similar situations, one that leads to an effect and one that does not. Look for something that was missing in one case and present in another—the single difference. The writer assumes that if everything is substantially alike in both cases, then the single difference is the (or a) cause. At the Battle of Midway in 1942, the major naval battle of World War II in the Pacific, the Japanese Navy had a 4-to-1 advantage over the U.S. Navy. Both fleets were commanded by competent, experienced leaders. But the U.S. commander, Admiral Nimitz, had a superior advantage in intelligence, which proved to be decisive.

- **Concomitant Variation.** This tongue twister is another favorite method of scientists. If an investigator finds that a possible cause and a possible effect have a similar pattern of variation, then one can suspect that a relationship exists. For example, scientists noticed that peaks in the 11-year sunspot cycle have predictable effects on high-frequency radio transmission on the earth.

- **Process of Elimination.** Many possible causes can be proposed for most trends and events. If you are a careful investigator, you have to consider all causes that you can think of and eliminate the ones that cannot be causes.

To understand how these methods might work for you, consider this example. Suppose you want to research the causes of the increase in legalized lotteries in the United States. You might discover that lotteries go back to colonial times. Harvard and Yale universities have been longtime rivals in football, but the schools' rivalry goes back much further. Both schools ran lotteries before the Revolutionary War! In 1747 the Connecticut legislature voted to allow Yale to conduct a lottery to raise money to build dormitories, and in 1765 the Massachusetts legislature gave Harvard permission for a lottery. Lotteries were common before and after the American Revolution, but they eventually ran into trouble because they were run by private companies that failed to pay the winners. After 1840, laws against lotteries were passed, but they came back in the South after the Civil War.

Finding Good Reasons
WHY ARE AMERICANS GAINING WEIGHT?

Eric Schlosser, author of *Fast Food Nation* (2001), chows down on a grilled cheese sandwich, fries, and a soda. *Fast Food Nation* traces the rise of fast food restaurants against the background of American culture based on the automobile. Schlosser claims that one of the effects of fast food is the increase of overweight Americans. For an example of his writing on another topic, see pages 520-523.

There is no doubt that Americans have grown larger. A 2004 survey of Americans published in *JAMA: The Journal of the American Medical Association* found that nearly one-third (32.5 percent) of adults are obese and two-thirds (66.3 percent) are overweight. An especially disturbing aspect of this trend is that children are increasingly obese. The Center for Disease Control and Prevention reports that the percentage of obese children aged 6 to 11 almost quadrupled from 4 percent in 1974 to 15 percent in 2000, and the percentage of obese children aged 12 to 19 increased from 6 percent in 1974 to 15 percent in 2000.

Write about it

To what extent do you think fast food is the cause of the trend toward excess weight? To what extent do you think lifestyle changes and the content of food are causes? In addition to the amount of fast food Americans consume, consider the following:

- more sedentary lifestyle with more driving and less walking
- more time spent watching television, using computers, and playing video games
- introduction of high-fructose corn syrup in many foods, from ketchup and peanut butter to chocolate milk and yogurt
- inadequate physical education and reduced outdoor recess periods in schools
- more food advertising directed at children

The defeated states of the Confederacy needed money to rebuild the bridges, buildings, and schools that were destroyed in the Civil War, and they turned to selling lottery tickets throughout the nation (ironically, the tickets were very popular in the North). Once again, the lotteries were run by private companies, and scandals eventually led to their being banned.

In 1964 the voters in New Hampshire approved a lottery as a means of funding education—in preference to an income tax or a sales tax. Soon other northeastern states followed this lead and establishing lotteries with the reasoning that if people were going to gamble, the money should remain at home. During the 1980s, other states approved not only lotteries but also other forms of state-run gambling such as keno and video poker. By 1993 only Hawaii and Utah had no legalized gambling of any kind.

If you are analyzing the causes of the spread of legalized gambling, you might use the **common factor method** to investigate what current lotteries have in common with earlier lotteries. That factor is easy to identify: It's economic. The early colonies and later the states have turned to lotteries again and again as a way of raising money that avoids unpopular tax increases. But why have lotteries spread so quickly and seemingly become so permanent since 1964, when before that, they were used only sporadically and were banned eventually? The **single difference method** points us to the major difference between the lotteries of today and those of previous eras: Lotteries in the past were run by private companies, and inevitably someone took off with the money instead of paying it out. Today's lotteries are owned and operated by state agencies or contracted under state control, and while they are not immune to scandals, they are much more closely monitored than lotteries were in the past.

The controversies over legal gambling now focus on casinos. In 1988 Congress passed the Indian Gaming Regulatory Act, which started a new era of casino gambling in the United States. The world's largest casino, Foxwoods Casino in Connecticut, owned by the Mashantucket Pequot Tribe, became a huge moneymaker. Along with nearby Mohegan Sun Casino, Foxwoods paid over $400 million into the Connecticut state treasury. Other tribes and other states were quick to cash in on casino gambling. Iowa legalized riverboat gambling in 1989, followed shortly by Louisiana, Illinois, Indiana, Mississippi, and Missouri. As with lotteries, the primary justification for approving casino gambling has been economic. States have been forced to fund various programs that the federal government used to pay for. Especially in states where lottery revenues had begun to sag, legislatures and voters turned to casinos to make up the difference.

Casinos, however, have been harder to sell to voters than lotteries. For many voters, casinos are a NIMBY ("not in my back yard") issue. They may believe that people should have the right to gamble, but they don't want a casino in their town. Casino proponents have tried to overcome these objections by arguing that casinos bring added tourist dollars, benefiting the community as a whole. Opponents argue the opposite: that people who go to casinos spend their money on gambling and not on tourist attractions. The cause-and-effect benefit of casinos to community businesses can be examined by **concomitant variation.** Casino supporters argue that people who come to gamble spend a lot of money elsewhere. Opponents of casinos claim that people who come for gambling don't want to spend money elsewhere. Furthermore, they point out that gambling represents another entertainment option for people within easy driving distance and can hurt area businesses such as restaurants, amusement parks, and bowling alleys. So far, the record has been mixed, some businesses being helped and others being hurt when casinos are built nearby.

Many effects don't have causes as obvious as the spread of legalized gambling. The **process of elimination method** can be a useful tool when several possible causes are involved. Perhaps you have had the experience of your computer not turning on. If you checked first to see if it was plugged in, then plugged it into another socket to make sure the socket was on, and then checked the surge suppressor to see if it worked, you used a process of elimination to diagnose the cause of the problem. Major advances in science and medicine have resulted from the process of elimination. For centuries soldiers on long campaigns and sailors on long sea voyages suffered horrible deaths from scurvy until 1747, when James Lind demonstrated that scurvy could be treated and prevented with a diet that includes lemons and limes. Nevertheless, people proposed various causes for scurvy including poor hygiene, lack of exercise, and tainted canned food. Finally, in 1932, the cause of scurvy was proven to be a vitamin C deficiency.

Build a Causal Argument

Effective causal arguments move beyond the obvious to get at underlying causes. The great causal mystery today is global warming. Scientists generally agree that the average surface temperature on Earth has gone up by 1 degree Fahrenheit or 0.6 degrees Celsius over the last hundred years and that the amount of carbon dioxide has increased by 25 percent. But the causes of those facts are much disputed. Some people believe that the rise in temperature is a naturally occurring climate variation and that the increase in carbon dioxide is only minimally the cause or not related at all. Others argue that the burning of fossil fuels and the cutting of tropical forests have led to the increase in carbon dioxide, which in turn traps heat in the atmosphere, thus increasing the temperature of the earth. The major problem for all participants in the global warming debate is that the causation is not simple and direct.

Arctic and subarctic regions have been affected more dramatically than elsewhere. In Iceland, average summer temperatures have risen by 0.5 to 1.0 degree Celsius since the early 1980s. All of Iceland's glaciers, except a few that surge and ebb independent of weather, are now in rapid retreat, a pattern observed throughout

Glaciers in many parts of the world are melting at rates faster than scientists thought possible just a few years ago. Even major oil companies have acknowledged that global warming is real. Yet the American public has taken little notice of world climate change— perhaps because it's difficult to get excited about the mean temperature rising a few degrees and the sea level rising a few feet. What would get Americans thinking seriously about global warming?

regions in the far north. Arctic sea ice shrank by 14 percent—an area the size of Texas—from 2004 to 2005, and Greenland's massive ice sheet has been thinning by more than 3 feet a year. Environmentalists today point to the melting of the glaciers and sea ice as proof that human-caused global warming is taking place.

Scientists, however, are not so certain. Their difficulty is to sort human causes from naturally recurring climate cycles. Much of the detailed data about the great melt in the north goes back only to the early 1990s—not long enough to rule out short-term climate cycles. If we are in a regular, short-term warming cycle, then the question becomes, how does greenhouse warming interact with that cycle? Computer models suggest there is a very low probability that such rapid change could occur naturally. But the definitive answers to the causes of the Great Melt are probably still a long way off.

Another pitfall common in causal arguments using statistics is mistaking correlation for causation. For example, the FBI reported that in 1995 criminal victimization rates in the United States dropped 13 percent for personal crimes and 12.4 percent for property crimes—the largest decreases ever. During that same year, the nation's prison and jail populations reached a record high of 1,085,000 and 507,000 inmates, respectively. The easy inference is that putting more people behind bars lowers the crime rate, but there are plenty of examples to the contrary. The drop in crime rates in the 1990s remains quite difficult to explain.

Others have argued that the decline in SAT verbal scores during the late 1960s and 1970s reflected a decline in literacy skills caused by an increase in television viewing. But the fact that the number of people who took the SAT during the 1970s greatly increased suggests that there was not an actual decline in literacy skills, only a great expansion in the population who wanted to go to college.

Annie Murphy Paul

The Real Marriage Penalty

Annie Murphy Paul is a freelance journalist who writes about mental health issues for publications such as Salon, Discover, *and* Self. *She is also the author of* The Cult of Personality: How Personality Tests Are Leading Us to Miseducate Our Children, Mismanage Our Companies, and Misunderstand Ourselves *(2004).*

In this article, which appeared in the New York Times Magazine *on November 19, 2006, Paul explores the possibility that the greater prevalence of egalitarian marriages in our society is leading to a less egalitarian society overall. She also asks why egalitarian marriages are on the rise: Are there more opportunities than ever before for singles to find a partner matched in education and earning potential? Or, has there been a change in the qualities women and men look for in a life partner?*

"Some of us are becoming the men we wanted to marry," Gloria Steinem proclaimed 25 years ago. She meant, of course, that women in large numbers were seizing the places in higher education and the professions that had formerly been closed to them, becoming the doctors, lawyers and executives that they once hoped only to wed. Over the past generation, the liberal notion of egalitarian marriage—in which wives are in every sense their husbands' peers—has gone from pie-in-the-sky ideal to unremarkable reality. But this apparently progressive shift has been shadowed by another development: America's growing gap between rich and poor. Even as husbands and wives have moved closer together on measures of education and income, the divide between well-educated, well-paid couples and their less-privileged counterparts has widened, raising an awkward possibility: are we achieving more egalitarian marriages at the cost of a more egalitarian society?

2   Once, it was commonplace for doctors to marry nurses and executives to marry secretaries. Now the wedding pages are stocked with matched sets, men and women who share a tax bracket and even an alma mater. People, like other members of the animal kingdom, have always been prone to "assortative mating," or choosing to have babies with a reassuringly similar partner. But observers like Geoffrey Miller, an evolutionary psychologist at the University of New Mexico and author of "The Mating Mind," suggest that the innovations of modern society—from greater geographic mobility to specialized work environments to Internet dating—have made this matching process much more efficient. "Assortative mating is driven by our personal preferences, but also by whom we meet, and these days we have many more opportunities to meet others like ourselves," he says. (As with most contemporary sociological phenomena, "Seinfeld" was there first: a 1996 episode featured the comedian finding "the female Jerry.")

3   In particular, Americans are increasingly pairing off by education level, according to the sociologists Christine Schwartz and Robert Mare. In an article published last year in the journal *Demography*, they reported that the odds of a high-school graduate marrying someone with a college degree declined by 43 percent between 1940 and the late 1970s. In our current decade, the researchers wrote, the percentage of couples who are "educationally homogamous"—that is, share the same level of schooling—reached its highest point in 40 years. Assortative mating by income also seems to be on the rise. In a 2004 study of couples wed in the 1970s through the early 1990s, the researchers Megan Sweeney and Maria Cancian found an increasingly strong association between women's wages before marriage and the occupational status and future earnings prospects of the men they married.

4   Why is this happening? For one thing, more couples are meeting in college and other educational settings, where prospective mates come prescreened by admissions committees as discerning as any yenta. Husbands and wives who begin their relationships during their school years are more likely to have comparable education (and, presumably, income) levels. Secondly, men and women have become more alike in what they want from a marriage partner. This convergence is both cultural—co-ed gyms and bars have replaced single-sex sewing circles and Elks clubs—and economic. Just as women have long sought to marry a good breadwinner, men, too, now find earning potential sexy. "There are fewer Cinderella marriages these days," says Stephanie Coontz, author of "Marriage, a History." "Men are less interested in rescuing a woman from poverty. They want to find someone who will pull her weight." For this reason, the "marriage penalty" once paid by highly educated women has all but disappeared: among women born after 1960, a college graduate is more likely to marry than her less-educated counterpart. And finally, there's

what Schwartz calls the growing "social and economic distance" between the well educated and the less so, a gulf even ardent romantics may find difficult to bridge.

5   This last theory holds that disparities in wealth influence whom we marry, but there's reason to think that our mating patterns could be producing economic inequality as well as reflecting it. A model constructed by the economists Raquel Fernandez and Richard Rogerson, published in 2001 in *The Quarterly Journal of Economics*, led them to conclude that "increased marital sorting"—high earners marrying high earners and low earners marrying low earners—"will significantly increase income inequality." A 2003 analysis by Gary Burtless, an economist at the Brookings Institution, found that a rising correlation of husband-and-wife earnings accounted for 13 percent of the considerable growth in economic inequality between 1979 and 1996.

6   Burtless himself does not think that assortative mating is necessarily becoming more prevalent. In fact, he says he believes that "the tendency of like to marry like has remained roughly unchanged over time. What have changed are the labor-market opportunities and behavior of women." In this conception, men have always married women of their own social class, but such stratification was obscured by the fact that the female halves of these couples often did not work or pursue advanced degrees. Now that women who are in a position to do so are attending college and graduate school and joining the professions, the economic consequences of Americans' assortative mating habits are becoming clearer.

7   If assortative mating does contribute to our growing gap between rich and poor, does that matter? Few people would question any individual's romantic preferences. And yet as the current clash over gay marriage demonstrates, private choices about whom we marry—or don't marry, or can't marry—can have loud public reverberations. Not long ago, the marriages of whites and blacks, and the lifting of laws that once prohibited such unions, revealed a nation beginning to open its mind on matters of race; likewise, rates of marriage across lines of education and income provide an index of social mobility. If there are fewer such marriages, then there are "fewer sources of intimate ties" between groups, Schwartz says, making marriage one more brick in the wall that separates America's haves and have-nots.

8   Of course, men and women don't choose each other on the basis of education and income alone. Putting love aside, as men's and women's roles continue to shift, other standards for selecting a partner may come to the fore. Indeed, the sociologist Julie Press recently offered what she called "a gynocentric theory of assortative mating," moving the focus from what men now desire in a marriage partner to the evolving preferences of women. What would-be wives may be seeking now, she proposed in *The Journal of Marriage and Family*, is "cute butts and housework"—that is, a man with an appealing physique and a willingness to wash dishes. Could this be a feminist slogan for our time? ∎

Emily Raine

Why Should I Be Nice to You? Coffeeshops and the Politics of Good Service

Emily Raine recently received a master's degree in communication studies at McGill University in Montreal. She also writes about graffiti and street art. This article appeared in the online journal Bad Subjects *in 2005.*

In this article, Raine explains why work in a coffee chain is worse than work in other kinds of service jobs. She also outlines the causes for what she sees as a destructive dynamic in the coffee chain culture and provides a possible alternative.

> "There is no more precious commodity than the relationship of trust and confidence a company has with its employees."
> —*Starbucks Coffee Company chairman Howard Schultz*

I actually like to serve. I'm not sure if this comes from some innate inclination to mother and fuss over strangers, or if it's because the movement and sociability of service work provides a much-needed antidote to the solitude of academic research, but I've always found something about service industry work satisfying. I've done the gamut of service jobs, from fine dining to cocktail waitressing to hip euro-bistro counter work, and the only job where I've ever felt truly whipped was working as a barista at one of the now-ubiquitous specialty coffee chains, those bastions of jazz and public solitude that have spread through urban landscapes over the last ten years or so. The pay was poor, the shifts long and oddly dispersed, the work boring and monotonous, the managers demanding, and the customers regularly displayed that unique spleen that emerges in even the most pleasant people before they've had the morning's first coffee. I often felt like an aproned Coke machine, such was the effect my sparkling personality had on the clientele. And yet, some combination of service professionalism, fear of termination and an imperative to be "nice" allowed me to suck it up, smile and continue to provide that intangible trait that the industry holds above all else, good service.

2   Good service in coffee shops doesn't amount to much. Unlike table service, where interaction with customers spans a minimum of half an hour, the average contact with a café customer lasts less than ten seconds. Consider how specialty cafés are laid out: the customer service counter is arranged in a long line that clients move along to "use" the café. The linear coffee bar resembles an assembly line, and indeed, café labor is heavily grounded in the rationalism of Fordist manufacturing principles, which had already been tested for use in hospitality services by fast food chains. Each of the café workers is assigned a specific stage in the service process to perform exclusively, such as taking orders, using the cash registers, or handing clients cups of brewed coffee.

3   The specialization of tasks increases the speed of transactions and limits the duration of any one employee's interaction with the clientele. This means that in a given visit a customer might order from one worker, receive food from the next, then brewed coffee or tea from yet another, then pay a cashier before proceeding down the line of the counter, finishing the trip at the espresso machine which is always situated at its end. Ultimately, each of the café's products is processed and served by a different employee, who repeats the same preparation task for hours and attends to each customer only as they receive that one product.

4   Needless to say, the productive work in cafés is dreary and repetitive. Further, this style of service severely curtails interaction with the clientele, and the very brevity of each transaction precludes much chance for authentic friendliness or conversation—even asking about someone's day would slow the entire operation. The one aspect of service work that can be unpredictable—people—becomes redundant, and interaction with customers is reduced to a fatiguing eight-hour-long smile and the repetition of sentiments that allude to good service, such as injunctions to enjoy their purchases or to have a nice day. Rather than friendly exchanges with customers, barista workers' good service is reduced to a quick rictus in the customer's direction between a great deal of friendly interaction with the espresso machine.

5   As the hospitality industry really took off in the sixties, good service became one of the trademarks of its advertising claims, a way for brands to distinguish themselves from the rest of the pack. One needn't think too hard to come up with a litany of service slogans that holler the good graces of their personnel—at Starbucks where the baristas make the magic, at Pacific Southwest Airlines where smiles aren't just painted on, or at McDonald's where smiles are free. Employee friendliness emerged as one of the chief distinguishing brand features of personal services, which means that the workers themselves become an aspect of the product for sale.

6   Our notions of good service revolve around a series of platitudes about professionalism—we're at your service, with a smile, where the customer's always right—each bragging the centrality of the customer to everything "we" do. Such claims imply an easy and equal exchange between two parties: the "we" that gladly serves and the "you" that happily receives. There is, however, always a third party involved in the service exchange, and that's whoever has hired the server, the body that ultimately decides just what the dimensions of good service will be.

7   Like most employees, a service worker sells labor to an employer at a set rate, often minimum wage, and the employer sells the product of that labor, the service itself, at market values. In many hospitality services, where gratuities make up the majority of employment revenue, the worker directly benefits from giving good service, which of course translates to good tips. But for the vast majority of service staff, and particularly those employed in venues yielding little or no gratuities—fast food outlets, café chains, cleaning and

maintenance operations—this promises many workers little more than a unilateral imperative to be perpetually bright and amenable.

8   The vast majority of service personnel do not spontaneously produce an unaffected display of cheer and good will continuously for the duration of a shift. When a company markets its products on servers' friendliness, they must then monitor and control employees' friendliness, so good service is defined and enforced from above. Particularly in chains, which are premised upon their consistent reproduction of the same experience in numerous locations, organizations are obliged to impose systems to manage employees' interaction their customers. In some chains, namely the fast food giants such as McDonald's and Burger King, employee banter is scripted into cash registers, so that as soon as a customer orders, workers are cued to offer, "would you like a dessert with that?" (an offer of dubious benefit to the customer) and to wish them a nice day. Ultimately, this has allowed corporations to be able to assimilate "good service"—or, friendly workers—into their overall brand image.

9   While cafés genuflect toward the notion of good service, their layouts and management styles preclude much possibility of creating the warmth that this would entail. Good service is, of course, important, but not if it interferes with throughput. What's more, these cafés have been at the forefront of a new wave of organizations that not only market themselves on service quality but also describe employees' job satisfaction as the seed from which this flowers.

10   Perhaps the most glaring example of this is Starbucks, where cheerful young workers are displayed behind elevated counters as they banter back and forth, calling out fancy Italian drink names and creating theatre out of their productive labor. Starbucks' corporate literature gushes not only about the good service its customers will receive, but about the great joy that its "partners" take in providing it, given the company's unique ability to "provide a great work environment and treat each other with respect and dignity," and where its partners are "emotionally and intellectually committed to Starbucks success." In the epigraph to this essay, Starbucks' chairman even describes the company's relationship with its workers as a commodity. Not only does Starbucks offer good service, but it attempts to guarantee something even better: good service provided by employees that are genuinely happy to give it.

11   Starbucks has branded a new kind of worker, the happy, wholesome, perfume-free barista. The company offers unusual benefits for service workers, including stock options, health insurance, dental plans and other perks such as product discounts and giveaways. Further, they do so very, very publicly, and the company's promotional materials are filled with moving accounts of workers who never dreamed that corporate America could care so much. With the other hand, though, the company has smashed unionization drives in New York, Vancouver and at its Seattle roaster; it schedules workers at oddly timed shifts that never quite add up to full-time hours; the company pays only

nominally more than minimum wage, and their staffs are still unable to subsist schlepping lattes alone.

12   Starbucks is not alone in marketing itself as an enlightened employer. When General Motors introduced its Saturn line, the new brand was promoted almost entirely on the company's good relations with its staff. The company's advertising spots often featured pictures of and quotes from the union contract, describing their unique partnership between manufacturer, workers and union, which allowed blue-collar personnel to have a say in everything from automobile designs to what would be served for lunch. The company rightly guessed that this strategy would go over well with liberal consumers concerned about the ethics of their purchases. Better yet, Saturn could market is cars based on workers' happiness whether personnel were satisfied or not, because very few consumers would ever have the chance to interact with them.

13   At the specialty coffee chains, however, consumers *have* to talk to employees, yet nobody ever really asks. The café service counter runs like a smooth piece of machinery, and I found that most people preferred to pretend that they were interacting with an appliance. In such short transactions, it is exceedingly difficult for customers to remember the humanity of each of the four to seven people they might interact with to get their coffees. Even fast food counters have one server who processes each customer's order, yet in cafés the workers just become another gadget in the well-oiled café machine. This is a definite downside for the employees—clients are much ruder to café staff than in any other sector of the industry I ever worked in. I found that people were more likely to be annoyed than touched by any reference to my having a personality, and it took no small amount of thought on my part to realize why.

14   Barista workers are hired to represent an abstract category of worker, not to act as individuals. Because of the service system marked by short customer interaction periods and a homogenous staff, the services rendered are linked in the consumer imagination to the company and not to any one individual worker. Workers' assimilation into the company image makes employees in chain service as branded as the products they serve. The chain gang, the workers who hold these eminently collegiate after-school jobs, are proscribed sales scripts and drilled on customer service scenarios to standardize interactions with customers. The company issues protocols for hair length, color and maintenance, visible piercings and tattoos as well as personal hygiene and acceptable odorific products. Workers are made more interchangeable by the use of uniforms, which, of course, serve to make the staff just that. The organization is a constant intermediary in every transaction, interjecting its presence in every detail of the service experience, and this standardization amounts to an absorption of individuals' personalities into the corporate image.

15   Many of the measures that chains take to secure the homogeneity of their employees do not strike us as particularly alarming, likely because similar

restrictions have been in place for several hundred years. Good service today has inherited many of the trappings of the good servant of yore, including prohibitions against eating, drinking, sitting or relaxing in front the served, entering and exiting through back doors and wearing uniforms to visually mark workers' status. These measures almost completely efface the social identities of staff during work hours, providing few clues to workers' status in their free time. Contact between service workers and their customers is thus limited to purely functional relations, so that the public only see them as workers, as makers of quality coffee, and never as possible peers.

16   Maintaining such divisions is integral to good service because this display of class distinctions ultimately underlies our notions of service quality. Good service means not only serving well, but also allowing customers to feel justified in issuing orders, to feel okay about being served—which, in turn, requires demonstrations of class difference and the smiles that suggest servers' comfort with having a subordinate role in the service exchange.

17   Unlike the penguin-suited household servant staffs whose class status was clearly defined, service industry workers today often have much more in common from a class perspective with those that they serve. This not only creates an imperative for them to wear their class otherness on their sleeves, as it were, but also to accept their subordinate role to those they serve by being unshakably tractable and polite.

18   Faith Popcorn has rather famously referred to the four-dollar latte as a "small indulgence," noting that while this is a lot to pay for a glass of hot milk, it is quite inexpensive for the feeling of luxury that can accompany it. In this service climate, the class status of the server and the served—anyone who can justify spending this much on a coffee—is blurry, indeed. Coffee shops that market themselves on employee satisfaction assert the same happy servant that allows politically conscientious consumers who are in many cases the workers' own age and class peers, to feel justified in receiving good service. Good service—as both an apparent affirmation of subordinate classes' desire to serve and as an enforced one-sided politeness—reproduces the class distinctions that have historically characterized servant-served relationships so that these are perpetuated within the contemporary service market.

19   The specialty coffee companies are large corporations, and for the twenty-somethings who stock their counters, barista work is too temporary to bother fighting the system. Mostly, people simply quit. Dissatisfied workers are stuck with engaging in tactics that will change nothing but allow them to make the best of their lot. These include minor infractions such as taking liberties with the uniforms or grabbing little bits of company time for their own pleasure, what Michel de Certeau calls *la perruque* and the companies themselves call "time theft." As my time in the chain gang wore on, I developed my own tactic, the only one I found that jostled the customers out of their complacency and allowed me to be a barista and a person.

20   There is no easy way to serve without being a servant, and I have always found that the best way to do so is to show my actual emotions rather than affecting a smooth display of interminable patience and good will. For café customers, bettering baristas' lots can be as simple as asking about their day, addressing them by name—any little gesture to show that you noticed the person behind the service that they can provide. My tactic as a worker is equally simple, but it is simultaneously an assertion of individual identity at work, a refusal of the class distinctions that characterize the service environment and a rebuttal to the companies that would promote my satisfaction with their system: be rude. Not arbitrarily rude, of course—customers are people, too, and nobody gains anything by spreading bad will. But on those occasions when customer or management behavior warranted a zinging comeback, I would give it.

21   Rudeness, when it is demanded, undermines companies' claims on workers' personal warmth and allows them to retain their individuality by expressing genuine rather than affected feelings in at-work interpersonal exchanges. It is a refusal of the class distinctions that underlie consumers' unilateral prerogative of rudeness and servers' unilateral imperative to be nice. It runs contrary to everything that we have been taught, not only about service but about interrelating with others. But this seems to be the only method of asserting one's person-hood in the service environment, where workers' personalities are all too easily reduced to a space-time, conflated with the drinks they serve. Baristas of the world, if you want to avoid becoming a green-aproned coffee dispensary, you're just going to have to tell people off about it. ■

Steps to Writing a Causal Argument

Step 1 Make a Claim

Make a causal claim on a controversial trend, event, or phenomenon.

Template

- SOMETHING does (or does not) cause SOMETHING ELSE.

  –or–

- SOMETHING causes SOMETHING ELSE, which, in turn, causes SOMETHING ELSE.

Examples

- One-parent families (or television violence, bad diet, and so on) are (or are not) the cause of emotional and behavioral problems in children.
- Firearms control laws (or right-to-carry-handgun laws) reduce (or increase) violent crimes.
- The trend toward home schooling (or private schools) is (or is not) improving the quality of education.
- The length of U.S. presidential campaigns forces candidates to become too much influenced by big-dollar contributors (or prepares them for the constant media scrutiny that they will endure as president).
- Putting grade school children into competitive sports teaches them how to succeed in later life (or puts undue emphasis on winning and teaches many who are slower to mature to have a negative self-image).

Step 2 What's at Stake in Your Claim?

- If the cause is obvious to everyone, then it probably isn't worth writing about.

Step 3 **Think of Possible Causes**

- Which are the immediate causes?
- Which are the background causes?
- Which are the hidden causes?
- Which are the causes that most people have not recognized?

Step 4 **Analyze Your Potential Readers**

- Who are your readers?
- How familiar will they be with the trend, event, or phenomenon that you're writing about?
- What are they likely to know and not know?
- How likely are they to accept your causal explanation?
- What alternative explanation might they argue for?

Step 5 **Write a Draft**

Introduction

- Describe the controversial trend, event, or phenomenon.
- Give the background that your intended readers will need.

Body

- Explain the cause or chain of causation of a trend, event, or phenomenon that is unfamiliar to your readers. Remember that providing facts is not the same thing as establishing causes, although facts can help to support your causal analysis.
- Set out the causes that have been offered and reject them one by one. Then you can present the cause that you think is most important.
- Treat a series of causes one by one, analyzing the importance of each.

Conclusion

- Do more than simply summarize. Consider describing additional effects beyond those that have been noted previously.

Step 6 Revise, Edit, Proofread

- For detailed instructions, see Chapter 4.
- For a checklist to use to evaluate your draft, see pages 61-62.

10

Evaluation Arguments

Why is it good to send humans on long space missions when probes and robots can gather the same data without risking lives?

Whenever people debate whether or not something is a good idea, like sending people into space, they are making an evaluation argument. People make evaluations all the time. Newspapers and magazines have picked up on this love of evaluation by running "best of" polls. They ask their readers to vote on the best Chinese restaurant, the best pizza, the best local band, the best coffeehouse, the best dance club, the best neighborhood park, the best swimming hole, the best bike ride (scenic or challenging), the best volleyball court, the best place to get married, and so on. If you ask one of your friends who voted in a "best" poll why she picked a particular restaurant as the best of its kind, she might respond by saying simply, "I like it." But if you ask her why she likes it, she might start offering good reasons such as these: the food is good, the service prompt, the prices fair, and the atmosphere comfortable. It's really not a mystery why these polls are often quite predictable or why the same restaurants tend to win year after year. Many people think that evaluations are matters of personal taste, but when we begin probing the reasons, we often discover that different people use similar criteria to make evaluations.

People opposed to sending humans into space, for example, use the criteria of cost and safety. Those who argue for sending people into space use the criteria of expanding human presence and human experience. The key to convincing other people that your judgment is sound is establishing the criteria you will use to make your evaluation. Sometimes it will be necessary to argue for the validity of the criteria that you think your readers should consider. If your readers accept your criteria, it's likely they will agree with your conclusions.

Understand How Evaluation Arguments Work

Evaluation arguments set out criteria and then judge something to be good or bad or best or worst according to those criteria.

> Something is a good (bad, the best, the worst) _____ if measured by certain criteria (practicality, aesthetics, ethics).

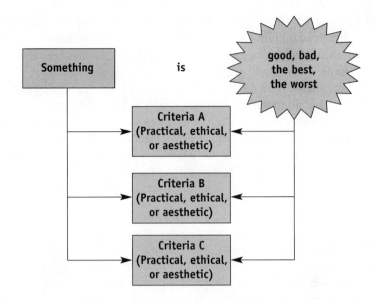

Google Maps is the best mapping program because it is easy to use, it is accurate, and it provides entertaining and educational features such as Google Earth.

Recognize Kinds of Evaluations

Arguments of evaluation are structured much like arguments of definition. Recall that the criteria in arguments of definition are set out in because clauses: SOME-THING is a _____ because it has these criteria. The key move in writing most evaluative arguments is first deciding what kind of criteria to use.

Imagine that the oldest commercial building in your city is about to be torn down. Your goal is to get the old store converted to a museum by making a proposal argument. First you will need to make an evaluative argument that will form the basis of your proposal. You might argue that a downtown museum would be much better than more office space because it would draw more visitors. You might argue that the stonework in the building is of excellent quality and deserves preservation. Or you might argue that it is only fair that the oldest commercial building be preserved because the oldest house and other historic buildings have been saved.

Each of these arguments uses different criteria. An argument that a museum is better than an office building because it would bring more visitors to the downtown area is based on **practical criteria.** An argument that the old building is beautiful and that beautiful things should be preserved uses **aesthetic criteria**. An argument that the oldest commercial building deserves the same treatment as the oldest house is based on fairness, a concept that relies on **ethical criteria**. The debate over the value of sending people versus sending robots into space employs all these criteria but with different emphases. Both those who favor and those who oppose human space travel make practical arguments that much scientific knowledge and many other benefits result from space travel. Those who favor sending humans use aesthetic arguments: space travel is essential to the way we understand ourselves as humans and Americans. Those who oppose sending humans question the ethics of spending so much money for manned space vehicles when there are pressing needs at home, and they point out that robots can be used for a fraction of the cost. (See Figure 10.1.)

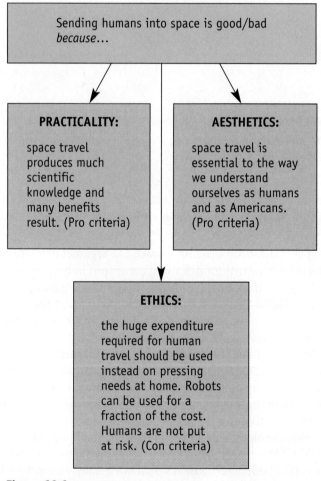

Figure 10.1

Finding Good Reasons
WHAT'S THE BEST ALTERNATIVE FUEL?

Since the 1990s automakers have produced flex-fuel cars, which burn ethanol (E-85) and gasoline, and hybrid vehicles, which combine electric and gasoline engines. More recently, spurred on by the federal government's 2003 $1.2-billion hydrogen initiative, automakers also have built fuel-cell prototypes. In a fuel-cell car, hydrogen reacts with oxygen to produce water and electricity, which then is used to power an electric motor. Hydrogen burns cleanly, emitting only water vapor, and can be produced from both renewable and nonrenewable energy sources, including solar, water, wind, and nuclear power.

But is hydrogen a realistic solution to the world's dependence on fossil fuels? The automaker Honda says yes. It plans to bring the first fuel-cell car, the FCX, to the market in 2008. Detractors say no. According to former U.S. Department of Energy official Joseph Romm, "A hydrogen car is one of the least efficient, most expensive ways to reduce greenhouse gases."

Write about it

1. One way to assess a complicated issue like alternative fuel technologies is to evaluate each technology against a set of common criteria. Which of the following criteria are useful for evaluating fuel-efficient cars? Why are they useful?

   - cost of development and production
   - sticker price of cars using the technology
   - how long it takes for cars to reach the market
   - efficiency and reliability of cars using the technology
   - environmental impact
   - convenience of refueling and maintenance
   - driver's aesthetic experience

2. Are any of the above criteria more important than the others? If so, how would you rank them? Why? Are there any criteria you would add?

Build an Evaluation Argument

Most people have a lot of practice making consumer evaluations, and when they have enough time to do their homework, they usually make an informed decision. Sometimes, criteria for evaluations are not so obvious, however, and evaluations are much more difficult to make. Sometimes one set of criteria favors one choice, while another set of criteria favors another. You might have encountered this problem when you chose a college. If you were able to leave home to go to school, you had a potential choice of over 1400 accredited colleges and universities. Until 20 years ago, there wasn't much information about choosing a college other than what colleges said about themselves. You could find out the price of tuition and what courses were offered, but it was hard to compare one college with another.

In 1983 the magazine *U.S. News & World Report* began ranking U.S. colleges and universities from a consumer's perspective. These rankings have remained highly controversial ever since. Many college officials have attacked the criteria that *U.S. News* uses to make its evaluations. In an August 1998 *U.S. News* article, Gerhard Casper, the president of Stanford University (which is consistently near the top of the rankings), writes, "Much about these rankings—particularly their specious formulas and spurious precision—is utterly misleading." Casper argues that using graduation rates as a criterion of quality rewards easy schools. Other college presidents have called for a national boycott of the *U.S. News* rankings (without much success).

U.S. News replies in its defense that colleges and universities themselves do a lot of ranking. Schools rank students for admissions, using SAT or ACT scores, high school GPA, high school class rank, quality of high school, and other factors, and then grade the students and rank them against each other when they are enrolled in college. Furthermore, schools also evaluate faculty members and take great interest in the national ranking of their departments. They care very much about where they stand in relation to each other. Why, then, *U.S. News* argues, shouldn't people be able to evaluate colleges and universities, since colleges and universities are so much in the business of evaluating people?

Arguing for the right to evaluate colleges and universities is one thing; actually doing comprehensive and reliable evaluations is quite another. *U.S. News* uses a formula in which 25 percent of a school's ranking is based on a survey of reputation in which the president, provost, and dean of admissions at each college rate the quality of schools in the same category, and the remaining 75 percent is based on statistical criteria of quality. These statistical criteria fall into six major categories: retention of students, faculty resources, student selectivity, financial resources, alumni giving, and (for national universities and liberal arts colleges only) graduation rate performance—the difference between the number of

Windmills produce energy without pollution and reduce dependence on foreign oil. Do you agree or disagree with people who do not want windmills built near them because they find them ugly?

students who are expected to graduate and the number that actually do. These major categories are made up of factors that are weighted according to their importance. For example, the faculty resources category is determined by the size of classes (the proportion of classes with fewer than 20 students to classes with 50 or more students), the average faculty pay weighted by the cost of living in different regions of the country, the percentage of professors with the highest degree in their field, the overall student–faculty ratio, and the percentage of faculty who are full-time.

Those who have challenged the *U.S. News* rankings argue that the magazine should use different criteria or weight the criteria differently. *U.S. News* explains its ranking system on its Web site (www.colleges.usnews.rankingsandreviews.com/college). If you are curious about where your school ranks, take a look.

Michael Eric Dyson

Gangsta Rap and American Culture

Michael Eric Dyson is a Baptist minister and professor of religious studies at the University of Pennsylvania. He is one of the first academics to defend rap music as an art form. This essay, from the 2004 collection The Michael Eric Dyson Reader, *is based on a 1994 editorial Dyson wrote for the* New York Times. *In this essay, Dyson responds to those in Congress and to social activists who wish to censor gangsta rap because of its tendency to feature violent and obscene lyrics.*

The recent attacks on the entertainment industry, especially gangsta rap, by Senator Bob Dole, former Education Secretary William Bennett, and political activist C. Delores Tucker, reveal the fury that popular culture can evoke in a wide range of commentators. As a thirty-five-year-old father of a sixteen-year-old son and as a professor and ordained Baptist minister who grew up in Detroit's treacherous inner city, I too am disturbed by many elements of gangsta rap. But I'm equally anguished by the way many critics have used its artists as scapegoats. How can we avoid the pitfall of unfairly attacking black youth for problems that bewitched our culture long before they gained prominence? First, we should understand what forces drove the emergence of rap. Second, we should place the debate about gangsta rap in the context of a much older debate about "negative" and "positive" black images. Finally, we should acknowledge that gangsta rap crudely exposes harmful beliefs and practices that are often maintained with deceptive civility in much of mainstream society, including many black communities.

If the fifteen-year evolution of hip-hop teaches us anything, it's that history is made in unexpected ways by unexpected people with unexpected results. Rap is now safe from the perils of quick extinction predicted at its humble start. But its birth in the bitter belly of the '70s proved to be a Rosetta stone of black popular culture. Afros, "blunts," funk music, and carnal eruptions define a "back-in-the-day" hip-hop aesthetic. In reality, the severe '70s busted the economic boom of the '60s. The fallout was felt in restructured automobile industries and collapsed steel mills. It was extended in exported employment to foreign markets. Closer to home, there was the depletion of social services to reverse the material ruin of black life. Later, public spaces for black recreation were gutted by Reaganomics or violently transformed by lethal drug economies.

3   Hip-hop was born in these bleak conditions. Hip-hoppers joined pleasure and rage while turning the details of their difficult lives into craft and capital. This is the world hip-hop would come to "represent": privileged persons speaking for less visible or vocal peers. At their best, rappers shape the tortuous twists of urban fate into lyrical elegies. They represent lives swallowed by too little love or opportunity. They represent themselves and their

peers with aggrandizing anthems that boast of their ingenuity and luck in surviving. The art of "representin" that is much ballyhooed in hiphop is the witness of those left to tell the afflicted's story.

4   As rap expands its vision and influence, its unfavorable origins and its relentless quest to represent black youth are both a consolation and challenge to hip-hoppers. They remind rappers that history is not merely the stuff of imperial dreams from above. It isn't just the sanitizing myths of those with political power. Representing history is within reach of those who seize the opportunity to speak for themselves, to represent their own interests at all costs. Even rap's largest controversies are about representation. Hip-hop's attitudes toward women and gays continually jolt in the unvarnished malevolence they reveal. The sharp responses to rap's misogyny and homophobia signify its central role in battles over the cultural representation of other beleaguered groups. This is particularly true of gangsta rap.

5   While gangsta rap takes the heat for a range of social maladies from urban violence to sexual misconduct, the roots of our racial misery remain buried beneath moralizing discourse that is confused and sometimes dishonest. There's no doubt that gangsta rap is often sexist and that it reflects a vicious misogyny that has seized our nation with frightening intensity. It is doubly wounding for black women who are already beset by attacks from outside their communities to feel the thrust of musical daggers to their dignity from within. How painful it is for black women, many of whom have fought valiantly for black pride, to hear the dissonant chord of disdain carried in the angry epithet "bitch."

6   The link between the vulgar rhetorical traditions expressed in gangsta rap and the economic exploitation that dominates the marketplace is real. The circulation of brutal images of black men as sexual outlaws and black females as "ho's" in many gangsta rap narratives mirrors ancient stereotypes of black sexual identity. Male and female bodies are turned into commodities. Black sexual desire is stripped of redemptive uses in relationships of great affection or love.

7   Gangsta rappers, however, don't merely respond to the values and visions of the marketplace; they help shape them as well. The ethic of consumption that pervades our culture certainly supports the rapacious materialism shot through the narratives of gangsta rap. Such an ethic, however, does not exhaust the literal or metaphoric purposes of material wealth in gangsta culture. The imagined and real uses of money to help one's friends, family, and neighborhood occupy a prominent spot in gangsta rap lyrics and lifestyles.

8   Equally troubling is the glamorization of violence and the romanticization of the culture of guns that pervades gangsta rap. The recent legal troubles of Tupac Shakur, Dr. Dre, Snoop Doggy Dogg, and other gangsta rappers chastens any defense of the genre based on simplistic claims that these artists are merely performing roles that are divorced from real life. Too often for gangsta rappers, life does indeed imitate and inform art.

9   But gangsta rappers aren't *simply* caving in to the pressure of racial stereotyping and its economic rewards in a music industry hungry to exploit

their artistic imaginations. According to this view, gangsta rappers are easily manipulated pawns in a chess game of material dominance where their consciences are sold to the highest bidder. Or else gangsta rappers are viewed as the black face of white desire to distort the beauty of black life. Some critics even suggest that white record executives discourage the production of "positive rap" and reinforce the desire for lewd expressions packaged as cultural and racial authenticity. ~ *rebuttal*

10   But such views are flawed. The street between black artists and record companies runs both ways. Even though black artists are often ripe for the picking—and thus susceptible to exploitation by white and black record labels—many of them are quite sophisticated about the politics of cultural representation. Many gangsta rappers helped to create the genre's artistic rules. Further, they have figured out how to financially exploit sincere and sensational interest in "ghetto life." Gangsta rap is no less legitimate because many "gangstas" turn out to be middle-class blacks faking homeboy roots. This fact simply focuses attention on the genre's essential constructedness, its literal artifice. Much of gangsta rap makes voyeuristic whites and naive blacks think they're getting a slice of authentic ghetto life when in reality they're being served colorful exaggerations. That doesn't mean, however, that the best of gangsta rappers don't provide compelling portraits of real social and economic suffering.

11   Critics of gangsta rap often ignore how hip-hop has been developed without the assistance of a majority of black communities. Even "positive" or "nation-conscious" rap was initially spurned by those now calling for its revival in the face of gangsta rap's ascendancy. Long before white record executives sought to exploit transgressive sexual behavior among blacks, many of us failed to lend support to politically motivated rap. For instance, when political rap group Public Enemy was at its artistic and popular height, most of the critics of gangsta rap didn't insist on the group's prominence in black cultural politics. Instead, Public Enemy, and other conscientious rappers, were often viewed as controversial figures whose inflammatory racial rhetoric was cause for caution or alarm. In this light, the hue and cry directed against gangsta rap by the new defenders of "legitimate" hip-hop rings false.

12   Also, many critics of gangsta rap seek to curtail its artistic freedom to transgress boundaries defined by racial or sexual taboo. That's because the burden of representation falls heavily on what may be termed the race artist in a far different manner than the one I've described above. The race artist stands in for black communities. She represents millions of blacks by substituting or sacrificing her desires and visions for the perceived desires and visions of the masses. Even when the race artist manages to maintain relative independence of vision, his or her work is overlaid with, and interpreted within, the social and political aspirations of blacks as a whole. Why? Because of the appalling lack of redeeming or nonstereotypical representations of black life that are permitted expression in our culture.

13   This situation makes it difficult for blacks to affirm the value of nontraditional or transgressive artistic expressions. Instead of viewing such cultural products through critical eyes—seeing the good and the bad, the productive and destructive aspects of such art—many blacks tend to simply dismiss such work with hypercritical disdain. A suffocating standard of "legitimate" art is thus produced by the limited public availability of complex black art. Either art is seen as redemptive because it uplifts black culture and shatters stereotypical thinking about blacks, or it is seen as bad because it reinforces negative perceptions of black culture.

14   That is too narrow a measure for the brilliance and variety of black art and cultural imagination. Black folk should surely pay attention to how black art is perceived in our culture. We must be mindful of the social conditions that shape perceptions of our cultural expressions and that stimulate the flourishing of one kind of art versus another. (After all, die-hard hip-hop fans have long criticized how gangsta rap is eagerly embraced by white record companies while "roots" hip-hop is grossly underfinanced.)

15   But black culture is too broad and intricate—its artistic manifestations too unpredictable and challenging—for us to be *obsessed* with how white folk view our culture through the lens of our art. And black life is too differentiated by class, sexual identity, gender, region, and nationality to fixate on "negative" or "positive" representations of black culture. Black culture is good and bad, uplifting and depressing, edifying and stifling. All of these features should be represented in our art, should find resonant voicing in the diverse tongues of black cultural expressions.

16   Gangsta rappers are not the first to face the grueling double standards imposed on black artists. Throughout African-American history, creative personalities have sought to escape or enliven the role of race artist with varying degrees of success. The sharp machismo with which many gangsta rappers reject this office grates on the nerves of many traditionalists. Many critics argue that since gangsta rap is often the only means by which many white Americans come into contact with black life, its pornographic representations and brutal stereotypes of black culture are especially harmful. The understandable but lamentable response of many critics is to condemn gangsta rap out of hand. They aim to suppress gangsta rap's troubling expressions rather than critically engage its artists and the provocative issues they address. Thus the critics of gangsta rap use it for narrow political ends that fail to enlighten or better our common moral lives.

17   Tossing a moralizing *j'accuse* at the entertainment industry may have boosted Bob Dole's standing in the polls over the short term. It did little, however, to clarify or correct the problems to which he has drawn dramatic attention. I'm in favor of changing the moral climate of our nation. I just don't believe that attacking movies, music, and their makers is very helpful. Besides, rightwing talk radio hosts wreak more havoc than a slew of violent films. They're the ones terrorist Timothy McVeigh was inspired by as he planned to bomb the federal building in Oklahoma City.

18   A far more crucial task lies in getting at what's wrong with our culture and what it needs to get right. Nailing the obvious is easy. That's why Dole, along with William Bennett and C. Delores Tucker, goes after popular culture, especially gangsta rap. And the recent attempts of figures like Tucker and Dionne Warwick, as well as national and local lawmakers, to censor gangsta rap or to outlaw its sale to minors are surely misguided. When I testified before the U.S. Senate's Subcommittee on Juvenile Justice, as well as the Pennsylvania House of Representatives, I tried to make this point while acknowledging the need to responsibly confront gangsta rap's problems. Censorship of gangsta rap cannot begin to solve the problems of poor black youth. Nor will it effectively curtail their consumption of music that is already circulated through dubbed tapes and without the benefit of significant airplay.

19   A crucial distinction needs to be made between censorship of gangsta rap and edifying expressions of civic responsibility and community conscientiousness. The former seeks to prevent the sale of vulgar music that offends mainstream moral sensibilities by suppressing the First Amendment. The latter, however, is a more difficult but rewarding task. It seeks to oppose the expression of misogynistic and sexist sentiments in hip-hop culture through protest and pamphleteering, through community activism, and through boycotts and consciousness raising.

20   What Dole, Bennett, and Tucker shrink from helping us understand—and what all effective public moralists must address—is why this issue now? Dole's answer is that the loss of family values is caused by the moral corruption of popular culture, and therefore we should hold rap artists, Hollywood moguls, and record executives responsible for our moral chaos. It's hard to argue with Dole on the surface, but a gentle scratch reveals that both his analysis and answer are flawed.

21   Too often, "family values" is a code for a narrow view of how families work, who gets to count as a legitimate domestic unit, and consequently, what values are crucial to their livelihood. Research has shown that nostalgia for the family of the past, when father knew best, ignores the widespread problems of those times, including child abuse and misogyny. Romantic portrayals of the family on television and the big screen, anchored by the myth of the Benevolent Patriarch, hindered our culture from coming to grips with its ugly domestic problems.

22   To be sure, there have been severe assaults on American families and their values, but they have not come mainly from Hollywood, but from Washington with the dismantling of the Great Society. Cruel cuts in social programs for the neediest, an upward redistribution of wealth to the rich, and an unprincipled conservative political campaign to demonize poor black mothers and their children have left latter-day D. W. Griffiths in the dust. Many of gangsta rap's most vocal black critics (such as Tucker) fail to see how the alliances they forge with conservative white politicians such as Bennett and Dole are plagued with problems. Bennett and Dole have put up roadblocks to many legislative and

political measures that would enhance the fortunes of the black poor they now claim in part to speak for. Their outcry resounds as crocodile tears from the corridors of power paved by bad faith. emo terms

23   Moreover, many of the same conservative politicians who support the attack on gangsta rap also attack black women (from Lani Guinier to welfare mothers), affirmative action, and the redrawing of voting districts to achieve parity for black voters. The war on gangsta rap diverts attention away from the more substantive threat posed to women and blacks by many conservative politicians. Gangsta rap's critics are keenly aware of the harmful effects that genre's misogyny can have on black teens. Ironically, such critics appear oblivious to how their rhetoric of absolute opposition to gangsta rap has been used to justify political attacks on poor black teens.

24   That doesn't mean that gratuitous violence and virulent misogyny should not be opposed. They must be identified and destroyed. I am wholly sympathetic, for instance, to sharp criticism of gangsta rap's ruinous sexism and homophobia though neither Dole, Bennett, nor Tucker has made much of the latter plague. "Fags" and "dykes" are prominent in the genre's vocabulary of rage. Critics' failure to make this an issue only reinforces the inferior, invisible status of gay men and lesbians in mainstream and black cultural institutions: Homophobia is a vicious emotion and practice that links mainstream middle-class and black institutions to the vulgar expressions of gangsta rap. There seems to be an implicit agreement between gangsta rappers and political elites that gays, lesbians, and bisexuals basically deserve what they get.

25   But before we discard the genre, we should understand that gangsta rap often reaches higher than its ugliest, lowest common denominator. Misogyny, violence, materialism, and sexual transgression are not its exclusive domain. At its best, this music draws attention to complex dimensions of ghetto life ignored by many Americans. Of all the genres of hip-hop—from socially conscious rap to black nationalist expressions, from pop to hardcore—gangsta rap has most aggressively narrated the pains and possibilities, the fantasies and fears, of poor black urban youth. Gangsta rap is situated in the violent climes of postindustrial Los Angeles and its bordering cities. It draws its metaphoric capital in part from the mix of myth and murder that gave the Western frontier a dangerous appeal a century ago.

26   Gangsta rap is largely an indictment of mainstream and bourgeois black institutions by young people who do not find conventional methods of addressing personal and social calamity useful. The leaders of those institutions often castigate the excessive and romanticized violence of this music without trying to understand what precipitated its rise in the first place. In so doing, they drive a greater wedge between themselves and the youth they so desperately want to help.

27   If Americans really want to strike at the heart of sexism and misogyny in our communities, shouldn't we take a closer look at one crucial source of these blights—religious institutions, including the synagogue, the temple,

and the church? For instance, the central institution of black culture, the black church, which has given hope and inspiration to millions of blacks, has also given us an embarrassing legacy of sexism and misogyny. Despite the great good it has achieved through a heroic tradition of emancipatory leadership, the black church continues to practice and justify *ecclesiastical apartheid*. More than 70 percent of black church members are female, yet they are generally excluded from the church's central station of power, the pulpit. And rarely are the few ordained female ministers elected pastors.

28   Yet black leaders, many of them ministers, excoriate rappers for their verbal sexual misconduct. It is difficult to listen to civil rights veterans deplore the hostile depiction of women in gangsta rap without mentioning the vicious sexism of the movements for racial liberation of the 1960s. And of course the problem persists in many civil rights organizations today.

29   Attacking figures like Snoop Doggy Dogg or Tupac Shakur—or the companies that record or distribute them—is an easy out. It allows scapegoating without sophisticated moral analysis and action. While these young black males become whipping boys for sexism and misogyny, the places in our culture where these ancient traditions are nurtured and rationalized—including religious and educational institutions and the nuclear family—remain immune to forceful and just criticism.

appeal to emotion

30   Corporate capitalism, mindless materialism, and pop culture have surely helped unravel the moral fabric of our society. But the moral condition of our nation is equally affected by political policies that harm the vulnerable and poor. It would behoove Senator Dole to examine the glass house of politics he abides in before he decides to throw stones again. If he really wants to do something about violence, he should change his mind about the ban on assault weapons he seeks to repeal. That may not be as sexy or self-serving as attacking pop culture, but it might help save lives.

31   Gangsta rap's greatest "sin" may be that it tells the truth about practices and beliefs that rappers hold in common with the mainstream and with black elites. This music has embarrassed mainstream society and black bourgeois culture. It has forced us to confront the demands of racial representation that plague and provoke black artists. It has also exposed our polite sexism and our disregard for gay men and lesbians. We should not continue to blame gangsta rap for ills that existed long before hip-hop uttered its first syllable. Indeed, gangsta rap's in-your-face style may do more to force our nation to confront crucial social problems than countless sermons or political speeches. ■

Sample Student Evaluation Argument

Rashaun Giddens
Professor Chen
English 1302
21 April 2009

Stop Loss or "Loss of Trust"

Looking back on my high school career, my social and extracurricular lives were filled with countless highs: hanging out with my friends, prom, and varsity track to name a few. My academic career, however, was a bit shakier. So busy with what I saw then as the important things in life, I often procrastinated or altogether avoided my schoolwork. My senior year, the recruiter from the U.S. Army Reserves spoke at a school assembly. He asked that we as seniors consider the prospect of becoming "weekend warriors." In the wake of September 11, we could help protect our country and simultaneously work toward paying for a college education, which seemed like a great idea to many students. For those who could not otherwise afford college, the prospect of receiving a higher education in return for patriotism and some good hard work sounded fair enough. My life, however, took a different turn. When I received my track scholarship, I decided to head off to college right away. Many of my friends, however, heeded the call to service. So far, their realities have been far from the lives that were pitched to them; rather, this was the beginning of a path to broken dreams and broken promises.

My cousin, moved to action by a charismatic recruiter, an Army announcement of fifteen-month active tours, and the prospect of a paid college education, chose to join the United States Army Reserves. The Army, suffering from a recruitment shortfall, had recently announced a policy that would allow recruits to serve in active duty for a mere fifteen months. For serving for just over a year, my cousin could do his national duty and put himself on a path to self-improvement. The recruiter did not, however, highlight the fine print to this new program. No one told my cousin that he could be called back to active duty for up to eight years under the government's "stop loss" policy. Further, no one told him that just one day after the Army announced the incentive program, an appeals court ruled that the Army could, under stop loss, compel soldiers to remain beyond the initial eight-year obligation (Wickham).

The stop loss policy forces thousands of soldiers to serve beyond their volunteer enlistment contracts. The all-volunteer army—on which the government prides itself—is slowly developing into a disgruntled mass of men and women being held against their will. These men and women wanted to serve their countries and their families, and they signed what they believed were binding agreements with a trustworthy employer—the United States government—only to find that their government didn't bargain in good faith.

As far back as the Civil War, the government needed incentives to retain its troops. (Although we all want freedom, few actually want to put our own lives on the line in the pursuit of that goal.) Both the Union and the Confederacy needed to make tough decisions to maintain strong armed forces when soldiers' contracts were expiring. The Union chose to offer financial incentives to keep its young men in uniform, while the Confederacy instituted a series of (not so) "voluntary" reenlistment policies (Robertson). During World War II all soldiers were forced to remain active until they reached a designated number of points. Vietnam saw the last stage of a mandatory draft, with soldiers serving one-year tours (Hockstader). Today's military relies on stop loss, making soldiers stay in the military after their commitment ends. Congress first gave the military the authority to retain soldiers after the Vietnam War when new volunteers were too few to replace departing soldiers. In November 2002, the Pentagon gave stop loss orders for Reserve and National Guard units activated to fight terrorism (Robertson).

This policy is neither forthcoming, safe, nor compassionate toward those most directly impacted—the soldiers and their families. As the United States became more and more entrenched in the conflict in Iraq, the military was stretched thinner and thinner. By 2004, approximately 40% of those serving in Iraq and Afghanistan came from the ranks of the part-time soldiers: the Reserves and the National Guard (Gerard). While these individuals did know that their countries could call if they enlisted, they continue to bear an inordinate burden of actual combat time, and this new policy continues to create situations further removed from the job for which they enlisted. Recruiters often pitch the military—including the Reserves and the Guard—to young, impressionable, and often underprivileged kids. I have experienced this pitch firsthand and have seen the eyes of my classmates as the recruiter promised them a better and richer tomorrow. Seeing a golden opportunity for self-respect and achievement, young men and women sign on the dotted line. Today, other young men and women are buying a bill of goods. These recruits—and those who came before them— deserve to have an honest relationship with the government they protect. As policymakers tout the all-volunteer Army, those who serve find their rights threatened. The military claims to teach soldiers respect and honor. Is misleading your employees honest?

Aside from being less than forthright, stop loss may be putting our soldiers in harm's way. The policy forces these soldiers to suffer the strain of combat for extended periods of time. Because of the way the policy works, troops may learn of tour extensions mere hours before they had planned to return stateside to lower-stress positions and their loved ones. These troops need to be ready, alert, and equipped with a morale which allows them to fight effectively. Stop loss instead forces these soldiers—often those trained for short stints—to work beyond their experience and training. This policy may prove to overextend, both emotionally and physically, our fighting men and women. As they repeatedly suffer disappointment because of changes in their orders and delays of departure, morale is likely to drop. Based on reports from families, this practice has been devastating to their soldiers. Nancy Durst, wife of United States Reservist Staff Sergeant Scott Durst, told *Talk of the Nation*'s Neal Conan that the military detained her husband's unit just thirty minutes before it was to board the bus scheduled to deliver it to a stateside flight. The unit was later informed that tours had been extended for another four months (Durst). War breeds stress, but how can soldiers be expected to function at an optimal level when forced to suffer disappointments at the hands of their own government?

Finally, this policy simply runs contrary to the current administration's stated interest in the preservation of family and the bolstering of small businesses. First (and most obviously), this less-than-forthright policy keeps families separated. Husbands, wives, and children find themselves separated for longer periods of time, left with uncertainty and ambiguity for comfort. How does this aid in preserving the family? Second, when the government deploys reservists, soldiers often take a severe pay cut. Forced to leave their regular jobs, soldiers—and their families—must survive on an often much smaller government wage. Stop loss extends tours of duty and consequently the economic struggles of the families in question. Third, the policy has proven detrimental to the small-business owner. Men and women have used their military experience, discipline, and training to further themselves economically. The United States prides itself on the power of the small businessman; however, individuals such as Chief Warrant Officer Ronald Eagle have been hurt by this policy. After twenty years of service, Eagle was set to retire from the Army and focus on his aircraft-maintenance business. Instead, the Army has indefinitely moved his retirement date. As a consequence, Eagle has taken a $45,000 pay cut and wonders whether his business will survive his hiatus (Hockstader). Is this the way the government and military fight to preserve the family—emotionally and economically?

Because American men and women risk their lives in the name of bettering those of Iraqis, the military should think about how their policy affects the lives of their soldiers and those back home. While the stop loss policy does allow the armed forces to build a larger active force without the public backlash (and political suicide) of instituting the draft, this policy comes at a cost. Those who have chosen to serve their country—whether for the training, educational possibilities, economic support, or expression of patriotism—are being bamboozled.

Watch the television commercials that, even now, tout training and part-time service. Read the stories of those serving and the families left behind. The sales pitch and the real picture do not match. The United States is undeniably one of the strongest nations in the world and a bastion of freedom. For these very reasons, the armed forces and the United States government, which represents all citizens, must find a way to lead this war (or conflict or crusade) honestly. If we have to pay soldiers double what they currently make in order to get them to reenlist, we should do so. Even a draft would at least be aboveboard and honest. But we cannot continue to trick people into risking their lives for our national security. Our country must show the

honor and respect deserved by those who fight, and stop loss
undeniably dishonors and shows disrespect to our soldiers. The military
must take a cue from its own advertising and "be all they can be."
Be honest.

Works Cited

Durst, Nancy. Interview by Neal Conan. *Talk of the Nation*. Natl. Public
　　　Radio. WNYC, New York. 19 Apr. 2004. Radio.

Gerard, Philip. "When the Cry Was 'Over the Hill in October.'" *Charleston
　　　Gazette* 16 May 2004: 1E. *LexisNexis Academic*. Web. 6 Apr. 2009.

Hockstader, Lee. "Army Stops Many Soldiers from Quitting; Orders
　　　Extend Enlistments to Curtail Troop Shortages." *Washington Post*
　　　29 Dec. 2003: A01. *LexisNexis Academic*. Web. 8 Apr. 2009.

Robertson, John. "The Folly of Stop Loss." *Pittsburgh Post-Gazette*
　　　19 Dec. 2004: J1. *LexisNexis Academic*. Web. 7 Apr. 2009.

Wickham, DeWayne. "A 15-Month Enlistment? Check Army's Fine Print."
　　　USA Today 17 May 2005: 13A. *LexisNexis Academic*. Web. 6 Apr.
　　　2009.

Steps to Writing an Evaluation Argument

Step 1 Make a Claim

Make an evaluative claim based on criteria.

Template

- SOMETHING is good (bad, the best, the worst) if measured by certain criteria (practicality, aesthetics, ethics).

Examples

- A book or movie review.
- A defense of a particular kind of music or art.
- An evaluation of a controversial aspect of sports (e.g., the current system of determining who is champion in Division I college football by a system of bowls and polls) or a sports event (e.g., this year's WNBA playoffs) or a team.
- An evaluation of the effectiveness of an educational program (such as your high school honors program or your college's core curriculum requirement) or some other aspect of your campus.
- An evaluation of the effectiveness of a social policy or law such as legislating 21 as the legal drinking age, current gun control laws, or environmental regulation.

Step 2 Think About What's at Stake

- Does nearly everyone agree with you? Then your claim probably isn't interesting or important. If you can think of people who disagree, then something is at stake.
- Who argues the opposite of your claim?
- Why do they make a different evaluation?

Step 3 List the Criteria

- Which criteria make something either good or bad?
- Which criteria are the most important?
- Which criteria are fairly obvious, and which will you have to argue for?

Step 4 Analyze Your Potential Readers

- Who are your readers?
- How familiar will they be with what you are evaluating?
- What are they likely to know and not know?
- Which criteria are they most likely to accept with little explanation, and which will they disagree with?

Step 5 Write a Draft

Introduction

- Introduce the person, group, institution, event, or object that you are going to evaluate. You might want to announce your stance at this point or wait until the concluding section.
- Give the background that your intended readers will need.

Body

- Describe each criterion and then analyze how well what you are evaluating meets that criterion.
- If you are making an evaluation according to the effects someone or something produces, describe each effect in detail.
- Anticipate where readers might question either your criteria or how they apply to your subject.
- Address opposing viewpoints by acknowledging how their evaluations might differ and by showing why your evaluation is better.

Conclusion

- If you have not yet announced your stance, conclude that, on the basis of the criteria you set out or the effects you have analyzed, something is good (bad, the best, the worst).
- If you have made your stance clear from the beginning, end with a compelling example or analogy.

Step 6 Revise, Edit, Proofread

- For detailed instructions, see Chapter 4.
- For a checklist to use to evaluate your draft, see pages 61–62.

11

Narrative Arguments

The U.S. Postal Service has issued a stamp to honor the AMBER Alert program, a system created in response to the abduction and murder of nine-year-old Amber Hagerman. The system seemed to be effective at first, but the number of false alarms, including numerous cases where a parent seized a child in a custody dispute, has undermined its credibility. To what extent can a large-scale solution be built on one case, no matter how tragic?

In 1996, nine-year-old Amber Hagerman was kidnapped while riding her bicycle in Arlington, Texas, and brutally murdered. Local police had information that might have saved her life, but they lacked a way to broadcast that information. Shortly after the tragedy, Dallas-Fort Worth broadcasters teamed with local police to develop a system to notify the public when a child is abducted. The program, AMBER (America's Missing: Broadcast Emergency Response), began in Texas and spread to all 50 U.S. states with federal government support. The story of Amber Hagerman's death appealed to shared community values in ways that statistics did not. It vividly demonstrated that something was very wrong if children could not be protected from abduction and exploitation.

A single, detailed personal story sometimes makes a stronger case than large-scale statistical evidence. The Annenberg Public Policy Center reported that an estimated 1.6 million of 17 million U.S. college students gambled on-line in 2005, but it was the story of Greg Hogan that made the problem real for many Americans. Hogan, the son of a Baptist minister, was an extraordinarily talented musician, playing onstage twice at Carnegie Hall by age 13. He chose to attend Lehigh University in Pennsylvania, where he was a member of the orchestra and class president. At Lehigh he also acquired an addiction to online poker. He lost $7,500, much of which he borrowed from fraternity brothers. To pay them back, he robbed a bank, only to be arrested a few hours later. Eventually he received a prison sentence of 22 months to 10 years. Hogan's story helped to influence Congress to pass the Unlawful Internet Gambling Enforcement Act, which requires financial institutions to stop money transfers to gambling sites.

Ronald Reagan and Martin Luther King Jr. are acknowledged as masters in using narratives to make arguments. Reagan once said that facts are stupid things until we give them meaning, which he supplied by putting facts in stories. In "Letter from Birmingham Jail," King relates in one sentence the pettiness of segregation laws and their effect on children:

> ...when you suddenly find your tongue twisted and your speech stammering as you seek to explain to your six-year-old daughter why she can't go to the public amusement park that has just been advertised on television, and see tears welling up in her eyes when she is told that Funtown is closed to colored children, and see ominous clouds of inferiority beginning to form in her little mental sky, and see her beginning to distort her personality by developing an unconscious bitterness toward white people.

This tiny story drives home King's point.

Understand How Narrative Arguments Work

Successful narrative arguments typically don't have a thesis statement but instead tell a compelling story. From the experience of one individual, readers infer a claim and the reasons that support the claim.

**A personal account illustrates the reasons that support a claim.
Sometimes the reader must infer these reasons, as well as the claim.**

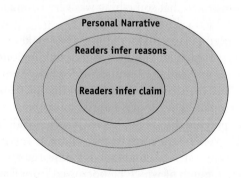

Personal Narrative

Readers infer reasons

Readers infer claim

Journalist Bob Woodruff's detailed account of his arduous recovery from a head injury suffered during a roadside bomb attack in Iraq illustrates the need for the U.S. military to reassess its methods of treating troops with brain injuries.

Recognize Kinds of Narrative Arguments

Using narratives to advocate for change is nothing new. As far back as we have records, we find people telling stories and singing songs that argue for change. Folk songs have always given voice to political protest and have celebrated marginalized people. When workers in the United States began to organize in the 1880s, they adapted melodies that soldiers had sung in the Civil War. In the 1930s, performers and songwriters such as Paul Robeson, Woody Guthrie, Huddie Ledbetter (Leadbelly), and Aunt Molly Jackson relied on traditions of hymns, folk songs, and African American blues to protest social conditions. In the midst of the politically quiet 1950s, folk songs told stories that critiqued social conformity and the dangers of nuclear war. In the 1960s, the

Folk singer/songwriter Shawn Colvin is one of many contemporary folk and blues singers who continue the tradition of making narrative arguments in their songs. Can you think of a song that makes a narrative argument?

civil rights movement and the movement against the Vietnam War brought a strong resurgence of folk music. The history of folk music is a continuous recycling of old tunes, verses, and narratives to engage new political situations. What can be said for folk songs is also true for any popular narrative genre, be it the short story, novel, drama, movies, or even rap music.

Narrative arguments work differently from arguments that spell out their criteria and argue for explicit links. A narrative argument succeeds if the experience being described invokes the life experiences of readers or listeners. Anyone who has ever been around children knows that most kids love amusement parks. When Martin Luther King Jr. describes the tears in his young daughter's eyes when he tells her she cannot go to a public amusement park because of the color of her skin, he does not have to explain to his readers why going to an amusement park advertised on television is so important for his daughter.

Likewise, the story of Amber Hagerman was effective because even if you have not known a child who was abducted and murdered or exploited, you will probably agree that children should be protected against these crimes. Narrative arguments allow readers to fill in the good reasons. In the cases of King's argument

Finding Good Reasons

CAN A STORY MAKE AN ARGUMENT?

This aerial photograph, taken on September 1, 2005, shows an evacuation point on Interstate 10 where victims of Hurricane Katrina were stranded. In the excerpt below, paramedics Larry Bradshaw and Lorrie Beth Slonsky describe what happened on the fourth day after the storm as they were forced to leave the hotel they were staying in and find a way out of New Orleans. Officials told them and a group of evacuees waiting for transportation that they were "on their own." Bradshaw and Slonsky describe what happened next:

> Our little encampment began to blossom. Someone stole a water delivery truck and brought it up to us. . . . A mile or so down the freeway, an army truck lost a couple of pallets of C-rations on a tight turn. We ferried the food back to our camp in shopping carts. Now secure with the two necessities, food and water, cooperation, community and creativity flowered. We organized a clean up, and hung garbage bags from the rebar poles. We made beds from wood pallets and cardboard. We designated a storm drain as the bathroom and the kids built an elaborate enclosure for privacy out of plastic, broken umbrellas, and other scraps.

Write about it

1. What argument might the authors be making about the official response to Katrina? What details reveal their argument?

2. How does the authors' account of their experience differ from media reports that you heard or saw about the evacuation effort after Katrina? Does their account change your thinking about the experiences of New Orleans evacuees? Why or why not?

against segregation laws and AMBER Alert's effort to protect children, that's exactly what happened. Public outcry led to changes in laws and public opinion.

Narrative arguments can be representative anecdotes, as with the previous examples, or they can be longer accounts of particular events that express larger ideas. One such story is George Orwell's account of a hanging in Burma (the country that is now known as Myanmar) while he was a colonial administrator in the late 1920s. In "A Hanging," first published in 1931, Orwell narrates an execution of a nameless prisoner who was convicted of a nameless crime. Everyone quietly and dispassionately performs his job—the prison guards, the hangman, the superintendent, and even the prisoner, who offers no resistance when he is bound and led to the gallows. All is totally routine until a very small incident makes Orwell aware of what is happening:

> It was about forty yards to the gallows. I watched the bare brown back of the prisoner marching in front of me. He walked clumsily with his bound arms, but quite steadily, with that bobbing gait of the Indian who never straightens his knees. At each step his muscles slid neatly into place, the lock of hair on his scalp danced up and down, his feet printed themselves on the wet gravel. And once, in spite of the men who gripped him by each shoulder, he stepped lightly aside to avoid a puddle on the path.
>
> It is curious; but till that moment I had never realized what it means to destroy a healthy, conscious man. When I saw the prisoner step aside to avoid the puddle, I saw the mystery, the unspeakable wrongness, of cutting a life short when it is in full tide. This man was not dying, he was alive just as we are alive. All the organs of his body were working—bowels digesting food, skin renewing itself, nails growing, tissues forming—all toiling away in solemn foolery. His nails would still be growing when he stood on the drop, when he was falling through the air with a tenth-of-a-second to live. His eyes saw the yellow gravel and gray walls, and his brain still remembered, foresaw, reasoned—even about puddles. He and we were a party of men walking together, seeing, hearing, feeling, understanding the same world; and in two minutes, with a sudden snap, one of us would be gone—one mind less, one world less.

Orwell's narrative leads to a dramatic moment of recognition, which gives this story its lasting power.

Build a Narrative Argument

The biggest problem with narrative arguments is that anyone can tell a story. On the one hand, there are compelling stories that argue against capital punishment. For example, a mentally retarded man who was executed in Arkansas refused a piece of pie at his last meal. He asked the guards to save the pie for later. On the other hand, there are also many stories about the victims of murder and other crimes. Many families have Web sites on which they call for killing the people responsible for murdering their loved ones. They too have compelling stories to tell.

Violent deaths of all kinds make for especially vivid narrative arguments. In the past decade we have witnessed several tragedies in which schoolchildren used guns taken from the family home to kill other students. In 2007 a mentally disturbed student at Virginia Tech was able to buy handguns that he used to kill 32 students and faculty members. Stories of these tragedies provided strong arguments for gun control. Gun rights organizations, including the National Rifle Association (NRA), counters these stories by claiming that they are not truly representative. The NRA argues that over 99 percent of all guns will not be used to commit crimes in any given year.

There are two keys to making effective narrative arguments: establishing that the narrative is truthful and representative of more than one person's experience. First, writing from personal experience can give you a great deal of impact, but that impact vanishes if your readers doubt that you are telling the truth. Second, the story you tell may be true enough, but it is important that the incident be representative. We don't ban bananas because someone once slipped on a banana peel.

Narratives are often useful for illustrating how people are affected by particular issues or events, but narrative arguments are more effective if you have more evidence than just one incident. The abduction and murder of Amber Hagerman was a personal tragedy for her family and community, but the fact that an average of 2100 children are reported missing each day made Amber Hagerman's story representative of a national tragedy. Thus, it had power because people understood it to be representative of a much larger—and preventable—problem.

Leslie Marmon Silko

The Border Patrol State

Leslie Marmon Silko (1948–) was born in Albuquerque and graduated from the University of New Mexico. She now teaches at the University of Arizona. She has received much critical acclaim for her writings about Native Americans. Her first novel, Ceremony *(1977), describes the struggles of a veteran returning home after World War II to civilian life on a New Mexico reservation. Her incorporation of Indian storytelling techniques in* Ceremony *drew strong praise. One critic called her "the most accomplished Indian writer of her generation." She has since published two more novels,* Almanac of the Dead *(1991) and* Gardens in the Dunes *(1999); a collection of essays,* Yellow Woman and a Beauty of the Spirit: Essays on Native American Life Today *(1996); two volumes of poems and stories; and many shorter works. Silko's talents as a storyteller are evident in this essay, which first appeared in the magazine* The Nation *in 1994.*

I used to travel the highways of New Mexico and Arizona with a wonderful sensation of absolute freedom as I cruised down the open road and across the vast desert plateaus. On the Laguna Pueblo reservation, where I was raised, the people were patriotic despite the way the U.S. government had treated Native Americans. As proud citizens, we grew up believing the freedom to travel was our inalienable right, a right that some Native Americans had been denied in the early twentieth century. Our cousin, old Bill Pratt, used to ride his horse 300 miles overland from Laguna, New Mexico, to Prescott, Arizona, every summer to work as a fire lookout.

2   In school in the 1950s, we were taught that our right to travel from state to state without special papers or threat of detainment was a right that citizens under communist and totalitarian governments did not possess. That wide open highway told us we were U.S. citizens; we were free. . . .

3   Not so long ago, my companion Gus and I were driving south from Albuquerque, returning to Tucson after a book promotion for the paperback edition of my novel *Almanac of the Dead*. I had settled back and gone to sleep while Gus drove, but I was awakened when I felt the car slowing to a stop. It was nearly midnight on New Mexico State Road 26, a dark, lonely stretch of two-lane highway between Hatch and Deming. When I sat up, I saw the headlights and emergency flashers of six vehicles—Border Patrol cars and a van were blocking both lanes of the highway. Gus stopped the car and rolled down the window to ask what was wrong. But the closest Border Patrolman and his companion did not reply; instead, the first agent ordered us to "step out of the car." Gus asked why, but his question seemed to set them off. Two more Border Patrol agents immediately approached our car, and one of them snapped, "Are you looking for trouble?" as if he would relish it.

4   I will never forget that night beside the highway. There was an awful feeling of menace and violence straining to break loose. It was clear that the uniformed men would be only too happy to drag us out of the car if we did not speedily comply with their request (asking a question is tantamount to resistance, it seems). So we stepped out of the car and they motioned for us to stand on the shoulder of the road. The night was very dark, and no other traffic had come down the road since we had been stopped. All I could think about was a book I had read—*Nunca Mas*—the official report of a human rights commission that investigated and certified more than 12,000 "disappearances" during Argentina's "dirty war" in the late 1970s.

5   The weird anger of these Border Patrolmen made me think about descriptions in the report of Argentine police and military officers who became addicted to interrogation, torture and the murder that followed. When the military and police ran out of political suspects to torture and kill, they resorted to the random abduction of citizens off the streets. I thought how easy it would be for the Border Patrol to shoot us and leave our bodies and car beside the highway, like so many bodies found in these parts and ascribed to "drug runners."

6   Two other Border Patrolmen stood by the white van. The one who had asked if we were looking for trouble ordered his partner to "get the dog," and from the back of the van another patrolman brought a small female German shepherd on a leash. The dog apparently did not heel well enough

to suit him, and the handler jerked the leash. They opened the doors of our car and pulled the dog's head into it, but I saw immediately from the expression in her eyes that the dog hated them, and that she would not serve them. When she showed no interest in the inside of the car, they brought her around back to the trunk, near where we were standing. They half-dragged her up into the trunk, but still she did not indicate any stowed-away human beings or illegal drugs.

7   The mood got uglier; the officers seemed outraged that the dog could not find any contraband, and they dragged her over to us and commanded her to sniff our legs and feet. To my relief, the strange violence the Border Patrol agents had focused on us now seemed shifted to the dog. I no longer felt so strongly that we would be murdered. We exchanged looks—the dog and I. She was afraid of what they might do, just as I was. The dog's handler jerked the leash sharply as she sniffed us, as if to make her perform better, but the dog refused to accuse us: She had an innate dignity that did not permit her to serve the murderous impulses of those men. I can't forget the expression in the dog's eyes; it was as if she were embarrassed to be associated with them. I had a small amount of medicinal marijuana in my purse that night, but she refused to expose me. I am not partial to dogs, but I will always remember the small German shepherd that night.

8   Unfortunately, what happened to me is an everyday occurrence here now. Since the 1980s, on top of greatly expanding border checkpoints, the Immigration and Naturalization Service and the Border Patrol have implemented policies that interfere with the rights of U.S. citizens to travel freely within our borders. I.N.S. agents now patrol all interstate highways and roads that lead to or from the U.S.–Mexico border in Texas, New Mexico, Arizona and California. Now, when you drive east from Tucson on Interstate 10 toward El Paso, you encounter an I.N.S. check station outside Las Cruces, New Mexico. When you drive north from Las Cruces up Interstate 25, two miles north of the town of Truth or Consequences, the highway is blocked with orange emergency barriers, and all traffic is diverted into a two-lane Border Patrol checkpoint—ninety-five miles north of the U.S.–Mexico border.

9   I was detained once at Truth or Consequences, despite my and my companion's Arizona driver's licenses. Two men, both Chicanos, were detained at the same time, despite the fact that they too presented ID and spoke English without the thick Texas accents of the Border Patrol agents. While we were stopped, we watched as other vehicles—whose occupants were white—were waved through the checkpoint. White people traveling with brown people, however, can expect to be stopped on suspicion they work with the sanctuary movement, which shelters refugees. White people who appear to be clergy, those who wear ethnic clothing or jewelry and women with very long hair or very short hair (they could be nuns) are also frequently detained; white men with beards or men with long hair are likely to be detained, too, because Border Patrol agents have "profiles" of "those sorts" of white people who may help

political refugees. (Most of the political refugees from Guatemala and El Salvador are Native American or mestizo because the indigenous people of the Americas have continued to resist efforts by invaders to displace them from their ancestral lands.) Alleged increases in illegal immigration by people of Asian ancestry mean that the Border Patrol now routinely detains anyone who appears to be Asian or part Asian, as well.

10   Once your car is diverted from the Interstate Highway into the checkpoint area, you are under the control of the Border Patrol, which in practical terms exercises a power that no highway patrol or city patrolman possesses: They are willing to detain anyone, for no apparent reason. Other law-enforcement officers need a shred of probable cause in order to detain someone. On the books, so does the Border Patrol; but on the road, it's another matter. They'll order you to stop your car and step out; then they'll ask you to open the trunk. If you ask why or request a search warrant, you'll be told that they'll have to have a dog sniff the car before they can request a search warrant, and the dog might not get there for two or three hours. The search warrant might require an hour or two past that. They make it clear that if you force them to obtain a search warrant for the car, they will make you submit to a strip search as well.

11   Traveling in the open, though, the sense of violation can be even worse. Never mind high-profile cases like that of former Border Patrol agent Michael Elmer, acquitted of murder by claiming self-defense, despite admitting that as an officer he shot an "illegal" immigrant in the back and then hid the body, which remained undiscovered until another Border Patrolman reported the event. (Last month, Elmer was convicted of reckless endangerment in a separate incident, for shooting at least ten rounds from his M-16 too close to a group of immigrants as they were crossing illegally into Nogales in March 1992.) Or that in El Paso a high school football coach driving a vanload of players in full uniform was pulled over on the freeway and a Border Patrol agent put a cocked revolver to his head. (The football coach was Mexican-American, as were most of the players in his van; the incident eventually caused a federal judge to issue a restraining order against the Border Patrol.) We've a mountain of personal experiences like that which never make the newspapers. A history professor at U.C.L.A. told me she had been traveling by train from Los Angeles to Albuquerque twice a month doing research. On each of her trips, she had noticed that the Border Patrol agents were at the station in Albuquerque scrutinizing the passengers. Since she is six feet tall and of Irish and German ancestry, she was not particularly concerned. Then one day when she stepped off the train in Albuquerque, two Border Patrolmen accosted her, wanting to know what she was doing, and why she was traveling between Los Angeles and Albuquerque twice a month. She presented identification and an explanation deemed "suitable" by the agents, and was allowed to go about her business.

12   Just the other day, I mentioned to a friend that I was writing this article and he told me about his 73-year-old father, who is half Chinese and who had

set out alone by car from Tucson to Albuquerque the week before. His father had become confused by road construction and missed a turnoff from Interstate 10 to Interstate 25; when he turned around and circled back, he missed the turnoff a second time. But when he looped back for yet another try, Border Patrol agents stopped him and forced him to open his trunk. After they satisfied themselves that he was not smuggling Chinese immigrants, they sent him on his way. He was so rattled by the event that he had to be driven home by his daughter.

13   This is the police state that has developed in the southwestern United States since the 1980s. No person, no citizen, is free to travel without the scrutiny of the Border Patrol. In the city of South Tucson, where 80 percent of the respondents were Chicano or Mexicano, a joint research project by the University of Wisconsin and the University of Arizona recently concluded that one out of every five people there had been detained, mistreated verbally or nonverbally, or questioned by I.N.S. agents in the past two years.

14   Manifest Destiny may lack its old grandeur of theft and blood—"lock the door" is what it means now, with racism a trump card to be played again and again, shamelessly, by both major political parties. "Immigration," like "street crime" and "welfare fraud," is a political euphemism that refers to people of color. Politicians and media people talk about "illegal aliens" to dehumanize and demonize undocumented immigrants, who are for the most part people of color. Even in the days of Spanish and Mexican rule, no attempts were made to interfere with the flow of people and goods from south to north and north to south. It is the U.S. government that has continually attempted to sever contact between the tribal people north of the border and those to the south.

15   Now that the "Iron Curtain" is gone, it is ironic that the U.S. government and its Border Patrol are constructing a steel wall ten feet high to span sections of the border with Mexico. While politicians and multinational corporations extol the virtues of NAFTA and "free trade" (in goods, not flesh), the ominous curtain is already up in a six-mile section at the border crossing at Mexicali; two miles are being erected but are not yet finished at Naco; and at Nogales, sixty miles south of Tucson, the steel wall has been all rubber-stamped and awaits construction likely to begin in March. Like the pathetic multimillion-dollar "antidrug" border surveillance balloons that were continually deflated by high winds and made only a couple of meager interceptions before they blew away, the fence along the border is a theatrical prop, a bit of pork for contractors. Border entrepreneurs have already used blowtorches to cut passageways through the fence to collect "tolls," and are doing a brisk business. Back in Washington, the I.N.S. announces a $300 million computer contract to modernize its record-keeping and Congress passes a crime bill that shunts $255 million to the I.N.S. for 1995, $181 million earmarked for border control, which is to include 700 new partners for the men who stopped Gus and me in our travels, and the history professor, and my friend's father, and as many as they could from South Tucson.

16   It is no use; borders haven't worked, and they won't work, not now, as the indigenous people of the Americas reassert their kinship and solidarity with

one another. A mass migration is already under way; its roots are not simply economic. The Uto–Aztecan languages are spoken as far north as Taos Pueblo near the Colorado border, all the way south to Mexico City. Before the arrival of the Europeans, the indigenous communities throughout this region not only conducted commerce, the people shared cosmologies, and oral narratives about the Maize Mothers, the Twin Brothers and their Grandmother, Spider Woman, as well as Quetzalcoatl the benevolent snake. The great human migration within the Americas cannot be stopped; human beings are natural forces of the Earth, just as rivers and winds are natural forces.

17   Deep down the issue is simple: The so-called "Indian Wars" from the days of Sitting Bull and Red Cloud have never really ended in the Americas. The Indian people of southern Mexico, of Guatemala and those left in El Salvador, too, are still fighting for their lives and for their land against the "cavalry" patrols sent out by the governments of those lands. The Americas are Indian country, and the "Indian problem" is not about to go away.

18   One evening at sundown, we were stopped in traffic at a railroad crossing in downtown Tucson while a freight train passed us, slowly gaining speed as it headed north to Phoenix. In the twilight I saw the most amazing sight: Dozens of human beings, mostly young men, were riding the train; everywhere, on flat cars, inside open boxcars, perched on top of boxcars, hanging off ladders on tank cars and between boxcars. I couldn't count fast enough, but I saw fifty or sixty people headed north. They were dark young men, Indian and mestizo; they were smiling and a few of them waved at us in our cars. I was reminded of the ancient story of Aztlán, told by the Aztecs but known in other Uto–Aztecan communities as well. Aztlán is the beautiful land to the north, the origin place of the Aztec people. I don't remember how or why the people left Aztlán to journey farther south, but the old story says that one day, they will return. ∎

Dagoberto Gilb

My Landlady's Yard

Dagoberto Gilb (1950-) was born in Los Angeles to a Mexican mother and a German father. After college, he worked as a journeyman carpenter in Los Angeles and El Paso, which allowed him to take off time to write between jobs. He published his first collection of stories, Winners on the Pass Line, in 1985, and a second collection, The Magic of Blood, in 1992. Despite the success of his first collection, Gilb initially could not get New York publishers interested in his nonstereotypical depictions of Mexican-American life. Nonetheless, The Magic of Blood was critically acclaimed, and his next work, Last Known Residence of Mickey Acuna, published by Grove Press in 1994, brought Gilb national recognition as a major literary talent.

Gilb's writing has appeared in The New Yorker, Harper's, and other publications. "My Landlady's Yard" is taken from his first collection of essays, Gritos (2003). Many of the essays in Gritos, including the one below, portray the complicated cultural mixings and way of life in the borderlands of Texas.

It's been a very dry season here. Not enough rain. And the sun's beginning to feel closer. Which, of course, explains why this is called the desert. Why the kinds of plants that do well enough in the region—creosote, mesquite, ocotillo, yucca—aren't what you'd consider lush, tropical blooms. All that's obvious, right? To you, I'm sure, it's obvious, and to me it is, too, but not to my landlady. My landlady doesn't think of this rock house I rent in central El Paso as being in the desert. To her, it's the big city. She's from the country, from a ranch probably just like the one she now calls home, a few miles up the paved highway in Chaparral, New Mexico, where the roads are graded dirt. She must still see the house as she did when she lived here as a young wife and mother, as part of the city's peaceful suburbs, which it certainly was thirty years ago. She probably planted the shrubs and evergreens that snuggle the walls of the house now, probably seeded the back- and front-yard grass herself. And she wants those Yankee plants and that imported grass to continue to thrive as they would in all other American, nondesert neighborhoods, even if these West Texas suburbs moved on to the east and west many years ago, even if the population has quadrupled and water is more scarce, and expensive, than back then.

2   So I go ahead and drag around a green hose despite my perception that *gold*, colorless and liquid, is pouring out onto this desert, an offering as unquenchable and ruthless as to any Aztec deity (don't water a couple of days and watch how fast it dries away). Superstitions, if you don't mind my calling them that, die hard, and property values are dependent on shared impressions. I'm not ready to rent and load another U-Haul truck.

3   With my thumb over the brass fitting and squeezed against the water, I use the digits on my other hand to pluck up loose garbage. You've heard, maybe, of West Texas wind. That explains why so much of it lands here on my front yard, but also a high school is my backyard: the school's rear exit is only a dirt alley and fence away from my garage, and teenagers pass by in the morning, during lunch, and when school lets out. I find the latest Salsa Rio brand of Doritos, Big Gulp Grande cups, paper (or plastic or both) bowls with the slimy remains of what goes for cheese on nachos from the smiley-faced Good Time Store two blocks away, used napkins, orange burger pouches, the new glossy-clean plastic soda containers, waxy candy wrappers from Mounds and Mars and Milky Way. Also beer cans and bottles, grocery-store bags both plastic and paper, and fragments from everything else (believe me) possible.

4   I'm betting you think I'm not too happy about accumulating such evidence. You're right. But I'm not mentioning it to complain. I want the image of all the trash, as well as the one of me spraying precious water onto this dusty alkaline soil, to get your attention. Because both stand for the odd way we live and think out here, a few hundred miles (at least) from everyplace else in the United States.

5   My green grass in the desert, for instance. My landlady wants thick, luxuriant grass because that's the way of this side of the border, and this side is

undeniably better, whatever misconception of place and history and natural resources the desire for that image depends on. It's not just her, and it's not just lawns. Take another example: a year ago about this time, police cars squealed onto the asphalt handball and basketball courts on the other side of the school fence to regain control of a hundred or so students lumped around a fight, most of them watching, some swinging baseball bats. What happened? According to the local newspaper, the fight broke out between a group of black students, all of them dependents of Fort Bliss military personnel (as their jargon has it), and a group of Hispanic students. "Hispanic" is the current media term for those of descent from South of the Border. Even around here. Which is the point: that even in this town—the other side of the concrete river considered the official land of Spanish-language history and culture—the latest minority-language terminology is used to describe its historic, multigenerational majority population. With the exception of one high school on the more affluent west side of town, Anglos are the overwhelming minority: at the high school behind my backyard the ratio must be ten to one. Though Mexico has been the mother of this region, and remains so, it's the language and understanding of The North that labels the account of the school incident: "Hispanic" students, black dependents of GIs.

6   If green grass is the aspiration, the realization of an American fantasy, then the trash is from the past, the husks of a frontier mentality that it took to be here, and stay, in the first place. Trash blowing by, snared by limbs and curbs and fences, is a display of what was the attitude of the West. The endlessness of its range. The ultimate principle of every man, woman, animal, and thing for itself. The meanness required to survive. The wild joy that could abandon rules. The immediacy of life. Or the stupidity of the non-Indian hunter eating one meal, then leaving behind the carcass. Except that vultures and coyotes and finally ants used to clean that mess up. The remains of the modernized hunt don't balance well in nature or its hybrid shrubs, do not biodegrade. And there are a lot more hunters than before.

7   Trash contradicts the well-tended lawn. And in my neighborhood, not all is Saint Augustine or Bermuda. Hardy weeds sprout and grow tall everywhere, gray-green century plants shoot stalks beside many homes. El Paso is still crossing cultures and times, the wind blows often, particularly this time of year, the sun will be getting bigger, but the pretty nights cool things off here on the desert. Let me admit this: I'd like it if grass grew well in my backyard. What I've got is patchy at best, and neglected, the brown dirt is a stronger color than the green. So the other day, I soaked that hard soil, dug it up, threw seed grown and packaged in Missouri, covered it with peat humus from Menard, Texas, and I'm waiting. ■

Steps to Writing a Narrative Argument

Step 1 Identify an Experience that Makes an Implicit Argument

Think about experiences that made you realize that something is wrong or that things need to be changed. The experience does not have to be one that leads to a moral lesson at the end, but it should be one that makes your readers think.

Examples

- Being accused of and perhaps even arrested and hauled to jail for something you didn't do or for standing up for something you believed in.
- Going through treatment for a serious medical condition, dealing with a complicated system of insurance and referrals, or having health care denied by an HMO.
- Moving from a well-financed suburban school to a much poorer rural or urban school in the same state.
- Experiencing stereotyping or prejudice in any way—for the way you look, the way you act, your age, your gender, your race, or your sexual orientation.

Step 2 List All the Details You Can Remember

- When did it happen?
- How old were you?
- Why were you there?
- Who else was there?
- Where did it happen? If the place is important, describe what it looked like.

Step 3 Examine the Significance of the Event

- How did you feel about the experience when it happened?
- How did it affect you then?
- How do you feel about the experience now?
- What long-term effects has it had on your life?

Step 4 Analyze Your Potential Readers

- Who are your readers?
- How much will your readers know about the background of the experience you are describing?
- Are they familiar with the place where it happened?
- Would anything similar ever likely have happened to them?
- How likely are they to agree with your feelings about the experience?

Step 5 Write a Draft

- You might need to give some background first, but if you have a compelling story, often it's best to launch right in.
- You might want to tell the story as it happened (chronological order), or you might want to begin with a striking incident and then go back to tell how it happened (flashback).
- You might want to reflect on your experience at the end, but you want your story to do most of the work. Avoid drawing a simple moral lesson. Your readers should share your feelings if you tell your story well.

Step 6 Revise, Edit, Proofread

- For detailed instructions, see Chapter 4.
- For a checklist to use to evaluate your draft, see pages 61–62.

12

Rebuttal Arguments

In May 2007, demonstrators in Lewes, Delaware, hung cloth strips with the names of dead soldiers to protest the Iraq War. Could their action be considered a rebuttal argument?

When you hear the word *rebuttal*, you might think of a debate team or the part of a trial when the attorney for the defense answers the plaintiff's accusations. Although rebuttal has those definitions, a rebuttal argument can be thought of in much larger terms. Indeed, much of what people know about the world today is the result of centuries of arguments of rebuttal.

In high school and college, you no doubt have taken many courses that required the memorization of facts, which you demonstrated by repeating these facts on tests. You probably didn't think much about how this knowledge came about. Once in a while, though, something happens that makes people think consciously about a fact they have learned. For example, in elementary school, you learned that the earth rotates on its axis once a day. Maybe you didn't think about it much at the time, but once, years later, you were outside on a clear night and noticed the Big Dipper in one part of the sky, and then you looked for it later and found it in another part of the sky. If you've ever spent a clear night out stargazing, you have observed that the North Star, called Polaris, stays in the same place. The stars near Polaris appear to move in a circle around it, and the stars farther away move from east to west until they sink below the horizon.

If you are lucky enough to live in a place where the night sky is often clear, you can see the same pattern repeated night after night. And if you stop to think about why you see the stars circling around Polaris, you remember what you were taught long ago—that you live on a rotating ball, so the stars appear to move across the sky, but in fact, stars are so distant from Earth that their actual movement is not visible to humans over a short period of time.

An alternative explanation for these facts is not only possible; it is the explanation that people believed from ancient times until about 500 years ago. People assumed that their position on Earth was fixed and that the entire sky rotated on an axis connecting Polaris and Earth. The flaw in this theory is the movement of the planets. If you watch the path of Mars over several nights, you will observe that it also moves across the sky from east to west, but it makes an anomalous backward movement during its journey and then goes forward again. The other planets also seem to wander back and forth as they cross the night sky. The ancient Greeks developed an explanation of the strange wanderings of the planets by theorizing that the planets move in small circles imposed on larger orbits. By graphing little circles on top of bigger circles, the courses of planets could be plotted and predicted. This theory culminated in the work of Ptolemy, who lived in Alexandria in the second century CE. Ptolemy proposed displaced centers for the small circles called epicycles, which provided a better fit for predicting the paths of planets.

Because Ptolemy's model of the universe was numerically accurate in its predictions, educated people assumed its validity for centuries, even though there was evidence to the contrary. For example, Aristarchus of Samos, who lived in the fourth century BCE, used the size of Earth's shadow cast on the Moon during a lunar eclipse to compute the sizes of the Moon and Sun and their distances from Earth. Even though his calculations were inaccurate, Aristarchus recognized that the Sun is much bigger than Earth, and he advanced the heliocentric hypothesis: that Earth orbits the Sun.

Many centuries passed, however, before educated people believed that the Sun, not Earth, was the center of the solar system. In the early sixteenth century, the Polish astronomer Nicolaus Copernicus recognized that Ptolemy's model could be greatly simplified if the Sun were at the center of the solar system. He kept his theory a secret for much of his life and saw the published account of his work only a few hours before his death in 1543. Even though Copernicus made a major breakthrough, he was not able to take full advantage of the heliocentric hypothesis because he followed the tradition that orbits are perfect circles: thus, he still needed circles on top of circles to explain the motion of the planets—but he needed far fewer circles than did Ptolemy.

The definitive rebuttal of Ptolemy's model came a century later with the work of the German astronomer Johannes Kepler. Kepler performed many tedious calculations, which were complicated by the fact that he first had to assume an orbit for Earth before he could compute orbits for the planets. Finally he made a stunning discovery: all the orbits of the planets could be described as an ellipse with the Sun at the center. The dominance of the Ptolemaic model of the universe was finally over.

Understand How Rebuttal Arguments Work

When you rebut the argument of someone else, you can do one of two things. You can refute the argument, or you can counterargue. In the first case, **refutation,** you emphasize the shortcomings of the argument that you wish to undermine without really making a positive case of your own. In the second case, **counterargument**, you emphasize not the shortcomings of the argument that you are rebutting but the strengths of the position you wish to support. Often there is considerable overlap between refutation and counterargument, and often both are present in a rebuttal.

Refutation: The opposing argument has serious shortcomings that undermine the claim.

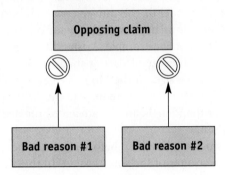

The great white shark gained a reputation as a "man eater" from the 1975 movie *Jaws*, but in fact attacks on humans are rare and most bites have been "test bites," which is a common shark behavior with unfamiliar objects.

Counterarguments: The opposing argument has some merit, but my argument is superior.

Those who argue for tariffs on goods from China claim that tariffs will protect American manufacturing jobs, but tariffs would increase prices on clothing, furniture, toys, and other consumer goods for everyone and would cause the loss of retailing jobs.

Finding Good Reasons

CAN THE WEB BE TRUSTED FOR RESEARCH?

Most Web users are familiar with the huge and immensely popular Wikipedia, the online encyclopedia. What makes Wikipedia so different from traditional, print encyclopedias is that entries can be contributed or edited by anyone.

In a recent edition of the *Wall Street Journal*, Jimmy Wales, president of Wikimedia and one of its founders, debated the legitimacy of Wikipedia with Dale Hoiberg, editor-in-chief of *Encyclopedia Britannica*. Hoiberg's main criticism of Wikipedia is that its structure—an open-source wiki without the formal editorial control that shapes traditional, print encyclopedias—allows for inaccurate entries.

In response, Wales argues that *Britannica* and newspapers also contain errors, but Wikipedia has the advantage that they are easily corrected. Furthermore, he asserts that Wikipedia's policy of using volunteer administrators to delete irrelevant entries and requiring authors of entries to cite reliable, published sources ensures quality. Nonetheless, some universities including UCLA and the University of Pennsylvania along with many instructors strongly discourage and even ban students from citing Wikipedia in their work. (Wikipedia also cautions against using its entries as a primary source for serious research.)

Write about it

1. If your college decided to ban the use of Wikipedia as a reference because it lacked the authority of a traditional encyclopedia, would you want to challenge it? Why or why not?

2. If you chose to challenge the college's policy, how would you do so? Would it be effective to refute the college's claims point by point, noting fallacies in logic and reasoning? Would it be effective to build a counterargument in which you examine the assumptions on which the college's claims are based? Which strategy would you choose, and why?

Recognize Kinds of Rebuttal Arguments

Refutation

There are two primary strategies for refutation arguments. First, you can challenge the assumptions on which a claim is based. Copernicus did not question Ptolemy's data concerning how the stars and planets appear in the sky to an observer on Earth. Instead, he questioned Ptolemy's central assumption that Earth is the center of the solar system.

Second, you can question the evidence supporting the claim. Sometimes the evidence presented is simply wrong. Sometimes the evidence is incomplete or unrepresentative, and sometimes counterevidence can be found. Often when you refute an argument, you make the case that your opponent has been guilty of one or more fallacies of arguments (see pages 27–28). A lively debate has developed in recent years over the impacts of Web 2.0, a term that has come to stand for a Web-based social phenomenon characterized by open communication and a decentralization of authority. Various new genre and software are associated with Web 2.0, including wikis, blogs, YouTube, MySpace, Facebook, eBay, craigslist, Second Life—anything that encourages participation and can exist only on the Internet.

From the beginning the Internet inspired grand visions of a better society through access to information and instant communication. The initial enthusiasm declined after the Web turned into a giant home-shopping network and the potential for dialog among different groups was lost in the proliferation of political and advocacy sites. But Web 2.0 rekindled that enthusiasm with the potential of connecting billions of human minds. Wikipedia is held up as a glorious example of the age of participation because it allows us to pool the collective wisdom of all our brains. Amateurism is celebrated. Anyone can publish writing, videos, songs, photographs, and other art for everyone else connected to the Internet to see and hear, and millions of people are doing just that.

One of Web 2.0's greatest proponents, Kevin Kelly, issued the manifesto "We Are the Web" in *Wired* magazine in August 2005, proclaiming the beginning of a new era of collective human consciousness (www.wired.com/wired/archive/13.08/tech_pr.html):

> There is only one time in the history of each planet when its inhabitants first wire up its innumerable parts to make one large Machine. Later that Machine may run faster, but there is only one time when it is born. You and I are alive at this moment. . . . Weaving nerves out of glass and radio waves, our species began wiring up all regions, all processes, all facts and notions into a grand network. From this embryonic neural net was born a collaborative interface for our civilization, a sensing, cognitive device with power that exceeded any previous invention. The Machine provided a new way of thinking (perfect search, total recall) and a new mind for an old species. It was the Beginning.

In case his readers miss the spiritual overtones, Kelly compares the present to the era of Jesus, Confucius, and the later Jewish prophets, when the world's great religions emerged.

Not surprisingly, the hype over Web 2.0 has drawn critics. In June 2007, Andrew Keen published *The Cult of the Amateur: How Today's Internet Is Killing Our Culture,* which upholds the authority of the expert against the thousands of amateurs who contribute to YouTube and Wikipedia. He challenges the assumptions of those who inflate the promise of Web 2.0:

> The Web 2.0 revolution has peddled the promise of bringing more truth to more people—more depth of information, more global perspective, more unbiased opinion from dispassionate observers. But this is all a smokescreen. What the Web 2.0 revolution is really delivering is superficial observations of the world around us rather than deep analysis, shrill opinion rather than considered judgment. The information business is being transformed by the Internet into the sheer noise of a hundred million bloggers all simultaneously talking about themselves. (16)

Keen repeats several of the frequent charges against the Internet: identity theft is made easy, pornographers and gamblers thrive, personal data is vulnerable, and political and corporate interests spread propaganda. What bothers him the most, however, is how all the "free information" will eventually destroy traditional media—magazines, newspapers, recording studios, and book publishers— with their resources of writers, editors, journalists, musicians, and reporters. Amateurs, according to Keen, do not have the resources to produce in-depth reporting or great music or great books, and even if they did, how could anyone find it? The sheer numbers of amateurs publishing on the Web makes it next to impossible to sort the good from the bad.

Keen begins by recalling the hypothetical example that if an infinite number of monkeys were given typewriters to pound, eventually one of them will type out a masterpiece. He writes, "today's amateur monkeys can use their networked computers to publish everything from uninformed political commentary, to unseemly home videos, to embarrassingly amateurish music, to unreadable poems, reviews, essays and novels" (3).

Keen's comparison of bloggers to millions of monkeys with typewriters drew the ire of bloggers even before the book appeared. Lawrence Lessig wrote in his blog (www.lessig.org/blog/) in May 2007 that Keen's book is no more reliable than the typical blog. Lessig goes after Keen's evidence:

> [W]hat is puzzling about this book is that it purports to be a book attacking the sloppiness, error and ignorance of the Internet, yet it itself is shot through with sloppiness, error and ignorance. It tells us that without institutions, and standards, to signal what we can trust (like the institution, Doubleday, that decided to print his book), we won't know what's true and what's false. But

the book itself is riddled with falsity—from simple errors of fact, to gross misreadings of arguments, to the most basic errors of economics.

If an edited book from a major publisher contains errors and misreadings, Lessig contends, it undermines Keen's claim that experts save us from these inaccuracies.

The Web 2.0 debate is a series of rebuttal arguments in which the debaters attempt to knock the evidence out from under the competing claims and thus to remove the good reasons.

Counterargument

Another way to rebut is to counterargue. In a counterargument, you do not really show the shortcomings of your opponent's point of view; you may not refer to the details of the other argument at all. Rather, you offer an argument of another point of view in the hope that it will outweigh the argument that is being rebutted. A counterarguer, in effect, says, "I hear your argument. But there is more to it than that. Now listen while I explain why another position is stronger."

The counterarguer depends on the wisdom of her or his audience members to hear all sides of an issue and to make up their minds about the merits of the case. In the following short poem, Wilfred Owen, a veteran of the horrors of World War I trench warfare, offers a counterargument to those who argue that war is noble, to those who believe along with the poet Horace that "dulce et decorum est pro patria mori"—that it is sweet and fitting to die for one's country. This poem gains in popularity whenever there is an unpopular war, for it rebuts the belief that it is noble to die for one's country in modern warfare.

Dulce Et Decorum Est

Bent double, like old beggars under sacks,
Knock-kneed, coughing like hags, we cursed through sludge,
Till on the haunting flares we turned our backs
And towards our distant rest began to trudge.
Men marched asleep. Many had lost their boots
But limped on, blood-shod. All went lame; all blind;
Drunk with fatigue; deaf even to the hoots
Of disappointed shells that dropped behind.

Gas! Gas! Quick, boys!—An ecstacy of fumbling,
Fitting the clumsy helmets just in time;
But someone still was yelling out and stumbling
And floundering like a man in fire or lime.—
Dim, through the misty panes and thick green light
As under a green sea, I saw him drowning.
In all my dreams, before my helpless sight,
He plunges at me, guttering, choking, drowning.

If in some smothering dreams you too could pace
Behind the wagon that we flung him in,
And watch the white eyes writhing in his face,
His hanging face, like a devil's sick of sin;
If you could hear, at every jolt, the blood
Come gargling from the froth-corrupted lungs,
Obscene as cancer, bitter as the cud
Of vile, incurable sores on innocent tongues,—
My friend, you would not tell with such high zest
To children ardent for some desperate glory,
The old Lie: Dulce et decorum est
Pro patria mori.

Owen does not summarize the argument in favor of being willing to die for one's country and then refute that argument premise by premise. Rather, his poem presents an opposing argument, supported by a narrative of the speaker's experience in a poison-gas attack, that he hopes will more than counterbalance what he calls "the old lie." Owen simply ignores the good reasons that people give for being willing to die for one's country and argues instead that there are also good reasons not to do so. And he hopes that the evidence that he summons for his countering position will outweigh for his audience ("My friend") the evidence in support of the other side.

This example shows that it can be artificial to oppose refutation and counterargument, particularly because all arguments, in a broad sense, are counterarguments. Rebuttal arguments frequently offer both refutation and counterargument. In short, people who write rebuttals work like attorneys do in a trial: they make their own cases with good reasons and hard evidence, but they also do what they can to undermine their opponent's argument. In the end the jury, the audience, decides.

Build a Rebuttal Argument

Rebuttal arguments begin with critical interrogations of the evidence underlying claims. In the era of the Internet, many writers use what turns up on the first page of a Google search. Google reports the most popular sites, however, not the most accurate ones. Mistakes and outright falsehoods are repeated because many writers on the Internet do not check their facts.

Look up a writer's sources to judge the quality of the evidence. Also, check if the writer is reporting sources accurately. Do your own fact checking. Having access to your library's databases gives you a great advantage because database sources are usually more reliable than the information you can find on the Internet.

Treat facts like a detective would. Sometimes there are alternative explanations. For example, arguments that schools are getting worse and students are

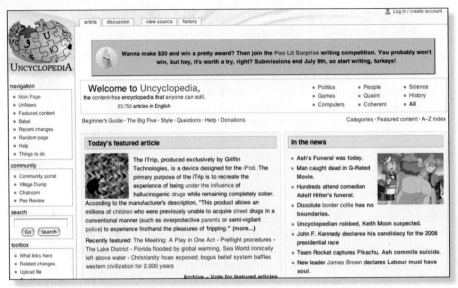

Uncyclopedia is a parody of Wikipedia that claims to be "an encyclopedia full of misinformation and utter lies." Is parody a rebuttal argument or something else?

getting dumber often use standardized test scores as evidence. On close inspection, however, you will find that writers often use these test scores selectively, quoting some scores and ignoring others that don't support their arguments. Furthermore, writers who quote test scores rarely take into account the population of test takers, which seldom remains constant from year to year.

When you write a counterargument with the goal of convincing readers that you have the stronger argument, your readers will appreciate your being fair about other arguments. Remember that you don't have to demolish the other person's argument, just establish that yours is better. Often you can be convincing by showing that you have thought about an issue in more depth and have taken into account more of its complexity.

Dan Stein

Crossing the Line

Dan Stein is president of the Federation for American Immigration Reform, a Washington D.C.-based nonprofit organization that seeks to stop illegal immigration. He frequently speaks and writes about immigration issues. He published "Crossing the Line" in the Los Angeles Business Journal *in February 2007.*

The timing could not have been worse for Bank of America to announce that it would begin issuing credit cards to illegal aliens in Los Angeles. News of Bank of America's decision was published in the *Wall Street Journal* on February 13, the same day that a new Harris Poll revealed that Americans perceive the two greatest threats to their security to be illegal immigration and the outsourcing of American jobs.

2   Even more than the prospect of the Iranians or the North Koreans with nukes, Americans believe that their security is threatened by millions of people pouring across our borders and by corporations that appear willing to sell out the interests of American workers. In one decision, Bank of America managed to pluck two raw nerves by appearing to encourage illegal immigration, while sending the message that it would not let any national interest stand in the way of it making a buck.

3   The Bank of America decision and the overwhelming negative public reaction to it illustrates the growing disconnect between the elite and everyone else in this country. To the elite—including the current occupant of the White House—the traditional idea of the nation has become a bothersome anachronism. To the extent that the entity known as the United States has any relevance at all to them, it is to secure their ability to conduct business and maximize their corporate bottom lines. Concepts of patriotism and loyalty are marketing tools and nothing more.

4   To Bank of America and other large corporations, illegal immigrants are a source of low wage labor and an untapped customer market. It matters not that illegal immigrants are breaking the laws of the United States, taking jobs from and driving down wages for middle class workers, burdening schools (not the ones the children of Bank of America executives attend, of course) and other vital public services. What matters to the banking industry is that the estimated 12 to 15 million illegal aliens living in the United States have purchasing power and that there is money to be made off of serving them.

5   It is true that Bank of America did not create the illegal immigration crisis in the United States, although banking industry decisions to allow illegal aliens to open bank accounts, take out home mortgages and now obtain credit cards has certainly added to the problem. But the fact that the federal government has done little to resolve the problem of illegal immigration does not mean that banks and other business interests have an unfettered right to profit from illegal immigration. Bank of America did not create the illegal drug problem in the United States, but that does not entitle it to market services to the drug cartels, even though it would be enormously profitable to do so.

Overtly discriminatory

The plan to issue credit cards to illegal aliens is also overtly discriminatory, giving a new meaning to their corporate slogan: "Bank of America, Higher Standards" (for some). While American citizens and legal U.S. residents are held to one standard in order to obtain credit, illegal aliens will be held to a lower standard. The plastic that any of us tote around in our wallets required us to open our entire lives to our creditors and to provide verification of our identities and credit-worthiness. In their hunger to make money off of illegal aliens Bank of America is prepared to accept easily counterfeited Mexican matricula cards as proof of identity, and maintaining a checking account for three months as a credit history.

7   Bank of America has obviously felt the sting of a public backlash, as evidenced by their sudden reluctance to discuss it in the media. Some people have gone so far as to pull their accounts out of Bank of America. But given the consolidation of the banking industry generally, and the fact that a handful of banks have corner on the credit card market, it will require government action to stop financial institutions from pursuing profits in blatant disregard of the law and the public interest.

8   Existing federal law clearly prohibits "encouraging or inducing unauthorized aliens to enter the United States, and engaging in a conspiracy or aiding and abetting" people who violate U.S. immigration laws. Products and services specifically marketed to illegal aliens, intended to make it easier to live and work in the U.S. illegally, violates the spirit if not the letter of the law.

9   To Bank of America, illegal aliens are just customers and the United States nothing more than a market. To the American people, illegal immigration and corporate greed are seen as serious threats to their security. Bank of America has provided the proof that both are inexorably intertwined. ■

Gregory Rodriguez

Illegal Immigrants—They're Money

Gregory Rodriguez is a Los Angeles-based Irvine Senior Fellow at the New America Foundation, a nonpartisan think tank in Washington, D.C. He has written widely about issues of national identity, social cohesion, assimilation, race relations, religion, immigration, demographics, and social and political trends. He published "Illegal Immigrants—They're Money," a rebuttal to Dan Stein's article about the Bank of America, as a column in the Los Angeles Times *on March 4, 2007.*

Dan Stein, the premier American nativist and president of the Federation for American Immigration Reform, is shocked, shocked. He's mad at Bank of America for issuing credit cards to illegal immigrants. He says that to Bank of America "and other large corporations, illegal immigrants are a source of low-wage labor and an untapped customer market." You bet they are, and that's the American way.

2   Sure, I'm proud to be a citizen of a nation that portrays itself as a refuge for the "tired," "the poor" and the "huddled masses yearning to breathe free." But let's face it, Emma Lazarus, the poet who wrote those

words, may have laid it on a bit thick. The truth, no less beautiful in its way, is a little more crass and self-serving. But it wouldn't have sounded nearly as poetic to say, "bring us your able-bodied, poor, hardworking masses yearning for a chance to climb out of poverty, establish a credit history and . . . ." We all love to rhapsodize about immigrants' embrace of the American dream, but it's more like a hard-nosed American deal — you come here, you work your tail off under grueling conditions, and you can try your damnedest to better your lot over time.

3   In their generational struggle for acceptance and security, from outsider to insider and, dare I say, from exploited to exploiter, immigrants could avail themselves of those inalienable rights that stand at the core of our national political philosophy—life, liberty and the pursuit of happiness.

4   But that, of course, was before the invention of illegal immigration.

5   Until the early 1900s, pretty much anybody who wasn't diseased, a criminal, a prostitute, a pauper, an anarchist or a Chinese laborer could gain entrance to the U.S. Between 1880 and 1914, only 1% of a total of 25 million European immigrants were excluded from this country. But after transatlantic crossings had already been halted by World War I, Congress buckled to anti-foreign sentiment and closed the proverbial Golden Door by passing a series of restrictionist laws in 1917, 1921 and 1924.

6   Yet even as the historical front door of the nation was being closed, business interests were busy prying open a new side-door. Only three months after the passage of the Immigration Act of 1917, which required all newcomers to pass a literacy test and pay a head tax, the U.S. Secretary of Commerce waived the regulations for Mexican workers. Thus began America's dishonorable relationship with Mexican immigrant labor.

7   For the next several decades, Mexican workers were brought in when the economy expanded and kicked out when times got bad. They were recruited in the 1920s, only to be deported in the 1930s. They were brought in again during the labor shortage in the 1940s. By the 1950s, one branch of the government recruited Mexican workers, under the illusion that they were "temporary," while another sought to keep them out.

8   The *piece de resistance* in the creation of the illegal immigrant is the Immigration Act of 1965. Although touted as a great piece of liberal legislation that ended discriminatory immigration barriers, it imposed an annual cap on migrants from the Western Hemisphere that was 40% less than the number that had been arriving yearly before 1965. A decade later, Congress placed a 20,000 limit per country in this hemisphere.

9   In other words, after importing millions of Mexicans over the decades, particularly during the bracero guest-worker program from 1942 to 1963, and establishing well-trod routes to employment north of the border, the U.S. drastically reduced the number of visas available to Mexicans. This reduction, of course, coincided with a rapid rise in Mexico's population. And guess what? When jobs were available on this side of the border, Mexicans just kept coming, whether they had papers or not.

10   Clearly, today as ever, mass migration to the U.S. is being driven by economic need—the immigrants' and our economy's. But the hard-nosed American deal has become unfair because, on top of the handicaps we have always imposed on new arrivals, we've added a rather brutal one—criminal status. Good luck with that pursuit of happiness as you engage in backbreaking labor when your place in society is summed up with that one cutting word, "illegal."

11   No, I'm not advocating open borders. Nor do I believe that immigrants should be guaranteed anything but a chance to achieve their end of the nation's cruel bargain. For hardworking illegal immigrants who've established roots here, we should uphold our end of the bargain and give them a chance to achieve their piece of the American dream. Bank of America is not wrong to give illegal immigrants the tools with which to compete legitimately in the marketplace. We as a nation are wrong for treating all these people as illegitimate. ■

Steps to Writing a Rebuttal Argument

Step 1 Identify an Argument to Argue Against as well as its Main Claim(s)

- What exactly are you arguing against?
- Are there secondary claims attached to the main claim?
- Include a fair summary of your opponent's position in your finished rebuttal.

Examples

- Arguing against raising taxes for the purpose of building a new sports stadium (examine how proponents claim that a new sports facility will benefit the local economy).
- Arguing for raising the minimum wage (examine how opponents claim that a higher minimum wage isn't necessary and negatively affects small-business owners).

Step 2 Examine the Facts on Which the Claim Is Based

- Are the facts accurate?
- Are the facts a truly representative sample?
- Are the facts current?
- Is there another body of facts that you can present as counterevidence?
- If the author uses statistics, is evidence for the validity of those statistics presented?
- Can the statistics be interpreted differently?
- If the author quotes from sources, how reliable are those sources?
- Are the sources treated fairly, or are quotations taken out of context?
- If the author cites outside authority, how much trust can you place in that authority?

Step 3 Examine the Assumptions on Which the Claim Is Based

- What is the primary assumption of the claim you are rejecting?
- What other assumptions support that claim?
- How are those assumptions flawed?
- If you are arguing against a specific piece of writing, how does the author fall short?
- Does the author resort to name calling, use faulty reasoning, or ignore key facts?
- What fallacies is the author guilty of committing?

Step 4 Analyze Your Potential Readers

- To what extent do your potential readers support the claim that you are rejecting?
- If they strongly support that claim, how might you appeal to them to change their minds?
- What common assumptions and beliefs do you share with them?

Step 5 Decide Whether to Write a Refutation, a Counterargument—or Both

- Make your aim clear in your thesis statement.

Examples

- For a refutation, your thesis statement might be as follows: Proponents of making the percentages of intercollegiate athletes proportionate to the number of male and female students ignore the facts that when participation is entirely voluntary, as in intramural sports, men participate at a far higher rate than women, and women participate at far higher rates in all activities but sports: student government, dance, band, orchestra, debate, and drama.

- For a counterargument, your thesis statement might be as follows: Critics of Title IX who focus only on the effects on men's sports neglect that women who play sports—especially minority women—make better grades, have higher self-esteem, are more likely to become community leaders, are less likely to smoke or to use drugs, and have higher graduation rates from high school and college than women who don't play sports.

Step 6 Write a Draft

Introduction

Identify the issue and the argument you are rejecting.

- Provide background if the issue is unfamiliar to most of your readers.
- Give a quick summary of the competing positions even if the issue is familiar to your readers.
- Remember that offering a fair and accurate summary is a good way to build credibility with your audience.

Body

Take on the argument that you are rejecting. Consider questioning the evidence that is used to support the argument by doing one or more of the following:

- Challenge the facts.
- Present counterevidence and countertestimony.
- Cast doubt on the representativeness of the sample or the currency and relevance of the examples.
- Challenge the credibility of any authorities cited.
- Question the way in which statistical evidence is presented and interpreted.
- Argue that quotations are taken out of context.

Conclusion

Conclude on a firm note by underscoring your objections.

- Consider closing with a counterargument or counterproposal.

Step 7 Revise, Edit, Proofread

- For detailed instructions, see Chapter 4.
- For a checklist to use to evaluate your draft, see pages 61–62.

13

Proposal Arguments

Manufactured goods from China move through the Panama Canal on their way to the United States. Do you agree or disagree with those who propose trade restrictions aimed at keeping manufacturing jobs in the U.S.?

At this moment, you might not think that you feel strongly enough about anything to write a proposal argument. But if you write a list of things that make you mad or at least a little annoyed, then you have a start toward writing a proposal argument. Some things on your list are not going to produce proposal arguments that many people would want to read. If your roommate is a slob, you might be able to write a proposal for that person to start cleaning up more, but who else would be interested? Similarly, it might be annoying to you that where you live is too far from the ocean, but it is hard to imagine making a serious proposal to move your city closer to the coast. Short of those extremes, however, are a lot of things that might make you think, "Why hasn't someone done something about this?" If you believe that others have something to gain if a problem is solved, or at least that the situation can be made a little better, then you might be able to develop a good proposal argument.

For instance, suppose you are living off campus, and you buy a student parking sticker when you register for courses so that you can park in the student lot. However, you quickly find out that there are too many cars and trucks for the number of available spaces, and unless you get to campus by 8:00 a.m., you aren't going to find a place to park in your assigned lot. The situation makes you angry because you believe that if you pay for a sticker, you should have a reasonable chance of finding a place to park. You see that there are unfilled lots reserved for faculty and staff next to the student parking lot, and you wonder why more spaces aren't allotted to students. You decide to write to the president of your college. You want her to direct parking and traffic services to give more spaces to students or else to build a parking garage that will accommodate more vehicles.

When you start talking to other students on campus, however, you begin to realize that the problem may be more complex than your first view of it. Your college has taken the position that if fewer students drive to campus, there will be less traffic on and around your campus. The administration wants more students to ride shuttle buses, to form car pools, or to bicycle to campus instead of driving alone. You also find out that faculty and staff members pay ten times as much as students for their parking permits, so they pay a very high premium for a guaranteed space—much too high for most students. If the president of your college is your primary audience, you first have to argue that a problem really exists. You have to convince the president that many students have no choice but to drive if they are to attend classes. You, for example, are willing to ride the shuttle buses, but they don't run often enough for you to make your classes, get back to your car that you left at home, and then drive to your job.

Next, you have to argue that your solution will solve the problem. An eight-story parking garage might be adequate to park all the cars of students who want to drive, but parking garages are very expensive to build. Even if a parking garage is the best solution, the question remains: who is going to pay for it? Many problems in life could be solved if you had access to unlimited resources, but very few people—or organizations—have such resources at their command. It's not enough to propose a solution that can resolve the problem. You have to be able to argue for the feasibility of your solution. If you want to argue that a parking garage is the solution to the parking problem on your campus, then you must also propose how to finance the garage.

Understand How Proposal Arguments Work

Proposal arguments call for some action to be taken (or not to be taken). The challenge for writers is to convince readers that they should take action, which usually involves their commitment of effort or money. It's always easier to do nothing and wait for someone else to act. Thus, the key is using good reasons to convince readers that good things will result if some action is taken and bad things can be avoided. If readers are convinced that the proposal serves their interests, they will take action. Proposal arguments take this form:

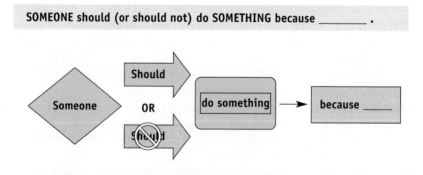

Recognize Components of Proposal Arguments

Proposal arguments are often complex and involve the kinds of arguments that are discussed in Chapters 8 through 12. Successful proposals have four major components:

- **Identifying the problem.** Sometimes, problems are evident to your intended readers. If your city is constantly tearing up the streets and then leaving them for months without doing anything to repair them, then you shouldn't have much trouble convincing the citizens of your city that streets should be repaired more quickly. But if you raise a problem that will be unfamiliar to most of your readers, first you will have to argue that the problem exists. Recall that in Chapter 1, Rachel Carson had to use several kinds of arguments in *Silent Spring* to make people aware of the dangers of pesticides, including narrative arguments, definition arguments, evaluation arguments, and arguments of comparison. Often, you will have to do similar work to establish exactly what problem you are attempting to solve. You will have to define the scope of the problem. Some of the bad roads in your city might be the responsibility of the state, not the city, government.

- **Stating a proposed solution.** You need a clear, definite statement of exactly what you are proposing. You might want to place this statement near the beginning of your argument, or later, after you have considered and rejected other possible solutions.

- **Using good reasons to convince readers that the proposed solution is fair and will work.** When your readers agree that a problem exists and a solution should be found, your next task is to convince them that your solution is the best one to resolve the problem. If you're writing about the problem your city has in getting streets repaired promptly, then you need to analyze carefully the process that is involved in repairing streets. Sometimes there are mandatory delays so that competing bids can be solicited, and sometimes there are unexpected delays when tax revenue falls short of expectations. You should be able to put your finger on the problem in a detailed causal analysis. You should be able to make an evaluation argument that your solution is fair to all concerned. You should also be prepared to make arguments of rebuttal against other possible solutions.

- **Demonstrating that the solution is feasible.** Your solution not only has to work; it must be feasible to implement. Malaysia effectively ended its drug problem by imposing mandatory death sentences for anyone caught selling even small amounts of drugs. Foreign nationals, teenagers, and grandmothers have all been hanged under this law. Malaysia came up with a solution for its

Finding Good Reasons
WHO SHOULD MAKE DECISIONS ABOUT
ECONOMIC DEVELOPMENT?

Northcross Mall in Austin, Texas, is a declining neighborhood shopping center with several empty stores. In 2006, Wal-Mart proposed taking over the site and building a Supercenter. Surrounding neighborhood associations rallied together and formed Responsible Growth for Northcross. They agreed that Northcross Mall should be re-developed, but they objected to Wal-Mart because of the traffic the Supercenter would generate and because the sprawling structure and large parking lot would not comply with the city's guidelines for redevelopment. Their opposition raises an important ques-tion: should surrounding neighborhoods have the right to decide on the kinds of busi-nesses that are appropriate for their neighborhood on commercially zoned property?

Write about it

1. If you were the spokesperson for Wal-Mart, what reasons would you give to the Austin City Council to persuade them to allow Wal-Mart to build a Supercenter on the site?

2. If you were the spokesperson for Responsible Growth for Northcross, what good reasons would you give to convince the city council to deny Wal-Mart permission to build a Supercenter?

3. If you were a member of the Austin City Council, what reasons might you expect to hear from these two groups? Draft a proposal that would win your vote.

purposes, but this solution probably would not work in most countries because the punishment seems too extreme. If you want a parking garage built on your campus and you learn that no college funds can be used to construct it, then you have to be able to argue that the potential users of the garage will be willing to pay greatly increased fees for the convenience of parking on campus.

Build a Proposal Argument

Proposal arguments often grow out of long histories of debate. An issue with a much shorter history can also quickly pile up mountains of arguments if it gains wide public attention. In 1972, President Richard Nixon signed into law the Education Amendments Act, including Title IX, which prohibits gender discrimination at schools and colleges that receive federal aid. Few people at the time guessed that Title IX would have the far-reaching consequences that it has. When Title IX was passed, 31,000 women participated in intercollegiate athletics. In the academic year 2002–2003, over 160,000 women athletes participated in varsity college sports. The 2006 data show the highest-ever participation by women in intercollegiate athletics programs. Even more striking is the increase in girls' participation in high school sports. The number of boy athletes rose gradually from about 3.6 million in 1971 to approximately 4 million in 2003–2004, while the number of girl athletes increased tenfold—from 294,000 in 1971 to over 2.9 million in 2006.

The participation of women in intercollegiate athletics has stalled since 2000. The proportion of female undergraduates was 55.8 percent in 2004–2005, but the percentage of women athletes was only 41.7 percent. Do you think women should participate in intercollegiate athletics at a level equal to men?

Proponents of Title IX are justifiably proud of the increased level of participation of women in varsity athletics. But for all the good that Title IX has done to increase athletic opportunities for women, critics blame Title IX for decreasing athletic opportunities for college men. According to the U.S. General Accounting Office (GAO), more than three hundred men's teams have been eliminated in college athletics since 1993. In 2000 the University of Miami dropped its men's swimming team, which had produced many Olympians, including Greg Louganis, who won gold medals in both platform and springboard diving in two consecutive Olympics. In 2001 the University of Nebraska also discontinued its men's swimming team, which had been in place since 1922, and the University of Kansas dropped men's swimming and tennis.

Wrestling teams have been especially hard hit, dropping from 363 in 1981 to 192 in 1999. The effects were noticeable at the 2000 Olympics in Australia, where U.S. freestyle wrestlers failed to win any gold medals for the first time since 1968.

College and university administrators claim that they have no choice but to drop men's teams if more women's teams are added. Their position comes not from the original Title IX legislation, which does not mention athletics, but from a 1979 clarification by the Office of Civil Rights (OCR), the agency that enforces Title IX. OCR set out three options for schools to comply with Title IX:

1. Bring the proportion of women in varsity athletics roughly equal to the percentage of women students.
2. Prove a "history and continuing practice" of creating new opportunities for women.
3. Prove that the school has done everything to "effectively accommodate" the athletic interests of women students.

University administrators have argued that the first option, known as proportionality, is the only one that can be argued successfully in a courtroom if the school is sued.

Proportionality is difficult to achieve at schools with football programs. Universities that play NCAA Division I-A football offer 85 football scholarships to men. Since there is no equivalent sport for women, football throws the gender statistics way out of balance. Defenders of football ask that it be exempted from Title IX because it is the cash cow that pays most of the bills for both men's and women's sports. Only a handful of women's basketball programs make money. All other women's sports are money losers and, like men's "minor" sports, depend on men's football and basketball revenues and student fees to pay their bills. College officials maintain that if they cut the spending for football, football will bring in less revenue, and thus all sports will be harmed.

Those who criticize Title IX argue that it assumes that women's interest in athletics is identical to men's. They point out that male students participate at much higher rates in intramural sports, which have no limitations on who can play. In contrast, women participate at much higher rates in music, dance, theater, and other extracurricular activities, yet Title IX is not being applied to those activities.

Defenders of Title IX argue that women's interest in athletics cannot be determined until they have had equal opportunities to participate. They claim Title IX is being used as a scapegoat for college administrators who do not want to make tough decisions. They point out that in 2004–2005, women made up 55.8 percent of all college students but only 41.7 percent of all college athletes. Without Title IX, in their view, schools would have no incentive to increase opportunities for women. The battle over Title IX is not likely to go away soon.

Thomas Homer-Dixon and S. Julio Freidmann

Coal in a Nice Shade of Green

Thomas Homer-Dixon is the director of the Center for Peace and Conflict Studies at the University of Toronto. His award-winning works include The Ingenuity Gap, *which won the 2001 Governor-General's Non-fiction Award, and* Environment, Scarcity, and Violence, *which received the 2000 Lynton Caldwell Prize from the American Political Science Association. His latest work is* The Upside of Down: Catastrophe, Creativity, and the Renewal of Civilization *(2006). S. Julio Friedmann directs the carbon sequestration project at Lawrence Livermore National Laboratory in Livermore, California. In this article, which appeared in the March 25, 2005, edition of the* New York Times, *Homer-Dixon and Friedmann argue for gasification as a solution to our reliance on costly crude oil.*

When it comes to energy, we are trapped between a rock and several hard places. The world's soaring demand for oil is pushing against the limits of production, lifting the price of crude nearly 90 percent in the last 18 months. Congress's vote in favor of drilling in the Arctic National Wildlife Refuge won't make much difference because the amount of oil there, at best, is tiny relative to global or even American needs. And relief isn't likely to come anytime soon from drilling elsewhere: oil companies spent $8 billion on exploration in 2003, but discovered only $4 billion of commercially useful oil.

2   Sadly, most alternatives to conventional oil can't give us the immense amount of energy we need without damaging our environment, jeopardizing our national security or bankrupting us. The obvious alternatives are other fossil fuels: natural gas and oil products derived from tar sands, oil shale and even coal. But natural gas supplies are tightening, at least in North America.

3   And, of course, all fossil fuels have a major disadvantage: burning them releases carbon dioxide, a greenhouse gas that may contribute to climate change. This drawback is especially acute for tar sands, oil shale and coal, which, joule for joule, release far more carbon dioxide than either conventional oil or natural gas.

4   As for energy sources not based on carbon, it would be enormously hard to meet a major percentage of America's energy needs at a reasonable cost, at least in the near term. Take nuclear power—a source that produces no greenhouse emissions. Even assuming we can find a place to dispose of nuclear waste and deal with the security risks, to meet the expected growth in total American energy demand over the next 50 years would require building 1,200 new nuclear power plants in addition to the current 104—or one plant every two weeks until 2050.

5   Solar power? To satisfy its current electricity demand using today's technology, the United States would need 10 billion square meters of photovoltaic panels; this would cost $5 trillion, or nearly half the country's annual gross domestic product.

6   How about hydrogen? To replace just America's surface transportation with cars and trucks running on fuel cells powered by hydrogen, America would have to produce 230,000 tons of the gas—or enough to fill 13,000 Hindenburg dirigibles—every day. This could be generated by electrolyzing water, but to do so America would have to nearly double its electricity output, and generating this extra power with carbon-free renewable energy would mean covering an area the size of Massachusetts with solar panels or of New York State with windmills.

7   Of course technology is always improving, and down the road some or all of these technologies may become more feasible. But for the near term, there is no silver bullet. The scale and complexity of American energy consumption are such that the country needs to look at many different solutions simultaneously. On the demand side, this means huge investments in conservation and energy efficiency—two areas that policy makers and consumers have sadly neglected.

8   On the supply side, the important thing is to come up with so-called bridge technologies that can power our cities, factories and cars with fewer emissions than traditional fossil fuels while we move to clean energy like solar, wind and safe nuclear power. A prime example of a bridge technology—one that exists right now—is gasification.

9   Here's how it works: in a type of power plant called an integrated gasification combined-cycle facility, we change any fossil fuel, including coal, into a superhot gas that is rich in hydrogen—and in the process strip out pollutants like sulfur and mercury. As in a traditional combustion power plant, the heat generates large amounts of electricity; but in this case, the gas byproducts can be pure streams of hydrogen and carbon dioxide.

10   This matters for several reasons. The hydrogen produced could be used as a transportation fuel. Equally important, the harmful carbon dioxide waste is in a form that can be pumped deep underground and stored, theoretically for millions of years, in old oil and gas fields or saline aquifers. This process is called geologic storage, or carbon sequestration, and recent field demonstrations in Canada and Norway have shown it can work and work safely.

11   The marriage of gasified coal plants and geologic storage could allow us to build power plants that produce vast amounts of energy with virtually no carbon dioxide emissions in the air. The Department of Energy is pursuing plans to build such a zero-emission power plant and is encouraging energy companies to come up with proposals of their own. The United States, Britain, and Germany are also collaborating to build such plants in China and India as part of an effort by the Group of 8. Moreover, these plants are very flexible: although coal is the most obvious fuel source, they could burn almost any organic material, including waste cornhusks and woodchips.

12   This is an emerging technology, so inevitably there are hurdles. For example, we need a crash program of research to find out which geological formations best lock up the carbon dioxide for the longest time, followed by global geological surveys to locate these formations and determine their

capacity. Also, coal mining is dangerous and strip-mining, of course, devastates the environment; if we are to mine a lot more coal in the future we will want more environmentally friendly methods.

13   On balance, though, this combination of technologies is probably among the best ways to provide the energy needed by modern societies—including populous, energy-hungry and coal-rich societies like China and India—without wrecking the global climate.

14   Fossil fuels, especially petroleum, powered the industrialization of today's rich countries and they still drive the world economy. But within the lifetimes of our grandchildren, the age of petroleum will wane. The combination of gasified coal plants and geologic storage can be our bridge to the clean energy—derived from renewable resources like solar and wind power and perhaps nuclear fusion—of the 22nd century and beyond. ■

Sample Student Proposal Argument

Kim Lee
Professor Patel
RHE 306
31 March 2009

Let's Make It a Real Melting Pot with Presidential Hopes for All

The image the United States likes to advertise is a country that embraces diversity and creates a land of equal opportunity for all. As the Statue of Liberty cries out, "give me your tired, your poor, your huddled masses yearning to breathe free," American politicians gleefully evoke such images to frame the United States as a bastion for all things good, fair, and equal. As a proud American, however, I must nonetheless highlight one of the cracks in this façade of equality. Imagine that an infertile couple decides to adopt an orphaned child from China. They follow all of the legal processes deemed necessary by both countries. They fly abroad and bring home their (once parentless) six-month-old baby boy. They raise and nurture him, and while teaching him to embrace his ethnicity, they also teach him to love Captain Crunch, baseball, and *The Three Stooges*. He grows and eventually attends an ethnically diverse American public school. One day his fifth-grade teacher tells the class that anyone can grow up to be president. To clarify her point, she turns to the boy, knowing his background, and states, "No, you could not be president, Stu, but you could still be a senator. That's something to aspire to!" How do Stu's parents explain this rule to this American-raised child? This scenario will become increasingly common, yet as the Constitution currently reads, only "natural-born" citizens may run for the offices of president and vice president. Neither these children nor the thousands of hardworking Americans who chose to make America their official homeland may aspire to the highest political position in the land. While the huddled masses may enter, it appears they must retain a second-class citizen ranking.

The "natural-born" stipulation regarding the presidency stems from the self-same meeting of minds that brought the American people the Electoral College. During the Constitutional Convention of 1787, the Congress formulated the regulatory measures associated with the office of the president. A letter sent from John Jay to George Washington during this period reads as follows:

> "Permit me to hint," Jay wrote, "whether it would not be wise and seasonable to provide a strong check to the admission of foreigners into the administration of our national government; and to declare expressly that the Commander in Chief of the American army shall not be given to, nor devolve on, any but a natural-born citizen." (Mathews A1)

Shortly thereafter, Article II, Section I, Clause V, of the Constitution declared that "No Person except a natural born Citizen, or a Citizen of the United States at the time of the Adoption of this Constitution, shall be eligible to the Office of President." Jill A. Pryor states in the *Yale Law Journal* that "some writers have suggested that Jay was responding to rumors that foreign princes might be asked to assume the presidency" (881). Many cite disastrous examples of foreign rule in the eighteenth century as the impetus for the "natural-born" clause. For example, in 1772—only 15 years prior to the adoption of the statute—Poland had been divided up by Prussia, Russia, and Austria (Kasindorf). Perhaps an element of self-preservation and not ethnocentrism led to the questionable stipulation. Nonetheless, in the twenty-first century this clause reeks of xenophobia.

The 2003 election of action-film star Arnold Schwarzenegger as governor of California stirred up a movement to change this Constitutional statute. Politicians such as Senators Orrin Hatch (R-Utah) and Ted Kennedy (D-Massachusetts and Arnold's uncle by marriage) have created a buzz for ratifying a would-be twenty-eighth amendment. In addition, grassroots campaigns like Amend for Arnold are trying to rally popular support as they dream of the Terminator-cum-president's political slogans ("I'll be back . . . for four more years" or "Hasta la vista, baby, and hasta la vista to high taxes"). Schwarzenegger has become the face—and the bulked-up body—of the viable *naturalized* president.

We as a nation should follow the lead set by those enamored of the action star, but distance the fight from this one extremely wealthy actor. We must instead take a stand against the discriminatory practice applied to all foreign-born American citizens by this obsolete provision of the Constitution. Congress has made minor attempts to update this biased clause. The Fourteenth Amendment clarified the difference between "natural-born" and "native-born" citizens by spelling out the citizenship status of children born to American parents outside of the United States (Ginsberg 929). (Such a clause qualifies individuals such as Senator John McCain—born in Panama—for presidency.) This change is not enough. I propose that the United States abolish the natural-born clause and replace it with a stipulation that allows naturalized citizens to run for president. This amendment would state that a candidate must have been naturalized and must have lived in residence in the United States for a period of at least twenty-five years. The present time is ideal for this change. This amendment could simultaneously honor the spirit of the Constitution, protect and ensure the interests of the United States, promote an international image of inclusiveness, and grant heretofore-withheld rights to thousands of legal and loyal United States citizens.

In our push for change, we must make clear the importance of this amendment. It would not provide special rights for would-be terrorists. To the contrary, it would fulfill the longtime promises of the nation. The United States claims to allow all people to blend into the great stew of citizenship. It has already suffered embarrassment and international cries of ethnic bias as a result of political moves such as Japanese-American internment and the Guantanamo Bay detention center. This amendment can help mend the national image as every American takes one more step toward equality. Naturalized citizens have been contributing to the United States for centuries. Many nameless Mexican, Irish, and Asian Americans sweated and toiled to build the American railroads. The public has welcomed naturalized Americans such as Bob Hope, Albert Pujols, and Peter Jennings into their hearts and living rooms. Individuals such as German-born Henry Kissinger and Czechoslovakian-born Madeleine Albright have held high posts in the American government and have served as respected aides to its presidents. The amendment must make clear that it is not about one man's celebrity. Approximately seven hundred foreign-born Americans have won the Medal of Honor and over sixty thousand proudly serve in the United States military today (Siskind 5). The "natural-born" clause must be removed to provide each of these people—over half a million naturalized in 2003 alone—with equal footing to those who were born into citizenship rather than working for it (U.S. Census Bureau).

Since the passing of the Bill of Rights, only 17 amendments have been ratified. This process takes time and overwhelming congressional

Lee 4

and statewide support. To alter the Constitution, a proposed amendment must pass with a two-thirds "super-majority" in both the House of Representatives and the Senate. In addition, the proposal must find favor in two-thirds (38) of state legislatures. In short, this task will not be easy. In order for this change to occur, a grassroots campaign must work to dispel misinformation regarding naturalized citizens and to force the hands of senators and representatives wishing to retain their congressional seats. We must take this proposal to ethnicity-specific political groups from both sides of the aisle, business organizations, and community activist groups. We must convince representatives that this issue matters. Only through raising voices and casting votes can the people enact change. Only then can every American child see the possibility for limitless achievement and equality. Only then can everyone find the same sense of pride in the possibility for true American diversity in the highest office in the land.

Lee 5

Works Cited

Epstein, Edward. "Doubt about a Foreign-Born President." *San Francisco Chronicle* 6 Oct. 2004: A5. *LexisNexis Academic*. Web. 6 Mar. 2009.

Ginsberg, Gordon. "Citizenship: Expatriation: Distinction between Naturalized and Natural Born Citizens." *Michigan Law Review* 50 (1952): 926-29. *JSTOR*. Web. 6 Mar. 2009.

Kasindorf, Martin. "Should the Constitution Be Amended for Arnold?" *USA Today* 2 Dec. 2004. *LexisNexis Academic*. Web. 8 Mar. 2009.

Mathews, Joe. "Maybe Anyone Can Be President." *Los Angeles Times* 2 Feb. 2005: A1. *LexisNexis Academic*. Web. 6 Mar. 2009.

Pryor, Jill A. "The Natural Born Citizen Clause and Presidential Eligibility: An Approach for Resolving Two Hundred Years of Uncertainty." *Yale Law Journal* 97.5 (1988): 881-99. Print.

Siskind, Lawrence J. "Why Shouldn't Arnold Run?" *Recorder* 10 Dec. 2004: 5. *LexisNexis Academic*. Web. 10 Mar. 2009.

United States. Dept. of Commerce. Census Bureau. "The Fourth of July 2005." *Facts for Features*. US Dept. of Commerce, 27 June 2005. Web. 17 Mar. 2009.

Steps to Writing a Proposal Argument

Step 1 Make a Claim

Make a proposal claim advocating a specific change or course of action.

Template

- *We should (or should not) do SOMETHING.* In an essay of five or fewer pages, it's difficult to propose solutions to big problems such as persistent poverty. Proposals that address local problems are more manageable, and sometimes they get actual results.

Examples

- Redesigning the process of registering for courses, getting email, or making appointments to be more efficient.
- Creating bicycle lanes to make cycling safer and to reduce traffic.
- Building a pedestrian overpass over a busy street to improve safety for walkers.
- Streamlining the rules for recycling newspapers, bottles, and cans to encourage increased participation.

Step 2 Identify the Problem

- What exactly is the problem?
- Who is most affected by the problem?
- What causes the problem?
- Has anyone tried to do anything about it? If so, why haven't they succeeded?
- What is likely to happen in the future if the problem isn't solved?

Step 3 Propose Your Solution

State your solution as specifically as you can.

- What exactly do you want to achieve?
- How exactly will your solution work?
- Can it be accomplished quickly, or will it have to be phased in over a few years?
- Has anything like it been tried elsewhere? If so, what happened?
- Who will be involved?
- Can you think of any reasons why your solution might not work?
- How will you address those arguments?
- Can you think of any ways to strengthen your proposed solution in light of those possible criticisms?

Step 4 Consider Other Solutions

- What other solutions have been or might be proposed for this problem, including doing nothing?
- What are the advantages and disadvantages of those solutions?
- Why is your solution better?

Step 5 Examine the Feasibility of Your Solution

- How easy is your solution to implement?
- Will the people most affected by your solution be willing to go along with it? (For example, lots of things can be accomplished if enough people volunteer, but groups often have difficulty getting enough volunteers to work without pay.)
- If your solution costs money, how do you propose to pay for it?
- Who is most likely to reject your proposal because it is not practical enough?
- How can you convince your readers that your proposal can be achieved?

Step 6 Analyze Your Potential Readers

- Whom are you writing for?
- How interested will your readers be in this problem?
- How much does this problem affect them?
- How would your solution benefit them directly and indirectly?

Step 7 Write a Draft

Introduction

- Set out the issue or problem, perhaps by telling about your experience or the experience of someone you know.
- Argue for the seriousness of the problem.
- Give some background about the problem if necessary.

Body

- Present your solution. Consider setting out your solution first, explaining how it will work, discussing other possible solutions, and arguing that yours is better. Or consider discussing other possible solutions first, arguing that they don't solve the problem or are not feasible, and then presenting your solution.
- Make clear the goals of your solution. Many solutions cannot solve problems completely. If you are proposing a solution for juvenile crime in your neighborhood, for example, you cannot expect to eliminate all juvenile crime.
- Describe in detail the steps in implementing your solution and how they will solve the problem you have identified. You can impress your readers with the care with which you have thought through this problem.
- Explain the positive consequences that will follow from your proposal. What good things will happen, and what bad things will be avoided, if your advice is taken?
- Argue that your proposal is feasible and can be put into practice.
- If people have to change the ways they are doing things now, explain why they would want to change. If your proposal costs money, you need to identify exactly where the money would come from.

Conclusion

- Issue a call to action—if your readers agree with you, they will want to take action.
- Restate and emphasize exactly what readers need to do to solve the problem.

Step 8 Revise, Edit, Proofread

- For detailed instructions, see Chapter 4.
- For a checklist to use to evaluate your draft, see pages 61–62.

Designing and Presenting Arguments

PART 4 **Designing and Presenting Arguments**

14. Designing Arguments 229

Think about your readers 229

Know when to use images and graphics 230

Compose and edit images 231

Create tables, charts, and graphs 234

Design pages for print 235

Design pages for the Web 236

15. Presenting Arguments 238

Plan in advance 238

Design effective visuals 240

Focus on your delivery 242

14

Designing Arguments

Arguments do not communicate with words alone. Even written arguments that do not contain graphics or images have a look and feel that also communicate meaning. In daily life we infer a great deal from what we see. Designers are well aware that, like people, writing has a body language that often communicates a strong message. It all has to do with understanding how particular effects can be achieved for particular readers in particular situations. Becoming more attentive to design will make your arguments more effective.

Think About Your Readers

Imagine yourself in the shoes of your reader. As a reader of an argument, you expect to find reasons supported by evidence. But you also expect the writer to do the little things that make it easier to read and understand the argument.

Telling readers what you are writing about

An accurate and informative title is critical for readers to decide whether they want to read what you have written. Furthermore, the title is critical to allow readers to return to something they read earlier.

Some kinds of writing require abstracts, which are short summaries of the overall document. Abstracts are required for scholarly articles in the sciences and social sciences as well as dissertations. Business reports and other reports often have executive summaries, which are similar to abstracts but often briefer.

Making your organization visible

Most longer texts and many shorter ones include headings, which give readers an at-a-glance overview and make the text easier to follow and remember. Readers increasingly expect you to divide what you write into sections and to label those sections with headings. A system of consistent headings should map the overall organization.

Use different levels of headings to show the hierarchy of your ideas. Determine the level of importance of each heading by making an outline to see what subpoint fits under what main point. Then make the headings conform to the different levels by choosing a font size and an effect such as boldfacing for each level. The type, the size, and the effect should signal the level of importance.

Helping readers navigate your text

Do the little things that help readers. Remember to include page numbers, which word-processing software can create for you automatically. Make cross-references to other parts of your document when a subject is covered elsewhere. If you are citing sources, make sure they are all in your list of works cited.

A traditional way to add information to a text without interrupting the main text is to add footnotes to the bottoms of pages or to include endnotes at the end of a paper. Today writers often use boxes or sidebars to supply extra information. If you use boxes or sidebars, indicate them with a different design or a different color. The key is to make what *is* different *look* different.

Know When to Use Images and Graphics

Personal computers, digital cameras, scanners, printers, and the Web have made it easy to include images and graphics in writing. But these technologies don't tell you if, when, or how images and graphics should be used.

Thinking about what an image or graphic communicates

- **What are your readers' expectations for the medium you are using?** Most essays don't include images; however, most Web sites and brochures do.
- **What is the purpose for an image or graphic?** Does it illustrate a concept? Does it highlight an important point? Does it show something that is hard to explain with words alone? If you don't know the purpose, you may not need the image.
- **Where should an image or graphic be placed in your text?** Images should be as close as possible to the relevant point in your text.
- **What will readers focus on when they see the image?** Will they focus on the part that matters? If not, you may need to crop the image.
- **What explanation do readers need in order to understand the image?** Provide informative captions for the images and graphics you use, and refer to them in your text.

Formatting images for the medium you are using

Images that you want to print need to be of higher quality than those intended for the Web or the screen. Pay attention to the settings on your camera or scanner.

- **Digital cameras** frequently make images with 72 dpi (dots per inch), which is the maximum you can display on the screen. Most printers use a resolution from 300 to 600 dpi. Use the high-quality setting on your camera for images you intend to print.

- **Scanners** typically offer a range of resolution from 72 to 1600 dpi. The higher the number, the finer the image, but the larger the file size. Images on the Web or a screen display at 72 dpi, so higher resolutions do not improve the quality but do make the image slow to load.

Compose and Edit Images

Photographs often provide evidence in arguments, especially involving local issues. For example, if you are proposing that your city should devote more money to park maintenance, photographs showing neglect help to document your case. Inexpensive digital cameras now can take high-quality photographs. Keeping a few principles in mind can give your photos more impact.

Taking better photographs

- **Nonessential elements:** Most people include too much in their photographs. Decide what is essential and concentrate on getting those elements in the frame.

- **Framing:** If you are taking a portrait, usually the closer you can get to your subject, the better. If your camera has a zoom lens, use it.

The boredom of waiting is expressed in the boys' faces.

Editing photographs

If you own a digital camera, you likely have an image-editing program that came with your camera. Image editors are now standard software on most new computers.

Decide what you want in a frame. If your goal is to show the habitat of sea lions, you'll need a wide shot. But if you want a portrait of a sea lion, get in tight.

■ **Cropping:** Most images can be trimmed to improve visual focus and file size. To crop an image, select the rectangle tool, draw the rectangle over the area you want to keep, and select the Crop or Trim command. The part of the image outside the rectangle will be discarded.

Cropping improves your photos by eliminating unnecessary elements and by allowing them to load faster on a computer.

- **Rotating:** Often you'll find that you held your camera at a slight angle when taking pictures, especially if your subjects were moving. You can make small adjustments by using the Rotate Image command. You can also rotate images 90 degrees to give them a vertical orientation.

- **Resizing:** Photo-editing programs will tell you the height and width of an image. You can resize images to fit in a particular area of a Web page or printed page. You can also change the resolution in the dpi window.

- **Adjusting color:** You can adjust color using controls for brightness, contrast, and saturation that are similar to those on your color TV. Be aware that colors look different on different monitors, and what you print may not look like the colors on your screen.

Create Tables, Charts, and Graphs

Tables are useful for presenting evidence in arguments if you have an array of statistical data that you want readers to take in at a glance. Charts and graphs are useful for visually representing statistical trends and for making comparisons.

Tables

Population Change for the Ten Largest U.S. Cities, 1990 to 2000

City and State	April 1, 2000	April 1, 1990	Number	Percentage
New York, NY	8,008,278	7,322,564	685,714	9.4
Los Angeles, CA	3,694,820	3,485,398	209,422	6.0
Chicago, IL	2,896,016	2,783,726	112,290	4.0
Houston, TX	1,953,631	1,630,553	323,078	19.8
Philadelphia, PA	1,517,550	1,585,577	−68,027	−4.3
Phoenix, AZ	1,321,045	983,403	337,642	34.3
San Diego, CA	1,223,400	1,110,549	112,851	10.2
Dallas, TX	1,188,580	1,006,877	181,703	18.0
San Antonio, TX	1,144,646	935,933	208,713	22.3
Detroit, MI	951,270	1,027,974	−76,704	−7.5

Source: U.S. Census Bureau, *Census 2000*; 1990 Census, Population and Housing Unit Counts, United States (1990 CPH-2-1).

A table is used to display numerical data and similar types of information. It usually includes several items as well as variables for each item.

Bar graphs

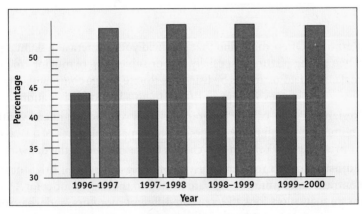

A bar graph compares the values of two or more items.

Line graphs

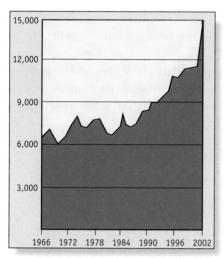

A line graph shows change over time.

Pie charts

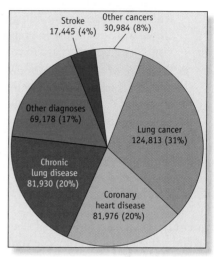

A pie chart shows the parts making up a whole.

Design Pages for Print

Word-processing programs design pages for you through default settings for margins, paragraph indentions, bullets, justification, and so on. Even if you use the default settings, you still have a range of options for designing a page that is appropriate to your assignment. Thinking about design will lead to a more effective presentation of your argument.

- **Choose the orientation, size of your page, and number of columns.** You can usually use the defaults on your word-processing program for academic essays (remember to select double-spacing for line spacing if the default is single-spaced). For other kinds of texts you may want a horizontal rather than a vertical orientation, a size other than a standard sheet of paper, and two or more columns rather than one.

- **Divide your text into units.** The paragraph is the basic unit of extended writing, but also think about when to use lists. This list is a bulleted list. You can also use a numbered list.

- **Use left-aligned text with a ragged-right margin.** Fully justified text aligns the right margin, which gives a more formal look but can also leave unsightly rivers of extra white space running through the middle of your text. Ragged-right text is easier to read.

- **Be conscious of white space.** White space can make your text more readable and set off more important elements. Headings stand out more with white space surrounding them. Leave room around graphics. Don't crowd words too close to graphics because both the words and the visuals will become hard to read.
- **Be aware of MLA and APA design specifications.** MLA and APA styles have specifications for margins, indentions, reference lists, and other aspects of paper formatting. See the sample paper on pages 297–303 for guidelines on designing a paper using MLA style.

Design Pages for the Web

If your argument calls for or might benefit from a Web site, a handsome, easy-to-read site is most likely to convince your readers that your argument is valid.

Creating a visual theme

A Web site does not need a loud background, an attention-grabbing image, or flashy animation to achieve a visual theme. Instead, a consistent look that supports the content and a simple set of colors for the text, headings, links, and background often work much better to create a unified visual theme. Similar graphics and images should be the same size, and often their placement can be repeated from page to page.

Keeping visuals simple

An uncomplicated site with simple elements is usually more friendly to readers because it loads faster, and if it is well designed, it can be elegant. Too many icons, bullets, horizontal rules, and other embellishments clutter the page. A simple, consistent design is always effective for pages that contain text.

Making text readable

Long stretches of text on the Web tend not to get read. You can make your text more readable on the Web if you do the following:

- **Divide your information into chunks.** If your information runs longer than a page, consider placing it on two Web pages.

- **Use shorter paragraphs when possible.** Long paragraphs are harder to read on screen than in print.
- **Use a sans serif typeface.** Consider using Arial, Helvetica, or Verdana, which are easier to read on screen. You can specify typefaces using the Font command on your Web-editing software.
- **Use white space to separate elements and to provide visual relief.**
- **Avoid dark backgrounds.** Dark backgrounds make your text hard to read.

Making navigation easy

People typically scan a Web site quickly and move around a lot. They are likely to click on links as they follow their interests. If you put content on more than one page, provide a navigation bar so readers can navigate easily. A navigation bar can be a simple text bar or icons that are easy to create with image-editing software.

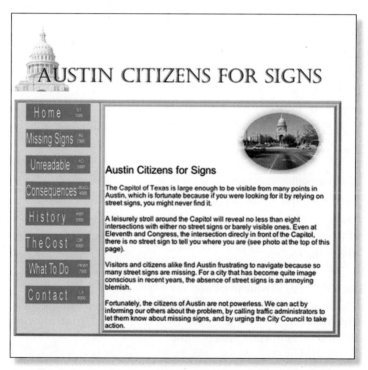

Kat Schwegel created the multi-page *Austin Citizens for Signs* for a proposal-argument assignment to address the problem of missing street signs. Her use of signs as navigation icons supports the visual theme of her site.

15

Presenting Arguments

Becoming effective in oral communication is just as important as in written communication. You likely will give many oral presentations in later life and perhaps in your college career. In the workplace and in public life, arguments are often both written and presented, and one is developed from the other using the same visuals.

Plan in Advance

A successful presentation, like successful writing, requires careful planning. Look closely at what you are being asked to present and how much time you will have to deliver your presentation. Decide early what kind of presentation you will give and what visuals you will incorporate.

Selecting your topic

Choosing and researching a topic for a presentation is similar to choosing and researching a written argument. Ask these questions:

- Will you enjoy speaking about this topic?
- Does the topic fit the assignment?
- Do you know enough to speak about this topic?
- If you do not know enough, are you willing to do research to learn more about the topic?

Remember that if your presentation requires you to do any research, then you will need to develop a written bibliography as you would for a research assignment. You will need to document the sources of your information and provide those sources in your presentation.

Thinking about your audience

Unlike writing, when you give a speech, you have your audience directly before you. They will give you concrete feedback during your presentation by smiling or frowning, by paying attention or losing interest, by asking questions or sitting passively. Ask these questions:

- Will your audience likely be interested in your topic?
- Are there ways you can get them more interested?
- What is your audience likely to know or believe about your topic?
- What does your audience probably not know about your topic?
- What key terms will you have to define or explain?
- Where is your audience most likely to disagree with you?
- What questions are they likely to ask?

Organizing your presentation

The steps for writing various kinds of arguments, listed at the ends of Chapters 8–13, can be used to organize an oral presentation. Decide first the best way to order your main points. Then begin building your presentation.

Support your argument

Look at your research notes and think about how best to incorporate the information you found. Consider using one or more of these strategies.

- **Facts:** Speakers who know their facts build credibility.
- **Statistics:** Good use of statistics gives the impression that the speaker has done his or her homework. Statistics also can indicate that a particular example is representative. One tragic car accident doesn't mean a road is dangerous, but an especially high accident rate relative to other nearby roads does make the case.
- **Statements by authorities:** Quotations from credible experts are another common way of supporting key points.
- **Narratives:** Narratives are small stories that can illustrate key points. Narratives are a good way of keeping the attention of the audience. Keep them short so they don't distract from your major points.
- **Humor:** In most situations audiences appreciate humor. Humor is a good way to convince an audience that you have common beliefs and experiences, and that your argument may be one they can agree with.

Plan your introduction

No part of your presentation is more critical than the introduction. You have to get the audience's attention, introduce your topic, convince the audience that the topic is important to them, present your thesis, and give your audience either an overview of your presentation or a sense of your direction. Accomplishing all this in a short time is a tall order, but if you lose your audience in the first two minutes, you won't recover their attention. You might begin with a compelling example or anecdote that both introduces your topic and indicates your stance.

Plan your conclusion

The next most important part of your speech is your conclusion. You want to end on a strong note. First, you need to signal that you are entering the conclusion. You can announce that you are concluding, but you also can give signals in other ways. Touching on your main points again will help your audience to remember them. Simply summarizing is a dull way to close, however. Think of an example or an idea that your audience can take away with them. If your argument is a proposal, end with a call for action.

Design Effective Visuals

Visual elements can both support and reinforce your major points. They give you another means of reaching your audience and keeping them stimulated. Visuals should communicate content and not just be eye candy. Some of the easier visuals to create are outlines, statistical charts, flow charts, photographs, and maps. Presentation software, such as Microsoft PowerPoint, allows you to import charts and other graphics that you have created in other programs, and it gives you several options for presentation, including printed handouts and Web pages.

At a minimum, consider putting an outline of your talk on a transparency or on a PowerPoint slide. An outline allows an audience to keep track of where you are in your talk and when you are moving to your next point.

Creating visuals

Follow these guidelines to create better visuals.

■ **Keep the text short.** You don't want your audience straining to read long passages on the screen and neglecting what you have to say. Except for quotations, use short words and phrases on transparencies and slides.

- **Use dark text on a white or light-colored background.** Light text on a dark background is hard to read.
- **Use graphics that reproduce well.** Some graphics do not show up well on the screen, often because there isn't enough contrast.
- **Avoid getting carried away with special effects.** Presentations with many special effects such as fade-ins, fade-outs, and sound effects often come off as heavy on style and light on substance. They also can be time-consuming to produce.
- **Plan your timing when using visuals.** Usually you can leave a slide on the screen for one to two minutes, which allows your audience time to read the slide and connect its points to what you are saying.
- **Always proofread.** Typos and misspelled words make you look careless and can distract the audience from your point.

Making an argument with slides

The organization of a presentation with visuals should be evident in the titles of the slides. Each title should give the main point of the slide and advance the story line of the presentation. If a slide has a box at the bottom with text, called a "take-away" box, it should either draw an implication from the body of the slide that isn't obvious or make the transition to the next slide.

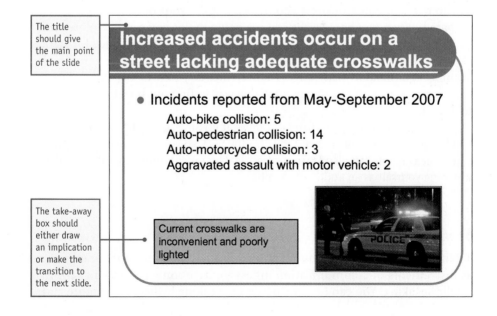

Generic titles like "Overview," "Problem," and "Solution" force readers to find the main point of the slide. Specific titles convey the story of the presentation. If you use a generic title, be sure to include a specific subtitle.

Overview: The success of First Thursday has created a major safety problem on South Congress Avenue
Problem: Increased accidents occur on a street lacking adequate crosswalks
Solution: Create temporary crosswalks with flashers

Focus on Your Delivery

The best speakers draw their inspiration from their audience, and they maintain contact with their audience by communicating with body language and presentation style in addition to content. Audience members leave feeling like they've had a conversation with the speaker even if they have been silent through the presentation.

The importance of practice

There is no substitute for rehearsing your speech several times in advance. You will become more confident and have more control over the content. The best way to overcome nervousness about speaking in front of others is to be well prepared. When you know what you are going to say, you can pay more attention to your audience, make eye contact, and watch body language for signals about how well you are making your points. When you rehearse you can also become comfortable with any visual elements you will be using. Finally, rehearsing your speech is the only reliable way to find out how long it will take to deliver.

Practice your speech in front of others. If possible, go to the room where you will be speaking and ask a friend to sit in the back so you can learn how well you can be heard. You can also learn a great deal by videotaping your rehearsal and watching yourself as an audience member.

Speaking effectively

Talking is so much a part of our daily lives that we rarely think about our voices as instruments of communication unless we have some training in acting or public speaking. You can become better at speaking by becoming more aware of your delivery. Pay attention to your breathing as you practice your speech. When you breathe at your normal rate, you will not rush your speech. Plan where you will pause during your speech. Pauses allow you to take a sip of water and give your audience a chance to sum up mentally what you have said. And don't be afraid to repeat key points. Repetition is one of the easiest strategies for achieving emphasis.

Most of the time nervousness is invisible. You can feel nervous and still impress your audience by appearing calm and confident. If you make mistakes while speaking, know that the audience understands and will be forgiving. Stage fright is normal; sometimes it can be helpful in raising the energy level of a presentation.

Nonverbal communication

While you are speaking, you are also communicating with your presence. Stand up unless you are required to sit. Move around instead of standing behind the podium. Use gestures to emphasize main points, and only main points; if you gesture continually, you may appear nervous.

Maintaining eye contact is crucial. Begin your speech by looking at the people directly in front of you and then move your eyes around the room, looking to both sides. Attempting to look at each person during a speech may seem unnatural, but it is the best way to convince all the members of your audience that you are speaking directly to them.

Handling questions

Your presentation doesn't end when you finish your planned talk. Speakers are usually expected to answer questions afterward. How you handle questions is also critical to your success. Speakers who are evasive or fail to acknowledge questions sometimes lose all the credibility they have built in their speech. But speakers who listen carefully to questions and answer them honestly build their credibility further. Have some strategies in mind for handling questions:

- **Repeat the question so that the entire audience can hear it and to confirm you understood it.**
- **Take a minute to reflect on the question.** If you do not understand the question, ask the questioner to restate it.
- **Avoid getting into a debate with audience members who make a small speech instead of asking a question.** Acknowledge their point of view and move on.

- **If you cannot answer a question, don't bluff and don't apologize.** You can offer to research the question or you can ask the audience if they know the answer.

- **If you are asked a question during your speech, answer it if it is a short, factual question or one of clarification.** Postpone questions that require long answers until the end to avoid losing the momentum of your speech.

PART 5

Researching Arguments

PART 5   Researching Arguments

16. Planning Research 247

Analyze the research task 247

Find a subject 247

Ask a research question 249

Gather information about the subject 249

Draft a working thesis 252

17. Finding Sources 254

Search with keywords 255

Find books 256

Find journal articles 256

Find Web sources 259

18. Evaluating and Recording Sources 263

Evaluate print sources 263

Find information to cite print sources 264

Evaluate database sources 266

Find information to cite a database source 266

Evaluate Web sources 267

Find information to cite a Web source 269

19. Writing the Research Paper 270

Review your goals and thesis 270

Determine your contribution 270

Determine your main points 271

Avoid plagiarism 271

Quote sources without plagiarizing 273

Summarize and paraphrase sources without plagiarizing 274

Incorporate quotations 276

Incorporate visuals 278

20. Documenting Sources in MLA Style 280

Elements of MLA documentation 280

MLA in-text citations 284

MLA works-cited list: Books 287

MLA works-cited list: Periodicals 291

MLA works-cited list: Library database sources 293

MLA works-cited list: Online sources 293

MLA works-cited list: Other sources 295

Brian Witkowski (student), Need a Cure for Tribe Fever? How about a Dip in the Lake? 297

21. Documenting Sources in APA Style 304

Elements of APA documentation 304

APA in-text citations 307

APA references list: Books 309

APA references list: Periodicals 310

APA references list: Library database sources 311

APA references list: Online sources 311

APA references list: Other sources 312

16

Planning Research

You do research every day. If you compare prices online before you buy an airline ticket, look up a detailed course description before registering for a class, or want to settle an argument about the first African American to win an Olympic gold medal, you need to do research. In college, research means both investigating existing knowledge that is stored on computers and in libraries, and creating new knowledge through original analysis, surveys, experiments, and theorizing. When you start a research task in a college course, you need to understand the different kinds of possible research and to plan your strategy in advance.

Analyze the Research Task

If you have an assignment that requires research, look closely at what you are being asked to do. The assignment may ask you to define, evaluate, analyze causes, rebut another's argument, or propose a course of action. You may be writing for experts, for students like yourself, or for the general public. The purpose of your research and your potential audience will help guide your strategies for research.

The key is understanding what is expected of you. You are being asked to do the following.

1. Find a subject.
2. Ask a question about the subject.
3. Find out what has been said about this subject.
4. Make a contribution to the discussion about this subject.

Find a Subject

Asking Questions

To find a subject that interests you, begin by asking meaningful questions about something that matters to you. Your courses may give you some ideas about questions to ask, such as are manufacturing jobs in the United States being lost primarily to outsourcing to other countries or to more efficient production?

STRATEGIES FOR RESEARCH

Find a subject that interests you. Research is more enjoyable if you are finding out new things rather than just confirming what you already know. The most exciting part of doing research is making small discoveries.

Make sure that you can do a thorough job of research. If you select a subject that is too broad, such as proposing how to end poverty, you will not be able to do an adequate job.

Develop a strategy for your research early on. If you are researching a campus issue such as a parking problem, then you probably will rely most on interviews, observations, and possibly a survey. But if you find out that one of the earliest baseball stadiums, Lakefront Park in Chicago (built in 1883), had the equivalent of today's luxury boxes and you want to make an argument that the trend toward building stadiums with luxury boxes is not a new development, then you will have to do library research.

Give yourself enough time to do a thorough job. As you conduct your research, expect to focus better on your subject, to find a few dead ends, and to spend more time on the project than you initially thought. Remember the first principle of doing research: things take longer than you think they will.

Personal experience is also often a good source of questions related to your research subject: What was the cause of something that happened to you? Was your experience typical or atypical? How can you solve a problem you have? What do experts think about the issues that concern you? Working with a subject that has already aroused your curiosity makes it more likely that your findings will interest others.

Browsing a subject directory

Another good way to begin exploring a research subject is by browsing, either in your library or on the Web. Browsing may lead you to subjects you hadn't yet considered; it may also show you a wide range of issues surrounding a potential subject. Subject directories can show you many different aspects of a single subject.

Browsing a general or specialized encyclopedia

Other ways to generate interesting subjects include consulting a general encyclopedia such as *Columbia Encyclopedia* (www.bartleby.com), Britannica Online (available on your library's Web site), or Wikipedia (en.wikipedia.org), or a specialized encyclopedia such as the *Encyclopedia of Crime and Justice*. The reference section of your library's Web site lists specialized encyclopedias and other specialized reference sources by subject.

Ask a Research Question

Often you'll be surprised by the amount of information your initial browsing uncovers. Your next task will be to identify a question for your research project within that mass of information. This **researchable question** will be the focus of the remainder of your research and ultimately of your research project or paper. Browsing on the subject of organic foods, for example, might lead you to one of the following researchable questions.

- How do farmers benefit from growing organic produce?
- Why are organic products more expensive than non-organic products?
- Are Americans being persuaded to buy more organic products?

Once you have formulated a research question, you should begin thinking about what kind of research you will need to do to address the question.

Gather Information About the Subject

Most researchers rely partly or exclusively on the work of others as sources of information. Research based on the work of others is called **secondary research**. In the past this information was contained almost exclusively in collections of print materials housed in libraries, but today enormous amounts of information are available through library databases and on the Web (see Chapter 17).

Much of the research done at a university creates new information through **primary research**—experiments, examination of historical documents—and **field research**, including data-gathering surveys, interviews, and detailed observations, described below.

Conducting field research

Sometimes you may be researching a question that requires you to gather first-hand information with field research. For example, if you are researching a campus issue such as the impact of a new library fee on students' budgets, you may need to conduct interviews, make observations, and give a survey.

Interviews

College campuses are a rich source of experts in many areas, including people on the faculty and in the surrounding community. Interviewing experts on your research subject can help build your knowledge base. You can use interviews to discover what the people most affected by a particular issue are thinking, such as why students object to some fees and not others.

Arrange interviews

Before you contact anyone, think carefully about your goals. Knowing what you want to find out through your interviews will help you determine whom you need to interview and what questions you need to ask. Use these guidelines to prepare for an interview.

- Decide what you want or need to know and who best can provide that for you.
- Schedule each interview in advance, and let the person know why you are conducting the interview. Estimate how long your interview will take, and tell your subject how much of her or his time you will need.
- Choose a location that is convenient for your subject but not too chaotic or loud. An office or study room is better than a noisy cafeteria.
- Plan your questions in advance. Write down a few questions and have a few more in mind.
- If you want to record the interview, ask for permission in advance. A recording device sometimes can intimidate the person you are interviewing.

Conduct interviews

- Come prepared with your questions, a notebook, and a pen or pencil.
- If you plan to record the interview (with your subject's permission), make sure whatever recording device you use has an adequate power supply and will not run out of tape, disk space, or memory.
- Listen carefully so you can follow up on key points. Make notes when important questions are raised or answered, but don't attempt to transcribe every word the person is saying.

■ When you are finished, thank your subject, and ask his or her permission to get in touch again if you have additional questions.

Surveys

Extensive surveys that can be projected to large populations, like the ones used in political polls, require the effort of many people. Small surveys, however, often can provide insight on local issues, such as what percentage of students might be affected if library hours were reduced.

Plan surveys

What information do you need for your research question? Decide what exactly you want to know and design a survey that will provide that information. Likely you will want both close-ended questions (multiple choice, yes or no, rating scale) and open-ended questions that allow detailed responses. To create a survey, follow these guidelines.

■ Write a few specific, unambiguous questions. People will fill out your survey quickly, and if the questions are confusing, the results will be meaningless.

■ Include one or two open-ended questions, such as "What do you like about X?" or "What don't you like about X?" Open-ended questions can be difficult to interpret, but sometimes they turn up information you had not anticipated.

■ Test the questions on a few people before you conduct the survey.

■ Think about how you will interpret your survey. Multiple-choice formats make data easy to tabulate, but often they miss key information. Open-ended questions will require you to figure out a way to sort responses into categories.

Administer surveys

■ Decide on who you need to survey and how many respondents your survey will require. For example, if you want to claim that the results of your survey represent the views of residents of your dormitory, your method of selecting respondents should give all residents an equal chance to be selected. Don't select only your friends.

■ Decide how you will contact participants in your survey. If you are conducting your survey on private property, you will need permission from the property owner. Likewise, email lists and lists of mailing addresses are usually guarded closely to preserve privacy. You will need to secure permission from the appropriate parties if you want to contact people via an email list.

- If you mail or email your survey, include a statement about what the survey is for.

Observations

Observing can be a valuable source of data. For example, if you are researching why a particular office on your campus does not operate efficiently, observe what happens when students enter and how the staff responds to their presence.

Make observations

- Choose a place where you can observe with the least intrusion. The less people wonder about what you are doing, the better.
- Carry a notebook and write extensive field notes. Record as much information as you can, and worry about analyzing it later.
- Record the date, exactly where you were, exactly when you arrived and left, and important details like the number of people present.
- Write on one side of your notebook so you can use the facing page to note key observations and analyze your data later.

Analyze observations

You must interpret your observations so they make sense in the context of your argument. Ask yourself the following questions:

- What patterns of behavior did you observe?
- How was the situation you observed unique? How might it be similar to other locations?
- What constituted "normal" activity during the time when you were observing? Did anything out of the ordinary happen?
- Why were the people there? What can you determine about the purposes of the activities you observed?

Draft a Working Thesis

Once you have done some preliminary research into your question, you can begin to craft a working thesis. Perhaps you have found a lot of interesting material about the increasing popularity of organic products, including meat, dairy products, and produce. You have discovered that due to this trend, large corporations such as Wal-Mart are beginning to offer organic products in their stores. However, the enormous demand for organic products that this creates is endangering smaller organic farmers and producers. As you research the question of why small farmers and producers in the United States are endangered and what small farmers and producers in other countries have done to protect themselves, a working thesis begins to emerge.

Write your subject, research question, and working thesis on a note card or sheet of paper. Keep your working thesis handy. You may need to revise it several times until the wording is precise. As you research, ask yourself, does this information tend to support my thesis? Information that does not support your thesis is still important! It may lead you to adjust your thesis or even to abandon it altogether. You may need to find another source or reason that shows your thesis is still valid.

> SUBJECT: Increased demand for organic products endangering smaller farmers and producers
>
> RESEARCH QUESTION: How can smaller organic farms and producers protect themselves from becoming extinct?
>
> WORKING THESIS: In order to meet the increasing demand for organic products that has been created by larger corporations such as Wal-Mart, smaller organic farmers and producers should form regional co-ops. These co-ops will work together to supply regional chains, much as co-ops of small farmers and dairies in Europe work together, thereby cutting transportation and labor costs and ensuring their survival in a much-expanded market.

17

Finding Sources

Newspapers

The distinction between doing research online and in the library is blurring as more and more libraries put their collections online. Many colleges and universities have made most of the major resources in their reference rooms available online. Still, your library is usually the best place to begin any research project because it contains some materials that are not available anywhere else. Moreover, professional librarians will help you locate sources quickly so you get the most out of your research time.

You will have a hard time finding the information you need if you don't know what you're looking for. To guide you in your library research, think about these questions.

Who are the parties involved in the issue?	Who are the experts? Who else is talking about it? Who is affected by the issue?
What is at stake?	How or why does this issue matter? What stands to be gained or lost? Who is likely to benefit or suffer?
What kinds of arguments are being made about the issue?	Are people making proposals? Are they trying to define terms? What kinds of reasons do they offer? What kinds of evidence do they present? What arguments are people *not* making that they could be making?
Who are the audiences for this debate?	Do people already have strong opinions? Are they still trying to make up their minds? How well informed are people about the issue?
What is your role?	What do you think? What else do you need to know? What do you think should be done?

Your answers to these questions will provide you with keywords and phrases to use as you begin your search for information.

Search with Keywords

For most research projects, you will begin with a subject search using one or more **keywords** or search terms that describe the subject.

Finding keywords

Entries for subjects in your library's online catalog and in databases will help you find keywords. If you find a book or article that is about your exact topic, use the subject terms to locate additional items. The sample below, for a book from an online catalog, shows the keywords under *subjects*. Try entering the subject terms individually and in combination in new subject searches to find more items similar to this one.

AUTHOR:

Solove, Daniel J., 1972-

TITLE:

The digital person: technology and privacy in the information age / Daniel J. Solove.

PUBLISHED:

New York: New York University Press, c2004.

SUBJECTS:

Data protection–Law and legislation–United States.

Electronic records–Access control–United States.

Public records–Law and legislation–United States.

Government information–United States.

Privacy, Right of–United States.

Single and multiple keyword searches

The simplest keyword searches return the most results, but often they are not the results you need. For example, imagine typing the word *capitalism* into the keyword search window on your library's online catalog and getting several thousand results, including subjects such as radicals and capitalism, global capitalism, American capitalism, new capitalism, women and capitalism, socialism and capitalism, slavery and capitalism, ethics and capitalism, and so on.

If you want to focus on how capitalism affects the natural world, however, then you can narrow your search using two or more keywords. For example, if you use the terms *capitalism* and *ecology* in the search window, you would likely receive a more manageable 25 or so results. You could then read through the titles and perhaps the brief abstracts provided and decide that a book such as *Wild Capitalism: Environmental Activists and Post-Socialist Political Ecology in Hungary* may not be as useful to you as a book titled *Ecology Against Capitalism*.

You can further limit your search by specifying what you don't want by using NOT. For example, if you are interested in air pollution control policies, but not those used in California, you would type *air pollution control policies* NOT *California*.

Find Books

Nearly all college libraries shelve books according to the Library of Congress Classification System, which uses a combination of letters and numbers to indicate the book's unique location in the library. The Library of Congress call number begins with a letter or letters that represent the broad subject area into which the book is classified.

The Library of Congress system groups books by subject, and you can often find other items relevant to your search shelved close to the particular one you are looking for. You can search the extensive Library of Congress online catalog (catalog. loc. gov) to find out how your subject might be indexed, or you can go straight to your own library's catalog and conduct a subject search. The call number will enable you to find the item in the stacks. You will need to consult the locations guide for your library to find the book on the shelves.

When you find a book in your library catalog, take time to notice the subject headings under which it is indexed. For example, if you locate Jeff Hawkins's *On Intelligence*, you will probably find it cross-listed under several subject categories, including the following.

Brain

Intellect

Artificial intelligence

Neural networks (Computer science)

Browsing within these categories, or using some of their keywords in a new search, may lead you to more useful sources.

Find Journal Articles

Searching for articles in scholarly journals and magazines works much the same way as searching for books. The starting point is your library's Web site. You should find a link to databases, which are listed by subject and by the name of the database.

Using databases

Databases are fully searchable by author, title, subject, or keywords. Many databases contain the full text of articles, allowing you to copy the contents onto your computer or email the article to yourself. To use databases effectively, make a list of keywords (see pages 255–256). For example, if you are researching the effects of hunting on deer populations, you could begin with the words *deer*, *hunting*, and *population*. If you are researching obesity in children, you might begin with *obesity*, *children*, and one more word such as *trend* or *United States* or *fast food*, depending on your focus.

Your next decision is to choose a database to begin your research. Newspapers might include stories on local deer populations and changes in hunting policy. Popular journals such as *Field and Stream* might have articles about national trends in deer hunting, and they might also summarize scholarly research about the subject. Scholarly journals, perhaps in the field of wildlife biology, would contain articles about formal research into the effects of deer hunting on population density, average size and weight of animals, range, and other factors.

To find newspaper stories, begin with LexisNexis Academic. To find popular and scholarly journal articles, go to Academic OneFile, Academic Search Premier or Academic Search Complete, InfoTrac OneFile, or MasterFILE Premier. If you have difficulty finding the right database, ask a librarian to help you.

Scholarly versus popular journals

Knowing what kinds of articles you want to look for—scholarly or popular—will help you select the right database. Many databases include more than one type of journal. Although the difference among journals is not always obvious, you should be able to judge whether a journal is scholarly or popular by its characteristics. Some instructors frown on using popular journals as sources in a research paper, but these journals can be valuable for researching current opinion on a particular topic. They cannot, however, be substituted for serious research articles written by accredited scholars.

Scholarly journals

Scholarly journals are excellent sources for research. They

- contain long articles typically written by scholars in the field, usually affiliated with a university or research center.
- usually include articles that report original research and have footnotes or a list of works cited at the end.
- are reviewed by other scholars in the field.
- assume that readers are also experts in the field.
- display few advertisements or illustrations.
- usually are published quarterly or biannually.

COMMON DATABASES

Academic OneFile	Indexes periodicals from the arts, humanities, sciences, social sciences, and general news, with full-text articles and images. (Formerly Expanded Academic ASAP.)
Academic Search Premier **or** **Academic Search Complete**	Provides full-text articles for thousands of scholarly publications, including social sciences, humanities, education, computer sciences, engineering, language and linguistics, literature, medical sciences, and ethnic-studies journals.
ArticleFirst	Indexes journals in business, the humanities, medicine, science, and social sciences.
EBSCOhost Research Databases	Gateway to a large collection of EBSCO databases, including Academic Search Premier, Academic Search Complete, and MasterFILE Premier.
Factiva	Provides full-text articles on business topics, including articles from *The Wall Street Journal*.
FirstSearch	Offers millions of full-text articles from many databases.
Google Scholar	Searches scholarly literature according to criteria of relevance.
InfoTrac OneFile	Contains millions of full-text articles about a wide range of academic and general-interest topics.
JSTOR	Provides scanned copies of scholarly journals.
LexisNexis Academic	Provides full text of a wide range of newspapers, magazines, government and legal documents, and company profiles from around the world.
MasterFILE Premier	Provides indexes and abstracts for business, consumer health, general science, and multicultural periodicals with many full-text articles.

Examples of scholarly journals include *American Journal of Mathematics, College English, JAMA: Journal of the American Medical Association, PMLA: Publication of the Modern Language Association,* and *Psychological Reports.*

Popular journals

Popular journals are found primarily on newsstands. They

- publish short articles aimed at the general public.
- contain many advertisements and photos.
- seldom include footnotes or the source of information.
- are published weekly or monthly.

Examples of popular journals include *Cosmopolitan*, *GQ*, *Rolling Stone*, *Sports Illustrated*, and *Time*.

Find Web Sources

You likely use the Web regularly to find information about products, restaurants, stores, services, jobs, people, maps, hobbies, music, films, and other entertainment. But researching an academic paper on the Web is different from such everyday tasks. The Web can be a powerful tool for research, but it also has many traps for the unwary.

Because anyone can publish on the Web, there is no overall quality control and there are no systems of organization as there are in a library. Nevertheless, the Web offers you some resources for current topics that would be difficult to find in a library. The keys to success are knowing where you are most likely to find current and accurate information about the particular question you are researching, and knowing how to access that information.

Using search engines

Search engines designed for the Web work in ways similar to library databases and your library's online catalog, but with one major difference. Databases typically do some screening of the items they list, but search engines potentially take you to every Web site that isn't password protected—millions of pages in all. Consequently, you have to work harder to limit searches on the Web or you can be deluged with tens of thousands of items.

Kinds of search engines

A search engine is a set of programs that sort through millions of items at incredible speed. There are four basic kinds of search engines.

- **Keyword search engines,** such as Ask.com, Answers.com, and Google, give unique results because they assign different weights to the information they find.
- **Web directories,** such as Yahoo! Directory, classify Web sites into categories and are the closest equivalent to the cataloging system used by libraries.

- **Metasearch agents,** such as Dogpile, Metacrawler, and WebCrawler, allow you to use several search engines simultaneously. While the concept is sound, metasearch agents are limited by the number of hits they can return and their inability to handle advanced searches.
- **Specialized search engines,** such as Froogle (shopping), Google Scholar (academic), Monster.com (jobs), Pubmed (medicine), Thomasnet (business), and WebMD (medicine), search specific subjects.

Advanced searches

Search engines often produce too many hits and are therefore not always useful. If you look only at the first few items, you may miss what is most valuable. The alternative is to refine your search. Most search engines offer you the option of an advanced search, which gives you the opportunity to limit numbers.

The advanced searches on Google and Yahoo! give you the options of using a string of words to search for sites that contain all the words, the exact phrase, or any of the words, or that exclude certain words. They also allow you to specify the language of the site, the date range, the file format, and the domain. For example, government statistics on crime are considered the most reliable, so if you want to find statistics on murder rates, you can specify the domain as *.gov* in an advanced search.

An advanced search on Google for government (.gov) sites only.

Finding discussion forums, groups, blogs, wikis, podcasts, and online video

Discussion forums and **discussion groups** are Internet sites for people to discuss thousands of specific topics. The Groups section of Google (groups.google.com) has an archive of several hundred million messages that can be searched. Much of the conversation on these sites is undocumented and highly opinionated, but you can still gather important information about people's attitudes and get tips about other sources, which you can verify later.

Web logs, better known as **blogs,** also are sources of public opinion. Several tools have been developed recently to search blogs: Blogdigger, Bloglines, Feedster, Google Blog Search, PubSub, Technorati, and IceRocket. Blogs are not screened and are not considered authoritative sources, but blogs can sometimes lead you to quality sources.

Wikis are web applications designed to let multiple authors write, edit, and review content. The best-known wiki is Wikipedia (en.wikipedia.org), a controversial online encyclopedia where any visitor can change an entry. Wikipedia can provide a useful introduction to many popular-culture topics, but do not rely on Wikipedia to be accurate. Many individual professors and teachers, as well as some colleges and universities, forbid the use of Wikipedia as a source in academic papers. If you include a Wikipedia entry in your works-cited list, prepare to be laughed at.

Podcasts are digital media files available on the Internet for playback on portable media players (such as the iPod). Many of these files are news, opinion, and entertainment broadcasts from major media outlets such as NPR (www.npr .org/rss/podcast/podcast_directory.php). Individuals can also create and distribute files for podcasts. Information from these podcasts should be treated with the same critical eye (and ear!) you use for blogs and personal Web pages.

Similarly, sites that offer **streaming video** such as YouTube (www.youtube .com) and Google Video (www.videogoogle.com) can be used to access videos from reputable sources, such as interviews and newscasts as well as eyewitness footage of events or situations around the world. Most videos on these sites, however, were created by a wide population of individuals—ranging from artists and video professionals to teenagers—strictly for entertainment purposes. Again, these video sites are not scholarly, but they can serve as examples or anecdotes if you are dealing with public opinion or popular-culture topics. Keep in mind also that videos originating from major media outlets appearing on these video sites are possibly there illegally.

Finding visual sources

You can find images published on the Web using Google and other search engines that allow you to specify searches for images. For example, if you are writing a research paper about invasive plant species, you might want to include an image of kudzu, an invasive vine common in the American South. In Google, choose Images and type *kudzu* in the search box. You'll find a selection of images of the plant, including several from the National Park Service.

Some search engines, such as Ditto (www.ditto.com), are designed specifically to find images. Yahoo! Picture Gallery has over 400,000 images that can be searched by subject (gallery.yahoo.com). In addition to images, you can find statistical data represented in charts and graphs on government Web sites. The Statistical Abstract of the United States is especially useful for finding charts and graphs of population statistics (www.census.gov/statab/www/). You can also find thousands of maps on the Web. (See www.lib.utexas.edu/maps/map_sites/map_sites.html for a directory of map sites.)

Kudzu

Pueraria montana var. *lobata* (Willd.) Maesen & S. Almeida
Pea family (Fabaceae)

NATIVE RANGE: Asia

DESCRIPTION: Kudzu ia a climbing, semi-woody, perennial vine in the pea family. Deciduous leaves are alternate and compound, with three broad leaflets up to 4 inches across. Leaflets may be entire or deeply 2-3 lobed with hairy margins. Individual flowers, about 1/2 inch long, are purple, highly fragrant and borne in long hanging clusters. Flowering occurs in late summer and is soon followed by production of brown, hairy, flattened, seed pods, each of which contains three to ten hard seeds.

Kudzu was planted widely in the South to reduce soil erosion but has itself become a major pest, smothering native trees and plants.

Just because images are easy to download from the Web does not mean that you are free to use every image you find. Look for the image creator's copyright notice and suggested credit line. This notice will tell you if you can reproduce the image. For example, the Cascades Volcano Observatory makes its images available to all: "The maps, graphics, images, and text found on our website, unless stated otherwise, are within the Public Domain. You may download and use them. Credit back to the USGS/Cascades Volcano Observatory is appreciated." Most images on government Web sites can be reproduced, but check the copyright restrictions. You should acknowledge the source of any image you use.

In many cases you will find a copyright notice that reads something like this: "Any use or re-transmission of text or images in this website without written consent of the copyright owner constitutes copyright infringement and is prohibited." You must write to the creator to ask permission to use an image from a site that is not in the public domain, even if you cannot find a copyright notice.

18

Evaluating and Recording Sources

A successful search for sources will turn up many more items than you can use in your final product. You have to make decisions about what is important and relevant. Return to your research question and working thesis (see Chapter 16) to determine which items are relevant and useful to your project.

Evaluate Print Sources

How reliable are your sources? Books are expensive to print and distribute, so book publishers generally protect their investment by providing some level of editorial oversight. Print sources in libraries have an additional layer of oversight because someone has decided that a book or journal is worth purchasing and cataloging. Web sites, in contrast, can be put up and changed quickly, so information can be—and often is—posted thoughtlessly.

But print sources contain their share of biased, inaccurate, and misleading information. Over the years librarians have developed a set of criteria for evaluating print sources. These criteria are summarized in the box below.

EVALUATING PRINT SOURCES	
Source	Who published the book or article? Scholarly books and articles in scholarly journals are reviewed by experts in the field before they are published. They are generally more reliable than popular magazines and books, which tend to emphasize what is entertaining at the expense of comprehensiveness.
Author	Who wrote the book or article? What are the author's qualifications?

(continued)

EVALUATING PRINT SOURCES *(continued)*

Timeliness	How current is the source? If you are researching a fast-developing subject such as vaccines for Asian bird flu, then currency is very important. Currency might not be as important for a historical subject, but even historical figures and events are often reinterpreted.
Evidence	Where does the evidence come from—facts, interviews, observations, surveys, or experiments? Is the evidence adequate to support the author's claims?
Biases	Can you detect particular biases of the author? How do the author's biases affect the interpretation offered?
Advertising	Is advertising a prominent part of the journal or newspaper? How might the ads affect what gets printed?

Find Information to Cite Print Sources

Recording the full bibliographic information for all of the articles, books, Web sites, and other materials you might want to use in your project will save you a great deal of time and trouble later. Determine which documentation style you should use (ask your instructor if you don't know). Two major documentation styles—Modern Language Association (MLA) and American Psychological Association (APA)—are explained in detail in Chapters 20 and 21 of this book.

For books you will need, at minimum, the following information. This information can typically be found on the front and back of the title page:

- Author's name
- Title of the book
- Place of publication
- Name of publisher
- Date of publication
- Medium of publication (Print)

You will also need the page numbers if you are quoting directly or referring to a specific passage, as well as the title and author of the individual chapter if your source is an edited book with contributions by several people. Add the call numbers for the book or journal so you can find it easily in the future. You can compile this information in a computer file, a notebook or on note cards.

HQ
799.7
K36
2006

Kamenetz, Anya. *Generation Debt: Why Now Is a Terrible
Time to Be Young*. New York: Penguin, 2006. Print.

For help with citing books, see pages 281–282 and 287–290 (MLA style) and 305
and 309–310 (APA style).

For journals you will need the following information:

- Author's name
- Title of the article
- Title of the journal
- Volume and issue of the journal
- Date of the issue
- Page numbers of the article
- Medium of publication (Print)

Brazina, Paul R. "On the Trail: How Financial Audits Mark
the Path for Forensic Teams." *Pennsylvania CPA
Journal* 77 (2006): 13–16. Print.

For help with citing journals, see pages 282 and 291–293 (MLA style) and 306 and
310–311 (APA style).

Evaluate Database Sources

Databases collect print sources and put them in digital formats. Evaluate database sources the same way you evaluate print sources, asking the questions above in addition to those below.

Source: Is the source a scholarly or popular journal?

Author: What are the author's qualifications?

Timeliness: How current is the source?

Evidence: Where does the evidence come from?

Biases: Can you detect particular biases?

Advertising: Is advertising prominent?

Find Information to Cite a Database Source

To cite a source from a database, you will need the following information:

- Author if listed
- Title of article
- Name of periodical
- Date of publication (and edition for newspapers)
- Section and page number
- Name of database
- Medium of publication (Web)
- Date of access (the day you found the article in the database)

Often you have to look carefully to distinguish the name of the vendor from the name of the database. In the screen shot on the facing page, the vendor's name (EBSCO) is at the top of the screen, making it look like the name of the database (Academic Search Premier). EBSCO the company that sells access to Academic Search Premier and many other databases.

Do not include the database URL or (for a library-based subscription) information about the library system. For help with citing database sources, see pages 282–283 and 293 (MLA style) and 311 (APA style).

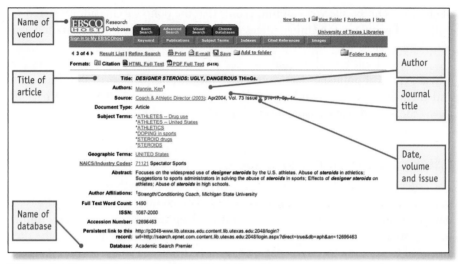

Citing a database article from Academic Search Premier.

Evaluate Web Sources

All electronic search tools share a common problem: They often give you too many sources. Web search engines pull up thousands of hits, and these hits may vary dramatically in quality. No one regulates or checks most information put on the Web, and it's no surprise that much of what is on the Web is highly opinionated or false.

Misleading Web sites

Some Web sites are put up as jokes. Other Web sites are deliberately misleading. Many prominent Web sites draw imitators who want to cash in on the commercial visibility. The Web site for the Campaign for Tobacco-Free Kids (www. tobaccofreekids.org), for example, has an imitator (www.smokefreekids.com) that sells software for antismoking education. The *.com* URL is often a tip-off that a site's main motive is profit.

Biased Web sites

Always approach Web sites with an eye toward evaluating their content. For example, Web sites with *.com* URLs that offer medical information often contain strong biases in addition to the motive to make money. The creators of the Web site Thinktwice.com, sponsored by the Global Vaccine Institute, oppose the vaccination of children. On the site you can find claims that the polio vaccine administered to millions of people in the United States causes cancer because it was contaminated with Simian Virus 40.

Always look for additional sources for verification. The U.S. Centers for Disease Control publishes fact sheets with the latest information about diseases and their prevention, including one on the polio vaccine and Simian Virus 40 (www.cdc.gov/od/science/iso/concerns/archive/polio_and_cancer.htm).

Criteria for evaluating Web sources

The criteria for evaluating print sources can be applied to Web sources if you keep in mind the special circumstances of the Web. For example, when you find a Web page by using a search engine, often you go deep into a complex site without having any sense of the context for that page. To evaluate the credibility of the site, you need to examine the home page, not just the first page you saw.

EVALUATING WEB SOURCES

Source	Look for the site's ownership in the Web address. If a Web site doesn't indicate ownership, attempt to discover who put it up and why. The domain can offer clues: *.gov* is used by government bodies and *.edu* is used by colleges and universities. In general, *.edu* sites are more reliable than *.com* sites.
Author	Often Web sites give no information about their authors other than an email address, if that. In such cases it is difficult or impossible to determine the author's qualifications. Look up the author on Google. If qualifications are listed, is the author an expert in the field? Some sites, such as Wikipedia, allow anyone to add or delete information. An entry on Wikipedia can (and often does) change from day to day, depending on who has edited the entry most recently.
Timeliness	Many Web pages do not list when they were last updated; thus you cannot determine their currency. Furthermore, there are thousands of deserted ghost sites on the Web—sites that the owners have abandoned but that search engines still turn up.
Evidence	The accuracy of any evidence found on the Web is often hard to verify. The most reliable information on the Web stands up to the tests of print evaluation, with clear indication of the sponsoring organization. Any factual information should be supported by indicating its source. Reliable Web sites list their sources.

(continued)

EVALUATING WEB SOURCES *(continued)*

Biases   Many Web sites announce their viewpoint on controversial issues, but others conceal their attitude with a reasonable tone and seemingly factual evidence such as statistics. Citations and bibliographies do not ensure that a site is reliable. Look carefully at the links and sources cited. Are the sources reliable?

Advertising Many Web sites are infomercials aimed at getting you to buy a product or service. While they might contain useful information, they are no more trustworthy than other forms of advertising.

Other Internet sources

Other Internet sources, such as online newsgroups, blogs, podcasts, wikis, and online videos, can give you useful ideas but are generally not considered authoritative. The use of Wikipedia for research is banned at some schools and by some instructors because many entries contain inaccuracies. If you do find facts on Wikipedia, be sure to confirm them with another source. Email communication from an expert in the field might be considered an authoritative source, but personal emails are generally not considered worthy of inclusion in a research paper. Remember that a key reason to cite sources is to allow other researchers to read and evaluate the sources you used.

Find Information to Cite a Web Source

To cite a Web site you will need the following information.

- Author (if listed)
- Title of the Web page
- Date the site was posted
- Sponsoring organization (if listed)
- Date you visited
- Complete URL

For help with citing Web sources, see pages 283–284 and 293–295 (MLA style) and 306–307 and 311–312 (APA style).

19

Writing the Research Paper

If you have chosen a subject you're interested in, asked questions about it, and researched it thoroughly, you have a wealth of ideas and information to communicate to your audience.

Review Your Goals and Thesis

Before you begin writing a research paper, review the assignment to remind you of the purpose of your argument, your potential readers, and the requested length.

By now you should have formulated a working thesis, which will be the focus of your paper. You also should have located, read, evaluated, and taken notes on enough source material to write your paper, and perhaps have conducted field research. At this stage in the writing process, your working thesis may be rough and may change as you write your draft, but having a working thesis will help keep your paper focused.

Determine Your Contribution

A convincing and compelling source-based argument does not make claims based solely on the word of you, the writer. To be persuasive, it must draw on the expertise and reputations of others as well. However, you must also demonstrate that you have thought about and synthesized the evidence you have gathered from your sources, and you must show your readers which elements of your paper represent your original thinking.

Determine exactly what you are adding to the larger conversation about your subject by answering these questions.

- Whom do you agree with?
- Whom do you disagree with?
- Whom do you agree with but have something else to add?
- What original analysis or theorizing do you have to offer?

See pages 42-44 for examples of how to identify your contribution in relation to your sources.

Determine Your Main Points

Look back over your notes on your sources and determine how to group the ideas you researched. Decide what your major points will be and how those points support your thesis. Group your research findings so that they match up with your major points.

Now it is time to create a working outline. Always include your thesis at the top of your outline as a guiding light. Some writers create formal outlines with roman numerals and the like; others compose the headings for the paragraphs of their paper and use them to guide their draft; still others may start writing and then determine how they will organize their draft when they have a few paragraphs written. Experiment and decide which method works best for you.

Avoid Plagiarism

Copying someone else's paper word for word or taking an article off the Internet and turning it in as yours is plagiarism. That's plain stealing, and people who take that risk should know that the punishment can be severe. But plagiarism also means using the ideas, melodies, or images of someone else without acknowledging them, and it is important to understand exactly what defines plagiarism.

What you don't have to document

Fortunately, common sense governs issues of academic plagiarism. The standards of documentation are not so strict that the source of every fact you cite must be acknowledged. Suppose you are writing about the causes of maritime disasters, and you want to know how many people drowned when the *Titanic* sank on the early morning of April 15, 1912. You check the Britannica Online and find that the death toll was around 1500. Since this fact is available in many other reference works, you would not need to cite Britannica Online as the source.

But let's say you want to challenge the version of the ship's sinking offered in the 1998 movie *Titanic*, which repeats the usual explanation that the *Titanic* sideswiped an iceberg, ripping a long gash along the hull that caused the ship to go down. Suppose that, in your reading, you discover that a September 1985 exploration of the wreck by an unmanned submersible did not find the long gash previously thought to have sunk the ship. The evidence instead suggested that the force of the collision with the iceberg broke the seams in the hull, allowing water to flood the ship's watertight compartments. You would need to cite the source of your information for this alternative version of the *Titanic*'s demise.

What you do have to document

For facts that are not easily found in general reference works, statements of opinion, and arguable claims, you should cite the source. You should also cite the sources of statistics, research findings, examples, graphs, charts, and illustrations. For example, if you state that the percentage of obese children aged 6 to 11 in the United States rose from 4 percent in 1974 to 15 percent in 2000, you need to cite the source.

As a reader you should be skeptical about statistics and research findings when the source is not mentioned. When a writer does not cite the sources of statistics and research findings, there is no way of knowing how reliable the sources are or whether the writer is making them up.

From the writer's perspective, careful citing of sources lends credibility. If you take your statistics from a generally trusted source, your readers are more likely to trust whatever conclusions or arguments you are presenting. When in doubt, always document the source.

Using caution with online source material

The best way to avoid unintentional plagiarism is to take care to distinguish source words from your own words.

- **Don't mix words from the source with your own words.** If you copy anything from a source when taking notes, place those words in quotation marks and note the page number(s) where those words appear.
- **Write down all the information you need for each source for a list of works cited or a list of references.** See Chapters 20 and 21.
- **If you copy words from an online source, take special care to note the source.** You could easily copy online material and later not be able to find where it came from.
- **Photocopy printed sources and print out online sources.** Having printed copies of sources allows you to double-check later that you haven't used words from the source by mistake and that any words you quote are accurate.

Quote Sources without Plagiarizing

Effective research writing builds on the work of others. You can summarize or paraphrase the work of others, but often it is best to let the authors speak in your text by quoting their exact words. Indicate the words of others by placing them inside quotation marks.

Most people who get into plagiarism trouble lift words from a source and use them without quotation marks. Where the line is drawn is easiest to illustrate with an example. In the following passage, Steven Johnson takes sharp issue with the metaphor of surfing applied to the Web:

> The concept of "surfing" does a terrible injustice to what it means to navigate around the Web. . . . What makes the idea of cybersurf so infuriating is the implicit connection drawn to television. Web surfing, after all, is a derivation of channel surfing—the term thrust upon the world by the rise of remote controls and cable panoply in the mid-eighties. . . . Applied to the boob tube, of course, the term was not altogether inappropriate. Surfing at least implied that channel-hopping was more dynamic, more involved, than the old routine of passive consumption. Just as a real-world surfer's enjoyment depended on the waves delivered up by the ocean, the channel surfer was at the mercy of the programmers and network executives. The analogy took off because it worked well in the one-to-many system of cable TV, where your navigational options were limited to the available channels.
>
> But when the term crossed over to the bustling new world of the Web, it lost a great deal of precision. . . . Web surfing and channel surfing are genuinely different pursuits; to imagine them as equivalents is to ignore the defining characteristics of each medium. Or at least that's what happens in theory. In practice, the Web takes on the greater burden. The television imagery casts the online surfer in the random, anesthetic shadow of TV programming, roaming from site to site like a CD player set on shuffle play. But what makes the online world so revolutionary is the fact that there *are* connections between each stop on a Web itinerant's journey. The links that join those various destinations are links of association, not randomness. A channel surfer hops back and forth between different channels because she's bored. A Web surfer clicks on a link because she's interested.
>
> —Steven Johnson. *Interface Culture: How New Technology Transforms the Way We Create and Communicate.* New York: Harper, 1997. 107–09.

If you were writing a paper or putting up a Web site that concerns Web surfing, you might want to mention the distinction that Johnson makes between channel surfing and surfing on the Web.

Quoting directly

If you quote directly, you must place quotation marks around all words you take from the original:

> One observer marks this contrast: "A channel surfer hops back and forth between different channels because she's bored. A Web surfer clicks on a link because she's interested" (Johnson 109).

Notice that the quotation is introduced and not just dropped in. This example follows MLA style, where the citation—(Johnson 109)—goes outside the quotation marks but before the final period. In MLA style, source references are made according to the author's last name, which refers you to the full citation in the list of works cited at the end. Following the author's name is the page number where the quotation can be located. (Notice that there is no comma after the name.)

Attributing every quotation

If the author's name appears in the sentence, cite only the page number, in parentheses:

> According to Steven Johnson, "A channel surfer hops back and forth between different channels because she's bored. A Web surfer clicks on a link because she's interested" (109).

Quoting words that are quoted in your source

Use single quotation marks to quote material that is already quoted in your source:

> Steven Johnson uses the metaphor of a Gothic cathedral to describe a computer interface: " ' The principle of the Gothic architecture,' Coleridge once said, 'is infinity made imaginable.' The same could be said for the modern interface" (42).

Summarize and Paraphrase Sources without Plagiarizing

Summarizing

When you summarize, you state the major ideas of an entire source or part of a source in a paragraph or perhaps even a sentence. The key is to put the summary in your own words. If you use words from the source, you must put those words within quotation marks.

Plagiarized

Steven Johnson argues in *Interface Culture* that the concept of "surfing" is misapplied to the Internet because channel surfers hop back and forth between different channels because they're bored, but Web surfers click on links because they're interested. [Most of the words are lifted directly from the original; see page 273.]

Acceptable summary

Steven Johnson argues in *Interface Culture* that the concept of "surfing" is misapplied to the Internet because users of the Web consciously choose to link to other sites while television viewers mindlessly flip through the channels until something catches their attention.

Paraphrasing

When you paraphrase, you represent the idea of the source in your own words at about the same length as the original. You still need to include the reference to the source of the idea. The following example illustrates an unacceptable paraphrase.

Plagiarized

Steven Johnson argues that the concept of "surfing" does a terrible injustice to what it means to navigate around the Web. What makes the idea of Web surfing infuriating is the association with television. Surfing is not a bad metaphor for channel hopping, but it doesn't fit what people do on the Web. Web surfing and channel surfing are truly different activities; to imagine them as the same is to ignore their defining characteristics. A channel surfer skips around because she's bored while a Web surfer clicks on a link because she's interested (107-09).

Even though the source is listed, this paraphrase is unacceptable. Too many of the words in the original are used directly here, including much or all of entire sentences. When a string of words is lifted from a source and inserted without quotation marks, the passage is plagiarized. Changing a few words in a sentence is not a paraphrase. Compare these two sentences:

Source

Web surfing and channel surfing are genuinely different pursuits; to imagine them as equivalents is to ignore the defining characteristics of each medium.

Unacceptable paraphrase

Web surfing and channel surfing are truly different activities; to imagine them as the same is to ignore their defining characteristics.

The paraphrase takes the structure of the original sentence and substitutes a few words. It is much too similar to the original.

> **A true paraphrase represents an entire rewriting of the idea from the source.**

Acceptable paraphrase

Steven Johnson argues that "surfing" is a misleading term for describing how people navigate on the Web. He allows that "surfing" is appropriate for clicking across television channels because the viewer has to interact with what the networks and cable companies provide, just as the surfer has to interact with what the ocean provides. Web surfing, according to Johnson, operates at much greater depth and with much more consciousness of purpose. Web surfers actively follow links to make connections (107-09).

Even though this paraphrase contains a few words from the original, such as *navigate* and *connections*, these sentences are original in structure and wording while accurately conveying the meaning of the source.

Incorporate Quotations

Quotations are a frequent problem area in research papers. Review every quotation to ensure that each is used effectively and correctly, and follow these guidelines.

- **Limit the use of long quotations.** If you have more than one blocked quotation on a page, look closely to see if one or more can be paraphrased or summarized.
- **Check that each quotation supports your major points rather than making major points for you.** If the ideas rather than the original wording are what's important, paraphrase the quotation and cite the source.
- **Check that each quotation is introduced and attributed.** Each quotation should be introduced and the author or title named. Check for verbs that signal a quotation: *Smith claims, Jones argues, Brown states.* (See page 277 for a list of verbs that introduce quotations and paraphrases.)

- **Check that each quotation is properly formatted and punctuated.** Prose quotations longer than four lines (MLA) or forty words (APA) should be indented ten spaces in MLA style or five spaces in APA style. Shorter quotations should be enclosed within quotation marks.

- **Check that you cite the source for each quotation.** You are required to cite the sources of all direct quotations, paraphrases, and summaries.

- **Check the accuracy of each quotation.** It's easy to leave out words or to mistype a quotation. Compare what is in your paper to the original source. If you need to add words to make the quotation grammatical, make sure the added words are in brackets.

- **Read your paper aloud to a classmate or a friend.** Each quotation should flow smoothly when you read your paper aloud. Put a check beside rough spots as you read aloud so you can revise later.

VERBS THAT INTRODUCE QUOTATIONS AND PARAPHRASES

acknowledge	concede	interpret
add	conclude	maintain
admit	contend	note
advise	criticize	object
agree	declare	observe
allow	describe	offer
analyze	disagree	point out
answer	discuss	refute
argue	dispute	reject
ask	emphasize	remark
assert	explain	reply
believe	express	report
charge	find	respond
claim	grant	show
comment	illustrate	state
compare	imply	suggest
complain	insist	write

Quoting directly vs. paraphrasing

Use direct quotations when the original wording is important.

Direct quotation

Smith notes that

> Although the public grew to accept film as a teaching tool, it was not always aware of all it was being taught. That was because a second type of film was also being produced during these years, the "attitude-building" film, whose primary purpose was to motivate, not instruct. Carefully chosen visuals were combined with dramatic story lines, music, editing, and sharply drawn characters to create powerful instruments of mass manipulation. (21)

Paraphrase

Smith points out that a second kind of mental-hygiene film, the attitude-building film, was introduced during the 1940s. It attempted to motivate viewers, whereas earlier films explicitly tried to teach something. The attitude-building films were intended to manipulate their audiences to feel a certain way (21).

Here, the original wording provides stronger description of the attitude-building films. The direct quotation is a better choice.

Often, you can paraphrase the main idea of a lengthy passage and quote only the most striking phrase or sentence.

Paraphrase combined with quotation

In his analysis of the rise of fascism in twentieth-century Europe, George Mosse notes that the fascist movement was built on pre-existing ideas like individualism and sacrifice. It "scavenged" other ideologies and made use of them. "Fascism was a new political movement but not a movement which invented anything new," Mosse explains (xvii).

Incorporate Visuals

Here are a few guidelines to keep in mind for incorporating visual sources into your research paper.

- **Use visuals for examples and supporting evidence, not for decoration.** For example, if the subject of your research is Internet crime in San Francisco, including a picture of the Golden Gate Bridge is irrelevant and will detract from your paper.

■ **Refer to images and other graphics in the body of your research paper.** Explain the significance of any images or graphics in the body of your paper. The relevance of the visual should not be left to the reader to guess.

■ **Respect the copyright of visual sources.** You may need to request permission to use a visual from the Web. Use your own photographs or public domain material whenever possible.

■ **Get complete citation information.** You are required to cite visual sources in your list of works cited just as you are for other sources.

■ **Describe the content of the image or graphic in the caption.**

20

Documenting Sources in MLA Style

The two styles of documentation used most frequently are APA style and MLA style. APA stands for American Psychological Association, which publishes a style manual used widely in the social sciences and education (see Chapter 21). MLA stands for the Modern Language Association, and its style is the norm for the humanities and fine arts, including English and rhetoric and composition. If you have questions that this chapter does not address, consult the *MLA Handbook for Writers of Research Papers*, Seventh Edition (2009), and the *MLA Style Manual and Guide to Scholarly Publishing*, Third Edition (2008).

Elements of MLA Documentation

Citing a source in your paper

Citing sources is a two-part process. When readers find a reference to a source (called an in-text or parenthetical citation) in the body of your paper, they can turn to the works-cited list at the end and find the full publication information. Place the author's last name and the page number inside parentheses at the end of the sentence.

> Anticipating the impact of Google's project of digitally scanning books in major research libraries, one observer predicts that "the real magic will come in the second act, as each word in each book is cross-linked, clustered, cited, extracted, indexed, analyzed, annotated, remixed, reassembled and woven deeper into the culture than ever before" (Kelly 43).

Author not mentioned in text

If you mention the author's name in the sentence, you do not have to put the name in the parenthetical reference at the end. Just cite the page number.

> Anticipating the impact of Google's project of digitally scanning books in major research libraries, Kevin Kelly predicts that "the real magic will come in the second act, as each word in each book is cross-linked, clustered, cited, extracted, indexed, analyzed, annotated, remixed, reassembled and woven deeper into the culture than ever before" (43).

Author mentioned in the text

The corresponding entry in the work-cited list at the end of your paper would be as follows.

Works Cited

> Kelly, Kevin. "Scan This Book!" *New York Times* 14 May 2006, late ed., sec 6: 43+. Print.

Entry in the works-cited list

Citing an entire work, a Web site, or another electronic source

If you wish to cite an entire work (a book, a film, a performance, and so on), a Web site, or an electronic source that has no page numbers or paragraph numbers, MLA style instructs that you mention the name of the person (for example, the author or director) in the text with a corresponding entry in the works-cited list. You do not need to include the author's name in parentheses. If you cannot identify the author, mention the title in your text.

Author mentioned in the text

> Joel Waldfogel discusses the implications of a study of alumni donations to colleges and universities, observing that parents give generously to top-rated colleges in the hope that their children chances for admission will improve.

Works Cited

> Waldfogel, Joel. "The Old College Try." *Slate*. Washington Post Newsweek Interactive, 6 July 2007. Web. 27 Jan. 2009.

MLA style now requires the medium of publication (print, Web, performance, etc.) to be included in each citation.

Creating an MLA-style works-cited list

To create your works-cited list, go through your paper and find every reference to the sources you consulted during your research. Each in-text reference must have an entry in your works-cited list.

Organize your works-cited list alphabetically by authors' last names or, if no author is listed, the first word in the title other than *a*, *an*, or *the*. (See pages 302–303 for a sample works-cited list.) MLA style uses four basic forms for entries in the works-cited list: books, periodicals (scholarly journals, newspapers, magazines), online library database sources, and other online sources (Web sites, discussion forums, blogs, online newspapers, online magazines, online government documents, and email messages).

Works-cited entries for books

Entries for books have three main elements.

> Poster, Mark. *Information Please: Culture and Politics in the Age of Digital Machines*. Durham: Duke UP, 2006. Print.

1. Author's name.
- List the author's name with the last name first, followed by a period.

2. *Title of book.*
- Find the exact title on the title page, not the cover.
- Separate the title and subtitle with a colon.
- Italicize the title and put a period at the end.

3. Publication information.
- Give the place (usually the city) of publication and a colon.
- Give the name of the publisher, using accepted abbreviations, and a comma.
- Give the date of publication, followed by a period.
- Give the medium of publication (Print), followed by a period.

Works-cited entries for periodicals

Entries for periodicals (scholarly journals, newspapers, magazines) have three main elements.

MacDonald, Susan Peck. "The Erasure of Language." *College Composition and Communication* 58 (2007): 585-625. Print.

1. Author's name.
- List the author's name with the last name first, followed by a period.

2. "Title of article."
- Place the title of the article inside quotation marks.
- Insert a period before the closing quotation mark.

3. Publication information.
- Italicize the title of the journal.
- Give the volume number.
- List the date of publication, in parentheses, followed by a colon.
- List the page numbers, followed by a period.
- Give the medium of publication (Print), followed by a period.

Works-cited entries for library database sources

Basic entries for library database sources have four main elements. See pages 266–267 for where to find this information.

Hede, Jesper. "Jews and Muslims in Dante's Vision." *European Review* 16.1 (2008): 101-14. *Academic Search Premier*. Web. 14 Apr. 2009.

1. Author's name.
■ List the author's name with the last name first, followed by a period.

2. "Title of article."
■ Place the title of the article inside quotation marks.
■ Insert a period before the closing quotation mark.

3. Print publication information.
■ Give the print publication information in standard format, in this case for a periodical (see page 282).

4. Database information.
■ Italicize the name of the database, followed by a period.
■ List the medium of publication, followed by a period. For all database sources, the medium of publication is *Web*.
■ List the date you accessed the source (day, month, and year), followed by a period.

Works-cited entries for other online sources

Basic entries for online sources (Web sites, discussion forums, blogs, online newspapers, online magazines, online government documents, and email messages) have three main elements. Sometimes information such as the author's name or the date of publication is missing from the online source. Include the information you are able to locate.

There are many formats for the different kinds of electronic publications. Here is the format of an entry for an online article.

Broudy, Oliver. "Air Head." *Salon.com*. Salon, 7 July 2007. Web. 6 Apr. 2009.

1. **Author's name.**
   - List the author's name with the last name first, followed by a period.

2. **"Title of work";** *Title of the overall Web site.*
   - Place the title of the work inside quotation marks if it is part of a larger Web site.
   - Italicize name of overall site if different from title of the work.
   - Some Web sites are updated periodically, so list the version if you find it (e.g., 2009 edition).

3. **Publication information.**
   - List the publisher or sponsor of the site, followed by a comma. If not available, use *N.p.* (for *no publisher*).
   - List the date of publication if available; if not, use *n.d.*
   - List the medium of publication (*Web*).
   - List the date you accessed the source (day, month, and year).

MLA In-Text Citations

1. Author named in your text

Put the author's name in a signal phrase in your sentence.

Sociologist Daniel Bell called this emerging U.S. economy the "postindustrial society" (3).

2. Author not named in your text

Put the author's last name and the page number inside parentheses at the end of the sentence.

In 1997, the Gallup poll reported that 55% of adults in the United States think secondhand smoke is "very harmful," compared to only 36% in 1994 (Saad 4).

3. Work by a single author

The author's last name comes first, followed by the page number. There is no comma.

(Bell 3)

4. Work by two or three authors

The authors' last names follow the order of the title page. If there are two authors, join the names with *and*. If there are three authors, use a comma between the first two names and a comma with *and* before the last name.

(Francisco, Vaughn, and Lynn 7)

5. Work by four or more authors

You may use the phrase *et al.* (meaning "and others") for all names but the first, or you may write out all the names. Make sure you use the same method for both the in-text citations and the works-cited list.

> (Abrams et al. 1653)

6. Work by an unnamed author

Use a shortened version of the title that includes at least the first important word. Your reader will use the shortened title to find the full title in the works-cited list.

> A review in the *New Yorker* of Ryan Adams's new album focuses on the artist's age ("Pure" 25).

Notice that "Pure" is in quotation marks because it is the shortened title of an article. If it were a book, the short title would be underlined.

7. Work by a group or organization

Treat the group or organization as the author, but try to identify the group author in the text and place only the page number in parentheses. Shorten terms that are commonly abbreviated.

> According to the *Irish Free State Handbook*, published by the Ministry for Industry and Finance, the population of Ireland in 1929 was approximately 4,192,000 (23).

8. Quotations longer than four lines

When using indented (block) quotations of more than four lines, place the period *before* the parentheses enclosing the page number.

> In her article "Art for Everybody," Susan Orlean attempts to explain the popularity of painter Thomas Kinkade:
>> People like to own things they think are valuable. . . . The high price of limited editions is part of their appeal: it implies that they are choice and exclusive, and that only a certain class of people will be able to afford them. (128)
>
> This same statement could possibly also explain the popularity of phenomena like PBS's *Antiques Road Show*.

If the source is longer than one page, provide the page number for each quotation, paraphrase, and summary.

9. **Web sources including Web pages, blogs, podcasts, wikis, videos, and other multimedia sources**

Give the author in the text instead of putting the author's name in parentheses.

> Andrew Keen ironically used his own blog to claim that "blogs are boring to write (yawn), boring to read (yawn) and boring to discuss (yawn)."

If you cannot identify the author, mention the title in your text.

> The podcast "Catalina's Cubs" describes the excitement on Catalina Island when the Chicago Cubs went there for spring training in the 1940s.

10. **Work in an anthology**

Cite the name of the author of the work within an anthology, not the name of the editor of the collection. Alphabetize the entry in the list of works cited by the author, not the editor.

> In "Beard," Melissa Jane Hardie explores the role assumed by Elizabeth Taylor as the celebrity companion of gay actors including Rock Hudson and Montgomery Cliff (278-79).

11. **Two or more works by the same author**

When an author has two or more items in the works-cited list, distinguish which work you are citing by using the author's last name and then a shortened version of the title of each source.

> The majority of books written about coauthorship focus on partners of the same sex (Laird, *Women* 351).

Note that *Women* is underlined because it is the name of a book; if an article were named, quotation marks would be used.

12. **Different authors with the same last name**

If your list of works cited contains items by two or more different authors with the same last name, include the initial of the first name in the parenthetical reference.

> Web surfing requires more mental involvement than channel surfing (S. Johnson 107).

Note that a period follows the initial.

13. Two or more sources within the same sentence
Place each citation directly after the statement it supports.

> In the 1990s, many sweeping pronouncements were made that the Internet is the best opportunity to improve education since the printing press (Ellsworth xxii) or even in the history of the world (Dyrli and Kinnaman 79).

14. Two or more sources within the same citation
If two sources support a single point, separate them with a semicolon.

> (McKibbin 39; Gore 92)

15. Work quoted in another source
When you do not have access to the original source of the material you wish to use, put the abbreviation *qtd. in* (quoted in) before the information about the indirect source.

> National governments have become increasingly what Ulrich Beck, in a 1999 interview, calls "zombie institutions"—institutions that are "dead and still alive" (qtd. in Bauman 6).

16. Literary works
To supply a reference to a literary work, you sometimes need more than a page number from a specific edition. Readers should be able to locate a quotation in any edition of the book. Give the page number from the edition that you are using, then a semicolon and other identifying information.

> "Marriage is a house" is one of the most memorable lines in *Don Quixote* (546; pt. 2, bk. 3, ch. 19).

MLA Works-Cited List: Books

One author

17. Book by one author
The author's last name comes first, followed by a comma, the first name, and a period.

> Doctorow, E. L. *The March*. New York: Random, 2005. Print.

18. Two or more books by the same author
In the entry for the first book, include the author's name. In the second entry, substitute three hyphens and a period for the author's name. List the titles of books by the same author in alphabetical order.

Grimsley, Jim. *Boulevard*. Chapel Hill: Algonquin, 2002. Print.

---. *Dream Boy*. New York: Simon, 1995. Print.

Multiple authors

19. Book by two or three authors
Second and subsequent authors' names appear first name first. A comma separates the authors' names.

Chapkis, Wendy, and Richard J. Webb. *Dying to Get High: Marijuana as Medicine*. New York: New York UP, 2008. Print

20. Book by four or more authors
You may use the phrase *et al.* (meaning "and others") for all authors but the first, or you may write out all the names. Use the same method in the in-text citation as you do in the works-cited list.

Zukin, Cliff, et al. *A New Engagement? Political Participation, Civic Life, and the Changing American Citizen*. New York: Oxford UP, 2006. Print.

Anonymous and group authors

21. Book by an unknown author
Begin the entry with the title.

Encyclopedia of Americana. New York: Somerset, 2001. Print.

22. Book by a group or organization
Treat the group as the author of the work.

United Nations. *The Charter of the United Nations: A Commentary*. New York: Oxford UP, 2000. Print.

23. Religious texts

Do not underline the title of a sacred text, including the Bible, unless you are citing a specific edition.

> *Holy Bible. King James Text: Modern Phrased Version*. New York:
> Oxford UP, 1980. Print.

Imprints, reprints, and undated books

24. Book with no publication date

If no year of publication is given, but can be approximated, put a *c*. ("circa") and the approximate date in brackets: [c. 1999]. Otherwise, put *n.d.* ("no date").

> O'Sullivan, Colin. *Traditions and Novelties of the Irish Country Folk*.
> Dublin, [c. 1793]. Print.

> James, Franklin. *In the Valley of the King*. Cambridge: Harvard UP, n.d. Print.

25. Reprinted works

For works of fiction that have been printed in many different editions or reprints, give the original publication date after the title.

> Wilde, Oscar. *The Picture of Dorian Gray*. 1890. New York: Norton, 2001. Print.

Parts of books

26. Introduction, foreword, preface, or afterword

Give the author and then the name of the specific part being cited. Next, name the book. Then, if the author for the whole work is different, put that author's name after the word *By*. Place inclusive page numbers at the end.

> Benstock, Sheri. Introduction. *The House of Mirth*. By Edith Wharton.
> Boston: Bedford-St. Martin's, 2002. 3-24. Print.

27. Single chapter written by same author as the book

> Ardis, Ann L. "Mapping the Middlebrow in Edwardian England." *Modernism
> and Cultural Conflict: 1880-1922*. Cambridge: Cambridge UP, 2002.
> 114-42. Print.

28. Selection from an anthology or edited collection

> Sedaris, David. "Full House." *The Best American Nonrequired Reading 2004.*
> Ed. Dave Eggers. Boston: Houghton, 2004. 350-58. Print.

29. Article in a reference work

You can omit the names of editors and most publishing information for an article from a familiar reference work. Identify the edition by date. There is no need to give the page numbers when a work is arranged alphabetically. Give the author's name, if known.

> "Utilitarianism." *The Columbia Encyclopedia.* 6th ed. 2001. Print.

Editions and translations

30. Book with an editor

List an edited book under the editor's name if your focus is on the editor. Otherwise, cite an edited book under the author's name as shown in the second example.

> Lewis, Gifford, ed. *The Big House of Inver.* By Edith Somerville and Martin
> Ross. Dublin: Farmar, 2000. Print.

> Somerville, Edith, and Martin Ross. *The Big House of Inver.* Ed. Gifford Lewis.
> Dublin: Farmar, 2000. Print.

31. Book with a translator

> Benjamin, Walter. *The Arcades Project.* Trans. Howard Eiland and Kevin
> McLaughlin. Cambridge: Harvard UP, 1999. Print.

32. Second or subsequent edition of a book

> Hawthorn, Jeremy, ed. *A Concise Glossary of Contemporary Literary Theory.*
> 3rd ed. London: Arnold, 2001. Print.

Multivolume works

33. Multivolume work

Identify both the volume you have used and the total number of volumes in the set.

> Samuel, Raphael. *Theatres of Memory.* Vol. 1. London: Verso, 1999. 2 vols.
> Print.

If you refer to more than one volume, identify the specific volume in your in-text citations, and list the total number of volumes in your list of works cited.

> Samuel, Raphael. *Theatres of Memory*. 2 vols. London: Verso, 1999. Print.

MLA Works-Cited List: Periodicals

Journal articles

34. Article by one author

> Mallory, Anne. "Burke, Boredom, and the Theater of Counterrevolution." *PMLA* 119 (2003): 329-43. Print.

35. Article by two or three authors

> Miller, Thomas P., and Brian Jackson. "What Are English Majors For?" *College Composition and Communication* 58 (2007): 825-31. Print.

36. Article by four or more authors

You may use the phrase *et al.* (meaning "and others") for all authors but the first, or you may write out all the names.

> Breece, Katherine E., et al. "Patterns of mtDNA Diversity in Northwestern North America." *Human Biology* 76 (2004): 33-54. Print.

Pagination in journals

37. Article in a scholarly journal

List the volume and issue number after the name of the journal.

> Duncan, Mike. "Whatever Happened to the Paragraph?" *College English* 69.5 (2007): 470-95. Print.

38. Article in a scholarly journal that uses only issue numbers

List the issue number after the name of the journal.

> McCall, Sophie. "Double Vision Reading." *Canadian Literature* 194 (2007): 95-97. Print.

Magazines

39. Monthly or seasonal magazines

Use the month (or season) and year in place of the volume. Abbreviate the names of all months except May, June, and July.

> Barlow, John Perry. "Africa Rising: Everything You Know about Africa Is
>   Wrong." *Wired* Jan. 1998: 142-58. Print.

40. Weekly or biweekly magazines

Give both the day and the month of publication, as listed on the issue.

> Brody, Richard. "A Clash of Symbols." *New Yorker* 25 June 2007: 16. Print.

Newspapers

41. Newspaper article by one author

The author's last name comes first, followed by a comma and the first name.

> Marriott, Michel. "Arts and Crafts for the Digital Age." *New York Times*
>   8 June 2006, late ed.: C13. Print.

42. Article by two or three authors

The second and subsequent authors' names are printed in regular order, first name first:

> Schwirtz, Michael, and Joshua Yaffa. "A Clash of Cultures at a Square in
>   Moscow." *New York Times* 11 July 2007, late ed.: A9. Print.

43. Newspaper article by an unknown author

Begin the entry with the title.

> "The Dotted Line." *Washington Post* 8 June 2006, final ed.: E2. Print.

Reviews, editorials, letters to the editor

44. Review

If there is no title, just name the work reviewed.

> Mendelsohn, Daniel. "The Two Oscar Wildes." Rev. of *The Importance of
>   Being Earnest*, dir. Oliver Parker. *The New York Review of Books*
>   10 Oct. 2002: 23-24. Print.

45. Editorial

"Hush-hush, Sweet Liberty." Editorial. *Los Angeles Times* 7 July 2007: A18. Print.

46. Letter to the editor

Doyle, Joe. Letter. *Direct* 1 July 2007: 48. Print.

MLA Works-Cited List: Library Database Sources

47. Work from a library database

Begin with the print publication information, then the name of the database (italicized), the medium of publication (*Web*), and the date of access.

Snider, Michael. "Wired to Another World." *Maclean's* 3 Mar. 2003: 23-24. *Academic Search Premier*. Web. 14 Jan. 2007.

MLA Works-Cited List: Online Sources

Web publications

When do you list a URL?

MLA style no longer requires including URLs of Web sources. URLs are of limited value because they change frequently and they can be specific to an individual search. Include the URL as supplementary information only when your readers probably cannot locate the source without the URL.

48. Publication by a known author

Boerner, Steve. "Leopold Mozart." *The Mozart Project: Biography*. The Mozart Project, 21 Mar. 1998. Web. 30 Oct. 2008.

49. Publication by a group or organization

If a work has no author's or editor's name listed, begin the entry with the title.

"State of the Birds." *Audubon*. National Audubon Society, 2008. Web. 19 Aug. 2008.

50. Article in a scholarly journal on the Web

Some scholarly journals are published on the Web only. List articles by author, title, name of journal in italics, volume and issue number, and year of publication. If the journal does not have page numbers, use *n. pag.* in place of page numbers. Then list the medium of publication (*Web*) and the date of access (day, month, and year).

> Fleckenstein, Kristie. "Who's Writing? Aristotelian Ethos and the Author
> Position in Digital Poetics." *Kairos* 11.3 (2007): n. pag. Web. 6 Apr.
> 2008.

51. Article in a newspaper on the Web

The first date is the date of publication; the second is the date of access.

> Brown, Patricia Leigh. "Australia in Sonoma." *New York Times.* New York Times,
> 5 July 2008. Web. 3 Aug. 2009.

52. Article in a magazine on the Web

> Brown, Patricia Leigh. "The Wild Horse Is Us." *Newsweek.* Newsweek, 1 July
> 2008. Web. 12 Dec. 2008.

53. Book on the Web

> Prebish, Charles S., and Kenneth K. Tanaka. *The Faces of Buddhism in America.*
> Berkeley: U of California P, 2003. *eScholarship Editions.* Web. 2 May
> 2009.

Other online sources

54. Blog entry

If there is no sponsor or publisher for the blog, use *N.p.*

> Arrington, Michael. "Think Before You Voicemail." *TechCrunch.* N.p., 5 July
> 2008. Web. 10 Sept. 2008.

55. E-mail

Give the name of the writer, the subject line, a description of the message, the date, and the medium of delivery (*E-mail*).

> Ballmer, Steve. "A New Era of Business Productivity and Innovation." Message to Microsoft Executive E-mail. 30 Nov. 2006. E-mail.

56. Video on the Web

Video on the Web often lacks a creator and a date. Begin the entry with a title if you cannot find a creator. Use *n.d.* if you cannot find a date.

> Wesch, Michael. *A Vision of Students Today. YouTube.* YouTube, 2007. Web. 28 May 2008.

57. Personal home page

List *Home page* without quotation marks in place of the title. If no date is listed, use *n.d.*

> Graff, Harvey J. Home page. Dept. of English, Ohio State U, n.d. Web. 15 Nov. 2008.

58. Wiki entry

A wiki is a collaborative writing and editing tool. Although some topic-specific wikis are written and carefully edited by recognized scholars, the more popular wiki sites—such as *Wikipedia*—are often considered unreliable sources for academic papers.

> "Snowboard." *Wikipedia.* Wikimedia Foundation, 2009. Web. 30 Jan. 2009.

59. Podcast

> Sussingham, Robin. "All Things Autumn." No. 2. *HighLifeUtah.* N.p., 20 Nov. 2006. Web. 28 Feb. 2009.

60. PDFs and digital files

PDFs and other digital files can often be downloaded through links. Determine the kind of work you are citing, include the appropriate information for the particular kind of work, and list the type of file.

> Glaser, Edward L., and Albert Saiz. "The Rise of the Skilled City." Discussion
> Paper No. 2025. Harvard Institute of Economic Research. Cambridge:
> Harvard U, 2003. PDF file.

MLA Works-Cited List: Other Sources

61. Sound recording

> McCoury, Del, perf. "1952 Vincent Black Lightning." By Richard Thompson.
> *Del and the Boys.* Ceili, 2001. CD.

62. Film

Begin with the title in italics. List the director, the distributor, the date, and the medium. Other data, such as the names of the screenwriters and performers, is optional.

> *Wanted.* Dir. Timur Bekmambetov. Perf. James McAvoy, Angelina Jolie, and
> Morgan Freeman. Universal, 2008. Film.

63. DVD

> *No Country for Old Men.* Dir. Joel Coen and Ethan Coen. Perf. Tommy Lee
> Jones, Javier Bardem, and Josh Brolin. Paramount, 2007. DVD.

64. Television or radio program

> "Kaisha." *The Sopranos.* Perf. James Gandolfini, Lorraine Bracco, and Edie
> Falco. HBO. 4 June 2006. Television.

Sample MLA paper

Include your last name and the page number as your page header, beginning with the first page, 1/2 inch from the top.

Brian Witkowski

Professor Mendelsohn

RHE 309K

2 May 2009

MLA style does not require a title page. Ask your instructor whether you need one.

Need a Cure for Tribe Fever?

How About a Dip in the Lake?

Center your title. Do not put the title inside quotation marks or type it in all capital letters.

Everyone is familiar with the Cleveland Indians' Chief Wahoo logo—and I do mean everyone, not just Clevelanders. Across America one can see individuals sporting the smiling mascot on traditional Indians caps and jerseys, and recent trends in sports merchandise have popularized new groovy multicolored Indians sportswear. In fact, Indians merchandise recently was ranked just behind the New York Yankees' merchandise in terms of sales (Adams). Because of lucrative merchandising contracts between Major League Baseball and Little League, youth teams all over the country don Cleveland's famous (or infamous) smiling Indian each season as fresh-faced kids scamper onto the diamonds looking like mini major leaguers ("MLBP"). Various incarnations of the famous Chief Wahoo—described by sportswriter Rick Telander as "the red-faced, big-nosed, grinning, drywall-toothed moron who graces the peak of every Cleveland Indians cap"—have been around since the 1940s (qtd. in Eitzen). Now redder and even more cartoonish than the original hook-nosed, beige Indian with a devilish grin, Wahoo often passes as a cheerful baseball buddy like the San Diego Chicken or the St. Louis Cardinals' Fredbird. (See Fig. 1.)

Double-space everything.

Cite sources without a named author by title.

Though defined by its distinctive logo, Cleveland baseball far preceded its famous mascot. The team changed from the Forest Citys to the Spiders to the Bluebirds/Blues to the Broncos to the Naps and finally to the Indians. Dubbed the Naps in 1903 in honor of its star player and manager Napoleon Lajoie, the team finally arrived at their current appellation in 1915. After Lajoie was traded, the team's president challenged sportswriters to devise a suitable "temporary" label for the floundering club. Publicity material has it that the writers decided on the Indians to celebrate Louis Sockalexis, a Penobscot Indian who played for the team from 1897 to 1899. With a heck of a

Indent each paragraph five spaces (1/2 inch on the ruler in your word-processing program).

Witkowski 2

batting average and the notability of being the first Native American in professional baseball, Sockalexis was immortalized by the new Cleveland label (Schneider 10-23). (Contrary to popular lore, some cite alternative—and less reverent—motivations behind the team's naming and point to a lack of Sockalexis publicity in period newspaper articles discussing the team's naming process [Staurowsky 95-97].) Almost ninety years later, the "temporary" name continues to raise eyebrows, in both its marketability and its ideological questionability.

> Cite sources by the author's last name, if possible.

Fig. 1.   Many youth baseball and softball teams use the Chief Wahoo logo, including teams with American Indian players.

Today the logo is more than a little embarrassing. Since the high-profile actions of the American Indian Movement (AIM) in the 1970s, sports teams around the country—including the Indians—have been criticized and cajoled over their less than racially sensitive mascots. Native American groups question the sensitivity of such caricatured displays—not just because of grossly stereotyped mascots, but also because of what visual displays of team support say about Native American culture. Across the country, professional sporting teams, as well as high schools and colleges, perform faux rituals in the name of team spirit. As Tim Giago, publisher of the *Lakota Times*, a weekly South Dakotan Native American newspaper, has noted, "The sham rituals, such as the wearing of feathers, smoking of so-called peace pipes, beating of tomtoms, fake dances, horrendous attempts at singing Indian songs, the so-called war whoops, and the painted faces, address more than the issues of racism. They are direct attacks upon the spirituality of the Indian people" (qtd. in Wulf).

Since 1969, when Oklahoma disavowed its "Little Red" mascot, more than 600 school and minor league teams have followed a more ethnically sensitive trend and ditched their "tribal" mascots for ones less publicly explosive (Price). High-profile teams such as Berkeley, St. Johns University, and Miami (Ohio) University have buckled to public pressure, changing their team names from the Indians to the Cardinals (1972), the Redmen to the Red Storm (1993), and the Redskins to the Redhawks (1996), respectively. While many people see such controversies as mere bowing to the pressures of the late twentieth and early twenty-first centuries, others see the mascot issue as a topic well worthy of debate.

Cleveland's own Chief Wahoo has far from avoided controversy. Protests regarding the controversial figure have plagued the city. Multiple conflicts between Wahoo devotees and dissenters have arisen around the baseball season. At the opening game of 1995, fifty Native Americans and supporters took stations around Jacobs Field to demonstrate against the use of the cartoonish smiling crimson mascot. While protestors saw the event as a triumph for First Amendment rights and a strike against negative stereotyping, one befuddled fan stated, "I never thought of [Chief Wahoo] that way. It's all how you think of it" (Kropk). Arrests were made in 1998 when demonstrators from the United Church of Christ burned a three-foot Chief Wahoo doll in effigy ("Judge"). Wedded to their memorabilia, fans proudly stand behind their Indian as others lobby vociferously for its removal. Splitting government officials, fans, and social and religious groups, this issue draws hostility from both sides of the argument.

In 2000 Cleveland mayor Michael White came out publicly against the team mascot, joining an already established group of religious leaders, laypersons, and civil rights activists who had demanded Wahoo's retirement. African-American religious and civic leaders such as Rev. Gregory A. Jacobs had been speaking out throughout the 1990s and highlighting the absurdity of minority groups who embrace the Wahoo symbol. "Each of us has had to fight its [sic] own battle, quite frankly," Jacobs stated. "We cannot continue to live in this kind of hypocrisy that says, Yes, we are in solidarity with my [sic] brothers and sisters, yet we continue to exploit them" (qtd. in Briggs). These words clash with those of individuals such as former Indians owner Dick Jacobs, who said amidst protest that the Wahoo logo would remain as long as he was principal owner of the club (Bauman 1) and a delegate of the East Ohio Conference of the United Methodist Church, who quipped, "I would cease being a United Methodist before I would cease wearing my Chief Wahoo clothing" (Briggs).

This controversy also swirls outside of the greater Cleveland area. Individual newspapers in Nebraska, Kansas, Minnesota, and Oregon have banned the printing of Native American sports symbols and team names such as the Braves, Indians, or Redmen (Wulf), while the *Seattle Times* went so far as to digitally remove the Wahoo symbol from images of the Cleveland baseball cap ("Newspaper"). As other teams make ethnically sensitive and image-conscious choices to change their mascots, Cleveland stands firm in its resolve to retain the chief. Despite internal division and public ridicule fueled by the team icon, the city refuses to budge. Clevelanders consequently appear as insensitive and backward as those who continue to support the Redmen, Redskins, or Illini.

As the city of Cleveland continues to enjoy its recent improved image and downtown revitalization, must the plague of the Wahoo controversy continue? As a native of Cleveland, I understand the power of "Tribe Fever" and the unabashed pride one feels when wearing Wahoo garb during a winning (or losing) season. Often it is not until we leave northeastern Ohio that we realize the negative image that Wahoo projects. What then can Cleveland do to simultaneously save face and bolster its burgeoning positive city image? I propose that the team finally change the "temporary" Indians label. In a city so proud of its diverse ethnic heritage—African American, Italian American, and Eastern European American to name a few examples—why stand as a bearer of retrograde ethnic politics? Cleveland should take this opportunity to link its positive Midwestern image to the team of which it is so proud. Why not take the advice of the 1915 Cleveland management and change the team's "temporary" name? I propose a shift to the Cleveland Lakers.

The city's revival in the last twenty years has embraced the geographic and aesthetic grandeur of Lake Erie. Disavowing its "mistake on the lake" moniker of the late 1970s, Cleveland has traded aquatic pollution fires for a booming lakeside business district. Attractions such

Witkowski 5

as the Great Lakes Science Center, the Rock and Roll Hall of Fame, and the new Cleveland Browns Stadium take advantage of the beauty of the landscape and take back the lake. Why not continue this trend through one of the city's biggest and highest-profile moneymakers: professional baseball? By changing the team's name to the Lakers, the city would gain national advertisement for one of its major selling points, while simultaneously announcing a new ethnically inclusive image that is appropriate to our wonderfully diverse city. It would be a public relations triumph for the city.

Of course this call will be met with many objections. Why do we have to buckle to pressure? Do we not live in a free country? What fans and citizens alike need to keep in mind is that ideological pressures would not be the sole motivation for this move. Yes, retiring Chief Wahoo would take Cleveland off AIM's hit list. Yes, such a move would promote a kinder and gentler Cleveland. At the same time, however, such a gesture would work toward uniting the community. So much civic division exists over this issue that a renaming could help start to heal these old wounds.

Additionally, this type of change could bring added economic prosperity to the city. First, a change in name will bring a new wave of team merchandise. Licensed sports apparel generates more than a 10-billion-dollar annual retail business in the United States, and teams have proven repeatedly that new uniforms and logos can provide new capital. After all, a new logo for the Seattle Mariners bolstered severely slumping merchandise sales (Lefton). Wahoo devotees need not panic; the booming vintage uniform business will keep him alive, as is demonstrated by the current ability to purchase replica 1940s jerseys with the old Indians logo. Also, good press created by this change will hopefully help increase tourism in Cleveland. If the goodwill created by the Cleveland Lakers can prove half as profitable as the Rock and Roll Hall of Fame, then local businesses will be humming a happy tune. Finally, if history repeats itself, a change to a more culturally inclusive logo could, in and of itself, prove to be a cash cow. When Miami University changed from the Redskins to the Redhawks, it saw alumni donations skyrocket to an unprecedented 25 million dollars (Price). Perhaps a less divisive mascot would prove lucrative to the ball club, the city, and the players themselves. (Sluggers with inoffensive logos make excellent spokesmen.)

Perhaps this proposal sounds far-fetched: Los Angeles may seem to have cornered the market on Lakers. But where is their lake? (The Lakers were formerly the Minneapolis Lakers, where the name makes sense in the "Land of 10,000 Lakes.") Various professional and collegiate sports teams—such as baseball's San Francisco Giants and football's New York Giants—share a team name, so licensing should not be an issue. If Los Angeles has qualms about sharing the name, perhaps Cleveland could persuade Los Angeles to become the Surfers or the Stars—after all, Los Angeles players seem to spend as much time on the big and small screens as on the court.

Now is the perfect time for Cleveland to make this jump. Sportscasters continue to tout the revitalized young Cleveland team as an up-and-coming contender. Perhaps a new look will help usher in a new era of Cleveland baseball. Like expansion teams such as the Florida Marlins and the Arizona Diamondbacks, Cleveland's new look could bring with it a vital sense of civic pride and a World Series ring to boot. Through various dry spells, the Cleveland Indians institution has symbolically turned to the descendants of Sockalexis, asking for goodwill or a latter-generation Penobscot slugger (Fleitz 3). Perhaps the best way to win goodwill, fortunes, and the team's first World Series title since 1948 would be to eschew a grinning life-size Chief Wahoo for the new and improved Cleveland Laker, an oversized furry monster sporting water wings, cleats, and a catcher's mask. His seventh-inning-stretch show could include an air-guitar solo with a baseball bat as he quietly reminds everyone that the Rock Hall is just down the street. Go Lakers and go Cleveland!

Works Cited ●————————————— Center "Works Cited" on a new page.

Adams, David. "Cleveland Indians Investors Watch Case on Native American Names." *Akron Beacon Journal* 6 Apr. 1999. *LexisNexis Academic*. Web. 20 Apr. 2009.

Witkowski 8

Works Cited

Bauman, Michael. "Indians Logo, Mascot Are the Real Mistakes." *Milwaukee Journal Sentinel* 23 Oct. 1997: Sports 1. Print.

Briggs, David. "Churches Go to Bat Against Chief Wahoo." *Cleveland Plain Dealer* 25 Aug. 2000: 1A. Print.

Eitzen, D. Stanley, and Maxine Baca Zinn. "The Dark Side of Sports Symbols." *USA Today Magazine* Jan. 2001: 48. Print.

Fleitz, David L. *Louis Sockalexis: The First Cleveland Indian*. Jefferson: McFarland, 2002. Print.

"Judge Dismisses Charges Against City in Wahoo Protest." *Associated Press* 6 Aug. 2001. *LexisNexis Academic*. Web. 19 Apr. 2009.

Kropk, M. R. "Chief Wahoo Protestors Largely Ignored by Fans." *Austin American Statesman* 6 May 1995: D4. Print.

Lefton, Terry. "Looks Are Everything: For New Franchises, Licensing Battles Must Be Won Long before the Team Even Takes the Field." *Sport* 89 (May 1998): 32. Print.

"MLBP Reaches Youth League Apparel Agreements with Majestic Athletic, Outdoor Cap." *MLB.com*. Major League Baseball, 25 June 2004. Web. 28 Apr. 2009.

"Newspaper Edits Cleveland Indian Logo from Cap Photo." *Associated Press* 31 Mar. 1997. *LexisNexis Academic*. Web. 17 Apr. 2009.

Price, S. L. "The Indian Wars." *Sports Illustrated* 4 Mar. 2002: 66+. *Academic OneFile*. Web. 20 Apr. 2009.

Schneider, Russell. *The Cleveland Indians Encyclopedia*. Philadelphia: Temple UP, 1996. Print.

Staurowsky, Ellen J. "Sockalexis and the Making of the Myth at the Core of the Cleveland's 'Indian' Image." *Team Spirits: The Native American Mascots Controversy*. Ed. C. Richard King and Charles Fruehling Springwood. Lincoln: U of Nebraska P, 2001. 82-106. Print.

Wulf, Steve. "A Brave Move." *Sports Illustrated* 24 Feb. 1992: 7. Print.

Double-space all entries. Indent all but the first line in each entry five spaces.

Alphabetize entries by the last names of the authors or by the first important word in the title if no author is listed.

Italicize the titles of books and periodicals.

Check to make sure all the sources you have cited in your text are in the list of works cited.

21

Documenting Sources in APA Style

Papers written for the social sciences, including government, linguistics, psychology, sociology, and education, frequently use the APA documentation style. For a detailed treatment of APA style, consult the *Publication Manual of the American Psychological Association*, fifth edition (2001), and the *APA Style Guide to Electronic References* (2007), available online.

Elements of APA Documentation

Citing a source in your paper

APA style emphasizes the date of publication. When you cite an author's name in the body of your paper, always include the date of publication. Notice too that APA style includes the abbreviation for page "(p.)" in front of the page number. A comma separates each element of the citation.

> Zukin (2004) observes that teens today begin to shop for themselves at age 13 or 14, "the same age when lower-class children, in the past, became apprentices or went to work in factories" (p. 50).

If the author's name is not mentioned in the sentence, cite the author, date, and page number inside parentheses.

> One sociologist notes that teens today begin to shop for themselves at age 13 or 14, "the same age when lower-class children, in the past, became apprentices or went to work in factories" (Zukin, 2004, p. 50).

The corresponding entry in the references list would be as follows.

> Zukin, S. (2004). *Point of purchase: How shopping changed American culture.* New York: Routledge.

Creating an APA-style references list

To create your references list, go through your paper and find every reference to the sources you consulted during your research. Each in-text citation must have an entry in your references list.

Organize your references list alphabetically by authors' last names or, if no author is listed, the first word in the title other than *a, an,* or *the.* APA style uses three basic forms for entries in the references list: books, periodicals (scholarly journals, newspapers, magazines), and online sources (online library database sources, Web sites, blogs, online newspapers, online magazines, and online government documents).

References entries for books

Orum, A. M. & Chen, X. (2003). *The world of cities: Places in comparative and historical perspective.* Malden, MA: Blackwell.

1. Author's or editor's name.
- List the author's name with the last name first, followed by a comma and the author's initials.
- Join two authors' names with an ampersand.
- If an editor, put "(Ed.)" after the name: Kavanaugh, P. (Ed.).

2. (Year of publication).
- Give the year of publication in parentheses. If no year of publication is given, write *(n.d.)* ("no date") : Smith, S. (n.d.).
- If it is a multivolume edited work, published over a period of more than one year, put the time span in parentheses: Smith, S. (1999–2001).

3. *Title of book.*
- Italicize the title.
- Capitalize only the first word, proper nouns, and the first word after a colon.
- If the title is in a foreign language, copy it exactly as it appears on the title page.

4. Publication information.
- List the city without a state abbreviation or country for major cities known for publishing (New York, Boston), but add the state abbreviation or country for other cities (as in this example). If the publisher is a university named for a state, omit the state abbreviation. If more than one city is given on the title page (as in this example), list only the first.
- Do not shorten or abbreviate words like *University* or *Press.* Omit words such as *Co., Inc.,* and *Publishers.*

References entries for periodicals

Lee, E. (2007). Wired for gender: Experientiality and gender-stereotyping in computer-mediated communication. *Media Psychology, 10, 182–210.*

1. Author's name.
- List the author's name, last name first, followed by the author's initials.
- Join two authors' names with a comma and an ampersand.

2. (Year of publication).
- Give the year the work was published in parentheses.

3. Title of article.
- Do not use quotation marks. If there is a book title in the article title, italicize it.
- Capitalize only the first word of the title, the first word of the subtitle, and any proper nouns in the title.

4. Publication information.
- Italicize the journal name.
- Capitalize all nouns, verbs, and pronouns, and the first word of the journal name. Do not capitalize any article, preposition, or coordinating conjunction unless it is the first word of the title or subtitle.
- Put a comma after the journal name.
- Italicize the volume number and follow it with a comma.
- Give page numbers of the article (see sample references 19 and 20 for more on pagination).

References entries for online sources

Department of Justice. Federal Bureau of Investigation. (2004). Hate crime statistics 2004: Report summary. Retrieved from http://www.fbi.gov/ucr/hc2004/openpage.htm

1. Author's name, associated institution, or organization.
- List the author's name, if given, with the last name first, followed by the author's initials.
- If the only authority you find is a group or organization (as in this example), list its name as the author.

■ If the author or organization is not identified, begin the reference with the title of the document.

2. (Date of publication).
■ List the date the site was produced, last revised, or copyrighted.

3. Title of page or article.
■ If you are citing a page or article that has a title, treat the title like an article in a periodical. If you are citing an entire Web site, treat the name like a book.
■ If the Web site has no title, list it by author or creator.

4. Retrieval date and URL
■ List the date of retrieval if the content may change or be updated. For published books and scholarly articles, do not list the date of retrieval.
■ Do not place angle brackets around the URL or end with a period.

APA In-Text Citations

1. Author named in your text

Influential sociologist Daniel Bell (1973) noted a shift in the United States to the "postindustrial society" (p. 3).

2. Author not named in your text

In 1997, the Gallup poll reported that 55% of adults in the United States think secondhand smoke is "very harmful," compared to only 36% in 1994 (Saad, 1997, p. 4).

3. Work by a single author

(Bell, 1973, p. 3)

4. Work by two authors

Notice that APA uses an ampersand (&) with multiple authors' names rather than *and*.

(Suzuki & Irabu, 2002, p. 404)

5. Work by three to five authors
The authors' last names follow the order of the title page.

(Francisco, Vaughn, & Romano, 2001, p. 7)

Subsequent references can use the first name and *et al.*

(Francisco et al., 2001, p. 17)

6. Work by six or more authors
Use the first author's last name and *et al.* for all in-text references.

(Swallit et al., 2004, p. 49)

7. Work by a group or organization
Identify the group author in the text and place only the page number in parentheses.

The National Organization for Women (2001) observed that this "generational shift in attitudes towards marriage and childrearing" will have profound consequences (p. 325).

8. Work by an unknown author
Use a shortened version of the title (or the full title if it is short) in place of the author's name. Capitalize all key words in the title. If it is an article title, place it in quotation marks.

("Derailing the Peace Process," 2003, p. 44)

9. Quotations of 40 words or longer
Indent long quotations five spaces and omit quotation marks. Note that the period appears before the parentheses in an indented block quote.

Orlean (2001) has attempted to explain the popularity of the painter Thomas Kinkade:

People like to own things they think are valuable. . . . The high price of limited editions is part of their appeal; it implies that they are choice and exclusive, and that only a certain class of people will be able to afford them. (p. 128)

APA References List: Books

10. Book by one author
The author's last name comes first, followed by a comma and the author's initials.

> Ball, E. (2000). *Slaves in the family*. New York: Ballantine Books.

If an editor, put "(Ed.)" in parentheses after the name.

> Kavanagh, P. (Ed.). (1969). *Lapped furrows*. New York: Hand Press.

11. Book by two authors
Join two authors' names with a comma and ampersand.

> Hardt, M., & Negri, A. (2000). *Empire*. Cambridge, MA: Harvard University Press.

If editors, use "(Eds.)" after the names.

> McClelland, D., & Eismann, K. (Eds).

12. Book by three or more authors
Write out all of the authors' names up to six. The seventh and subsequent authors can be abbreviated to "et al."

> Anders, K., Child, H., Davis, K., Logan, O., Petersen, J., Tymes, J., et al.

13. Chapter in an edited collection
Add "In" after the selection title and before the names of the editor(s).

> Howard, A. (1997). Labor, history, and sweatshops in the new global economy. In A. Ross (Ed.), *No sweat: Fashion, free trade, and the rights of garment workers* (pp. 151–72). New York: Verso.

14. Published dissertation or thesis
If the dissertation you are citing is published by University Microfilms International (UMI), provide the order number as the last item in the entry.

> Price, J. J. (1998). Flight maps: Encounters with nature in modern American culture. *Dissertation Abstracts International, 59*(5), 1635. (UMI No. 9835237)

15. Government document
When the author and publisher are identical, use "Author" as the name of the publisher.

> U.S. Environmental Protection Agency. (2002). *Respiratory health effects of passive smoking: Lung cancer and other disorders.* (EPA Publication No. 600/6-90/006 F). Washington, DC: Author.

APA References List: Periodicals

16. Article by one author

> Kellogg, R. T. (2001). Competition for working memory among writing processes. *American Journal of Psychology, 114,* 175–192.

17. Article by multiple authors
Write out all of the authors' names, up to six authors. The seventh and subsequent authors can be abbreviated to "et al."

> Blades, J., & Rowe-Finkbeiner, K. (2006). The motherhood manifesto. *The Nation, 282*(20) 11–16.

18. Article by a group or organization

> National Organization for Women (2002). Where to find feminists in Austin. *The NOW guide for Austin women.* Austin, TX: Chapter Press.

19. Article in a journal with continuous pagination
Include the volume number and the year, but not the issue number.

> Engen, R., & Steen, S. (2000). The power to punish: Discretion and sentencing reform in the war on drugs. *American Journal of Sociology, 105,* 1357–1395.

20. Article in a journal paginated by issue
List the issue number in parentheses (not italicized) after the volume number. For a popular magazine that does not commonly use volume numbers, use the season or date of publication.

> McGinn, D. (2006, June 5). Marriage by the numbers. *Newsweek,* 40–48.

21. Monthly publication

> Barlow, J. P. (1998, January). Africa rising: Everything you know about Africa
> is wrong. *Wired, 142–158.*

22. Newspaper article

> Hagenbaugh, B. (2005, April 25). Grads welcome an uptick in hiring. *USA
> Today,* p. A1.

APA References List: Library Database Sources

23. Document from a library database

Increasingly, articles are accessed online. Because URLs frequently change, many scholarly publishers have begun to use a Digital Object Identifier (DOI), a unique alphanumeric string that is permanent. If a DOI is available, use the DOI.

APA no longer requires listing the names of well-known databases. The article below was retrieved from the PsychARTICLES database, but there is no need to list the database, the retrieval date, or the URL if the DOI is listed.

> Erdfelder, E. (2008). Experimental psychology: Good news. *Experimental
> Psychology, 55*(1), 1–2. doi: 0.1027/1618-3169.55.1.1

APA References List: Online Sources

24. Online publication by a known author

Authorship is sometimes hard to discern for online sources. If you do have an author or creator to cite, follow the rules for periodicals and books.

> Carr, A. (2003. May 22). AAUW applauds senate support of title IX resolution.
> Retrieved from http://www.aauw.org/about/newsroom/press_releases
> /030522. cfm

25. Online publication by a group or organization

If the only authority you find is a group or organization, list its name as the author.

> Girls Incorporated. (2003). Girls' bill of rights. Retrieved from
> http://www.girlsinc.org/gc/page.php?id=9

26. Article in an online scholarly journal

Brown, B. (2004). The order of service: the practical management of customer interaction. *Sociological Research Online, 9*(4). Retrieved from http://www.socresonline.org.uk/9/4/brown.html

27. Article in an online newspaper

Slevin, C. (2005, April 25). Lawmakers want to put limits on private toll roads. *Boulder Daily Camera*. Retrieved from http:// www.dailycamera.com

28. Article in an online magazine

Pein, C. (2005, April 20). Is Al-Jazeera ready for prime time? *Salon*. Retrieved from http://www.salon.com

APA References List: Other Sources

29. Television program

Burgess, M., & Green, M. (Writers). (2004). Irregular around the margins. [Television series episode]. In D. Chase (Producer), *The sopranos*. New York: HBO.

30. Film, Video, or DVD

Kaurismäki, A. (Director). (1999). *Leningrad cowboys go America* [DVD]. United States: MGM.

31. Musical recording

List both the title of the song and the title of the album or CD. In the in-text citation, include side or track numbers.

Lowe, N. (2001). Lately I've let things slide. On *The convincer* [CD]. Chapel Hill, NC: Yep Roc Records.

PART 6

Contemporary Arguments

PART 6　Contemporary Arguments

22. Negotiating
    the Environment 315

23. Confronting Sexual Difference
    353

24. Globalization: Importing
    and Exporting America 400

25. Science and Ethics 427

26. Privacy 472

27. Regulating Substances/
    Regulating Bodies 515

28. New Media 574

22

Negotiating the Environment

Dams on the Klamath River in Oregon provide water to power plants, which in turn supply clean electricity. But dams also affect fish and other wildlife, farmers, and Native Americans who live along the river. When people decide to build a dam, whose priorities should be considered?

American Environmentalism

As noted in the first chapter, Rachel Carson's *Silent Spring* in 1962 stimulated the environmental movement in the United States. Carson's book explicitly indicted pesticides commonly used in the agriculture industry, particularly DDT, but implicitly she was arguing for something broader—for a new sense of our relationship to our environment, for the conviction that we should be living in balance with nature, not in domination over it. Thus, Carson's book ultimately influenced not only agricultural practice but also efforts to protect endangered species, to regulate population growth, and to clean up our air and water resources. When President Richard Nixon created the Environmental Protection Agency in 1973, environmental concern became institutionalized in the United States; most states created their own departments of natural resources or environmental protection soon afterward.

> We are the most dangerous species of life on the planet, and every other species, even the earth itself, has cause to fear our power to exterminate. But we are also the only species which, when it chooses to do so, will go to great effort to save what it might destroy.
>
> —WALLACE STEGNER

In part, Rachel Carson was successful because her appeals struck a chord deep within many Americans. For in a very real sense environmentalism is ingrained within the American character. It derives from a respect for the land—the American Eden—that is evident in the legend of Rip Van Winkle, in the work of Hudson River painters such as Thomas Cole, in the landscape architecture of Frederick Law Olmsted, in Henry David Thoreau's *Walden* and in Ralph Waldo

315

Emerson's Transcendentalist writings in the 1850s, in John Muir's testimonials about Yosemite, and in Theodore Roosevelt's withdrawals into the Badlands and campaign to begin a system of national parks. Of course, the exploitation of the American green world for profit is also ingrained in our national character. Even as some Americans were revering the land as a special landscape that sustained them physically and spiritually, pioneers moving westward were subduing it for their own purposes, in the process spoiling rivers and air and virgin forests—and native peoples—in the name of development.

In this photograph of an environmental rally in Washington, D.C., what images evoke environmental themes?

Contemporary Arguments

Today, tensions between preserving nature and using nature are perhaps as high as they have ever been. These tensions help to explain why environmental issues remain so prevalent in public discourse.

- What are—and what should be—the relationships among science, technology, and the environment?
- What is the proper relationship between people and the natural environment?
- How can humans balance resource development and resource protection—with resources including everything from timber and coal to streams and animals?
- What are the nature and extent of global warming, and what human actions does it require?
- How can poorer nations develop economically without negative global environmental repercussions?

Such questions are debated each day in all media, especially as organized environmental groups are legion, ranging from the activist Earth First! (whose

10,000 members sometimes advocate direct action in support of environmental aims) to more mainstream groups such as the Sierra Club or the Nature Conservancy. The Nature Conservancy has created a membership of nearly a million in an explicit effort to create partnerships between scientists and businesspeople in the interests of environmental reform. On the other hand, conservatives such as Rush Limbaugh have often ridiculed the efforts of environmentalists in the interest of a relatively unbridled developmentalism that is in the optimistic tradition of nineteenth-century free enterprise.

Debates about environmental issues are part and parcel of American culture. In the following pages you will find a sampling of the arguments concerning our relationship to the natural world. The first selections (by Edward O. Wilson, N. Scott Momaday,

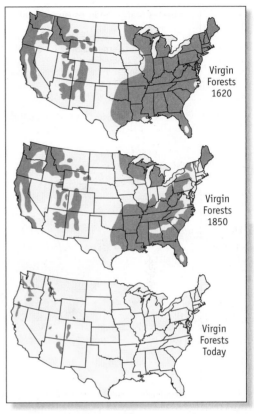

How virgin forests have diminished in the continental united states.

Richard Bullard, and Wendell Berry) discuss philosophical issues and relate environmental ethics to human societies and practices—thereby providing context for specific arguments, such as those about global warming.

Next, this chapter focuses on different perspectives about global warming, from Al Gore's moral appeal to Americans to dramatically change their energy habits to Christopher Horner's exhortation that global warming is merely a phenomenon in Earth's history that bears little or no relationship to human practices. How reliable is the scientific evidence that shows warming in the Earth's atmosphere? How responsible are humans for climate changes? This section also discusses causal relationships and how to show causality. Do some creature comforts have to be given up in order for people to survive in a healthy environment? What choices must we make among economic growth, technological advancement and innovation, the preservation of green spaces, environmental quality, and biodiversity—and what should be our priorities?

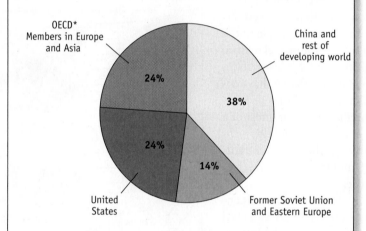

The United States Produces Most Greenhouse Gases

The United States produces about a quarter of the world's carbon dioxide emissions—the major cause of global warming. While U.S. emissions are expected to drop to 21 percent of the total by 2020, those from China and the rest of the developing world will rise from the current 38 percent to 50 percent.

Worldwide Carbon Emissions by Region, 1996

OECD* Members in Europe and Asia — 24%

China and rest of developing world — 38%

United States — 24%

Former Soviet Union and Eastern Europe — 14%

* Organization for Economic Cooperation and Development

Source: Environmental Protection Agency Web site on global warming: www.epa.gov/global_missions/international/projections.html. Reproduced in *CQ Researcher* issue on global warming, January 26, 2001.

Edward O. Wilson

The Conservation Ethic

Edward O. Wilson, a long-time Harvard professor and an entomologist with a special interest in ants, is one of the world's leading naturalists. He has won the Pulitzer Prize (twice) and the National Medal of Science, among other awards. Many of his books, including The Diversity of Life, Naturalist, *and* Biophilia, *emphasize the vitality of species diversity and decry activities that cause the extinction of particular species. Wilson points out the value of even the smallest bugs and plants as integral parts of life systems. The following text, from* Biophilia *(1984), outlines important connections between ecology and ethics.*

When very little is known about an important subject, the questions people raise are almost invariably ethical. Then as knowledge grows, they become more concerned with information and amoral, in other words more narrowly intellectual. Finally, as understanding becomes sufficiently complete, the questions turn ethical again. Environmentalism is now

[handwritten marginalia at top: environmentalism is now about facts, but is moving to "do what is right" again]

passing from the first to the second phase, and there is reason to hope that it will proceed directly on to the third.

2   The future of the conservation movement depends on such an advance in moral reasoning. Its maturation is linked to that of biology and a new hybrid field, bioethics, that deals with the many technological advances recently made possible by biology. Philosophers and scientists are applying a more formal analysis to such complex problems as the allocations of scarce organ transplants, heroic but extremely expensive efforts to prolong life, and the possible use of genetic engineering to alter human heredity. They have only begun to consider the relationships between human beings and organisms with the same rigor. It is clear that the key to precision lies in the understanding of motivation, the ultimate reasons why people care about one thing but not another—why, say, they prefer a city with a park to a city alone. The goal is to join emotion with the rational analysis of emotion in order to create a deeper and more enduring conservation ethic.

[handwritten marginalia: people must care, but also see factual evidence]

Aldo Leopold, the pioneer ecologist and author of *A Sand County Almanac*, defined an ethic as a set of rules invented to meet circumstances so new or intricate, or else encompassing responses so far in the future, that the average person cannot foresee the final outcome. What is good for you and me at this moment might easily sour within ten years, and what seems ideal for the next few decades could ruin future generations. That is why any ethic worthy of the name has to encompass the distant future. The relationships of ecology and the human mind are too intricate to be understood entirely by unaided intuition, by common sense—that overrated capacity composed of the set of prejudices we acquire by the age of eighteen.

[handwritten marginalia: appeal for ethos]

4   Values are time-dependent, making them all the more difficult to carve in stone. We want health, security, freedom, and pleasure for ourselves and our families. For distant generations we wish the same but not at any great personal cost. The difficulty created for the conservation ethic is that natural selection has programmed people to think mostly in physiological time. Their minds travel back and forth across hours, days, or at most a hundred years. The forests may all be cut, radiation slowly rise, and the winters grow steadily colder, but if the effects are unlikely to become decisive for a few generations, very few people will be stirred to revolt. Ecological and evolutionary time, spanning centuries and millennia, can be conceived in an intellectual mode but has no immediate emotional impact. Only through an unusual amount of education and reflective thought do people come to respond emotionally to far-off events and hence place a high premium on posterity.

5   The deepening of the conservation ethic requires a greater measure of evolutionary realism, including a valuation of ourselves as opposed to other people. What do we really owe our remote descendants? At the risk of offending some readers I will suggest: Nothing. Obligations simply lose their meaning across centuries. But what do we owe ourselves in planning for them? Everything. If human existence has any verifiable meaning, it is that our passions and toil are enabling mechanisms to continue that existence unbroken, unsullied, and progressively secure. It is for ourselves, and not for them or any

abstract morality, that we think into the distant future. The precise manner in which we take this measure, how we put it into words, is crucially important. For if the whole process of our life is directed toward preserving our species and personal genes, preparing for future generations is an expression of the highest morality of which human beings are capable. It follows that the destruction of the natural world in which the brain was assembled over millions of years is a risky step. And the worst gamble of all is to let species slip into extinction wholesale, for even if the natural environment is conceded more ground later, it can never be reconstituted in its original diversity. The first rule of the tinkerer, Aldo Leopold reminds us, is to keep all the pieces.

6   This proposition can be expressed another way. What event likely to happen during the next few years will our descendants most regret? Everyone agrees, defense ministers and environmentalists alike, that the worst thing possible is global nuclear war. If it occurs the entire human species is endangered; life as normal human beings wish to live it would come to an end. With that terrible truism acknowledged, it must be added that if no country pulls the trigger the worst thing that will *probably* happen—in fact is already

Aldo Leopold

Excerpts from "The Land Ethic"

Aldo Leopold (1887–1948) was one of the most influential nature writers of the twentieth century and one of the founders of modern ecology. He was completing his essay "The Land Ethic" when he died while fighting a brushfire in a neighbor's field. It appeared in Leopold's posthumously published A Sand County Almanac *(1949). As the following excerpts illustrate, the essay offers a new way of understanding our relationship with the environment—an understanding that has powerfully influenced environmental policy debates in the United States.*

The Ethical Sequence
The first ethics dealt with the relation between individuals; the Mosaic Decalogue is an example. Later accretions dealt with the relation between the individual and society. The Golden Rule tries to integrate the individual to society; democracy to integrate social organization to the individual.

There is as yet no ethic dealing with man's relation to land and to the animals and plants which grow upon it.

The Community Concept
All ethics so far evolved rest upon a single premise: that the individual is a member of a community of interdependent parts. His instincts prompt him to compete for his place in that community, but his ethics prompt him also to cooperate (perhaps in order that there may be a place to compete for).

The land ethic simply enlarges the boundaries of the community to include soils, waters, plants, and animals, or collectively: the land.

well underway—is not energy depletion, economic collapse, conventional war, or even the expansion of totalitarian governments. As tragic as these catastrophes would be for us, they can be repaired within a few generations. The one process now going on that will take millions of years to correct is the loss of genetic and species diversity by the destruction of natural habitats. This is the folly our descendants are least likely to forgive us.

7   Extinction is accelerating and could reach ruinous proportions during the next twenty years. Not only are birds and mammals vanishing but such smaller forms as mosses, insects, and minnows. A conservative estimate of the current extinction rate is one thousand species a year, mostly from the destruction of forests and other key habitats in the tropics. By the 1990s the figure is expected to rise past ten thousand species a year (one species per hour). During the next thirty years fully one million species could be erased.

8   Whatever the exact figure—and the primitive state of evolutionary biology permits us only to set broad limits—the current rate is still the greatest in recent geological history. It is also much higher than the rate of production of new species by ongoing evolution, so that the net result is a steep decline in

The Ecological Conscience
Obligations have no meaning without conscience, and the problem we face is the extension of the social conscience from people to land.

Substitutes for a Land Ethic
A system of conservation based solely on economic self-interest is hopelessly lopsided. It tends to ignore, and thus eventually to eliminate, many elements in the land community that lack commercial value, but that are (as far as we know) essential to its healthy functioning.

The Land Pyramid
Land, then, is not merely soil; it is a fountain of energy flowing through a circuit of soils, plants, and animals. Food chains are the living channels which conduct energy upward; death and decay return it to the soil.

Land Health and the A–B Cleavage
We see repeated the same basic paradoxes: man the conqueror *versus* man the biotic citizen; science the sharpener of his sword *versus* science the searchlight on his universe; land the slave and servant *versus* land the collective organism.

The Outlook
Examine each question in terms of what is ethically and esthetically right, as well as what is economically expedient. A thing is right when it tends to preserve the integrity, stability, and beauty of the biotic community. It is wrong when it tends otherwise. ■

the world's standing diversity. Whole categories of organisms that emerged over the past ten million years, among them the familiar condors, rhinoceros, manatees, and gorillas, are close to the end. For most of their species, the last individuals to exist in the wild state could well be those living there today. It is a grave error to dismiss the hemorrhaging as a "Darwinian" process, in which species autonomously come and go and man is just the latest burden on the environment. Human destructiveness is something

The plight of the bonobo, an endangered species found only in the Congo (shown here in a sanctuary in Kinshasa, the Congo), raises questions about the impact of war on the ecosystems of the Congo. What sort of argument is implied by the photograph?

new under the sun. Perhaps it is matched by the giant meteorites thought to smash into the Earth and darken the atmosphere every hundred million years or so (the last one apparently arrived 65 million years ago and contributed to the extinction of the dinosaurs). But even that interval is ten thousand times longer than the entire history of civilization. In our own brief lifetime humanity will suffer an incomparable loss in aesthetic value, practical benefits from biological research, and worldwide biological stability. Deep mines of biological diversity will have been dug out and carelessly discarded in the course of environmental exploitation, without our even knowing fully what they contained.

9   The time is late for simple answers and divine guidance, and ideological confrontation has just about run its course. Little can be gained by throwing sand in the gears of industrialized society, even less by perpetuating the belief that we can solve any problem created by earlier spasms of human ingenuity. The need now is for a great deal more knowledge of the true biological dimensions of our problem, civility in the face of common need, and the style of leadership once characterized by Walter Bagehot as agitated moderation.

10   Ethical philosophy is a much more important subject than ordinarily conceded in societies dominated by religious and ideological orthodoxy. It faces an especially severe test in the complexities of the conservation problem. When the time scale is expanded to encompass ecological events, it becomes far more difficult to be certain about the wisdom of any particular decision. Everything is riddled with ambiguity; the middle way turns hard and general formulas fail with dispiriting consistency. Consider that a man who is a villain to his contemporaries can become a hero to his descendants. If a tyrant were to carefully preserve his nation's land and natural resources for his personal needs while keeping his people in poverty, he might unintentionally bequeath a rich,

healthful environment to a reduced population for enjoyment in later, democratic generations. This caudillo will have improved the long-term welfare of his people by giving them greater resources and more freedom of action. The exact reverse can occur as well: today's hero can be tomorrow's destroyer. A popular political leader who unleashes the energies of his people and raises their standard of living might simultaneously promote a population explosion, overuse of resources, flight to the cities, and poverty for later generations. Of course these two extreme examples are caricatures and unlikely to occur just so, but they suffice to illustrate that, in ecological and evolutionary time, good does not automatically flow from good or evil from evil. To choose what is best for the near future is easy. To choose what is best for the distant future is also easy. But to choose what is best for both the near and distant futures is a hard task, often internally contradictory, and requiring ethical codes yet to be formulated. ■

N. Scott Momaday

The Way to Rainy Mountain

N. Scott Momaday (1934–) tells us something about himself in the following introductory chapter from his 1969 book The Way to Rainy Mountain, *an account of his homeland in the Wichita Mountains of Oklahoma. Momaday's father was a Kiowa and his mother was a descendant of white pioneers, and hence a concern with the uneasy relationships among American subcultures has always permeated his work. In addition to essays and fiction, Momaday has created paintings, memoirs, and plays. He is currently the poet laureate of Oklahoma.*

A single knoll rises out of the plain in Oklahoma, north and west of the Wichita Range. For many people, the Kiowas, it is an old landmark, and they gave it the name Rainy Mountain. The hardest weather in the world is there. Winter brings blizzards, hot tornadic winds arise in the spring, and in summer the prairie is an anvil's edge. The grass turns brittle and brown, and it cracks beneath your feet. There are green belts along the rivers and creeks, linear groves of hickory and pecan, willow and witch hazel. At a distance in July or August the steaming foliage seems almost to writhe in fire. Great green and yellow grasshoppers are everywhere in the tall grass, popping up like corn to sting the flesh, and tortoises crawl about on the red earth, going nowhere in the plenty of time. Loneliness is an aspect of the land. All things in the plain are isolate; there is no confusion of objects in the eye, but *one* hill or *one* tree or *one* man. To look upon that landscape in the early morning, with the sun at your back, is to lose the sense of proportion. Your imagination comes to life, and this, you think, is where Creation was begun.

2   I returned to Rainy Mountain in July. My grandmother had died in the spring, and I wanted to be at her grave. She had lived to be very old and at last infirm. Her only living daughter was with her when she died, and I was told that in death her face was that of a child.

3   I like to think of her as a child. When she was born, the Kiowas were living that last great moment of their history. For more than a hundred years they had controlled the open range from the Smoky Hill River to the Red, from the headwaters of the Canadian to the fork of the Arkansas and Cimarron. In alliance with the Comanches, they had ruled the whole of the southern plains. War was their sacred business, and they were among the finest horsemen the world has ever known. But warfare for the Kiowas was preeminently a matter of disposition rather than of survival, and they never understood the grim, unrelenting advance of the U.S. Cavalry. When at last, divided and ill-provisioned, they were driven onto the Staked Plains in the cold rains of autumn, they fell into panic. In Palo Duro Canyon they abandoned their crucial stores to pillage and had nothing then but their lives. In order to save themselves, they surrendered to the soldiers at Fort Sill and were imprisoned in the old stone corral that now stands as a military museum. My grandmother was spared the humiliation of those high gray walls by eight or ten years, but she must have known from birth the affliction of defeat, the dark brooding of old warriors.

4   Her name was Aho, and she belonged to the last culture to evolve in North America. Her forebears came down from the high country in western Montana nearly three centuries ago. They were a mountain people, a mysterious tribe of hunters whose language has never been positively classified in any major group. In the late seventeenth century they began a long migration to the south and east. It was a journey toward the dawn, and it led to a golden age. Along the way the Kiowas were befriended by the Crows, who gave them the culture and religion of the Plains. They acquired horses, and their ancient nomadic spirit was suddenly free of the ground. They acquired Tai-me, the sacred Sun Dance doll, from that moment the object and symbol of their worship, and so shared in the divinity of the sun. Not least, they acquired the sense of destiny, therefore courage and pride. When they entered upon the southern Plains they had been transformed. No longer were they slaves to the simple necessity of survival; they were a lordly and dangerous society of fighters and thieves, hunters and priests of the sun. According to their origin myth, they entered the world through a hollow log. From one point of view, their migration was the fruit of an old prophecy, for indeed they emerged from a sunless world.

5   Although my grandmother lived out her long life in the shadow of Rainy Mountain, the immense landscape of the continental interior lay like memory in her blood. She could tell of the Crows, whom she had never seen, and of the Black Hills, where she had never been. I wanted to see in reality what she had seen more perfectly in the mind's eye, and traveled fifteen hundred miles to begin my pilgrimage.

6   Yellowstone, it seemed to me, was the top of the world, a region of deep lakes and dark timber, canyons and waterfalls. But, beautiful as it is, one might have the sense of confinement there. The skyline in all directions is

close at hand, the high wall of the woods and deep cleavages of shade. There is a perfect freedom in the mountains, but it belongs to the eagle and the elk, the badger and the bear. The Kiowas reckoned their stature by the distance they could see, and they were bent and blind in the wilderness.

7   Descending eastward, the highland meadows are a stairway to the plain. In July the inland slope of the Rockies is luxuriant with flax and buckwheat, stonecrop and larkspur. The earth unfolds and the limit of the land recedes. Clusters of trees, and animals grazing far in the distance, cause the vision to reach away and wonder to build upon the mind. The sun follows a longer course in the day, and the sky is immense beyond all comparison. The great billowing clouds that sail upon it are shadows that move upon the grain like water, dividing light. Farther down, in the land of the Crows and Blackfeet, the plain is yellow. Sweet clover takes hold of the hills and bends upon itself to cover and seat the soil. There the Kiowas paused on their way; they had come to the place where they must change their lives. The sun is at home on the plains. Precisely there does it have the certain character of a god. When the Kiowas came to the land of the Crows, they could see the dark lees of the hills at dawn across the Bighorn River, the profusion of light on the grain shelves, the oldest deity ranging after the solstices. Not yet would they veer southward to the caldron of the land that lay below; they must wean their blood from the northern winter and hold the mountains a while longer in their view. They bore Tai-me in procession to the east.

8   A dark mist lay over the Black Hills, and the land was like iron. At the top of a ridge I caught sight of Devil's Tower upthrust against the gray sky as if in the birth of time the core of the earth had broken through its crust and the motion of the world was begun. There are things in nature that engender an awful quiet in the heart of man; Devil's Tower is one of them. Two centuries ago, because they could not do otherwise, the Kiowas made a legend at the base of the rock. My grandmother said:

> Eight children were there at play, seven sisters and their brother. Suddenly the boy was struck dumb; he trembled and began to run upon his hands and feet. His fingers became claws, and his body was covered with fur. Directly there was a bear where the boy had been. The sisters were terrified; they ran, and the bear after them. They came to the stump of a great tree, and the tree spoke to them. It bade them climb upon it, and as they did so it began to rise into the air. The bear came to kill them, but they were just beyond its reach. It reared against the tree and scored the bark all around with its claws. The seven sisters were borne into the sky, and they became the stars of the Big Dipper.

From that moment, and so long as the legend lives, the Kiowas have kinsmen in the night sky. Whatever they were in the mountains, they could be no more. However tenuous their well-being, however much they had suffered and would suffer again, they had found a way out of the wilderness.

9   My grandmother had a reverence for the sun, a holy regard that now is all but gone out of mankind. There was a wariness in her, and an ancient awe. She

was a Christian in her later years, but she had come a long way about, and she never forgot her birthright. As a child she had been to the Sun Dances; she had taken part in those annual rites, and by them she had learned the restoration of her people in the presence of Tai-me. She was about seven when the last Kiowa Sun Dance was held in 1887 on the Washita River above Rainy Mountain Creek. The buffalo were gone. In order to consummate the ancient sacrifice—to impale the head of a buffalo bull upon the medicine tree—a delegation of old men journeyed into Texas, there to beg and barter for an animal from the Goodnight herd. She was ten when the Kiowas came together for the last time as a living Sun Dance culture. They could find no buffalo; they had to hang an old hide from the sacred tree. Before the dance could begin, a company of soldiers rode out from Fort Sill under orders to disperse the tribe. Forbidden without cause the essential act of their faith, having seen the wild herds slaughtered and left to rot upon the ground, the Kiowas backed away forever from the medicine tree. That was July 20, 1890, at the great bend of the Washita. My grandmother was there. Without bitterness, and for as long as she lived, she bore a vision of deicide.

10   Now that I can have her only in memory, I see my grandmother in the several postures that were peculiar to her: standing at the wood stove on a winter morning and turning meat in a great iron skillet; sitting at the south window, bent above her beadwork, and afterwards, when her vision failed, looking down for a long time into the fold of her hands; going out upon a cane, very slowly as she did when the weight of age came upon her; praying. I remember her most often at prayer. She made long, rambling prayers out of suffering and hope, having seen many things. I was never sure that I had the right to hear, so exclusive were they of all mere custom and company. The last time I saw her she prayed standing by the side of her bed at night, naked to the waist, the light of a kerosene lamp moving upon her dark skin. Her long, black hair, always drawn and braided in the day, lay upon her shoulders and against her breasts like a shawl. I do not speak Kiowa, and I never understood her prayers, but there was something inherently sad in the sound, some merest hesitation upon the syllables of sorrow. She began in a high and descending pitch, exhausting her breath to silence then again and again—and always the same intensity of effort, of something that is, and is not, like urgency in the human voice. Transported so in the dancing light among the shadows of her room, she seemed beyond the reach of time. But that was illusion; I think I knew then that I should not see her again.

11   Houses are like sentinels in the plain, old keepers of the weather watch. There, in a very little while, wood takes on the appearance of great age. All colors wear soon away in the wind and rain, and then the wood is burned gray and the grain appears and the nails turn red with rust. The windowpanes are black and opaque; you imagine there is nothing within, and indeed there are many ghosts, bones given up to the land. They stand here and there against the sky, and you approach them for a longer time than you expect. They belong in the distance; it is their domain.

12   Once there was a lot of sound in my grandmother's house, a lot of coming and going, feasting and talk. The summers there were full of excitement and reunion. The Kiowas are a summer people; they abide the cold and keep to themselves, but when the season turns and the land becomes warm and vital they cannot hold still; an old love of going returns upon them. The aged visitors who came to my grandmother's house when I was a child were made of lean and leather, and they bore themselves upright. They wore great black hats and bright ample shirts that shook in the wind. They rubbed fat upon their hair and wound their braids with strips of colored cloth. Some of them painted their faces and carried the scars of old and cherished enmities. They were an old council of warlords, come to remind and be reminded of who they were. Their wives and daughters served them well. The women might indulge themselves; gossip was at once the mark and compensation of their servitude. They made loud and elaborate talk among themselves, full of jest and gesture, fright and false alarm. They went abroad in fringed and flowered shawls, bright beadwork and German silver. They were at home in the kitchen, and they prepared meals that were banquets.

13   There were frequent prayer meetings, and great nocturnal feasts. When I was a child I played with my cousins outside, where the lamplight fell upon the ground and the singing of the old people rose up around us and carried away into the darkness. There were a lot of good things to eat, a lot of laughter and surprise. And afterwards, when the quiet returned, I lay down with my grandmother and could hear the frogs away by the river and feel the motion of the air.

14   Now there is a funeral silence in the rooms, the endless wake of some final word. The walls have closed in upon my grandmother's house. When I returned to it in mourning, I saw for the first time in my life how small it was. It was late at night, and there was a white moon, nearly full. I sat for a long time on the stone steps by the kitchen door. From there I could see out across the land; I could see the long row of trees by the creek, the low light upon the rolling plains, and the stars of the Big Dipper. Once I looked at the moon and caught sight of a strange thing. A cricket had perched upon the handrail, only a few inches away from me. My line of vision was such that the creature filled the moon like a fossil. It had gone there, I thought, to live and die, for there, of all places, was its small definition made whole and eternal. A warm wind rose up and purled like the longing within me.

15   The next morning I awoke at dawn and went out on the dirt road to Rainy Mountain. It was already hot, and the grasshoppers began to fill the air. Still, it was early in the morning, and the birds sang out of the shadows. The long yellow grass on the mountain shone in the bright light, and a scissortail hied above the land. There, where it ought to be, at the end of a long and legendary way, was my grandmother's grave. Here and there on the dark stones were ancestral names. Looking back once, I saw the mountain and came away. ■

Robert Bullard

How Race Affected the Federal Government's Response to Katrina

Dr. Robert Bullard serves as director of the Environmental Justice Resource Center at Clark Atlanta University. As an African-American lawyer, he became interested in environmental justice during the 1970s when he recognized that environmental resources were inequitably distributed and that environmental burdens were inequitably placed upon impoverished and minority social groups. In the following talk (notice how the language use reflects the oral delivery), Bullard speaks about ongoing issues of environmental racism in Louisiana in the aftermath of Hurricane Katrina. He raises questions about race, the communities' distrust of federal and local agencies, and housing laws and discrimination.

We've documented at least a dozen hurricanes in the South and how African-American communities have fared when it comes to the response, the post-response, in terms of how government has actually dealt with aid, insurance, small business loans, how the Red Cross has dealt with it, etc. But I'm going to get to that in the next couple of minutes.

2 First I want to get to how government has responded when it comes to terrorism, as related to the threat posed by the possibility of the release of some type of bacteria or bioterrorist threat. I'm sure you remember the case of the anthrax threat in Washington, D.C. It's where, in 2001, letters were sent and threats were sent to the U.S. Senate, and they were also sent through the U.S. Post Office, the Brentwood Section Post Office. And the Senate was immediately evacuated, and the Senate staff—predominantly white—were immediately given health clearance and medical exams and the Hart Senate Office Building was quarantined, and the senators were just cordoned, you know, pushed off and looked at, and everything was done in a way that was very efficient and thorough.

3 But the Brentwood Post Office—and we know who works at the post office, mostly people who look like me—was not notified until several days later. Two postal workers died. So you get treatment from one way in terms of how the government responds, in terms of health and protection of health in terms of the Senate, mostly white, and the post office, postal workers, mostly black, night and day.

4 So, if you talk about homeland security and emergency response, consider the fact that the government has historically responded in very different ways if the threat, the imminent threat, is against white people versus black people and other people of color. Let me just go through hurricanes. And what we did is we looked at various hurricanes, how and what happened and the damage and what the response was.

5 Hurricane Betsy was a hurricane that hit New Orleans, and a lot of people like to refer to Betsy. This is 1965—what happened in New Orleans and in

terms of the levee breaching and the Lower Ninth Ward being flooded and the fact that there are still people in the Lower Ninth Ward who believe that the levee was breached on purpose by the mayor and his officials to save the white areas. And so, it's—in some cases—it is an urban myth. In other cases, people believe it, and therefore, it becomes real. And probably the reason why there were fewer deaths in the Lower Ninth Ward [after Katrina] is because people, older people, remember Betsy and remember being trapped in their attics with no way to get through, and so a lot of people during Katrina in the Lower Ninth Ward had hatchets and axes in their attics and were able to chop through, and other places as well. So we have the story of the breaching of the Ninth Ward—of the levee and flooding of the Ninth Ward on purpose. *Person saying you believe it*

6   Hurricane Betsy created not only devastation, but it also created a landfill that created a Superfund site in a black neighborhood, the Agriculture Street Landfill. Most of the debris from Hurricane Betsy in 1965 was put in a landfill in a black neighborhood in New Orleans, and so the people in the Agriculture Street community, Press Park area, have been fighting for decades to get their community relocated away from this Superfund site. And it's ironic that they may get their neighborhood cleaned up from this Superfund site because of Katrina. Just before December 2004, there was a major lawsuit—the lawsuit actually went to trial, and the case was declared a class action, and it's still pending in court right now, even though the area where the landfill is located, the Superfund site, or the contamination, is much wider than the site itself.

7   There are many neighborhoods in New Orleans now that are contaminated; whether they are Brownfields or whether they are Superfund sites is to be determined by the EPA and the federal government. And so, there are concerns now—where will all the debris go for Katrina? Will it be another Betsy, where the dump is put in another area, and the debris from the hurricane is going to be creating more and more sites for devastation? *transs?*

8   I'll give you an example of the way that black farmers, for example, were mistreated and discriminated against when it comes to hurricane disaster relief and loans and for droughts and floods. The black farmers sued the United States USDA, the United States Department of Agriculture, because black farmers and white farmers are treated very differently. And they won their lawsuit, and again, the fact is that this is the government. This is not some entity. This is not a corporation. This is the U.S. government, who you expect to treat everybody the same, but after natural disasters, like a flood or a drought, black farmers were not able to get their loans. They were not able to get grants. They were not able to recover from disaster, because of just in-your-face, slam-dunk discrimination. *authr pnons*

9   The case of Hurricane Hugo: Hurricane Hugo struck South Carolina in 1989. And following Hugo, clear documentation in a number of reports showed that African Americans received less help than whites when it comes to this whole idea of loans, grants, something as simple as ice and something as simple as shelter. Studies show that African Americans and poor people are

[handwritten: personal experience undocumented sources?]

most likely to spend longer times in shelter; they're most likely to receive smaller grants and loans, even when you control for income and social class.

10   We have investigated this whole idea of who provides assistance in the initial hours of disasters. And we've shown clear documentation that oftentimes the Red Cross is not on the scene when it comes to many African-American communities in many of these disasters. And Katrina is no exception. There are many communities—for example, in Mississippi right now, in many of the parts of Mississippi that were hit, in Biloxi, Gulfport and some of the other areas, that are not—where it was days before the Red Cross was seen on the scene, and so it basically was our organizations, our churches, etc., that provided the assistance. And in many cases communities basically say, "Well we don't trust the government, and we don't trust FEMA, we don't trust the Red Cross." And in some cases, that trust is not based on any paranoia, it's based on trust—it's based on survival. The mere fact that in some cases—in many of our communities in Mississippi—the Red Cross was not the Red Cross, it was the White Cross. *[handwritten: → negative]*

[handwritten left margin: Then how can they help?]

11   When we look at this whole pattern, what do we see? For example, I lived in Houston in the 1980s, and there was a huge hurricane that hit Houston in 1983, Hurricane Alicia. And I had lots of damage, and I dealt with this in a book that I wrote called *Invisible Houston: The Black Experience in Boom and Bust*. That book was written in 1987. And we documented the fact that in the black wards, in Third Ward, Fourth Ward, Fifth Ward, Sedigas, Northwood Manor, Carverdale—these are all black neighborhoods, historically black neighborhoods—these areas were allowed to have debris not picked up. And there was so much debris, hurricane debris there, so much destruction, that black people started complaining. They started protesting, because debris was piling up and they needed a place to dump this debris. And so, the officials had to come up with this emergency site for this debris. And so, the place that they picked was a very poor African-American community in Northeast Houston near the airport called Bordersville. It was a poor community that didn't even have paved streets, didn't have running water. It was basically a sawmill community. And that's where they took all of this debris. They started burning it, created lots of problems in that area, and people were saying, "Well, we've been hit by a hurricane. Now we've been hit by the city and government officials, in terms of debris being dumped on." *[handwritten: emotional appeal]*

12   What does all of this mean? It means that the disasters that hit communities oftentimes are less, in terms of their damage, than the postdisaster kinds of activities. The fact is that right now communities are struggling with housing, and they are—you know, the people before, the witnesses before, testified about racism as it exists in the parishes in Louisiana. There are parishes now that are passing ordinances—that have already passed ordinances limiting the concentration of mobile homes and trailers, and in some cases, banning trailers. Well, that's what FEMA uses for temporary housing in many cases. If you look at the fact that in many cases, communities that are struggling, trying to

find housing, African Americans are meeting with discrimination in housing. I've worked with a lot of people in Louisiana, particularly around Baton Rouge, who are meeting with housing discrimination. You know, black people show up for a unit that has been posted for rent, and then when they show up, "Oh, we've already rented that." White person shows up, "OK, come on in, rent it." And so, using testing we can show that there's clear racial discrimination, in terms of fair housing not being enforced.

13   So it's not just FEMA and not just the federal government. In terms of the agencies, there are also local entities that need to enforce the laws as relates to housing. In terms of price-gouging, in terms of insurance red-lining, there are many cases of communities that can't get insurance. And this happened before. And so what needs to happen? There has to be strict enforcement of fair housing laws. There has to be monitoring, independent monitoring, of FEMA and how resources get distributed in terms of loans, in terms of grants.

proposing solution

14   There have to be uniform cleanup standards, in terms of the Gulf Coast. In many communities of color, our communities get less cleaned up. And so, the way you can kill a community easily is to not clean it up. If the Lower Ninth Ward is not cleaned up to residential standards, and if basically [authorities] say, "Oh, it's not feasible to clean it up. It's going to be industrial now," you've eliminated one of the strongest voting blocks in the area and one of the strongest African-American communities in the area. If you say that East New Orleans, where mostly affluent, middle-income African Americans live, is not going to be cleaned up to residential standards, you have basically eliminated politically one of the strongest parts of the city. And so environmental racism cannot only affect health, it can affect political strength and political power.

15   And finally, I think it's important that people understand that the issues that I've looked at and that we're looking at did not just happen in August 2005. These are issues that have been around for a long time. And the federal government, the state government, and local government oftentimes have not operated in the best interest of people of color and poor people and disenfranchised people. ■

Wendell Berry

Manifesto: The Mad Farmer Liberation Front

Writer, teacher, and land lover Wendell Berry (born 1934) grew up (and still lives) on a farm in Kentucky. His poetry and essays explore the connections between people and nature and typically endorse a simple lifestyle, at odds with new technologies that threaten agrarian ways. His many published works include the essays "What Are People For?" and "Why I Am Not Going to Buy a Computer." His books of poetry include Sabbaths *and* The Country of Marriage *(1973), from which the following poetic argument is taken.*

Love the quick profit, the annual raise,
vacation with pay. Want more
of everything ready-made. Be afraid
to know your neighbors and to die.

5   And you will have a window in your head.
Not even your future will be a mystery
any more. Your mind will be punched in a card
and shut away in a little drawer.

When they want you to buy something
10 they will call you. When they want you
to die for profit they will let you know.
So, friends, every day do something
that won't compute. Love the Lord.
Love the world. Work for nothing.
15 Take all that you have and be poor.
Love someone who does not deserve it.

Denounce the government and embrace
the flag. Hope to live in that free
republic for which it stands.
20 Give your approval to all you cannot
understand. Praise ignorance, for what man
has not encountered he has not destroyed.

Ask the questions that have no answers.
Invest in the millennium. Plant sequoias.
25 Say that your main crop is the forest
that you did not plant,
that you will not live to harvest.

Say that the leaves are harvested
when they have rotted into the mold.
30 Call that profit. Prophesy such returns.
Put your faith in the two inches of humus
that will build under the trees
every thousand years.

Listen to carrion—put your ear
35 close, and hear the faint chattering
of the songs that are to come.
Expect the end of the world. Laugh.

Laughter is immeasurable. Be joyful
though you have considered all the facts.
40 So long as women do not go cheap
for power, please women more than men.

Ask yourself: Will this satisfy
a woman satisfied to bear a child?
Will this disturb the sleep
45   of a woman near to giving birth?

Go with your love to the fields.
Lie down in the shade. Rest your head
in her lap. Swear allegiance
to what is nighest your thoughts.

50   As soon as the generals and the politicos
can predict the motions of your mind,
lose it. Leave it as a sign
to mark the false trail, the way
you didn't go.

55   Be like the fox
who makes more tracks than necessary,
some in the wrong direction.
Practice resurrection. ■

Issue in Focus
CLIMATE CHANGE

Climate change gets considerable attention in political and social debates to-day. The broad term *climate change* refers to variability over time within Earth's atmospheric conditions as well as to recorded alterations within regional temperatures and climate patterns. While the vast majority of scientists agree that climates are always changing, debates nevertheless still arise about the consequences of those changes and their causes: are the changes serious, and are they the result of natural causes and cycles or human activities? Scientists, activists, and policy makers also dispute about the degree of damage (if any) that is caused by climate change, and about the kinds of changes humans need to make in response to climate change.

Some scientists and political leaders assert the need to completely overhaul human habits—from our dependency on fossil fuels to heat our homes and the kinds of cars we drive to the kinds of lightbulbs we use and the kinds of clothes we wear. Other voices publicly assert that global warming, with its emphasis on endangered species, severe storms, and devastation to impoverished regions, is simply stirring up drama and debate when we're actually seeing merely the cyclical and natural patterns of Earth.

Sawyer Glacier, Alaska

The most visible public figure to emerge in the climate change conversation is former U.S. vice president Al Gore. In his 2006 film *An Inconvenient Truth,* Gore strives to make the complex science behind this issue clear and spur his audience to action. Certainly, the widespread distribution, compelling visuals (particularly the footage of a polar bear stranded on melting ice), and impassioned arguments of the film make *An Inconvenient Truth* a stirring statement of the position of many environmentalists on climate change and its negative consequences. This issue reached a public milestone at the 2007 Academy Awards ceremony (where *An Inconvenient Truth* won an Oscar for best documentary) as Gore and actor Leonardo DiCaprio bantered about politics and climate change—demonstrating very visible faces in the conversation about climate change. It reached an additional milestone when Gore was awarded the Nobel Peace Prize in recognition of his efforts. (He shared the prize with the Intergovernmental Panel on Climate Change, a United Nations network of scientists, in October, 2007.)

In short, the debates about climate change continue—debates not only about whether or not it exists, but also about whether and to what extent people should respond. Skeptics argue that there is not enough measurable data to support *any* action. They contend that scientists have captured only a glimpse of Earth's long-standing history of temperature, atmospheric, and climate variation. They wonder whether global warming is natural and inevitable—not the result of human activity after all. If human activity is the primary cause, then why did global temperatures seem to decrease in the 1950s and 1960s, when carbon dioxide emissions were already increasing greatly—and why did *Time* publish a cover story on global *cooling* in the late 1970s? If temperature changes occur cyclically, why worry, particularly because attempted interventions on such a large phenomenon would only be futile—and because there could be as many benefits to global warming as problems associated with it? Skeptics on the subject of climate change question scientists' ability to forecast vast, long-term climatic conditions when even highly trained meteorologists sometimes struggle to predict the next day's weather. They question the motivations of politicians like Gore, the costs of a "cleanup," and the impact of those costs on the poor.

Perhaps there is only one thing that everyone can agree on: the debate will continue. In this section, you'll find images and words that illustrate the arguments in the complicated conversations about climate change. On the one hand, we include Christopher Horner's "Top Ten 'Global-Warming' Myths" and Glenn McCoy's meteorologist cartoon to demonstrate the arguments of the skeptics. On the other hand, to represent the arguments of those concerned about climate change, we include a feature from Al Gore's "climate crisis" Web site, an essay by Philip Jenkins on how climate change might influence global politics and even religious movements, and a conversation about how even the fashion industry factors into climate change. At their heart, all of these arguments require us to think about how we live on our planet and how we care for it, as well as the legacy we wish to leave future generations. As readers and writers, you too may feel strongly about humans' influence and your own role in climate change. Pay attention to how the authors that follow construct their arguments. Focus on what makes a text effective or ineffective, regardless of what position you take with regard to climate change.

Al Gore

What Is Global Warming?

Carbon dioxide and other gases warm the surface of the planet naturally by trapping solar heat in the atmosphere. This is a good thing because it keeps our planet habitable. However, by burning fossil fuels such as coal, gas and oil and clearing forests we have dramatically increased the amount of carbon dioxide in the Earth's atmosphere and temperatures are rising.

The vast majority of scientists agree that global warming is real, it's already happening, and that it is the result of our activities and not a natural occurrence.[1] The evidence is overwhelming and undeniable.

We're already seeing changes. Glaciers are melting, plants and animals are being forced from their habitat, and the number of severe storms and droughts is increasing.

The number of Category 4 and 5 hurricanes has almost doubled in the last 30 years.[2]

Malaria has spread to higher altitudes in places like the Colombian Andes, 7,000 feet above sea level.[3]

"What Is Global Warming?" from www.climatecrisis.net. Courtesy of Participant Productions.

The flow of ice from glaciers in Greenland has more than doubled over the past decade.[4]

At least 279 species of plants and animals are already responding to global warming by moving closer to the poles.[5]

If the warming continues, we can expect catastrophic consequences.

Deaths from global warming will double in just 25 years—to 300,000 people a year.[6]

Global sea levels could rise by more than 20 feet with the loss of shelf ice in Greenland and Antarctica, devastating coastal areas worldwide.[7]

Heat waves will be more frequent and more intense.

Droughts and wildfires will occur more often.

The Arctic Ocean could be ice-free in summer by 2050.[8]

More than a million species worldwide could be driven to extinction by 2050.[9]

There is no doubt we can solve this problem. In fact, we have a moral obligation to do so. Small changes to your daily routine can add up to big differences in helping to stop global warming. The time to come together to solve this problem is now—TAKE ACTION.

[1]According to the Intergovernmental Panel on Climate Change (IPCC), this era of global warming "is unlikely to be entirely natural in origin" and "the balance of evidence suggests a discernible human influence of the global climate."

[2]Emanuel, K. 2005. Increasing destructiveness of tropical cyclones over the past 30 years. *Nature* 436: 686–688.

[3]World Health Organization.

[4]Krabill, W., E. Hanna, P. Huybrechts, W. Abdalati, J. Cappelen, B. Csatho, E. Frefick, S. Manizade, C. Martin, J, Sonntag, R. Swift, R. Thomas and J. Yungel. 2004. Greenland Ice Sheet: Increased coastal thinning. *Geophysical Research Letters* 31.

[5]*Nature.*

[6]World Health Organization.

[7]*Washington Post*, Debate on Climate Shifts to Issue of Irreparable Change, Juliet Eilperin, January 29, 2006, Page A1.

[8]Arctic Climate Impact Assessment. 2004. Impacts of a Warming Arctic. Cambridge, UK: Cambridge University Press. Also quoted in *Time Magazine*, Vicious Cycles, Missy Adams, March 26, 2006.

[9]*Time Magazine*, Feeling the Heat, David Bjerklie, March 26, 2006. ■

Al Gore

Ten Things to Do to Help Stop Global Warming

tenthingstodo

Want to do something to help stop global warming?
Here are 10 simple things you can do and how much carbon dioxide you'll save doing them.

Change a light
Replacing one regular light bulb with a compact fluorescent light bulb will save 150 pounds of carbon dioxide a year.

Drive less
Walk, bike, carpool or take mass transit more often. You'll save one pound of carbon dioxide for every mile you don't drive!

Recycle more
You can save 2,400 pounds of carbon dioxide per year by recycling just half of your household waste.

Check your tires
Keeping your tires inflated properly can improve gas mileage by more than 3%.

Every gallon of gasoline saved keeps 20 pounds of carbon dioxide out of the atmosphere!

Use less hot water
It takes a lot of energy to heat water. Use less hot water by installing a low flow showerhead

(350 pounds of CO2 saved per year) and washing your clothes in cold water or warm water (500 pounds saved per year).

Avoid products with a lot of packaging
You can save 1,200 pounds of carbon dioxide if you cut down your garbage by 10%.

Adjust your thermostat
Moving your thermostat just 2 degrees in winter and up 2 degrees in summer
You could save about 2,000 pounds of carbon dioxide a year with this simple adjustment.

Plant a tree
A single tree will absorb one ton of carbon dioxide over it's lifetime

Turn off electronic devices
Simply turning off your television, DVD player, stereo, and computer when you're
not using them will save you thousands of pounds of carbon dioxide a year.

Spread the word! Encourage your friends to buy An Inconvenient Truth

aninconvenienttruth

available on DVD
November 21

www.climatecrisis.net

"The Ten Things to Do to Stop Global Warming" from www.climatecrisis.net. Courtesy of Participant Productions.

Christopher C. Horner

Top Ten "Global-Warming" Myths

1. It's hot in here!

2   In fact, "It's the baseline, stupid." Claiming that present temperatures are warm requires a starting point at, say, the 1970s, or around the Little Ice Age (approximately 1200 A.D. to the end of the 19th century), or thousands of years ago. Select many other baselines, for example, such as the 1930s, or 1000 A.D.—or 1998—and it is presently cool. Cooling does paint a far more frightening picture, given that another ice age would be truly catastrophic, while throughout history, warming periods have always ushered in prosperity. Maybe that's why the greens tried "global cooling" first.

3   The claim that the 1990s were the hottest decade on record specifically targets the intellectually lazy and easily frightened, ignoring numerous obvious factors. "On record" obviously means a very short period, typically the past 100-plus years, or since the end of the Little Ice Age. The National Academies of Science debunked this claim in 2006. Previously, rural measuring stations registered warmer temps after decades of "sprawl" (growth), cement being warmer than a pasture.

4   ### 2. The science is settled—CO_2 causes global warming.

5   Al Gore shows his audience a slide of CO_2 concentrations, and a slide of historical temperatures. But for very good reason he does not combine them in one overlaid slide: historically, atmospheric CO_2, as often as not, increases after warming. This is typical in the campaign of claiming "consensus" to avoid debate (consensus about what is being left unspoken or distorted).

6   What scientists do agree on is little and says nothing about man-made global warming, to wit: (1) that global average temperature is probably about 0.6 degree Celsius—or 1 degree Fahrenheit—higher than a century ago; (2) that atmospheric levels of carbon dioxide have risen by about 30 percent over the past 200 years; and (3) that CO_2 is one greenhouse gas, some level of an increase of which presumably would warm the Earth's atmosphere were all else equal, which it demonstrably is not.

7   Until scientists are willing to save the U.S. taxpayers more than $5 billion per year thrown at researching climate, it is fair to presume the science is not settled.

8   ### 3. Climate was stable until man came along.

9   Swallowing this whopper requires burning every basic history and science text, just as "witches" were burned in retaliation for changing climates in ages (we had thought) long past. The "hockey stick" chart—poster child for this concept—has been disgraced and air-brushed from the UN's alarmist repertoire.

10   **4. The glaciers are melting!**

11   As good fortune has it, frozen things do in fact melt or at least recede after cooling periods mercifully end. The glacial retreat we read about is selective, however. Glaciers are also advancing all over, including lonely glaciers nearby their more popular retreating neighbors. If retreating glaciers were proof of global warming, then advancing glaciers are evidence of global cooling. They cannot both be true, and in fact, neither is. Also, retreat often seems to be unrelated to warming. For example, the snow-cap on Mount Kilimanjaro is receding—despite decades of cooling in Kenya due to regional land use and atmospheric moisture.

12   **5. Climate change is raising the sea levels.**

13   Sea levels rise during interglacial periods such as that in which we (happily) find ourselves. Even the distorted United Nations Intergovernmental Panel on Climate Change reports refute the hysteria, finding no statistically significant change in the rate of increase over the past century of man's greatest influence, despite green claims of massive melting already occurring. Small island nations seeking welfare and asylum for their citizens such as in socially generous New Zealand and Australia have no sea-level rise at all and in some cases see instead a drop. These societies' real problem is typically that they have made a mess of their own situation. One archipelago nation is even spending lavishly to lobby the European Union for development money to build beachfront hotel resorts, at the same time it shrieks about a watery and imminent grave. So, which time are they lying?

Images of polar bears have become popular in the arguments made by those working to spur people to take action to slow global warming. As large predators, polar bears need vast ice scapes for hunting, but these icy spaces are dwindling.

AND LOOKING AT OUR EXTENDED FORECAST, THERE'S A FIFTY-FIFTY CHANCE OF RAIN TOMORROW, POSSIBLE WARM OR COLD WEATHER WEDNESDAY, THURSDAY LOOKS IFFY. THE WEEKEND'S JUST TOO CLOSE TO CALL... OH YEAH... AND OVER THE NEXT SEVERAL DECADES LOOK FOR DEFINITE GLOBAL WARMING TO OCCUR.

6. Global warming has doomed the polar bears!

For some reason, Al Gore's computerized polar bear can't swim, unlike the real kind, as one might expect of an animal named Ursa Maritimus. On the whole, these bears are thriving, if a little less well in those areas of the Arctic that are cooling (yes, cooling). Their biggest threat seems to be computer models that air-brush them from the future, the same models that tell us it is much warmer now than it is. As usual in this context, you must answer the question: Who are you going to believe—me or your lying eyes?

7. Global warming means more frequent, more severe storms.

Here again the alarmists cannot even turn to the wildly distorted and politicized "Summary for Policy Makers" of the UN's IPCC to support this favorite chestnut of the press.

8. Climate change is the greatest threat to the world's poor.

Climate—or more accurately, weather—remains one of the greatest challenges facing the poor. Climate change adds nothing to that calculus, however. Climate and weather patterns have always changed, as they always will. Man has always best dealt with this through wealth creation and technological advance—a.k.a. adaptation—and most poorly through superstitious casting of blame, such as burning "witches." The wealthiest societies have always adapted best. One would prefer to face a similar storm in Florida than Bangladesh. Institutions, infrastructure and affordable energy are key to dealing with an ever-changing climate, not rationing energy.

20 **9. Global-warming proposals are about the environment.**

21   Only if this means that they would make things worse, given that "wealthier is healthier and cleaner." Even accepting every underlying economic and alarmist environmentalist assumption, no one dares say that the expensive Kyoto Protocol would detectably affect climate. Imagine how expensive a pact must be—in both financial and human costs—to so severely ration energy use as the greens demand. Instead, proponents candidly admit desires to control others' lifestyles, and supportive industries all hope to make millions off the deal. Europe's former environment commissioner admitted that Kyoto is "about leveling the playing field for big businesses worldwide" (in other words, bailing them out).

22 **10. The U.S. is going it alone on Kyoto and global warming.**

23   Nonsense. The U.S. rejects the Kyoto Protocol's energy-rationing scheme, along with 155 other countries, representing most of the world's population, economic activity, and projected future growth. Kyoto is a European treaty with one dozen others, none of whom is in fact presently reducing its emissions. Similarly, claims that Bush refused to sign Kyoto, and/or he withdrew, not only are mutually exclusive but also false. We signed it, Nov. 11, 1998. The Senate won't vote on it. Ergo, the (Democratic) Senate is blocking Kyoto. Gosh.

24   Don't demand they behave otherwise, however. Since Kyoto was agreed, Europe's CO_2 emissions are rising twice as fast as those of the climate-criminal United States, a gap that is widening in more recent years. So we should jump on a sinking ship?

25   Given Al Gore's proclivity for invoking Winston Churchill in this drama, it is only appropriate to summarize his claims as such: Never in the field of political conflict has so much been asked by so few of so many . . . for so little. ∎

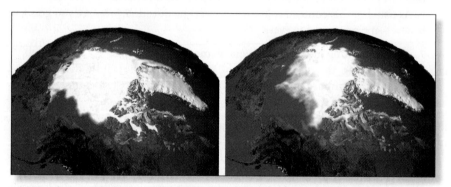

Sea ice in the Arctic Ocean has been shrinking at a rate of 9% per decade. The image on the left shows the minimum sea ice concentration for the year 1979, and the image on the right shows the minimum sea ice concentration in 2003. Are these photographs more or less effective than the photographs of polar bears, such as the one on page 340, in getting people to take action to slow global warming?

Philip Jenkins

Burning at the Stake

When John of Patmos listed the four horsemen of the apocalypse, he didn't have access to climate-modeling software or any of the technology used by the Intergovernmental Panel on Climate Change. If he had, he might have described the end of times in slightly more specific terms. And, to know what those terms would be, you just have to look at the area approximately between the latitudes of 23 degrees north and 23 degrees south over the next 50 or so years.

2   Over the next half-century, this equatorial swath will be broiling from global warming. Droughts will kill crops, and warming oceans will cripple the fishing industry (decimating the populations of fishing villages that will be disappearing, anyway, because water from the melting ice caps will drown them). By mid-century, water shortages could force countries already suffering from generations of ethnic and religious conflict to explode. A country like Nigeria, for example, where Christians and Muslims have self-segregated to the Southeast and the North, might erupt in a violent tug-of-war over limited water supplies. The Coptic Christians in Egypt could become a lost people, as ethnic cleansing in the name of resource protection becomes common. By the same token, Muslim minorities in places like Uganda and Kenya might be annihilated or driven out, creating vast waves of refugees that will swarm the more prosperous countries looking for aid (in response to which Western countries could see a new era of harsh border enforcement). Gradually, whole areas would become arid, uninhabitable wastelands.

3   The ramifications for the global warming-driven destruction of equatorial nations are frightening for everyone—but they should be especially frightening for Christians, whose numbers have been growing so explosively in those very areas. By 2050, although the world's largest Christian population will still be found in the United States, many of the other most populous communities will belong to the global South, in places like Brazil, Mexico, Nigeria, the Congo, Ethiopia, Uganda, and the Philippines. Christianity is no longer synonymous with the West, and that equation will become ever less plausible as time passes. What Christianity is becoming synonymous with, however, is the most volatile and the most ecologically threatened area of the world—and the coming temperature changes could have serious consequences for the future of the religion.

4   The connection between climate change and religious violence is not that tenuous—in fact, there's a historical indicator of how it could unfold, the Little Ice Age. Between the ninth and thirteenth centuries, the Northern Hemisphere actually went through a modest warming phase: With a longer growing season, harvests were bountiful, Europe's population boomed, and the relative prosperity inspired a burst of creativity in the arts and in the new university system. But, in the late thirteenth century, what's known as the Little Ice Age began: Pack ice grew in the oceans, making trade routes more dangerous, and

summers became cooler and wetter, harming crops. Populations swollen by the earlier boom came up against steep food shortages. The Great Famine, beginning in 1315, led to rumors of widespread cannibalism within a few years. At least one-third of Eurasia's weakened population died in the Black Death of the 1340s.

5   In a climate of death and horror, people cast about for scapegoats, even before the Black Death struck. The Church formally declared witchcraft a heresy in 1320, and people were soon being executed for devil-worship and black magic. And governments, desperate to find a safe outlet for their subjects' rage, condoned mob attacks on religious minorities.

6   Bigots of whatever faith rarely referred explicitly to the climatic catastrophe in progress around them, but the very close correlation between the cooling and a regionwide heightening of violent intolerance makes such a linkage likely. Jews were among the favorite targets of the Little Ice Age's hate criminals: England expelled its Jews in the 1290s, and pogroms were common in the 1320s and '30s and accelerated during the Black Death, forcing an eastward migration that ended up concentrating most of Europe's Jews in modern-day Poland, Lithuania, and Russia by the end of the fourteenth century.

7   But Christians suffered as well, at the hands of Muslims in Asia and the Middle East strained by some of the same circumstances that were affecting Europe. In 1250, Christians were still substantial minorities in many African and Asian countries. But, during the Little Ice Age, old-established Christian communities began to get the same treatment their coreligionists were dishing out to Jews in Europe. Egyptian Muslims accused Christians of arson and plotting terrorist attacks against mosques, using the newly popular weapon of gunpowder. Elsewhere, in Mesopotamia and modern-day Turkey, churches were destroyed and Christians were massacred. When modern jihadis look for intellectual role models, they turn back to precisely this era, to hard-line scholars like Ibn Taymiyya, who loathed infidels and condemned moderate Muslim regimes for not being tough enough on them.

8   It is not outlandish to say that we are heading toward a future very much like our fourteenth-century past, particularly in the areas of the global South where Christian populations are rising drastically. As the Little Ice Age did in the fourteenth century, global warming will redraw the world's religious maps, making it more and more difficult for religious or ethnic minorities to survive under a majority-led government and forcing splinter groups to concentrate in nations with sympathetic governments. The resource-driven genocide in Darfur, for example, although it involves competing Muslim communities and not Muslim-Christian warfare, is a foretaste of conflicts that could soon be sweeping the whole area, as nations implode in sectarian violence, pulling neighboring countries down with them.

9   But the greater globalization of Christianity, while it heightens some of the religious tensions in resource-poor countries and may put the religion at risk of pogroms and genocides, might also help prevent some of the worst

scenarios. As morally conservative churches in America form relationships with like-minded churches in the global South, especially Africa, they are becoming vastly more sensitive to African and Asian issues and values, and among these is a greater sympathy toward international cooperation on climate change.

10   In fact, the looming crisis has provoked some surprisingly radical actions by conservative Christians. The most famous of these is probably Richard Cizik, vice president of governmental affairs for the National Association of Evangelicals, an umbrella organization whose affiliate groups claim 30 million members. In the past five years, Cizik has become an outspoken advocate of "creation care," a doctrine rooted in the Bible that urges environmental protection, with global climate change as the clear and present danger. Cizik has called climate change "a phenomenon of truly Biblical proportions"—and one, therefore, that demands action on a similarly Biblical scale. Recognizing the pivotal importance of Africa in the Christian future, prominent evangelicals such as Rick Warren have become deeply committed to global South issues.

11   Once the connection between climate change and the fate of many of the world's Christians becomes self-evident (as, sadly, it will begin to before very long), we can expect an even greater involvement from the Christian community. Combining the themes of world stewardship and protecting Christian minorities could lead to a whole new synthesis of religious and political action, a kind of latitude politics that could represent a potent new element in U.S. foreign affairs. It's that, of course, or a return to medieval levels of misery and doom for the majority of Christians worldwide. ■

Alex Williams

Buying into the Green Movement

Here's one popular vision for saving the planet: Roll out from under the sumptuous hemp-fiber sheets on your bed in the morning and pull on a pair of $245 organic cotton Levi's and an Armani biodegradable knit shirt. Stroll from the bedroom in your eco-McMansion, with its photovoltaic solar panels, into the kitchen remodeled with reclaimed lumber. Enter the three-car garage lighted by energy-sipping fluorescent bulbs and slip behind the wheel of your $104,000 Lexus hybrid. Drive to the airport, where you settle in for an 8,000-mile flight—careful to buy carbon offsets beforehand—and spend a week driving golf balls made from compacted fish food at an eco-resort in the Maldives.

2   That vision of an eco-sensitive life as a series of choices about what to buy appeals to millions of consumers and arguably defines the current environmental movement as equal parts concern for the earth and for making a stylish statement. Some 35 million Americans regularly buy products that claim to be

earth-friendly, according to one report, everything from organic beeswax lipstick from the west Zambian rain forest to Toyota Priuses. With baby steps, more and more shoppers browse among the 60,000 products available under Home Depot's new Eco Options program.

3   Such choices are rendered fashionable as celebrities worried about global warming appear on the cover of *Vanity Fair's* "green issue," and pop stars like Kelly Clarkson and Lenny Kravitz prepare to be headline acts on July 7 at the Live Earth concerts at sites around the world. Consumers have embraced living green, and for the most part the mainstream green movement has embraced green consumerism. But even at this moment of high visibility and impact for environmental activists, a splinter wing of the movement has begun to critique what it sometimes calls "light greens."

A shopper looks at a display of high-efficiency lightbulbs at a Home Depot store. Products accepted for Home Depot's new Eco Options marketing campaign include solar-powered landscape lighting, biodegradable peat pots, and paints that discharge fewer pollutants. Is buying green the answer or do we need to make due with less?

4   Critics question the notion that we can avert global warming by buying so-called earth-friendly products, from clothing and cars to homes and vacations, when the cumulative effect of our consumption remains enormous and hazardous. "There is a very common mind-set right now which holds that all that we're going to need to do to avert the large-scale planetary catastrophes upon us is make slightly different shopping decisions," said Alex Steffen, the executive editor of Worldchanging.com, a Web site devoted to sustainability issues. The genuine solution, he and other critics say, is to significantly reduce one's consumption of goods and resources. It's not enough to build a vacation home of recycled lumber; the real way to reduce one's carbon footprint is to only own one home. Buying a hybrid car won't help if it's the aforementioned Lexus, the luxury LS 600h L model, which gets 22 miles to the gallon on the highway; the Toyota Yaris ($11,000) gets 40 highway miles a gallon with a standard gasoline engine. It's as though the millions of people whom environmentalists have successfully prodded to be concerned about climate change are experiencing a SnackWell's moment: confronted with a box of fat-free devil's food chocolate cookies, which seem deliciously guilt-free, they consume the entire box, avoiding any fats but loading up on calories.

5   The issue of green shopping is highlighting a division in the environmental movement: "the old-school environmentalism of self-abnegation versus this camp of buying your way into heaven," said Chip Giller, the founder of Grist.org, an online environmental blog that claims a monthly readership of 800,000. "Over even the last couple of months, there is more concern growing within the traditional camp about the Cosmo-izing of the green movement—'55 great ways

to look eco-sexy,'" he said. "Among traditional greens, there is concern that too much of the population thinks there's an easy way out."

6 The criticisms have appeared quietly in some environmental publications and on the Web. George Black, an editor and a columnist at *OnEarth*, a quarterly journal of the Natural Resources Defense Council, recently summed up the explosion of high-style green consumer items and articles of the sort that proclaim "green is the new black," that is, a fashion trend, as "eco-narcissism." Paul Hawken, an author and longtime environmental activist, said the current boom in earth-friendly products offers a false promise. "Green consumerism is an oxymoronic phrase," he said. He blamed the news media and marketers for turning environmentalism into fashion and distracting from serious issues. "We turn toward the consumption part because that's where the money is," Mr. Hawken said. "We tend not to look at the 'less' part. So you get these anomalies like 10,000-foot 'green' homes being built by a hedge fund manager in Aspen. Or 'green' fashion shows. Fashion is the deliberate inculcation of obsolescence." He added: "The fruit at Whole Foods in winter, flown in from Chile on a 747—it's a complete joke. The idea that we should have raspberries in January, it doesn't matter if they're organic. It's diabolically stupid."

7 Environmentalists say some products marketed as green may pump more carbon into the atmosphere than choosing something more modest, or simply nothing at all. Along those lines, a company called PlayEngine sells a 19-inch widescreen L.C.D. set whose "sustainable bamboo" case is represented as an earth-friendly alternative to plastic. But it may be better to keep your old cathode-tube set instead, according to "The Live Earth Global Warming Survival Handbook," because older sets use less power than plasma or L.C.D. screens. (Televisions account for about 4 percent of energy consumption in the United States, the handbook says.) "The assumption that by buying anything, whether green or not, we're solving the problem is a misperception," said Michael Ableman, an environmental author and long-time organic farmer. "Consuming is a significant part of the problem to begin with. Maybe the solution is instead of buying five pairs of organic cotton jeans, buy one pair of regular jeans instead."

8 For the most part, the critiques of green consumption have come from individual activists, not from mainstream environmental groups like the Sierra Club, Greenpeace and the Rainforest Action Network. The latest issue of *Sierra*, the magazine of the Sierra Club, has articles hailing an "ecofriendly mall" featuring sustainable clothing (under development in Chicago) and credit cards that rack up carbon offsets for every purchase, as well as sustainably harvested caviar and the celebrity-friendly Tango electric sports car (a top-of-the-line model is $108,000).

9 One reason mainstream groups may be wary of criticizing Americans' consumption is that before the latest era of green chic, these large organizations endured years in which their warnings about climate change were scarcely heard. Much of the public had turned away from the Carter-era environmental

message of sacrifice, which included turning down the thermostat, driving smaller cars and carrying a cloth "Save-a-Tree" tote to the supermarket.

10   Now that environmentalism is high profile, thanks in part to the success of *An Inconvenient Truth,* the 2006 documentary featuring Al Gore, mainstream greens, for the most part, say that buying products promoted as eco-friendly is a good first step. "After you buy the compact fluorescent bulbs," said Michael Brune, the executive director of the Rainforest Action Network, "you can move on to greater goals like banding together politically to shut down coal-fired power plants." John Passacantando, the executive director of Greenpeace USA, argued that green consumerism has been a way for Wal-Mart shoppers to get over the old stereotypes of environmentalists as "tree-hugging hippies" and contribute in their own way. This is crucial, he said, given the widespread nature of the global warming challenge. "You need Wal-Mart and Joe Six-Pack and mayors and taxi drivers," he said. "You need participation on a wide front."

11   It is not just ecology activists with one foot in the 1970s, though, who have taken issue with the consumerist personality of the "light green" movement. Anti-consumerist fervor burns hotly among some activists who came of age under the influence of noisy, disruptive anti-globalization protests. Last year, a San Francisco group called the Compact made headlines with a vow to live the entire year without buying anything but bare essentials like medicine and food. A year in, the original 10 "mostly" made it, said Rachel Kesel, 26, a founder. The movement claims some 8,300 adherents throughout the country and in places as distant as Singapore and Iceland. "The more that I'm engaged in this, the more annoyed I get with things like 'shop against climate change' and these kind of attitudes," said Ms. Kesel, who continues her shopping strike and counts a new pair of running shoes—she's a dog-walker by trade—as among her limited purchases in 18 months. "It's hysterical," she said. "You're telling people to consume more in order to reduce impact."

12   For some, the very debate over how much difference they should try to make in their own lives is a distraction. They despair of individual consumers being responsible for saving the earth from climate change and want to see action from political leaders around the world. Individual consumers may choose more fuel-efficient cars, but a far greater effect may be felt when fuel-efficiency standards are raised for all of the industry, as the Senate voted to do on June 21, the first significant rise in mileage standards in more than two decades. "A legitimate beef that people have with green consumerism is, at end of the day, the things causing climate change are more caused by politics and the economy than individual behavior," said Michel Gelobter, a former professor of environmental policy at Rutgers who is now president of Redefining Progress, a nonprofit policy group that promotes sustainable living. "A lot of what we need to do doesn't have to do with what you put in your shopping basket," he said. "It has to do with mass transit, housing density. It has to do with the war and subsidies for the coal and fossil fuel industry."

13   In fact, those light-green environmentalists who chose not to lecture about sacrifice and promote the trendiness of eco-sensitive products may be on to

something. Michael Shellenberger, a partner at American Environics, a market research firm in Oakland, California, said that his company ran a series of focus groups in April for the environmental group Earthjustice, and was surprised by the results. People considered their trip down the Eco Options aisles at Home Depot a beginning, not an end point. "We didn't find that people felt that their consumption gave them a pass, so to speak," Mr. Shellenberger said. "They knew what they were doing wasn't going to deal with the problems, and these little consumer things won't add up. But they do it as a practice of mindfulness. They didn't see it as antithetical to political action. Folks who were engaged in these green practices were actually becoming more committed to more transformative political action on global warming." ■

Chicago Tribune Editorial

Fast Clothes vs. Green Clothes

There's a new term for those ever-changing racks of low-cost, high-fashion duds at places such as Target and Old Navy: fast clothes. Not fast, as in racy. Fast, as in fast food. Like a Big Mac, fast clothes—we used to call them "affordable"—are cheap, appealing and morally suspect in some circles. Sure, there's short-term gratification in scoring a fashion-forward hoodie pullover for $6.99. But unless you wear it dozens of times—and wash it far less often—then you're not doing the planet any favors.

2   A simple T-shirt is fraught with eco-peril, beginning in the cotton field and ending in the landfill. Pesticides, tractor emissions, resources used in manufacturing and packaging, energy costs to wash, dry and iron it. Most clothes go out of style so fast they're practically disposable, which explains the appeal of bargain labels.

3   Researchers at Cambridge University's Institute for Manufacturing are all over the problem. A recent study envisions a clothing industry that is both sustainable and profitable. It urges consumers to choose "green" clothing. Organic fibers are good, if you wash them sparingly and at low temperatures, use a clothesline instead of a dryer and avoid ironing. Synthetics like polyester take more energy to make, but they clean easier and dry faster. Consumers should buy fewer, but more durable clothes and wear them until they're worn out, or recycle them. The report even suggests leasing clothes for a month or a season and returning them, like library books, to be used by someone else.

4   For manufacturers and retailers, the researchers recommend new business models based on durability and longevity (and higher prices) instead of volume. Clothing should emphasize classic styling, and businesses should offer repair, maintenance and upgrading. The report also recommends "eco-tagging," reasoning that customers will pay more for earth-friendly clothing, just as they pay premiums for organic produce and free-range chicken breasts.

5   Governments could charge a sin tax on non-green textiles and promote recycling of clothing alongside paper, glass and aluminum.

6   If this doesn't sound like the world you live in, remember that you can do your part by taking it one step at a time. You could start by giving up ironing. ■

Elisabeth Rosenthal

Environmentally Unfriendly Trend: Fast Fashion

Josephine Copeland and her 20-year-old daughter, Jo Jo, visited Primark at the Peacock Center mall in the London, England suburbs to buy presents for friends, but they ended up loaded with clothes for themselves: boots, a cardigan, a festive blouse and a long silver coat with faux-fur trim, which cost 12 pounds but looked like a million bucks. "If it falls apart, you just toss it away!" said Jo Jo, proudly wearing her purchase.

2   Environmentally, that is more and more a problem. With rainbow piles of sweaters and T-shirts that often cost less than a sandwich, stores like Primark are leaders in the quick-growing "fast fashion" industry, selling cheap garments that can be used and discarded without a second thought. Consumers, especially teenagers, love the concept, pioneered also by stores like H&M internationally and by Old Navy and Target in the United States, since it allows them to shift styles with speed on a low budget.

3   But clothes—and fast clothes in particular—are a large and worsening source of the carbon emissions that contribute to global warming, because of how they are both produced and cared for, concludes a new report from researchers at Cambridge University titled "Well Dressed?" The global textile industry must become eco-conscious, the report concludes. It explores how to develop a "sustainable clothing" industry—a seeming oxymoron in a world where fashions change every few months.

4   "Hmmm," said Sally Neild, 44, dressed in casual chic jeans and boots as she pondered such alien concepts, shopping bags in hand. "People now think a lot about green travel and green food. But I think we are a long way from there in terms of clothes. People are mad about those stores."

5   It is hard to imagine how customers who rush after trends, or the stores that serve them, will respond to the report's suggestions: that people lease clothes and return them at the end of a month or a season so the garments can be lent again to someone else—like library books—and that they buy more expensive and durable clothing that can be worn for years.

6   As for care, the report highlights the benefits of synthetic fabrics that require less hot water to wash and less ironing. It suggests that consumers air-dry clothes and throw away their tumble dryers, which require huge amounts of energy.

7   But some big retailers are starting to explore their options. "Our research shows that customers are getting very concerned about environmental issues, and

we don't want to get caught between the eyes," said Mike Barry, head of corporate social responsibility at Marks & Spencer, one of Britain's largest retailers, which helped pay for the Cambridge study. "It's a trend that we know won't go away after a season, like a poncho." Customers "will ask, 'What are you doing?'" Barry said, noting that 70 percent of Britons shop at his chain. "So we're doing a lot of thinking about what a sustainable-clothing industry could look like in five years."

8   Consumers spend more than $1 trillion a year on clothing and textiles, an estimated one-third of that in Western Europe, another third in North America and about a quarter in Asia. In many places, cheap, readily disposable clothes have displaced hand-me-downs as the mainstay of dressing. "My mother had the same wardrobe her entire life," Neild said. "For my daughter, styles change every six months, and you need to keep up." As a result, women's clothing sales in Britain rose by 21 percent between 2001 and 2005 alone to about 24 billion pounds ($47.6 billion), spurred by lower prices, according to the Cambridge report.

9   And while many people have grown accustomed to recycling cans, bottles and newspapers, used clothes are generally thrown away. "In a wealthy society, clothing and textiles are bought as much for fashion as for function," the report says, and that means that clothes are replaced "before the end of their natural life." ■

How "Green" Is Your T-Shirt?

Cotton is cheaper and takes less energy to manufacture than synthetic fibers. But over its lifetime, a cotton T-shirt requires more than twice the energy than is necessary to manufacture and maintain a polyester blouse. The main difference: polyester garments can be washed at a lower temperature, can hang dry and need no ironing.

The list below shows energy used over the lifetime of the garment, in kilowatt hours.*

COTTON T-SHIRT	POLYESTER BLOUSE
Raw material: 4	Raw material: 9
Manufacturing: 7	Manufacturing: 3
Transportation: 2	Transportation: 1
Use: 18	Use: 2

Use assumes 25 washes per garment. The cotton T-shirt is washed at 140 degrees Fahrenheit, followed by tumble-drying and ironing. The polyester blouse is washed at 104 degrees Fahrenheit, hung dry, and not ironed.

*The energy of one kilowatt hour will operate a 40-watt lightbulb for a full day or a 19-inch color television for about four hours.

(*Source:* University of Cambridge Institute for Manufacturing.)

From Reading to Writing

1. Analyze the argument by either Al Gore or Christopher Horner: how is each argument the product of its audience and purpose? What sources of argument (ethical appeals, emotional appeals, and logical appeals) does each author choose and why? (See Chapter 5 for more on rhetorical analysis.)

2. Compare the various photos and charts that appear on the preceding pages. What visual argument does each photo seem to make? (See Chapter 6 for guidance on analyzing visuals.)

3. Write an argument that makes its point by defining a key term related to environmental concerns. You might choose to change someone's attitude toward a particular practice or concept in order to defend or challenge it, for instance, by defining it in a certain way. For example, you might start with the claim that "Green clothes are just a marketing ploy for the fashion industry to cash in on consumers' increased environmental awareness" or "Global warming is actually a blessing in disguise for some of the world." (See Chapter 8 for strategies for writing definition arguments.)

4. Propose a change in policy related to an environmental issue in your community. (See Chapter 13 for help with writing a proposal argument.)

5. Write a rebuttal of an article related to the environment in your local or school newspaper. (See Chapter 12 for advice on rebuttals.) Consider whether you wish to show the weaknesses in the article, whether you wish to counterargue, or both.

6. Write an essay that recounts a personal experience of yours to make an argumentative point related to the environment. It could be a story about camping or hiking, for example, or a tale of your encounter with some environmental problem or challenge. (See Chapter 11 for advice on writing narrative arguments.)

23

Confronting Sexual Difference

How might these wedding cake-toppers make different arguments about who should be allowed to marry legally?

Sexual Difference in American Culture

It happened a decade ago, but people still talk about it: in 1998 University of Wyoming political science major Matthew Shepard was beaten to a pulp and pistol-whipped to death in the town of Laramie, Wyoming. Russell Henderson, 21, and

Matthew Shepard

Aaron McKinney, 20, lured Shepard from a bar (they knew he was gay), drove him to a deserted area, beat him as he begged for mercy, and removed his shoes and tied him to a post, like a coyote, to warn off others. Henderson and McKinney took Shepard's wallet, left him to die, and then attacked two Latino men before they were arrested. Shepard, buried two days later before a crowd of 650 mourners (and a small group of protesters holding signs ridiculing "fags"), became a symbol of growing violence against gays in the United States. His murder and the subsequent trial of the perpetrators led many citizens and legislators to advocate a range of measures to protect gay, lesbian, and bisexual citizens, and to expand the rights and responsibilities that those citizens might enjoy.

A year before, in 1997, Ellen DeGeneres, star of the comedy series *Ellen*, made public her character's (and her own) lesbianism and redirected her show toward an exploration of gay and lesbian identity. Before the series closed two years later, it consistently treated (typically as the material of comedy) the social and cultural tribulations faced by gays and lesbians, and challenged viewers to confront those tribulations in their own communities. Since then, a number of other television series have pursued the same end—most prominently *Will and Grace, Six Feet Under*, and *Queer as Folk*, but also soap operas, documentaries, variety shows (such as *Saturday Night Live*), and reality shows such as *Survivor* and *Boy Meets Boy*. Television shows like these, as well as a range of movies, ads, and Web sites, have required American citizens to confront a range of cultural practices involving gay, lesbian, and bisexual people—practices including service in the military, same-sex marriage and other domestic issues, and even the ordination of priests.

Contemporary Arguments

This section of *Good Reasons* contains a range of arguments related to just those issues. In recent years hate crimes in various communities have focused great attention on the violence that is often leveled at gays and on the issue of rights and protections for gay, lesbian, and bisexual citizens. The question of passing legislation to protect the rights, property, and bodies of gays, lesbians, and bisexuals has animated citizens in many communities. Thus we present an argument by Carmen Vazquez about the predicament of gay and lesbian citizens in the United States, an argument that might have implications for legislation.

In 2003 the Supreme Court struck down a Texas law criminalizing consensual sexual relations between people of the same sex. While proponents of such legal maneuvers feel that criminal conduct based on prejudice not only terrorizes victims and strips them of civil rights but also debilitates entire communities, critics note that law enforcement officials may remain indifferent to violence based on sexual orientation—no matter what the laws state. Critics of legislation protecting gays, lesbians, and bisexuals also raise other objections: laws already prohibit violence and excessive harassment; gay rights legislation is really "special rights" legislation as opposed to "civil rights" legislation; sexual preference relates to social behaviors, not inherent and immutable characteristics like gender or race that require protection, and homosexual behaviors can be modified through therapy or even religion; and legal protections might somehow grow into affirmative action for gays, lesbians, and bisexuals. We present here an argument by Peter J. Gomes asserting that appropriate interpretation of culture and the Bible should lead not to persecution of homosexuals, but to understanding and tolerance of sexual differences. On the other hand, Ryan T. Anderson explores the challenge (and what he sees as the necessity) of homosexuals using disciplined faith to avoid "immoral" behavior such as same-sex intimacy.

At most, so-called gay rights legislation might extend the rights of gays, lesbians, and bisexuals to permit a number of practices: serving in the military, getting married, becoming ordained into the clergy, adopting and raising children, sexual freedom, and protection against discrimination based on AIDS.

The question of same-sex marriage is the most prominent of those issues right now, and so we devote an Issue in Focus segment to it here. The current controversy over gay marriage derives from years of efforts by gay, lesbian, and bisexual activists to achieve family rights on a piecemeal basis—through pressing for domestic partnership laws, for example, or through lawsuits to permit adoption by single persons. In 1993, the Hawaii Supreme Court suddenly ruled in support of the recognition of same-sex marriage. Since marriages in one state are usually recognized in all states, the ruling in Hawaii made same-sex marriage into a national issue immediately. A federal law—the Defense of Marriage Act—soon was passed. It said that states are not required to recognize Hawaiian marriages.

The issue has remained significant in many states, however, because each must now decide whether to permit or at least recognize same-sex marriage. Subsequent court decisions, voter referenda, and new laws have only created additional controversies.

Since 2004, a number of states have introduced legislation to define marriage as strictly between one man and one woman; all of these measures have passed except Arizona's, which failed in 2006. No constitutional amendment has been ratified, though it has been publicly and persistently debated.

We include the Defense of Marriage Act, which advocates traditional family arrangements, followed by Anna Quindlen and Sonya Geis's cases for a variety of family arrangements and the social benefits for all of legally recognizing commitments beyond traditional heterosexual marriage.

We conclude our sampling of arguments with a variety of articles relating to culture, sexuality, and gender—including Andrew Sullivan's "The End of Gay Culture" and Alexa Hackbarth's lighthearted thoughts on the "metrosexual phenomenon." Each of the pieces in this chapter takes up fundamental questions of identity and sexual difference and asks us to think carefully and critically about the influence of sex and gender on our lives.

SOME GAY RIGHTS WEB SITES

www.thetaskforce.org	The National Gay and Lesbian Task Force
www.glaad.org	Gay and Lesbian Alliance Against Defamation
www.aclu.org/lgbt/index.html	American Civil Liberties Union
www.advocate.com	The *Advocate* magazine
www.lambdalegal.org	Lambda Legal
www.theweddingparty.org	Seeks to secure equal marriage rights for same-sex couples
www.hrc.org	Human Rights Campaign
www.gmhc.org	Gay Men's Health Crisis organization
www.glsen.org	Gay, Lesbian and Straight Education Network
www.buddybuddy.com	Partners Task Force for Gay and Lesbian Couples
www.actwin.com/cahp	Citizens Against HomoPhobia
www.planetout.com	Collects news and commentary

Carmen Vazquez

Appearances

Carmen Vazquez (1949–) was born in Puerto Rico and raised in Harlem, a predominantly African-American community in New York City. Active in the gay and lesbian movement for years, she has published many essays. The following piece was included in Warren J. Blumenfeld's 1992 book called Homophobia: How We All Pay the Price.

North of Market Street and east of Twin Peaks, where you can see the white fog mushroom above San Francisco's hills, is a place called the Castro. Gay men, lesbians, and bisexuals stroll leisurely up and down the bustling streets. They jaywalk with abandon. Night and day they fill the cafés and bars, and on weekends they line up for a double feature of vintage classics at their ornate and beloved Castro theater.

2   The 24 bus line brings people into and out of the Castro. People from all walks of life ride the electric-powered coaches. They come from the opulence of San Francisco's Marina and the squalor of Bayview projects. The very gay Castro is in the middle of its route. Every day, boys in pairs or gangs from either end of the city board the bus for a ride through the Castro and a bit of fun. Sometimes their fun is fulfilled with passionately obscene derision: "Fucking cocksucking faggots." "Dyke cunts." "Diseased butt fuckers." Sometimes, their fun is brutal.

3   Brian boarded the 24 Divisadero and handed his transfer to the driver one late June night. Epithets were fired at him the moment he turned for a seat. He slid his slight frame into an empty seat next to an old woman with silver blue hair who clutched her handbag and stared straight ahead. Brian stuffed his hands into the pockets of his worn brown bomber jacket and stared with her. He heard the flip of a skateboard in the back. The taunting shouts grew louder. "Faggot!" From the corner of his eye, he saw a beer bottle hurtling past the window and crash on the street. A man in his forties, wearing a Giants baseball cap and warmup jacket, yelled at the driver to stop the bus and get the hoodlums off. The bus driver ignored him and pulled out.

4   Brian dug his hands deeper into his pockets and clenched his jaw. It was just five stops to the top of the hill. When he got up to move toward the exit, the skateboard slammed into his gut and one kick followed another until every boy had got his kick in. Despite the plea of the passengers, the driver never called the police.

5   Brian spent a week in a hospital bed, afraid that he would never walk again. A lawsuit filed by Brian against the city states, "As claimant lay crumpled and bleeding on the floor of the bus, the bus driver tried to force claimant off the bus so that the driver could get off work and go home. Claimant was severely beaten by a gang of young men on the #24 Divisadero Bus who perceived that he was gay."

6   On the south side of Market Street, night brings a chill wind and rough trade. On a brisk November night, men with sculptured torsos and thighs wrapped in leather walked with precision. The clamor of steel on the heels of their boots echoed in the darkness. Young men and women walked by the men in leather, who smiled in silence. They admired the studded bracelets on Mickey's wrists, the shine of his flowing hair, and the rise of his laughter. They were, each of them, eager to be among the safety of like company where they could dance with abandon to the pulse of hard rock, the hypnotism of disco, or the measured steps of country soul. They looked forward to a few drinks, flirting with strangers, finding Mr. or Ms. Right or, maybe someone to spend the night with.

7   At the end of the street, a lone black street lamp shone through the mist. The men in leather walked under the light and disappeared into the next street. As they reached the corner, Mickey and his friends could hear the raucous sounds of the Garden spill onto the street. They shimmied and rocked down the block and through the doors.

8   The Garden was packed with men and women in sweat-stained shirts. Blue smoke stung the eyes. The sour and sweet smell of beer hung in the air. Strobe lights pulsed over the dancers. Mickey pulled off his wash-faded black denim jacket and wrapped it around his waist. An iridescent blue tank top hung easy on his shoulders. Impatient with the wait for a drink, Mickey steered his girlfriend onto the crowded dance floor.

9   Reeling to the music and immersed in the pleasure of his rhythms Mickey never saw the ice pick plunge into his neck. It was just a bump with a drunk yelling, "Lame-assed faggot." "Faggot. Faggot. Faggot. Punk faggot." Mickey thought it was a punch to the neck. He ran after the roaring drunk man for seven steps, then lurched and fell on the dance floor, blood gushing everywhere. His girlfriend screamed. The dance floor spun black.

10   Mickey was rushed to San Francisco General Hospital, where thirty-six stitches were used by trauma staff to close the wound on his neck. Doctors said the pick used in the attack against him was millimeters away from his spinal cord. His assailant, charged with attempted murder, pleaded innocent.

11   Mickey and Brian were unfortunate stand-ins for any gay man. Mickey was thin and wiry, a great dancer clad in black denim, earrings dangling from his ear. Brian was slight of build, wore a leather jacket, and boarded a bus in the Castro. Dress like a homo, dance like a homo, must be a homo. The homophobic fury directed at lesbians, gay men, and bisexuals in America most often finds its target. Ironclad evidence of sexual orientation, however, is not necessary for someone to qualify as a potential victim of deadly fury. Appearances will do.

12   The incidents described above are based on actual events reported to the San Francisco Police and Community United Against Violence (CUAV), an agency serving victims of antilesbian and antigay violence where I worked for

four years. The names of the victims have been changed. Both men assaulted were straight.

13   Incidents of antilesbian and antigay violence are not uncommon or limited to San Francisco. A *San Francisco Examiner* survey estimates that over one million hate-motivated physical assaults take place each year against lesbians, gays, and bisexuals. The National Gay and Lesbian Task Force conducted a survey in 1984 that found that 94 percent of all lesbians and gay men surveyed reported being physically assaulted, threatened, or harassed in an antigay incident at one time or another. The great majority of these incidents go unreported.

14   To my knowledge, no agency other than CUAV keeps track of incidents of antigay violence involving heterosexuals as victims. An average of 3 percent of the over three hundred victims seen by CUAV each year identify as heterosexuals. This may or may not be an accurate gauge of the actual prevalence of antigay violence directed at heterosexuals. Most law enforcement agencies, including those in San Francisco, have no way of documenting this form of assault other than under a generic "harassment" code. The actual incidence of violence directed at heterosexuals that is motivated by homophobia is probably much higher than CUAV's six to nine victims a year. Despite the official paucity of data, however, it is a fact that incidents of antigay and antilesbian violence in which straight men and women are victimized do occur. Shelters for battered women are filled with stories of lesbian baiting of staff and of women whose husbands and boyfriends repeatedly called them "dykes" or "whores" as they beat them. I have personally experienced verbal abuse while in the company of a straight friend, who was assumed to be my lover.

15   Why does it happen? I have no definitive answers to that question. Understanding homophobic violence is no less complex than understanding racial violence. The institutional and ideological reinforcements of homophobia are myriad and deeply woven into our culture. I offer one perspective that I hope will contribute to a better understanding of how homophobia works and why it threatens all that we value as humane.

16   At the simplest level, looking or behaving like the stereotypical gay man or lesbian is reason enough to provoke a homophobic assault. Beneath the veneer of the effeminate gay male or the butch dyke, however, is a more basic trigger for homophobic violence. I call it *gender betrayal*.

17   The clearest expression I have heard of this sense of gender betrayal comes from Doug Barr, who was acquitted of murder in an incident of gay bashing in San Francisco that resulted in the death of John O'Connell, a gay man. Barr is currently serving a prison sentence for related assaults on the same night that O'Connell was killed. He was interviewed for a special report on homophobia produced by ABC's 20/20 (10 April 1986). When asked what he and his friends thought of gay men, he said, "We hate homosexuals. They degrade our manhood. We was brought up in a high school where guys are football players,

mean and macho. Homosexuals are sissies who wear dresses. I'd rather be seen as a football player."

18   Doug Barr's perspective is one shared by many young men. I have made about three hundred presentations to high school students in San Francisco, to boards of directors and staff of nonprofit organizations, and at conferences and workshops on the topic of homophobia or "being lesbian or gay." Over and over again, I have asked, "Why do gay men and lesbians bother you?" The most popular response to the question is, "Because they act like girls," or, "Because they think they're men." I have even been told, quite explicitly, "I don't care what they do in bed, but they shouldn't act like that."

19   They shouldn't act like that. Women who are not identified by their relationship to a man, who value their female friendships, who like and are knowledgeable about sports, or work as blue-collar laborers and wear what they wish are very likely to be "lesbian baited" at some point in their lives. Men who are not pursuing sexual conquests of women at every available opportunity, who disdain sports, who choose to stay at home and be a househusband, who are employed as hairdressers, designers, or housecleaners, or who dress in any way remotely resembling traditional female attire (an earring will do) are very likely to experience the taunts and sometimes the brutality of "fag bashing."

20   The straitjacket of gender roles suffocates many lesbians, gay men, and bisexuals, forcing them into closets without an exit and threatening our very existence when we tear the closet open. It also, however, threatens all heterosexuals unwilling to be bound by their assigned gender identity. Why, then, does it persist?

21   Suzanne Pharr's examination of homophobia as a phenomenon based in sexism and misogyny offers a succinct and logical explanation for the virulence of homophobia in Western civilization:

> It is not by chance that when children approach puberty and increased sexual awareness they begin to taunt each other by calling these names: "queer," "faggot," "pervert." It is at puberty that the full force of society's pressure to conform to heterosexuality and prepare for marriage is brought to bear. Children know what we have taught them, and we have given clear messages that those who deviate from standard expectations are to be made to get back in line. . . .
>
> To be named as lesbian threatens all women, not just lesbians, with great loss. And any woman who steps out of role risks being called a lesbian. To understand how this is a threat to all women, one must understand that any woman can be called a lesbian and there is no real way she can defend herself: there is no real way to credential one's sexuality. (*The Children's Hour*, a Lillian Hellman play, makes this point when a student asserts two teachers are lesbians and they have no way to disprove it.) She may be married or divorced, have children, dress in the most feminine manner, have sex with men, be celibate—but there are lesbians who do all these things. *Lesbians look like all women and all women look like lesbians.*[1]

[1]Pharr, Suzanne. *Homophobia: A Weapon of Sexism* (Inverness, CA: Chardon, 1988), 17–19.

I would add that gay men look like all men and all men look like gay men. There is no guaranteed method for identifying sexual orientation. Those small or outrageous deviations we sometimes take from the idealized mystique of "real men" and "real women" place all of us—lesbians, gay men, bisexuals, and heterosexuals alike—at risk of violence, derision, isolation, and hatred.

22   It is a frightening reality. Dorothy Ehrlich, executive director of the Northern California American Civil Liberties Union (ACLU), was the victim of a verbal assault in the Castro several years ago. Dorothy lives with her husband, Gary, and her two children, Jill and Paul, in one of those worn and comfortable Victorian homes that grace so many San Francisco neighborhoods. Their home is several blocks from the Castro, but Dorothy recalls the many times she and Gary could hear, from the safety of their bedroom, shouts of "faggot" and men running in the streets.

23   When Jill was an infant, Gary and Dorothy had occasion to experience for themselves how frightening even the threat of homophobic violence can be. One foggy, chilly night they decided to go for a walk in the Castro. Dorothy is a small woman whom some might call petite; she wore her hair short at the time and delights in the comfort of jeans and oversized wool jackets. Gary is very tall and lean, a bespectacled and bearded cross between a professor and a basketball player who wears jean jackets and tweed jackets with the exact same slouch. On this night they were crossing Castro Street, huddled close together with Jill in Dorothy's arms. As they reached the corner, their backs to the street, they heard a truck rev its engine and roar up Castro, the dreaded "faggot" spewing from young men they could not see in the fog. They looked around them for the intended victims, but there was no one else on the corner with them. They were the target that night: Dorothy and Gary and Jill. They were walking on "gay turf," and it was reason enough to make them a target. "It was so frightening." Dorothy said. "So frightening and unreal."

24   But it is real. The *20/20* report on homophobia ends with the story of Tom and Jan Matarrase, who are married, have a child, and lived in Brooklyn, New York, at the time of their encounter with homophobic violence. On camera, Tom and Jan are walking down a street in Brooklyn lined with brown townhouses and black wrought-iron gates. It is snowing, and, with hands entwined, they walk slowly down the street where they were assaulted. Tom is wearing a khaki trenchcoat, slacks, and loafers. Snowflakes melt into the tight dark curls on his head. Jan is almost his height, her short bobbed hair moving softly as she walks. She is wearing a black leather jacket, a red scarf, and burnt orange cords. The broadness of her hips and softness of her face belie the tomboy flavor of her carriage and clothes, and it is hard to believe that she was mistaken for a gay man. But she was.

25   They were walking home, holding hands and engrossed with each other. On the other side of the street, Jan saw a group of boys moving toward them. As the gang approached, Jan heard a distinct taunt meant for her and

Tom: "Aw, look at the cute gay couple." Tom and Jan quickened their step but it was too late. Before they could say anything, Tom was being punched in the face and slammed against a car. Jan ran toward Tom and the car, screaming desperately that Tom was her husband. Fists pummeled her face as well. Outnumbered and in fear for their lives, Tom yelled at Jan to please open her jacket and show their assailants that she was a woman. The beating subsided only when Jan was able to show her breasts.

26   For the *20/20* interview, Jan and Tom sat in the warmth of their living room, their infant son in Jan's lap. The interviewer asked them how they felt when people said they looked like a gay couple. "We used to laugh," they said. "But now we realize how heavy the implications are. Now we know what the gay community goes through. We had no idea how widespread it was. It's on every level."

27   Sadly, it *is* on every level. Enforced heterosexism and the pressure to conform to aggressive masculine and passive feminine roles place fag bashers and lesbian baiters in the same psychic prison with their victims, gay or straight. Until all children are free to realize their full potential, until all women and men are free from the stigma, threats, alienation, or violence that come from stepping outside their roles, we are all at risk.

28   The economic and ideological underpinnings of enforced heterosexism and sexism or any other form of systematic oppression are formidable foes and far too complex for the scope of this essay. It is important to remember, however, that bigots are natural allies and that poverty or the fear of it has the power to seduce us all into conformity. In Castro graffiti, *faggot* appears right next to *nigger* and *kike*. Race betrayal or any threat to the sanctimony of light-skinned privilege engenders no less a rage than gender betrayal, most especially when we have a great stake in the elusive privilege of proper gender roles or the right skin color. *Queer lover* and *fag hag* are cut from the same mold that gave us *nigger lover*, a mold forged by fears of change and a loss of privilege.

29   Unfortunately, our sacrifices to conformity rarely guarantee the privilege or protection we were promised. Lesbians, gay men, and bisexuals who have tried to pass know that. Heterosexuals who have been perceived to be gay know that. Those of us with a vision of tomorrow that goes beyond tolerance to a genuine celebration of humanity's diversity have innumerable fronts to fight on. Homophobia is one of them.

30   But how will this front be won? With a lot of help, and not easily. Challenges to homophobia and the rigidity of gender roles must go beyond the visible lesbian and gay movement. Lesbians, gay men, and bisexuals alone cannot defuse the power of stigmatization and the license it gives to frighten, wound, or kill. Literally millions of us are needed on this front, straight and gay alike. We invite any heterosexual unwilling to live with the damage that "real men" or "real women" messages wreak on them, on their children, and on lesbians, gay men, and bisexuals to join us. We ask that you not let queer jokes go unchallenged at work, at home, in the media, or anywhere. We ask that you foster in your children a genuine respect for themselves and their right to be who

and what they wish to be, regardless of their gender. We ask that you embrace your daughter's desire to swing a bat or be a carpenter, that you nurture your son's efforts to express affection and sentiment. We ask that you teach your children how painful and destructive words like *faggot* or *bulldyke* are. We ask that you invite your lesbian, gay, and bisexual friends and relatives into the routine of your lives without demanding silence or discretion from them. We invite you to study our history, read the literature written by our people, patronize our businesses, come into our homes and neighborhoods. We ask that you give us your vote when we need it to protect our privacy or to elect open lesbians, gay men, and bisexuals to office. We ask that you stand with us in public demonstrations to demand our right to live as free people, without fear. We ask that you respect our dignity by acting to end the poison of homophobia.

31   Until individuals are free to choose their roles and be bound only by the limits of their own imagination, *faggot*, *dyke*, and *pervert* will continue to be playground words and adult weapons that hurt and limit far many more people than their intended victims. Whether we like it or not, the romance of virile men and dainty women, of Mother, Father, Dick, Jane, Sally, and Spot is doomed to extinction and dangerous in a world that can no longer meet the expectations conjured by history. There is much to be won and so little to lose in the realization of a world where the dignity of each person is worthy of celebration and protection. The struggle to end homophobia can and must be won, for all our sakes. Personhood is imminent. ∎

Peter J. Gomes

Homophobic? Read Your Bible

Peter J. Gomes (1942–) is an American Baptist minister. Widely regarded as one of the most distinguished preachers in the nation, he has served since 1970 in the Memorial Church at Harvard University. Since 1974 he has been Plummer Professor of Christian Morals at Harvard Divinity School as well. He wrote the following essay for the New York Times *in 1992.*

Opposition to gays' civil rights has become one of the most visible symbols of American civic conflict this year, and religion has become the weapon of choice. The army of the discontented, eager for clear villains and simple solutions and ready for a crusade in which political self-interest and social anxiety can be cloaked in morality, has found hatred of homosexuality to be the last respectable prejudice of the century.

2   Ballot initiatives in Oregon and Maine would deny homosexuals the protection of civil rights laws. The Pentagon has steadfastly refused to allow gays into the armed forces. Vice President Dan Quayle is crusading for "traditional family values." And Pat Buchanan, who is scheduled to speak at the Republican

National Convention this evening, regards homosexuality as a litmus test of moral purity.

3   Nothing has illuminated this crusade more effectively than a work of fiction, *The Drowning of Stephan Jones*, by Bette Greene. Preparing for her novel, Ms. Greene interviewed more than 400 young men incarcerated for gay-bashing, and scrutinized their case studies. In an interview published in *The Boston Globe* this spring, she said she found that the gay-bashers generally saw nothing wrong in what they did, and, more often than not, said their religious leaders and traditions sanctioned their behavior. One convicted teen-age gay-basher told her that the pastor of his church had said, "Homosexuals represent the devil, Satan," and that the Rev. Jerry Falwell had echoed that charge.

4   Christians opposed to political and social equality for homosexuals nearly always appeal to the moral injunctions of the Bible, claiming that Scripture is very clear on the matter and citing verses that support their opinion. They accuse others of perverting and distorting texts contrary to their "clear" meaning. They do not, however, necessarily see quite as clear a meaning in biblical passages on economic conduct, the burdens of wealth, and the sin of greed.

5   Nine biblical citations are customarily invoked as relating to homosexuality. Four (Deuteronomy 23:17, I Kings 14:24, I Kings 22:46, and II Kings 23:7) simply forbid prostitution, by men and women.

6   Two others (Leviticus 18:19–23 and Leviticus 20:10–16) are part of what biblical scholars call the Holiness Code. The code explicitly bans homosexual acts. But it also prohibits eating raw meat, planting two different kinds of seed in the same field, and wearing garments with two different kinds of yarn. Tattoos, adultery, and sexual intercourse during a woman's menstrual period are similarly outlawed.

7   There is no mention of homosexuality in the four Gospels of the New Testament. The moral teachings of Jesus are not concerned with the subject.

8   Three references from St. Paul are frequently cited (Romans 1:26–2:1, I Corinthians 6:9–11, and I Timothy 1:10). But St. Paul was concerned with homosexuality only because in Greco-Roman culture it represented a secular sensuality that was contrary to his Jewish-Christian spiritual idealism. He was against lust and sensuality in anyone, including heterosexuals. To say that homosexuality is bad because homosexuals are tempted to do morally doubtful things is to say that heterosexuality is bad because heterosexuals are likewise tempted. For St. Paul, anyone who puts his or her interest ahead of God's is condemned, a verdict that falls equally upon everyone.

9   And lest we forget Sodom and Gomorrah, recall that the story is not about sexual perversion and homosexual practice. It is about inhospitality, according to Luke 10:10–13, and failure to care for the poor, according to Ezekiel 16:49–50: "Behold, this was the iniquity of thy sister Sodom, pride, fullness of bread, and abundance of idleness was in her and in her daughters, neither did she strengthen the hand of the poor and needy." To suggest that Sodom and Gomorrah is about homosexual sex is an analysis of about as much worth as suggesting that the story of Jonah and the whale is a treatise on fishing.

10   Part of the problem is a question of interpretation. Fundamentalists and literalists, the storm troopers of the religious right, are terrified that Scripture, "wrongly interpreted," may separate them from their values. That fear stems from their own recognition that their "values" are not derived from Scripture, as they publicly claim.

11   Indeed, it is through the lens of their own prejudices that they "read" Scripture and cloak their own views in its authority. We all interpret Scripture: Make no mistake. And no one truly is a literalist, despite the pious temptation. The questions are, By what principle of interpretation do we proceed, and by what means do we reconcile "what it meant then" to "what it means now"?

12   These matters are far too important to be left to scholars and seminarians alone. Our ability to judge ourselves and others rests on our ability to interpret Scripture intelligently. The right use of the Bible, an exercise as old as the church itself, means that we confront our prejudices rather than merely confirm them.

13   For Christians, the principle by which Scripture is read is nothing less than an appreciation of the work and will of God as revealed in that of Jesus. To recover a liberating and inclusive Christ is to be freed from the semantic bondage that makes us curators of a dead culture rather than creatures of a new creation.

14   Religious fundamentalism is dangerous because it cannot accept ambiguity and diversity and is therefore inherently intolerant. Such intolerance, in the name of virtue, is ruthless and uses political power to destroy what it cannot convert.

15   It is dangerous, especially in America, because it is antidemocratic and is suspicious of "the other," in whatever form that "other" might appear. To maintain itself, fundamentalism must always define "the other" as deviant.

16   But the chief reason that fundamentalism is dangerous is that, at the hands of the Rev. Pat Robertson, the Rev. Jerry Falwell, and hundreds of lesser-known but equally worrisome clerics, preachers, and pundits, it uses Scripture and the Christian practice to encourage ordinarily good people to act upon their fears rather than their virtues.

17   Fortunately, those who speak for the religious right do not speak for all American Christians, and the Bible is not theirs alone to interpret. The same Bible that the advocates of slavery used to protect their wicked self-interests is the Bible that inspired slaves to revolt and their liberators to action.

18   The same Bible that the predecessors of Mr. Falwell and Mr. Robertson used to keep white churches white is the source of the inspiration of the Rev. Martin Luther King. Jr., and the social reformation of the 1960's.

19   The same Bible that antifeminists use to keep women silent in the churches is the Bible that preaches liberation to captives and says that in Christ there is neither male nor female, slave nor free.

20   And the same Bible that on the basis of an archaic social code of ancient Israel and a tortured reading of Paul is used to condemn all homosexuals and

homosexual behavior includes metaphors of redemption, renewal, inclusion, and love—principles that invite homosexuals to accept their freedom and responsibility in Christ and demands that their fellow Christians accept them as well.

21   The political piety of the fundamentalist religious right must not be exercised at the expense of our precious freedoms. And in this summer of our discontent, one of the most precious freedoms for which we must all fight is freedom from this last prejudice. ■

Ryan T. Anderson

Struggling Alone

Ryan T. Anderson serves as a junior fellow for First Things—*a magazine published by the Institute on Religion and Public Life, a conservative thinktank that offers religious perspectives on social issues. In his work, Anderson has written about issues ranging from stem cell research to Amnesty International's statement on abortion to adoption laws in the United Kingdom. In "Struggling Alone," published in the February 2007 edition of* First Things, *Anderson discusses the loneliness that often challenges homosexuals who strive to live according to the doctrines of their faith.*

He came out to me in an email. I've known him for years, long enough that I can't remember when we first met, and we were recently emailing back and forth about our lives, our futures—the kind of stuff separated friends discuss. Along the way he mentioned, in an aside, that he had some lingering troubles he had to work his way through. My reply asked for an explanation—and that's when he told me.

2   Over the past three years, "Chris" (let's call him) has experienced a pronounced attraction to other males—for one old friend from high school in particular. A crush, maybe, or an infatuation. Whatever it was, he knew it wasn't healthy. And though he had never acted on the attraction, he explained, it led to fantasies and lusts he didn't want. So he made a resolution never to embrace them as essential to his identity or accept them as permanent or untreatable—a resolution he has kept practically alone, without the support of community, family, or friends. Over the course of many phone calls and emails, he shared with me his reflections on what he thought had created his problem of same-sex attractions. He described an "exceedingly close, best-friendly relationship" to his mother, often serving the role of her sole confidant, and a subsequent alienation from his father. Relationships with his friends, he thought, also contributed, as he suffered through "deeply hurtful rejection" by male peers, along with "oscillations between reverence for and fear of typically masculine" classmates. Once puberty hit, this took on sexual connotations, as Chris began experiencing "eroticized desire" for traits he found in other males that he himself lacked.

3   All this resulted in his dividing males into those he found "superior and feared (because of their strongly masculine features)," and those he found "inferior and disdained (because of their lack thereof)." But it affected his overall personality, too. He developed, he wrote, a "passive-aggressive, detachedly defensive and otherwise manipulative behavior toward males" and a "woeful inability" to assert himself as others do. The overarching weakness, he thought, was "a deep need to fulfill the emasculating and benign-to-a-fault role of the good little boy who pleases Mom by following all rules (the civil law, school rules, conventional morality, politeness, etc.) [while] remaining unthreatening and unphysical."

4   What he described seemed an accurate summary of the person I have known for years. So when he pointed to the likely causes and said he was seeking help in addressing them, I was supportive. "I would be untrue to myself if I simply accepted this condition right now," he wrote. "I would be denying what I've come to believe—what I believe I know—to be the causes and potential cures of this condition in my case." Some people say that change isn't possible, but he thinks that with God all things are, and he at least wants to try to do his part.

5   Chris' situation is sad, but it seems to be moving somewhere. He told me how he had cried daily for the first two years of his same-sex attractions, knowing that he was becoming someone he didn't want to be. But during the third year he found a good therapist and began making progress. He set out to find "healthy male affirmation through deep, nonerotic same-sex friendships"— along with a "purification of memory regarding the hurts of the past" and a more masculine view of himself. Without any reason to exaggerate his progress, he assured me he is "100 times happier and healthier than before— though not yet whole." Even friends and relatives who do not know about his struggles have remarked on his increased serenity and joy.

6   Other than his confessor and therapist, I'm the only person who knows. His parents would be devastated—his mother wondering whether she had caused it, his father fearing he had failed his son. His roommates and friends wouldn't know how to take it. Others on campus would encourage him to embrace his true self: They'd label him a homosexual and call him gay. But he's not—and neither does he want to be: Sexual attraction, he thinks, doesn't define a person. Indeed, he particularly fears coming out about his attractions while struggling against them, which would get him labeled a repressed homosexual, the gay-basher who himself is queer, the gay kid who thinks it's just some disorder. All he wants is to live chastely and try to make progress in addressing the causes of his same-sex attractions. But at the modern American university, this is anathema. For all their celebrations of diversity and pledges of tolerance, this choice is not to be celebrated or even tolerated.

7   Like many schools, Chris' university has an LGBTQA center (an official office supporting "lesbian, gay, bisexual, transgendered, queer, and allied" students). Had he been seeking advice on how to embrace his same-sex attractions, perform sexually as a gay man, or develop a romantic homosexual relationship, he would have been welcomed. Wanting instead help to live chastely, he found nothing. Worse than nothing, he found rejection. Such

centers routinely sponsor public lectures attacking Christian responses to same-sex attractions, calls to chastity, and attempts to seek therapy.

8   You might think Chris could find help at the university's religious-life center. But with pink pride triangles on every interior door, that office, too, has embraced the gay-pride movement. The college hosts an annual Pride Sunday Liturgy in lieu of regular chapel worship—for pride, apparently, is the proper liturgical response to homosexuality—and sponsors public lectures with titles such as "Overcoming Christian Fear of Homosexuality."

9   Fortunately, the Catholic chaplaincy on campus is vibrant and orthodox. The chaplain gave Chris solid if general spiritual advice—regular prayer, reception of the sacraments, and a life of charity—but he wasn't sure how to tailor it to a young Christian experiencing same-sex attractions. So he suggested Chris work with a therapist to address the psychological causes of his attractions.

10   And Chris tried. He went to his school's health center to see a psychologist, but she was hostile. When he asked for a referral to see a Catholic therapist, she all but called him crazy for refusing to give in to his nature as homosexual. In the end, his university health insurance wouldn't cover all the cost of an outside therapist, and he obviously couldn't turn to his parents.

11   Sexual confusion can be found anywhere, but it is particularly pronounced on college campuses, where to the general human confusion is added approved promiscuity and an institutional rejection of anything traditionally Christian or conservative. Is there any student more alienated or marginalized on campus than one who experiences same-sex attractions but who doesn't embrace them? Silence is forced upon him, and his entire life experience is discounted: He suffers same-sex attractions, he doesn't want to, and he seeks to be made whole again. This doesn't seem so extreme a narrative, and yet there are very few, if any, campus groups devoted to supporting these students.

12   While listening to Chris, I grew angrier and angrier about our troubled culture, the sexual chaos our parents' generation bequeathed us, the lack of support the Church provides, and the hostile environment the university maintains. Gradually, however, my anger gave way to sadness. A sadness that Chris struggles almost alone. A sadness that others like him have no one to turn to. A sadness that universities deliberately reject chaste students with same-sex attractions.

13   In the end, though, I found myself feeling grateful. Grateful for knowing Chris. Grateful for the chance to see him carry a cross he did not choose. Offering up his daily struggles, he strives for holiness, refuses surrender, and resists temptations. He labors to remedy the unwanted causes and side effects of attractions he never desired, aware all the while that a cure isn't certain, that in this fallen world some disorders may always be with us.

14   I am witnessing my friend's unique path to holiness: a remarkable instance of grace working through a broken earthly vessel, making all things new, and leading to fullness of life. I think how blessed I am that I've been fortunate enough to witness it and find inspiration for my life in his struggles.

15   How sad, though, that the rest of the world will never know. ■

Issue in Focus
SAME-SEX MARRIAGE

Although the question of whether to allow same-sex marriages in the United States has been debated for at least two decades, the conversations surrounding the practice became especially impassioned in the first few years of the twenty-first century. In February 2004, the newly elected mayor of San Francisco, Gavin Newsom, ordered the issuance of marriage licenses to same-sex couples in defiance of California's Proposition 22 (which defined marriage as exclusively between one man and one woman and passed by 61 percent in 2000). Gay couples rushed to obtain licenses as they seized a short-lived chance to marry; ultimately, the California Supreme Court ordered a halt to the marriages.

In 2004, Massachusetts became the first state to legally sanction gay marriage. While some gay couples celebrated on the steps of Boston's City Hall, other citizens fought the decision. These marriages were stopped temporarily through court actions, but only temporarily, and a subsequent effort to amend the state constitution to forbid same-sex marriage was defeated in 2007. These legal actions drew national attention to the issue of defining and regulating marriages.

Phyllis Lyon, 79 (left), and Del Martin, 83, in San Francisco were the first same-sex couple to be officially married in California. (Photo: Liz Margelsdorf in the *San Francisco Chronicle*.)

Proponents of gay marriage, like former *New York Times* columnist and author Anna Quindlen (whose essay, "Evan's Two Moms," is reprinted here), emphasize the practicality of legalizing same-sex marriages. They argue that legal marriage would recognize and protect personal, lasting, and loving monogamous relationships; shield marital partners from prosecution for sexual behavior; help partners share pensions, insurance, taxes, and inheritances; and guard partners from custody battles. As described by *Washington Post* reporter Sonya Geis, other proponents of legal gay unions are choosing to take a new approach that emphasizes the benefits of same-sex unions for straight couples (namely through civil unions and domestic partnerships). Geis reports on a burning question: what kinds of relationships ought to be legally validated within the United States? As you read, consider whether the article is a balanced news account or an argument favoring a particular side.

Opponents of same-sex marriage, including President George W. Bush, call for a constitutional amendment that strictly endorses heterosexual marriage. They seek to defend traditional perspectives on marriage, to protect children by providing male and female role models within the immediate family unit, to uphold Biblical interpretations of marriage, and to sustain traditional heterosexual marriages already threatened by skyrocketing divorce rates. In the previous essay, "Struggling Alone," for example, Ryan Anderson articulates the belief that people with homosexual impulses and attractions need not act on those feelings, and his argument fits within many contemporary religious perspectives on homosexuality.

The proposed constitutional amendment (reprinted here) failed to reach the Senate floor for debate, but opponents of same-sex marriage have fared quite well in some state legislatures—at least 37 states and the federal government legally define marriage as between one man and one woman. Similar legislation is pending in other states. These laws, as well as the images and essays you see excerpted in this section, hinge on fundamental social concerns: how is and should marriage be defined? What are and should be social norms in sexual relationships? What kinds of relationships are viable legally and socially—and for whom? As you read, consider how these writers construct their arguments, and consider entering into these conversations based on what you read here and what you've encountered in your own communities.

Davis Wilson (left) and Robert Compton were married at the Arlington Street Church in Boston. (Photo: Deanne Fitzmaurice in the *San Francisco Chronicle*)

PROPOSED AMENDMENT TO THE U.S. CONSTITUTION

108th CONGRESS, 1st Session

RESOLUTION 56 Proposing an amendment to the Constitution of the United States relating to marriage.

Resolved by the Senate and House of Representatives of the United States of America in Congress assembled (two-thirds of each House concurring therein). That the following article is proposed as an amendment to the Constitution of the United States, which shall be valid to all intents and purposes as part of the Constitution when ratified by the legislatures of three-fourths of the several States within seven years after the date of its submission for ratification:

"Article—

"SECTION 1. Marriage in the United States shall consist only of the union of a man and a woman. Neither this Constitution or the constitution of any State, nor state or federal law, shall be construed to require that marital status or the legal incidents thereof be conferred upon unmarried couples or groups."

House of Representatives

The Defense of Marriage Act

Congress of the United States
House of Representatives
AS INTRODUCED ON MAY 7, 1996

Summary of the Act:

T he Defense of Marriage Act (DOMA) does two things. First, it provides that no State shall be required to give effect to a law of any other State with respect to a same-sex "marriage." Second, it defines the words "marriage" and "spouse" for purposes of Federal law.

2   The first substantive section of the bill is an exercise of Congress' power under the "Effect" clause of Article IV, section I of the Constitution (the Full Faith and Credit Clause) to allow each State (or other political jurisdiction) to decide for itself whether it wants to grant legal status to same-sex "marriage." This provision is necessary in light of the possibility of Hawaii giving sanction to same-sex "marriage" under its state law, as interpreted by its state courts, and other states being placed in the position of having to give "full faith and credit" to Hawaii's interpretation of what constitutes "marriage." Although so-called "conflicts of law" principles do not necessarily compel such a result, approximately 30 states of the union are sufficiently alarmed by such a prospect to have initiated legislative efforts to defend themselves against any compulsion to acknowledge same-sex "marriage."

3   This is a problem most properly resolved by invoking Congress' authority under the Constitution to declare what "effect" one State's acts, records, and judicial proceedings shall have in another State. Congress has invoked this authority recently on two other occasions: in the Parental Kidnapping Prevention Act of 1980, which required each State to enforce child custody determinations made by the home State if made consistently with the provisions of the Act; and in the Full Faith and Credit for Child Support Order Act of 1994, which required each State to enforce child support orders made by the child's State if made consistently with the provisions of the Act.

4   The second substantive section of the bill amends the U.S. Code to make explicit what has been understood under federal law for over 200 years: that a marriage is the legal union of a man and a woman as husband and wife, and a spouse is a husband or wife of the opposite sex. The DOMA definition of marriage is derived most immediately from a Washington state case from 1974, Singer v. Hara, which is included in the 1990 edition of Black's Law Dictionary. More than a century ago, the U.S. Supreme Court spoke of the "union for life of one man and one woman in the holy estate of matrimony." Murphy v. Ramsey, 114 U.S. 15, 45 (1885).

5   DOMA is not meant to affect the definition of "spouse" (which under the Social Security law, for example, runs to dozens of lines). It ensures that whatever definition of "spouse" may be used in Federal law, the word refers only to a person of the opposite sex.

Provisions of the Act

4th CONGRESS 2D SESSION

H.R. 3396

IN THE HOUSE OF REPRESENTATIVES

Mr. BARR of Georgia (for himself, Mr. LARGENT, Mr. SENSENBRENNER, Ms. MYRICK, Mr. VOLKMER, Mr. SKELTON, Mr. BRYANT, and Mr. EMERSON) introduced the following bill, which was referred to the Committee

A BILL To define and protect the institution of marriage.

Be it enacted by the Senate and House of Representatives of the United States of America in Congress assembled,

SECTION 1. SHORT TITLE.

This Act may be cited as the "Defense of Marriage Act."

SECTION 2. POWERS RESERVED TO THE STATES.

(a)   IN GENERAL.—Chapter 115 of title 28, United States Code, is amended by adding after section 1738B the following:
Section 1738C. Certain acts, records, and proceedings and the effect thereof "No State, territory, or possession of the United States, or Indian tribe, shall be required to give effect to any public act, record, or judicial proceeding of any other State, territory, possession, or tribe respecting a relationship between persons of the same sex that is treated as a marriage under the laws of such other State, territory, possession, or tribe, or a right or claim arising from such relationship."

(b)   CLERICAL AMENDMENT.—The table of sections at the beginning of Chapter 115 of title 28, United States Code, is amended by inserting after the item relating to section 1738B the following new item: "1738C. Certain acts, records, and proceedings and the effect thereof."

SECTION 3. DEFINITION OF MARRIAGE.

(a)   IN GENERAL.—Chapter 1 of title 1, United States Code, is amended by adding at the end the following:

"Section 7. Definition of 'marriage' and 'spouse'

"In determining the meaning of any Act of Congress, or of any ruling, regulation, or interpretation of the various administrative bureaus and agencies of the United States, the word 'marriage' means only a legal union between one man and one woman as husband and wife, and the word 'spouse' refers only to a person of the opposite sex who is a husband or a wife." ■

Anna Quindlen

Evan's Two Moms

Evan has two moms. This is no big thing. Evan has always had two moms in his school file, on his emergency forms, with his friends. "Ooooh, Evan, you're lucky," they sometimes say. "You have two moms." It sounds like a sit-com, but until last week it was emotional truth without legal bulwark. That was when a judge in New York approved the adoption of a six-year-old boy by his biological mother's lesbian partner. Evan. Evan's mom. Evan's other mom. A kid, a psychologist, a pediatrician. A family.

2   The matter of Evan's two moms is one in a series of events over the last year that led to certain conclusions. A Minnesota appeals court granted guardianship of a woman left a quadriplegic in a car accident to her lesbian lover, the culmination of a seven-year battle in which the injured woman's parents did everything possible to negate the partnership between the two. A lawyer in Georgia had her job offer withdrawn after the state attorney general found out that she and her lesbian lover were planning a marriage ceremony: she's brought suit. The computer company Lotus announced that the gay partners of employees would be eligible for the same benefits as spouses.

3   Add to these public events the private struggles, the couples who go from lawyer to lawyer to approximate legal protections their straight counterparts take for granted, the AIDS survivors who find themselves shut out of their partners' dying days by biological family members and shut out of their apartments by leases with a single name on the dotted line, and one solution is obvious.

4   Gay marriage is a radical notion for straight people and a conservative notion for gay ones. After years of being sledge-hammered by society, some gay men and lesbian women are deeply suspicious of participating in an institution that seems to have "straight world" written all over it.

5   But the rads of twenty years ago, straight and gay alike, have other things on their minds today. Family is one, and the linchpin of family has commonly been a loving commitment between two adults. When same-sex couples set out to make that commitment, they discover that they are at a disadvantage: No joint tax returns. No health insurance coverage for an uninsured partner. No survivor's benefits from Social Security. None of the automatic rights, privileges, and responsibilities society attaches to a marriage contract. In Madison, Wisconsin, a couple who applied at the Y with their kids for a family membership were turned down because both were women. It's one of those small things that can make you feel small.

6   Some took marriage statutes that refer to "two persons" at their word and applied for a license. The results were court decisions that quoted the Bible and embraced circular argument: marriage is by definition the union of a man and a woman because that is how we've defined it.

7   No religion should be forced to marry anyone in violation of its tenets, although ironically it is now only in religious ceremonies that gay people can
marry, performed by clergy who find the blessing of two who love each other
no sin. But there is no secular reason that we should take a patchwork approach
of corporate, governmental, and legal steps to guarantee what can be done simply, economically, conclusively, and inclusively with the words "I do."

8   "Fran and I chose to get married for the same reasons that any two people
do," said the lawyer who was fired in Georgia. "We fell in love; we wanted to
spend our lives together." Pretty simple.

9   Consider the case of *Loving* v. *Virginia*, aptly named. At the time, sixteen
states had laws that barred interracial marriage, relying on natural law, that
amorphous grab bag for justifying prejudice. Sounding a little like God throwing Adam and Eve out of paradise, the trial judge suspended the one-year sentence of Richard Loving, who was white, and his wife, Mildred, who was black,
provided they got out of the State of Virginia.

10   In 1967 the Supreme Court found such laws to be unconstitutional. Only
twenty-five years ago it was a crime for a black woman to marry a white man.
Perhaps twenty-five years from now we will find it just as incredible that two
people of the same sex were not entitled to legally commit themselves to each
other. Love and commitment are rare enough; it seems absurd to thwart them
in any guise. ■

Sonya Geis

A New Tactic in Fighting Marriage Initiatives

A pair of retirees keeping house in a concrete bungalow, with snapshots of
their 30 grandchildren and great-grandchildren in the living room and an
American flag out front, may not look like the face of gay America. But this
month Al Breznay, 79, and Maxine Piatt, 75, were pivotal in defeating an Arizona
initiative that defined marriage as the union of one man and one woman—the
only one of 28 such state measures ever to fail. Breznay, a retired mechanic who
still does odd jobs to bring in extra cash, and Piatt, a former bank teller, are at
the forefront of a strategy to defeat a tide of same-sex marriage bans by talking
about straight people.

2   Of those 28 state marriage initiatives, 17 have included language outlawing
domestic partnerships. Gay rights advocates see this as an opening to highlight
for heterosexual voters the impact such initiatives may have on them, and in
Arizona, activists kept the spotlight on couples such as Breznay and Piatt, registered domestic partners whose faces appeared on fliers and television ads.

3   "The majority of people in Arizona don't support gay marriage. That's clear,
they do not," said Marty Rouse, national field director of the Human Rights
Campaign, a gay advocacy group. "Once you say gay and lesbian, people hone in

on that. We have to focus on the majority of people that will be affected by this. And the majority of people are straight couples."

4   The campaign against the Arizona measure, Proposition 107, avoided almost any mention of gay marriage, except in small liberal pockets of the state. Instead, the message was about the section of the measure that would have banned government agencies from recognizing civil unions or domestic partnerships. That apparently struck home in the state's sizable senior-citizen enclaves, where many older couples do not marry because their retirement income would be affected. The initiative was defeated, 52 percent to 48 percent.

5   "It's not a liberal-versus-conservative issue," said Steve May, a former Republican state representative who is gay and who served as treasurer of the campaign against Proposition 107. "It's about, 'I don't need to take away health care from Al and Maxine, this nice old couple in Tucson.'" In fact, the couple's health coverage would not have been affected by the measure's passage, although their ability to pay for the coverage or to visit each other in intensive care would change, as they discovered when Piatt got sick two years ago.

6   Such generalizing upsets supporters of the initiative, who accuse opponents of fear-mongering. "They misled voters. They scared seniors into believing they would lose Social Security benefits," said Cathi Herrod, spokeswoman for the pro-107 campaign. "Our problem was we did not have funds to respond to the attacks." Her campaign spent about $1 million, she said, compared with the $2.1 million spent by the measure's opponents.

7   Talking to straight couples does not always work; the strategy failed in Virginia this year, where a marriage law passed with 57 percent of the vote. The differences in Arizona were a longer campaign and a relentless focus on benefits and health care, Rouse said. In Virginia, "most of the media coverage talked about a gay marriage ban," he said, "whereas in Arizona, you did hear about a ban on same-sex marriage, but it was still focused on health care."

8   The Arizona results may prove instructive in setting the debate in the next state where same-sex marriage is likely to appear on the ballot: Florida, in 2008. "Florida might be able to learn from Arizona," Rouse said. But "campaigns are campaigns. If you do your research and you find out what voters care about, then you know what to focus on."

9   For some gay activists, it was bittersweet to defeat a same-sex marriage ban by avoiding the subject of homosexuality. "To truly win the freedom to marry and end discrimination, we can't just play defense," said Evan Wolfson, executive director of the gay rights group Freedom to Marry. He added that proponents of same-sex marriage must "avoid messaging that blocks further attacks and does not move us further ahead."

10   Wolfson says he takes heart in the re-election of legislators who support same-sex marriage and in the narrowing margins by which initiatives banning same-sex marriage have passed. In 2004, 71 percent of voters voted for such initiatives on average; that dropped to 56 percent this year. "Even if, in the short-term battles, we may have to emphasize the overbreadth, the dangers to non-gay people and the general unfairness, the trend is in our favor," Wolfson said.

11   That is not how it looks to Bill Maier, vice president and psychologist in residence at Focus on the Family, a proponent of state same-sex marriage bans. "Voters in states with marriage initiatives this year tended to be more libertarian than those voting in 2004, so they shied away from constitutional changes," he said. "When you see more of these amendments pop up in 'red states,' I think you're going to see more of those large percentages," Maier said. Maier also sees a backlash on the horizon. He points to New Jersey, where civil unions or same-sex marriage could be legalized in the next six months after an order by the state Supreme Court. "When people see gay people standing on the courthouse steps saying, 'I'm getting married come hell or high water,' among the general population there tends to be a recoil," Maier said.

12   For their part, Breznay and Piatt are pleased that Arizona's initiative lost, though same-sex marriage has never been their cause. "We didn't care one way or the other. It didn't involve us," Piatt said. "That's what makes me so angry, is that people linked this gay marriage to domestic partnerships." Breznay added, "We got involved because it was affecting us personally." ■

From Reading to Writing

1. Write an essay defining the ideal marriage in order to support or undermine the concept of same-sex marriage. Just what is marriage, anyway? (Chapter 8 has advice on definition arguments.)

2. Like Anna Quindlen, write an essay that describes a particular, monogamous, same-sex couple that you know. In your essay, support or undermine the notion of legal same-sex unions.

3. Write a proposal argument (like the ones discussed in Chapter 13) that is based on the positive or negative consequences that would follow from legalizing same-sex unions.

4. Do a rhetorical analysis of an essay or image associated with same-sex marriage. You might use an argument, photo, or cartoon reprinted here; or, you could use another argument with which you are familiar. Consider how the author uses good reasons to support his or her perspective, as well as the completeness of the argument and the credibility of the arguer. (Look again at Chapters 5 and 6 for reminders on effective rhetorical and visual analyses.)

5. Evaluate the Defense of Marriage Act or the proposed constitutional amendment banning same-sex marriage. Based on aesthetic, ethical, and practical criteria, are these good laws or not? Why? (See Chapter 10 for information on forming evaluative arguments.)

William F. Jasper

Subversion Through Perversion

William F. Jasper is a senior editor of The New American, *a biweekly magazine that is owned by the radically conservative John Birch Society, which claims to be "a valuable tool in confronting the liberal, mainstream media." It is a news and opinion publication focusing on national issues. Jasper is the author of* Global Tyranny . . . Step by Step: The United Nations and the Emerging New World Order *(1992) and* The United Nations Exposed *(2001). "Subversion Through Perversion" appeared in the March 21, 2005, edition of* The New American.

Maybe you're like this writer and rarely sample the toxic television fare that parades under the false label of "entertainment." Even so, it's impossible to conduct even a brief, occasional audit of the tube without confronting the hard fact that the forces in control of this omnipresent and potent medium are hell-bent themselves, and are determined to take our whole society there with them.

2 Nowhere is this more evident than in the incredible brazenness of the full-tilt campaign to homosexualize American culture. The organized sodomites, who constitute a tiny fraction of our society—1 to 2 percent, not the 10 percent they claim—have been given carte blanche to "overhaul straight America." You may not know it, but you are being psychologically overhauled to accept the homosexual revolution "whether you like it or not."

3 Welcome to the "queering of America." That's how the radical homosexual strategies themselves refer to their insidious crusade to remake our society and our entire culture in their image. They know they cannot succeed totally in the legislatures and the courts unless and until they have transformed our culture. This means saturating our popular cultural media with homosexual and lesbian characters, themes, styles, and symbols.

4 This also means placing homosexual and lesbian characters into virtually every sitcom, soap, and drama on television. And it has gone far beyond that, of course. Programs like *Queer Eye for the Straight Guy, Queer Eye for the Straight Girl,* and *The L Word* are total propaganda platforms for the superiority of homosexuals over straights.

"Velvet Mafia"

5 This subversive crafting of the program content of network and cable TV is dictated by a contingent of homo-lesbo executives, artists, and consultants known in the trade as the Velvet Mafia or the Lavender Mob.

6 When the Velvet Mafia determines that it's time to inoculate the American public with a few more doses of "gay" culture, we get another spate of "coming out" episodes or homo-lesbo kissing scenes. Thus, on February 10,

New York Times writer Virginia Heffernan approvingly noted the recent wave of lesbian smooching during the network sweeps: "On *One Tree Hill, The O.C.* and even *Wife Swap,* Sapphic love is in the air. And why not? It's that extended prom night for television lesbians—sweeps."

7   According to Heffernan, "in the last decade television's masterminds have discovered the lesbian kiss" as a gimmick to gain viewership. Lesbian kisses, she claims, "offer something for everyone, from advocacy groups looking for role models to indignation-seeking conservatives, from goggle-eyed male viewers to progressive female ones, from tyrants who demand psychological complexity to plot buffs. Hooray for the all-purpose lesbian kiss, then, cynical though it may be."

8   Heffernan then runs through a historical list of television's lesbian kisses, from *L.A. Law* in 1991, up through *Picket Fences, Roseanne, Ellen, Ally McBeal,* and *Buffy the Vampire Slayer.* Next up, then, are Marissa (Mischa Barton) and Alex (Olivia Wilde) on *The O.C.* (Fox), Heffernan reports, in apparent breathless anticipation. "The gorgeous California girls will finally kiss tonight."

9   Heffernan hit on the key element of the Velvet Mafia strategy when she said "gorgeous California girls." To sell their perversion to the targeted teen and young adult audiences, they have gone to great lengths to package lesbians as gorgeous, cool, hip, smart, chic. That is especially obvious in the new lesbian series, *The L Word,* now in its second season on the Showtime network. Giant billboards for *The L Word* show a bevy of beautiful actress/models posing naked in a group huddle.

10   Now comes Homer Simpson to further the revolution. In a special episode of *The Simpsons* on February 20, Homer, who has become a beloved cartoon icon, conducted "gay marriages" and one of the regular characters on the series, Patty, came out of the closet.

Televised Revolution

11   The revolutionary nature of these recent events was noted by the *Chicago Tribune*'s Web Behrens. "You probably didn't notice it at the time, but a revolution quietly took place a week and a half ago—and, yes, it was televised." After reciting a string of recent "gay" TV episodes, including *The Simpsons,* Behrens wrote: "When you consider that, just a decade ago, any one of these recent episodes would have been cause for much hand-wringing, protests and even boycotts, the word 'revolution' is no exaggeration. So how did American culture arrive at this place?"

12   Behrens only partially answers that important question by reciting, like Heffernan, the chronology of landmark homo-lesbo TV episodes over the past decade. But those episodes did not appear out of thin air; they were part of a long-term, revolutionary program planned by militant homosexuals and their insider sponsors in the industry. Their entire strategy was laid out in minute

detail in 1989, in a book entitled *After the Ball: How America Will Conquer Its Fear and Hatred of Gays in the 90's.*

13   The authors, Marshall Kirk and Hunter Madsen, boasted that this was an operational manual for the "overhauling of straight America," by which they meant "converting" America. Kirk and Madsen state: "By conversion we actually mean something far more profoundly threatening to the American way of life. We mean conversion of the average American's emotions, mind and will, through a planned psychological attack. We mean 'subverting' the mechanism of prejudice to our own ends—using the very process that made America hate us to turn their hatred into warm regard—whether they like it or not."

14   And how would this be accomplished? Through a massive media, public relations, and advertising "propaganda campaign." "Gays must launch a large-scale campaign—we've called it the Waging Peace campaign—to reach straights through the mainstream media," the coauthors wrote. "We're talking about propaganda." They explained to their deviate cohorts that "propaganda relies more upon emotional manipulation than upon logic, since its goal is, in fact, to bring about a change in the public's feelings."

15   "The main thing," they asserted, "is to talk about gayness until the issue becomes thoroughly tiresome." Accordingly, they said, the "free and frequent discussion of gay rights by a variety of persons in a variety of places gives the impression that homosexuality is commonplace. That impression is essential, because . . . the acceptability of any new behavior ultimately hinges on the proportion of one's fellows accepting or doing it." And, the deviate duo opined, the "fastest way to convince straights that homosexuality is commonplace is to get a lot of people talking about the subject in a neutral or supportive way. Open, frank talk makes gayness seem less furtive, alien, and sinful; more aboveboard."

16   "At least at the outset," say Kirk and Madsen, "we seek desensitization and nothing more." The purpose of that phase is simply to get straight folks to the "shoulder-shrug stage." The radical homo duo write that "If you can get them to think that [homosexuality] is just another thing—meriting no more than a shrug of the shoulders—then your battle for legal and social rights is virtually won."

17   However, the Kirk-Madsen program does not stop with mere societal acceptance of homosexuality. It goes on to "paint gay men and lesbians as superior—veritable pillars of society." That is what we are seeing now, with programming that portrays the homo-lesbo community as superior to the straight community.

18   Yes, Mr. Behrens was correct to use the word "revolution." That is precisely what Communist theoretician Antonio Gramsci intended in his strategy to achieve complete transformation of society through a complete transformation of the culture. For the past several decades, Gramsci's disciples have been applying his subversive strategy to undermine the moral foundations that provide the bulwark of protection against that revolution. ■

Marc Haeringer

Coming Out in the Line of Fire

The article below was published in the July 3, 2007, issue of The Advocate, *a nationwide U.S. news magazine for gays and lesbians that includes personal ads, updates on political developments, celebrity gossip, and features on special-interest issues like surrogacy and gay adoption. In "Coming Out in the Line of Fire," Haeringer tackles the long-standing prohibition against homosexuals in the military being "out." He calls into question the "don't ask, don't tell" policy and proposes that units may be able to handle, and thrive with, openly gay members in their midst.*

I n many ways, Army Private Karissa Urmanita is a typical U.S. soldier. The Pomona, California, native joined the Army to take advantage of its generous college tuition assistance program and to help support her family. She's close with her colleagues (calling them her "battle buddies"), and in her downtime from stocking the combat support hospital at Camp Bucca in southern Iraq, she likes to play cards and talk. But Urmanita, now 20, is an atypical soldier in at least one respect—she's an out lesbian.

2   In direct violation of "don't ask, don't tell," Urmanita was deployed to Iraq in March—two weeks after she came out to her command. And challenging the belief that open homosexuality would undermine unit cohesion and morale in combat, Urmanita says being out has had no negative impact. "My command seems to act as if I never came out to them," Urmanita writes in an e-mail from Iraq. "Work is still the same, and off time didn't change."

3   "I'm open about talking to my girlfriend over the phone," she continues. "I know other lesbians, and I've been seen hanging out with them. I'm just in a more comfortable environment because [my colleagues] know it's hard for me to be honest and open to the whole Army."

4   It's not just hard; it's forbidden. If the whole Army—or, particularly, the Pentagon—were to find out how open Urmanita is about her sexuality, she would be sent back to the United States immediately, like the more than 2,500 gay and lesbian soldiers who've been dismissed since the war began in 2003. In May, three linguists specializing in Arabic dialects were discharged under "don't ask, don't tell," bringing the total number of expelled specialists in that key language to 58 and prompting calls in Congress for an explanation.

5   Fourteen years ago, in debate leading up to the passage of "don't ask, don't tell," congressional witnesses testified that "the presence in the armed forces of persons who demonstrate a propensity or intent to engage in homosexual acts would create an unacceptable risk to the high standards of morale, good order and discipline, and unit cohesion that are the essence of military capability." Since then the American public's negative attitudes toward gays and lesbians have softened in many respects, but the Pentagon and a diminishing breed of politicians refuse to evolve.

6   Case in point: In April, U.S. senator from Arizona and 2008 Republican presidential candidate John McCain reinforced the military status quo, saying, "Open homosexuality within the military services presents an intolerable risk to morale, cohesion, and discipline." *The Advocate* spoke to some openly gay U.S. servicemen and women on active duty, only to find that the "intolerable risk" of their being out actually posed no risk at all.

7   This spring, Navy petty officer second class Jason Knight, then serving his second Middle East tour in Kuwait, was told he would be discharged after he spoke openly about his sexuality in the military paper *Stars and Stripes*. It was a bold move and not his first. Knight had previously come out to his command in 2005, just before the end of his first tour of duty, during which he served in Iraq as a linguist specializing in Hebrew. In response to his admission, he was told that, per "don't ask, don't tell" policy, discharge orders would be prepared, but—somewhat mysteriously—the paperwork failed to reach Knight's file, allowing him to complete his tour and remain in the inactive reserve. A year after he returned home, the Navy recalled him for a one-year deployment, and Knight reported for duty—with no plans to return to the closet. "I wasn't going to go back to that life," says Knight, now 24, via telephone from his home in San Diego. "My coworkers and direct chain of command were all aware of my sexuality, and it really didn't bother them."

8   It clearly bothered higher-ups, though. Within days of the *Stars and Stripes* article Knight was told he would be discharged—again—under "don't ask, don't tell," and the article was cited as one of the reasons. Knight's decision to go public was motivated by Joint Chiefs of Staff chairman Gen. Peter Pace's statement in March that homosexuality is "immoral," and his valor cost him his job. "I don't have any regrets," says Knight, who officially received his "don't ask, don't tell" discharge in late May, just before his latest military commitment was due to end. He has since joined the Servicemembers Legal Defense Network's national speakers' bureau and has met with congressional staffers. "This is a good opportunity for me to help lift the ban."

9   As soldiers like Urmanita and Knight are finding out, being gay in the service is often OK—as long as the Pentagon brass don't know. While simply being out is grounds for dismissal under "don't ask, don't tell," and certainly not all commands are accepting of gays and lesbians, in many cases the ban against openly gay service members is not being enforced. Dismissals under "don't ask, don't tell" have dropped significantly since peaking in 2001, with 2006 discharges just barely topping half the number handed down in '01.

10   Urmanita realizes that telling her story to the press could be grounds for discharge—and the decision to do so hasn't been easy. She had agreed to speak on the record for this story, but when news broke about Knight's discharge—the sailor has been interviewed by numerous media outlets, including *Good Morning America*—Urmanita reconsidered. She didn't specify why she didn't want to be a source any longer, but the reason seemed clear. Then she changed her mind again. "I'm sorry if I keep going back and forth

on this, but this time I'm sure," she writes in an e-mail. "I will take whatever consequences this article comes with, whether I do get discharged or I am kept in the Army. I want my story out."

11   Urmanita knew she was a lesbian before she enlisted with the Army in June 2006. Nevertheless, she says, "don't ask, don't tell" didn't concern her—until she discovered that the policy required her to make sacrifices most of her fellow soldiers didn't have to make. Concealing her personal life demanded forfeiture of the very values the Army reinforces from the first day of boot camp: loyalty, duty, respect, selfless service, honor, integrity, and personal courage. Hiding her sexuality, she says, meant "breaking the seven Army values every single day."

12   Rumors of her sexuality spread in her company, hastening her decision to come out. "I am not the type to lie or keep secrets from people, so I came clean," she writes. "I want to be open and honest about my sexuality, the same as everyone else." Today, almost everyone in Urmanita's unit knows she's a lesbian. And the revelation has had a beneficial effect on her relationship with comrades. "Before they knew about me, I was cool with them, but I didn't really talk to them or hang out with them," she explains. "Once they found out, it was like there are no secrets between us anymore. I can actually talk about my life with them."

13   It was the same for Army sergeant Darren Manzella, currently on his second deployment to the Middle East, when he came out to his unit in 2006. "For the most part, my peers have been supportive—or at the very least, indifferent—toward me," he says by phone from his home in Austin, where he was on leave from his station in Kuwait. The only change he's noticed is that closeted soldiers sometimes avoid him, "as if talking to me would automatically out them."

14   Manzella, now 29, joined the Army in 2002. He came under attack two years later while helping a field surgeon treat wounded soldiers in Iraq. In recognition of the valor he demonstrated while administering aid under fire he was awarded the Combat Medical Badge. Manzella returned to the United States in March 2005 at the completion of his first tour, and in the summer of 2006 he began receiving e-mails and phone calls from an anonymous individual who claimed to be a fellow soldier and who warned that an investigation into Manzella's sexuality was under way. To head off what he expected to be a painful inquiry and discharge, Manzella came out to his supervisors that August. In response, an official investigation into his sexual orientation was launched, but despite his own admission that he's gay, which is by itself enough to trigger a discharge, Manzella's command found no compelling evidence of his homosexuality and took no action.

15   Yet after he was sent to Iraq for a second tour in October 2006, Manzella was quickly moved to Kuwait to serve in a different section of his battalion. His superiors refused to give him a reason, but Manzella assumes the transfer was the Army's way of responding to his coming out. Still, he was not discharged, and he continues to be open about being gay.

16   Indeed, prior to his current deployment, Manzella introduced his military peers to his boyfriend. "There was some uncomfortable feelings among some of the males," he says. "But the majority showed no hostility or ill feelings." He remains close with a number of friends from his original section, who continue to be "very supportive." But like Urmanita, Manzella knows that publicly discussing his story could mean trouble. "It's worth it to me," he says. "I hope that putting my name to this story will make it possible for people to relate to this issue."

17   Many service members who are out within their units can't go public in a larger sense for fear of severing financial ties to the military. One sailor tells *The Advocate* that while he's happy to be out to his peers, he can't allow his name to be used in this article because he would have to repay all the college tuition reimbursements he's received from the military if he were discharged. "I've become even closer to most people than I was before being out, so I guess it's been lots better," he writes in an e-mail from his current station on a U.S. aircraft carrier. In fact, he says, he "would've come out sooner" had he known how well his colleagues would take the news (though he has not told his commander). An intelligence analyst, the sailor joined the Navy six years ago to see the world and to contribute to something bigger than himself, and he recently reenlisted for another four years of service.

18   "Plain and simple, we, as gay Americans, just want to serve, defend, and be a part of something that's been around longer than all of us and will be around for many years after us," he writes of his desire to be in the military. But he is obviously frustrated by "don't ask, don't tell"—an outdated and discriminatory policy if ever there were one. "Here's some irony," he writes in an e-mail. "As I sit here and type this message, I am also working on a classified briefing concerning terrorists who we are helping to track down. How funny is it that I'm here trying to help inform people of bad guys who are trying to kill innocents of their own country as well as many Americans, but if I was found out to be gay I'd be yanked out of here so fast?" Indeed. Under "don't ask, don't tell," he'd be the bad guy. ∎

Emily Martin and Katie Schwartzmann

Bad for Both Boys and Girls

Emily Martin works as deputy director of the Women's Rights Project of the American Civil Liberties Union (ACLU), and Katie Schwartzmann serves the ACLU as an attorney in Louisiana. The ACLU dedicates itself to preserving the Bill of Rights and ensuring personal freedoms for all Americans. It focuses much of its attention on citizens who are most often denied civil rights, such as women and minorities. In their opinion essay, which originally appeared on August 17, 2006, in USA Today, *Martin and Schwartzmann rebut the recent revival of sex-segregated schooling, arguing that single-sex education simply buys into traditional stereotypes about boys and girls and, in fact, harms both sexes more than it helps either.*

This summer, after receiving a complaint from parents told they faced a mandatory sex-segregated educational program at a public school in Livingston Parish, Louisiana, the ACLU filed a lawsuit and the school board quickly withdrew the plan. This was an exciting victory, but unfortunately, the Livingston school is not unique.

2   The U.S. Department of Education plans to release new rules that will allow for expanded use of single-sex education in public schools. Across the country, proponents of gender-segregation are touting boys- or girls-only classrooms as a fix-all solution to the woes of many struggling school districts. In addition to being unlawful, the rationale behind these programs is bad for kids.

3   Advocates of sex-segregated schools offer pseudo-scientific workshops where educators learn about alleged brain differences between boys and girls. According to some advocates: When establishing authority, teachers should not smile at boys because they're biologically programmed to read this as a sign of weakness; they should only look boys in the eyes when disciplining them; girls should not have time limits on tests or be put under stress because unlike boys, girls' brains cannot function well under these conditions; and girls don't understand mathematical theory very well except for a few days a month when their estrogen is surging. Although these ideas are hyped as "new discoveries" about brain differences, they are, in fact, only dressed up versions of old stereotypes—that boys must be bullied and girls must be coddled.

4   In the coming months, many school districts may introduce such programs. Rather than offering choice, sex-segregated programs limit the education of both boys and girls. Parents and students facing sex segregation in public schools should ask themselves whether these new claims about biological differences look much different from the old stereotypes that have always limited the choices of girls and boys.

5   The most reliable evidence available shows that proven approaches to educational reform—such as smaller classes, teachers with decent salaries and parental involvement—make much more sense than separating boys and girls based on outmoded stereotypes. ■

Andrew Sullivan

The End of Gay Culture

Andrew Sullivan is one of the leading commentators on gay, lesbian, and bisexual issues in the nation. Openly gay himself, devoutly Catholic, critical of certain aspects of the gay community, and outspokenly politically conservative in many respects, he nevertheless argues for full integration of gays and lesbians into American life. In 1996, Sullivan

disclosed that he was receiving treatment for AIDS and entered graduate studies in
government at Harvard University, where he eventually completed a PhD in political
science. One-time editor of The New Republic, *where this piece appeared in October*
2005, Sullivan now blogs extensively for The Atlantic.

For the better part of two decades, I have spent much of every summer in the small resort of Provincetown, at the tip of Cape Cod. It has long attracted artists, writers, the off-beat, and the bohemian; and, for many years now, it has been to gay America what Oak Bluffs in Martha's Vineyard is to black America: a place where a separate identity essentially defines a separate place. No one bats an eye if two men walk down the street holding hands, or if a lesbian couple pecks each other on the cheek, or if a drag queen dressed as Cher careens down the main strip on a motor scooter. It's a place, in that respect, that is sui generis. Except that it isn't anymore. As gay America has changed, so, too, has Provincetown. In a microcosm of what is happening across this country, its culture is changing.

2   Some of these changes are obvious. A real-estate boom has made Provincetown far more expensive than it ever was, slowly excluding poorer and younger visitors and residents. Where, once, gayness trumped class, now the reverse is true. Beautiful, renovated houses are slowly outnumbering beach shacks, once crammed with twenty-something, hand-to-mouth misfits or artists. The role of lesbians in the town's civic and cultural life has grown dramatically, as it has in the broader gay world. The faces of people dying from or struggling with AIDS have dwindled to an unlucky few. The number of children of gay couples has soared, and, some weeks, strollers clog the sidewalks. Bar life is not nearly as central to socializing as it once was. Men and women gather on the beach, drink coffee on the front porch of a store, or meet at the Film Festival or Spiritus Pizza.

3   And, of course, week after week this summer, couple after couple got married—well over a thousand in the year and a half since gay marriage has been legal in Massachusetts. Outside my window on a patch of beach that somehow became impromptu hallowed ground, I watched dozens get hitched—under a chuppah or with a priest, in formalwear or beach clothes, some with New Age drums and horns, even one associated with a full-bore Mass. Two friends lit the town monument in purple to celebrate; a tuxedoed male couple slipping onto the beach was suddenly greeted with a huge cheer from the crowd; an elderly lesbian couple attached cans to the back of their Volkswagen and honked their horn as they drove up the high street. The heterosexuals in the crowd knew exactly what to do. They waved and cheered and smiled. Then, suddenly, as if learning the habits of a new era, gay bystanders joined in. In an instant, the difference between gay and straight receded again a little.

4   But here's the strange thing: These changes did not feel like a revolution. They felt merely like small, if critical, steps in an inexorable evolution toward

the end of a distinctive gay culture. For what has happened to Provincetown this past decade, as with gay America as a whole, has been less like a political revolution from above than a social transformation from below. There is no single gay identity anymore, let alone a single look or style or culture. Memorial Day sees the younger generation of lesbians, looking like lost members of a boy band, with their baseball caps, preppy shirts, short hair, and earrings. Independence Day brings the partiers: the "circuit boys," with perfect torsos, a thirst for nightlife, designer drugs, and countless bottles of water. For a week in mid-July, the town is dominated by "bears"—chubby, hairy, unkempt men with an affinity for beer and pizza. Family Week heralds an influx of children and harried gay parents. Film Festival Week brings in the artsy crowd. Women's Week brings the more familiar images of older lesbians: a landlocked flotilla of windbreakers and sensible shoes. East Village bohemians drift in throughout the summer; quiet male couples spend more time browsing gourmet groceries and realtors than cruising nightspots; the predictable population of artists and writers—Michael Cunningham and John Waters are fixtures—mix with openly gay lawyers and cops and teachers and shrinks.

5   Slowly but unmistakably, gay culture is ending. You see it beyond the poignant transformation of P-town: on the streets of the big cities, on university campuses, in the suburbs where gay couples have settled, and in the entrails of the Internet. In fact, it is beginning to dawn on many that the very concept of gay culture may one day disappear altogether. By that, I do not mean that homosexual men and lesbians will not exist—or that they won't create a community of sorts and a culture that sets them in some ways apart. I mean simply that what encompasses gay culture itself will expand into such a diverse set of subcultures that "gayness" alone will cease to tell you very much about any individual. The distinction between gay and straight culture will become so blurred, so fractured, and so intermingled that it may become more helpful not to examine them separately at all.

6   For many in the gay world, this is both a triumph and a threat. It is a triumph because it is what we always dreamed of: a world in which being gay is a nonissue among our families, friends, and neighbors. But it is a threat in the way that all loss is a threat. For many of us who grew up fighting a world of now-inconceivable silence and shame, distinctive gayness became an integral part of who we are. It helped define us not only to the world but also to ourselves. Letting that go is as hard as it is liberating, as saddening as it is invigorating. And, while social advance allows many of us to contemplate this gift of a problem, we are also aware that in other parts of the country and the world, the reverse may be happening. With the growth of fundamentalism across the religious world—from Pope Benedict XVI's Vatican to Islamic fatwas and American evangelicalism—gayness is under attack in many places, even as it wrests free from repression in others. In fact, the two phenomena are related. The new anti-gay fervor is a response to the growing probability that the world will one day treat gay and straight as interchangeable humans and citizens rather than as estranged others. It is the end of gay culture—not its

endurance—that threatens the old order. It is the fact that, across the state of Massachusetts, "gay marriage" has just been abolished. The marriage licenses gay couples receive are indistinguishable from those given to straight couples. On paper, the difference is now history. In the real world, the consequences of that are still unfolding.

7   Quite how this has happened (and why) are questions that historians will fight over someday, but certain influences seem clear even now—chief among them the HIV epidemic. Before AIDS hit, a fragile but nascent gay world had formed in a handful of major U.S. cities. The gay culture that exploded from it in the 1970s had the force of something long suppressed, and it coincided with a more general relaxation of social norms. This was the era of the post-Stonewall New Left, of the Castro and the West Village, an era where sexuality forged a new meaning for gayness: of sexual adventure, political radicalism, and cultural revolution.

8   The fact that openly gay communities were still relatively small and geographically concentrated in a handful of urban areas created a distinctive gay culture. The central institutions for gay men were baths and bars, places where men met each other in highly sexualized contexts and where sex provided the commonality. Gay resorts had their heyday—from Provincetown to Key West. The gay press grew quickly and was centered around classified personal ads or bar and bath advertising. Popular culture was suffused with stunning displays of homosexual burlesque: the music of Queen, the costumes of the Village People, the flamboyance of Elton John's debut; the advertising of Calvin Klein; and the intoxication of disco itself, a gay creation that became emblematic of an entire heterosexual era. When this cultural explosion was acknowledged, when it explicitly penetrated the mainstream, the results, however, were highly unstable: Harvey Milk was assassinated in San Francisco and Anita Bryant led an anti-gay crusade. But the emergence of an openly gay culture, however vulnerable, was still real.

9   And then, of course, catastrophe. The history of gay America as an openly gay culture is not only extremely short—a mere 30 years or so—but also engulfed and defined by a plague that struck almost poignantly at the headiest moment of liberation. The entire structure of emergent gay culture—sexual, radical, subversive—met a virus that killed almost everyone it touched. Virtually the entire generation that pioneered gay culture was wiped out—quickly. Even now, it is hard to find a solid phalanx of gay men in their fifties, sixties, or seventies—men who fought from Stonewall or before for public recognition and cultural change. And those who survived the nightmare of the 1980s to mid-'90s were often overwhelmed merely with coping with plague; or fearing it themselves; or fighting for research or awareness or more effective prevention.

10   This astonishing story might not be believed in fiction. And, in fiction, it might have led to the collapse of such a new, fragile subculture. AIDS could

have been widely perceived as a salutary retribution for the gay revolution; it could have led to quarantining or the collapse of nascent gay institutions. Instead, it had the opposite effect. The tens of thousands of deaths of men from every part of the country established homosexuality as a legitimate topic more swiftly than any political manifesto could possibly have done. The images of gay male lives were recorded on quilts and in countless obituaries; men whose homosexuality might have been euphemized into nonexistence were immediately identifiable and gone. And those gay men and lesbians who witnessed this entire event became altered forever, not only emotionally, but also politically—whether through the theatrical activism of Act-Up or the furious organization of political gays among the Democrats and some Republicans. More crucially, gay men and lesbians built civil institutions to counter the disease; they forged new ties to scientists and politicians; they found themselves forced into more intense relations with their own natural families and the families of loved ones. Where bath houses once brought gay men together, now it was memorial services. The emotional and psychic bonding became the core of a new identity. The plague provided a unifying social and cultural focus.

11   But it also presaged a new direction. That direction was unmistakably outward and integrative. To borrow a useful distinction deployed by the writer Bruce Bawer, integration did not necessarily mean assimilation. It was not a wholesale rejection of the gay past, as some feared and others hoped. Gay men wanted to be fully part of the world, but not at the expense of their own sexual freedom (and safer sex became a means not to renounce that freedom but to save it). What the epidemic revealed was how gay men—and, by inference, lesbians—could not seal themselves off from the rest of society. They needed scientific research, civic support, and political lobbying to survive, in this case literally. The lesson was not that sexual liberation was mistaken, but rather that it wasn't enough. Unless the gay population was tied into the broader society; unless it had roots in the wider world; unless it brought into its fold the heterosexual families and friends of gay men and women, the gay population would remain at the mercy of others and of misfortune. A ghetto was no longer an option.

12   So, when the plague receded in the face of far more effective HIV treatments in the mid-'90s and gay men and women were able to catch their breath and reflect, the question of what a more integrated gay culture might actually mean reemerged. For a while, it arrived in a vacuum. Most of the older male generation was dead or exhausted; and so it was only natural, perhaps, that the next generation of leaders tended to be lesbian—running the major gay political groups and magazines. Lesbians also pioneered a new baby boom, with more lesbian couples adopting or having children. HIV-positive gay men developed different strategies for living suddenly posthumous lives. Some retreated into quiet relationships; others quit jobs or changed their careers completely; others chose the escapism of what became known as "the circuit," a series of rave parties around the country and the world where fears could be lost on the drug-enhanced dance floor; others still became lost in a suicidal vortex of crystal meth, Internet hook-ups, and sex addiction. HIV-negative

men, many of whom had lost husbands and friends, were not so different. In some ways, the toll was greater. They had survived disaster with their health intact. But, unlike their HIV-positive friends, the threat of contracting the disease still existed while they battled survivors' guilt. The plague was over but not over; and, as they saw men with HIV celebrate survival, some even felt shut out of a new sub-sub-culture, suspended between fear and triumph but unable to experience either fully.

13   Then something predictable and yet unexpected happened. While the older generation struggled with plague and post-plague adjustment, the next generation was growing up. For the first time, a cohort of gay children and teens grew up in a world where homosexuality was no longer a taboo subject and where gay figures were regularly featured in the press. If the image of gay men for my generation was one gleaned from the movie *Cruising* or, subsequently, *Torch Song Trilogy*, the image for the next one was MTV's "Real World," Bravo's "Queer Eye," and Richard Hatch winning the first "Survivor." The new emphasis was on the interaction between gays and straights and on the diversity of gay life and lives. Movies featured and integrated gayness. Even more dramatically, gays went from having to find hidden meaning in mainstream films—somehow identifying with the aging, campy female lead in a way the rest of the culture missed—to everyone, gay and straight, recognizing and being in on the joke of a character like "Big Gay Al" from "South Park" or Jack from "Will & Grace."

14   There are now openly gay legislators. Ditto Olympic swimmers and gymnasts and Wimbledon champions. Mainstream entertainment figures—from George Michael, Ellen DeGeneres, and Rosie O'Donnell to edgy musicians, such as the Scissor Sisters, Rufus Wainwright, or Bob Mould—now have their sexual orientation as a central, but not defining, part of their identity. The National Lesbian and Gay Journalists Association didn't exist when I became a journalist. Now it has 1,300 dues-paying members in 24 chapters around the country. Among Fortune 500 companies, 21 provided domestic partner benefits for gay spouses in 1995. Today, 216 do. Of the top Fortune 50 companies, 49 provide nondiscrimination protections for gay employees. Since 2002, the number of corporations providing full protections for openly gay employees has increased sevenfold, according to the Human Rights Campaign (HRC). Among the leaders: the defense giant Raytheon and the energy company Chevron. These are not traditionally gay-friendly work environments. Nor is the Republican Party. But the offspring of such leading Republican lights as Dick Cheney, Alan Keyes, and Phyllis Schlafly are all openly gay. So is the spokesman for the most anti-gay senator in Congress, Rick Santorum.

15   This new tolerance and integration—combined, of course, with the increased ability to connect with other gay people that the Internet provides—has undoubtedly encouraged more and more gay people to come out. The hard data for this are difficult to come by (since only recently have we had studies

that identified large numbers of gays) and should be treated with caution. Nevertheless, the trend is clear. If you compare data from, say, the 1994 National Health and Social Life Survey with the 2002 National Survey of Family Growth, you will find that women are nearly three times more likely to report being gay, lesbian, or bisexual today than they were eight years ago, and men are about 1.5 times more likely. There are no reliable statistics on openly gay teens, but no one doubts that there has been an explosion in visibility in the last decade—around 3,000 high schools have "gay-straight" alliances. The census, for its part, recorded a threefold increase in the number of same-sex unmarried partners from 1990 to 2000. In 2000, there were close to 600,000 households headed by a same-sex couple, and a quarter of them had children. If you want to know where the push for civil marriage rights came from, you need look no further. This was not an agenda invented by activists; it was a movement propelled by ordinary people.

16   So, as one generation literally disappeared and one generation found itself shocked to still be alive, a far larger and more empowered one emerged on the scene. This new generation knew very little about the gay culture of the '70s, and its members were oblivious to the psychically formative experience of plague that had shaped their elders. Most came from the heart of straight America and were more in tune with its new, mellower attitude toward gayness than the embattled, defensive urban gay culture of the pre-AIDS era. Even in evangelical circles, gay kids willing to acknowledge and struggle publicly with their own homosexuality represented a new form of openness. The speed of the change is still shocking. I'm only 42, and I grew up in a world where I literally never heard the word "homosexual" until I went to college. It is now not uncommon to meet gay men in their early twenties who took a boy as their date to the high school prom. When I figured out I was gay, there were no role models to speak of; and, in the popular culture, homosexuality was either a punch line or an embarrassed silence. Today's cultural climate could not be more different. And the psychological impact on the younger generation cannot be overstated.

17   After all, what separates homosexuals and lesbians from every other minority group is that they are born and raised within the bosom of the majority. Unlike Latino or Jewish or black communities, where parents and grandparents and siblings pass on cultural norms to children in their most formative stages, each generation of gay men and lesbians grows up being taught the heterosexual norms and culture of their home environments or absorbing what passes for their gay identity from the broader culture as a whole. Each shift in mainstream culture is therefore magnified exponentially in the next generation of gay children. To give the most powerful example: A gay child born today will grow up knowing that, in many parts of the world and in parts of the United States, gay couples can get married just as their parents did. From the very beginning of their gay lives, in other words, they will have internalized a sense of normality, of human potential, of self-worth—something that my generation never had and that previous generations would have found unimaginable. That shift in consciousness is as profound as it is irreversible.

18   To give another example: Black children come into society both uplifted and burdened by the weight of their communal past—a weight that is transferred within families or communities or cultural institutions, such as the church, that provide a context for self-understanding, even in rebellion. Gay children have no such support or burden. And so, in their most formative years, their self-consciousness is utterly different than that of their gay elders. That's why it has become increasingly difficult to distinguish between gay and straight teens today—or even young gay and straight adults. Less psychologically wounded, more self-confident, less isolated, young gay kids look and sound increasingly like young straight kids. On the dozens of college campuses I have visited over the past decade, the shift in just a few years has been astounding. At a Catholic institution like Boston College, for example, a generation ago there would have been no discussion of homosexuality. When I visited recently to talk about that very subject, the preppy, conservative student president was openly gay.

19   When you combine this generational plasticity with swift demographic growth, you have our current explosion of gay civil society, with a disproportionately young age distribution. I use the term "civil society" in its classic Tocquevillean and Burkean sense: the little platoons of social organization that undergird liberal democratic life. The gay organizations that erupted into being as AIDS killed thousands in the '80s—from the Gay Men's Health Crisis to the AIDS Project Los Angeles to the Whitman-Walker Clinic in Washington—struggled to adapt to the swift change in the epidemic in the mid-'90s. But the general principle of communal organization endured. If conservatives had been open-minded enough to see it, they would have witnessed a classic tale of self-help and self-empowerment.

20   Take, for example, religious life, an area not historically associated with gay culture. One of the largest single gay organizations in the country today is the Metropolitan Community Church, with over 40,000 active members. Go to, yes, Dallas, and you'll find the Cathedral of Hope, one of the largest religious structures in the country, with close to 4,000 congregants—predominantly gay. Almost every faith now has an explicitly gay denomination associated with it—Dignity for gay Catholics, *Bet Mishpachah* for gay Jews, and so on. But, in many mainstream Protestant churches and among Reform Jews, such groups don't even exist because the integration of gay believers is now mundane. These groups bring gays together in a context where sexuality is less a feature of identity than faith, where the interaction of bodies is less central than the community of souls.

21   In contrast, look at bar life. For a very long time, the fundamental social institution for gay men was the gay bar. It was often secluded—a refuge, a safe zone, and a clearinghouse for sexual pickups. Most bars still perform some of those functions. But the Internet dealt them a body-blow. If you are merely looking for sex or a date, the Web is now the first stop for most gay men. The result has been striking. Only a decade ago, you could wander up the West

Side Highway in New York City and drop by several leather bars. Now, only one is left standing, and it is less a bar dedicated to the ornate codes of '70s leather culture than a place for men who adopt a more masculine self-presentation. My favorite old leather bar, the Spike, is now the "Spike Gallery." The newer gay bars are more social than sexual, often with restaurants, open windows onto the street, and a welcoming attitude toward others, especially the many urban straight women who find gay bars more congenial than heterosexual pickup joints.

22   Even gay political organizations often function more as social groups than as angry activist groups. HRC, for example, raises funds and lobbies Congress. Around 350,000 members have contributed in the last two years. It organizes itself chiefly through a series of formal fund-raising dinners in cities across the country—from Salt Lake City to Nashville. These dinners are a social venue for the openly gay bourgeoisie: In tuxedos and ballgowns, they contribute large sums and give awards to local businesses and politicians and community leaders. There are silent auctions, hired entertainers, even the occasional bake-sale. The closest heterosexual equivalent would be the Rotary Club. These dinners in themselves are evidence of the change: from outsider rebellion to bourgeois organization.

23   Take a look at the gay press. In its shallower forms—glossy lifestyle magazines—you are as likely to find a straight Hollywood star on the cover as any gay icon. In its more serious manifestations, such as regional papers like the *Washington Blade* or *Southern Voice*, the past emphasis on sex has been replaced with an emphasis on domesticity. A recent issue of the *Blade* had an eight-page insert for escort ads, personals, and the kind of material that, two decades ago, would have been the advertising mainstay of the main paper. But in the paper itself are 23 pages of real-estate ads and four pages of home-improvement classifieds. There are columns on cars, sports, DVDs, and local plays. The core ad base, according to its editor, Chris Crain, now comprises heterosexual-owned and operated companies seeking to reach the gay market. The editorial tone has shifted as well. Whereas the *Blade* was once ideologically rigid—with endless reports on small activist cells and a strident left-wing slant—now it's much more like a community paper that might be published for any well-heeled ethnic group. Genuine ideological differences are now aired, rather than bitterly decried as betrayal or agitprop. Editorials regularly take Democrats to task as well as Republicans. The maturation has been as swift as it now seems inevitable. After all, in 2004, one-quarter of self-identified gay voters backed a president who supported a constitutional ban on gay marriage. If the gay world is that politically diverse under the current polarized circumstances, it has obviously moved well beyond the time it was synonymous with radical left politics.

24   How gay men and lesbians express their identity has also changed. When openly gay identity first emerged, it tended toward extremes of gender expression. When society tells you that gay men and lesbians are not fully male or female, the response can be to overcompensate with caricatures of each gender or to rebel by

blurring gender lines altogether. Effeminate "queens" were balanced by hyper-masculine bikers and muscle men; lipstick lesbians were offset by classically gruff "bull-dykes." All these sub-sub-cultures still exist. Many feel comfortable with them; and, thankfully, we see fewer attempts to marginalize them. But the polarities in the larger gay population are far less pronounced than they once were; the edges have softened. As gay men have become less defensive about their masculinity, their expression of it has become subtler. There is still a pronounced muscle and gym culture, but there are also now openly gay swimmers and artists and slobs and every body type in between. Go watch a gay rugby team compete in a regional tournament with straight teams and you will see how vast but subtle the revolution has been. And, in fact, this is the trend: gay civil associations in various ways are interacting with parallel straight associations in a way that leaves their gay identity more and more behind. They're rugby players first, gay rugby players second.

25   One of the newest reflections of this is what is known as "bear" culture: heavy, hirsute, unkempt guys who revel in their slovenliness. Their concept of what it means to be gay is very different than that of the obsessive gym-rats with torsos shaved of every stray hair. Among many younger gay men, the grungy look of their straight peers has been adopted and tweaked to individual tastes. Even among bears, there are slimmer "otters" or younger "cubs" or "musclebears," who combine gym culture with a bear sensibility. The varieties keep proliferating; and, at the rate of current change, they will soon dissipate into the range of identities that straight men have to choose from. In fact, these variations of masculinity may even have diversified heterosexual male culture as well. While some gay men have proudly adopted some classically straight signifiers— beer bellies and back hair—many straight men have become "metrosexuals." Trying to define "gay culture" in this mix is an increasingly elusive task.

26   Among lesbians, Ellen DeGeneres's transition from closeted sitcom star to out-lesbian activist and back to appealingly middle-brow daytime talk-show host is almost a microcosm of diversifying lesbian identity in the past decade. There are still classic butch-femme lesbian partnerships, but more complex forms of self-expression are more common now. With the abatement in many places of prejudice, lesbian identity is formed less by reaction to hostility than by simple self-expression. And this, after all, is and was the point of gay liberation: the freedom not merely to be gay according to some preordained type, but to be yourself, whatever that is.

27   You see this even in drag, which once defined gayness in some respects but now is only one of many expressions. Old-school drag, the kind that dominated the '50s, '60s, and '70s, often consisted of female impersonators performing torch songs from various divas. The more miserable the life of the diva, the better able the performer was to channel his own anguish and drama into the show. After all, gayness was synonymous with tragedy and showmanship. Judy Garland, Marilyn Monroe, Bette Davis: these were the models. But today's drag looks and feels very different. The drag impresario of Provincetown, a

twisted genius called Ryan Landry, hosts a weekly talent show for local drag performers called "Showgirls." Attending it each Monday night is P-town's equivalent of weekly Mass. A few old-school drag queens perform, but Landry sets the tone. He makes no attempt to look like a woman, puts on hideous wigs (including a horse mask and a pair of fake boobs perched on his head), throws on ill-fitting dresses, and performs scatological song parodies. Irony pervades the show. Comedy defines it. Gay drag is inching slowly toward a version of British pantomime, where dada humor and absurd, misogynist parodies of woman-hood are central. This is post-drag; straight men could do it as well. This year, the longest-running old school drag show—"Legends"—finally closed down. Its audience had become mainly heterosexual and old.

28   This new post-gay cultural synthesis has its political counterpart. There was once a ferocious debate among gays between what might be caricatured as "separatists" and "assimilationists." That argument has fizzled. As the gay popu-lation has grown, it has become increasingly clear that the choice is not either/or but both/and. The issue of civil marriage reveals this most graphically. When I first argued for equal marriage rights, I found myself assailed by the gay left for social conservatism. I remember one signing for my 1995 book, *Virtually Normal*, the crux of which was an argument for the right to marry. I was picketed by a group called "Lesbian Avengers," who depicted my argument as patriarchal and reactionary. They crafted posters with my face portrayed within the crosshairs of a gun. Ten years later, lesbian couples make up a majority of civil marriages in Massachusetts and civil unions in Vermont; and some of the strongest voices for marriage equality have been lesbians, from the pioneering lawyer Mary Bonauto to writer E. J. Graff. To its credit, the left—gay male and lesbian—recognized that what was at stake was not so much the corralling of all gay individuals into a con-formist social institution as a widening of choice for all. It is still possible to be a gay radical or rigid leftist. The difference now is that it is also possible to be a gay conservative, or traditionalist, or anything else in between.

29 Who can rescue a uniform gay culture? No one, it would seem. The generation most psychologically wedded to the separatist past is either dead from HIV or sidelined. But there are still enclaves of gay distinctiveness out there. Para-doxically, gay culture in its old form may have its most fertile ground in those states where homosexuality is still unmentionable and where openly gay men and women are more beleaguered: the red states. Earlier this year, I spoke at an HRC dinner in Nashville, Tennessee, where state politicians are trying to bar gay couples from marrying or receiving even basic legal protections. The younger gay generation is as psychologically evolved there as any place else. They see the same television and the same Internet as gay kids in New York. But their social space is smaller. And so I found a vibrant gay world, but one far more cohesive, homogeneous, and defensive than in Massachusetts. The strip of gay bars—crammed into one place rather than diffuse, as in many blue-state cities—was packed on a Saturday night. The mix of old and young, gay and lesbian, black, white, and everything in between reminded me of

Boston in the '80s. The tired emblems of the past—the rainbow flags and leather outfits—retained their relevance there.

30   The same goes for black and Latino culture, where homophobia, propped up by black churches and the Catholic hierarchy respectively, is more intense than in much of white society. It's no surprise that these are the populations also most at risk for HIV. The underground "down-low" culture common in black gay life means less acknowledgment of sexual identity, let alone awareness or disclosure of HIV status. The same repression that facilitated the spread of HIV among gay white men in the '70s now devastates black gay America, where the latest data suggest a 50 percent HIV infection rate. (Compare that with largely white and more integrated San Francisco, where recent HIV infection rates are now half what they were four years ago.) The extremes of gender expression are also more pronounced among minorities, with many gay black or Latino men either adopting completely female personalities or refusing to identify as gay at all. Here the past lives on. The direction toward integration is clear, but the pace is far slower.

31   And, when you see the internalized defensiveness of gays still living in the shadow of social hostility, any nostalgia one might feel for the loss of gay culture dissipates. Some still echo critic Philip Larkin's jest that he worried about the American civil rights movement because it was ruining jazz. But the flipness of that remark is the point, and the mood today is less genuine regret—let alone a desire to return to those days—than a kind of wistfulness for a past that was probably less glamorous or unified than it now appears. It is indeed hard not to feel some sadness at the end of a rich, distinct culture built by pioneers who braved greater ostracism than today's generation will ever fully understand. But, if there is a real choice between a culture built on oppression and a culture built on freedom, the decision is an easy one. Gay culture was once primarily about pain and tragedy, because that is what heterosexuals imposed on gay people, and that was, in part, what gay people experienced. Gay culture was once primarily about sex, because that was how heterosexuals defined gay lives. But gay life, like straight life, is now and always has been about happiness as well as pain; it is about triumph as well as tragedy; it is about love and family as well as sex. It took generations to find the self-worth to move toward achieving this reality in all its forms—and an epidemiological catastrophe to accelerate it. If the end of gay culture means that we have a new complexity to grapple with and a new, less cramped humanity to embrace, then regret seems almost a rebuke to those countless generations who could only dream of the liberty so many now enjoy.

32   The tiny, rich space that gay men and women once created for themselves was, after all, the best they could do. In a metaphor coined by the philosopher Michael Walzer, they gilded a cage of exclusion with magnificent ornaments; they spoke to its isolation and pain; they described and maintained it with dignity and considerable beauty. But it was still a cage. And the thing that kept gay people together, that unified them into one homogeneous unit, and that defined the parameters of their culture and the limits of their dreams,

were the bars on that cage. Past the ashes of thousands and through the courage of those who came before the plague and those who survived it, those bars are now slowly but inexorably being pried apart. The next generation may well be as free of that cage as any minority ever can be; and they will redefine gayness on its own terms and not on the terms of hostile outsiders. Nothing will stop this, since it is occurring in the psyches and souls of a new generation: a new consciousness that is immune to any law and propelled by the momentum of human freedom itself. While we should treasure the past, there is no recovering it. The futures—and they will be multiple—are just beginning. ■

Alexa Hackbarth

Vanity, Thy Name Is Metrosexual

In the last several years a new term, metrosexual, *has moved toward the center of discussions about sexuality and masculinity. Most likely coined by journalist Mark Simpson in 1994, the term* metrosexual *has been the subject of many definition arguments on talk radio and TV and in the print media. Alexa Hackbarth, a research assistant and photo technician at the* Washington Post *who has done freelance writing since 1999, invokes the term in her discussion of dating protocols that is reprinted below from the November 17, 2003,* Post.

A t dinner the other night, my date listed the calorie count of the main entrees, raising an eyebrow at my chicken Alfredo selection after he had ordered a salad. I saw him check his reflection in the silver water pitcher three times. During dessert, he looked deeply into my eyes and told me he thought what we have together is very special. It was our third date.

2   It was then that I realized why my dating life has been as mysterious as the Bermuda Triangle since I arrived in Washington. This city, unlike any other place I've lived, is a haven for the metrosexual. A metrosexual, in case you didn't catch any of several newspaper articles about this developing phenomenon (or the recent "South Park" episode on Comedy Central), is a straight man who styles his hair using three different products (and actually calls them "products"), loves clothes and the very act of shopping for them, and describes himself as sensitive and romantic. In other words, he is a man who seems stereotypically gay except when it comes to sexual orientation.

3   Gay men say they actually have a bit of trouble telling the straight from the gay anymore. But at least this new breed of man is more likely to thank the gay man for the compliment than punch him in the face after being approached, which may indicate that metrosexuals are more accepting of other people's sexual preferences. Either that or they're afraid of breaking a nail when their fist makes contact.

4   My primary concern, however, is that women are also having a difficult time telling straight men from gay men. Maybe city girls really do want a boyfriend who can pick out a purse that goes with her outfit, who likes to talk about calorie intake and celebrity hook-ups. But there are just too many men in this city who know all the soap opera story lines and designer labels and too few who associate sweat with hard work instead of a stint in the sauna.

5   In the small western ranching town where I grew up, men wrangle cattle before sitting down to a breakfast of bacon and eggs. They're the strong and silent type, capable and calm in a crisis. They know how to fix a leaky faucet or rewire an electrical outlet. They drive pickup trucks. And when they cook, it's steak and potatoes, not wine-braised duck. They sure don't spend hours in front of the mirror only to emerge with prettier hair than mine.

6   Metrosexuals are overwhelmingly city-dwellers, which makes sense since Diesel, Banana Republic, Gap and Express Men are rarely found down dirt roads. The source of my confusion, however, is the overwhelming abundance of this type of man in Washington. This is a city of transplants, rural and urban alike. But for some reason, each of the nearly two dozen men I have dated over the past eight months has displayed metrosexual traits. I met quite a few of them in bars, some in coffeeshops and grocery stores, and one or two through mutual friends. I figure I've experienced a decent cross-section of the city's dating pool. So where, as Paula Cole sings, have all the cowboys gone?

7   I understand that men, like women, want to look their best in order to convey professionalism, attract lovers and improve their self-image. I just don't think they're going about it the right way. It's as if, in an effort to move far away from the image of a smelly, unshaven man smashing beer cans on his forehead and wiping his nacho cheese down the front of his stained T-shirt, these guys have swung too far in the opposite direction. It makes me uncomfortable when a man can discuss the new season's fashions in intimate detail. Perhaps I am unusually insensitive, but I don't want a man who pours out his heart on the fourth date. I lose interest in men who not only won't make the first move, but hesitate to make the second and third. I don't want my date to be tearing up at the end of a movie when I'm sitting there dry-eyed.

8   We're living in an exciting time. America's social fabric is being unraveled and rewoven as we become more accepting of the differences that make each individual unique and our country so great. I have no arguments with expressions of individuality. But I will admit to worrying when I read the results of a survey of American men aged 21 to 48, conducted by Euro RSCG Worldwide, that says more than two-thirds of men value love over professional success. As it should be, you say. Perhaps. But only if the men surveyed were just those with families.

9   Who are the young, single men who say they value love over anything else? My guess is they're predominantly members of this new breed called metrosexuals: men in touch with their so-called feminine side who would rather "grow old with the woman they love," even if they haven't met her yet,

than "head up a Fortune 500 company." This might be endearing and romantic, but it's not very productive. It doesn't make scientific and medical advances, it doesn't help develop solid foreign policy and it doesn't contribute to the gross national product.

10   So what is the motivation behind this metrosexual trend? A number of close male friends have told me that any secondary reasons for a straight man's behavior are completely overshadowed by their central motivation: to attract women. Men, they tell me, acquire money, status and distinguished job titles to impress and win the ladies, whether in droves or in terms of "till death do us part." They hear women describe the perfect man as being sensitive, sweet and romantic and aspire to that description.

11   But frank, open confessions of emotions on the first date? Poorly written poetry and a closet full of shoes? Plot-line knowledge of "The Bold and the Beautiful"? This just seems like way too much work to get a woman's attention, especially if the man is, indeed, looking to grow old with her. That's a long time to keep up the act. And while the theory that men are changing their images and priorities for love seems terribly flattering to us women, I find it hard to believe.

12   I'd hate to think that this is all the result of marketing and advertising pressure.

13   We all recognize the influence these methods have on people, both individually and en masse. That's why propaganda is an essential part of every war. That's why anorexia and bulimia were, and still are, such a problem in young girls. It is interesting to note that the term "metrosexual" was actually coined a few years ago by a writer in a satirical comment on "consumerism's toll on traditional masculinity." Marketers, like sharks in a feeding frenzy, grabbed on to the term and are currently masticating their way through the attached school of consumers who are willing to pay $150 for a pair of jeans. But even if this explains how a man can rationalize spending $75 on moisturizing cream, it still doesn't explain the mind-set that goes with it.

14   The metrosexual movement can't just be about love. Commercialism also can't be held solely responsible. And it's not just a heightened appreciation of the finer things in life.

15   These are all aspects of what drives this type of man, just as it motivates the women who consider shopping to be a form of therapy, who fall in love every other week, who live vicariously through the characters on TV. We all do this to some extent. But there's something more to it.

16   Perhaps this metrosexual trend indicates how far removed we've become from the real world.

17   Concrete cause-and-effect is becoming more and more disconnected from the lives of those of us fortunate enough to have the resources to be extravagant. Impracticality has become an indicator of progress. Money can provide every creature comfort, without requiring any skill or knowledge except that which earned the money in the first place. A man with money doesn't need to know how to install a water heater. He doesn't need to know his way around a

sawhorse; he can pay some- one else to build his cabinets.

18 Maybe the lack of a vis- ible connection between hard work and the fruits of labor means that satisfaction in a job well done is much more elusive today than it used to be. And maybe, if fulfillment isn't being found in work, we end up looking to relation- ships to provide this sense of satisfaction and contented- ness. But while I enjoy being

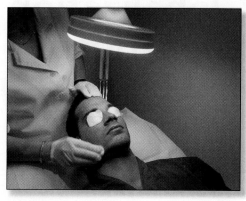

Spas for men.

in love as much as the next person, perhaps we shouldn't force its existence sim- ply because we feel disconnected and adrift. It almost seems as if love and money and status are all just flimsy stand-ins for something more.

19 The emergence of metrosexuals, prevalent enough both to warrant a label and provoke discussion, indicates that something has been missing in the lives of these men. I just hope they find what they're looking for. ■

24

Globalization: Importing and Exporting America

In June 2007, a group called the Fair Immigration Reform Movement organized a march on Washington, D.C., to protest immigration laws that force families to live apart. By using the strollers and the posters, what values are the protesters appealing to?

America's Place in the World

The place of America and Americans in relation to the rest of the world has always been an important topic in the national conversation. As a nation of immigrants, the United States has taken an increasing role in international affairs since its founding. But that topic has only grown more important, it seems, since the end of the Cold War (which seemed to leave the United States as the world's only superpower); since the development of economic reforms in China, in the European Union, and in other parts of the world (which are challenging the primacy of American economic power); and especially since the events of September 11 and the subsequent war in Iraq (which have underscored the limits of the American military and compromised our will to work cooperatively with traditional allies). Indeed, according to a survey released on August 18, 2004, by the Pew Research Center for the People and the Press, the American public has a divided, even paradoxical opinion about the place of the United States in the world. On the one hand, Americans agree that the United States has assumed a more powerful role as a world leader, but, on the other hand, they concede that America also seems less respected around the world. Americans reject the role of the United States as a single world leader, but they also reject the pull toward isolation. More generally, then, Americans are confronting the issue of what has come to be known as globalization—that is, the general impact of various nations on each other and more particularly the impact of American culture on other nations and cultures, and their impact on the United States.

Some of those impacts are economic, as the United States outsources manufacturing jobs to other nations and shifts in the direction of a service economy. Other impacts are military and political, as leaders and citizens debate the wisdom of various options. (For example, should our nation behave as a kind of American

"THE BAD NEWS IS OPERATION ANACONDA DEVASTATED OUR FORCES. THE GOOD NEWS IS THE AMERICAN INS APPROVED YOUR VISA."

Source: Henry Payne reprinted by permission of United Feature Syndicate, Inc.

empire, free to impose its wishes and will on others? Should our foreign policy be an effort to export democracy, even at the point of a gun? Or should we cooperate more broadly with allies, cultivate new friends, and respect the right of each nation to self-determination? Should the United States close off its borders, literally and figuratively, to follow a kind of neo-isolationism?) Yet other impacts are broadly cultural, as Americans import some of the cultural practices and values of others (as in popular songs, films, restaurants, fashions, and so forth) and export our own cultural values and traditions to others. This chapter of *Good Reasons with Contemporary Arguments* offers arguments about one or another aspect of these questions related to globalization.

Contemporary Arguments

The chapter begins with immigration. Just about everyone can quote the famous words that Emma Lazarus wrote for the pedestal of the Statue of Liberty ("Give me your tired, your poor, your huddled masses yearning to breathe free, the wretched refuse of your teeming shore. Send these, the homeless, tempest-tost to me") because the United States prides itself on being a nation of immigrants. And recently we have made good on the promise: more than 10 percent of our people, over 30 million in all (up from 10 million in 1970), were born in other countries. Indeed, according to the 2000 census, one in five U.S. citizens was born either abroad or to foreign-born parents. Steady increases in immigration after World War II developed into a boom during the 1980s and 1990s in part because the 1965 Immigration Act (amended in 1990) looked favorably on the immigration of relatives of U.S. citizens; repealed quotas on immigrants from certain nations; and therefore encouraged immigration from Asia, Latin America, and Africa. As a result, in 2000 and 2001 over a million people immigrated to the United States. While immigrants in the late nineteenth and early twentieth centuries mostly came from southern and central Europe, most of today's immigrants come from Mexico; the Caribbean islands; the former Soviet Union; and Asian nations such as China, Vietnam, the Philippines, and India. While earlier immigrants typically passed by the Statue of Liberty and were processed at Ellis Island before going on to northern cities, more than half of recent immigrants have been attracted to Florida, Texas, and California.

The Statue of Liberty

Nevertheless, there has also been a long history of resistance to immigration in the United States, dating at least to those who proudly enrolled in the Know Nothing political party of the 1840s and 1850s. Members of that political faction resisted the immigrants from Ireland and Germany who were arriving in waves, and they tended to blame all the nation's ills on immigration—crime, economic problems, and social stresses. The questions (and fears) raised by those early critics persist today, except that now they are raised in connection with Asians, Arabs, and Latin Americans. Just what are the social and economic effects of immigration? How quickly and how completely do immigrants become assimilated—learning the majority language, identifying themselves with American cultural values, and participating in American political life? What is our national responsibility to support, educate, and help assimilate immigrants? Do immigrants constitute a threat to the nation's economic well-being because they are commonly poor and less educated, because they take jobs away from native workers, and because they require expensive social services, such as welfare, education, and health? Or do immigrants actually increase the nation's wealth because they are highly motivated and because they supply labor to a perennially labor-hungry economy? Do immigrants endanger our democracy because they cling to their original national identities, are slow to learn English, and participate only fitfully in political life—or do immigrants enrich the nation with their values and beliefs, ideas and ideals, and hopes and hard work? Do immigrants pose a threat to national security?

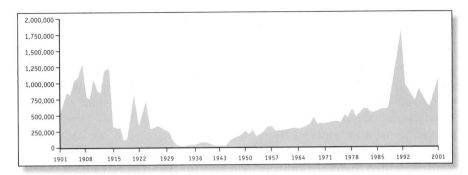

Legal Immigration, 1991–2001
Source: "Legal Immigration, Fiscal Year 2001." Immigration and Naturalization Service,
U.S. Department of Justice.

This section provides diverse perspectives on immigration. In "No Human Being Is Illegal," Mae Ngai takes a balanced look at the stereotypes of immigrants in the United States, while keeping individual differences central. Meanwhile, Michelle Malkin offers a politically conservative perspective on the risks of immigrants as potential terrorist threats. Helen Epstein uses her personal narrative as a jumping-off point to pose questions about the effectiveness and purposes of immigration policies at work in the United States today.

Elsewhere in this book, you may already have read about the serious debates that surround immigration. In "Crossing the Line" (page 200), Dan Stein argues that illegal immigrants are being dangerously welcomed when banks issue them

Waiting on the Mexican side of the Rio Grande.

credit cards. Responding to Stein, Gregory Rodriguez argues in "Illegal Immigrants—They're Money" (page 202) that people who have come to the United States to work should not be denied the opportunity for credit that other Americans enjoy. For narrative arguments about immigration, turn to "My Landlady's Yard" (page 187), Dagoberto Gilb's essay on immigration and community, or Leslie Marmon Silko's "The Border Patrol State (page 182), which relates the experience of being pulled over by the border police.

The final arguments in this chapter shift the focus to the exchange of economies and cultural goods between the United States and other nations. Todd Gitlin's essay uses iconic American cultural signs to argue that the global village today has a distinctly American flavor—though that flavor blends and changes in its new environments. Urvashi Butalia looks at young Indian women and the ways in which their entrepreneurship and demand for increased financial and educational opportunities challenge traditional Indian values. In an essay about Wal-Mart and Mexico, Laura Carlsen discusses her concern about the broader impact of American

IMMIGRATION WEB SITES

You can learn more about immigration and read more arguments about it at a number of places on the World Wide Web. Here are a few:

U.S. Department of Homeland Security, U.S. Citizenship and Immigration Services, administers and enforces U.S. immigration policy. For information check the Office of Immigration Statistics at uscis.gov/graphics/shared/statistics/index.htm.

For information about immigration from the U.S. Census Bureau, see www. census.gov/main/www/cen2000.html.

The Cato Institute offers demographic and economic statistics about immigrants: www. cato.org.

The Alexis de Tocqueville Institution works to increase public understanding of the cultural and economic benefits of immigration: www.adti.net.

The Center for Immigration Studies conducts research on the impact of immigration: www.cis.org.

The Federation for American Immigration Reform (FAIR) lobbies in favor of placing restrictions on immigration: www.fairus.org.

The National Council of La Raza lobbies on behalf of Latinos in the United States: www.nclr.org.

The National Immigration Forum builds public support for immigration: www. immigrationforum.org.

The Immigration History Research Center, based at the University of Minnesota, is a substantial resource on American immigration and ethnic history: www. ihrc.umn.edu.

A TIME LINE ON IMMIGRATION

1607. The first permanent English settlement at Jamestown, Virginia, is established.

1607–1776. "Open Door" era: individual colonies encourage immigration, restricting only criminals and "undesirables."

1776–1835. The "First Great Lull" in immigration: immigration numbers are low.

1808. Importation of slaves is halted.

1840s. Irish immigration (as a result of famine) initiates an era of mass immigration that lasts until World War I.

1875. The Supreme Court decides that immigration policy is the responsibility of the federal government, not the states.

1882–1917. Asian immigration is effectively interdicted. The 1882 Chinese Exclusion Act bars Chinese in particular.

1892. Ellis Island in New York Harbor becomes the leading entry point for immigrants.

1890–1920. A wave of immigration from southern and eastern Europe peaks at 1.3 million in 1907.

1921. Quotas are initiated to reduce immigration sharply and to make

immigration reflect the established face of the American community (i.e., white and European).

1920–1945. Second "Great Lull" in immigration: more restrictive immigration policies, the effects of the Great Depression, and the Second World War limit the number of immigrants who settle in the United States.

1940s. Restrictions on Asian immigration are dropped.

1954. Operation Wetback effectively stops illegal immigration.

1965. The Immigration and Nationality Act increases immigration quotas, abolishes the principle of taking into account immigrants' national origins, and emphasizes family unification.

1986. The Immigration Reform and Control Act provides amnesty for many illegal immigrants.

1990s and 2000s. Immigration numbers increase substantially—for both legal and illegal immigrants.

Basic sources: Peter Brimelow, *Alien Nation; CQ Researcher*

economic power on the cultures of other nations. Finally, Darla Deardorff explains the concept of intercultural competence and explores ways that different cultural communities can effectively communicate with one another.

While the topics discussed in this chapter are varied, all of the readings bring up similar questions about the movement between cultures—of people, goods, values, images, and communication. What do you think about American importation of cultural forms from other nations? What about exportation of American culture that is welcomed—even sought out—by people in other nations? Is this importation and exportation dangerous, enriching, or some complicated mixture of the two?

Mae M. Ngai

No Human Being Is Illegal

Mae M. Ngai is a professor of history at the University of Chicago, where she specializes in immigration studies. Her 2005 book, Impossible Subjects: Illegal Aliens and the Making of Modern America, *provides a fresh perspective on the vital role that immigrants play in U.S. history and culture. She emphasizes how vital immigrants are to U.S. economic growth, even when immigrants come from very difficult backgrounds. "No Human Being Is Illegal," published in* Women's Studies Quarterly *in 2006, takes a similar stance. The essay challenges readers to rethink the stereotypes we use to label immigrants and raises fundamental questions about what it means to participate in American society with and without the privilege of citizenship.*

L ike abortion and guns, immigration has emerged as a hot-button issue in American politics. Because immigration involves concerns in
different registers, economic and cultural, it is strangely and perhaps
uniquely misaligned in traditional partisan terms (Wong 2006; Zolberg
2006). President Bush cannot manage the split in his own party, between
those Republicans who want to exploit immigrants and those who want to
expel them. Among Democratic voters, some support cultural diversity and
inclusion while others worry that cheaper immigrant labor depresses domestic wages. Political consultants, sensing a no-win situation, are advising
Democrats with presidential aspirations to stay clear of the issue altogether.

2   The lack of partisan coherence, however, does not explain why immigration evokes such heated debate. There is a dimension to the debate that
seems irrational, impervious to arguments involving empirical data, historical experience, or legal precedent. This was brought home to me after
I wrote an op-ed in a major newspaper about how, during the first half of
the twentieth century, the U.S. government legalized tens of thousands of
illegal European immigrants (Ngai 2006). I received postcards with invec-
tives like, "stupid professor!" I faced similar hostility during a live call-in
show on public radio. Confronted with ranting about how immigrants are
bad for the United States, I wanted to counter that immigrants are good for
the United States. At one level, negative generalizations about immigrants
can be refuted point by point: they do not hurt the economy, they expand
it; they are more law abiding than the native-born population; they want to
learn English and their children all do (Smith and Edmonston 1997; Alba
and Nee 2003).

3   But this approach is risky. Generalizations reproduce stereotypes and
efface the complexity and diversity of immigrant experience. As Bonnie
Honig (2001) has argued, xenophilia is the flip side of xenophobia. In both

cases citizens use "immigrants" as a screen onto which they project their own aspirations or frustrations about American democracy. Casting immigrants as bearers of the work ethic, family values, and consensual citizenship renews the tired citizen's faith-liberal capitalism. But when the immigrants disappoint or when conditions change, they become easy scapegoats.

4   As Honig suggests, this kind of immigration discourse is an exercise in nationalism. In an important sense, "Are immigrants good or bad for us?" is the wrong question. It takes as its premise that immigrants are not part of "us." The idea falsely posits that non-citizens are not part of American society and leaves them out of the discussion. The mass demonstrations of Mexicans and other immigrants last spring were significant because they showed that immigrants are no longer content to be the object of discussion but have emerged as subjects with voice and agency. It was particularly noteworthy but perhaps not surprising that so many of the participants were female, from older hotel workers to high school students, giving lie to the stereotypes that the "illegal alien" is a solo male laborer or that immigrants are meek. Undocumented immigration involves men, women, and families, and they are all standing up.

5   Further, the question assumes that "we" (the United States, defined by its citizens) have a singular interest above and against the interests of "them" (all non-citizens and the foreign countries from whence they came). To be sure, while human migration is as old as human history, immigration and naturalization are modern phenomena, part of the international system based on nation-states that was consolidated in the period between the late nineteenth century and World War I. In this system, sovereign nations assert their absolute right to determine, in the first instance, who shall be admitted to territory and membership and who shall not.

6   In the United States, immigration was not regulated by the federal government until after the civil war, and not until the late 1880s and 1890s did the U.S. Supreme Court invoke the sovereign principle as the basis for immigration policy. Before that, it considered immigration part of the commerce clause of the Constitution; as laborers, immigrants were easily imagined as "articles of commerce" (Bilder 1996).

7   But Chinese exclusion, first legislated in 1882, required the Court to justify why some laborers were desired and others were not. Was the claim that Chinese were racially inassimilable an acceptable reason? The Court said yes; in fact, it said that Congress did not have to justify itself in terms of the Constitution. In the Chinese Exclusion Case (130 U.S. 518 [1889]) the Court recognized Congress's plenary, or absolute power to regulate immigration as part of its authority over foreign relations, in the same realm as declaring war and making treaties. "Aliens enter and remain in the United States only with the license, permission, and sufferance of Congress," it opined (Fong Yue Ting v. U.S., 149 U.S. 698 [1893]). To this day the plenary power doctrine over immigration stands.

8   American political culture has thoroughly normalized the primacy of national sovereignty in immigration affairs, and with important consequences. Nationalism generates the view that immigration is a zero-sum game among competitive nation-states. Americans like to believe that immigration to the United States proves the superiority of liberal capitalism, that "America" is the object of global envy; we resist examining the role that American world power has played in global structures of migration, including the gendered dimensions of migrant exploitation. Increasing numbers of women from the global south are leaving their families behind as they migrate to the affluent countries to work as caretakers for other people's children, as hotel-room cleaners, or as indentured sex-workers. We prefer to ignore these realities and to think, instead, that our immigration policy is generous—indeed, too generous, as we also resent the demands made upon us by others and we think we owe outsiders nothing (Ngai 2004).

9   The emphasis on national sovereignty is the basis for the alarm that we've "lost control" of the border and for the draconian proposals against unauthorized immigration: more fencing, criminalization of the undocumented and those who hire or assist them, mass deportations. But many liberals who are sympathetic to Mexican immigrants also want "something done" to stop illegal immigration, although few would actually support turning the entire country into a police state, which is what would be necessary to truly seal the border from unauthorized entry. The cost of viewing sovereignty as the exclusive grounds for immigration policy is that we push to the margins other

Emma Lazarus

The New Colossus

Emma Lazarus (1849–1887) wrote poetry and essays on a wide variety of topics. Her works were were published in the best-known magazines of her time, and she became an influential figure in the rapidly changing New York art scene. She was born into a well-established Jewish family in New York City, was well educated, and worked to improve the conditions of Jews both at home and abroad by establishing programs to educate new immigrants and by founding the Society for the Improvement and Colonization of Eastern European Jews. Her most famous sonnet, reprinted here, was written in 1883 to help raise money for the Statue of Liberty Pedestal, and in 1903 it was engraved on a tablet within the pedestal on which the Statue of Liberty now stands.

considerations, such as human rights and global distributive justice. The current debate over immigration policy reform reminds us that sovereignty is not just a claim to national right; it is a theory of power (Carens 1998).

10   Just two months before September 11, 2001, it will be recalled, President Bush announced his intention to legalize undocumented Mexican immigrants and institute a guest-worker program that would offer a path to permanent residency and citizenship. In its details it was not particularly generous and it faced a complex process of legislative negotiation, as have all efforts to reform the immigration laws. But it did not provoke the kind of emotional controversy that we hear today.

11   However, after 9/11 the immigration issue disappeared from the Washington scene. It resurfaced a couple of years ago, with Bush's proposal receiving support from then-president of Mexico, Vicente Fox. But only in the last year has it become an explosive issue in national politics, with vociferous rhetoric like "stop the invasion" and "no amnesty for lawbreakers." It seems no accident that immigration restriction has moved to the fore as public disaffection with the war in Iraq grows. According to Republican strategist Don Allen, immigration is an issue that "gets us talking about security and law and order" (Hulse 2006). House majority leader Dennis Hastert deploys flexible rhetoric of popular sovereignty most succinctly: "We're at war. Our borders are a sieve" (Swarns 2006). Whether mongering terrorism and illegal immigration will result in greater mass support for U.S. wars against both will succeed remains to be seen. But the very connections made between them suggest broad ground for oppositional action.

Not like the brazen giant of Greek fame,
With conquering limbs astride from land to land;
Here at our sea-washed, sunset gates shall stand
A mighty woman with a torch, whose flame
5   Is the imprisoned lightning, and her name
Mother of Exiles. From her beacon-hand
Glows world-wide welcome; her mild eyes command
The air-bridged harbor that twin cities frame.
"Keep ancient lands, your storied pomp!" cries she
10   With silent lips. "Give me your tired, your poor,
Your huddled masses yearning to breathe free,
The wretched refuse of your teeming shore.
Send these, the homeless, tempest-tost to me,
I lift my lamp beside the golden door!" ∎

Works Cited

Alba, Richard, and Victor Nee. 2003. *Remaking the American Mainstream*. Cambridge: Harvard University Press.

Bilder, Mary Sarah. 1996. "The Struggle over Immigration: Indentured Servants, Slaves, and Articles of Commerce," *Missouri Law Review*.

Carens, Joseph. 1998. "Aliens and Citizens: The Case for Open Borders," in *The Immigration Reader: America in Multidisciplinary Perspective*, ed. David Jacobson. Malden, MA: Blackwell Publications.

Honig, Bonnie. 2001. *Democracy and the Foreigner*. Princeton: Princeton University Press.

Hulse, Carl. 2006. "In Bellweather District, GOP Runs on Immigration," *New York Times*, September 6, A1.

Ngai, Mae M. 2004. *Impossible Subjects: Illegal Aliens and the Making of Modern America*. Princeton: Princeton University Press.

———. 2006. "How Granny Got Legal." *Los Angeles Times*, May 18.

Smith, James P., and Barry Edmonston, eds. 1997. *The New Americans: Economic, Demographic, and Fiscal Effects of Immigration*. Washington, DC: National Academy Press.

Swarns, Rachel. 2006. "Immigration Overhaul Takes a Backseat as Campaign Season Begins," *New York Times*, September 8, A1.

Wong, Carolyn. 2006. *Lobbying for Inclusion*. Stanford: Stanford University Press.

Zolberg, Aristide. 2006. *A Nation by Design*. New York: Russell Sage Foundation; Cambridge: Harvard University Press. ■

Thomas Bailey Aldrich

The Unguarded Gates

Thomas Bailey Aldrich (1836–1907) provides a poetic argument from the same time period as Emma Lazarus (his poem was published in 1895—two years after hers), but with a more guarded viewpoint. Aldrich was a prominent and prolific New England writer originally from Portsmouth, New Hampshire; his 1883 book An Old Town by the Sea *was an important regional book. Aldrich's 1870 novel* Story of a Bad Boy *served as one inspiration for Mark Twain's* Tom Sawyer.

    Wide open and unguarded stand our gates.
    And through them press a wild, a motley throng—
    Men from the Volga and the Tartar steppes,
    Featureless figures of the Hoang Ho,
5   Malayan, Seythian, Teuton, Kelt, and Slav,
    Flying the Old World's poverty and scorn;

Michelle Malkin

Beware of Illegal Aliens Seeking Hazmat Licenses

Michelle Malkin, a self-described conservative, works as a wife, mother, writer, blogger, and contributor to the Fox News Channel (see her Web site at michellemalkin.com). Her book, Unhinged: Exposing Liberals Gone Wild *(2005) is an instance of what she has become known for—that is, attacking the hypocrisies of liberals. In the blog entry below— posted to a number of politically conservative Internet sites in 2006—Malkin asserts that liberals who allow immigrants to possess driver's licenses are in danger of allowing terrorists to move freely around the United States.*

What's the harm in allowing illegal aliens to have driver's licenses? After all, they're just all here innocently doing the jobs Americans won't do, right? And since they're already here, we might as well let them drive legally, right? We'll all be safer, right? Wrong.

2   Last week, law enforcement officials arrested an illegal alien enrolled at a Smithfield, R.I., tractor-trailer training school who was trying to obtain a commercial driver's license and permit to haul hazardous materials. Not many people paid attention. You should. Illegal alien Mohammed Yusef Mullawala. 28, of Jamaica, New York, had obtained drivers' licenses from New York, New Jersey and Rhode Island. He was reportedly in a hurry to get a commercial driver's license and a permit to haul hazardous cargo.

These bringing with them unknown gods and rites,
Those tiger passions, here to stretch their claws.
In street and alley what strange tongues are these.
10 Accents of menace alien to our air,
Voices that once the tower of Babel knew!
O, Liberty, white goddess, is it well
To leave the gate unguarded? On thy breast
Fold sorrow's children, soothe the hurts of fate,
15 Lift the downtrodden, but with the hand of steel
Stay those who to thy sacred portals come
To waste the fight of freedom. Have a care
Lest from thy brow the clustered stars be torn
And trampled in the dust. For so of old
20 The thronging Goth and Vandal trampled Rome,
And where the temples of the Caesars stood
The lean wolf unmolested made her lair. ∎

3   An investigation was initiated after driver's school officials became concerned about his suspicious behavior. "His behavior was consistent with terrorist-
type activity," Maj. Steve O'Donnell of the Rhode Island state police told the press.
"He showed no interest in learning the fine art of driving a tractor-trailer. He had
no interest in learning how to back up." Sort of like learning how to steer a plane,
but not take off or land.

4   As in several other cases since 9/11, it was alert private citizens who notified the Department of Homeland security of Mullawala's suspicious behavior.
And once again, it was enforcement of immigration laws that played a critical
role in detaining him. Like some of the 9/11 hijackers and several al Qaeda
operatives identified in the United States over the past decade, Mullawala was
here on a temporary student visa that he had overstayed.

5   The 9/11 hijackers obtained some 364 separate pieces of identification, including drivers' licenses, in order to conduct their murderous business. Hijackers
Hani Hanjour and Khalid Almihdhar conspired with illegal alien day laborers at
a Falls Church, Virginia, 7-Eleven to obtain government-issued photo IDs. Three
other hijackers obtained IDs at an Arlington, Virginia, DMV. Terrorist truck
bombs have killed hundreds of Americans in Beirut, at the Khobar Towers, and
Iraq. For the operatives behind the wheel, a license to drive is a license to kill.
Over the past two years, the FBI has put law enforcement officials on high alert
for U.S.-based operatives connected to al Qaeda who may be in possession of
commercial driver's licenses and may be planning to use truck bombs.

This tower, near Arivaca, Arizona, is one of many equipped with
radar and cameras designed to detect people entering the U.S.
illegally. The tower and the fence (in the background) are designed
to discourage illegal immigrants: What feelings does the image of
this surveillance technology and the desert sunset evoke?

6 In Boston, suspected al Qaeda agent and illegal alie[...] obtained a license permitting him to drive semi-trucks con[...] materials, including explosives and caustic materials.

7 In Minneapolis, suspected al Qaeda operative Mohamad Elzahabi, who obtained a green card through a fake marriage, was able to obtain a commercial driver's license to drive a school bus and to haul hazardous materials—despite FBI knowledge that Elzahabi had been tied to terrorism.

8 Earlier this year, more than 200 Somalian and Bosnian immigrants illegally obtained Missouri commercial driver's licenses or certifications to handle hazardous materials through a West Plains truck-driving school that had a contract with the state, according to federal prosecutors. In just a few short weeks, Democrats led by Nancy Pelosi will reassume power in Washington. An open borders-friendly White House has expressed willingness to deal with them. So we know who supports illegal alien workers and potential terrorist drivers waiting for amnesty. But who will stand up for us? ■

Helen Epstein

Immigration Maze

Born in Prague, raised in New York City, and educated for several years in Jerusalem, Helen Epstein uses her travels and worldly experiences to inform her writing—including her first published article, which discusses the 1968 Soviet invasion of Czechoslovakia. Epstein has written numerous articles and five books, three of which were named on the prestigious New York Times *list of Notable Books of the Year. The article that follows was originally published in a 2004 issue of* The Washington Post.

I n 1999 my husband and I moved to New York from Europe. He is Czech, and in 2000 we submitted a green card application to what was then known as the Immigration and Naturalization Service. This should have been routine. I am an American citizen, and my spouse has a right to reside here with me as long as he is not a common criminal or a terrorist. After three years, my husband's green card application had still not been approved. During this time, his grandmother became ill and died, but he was unable to visit her. Had he done so, he might never have been allowed to return to the United States.

2 Our venture through the bureaucracy of what is now known as the Bureau of Citizenship and Immigration Services (BCIS) and the FBI, which, since November 2001 has been conducting background checks on all potential immigrants, has been so bizarre that it raises questions about whether these agencies are up to the simplest of tasks, much less protecting the country against foreign terrorists.

3 The number of people suffering ordeals similar to ours is enormous and grows every day. Lawyers, immigration officers and other insiders have told me that the immigration services were thrown into chaos by the reorganization fol-

lowing the creation of the Department of Homeland Security after Sept. 11, 2001. Many officers in both the BCIS and the FBI have been given new duties. Many lines of communication—between headquarters and district offices, for example, and between congressional offices and district offices—have been rerouted so that information about particular cases is now harder than ever to obtain. Phone numbers have been changed, personnel moved and immigration and FBI officers overwhelmed with complaints and new paperwork and other distractions—none of which are likely to make us any safer.

4   The piles of unattended green-card applications at the FBI and the BCIS suggest that the "streamlining" of immigration services that the administration predicted would follow the establishment of the DHS has not taken place. BCIS officers themselves complained to me about the turmoil they confront daily. This may partly explain, though it does not excuse, their legendary unhelpfulness, which borders on, and often exceeds, the boundaries of etiquette. This does not sound like "streamlining" to me.

5   At times, I feared I would be calling the BCIS customer information line from my grave, and they still wouldn't tell me what was going on with our green-card application. I wrote to both New York senators, as well as to the secretary of homeland security at the time, Tom Ridge, and to acting BCIS commissioner Eduardo Aguirre. None ever acknowledged my letters. When I called Sen. Hillary Clinton's office six months later, I was told that she receives so many complaints

Wiley Miller has been writing *Non Sequitur* since 1991 and has won four National Cartoonist Society awards. This cartoon appeared in 2002.

about the BCIS that her assistants are unable to keep up with the correspondence. Thus another heap of paper grows in her office, this one a child of the heaps of unattended applications at the BCIS and the FBI. I asked what sort of legislative remedies the senator or anyone else had proposed to address this dire situation, but no one in Clinton's office could provide an answer. In desperation, I finally appealed to a close relative who holds a senior position in the State Department. One month later my husband's green card was approved.

6   But most of the people suffering because of this situation have no political voice in this country. This probably explains why so many bureaucrats and lawmakers don't take the issue seriously.

7   Many immigrants take low-paying jobs Americans refuse. They drive our taxis, build our houses, weed our gardens, serve our fast-food breakfasts, lunches and dinners. Without them, the service industries, the backbone of America's economy right now, would collapse. They deserve better than this, and so do we. ■

Todd Gitlin

Under the Sign of Mickey Mouse & Co.

Todd Gitlin is a professor of journalism and sociology at Columbia University. A leading and longtime culture critic who writes for a variety of publications (including Mother Jones, *a popular magazine with a left-of-center appeal, especially to younger readers), he has received several prestigious grants and fellowships, including one from the MacArthur Foundation. His books include* Media Unlimited: How the Torrent of Images and Sounds Overwhelms Our Lives *(2002),* Letters to a Young Activist *(2003), and* The Bulldozer and the Big Tent: Blind Republicans, Lame Democrats, and the Recovery of American Ideals *(2007). The selection below comes from the last chapter of* Media Unlimited.

Everywhere, the media flow defies national boundaries. This is one of its obvious, but at the same time amazing, features. A global torrent is not, of course, the master metaphor to which we have grown accustomed. We're more accustomed to Marshall McLuhan's *global village.* Those who resort to this metaphor casually often forget that if the world is a global village, some live in mansions on the hill, others in huts. Some dispatch images and sounds around town at the touch of a button; others collect them at the touch of *their* buttons. Yet McLuhan's image reveals an indispensable half-truth. If there is a village, it speaks American. It wears jeans, drinks Coke, eats at the golden arches, walks on swooshed shoes, plays electric guitars, recognizes Mickey Mouse, James Dean, E.T., Bart Simpson, R2-D2, and Pamela Anderson.

2   At the entrance to the champagne cellar of Piper-Heidsieck in Reims, in eastern France, a plaque declares that the cellar was dedicated by Marie Antoinette. The tour is narrated in six languages, and at the end you walk back upstairs into a museum featuring photographs of famous people drinking champagne. And who are they? Perhaps members of today's royal houses,

presidents or prime ministers, economic titans or Nobel Prize winners? Of course not. They are movie stars, almost all of them American—Marilyn Monroe to Clint Eastwood. The symmetry of the exhibition is obvious, the premise unmistakable: Hollywood stars, champions of consumption, are the royalty of this century, more popular by far than poor doomed Marie.

3   Hollywood is the global cultural capital—capital in both senses. The United States presides over a sort of World Bank of styles and symbols, an International Cultural Fund of images, sounds, and celebrities. The goods may be distributed by American-, Canadian-, European-, Japanese-, or Australian-owned multinational corporations, but their styles, themes, and images do not detectably change when a new board of directors takes over. Entertainment is one of America's top exports. In 1999, in fact, film, television, music, radio, advertising, print publishing, and computer software together *were* the top export, almost $80 billion worth, and while software alone accounted for $50 billion of the total, some of that category also qualifies as entertainment—video games and pornography, for example. Hardly anyone is exempt from the force of American images and sounds. French resentment of Mickey Mouse, Bruce Willis, and the rest of American civilization is well known. Less well known, and rarely acknowledged by the French, is the fact that *Terminator 2* sold 5 million tickets in France during the month it opened—with no submachine guns at the heads of the customers. The same culture minister, Jack Lang, who in 1982 achieved a moment of predictable notoriety in the United States for declaring that *Dallas* amounted to cultural imperialism, also conferred France's highest honor in the arts on Elizabeth Taylor and Sylvester Stallone. The point is not hypocrisy pure and simple but something deeper, something obscured by a single-minded emphasis on American power: dependency. American popular culture is the nemesis that hundreds of millions—perhaps billions—of people love, and love to hate. The antagonism and the dependency are inseparable, for the media flood—essentially American in its origin, but virtually unlimited in its reach—represents, like it or not, a common imagination.

4   How shall we understand the Hong Kong T-shirt that says "I Feel Coke"? Or the little Japanese girl who asks an American visitor in all innocence, "Is there really a Disneyland in America?" (She knows the one in Tokyo.) Or the experience of a German television reporter sent to Siberia to film indigenous life, who after flying out of Moscow and then traveling for days by boat, bus, and jeep, arrives near the Arctic Sea where live a tribe of Tungusians known to ethnologists for their bearskin rituals. In the community store sits a grandfather with his grandchild on his knee. Grandfather is dressed in traditional Tungusian clothing. Grandson has on his head a reversed baseball cap.

5   American popular culture is the closest approximation today to a global lingua franca, drawing the urban and young in particular into a common cultural zone where they share some dreams of freedom, wealth, comfort, innocence, and power—and perhaps most of all, youth as a state of mind. In general, despite the rhetoric of "identity," young people do not live in monocultures. They are not monocular. They are both local and cosmopolitan. Cultural

bilingualism is routine. Just as their "cultures" are neither hard-wired nor uniform, so there is no simple way in which they are "Americanized," though there are American tags on their experience—low-cost links to status and fun. Everywhere, fun lovers, efficiency seekers, Americaphiles, and Americaphobes alike pass through the portals of Disney and the arches of McDonald's wearing Levi's jeans and Gap jackets. Mickey Mouse and Donald Duck, John Wayne, Marilyn Monroe, James Dean, Bob Dylan, Michael Jackson, Madonna, Clint Eastwood, Bruce Willis, the multicolor chorus of Coca-Cola, and the next flavor of the month or the universe are the icons of a curious sort of one-world sensibility, a global semiculture. America's bid for global unification surpasses in reach that of the Romans, the British, the Catholic Church, or Islam; though without either an army or a God, it requires less. The Tungusian boy with the reversed cap on his head does not automatically think of it as "American," let alone side with the U.S. Army.

6   The misleadingly easy answer to the question of how American images and sounds became omnipresent is: American imperialism. But the images are not even faintly force-fed by American corporate, political, or military power. The empire strikes from inside the spectator as well as from outside. This is a conundrum that deserves to be approached with respect if we are to grasp the fact that Mickey Mouse and Coke are everywhere recognized and often enough *enjoyed.* In the peculiar unification at work throughout the world, there is surely a supply side, but there is not only a supply side. Some things are true even if multinational corporations claim so: there is demand.

7   What do American icons and styles mean to those who are not American? We can only imagine—but let us try. What young people graced with disposable income encounter in American television shows, movies, soft drinks, theme parks, and American-labeled (though not American-manufactured) running shoes, T-shirts, baggy pants, ragged jeans, and so on, is a way of being in the world, the experience of a flow of ready feelings and sensations bobbing up, disposable, dissolving, segueing to the next and the next after that. It is a quality of immediacy and casualness not so different from what Americans desire. But what the young experience in the video game arcade or the music megastore is more than the flux of sensation. They flirt with a loose sort of social membership that requires little but a momentary (and monetary) surrender. Sampling American goods, images, and sounds, they affiliate with an empire of informality. Consuming a commodity, wearing a slogan or a logo, you affiliate with disaffiliation. You make a limited-liability connection, a virtual one. You borrow some of the effervescence that is supposed to emanate from this American staple, and hope to be recognized as one of the elect. When you wear the Israeli version that spells *Coca-Cola* in Hebrew, you express some worldwide connection with unknown peers, or a sense of irony, or both—in any event, a marker of membership. In a world of ubiquitous images, of easy mobility and casual tourism, you get to feel not only local or national but global—without locking yourself in a box so confining as to deserve the name "identity."

8   We are seeing on a world scale the familiar infectious rhythm of modernity. The money economy extends its reach, bringing with it a calculating mentality. Even in the poor countries it stirs the same hunger for private feeling, the same taste for disposable labels and sensations on demand, the same attention to fashion, the new and the now, that cropped up earlier in the West. Income beckons; income rewards. The taste for the marketed spectacle and the media-soaked way of life spreads. The culture consumer may not like the American goods in particular but still acquires a taste for the media's speed, formulas, and frivolity. Indeed, the lightness of American-sponsored "identity" is central to its appeal. It imposes few burdens. Attachments and affiliations coexist, overlap, melt together, form, and re-form.

9   Marketers, like nationalists and fundamentalists, promote "identities," but for most people, the melange is the message. Traditional bonds bend under pressure from imports. Media from beyond help you have your "roots" and eat them, too. You can watch Mexican television in the morning and American in the afternoon, or graze between Kurdish and English. You can consolidate family ties with joint visits to Disney World—making Orlando, Florida, the major tourist destination in the United States, and the Tokyo and Marne-la-Vallée spin-offs massive attractions in Japan and France. You can attach to your parents, or children, by playing oldie music and exchanging sports statistics. You plunge back into the media flux, looking for—what? Excitement? Some low-cost variation on known themes? Some next new thing? You don't know just what, but you will when you see it—or if not, you'll change channels.

A McDonald's in Saudi Arabia shows the more obvious side of social change. What deeper changes might it signify?

10   As devotees of Japanese video games, Hong Kong movies, and Mexican *telenovelas* would quickly remind us, the blends, juxtapositions, and recombinations of popular culture are not just American. American and American-based models, styles, and symbols are simply the most far-flung, successful, and consequential. In the course of a century, America's entertainment corporations succeeded brilliantly in cultivating popular expectations for entertainment—indeed, the sense of a *right* to be entertained, a right that belongs to the history of modernity, the rise of market economies and individualism. The United States, which began as Europe's collective fantasy, built a civilization to deliver the goods for playing, feeling, and meaning. Competitors ignore its success at their own peril, financial and otherwise. ■

Urvashi Butalia

Living the Dream

Urvashi Butalia was born in India and was educated in India and London. Her work spans many disciplines, including sociology, South Asian studies, and women's studies. She is particularly noted for starting India's first feminist press, Kali for Women. Butalia's best known book, The Other Side of Silence, *features interviews with more than seventy of the people dislocated by the 1948 partition that divided India and Pakistan, a political situation that caused the largest migration in history. In "Living the Dream," Butalia continues her feminist work by exploring the challenges and opportunities of young women striving to break patriarchal traditions in India.*

At 16, Bina, daughter of the presswaala across the road, ran away from home. It took her parents three days to track her down and shortly after she returned, she was found to be pregnant. An abortion was swiftly arranged and soon after, Bina was "safely" married. At 16, her younger sister Priyanka decided to follow a different path. Aware of her parents' anxiety about her future and their worry for her present, Priyanka took her life in her hands. Alongside school, she joined a neighbourhood beauty course. Three months later, she "graduated" and found work in a local parlour.

2   But that was only a stopgap arrangement. Having learned the ropes of the job, Priyanka set out to become a freelance beautician. She would attend school in the morning, and the rest of the day was spent in going from home to home, offering manicures and pedicures, face and body massages, and a range of other services to women in the neighbourhood—a relatively low income area in Delhi. A new job, and a new, hitherto unexplored, market.

3   The enterprise did not stop there. Priyanka's earnings started supplementing the family income. Her sister-in-law helped in the preparation of the materials she used in her work. Her brother helped to ferry her around, and

with this support structure in place, Priyanka began to approach clients who were better-off in the residential South Delhi area where her father and mother still iron clothes. Soon, she had a pricier Sunday clientele. Now, confident, smart and intelligent, Priyanka laughs and asserts that when she is ready, she will find a man she wishes to marry. Till then and after, she will continue to be her own mistress.

4   Are there other Priyankas out there? My guess is there are, and hundreds of them (even though they will not make it to Page 3 of any newspaper). They are the young women between 18 and 30, living in semi-urban situations, who come from the less well-off households, but who dare to dream, and work to fulfill their dreams. It's probably too early to say why this is happening, but if one were to speculate, it's a fair guess that this change would have something to do with the growth of television, its constant barrage of advertising for the tools of the beauty trade and its ability to create dreams. Like many other girls, Priyanka too wants to have clear skin and beautiful hair and she wants to be successful. That's the positive side.

5   Today, opportunities have sprung up for young women for whom earlier, marriage would have been the logical step after school, or at the most after college. These numbers are not huge but they're significant. Walk into a neighbourhood grocery shop and chances are there will be young female salespersons there. Stop by for a morning coffee and the attendant at barista will very likely be a female. The numbers of young women in BPOs and call centres is by now a legion. Even petrol pump attendants are now women.

6   And then there are others, like Nirmala, seven years out of the village, mother of two small boys, not yet 30: she has sold her ancestral land in the village—there's no one to work on it now—and put her savings into a car that she now rents out to mobile phone operators and earns enough to pay back the loan and make a little extra. Or still, the young sex worker in Kolkata who has put aside enough to buy herself a small truck and earn a second income. Clearly, enterprise has a female, and now youthful face.

7   But, as always, there's another side too: while Priyanka represents one kind of transformation among the young, not-so-well-off women in India, for every Priyanka there are hundreds of others who continue to face the worst kind of discrimination—that is, if they are not murdered before they are born. And more, while the new globalised world offers the Priyankas across urban India some opportunities—however limited—to reshape their lives, it also constrains them in many ways. For Priyanka, beauty now equals a flat stomach, a pair of blue jeans, fair and lovely skin, streaked hair and pencil thin eyebrows. It's difficult to balance what has been lost with what has been gained.

8   And that's the rub. India is today a young country—one of the few in the world to have a large young population (and for the first time India's population is, in the official discourse, seeming like an asset rather than otherwise). It's also a country going through tremendous upheaval and change. The young are bound to be caught up in this revolution.

Globalization in India—what the jobs look like.

9   For young women, particularly the poor classes, who have been denied opportunities because of the heavy hand of patriarchy and tradition, new spaces are beginning to open up. And especially if these are opportunities that bring some income into the family, then money speaks its own language. This is why today one sees many more young women working as sales assistants in shops than, say, 10 years back. But whether this will mean that women are given the space—for they certainly don't lack the ability—to become more independent and enterprising is something only society at large can ensure by embracing, not rejecting, their metamorphosis. ■

National Readership Survey 2006: Women's Attitudes in India

The National Readership Survey (NRS) of India, one of the largest surveys in the world, is given to readers of many newspapers and magazines to collect data on Indians' attitudes.

- 67% of women like new products, but 78% say they would not blindly buy expensive commodities.
- 69% of women love excitement and would want to have a lot of variety in their lives.
- 32% of women today are unafraid of breaking rules, while 44% like taking risks.
- 19% of women do not always take the advice and recommendations of parents and friends.
- 70% of women insist they will live life on their own terms.

Laura Carlsen

Wal-Mart vs. Pyramids

Laura Carlsen is the director of the Americas Program for the International Relations Center (formerly the Interhemispheric Resource Center), which provides policy analysis and options for economic policy involving North, Central, and South America. A graduate of Stanford University, in 1986 she received a Fulbright Scholarship to study the impact on women of the Mexican economic crisis. She continues to reside in Mexico City. Carlsen has also written about trade agreements and other economic issues impacting Mexico. The article reprinted below appeared in several places in October and November of 2004, including New York University's Global Beat Syndicate, *the Common Dreams Web site (www.commondreams.org), and* Human Quest, *an academic journal of religion and philosophy.*

The showdown is rife with symbolism. Wal-Mart's expansion plans in Mexico have brought about a modern-day clash of passions and principles at the site of one of the earth's first great civilizations.

2　　Several months ago Wal-Mart, the world's largest retail chain, quietly began constructing a new store in Mexico—the latest step in a phenomenal takeover of Mexico's supermarket sector. But the expansion north of Mexico City is not just part of Wal-Mart's commercial conquest of Mexico. It is infringing on the cultural foundations of the country. The new store is just 3,000 meters from the Pyramid of the Sun, the tallest structure in the ancient city of Teotihuacan.

3　　The Teotihuacan Empire is believed to have begun as early as 200 B.C. Its dominion stretched deep into the heart of Mayan country in Guatemala and throughout present-day Mexico. At its peak, Teotihuacan was a thriving city of about 200,000 inhabitants, but the civilization declined in 700 A.D. under circumstances still shrouded in mystery.

4　　Since then, other tribes and civilizations, including the Aztecs and contemporary Mexican society, have claimed the "City of the Gods" as their heritage. The grand human accomplishment it represents and the power of its architectural, historical and, for many, spiritual legacy is central to Mexico's history and culture.

5　　While little is known for certain about the rise and fall of Teotihuacan, much is known about the rise of the Wal-Mart empire. From a store in Rogers, Arkansas founded by the Walton brothers in 1962, the enterprise grew in the breathtakingly short period of 42 years into the world's largest company.

6　　In Mexico, its conquest of the supermarket sector began by buying up the nation's extensive chain, Aurrerá, beginning in 1992. Today, with 657 stores, Mexico is home to more Wal-Marts and their affiliates than any other country outside the United States. Wal-Mart is now Mexico's largest private employer, with over 100,000 employees. But recent studies in the United

States, where resistance to the megastores has been growing, show that job creation is often job displacement, because Wal-Marts put local stores out of business, leading to net job losses.

7   Wal-Mart has revolutionized the labor and business world by working cheap and growing big. Labor costs are held down through anti-union policies, the hiring of undocumented workers in the United States, alleged discrimination against women and persons with disabilities, and cutbacks in benefits. Prices paid suppliers are driven down by outsourcing competition. Buoyed by $244.5 billion dollars in annual net sales, the chain can afford to make ever deeper incursions into Mexico's retail sector.

8   A diverse group of local merchants, artists, actors, academics and indigenous organizations are leading the opposition, protesting that the store damages Mexico's rich cultural heritage. Through ceremonies, hunger strikes, demonstrations and press coverage, the movement to defend the site has kept the conflict in the public eye and heightened the public-opinion costs to Wal-Mart. Now opponents have taken their concerns to the Mexican Congress and UNESCO.

9   Some ancient ruins have already been found on the store's new site, and Wal-Mart construction workers told the national daily, *La Jornada,* that they had orders to hide any archaeological relics they found. Normally, the presence of relics requires that further excavation be carried out painstakingly or halted altogether. But the booming Wal-Mart corporation clearly has no time for such delays.

10   The dispute in Teotihuacan today is not a battle between the past and the future. It is a struggle over a country's right to define itself. For defenders of the ancient site, the foremost symbol of the nation's cultural heritage also constitutes part of its contemporary integrity. Modern Mexico is still a country that defines itself by legends, and whose collective identity—unlike its neophyte northern neighbor—reaches back thousands of years.

11   In this context, Wal-Mart is a symbol of the cultural insensitivity of rampant economic integration. While its actions may be technically legal, in the end Wal-Mart could pay a high price for this insensitivity . . . and if there is anything Wal-Mart hates, it is high prices. ■

Darla K. Deardorff

From *In Search of Intercultural Competence*

Darla Deardorff serves as the executive director of the Association of International Education Administrators, where she fuels her passion for "intercultural competence," a concept that focuses on successful communication among people of different cultures. Deardorff's experiences include ESL teaching and tutoring, studying and working abroad (in Germany, Switzerland, and Japan), and working with international students. In In Search of Intercultural Competence, *published in the spring 2004 edition of* NAFSA'S

International Educator, Deardorff tries to define what it means to be interculturally competent, and then discusses how institutions of higher learning can help students to achieve that goal.

U.S. institutions of higher education face many challenges at the beginning of the twenty-first century, including the tasks of remaining intellectually and culturally viable in a rapidly changing world, preparing students to vie competitively in the global marketplace, and staying abreast of the electronic deluge of information and globalized knowledge. The internationalization of higher education has become one possible response to such challenges. Yet the specification of anticipated outcomes of internationalization are often general and vague, with goals stated broadly that the institution will "become internationalized" or that a goal is to graduate "cross-culturally competent students" or "global citizens" without giving further meaning to these phrases.

2 Few U.S. universities address the development of interculturally competent students as an anticipated outcome of internationalization in which the concept of "intercultural competence" is specifically defined. This lack of specificity in further defining intercultural competence is due presumably to the difficulty of identifying the specific components of this concept. Even fewer institutions have designated methods for documenting or measuring intercultural competence. So, while the purpose of having an internationalized campus is obvious enough that funds are being directed accordingly, it is unclear how these institutions know, or even if they can know, that they are graduating interculturally competent students and what it means to be interculturally competent.

3 A new doctoral research study has been undertaken to address these key questions through the collection and analysis of data on the identification and assessment of intercultural competence as a student outcome of internationalization in higher education. This research study seeks to provide administrators with a more definitive meaning of intercultural competence, as well as with suggestions regarding the effective assessment of students' intercultural competence. At a minimum, this study will help generate discussion around the complex phenomenon of intercultural competence, as well as discussions on how to assess meaningful outcomes of internationalization.

A Barometer

4 Institutions of higher education rely heavily on numbers to demonstrate success in internationalization—numbers such as how many of their students study abroad, how many international students study on their campus, how many foreign faculty teach courses, how many courses are included in the internationalized curriculum, and so on. While such numbers are certainly an important element to evaluation, what do they indicate about the meaningful outcomes

of internationalization, such as developing interculturally competent graduates who can compete successfully in the global workforce? In answer to this question, a report by the American Council on Education (ACE) stated, "Such measures are silent on student learning and attitudes. While this "supply-side" approach to internationalization provides a starting point, institutions that are serious about its effect on students should take a closer look at learning goals, course content, pedagogy, campus life, enrollment pattern, and institutional policies and practices to get a more complete picture of their success" (Engberg and Green 2002). There is a need to move beyond numbers (outputs) to meaningful outcomes of internationalization. Given increasing pressure on institutions to evaluate the effectiveness of their internationalization efforts, questions often arise as to what specifically to evaluate in regard to internationalization and more importantly, how to evaluate. And quite often, intercultural competence is being looked at as an indicator of internationalization.

5   There is little agreement, however, as to specifically what constitutes intercultural competence. For example, if intercultural competence comprises knowledge, skills, attitudes, and awareness to enable a person to interact effectively with those from other cultures, what actually comprises intercultural knowledge? Intercultural skills? Intercultural attitudes? Intercultural awareness? While there has been some effort to research and write about this in the field, there has been no real agreement on the specifics. Furthermore, how can intercultural competence be assessed? How can this demonstrate effective implementation of internationalization strategy? As Terenzini and Upcraft (1996) observed, ". . . while assessing the purported outcomes of our efforts with students is probably the most important assessment we do, it is seldom done, rarely done well, and when it is done, the results are seldom used effectively." Yet, there is a correct way to do it, if a definition is clear and accepted: ". . . Competence can be measured, But its measurement depends first on its definition . . ." (Klemp 1979).

Defining the Term

6   What exactly is intercultural competence? This question has been debated by experts for decades and a myriad of terminology has been used including global competence, global citizenship, cross-cultural competence, international competence, intercultural effectiveness, and intercultural sensitivity, to name a few. (Global competence, as explained by William Hunter, indicates that intercultural competence is a significant part of global competence.) Yet, how do institutions of higher education define intercultural competence?

Previous Research

7   Definitions have cited some of the same general components of intercultural competence such as empathy, flexibility, cross-cultural awareness, and managing stress, while some definitions of intercultural competence specifically note other elements such as technical skills, foreign language proficiency, and situational factors. Other scholars have written that intercultural competence

does not comprise individual traits but is rather the characteristic of the association between individuals and that no prescriptive set of characteristics guarantees competence in all intercultural situations (Lustig and Koester 2003). Chen and Starosta (1996), in their definition of intercultural competence, stress that cross-culturally competent persons are those who can interact effectively and appropriately with people who have multilevel cultural identities. When presented with various definitions of intercultural competence, administrators who participated in this study selected the following summarized definition as the one that is most applicable to their institution's internationalization strategies: Knowledge of others; knowledge of self; skills to interpret and relate; skills to discover and/or to interact; valuing others' values, beliefs, and behaviors; and relativizing one's self. Linguistic competence also plays a key role (Byram 1997). Nearly all definitions of intercultural competence include more than knowledge of other cultures, since knowledge alone is not enough to constitute intercultural competence. Intercultural competence also involves the development of one's skills and attitudes in successfully interacting with persons of diverse backgrounds.

8   The following are some additional questions and issues that scholars have wrestled during the search for a definition. Should intercultural competence be defined more generally or more specifically? Should intercultural competence be measured holistically or in separate components? What role does language play in intercultural competence? Should intercultural competence be measured in degrees and if so, what are the implications for those deemed interculturally incompetent? Is intercultural competence context-specific or is it possible to identify comprehensive elements that are applicable to many different contexts? How does intercultural competence fit with global competence?

References

Byram, M. 1997. *Teaching and Assessing Intercultural Communicative Competence.* Clevedon: Multilingual Matters Ltd.

Chen, G. M. and W. J. Starosta. 1996. "Intercultural Communication Competence: A Synthesis." *Communication Yearbook* 19.

Engberg, D. and M. Green. 2002. *Promising Practices: Spotlighting Excellence in Comprehensive Internationalization.* Washington, D.C.: American Council on Education.

Hayward, F. M. 2000. *Preliminary Status Report 2000: Internationalization of U.S. Higher Education.* Washington, D.C.: American Council on Education.

Klemp, G. O., Jr. 1979. "Identifying, Measuring and Integrating Competence." In P. S. Pottinger and J. Goldsmith. (Eds.) *Defining and Measuring Competence.* San Francisco: Jossey-Bass.

Lustig, M. W. and J. Koester. 2003. *Intercultural Competence: Interpersonal Communication Across Cultures,* fourth edition. Boston: Allyn and Bacon.

Terenzini, P. T. and M. L. Upcraft. 1996. "Assessing Programs and Service Outcomes." In M. L. Upcraft and J. H. Schuh (Eds). *Assessment in Student Affairs: A Guide for Practitioners,* San Francisco: Jossey-Bass Publishers. ■

25

Science and Ethics

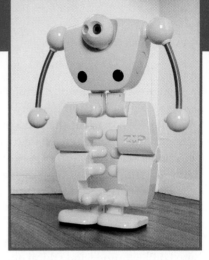

How does the Nuvo robot's appearance meet—or not meet—your notions of what a household robot might look like? What are some of the ethical concerns associated with having robots "living" in the home?

The Ethics of Science and Technology

Item: In November 2004, couples with a family history of cancer were given an unusual permission by the Human Fertilization and Embryology Authority in Great Britain—they were allowed to select for human fertilization embryos free of cancer-causing genes. Critics immediately complained about this effort to create "designer babies." They drew comparisons with Adolph Hitler's interest in creating a "super-race" of genetically enhanced Aryans and raised concerns about the possibility that "better" human beings might have advantages over "natural" people.

Item: Early in 2005 in the United States, members of the National Academy of Sciences were finishing a recommendation report on the legal and ethical status of "chimeras"—hybrid creatures created by implanting one animal's stem cells into the fetal matter of a different species. Several living creatures have been "invented" and patented in recent years, raising the question of the possibility of others—mice with human brains? Pigs bioengineered to produce human blood? Or even a genetically plausible hybrid between humans and chimpanzees?

> "Twenty-first century technologies—genetics, nanotechnology, and robotics—are so powerful they can spawn whole new classes of accidents and abuses."
>
> —BILL JOY, SUN MICROSYSTEMS

Item: On Thanksgiving Day 2001, teenager Shawn Woolley committed suicide after (his mother claims) weeks of twelve-hour stints playing the online role-playing game EverQuest addled his neurochemical condition. Do electronically mediated experiences like playing

EverQuest—not to mention similar experiences that may soon make the transition from science fiction to reality—have mind-and-body effects on the human condition? What about the widespread use of Prozac and other mind-altering drugs: do they threaten to change our sense of what human nature is at its core? No wonder science fiction movies and narratives are so popular—characters like the Terminator (hybrids of human and nonhuman) seem possible in the not-so-very-distant future.

These three items, brought to our attention by Jeffrey Pruchnic, highlight some of the ethical issues related to science and technology that people are grappling with these days. Science and technology, as central enterprises in our culture, have always raised difficult moral and ethical questions. Whether it is environmental protection (the subject of Chapter 22), medicine, genetic engineering, animal rights, the teaching of evolution, computer technologies, space exploration, or military weapons technology, science and technology command our attention and our committed arguments because they challenge our assumptions about what is possible and push the limits of what we think of as ethical.

Contemporary Arguments

The items we have cited point to something new, however: new technologies are calling into question human nature itself. What are we to make of scientific developments that offer the potential for tremendous human benefits if they also have the potential to change our very natures? Here we include arguments on three especially important and compelling developments related to science and human nature.

The first is nanotechnology. MIT researcher K. Eric Drexler coined the term because *nano* literally means "one billionth": nanotechnology refers to the science of creating molecule-sized materials and machines. Occupying the space between biology and engineering, nanotechnologists promise to create new things that fundamentally change the ways we work and live. As *Spiderman, Star-Trek: The Next Generation,* and popular magazines such as *Forbes* and *Wired* all indicate, nanotechnology promises to be the next big thing. Nano skin creams are on the market, nano-enhanced tennis balls are used in the Davis Cup, and microscopic silicon chips run computer games. More important, nanotechnologists are developing micromachines that might radically improve water quality, benefit agriculture, clean up toxic waste, or make obsolete our reliance on oil by improving the efficiency of solar power. Others might enter the human body to repair tissue. Nanomaterials hundreds of times stronger than steel might make possible ten-pound automobiles or airplanes.

But is nanotechnology safe? Could dangerous nanoparticles escape and cause great damage? And what about nanotechnology's implications for the way human beings think of themselves? Will nanotechnology widen the gap between haves and have-nots around the globe? Those very serious questions are raised here in essays by Bill Joy and Francis Fukuyama. We also include a response to Joy and Fukuyama by Ralph C. Merkle, in the form of an interview.

The second new technology under watch is robotics. According to Bill Gates, robotics hold the potential to become as ubiquitous as computers—although he acknowledges that there are as many naysayers about today's robotics developments as there once were about the possibilities of bringing computers into nearly every home. In "A Robot in Every Home," Gates discusses the potential for robotics with enthusiasm; detractors raise questions about the ethics of replacing humans and human labor with robots and robotic labor. The rise of robotics lends an almost science-fiction quality to technology and gives rise in the popular imagination to sci-fi's greatest dreams and fears.

Meanwhile, Ursula Franklin philosophizes about science. She asserts that every scientific discovery includes the three adjectives that comprise her title: beautiful, functional, and frugal. In this essay, Franklin considers the attributes that make "good science"—ultimately the foundation of the technologies on which this chapter focuses. In "Attitude Screen," Christine Soares ties together the hopes and the anxieties about new genetic information and its uses (especially in medicine) and raises a critical question for all scientific and technological developments: how do we ethically balance the risks and responsibilities of tampering with the "natural"?

Finally, to conclude this chapter, we offer an Issue in Focus on embryonic stem cell research. No doubt you have read and heard a great deal about stem cell research because of highly publicized appeals on its behalf by the late Christopher Reeve and Ron Reagan (the latter at the 2004 Democratic National Convention). Here we provide not only Reagan's speech and responses to it, but also background information that you will need to understand the issue—and perhaps to write about it yourself.

Bill Joy

Why the Future Doesn't Need Us

Bill Joy is a cofounder of Sun Microsystems and was the chief scientist there until 2003. He played a major role in developing an early form of UNIX, a computer operating system, as well as other computer technologies, such as the JAVA programming language. "Why the Future Doesn't Need Us" appeared in the April 2000 issue of Wired *magazine, a monthly periodical that covers cultural, political, and economic impacts of technology. The article, which expresses a surprisingly critical position on technology, created a large stir—see the interview with Ralph C. Merkle that follows the next selection.*

From the moment I became involved in the creation of new technologies, their ethical dimensions have concerned me, but it was only in the autumn of 1998 that I became anxiously aware of how great are the dangers facing us in the 21st century. I can date the onset of my unease to the day I met Ray Kurzweil, the deservedly famous inventor of the first reading machine for the blind and many other amazing things.

2   Ray and I were both speakers at George Gilder's Telecosm conference, and I encountered him by chance in the bar of the hotel after both our sessions were over. I was sitting with John Searle, a Berkeley philosopher who studies consciousness. While we were talking, Ray approached and a conversation began, the subject of which haunts me to this day.

3   I had missed Ray's talk and the subsequent panel that Ray and John had been on, and they now picked right up where they'd left off, with Ray saying that the rate of improvement of technology was going to accelerate and that we were going to become robots or fuse with robots or something like that, and John countering that this couldn't happen, because the robots couldn't be conscious.

4   While I had heard such talk before, I had always felt sentient robots were in the realm of science fiction. But now, from someone I respected, I was hearing a strong argument that they were a near-term possibility. I was taken aback, especially given Ray's proven ability to imagine and create the future. I already knew that new technologies like genetic engineering and nanotechnology were giving us the power to remake the world, but a realistic and imminent scenario for intelligent robots surprised me.

5   It's easy to get jaded about such breakthroughs. We hear in the news almost every day of some kind of technological or scientific advance. Yet this was no ordinary prediction. In the hotel bar, Ray gave me a partial preprint of his then-forthcoming book *The Age of Spiritual Machines,* which outlined a utopia he foresaw—one in which humans gained near immortality by becoming one with robotic technology. On reading it, my sense of unease only intensified; I felt sure he had to be understating the dangers, understating the probability of a bad outcome along this path.

6   I found myself most troubled by a passage detailing a *dys*topian scenario:

> First let us postulate that the computer scientists succeed in developing intelligent machines that can do all things better than human beings can do them. In that case presumably all work will be done by vast, highly organized systems of machines and no human effort will be necessary. Either of two cases might occur. The machines might be permitted to make all of their own decisions without human oversight, or else human control over the machines might be retained.
>
> If the machines are permitted to make all their own decisions, we can't make any conjectures as to the results, because it is impossible to guess how such machines might behave. We only point out that the fate of the human race would be at the mercy of the machines. It might be argued that the human race would never be foolish enough to hand over

all the power to the machines. But we are suggesting neither that the human race would voluntarily turn power over to the machines nor that the machines would willfully seize power. What we do suggest is that the human race might easily permit itself to drift into a position of such dependence on the machines that it would have no practical choice but to accept all of the machines' decisions. As society and the problems that face it become more and more complex and machines become more and more intelligent, people will let machines make more of their decisions for them, simply because machine-made decisions will bring better results than man-made ones. Eventually a stage may be reached at which the decisions necessary to keep the system running will be so complex that human beings will be incapable of making them intelligently. At that stage the machines will be in effective control. People won't be able to just turn the machines off, because they will be so dependent on them that turning them off would amount to suicide.

On the other hand it is possible that human control over the machines may be retained. In that case the average man may have control over certain private machines of his own, such as his car or his personal computer, but control over large systems of machines will be in the hands of a tiny elite—just as it is today, but with two differences. Due to improved techniques the elite will have greater control over the masses; and because human work will no longer be necessary the masses will be superfluous, a useless burden on the system. If the elite is ruthless they may simply decide to exterminate the mass of humanity. If they are humane they may use propaganda or other psychological or biological techniques to reduce the birth rate until the mass of humanity becomes extinct, leaving the world to the elite. Or, if the elite consists of soft-hearted liberals, they may decide to play the role of good shepherds to the rest of the human race. They will see to it that everyone's physical needs are satisfied, that all children are raised under psychologically hygienic conditions, that everyone has a wholesome hobby to keep him busy, and that anyone who may become dissatisfied undergoes "treatment" to cure his "problem." Of course, life will be so purposeless that people will have to be biologically or psychologically engineered either to remove their need for the power process or make them "sublimate" their drive for power into some harmless hobby. These engineered human beings may be happy in such a society, but they will most certainly not be free. They will have been reduced to the status of domestic animals.[1]

7   In the book, you don't discover until you turn the page that the author of this passage is Theodore Kaczynski—the Unabomber. I am no apologist for Kaczynski. His bombs killed three people during a 17-year terror campaign and wounded many others. One of his bombs gravely injured my friend David Gelernter, one of the most brilliant and visionary computer scientists of our time. Like many of my colleagues, I felt that I could easily have been the Unabomber's next target.

8   Kaczynski's actions were murderous and, in my view, criminally insane. He is clearly a Luddite, but simply saying this does not dismiss his argument;

as difficult as it is for me to acknowledge, I saw some merit in the reasoning in this single passage. I felt compelled to confront it.

9   Kaczynski's dystopian vision describes unintended consequences, a well-known problem with the design and use of technology, and one that is clearly related to Murphy's law—"Anything that can go wrong, will." (Actually, this is Finagle's law, which in itself shows that Finagle was right.) Our overuse of antibiotics has led to what may be the biggest such problem so far: the emergence of antibiotic-resistant and much more dangerous bacteria. Similar things happened when attempts to eliminate malarial mosquitoes using DDT caused them to acquire DDT resistance; malarial parasites likewise acquired multi-drug-resistant genes.[2]

10   The cause of many such surprises seems clear: The systems involved are complex, involving interaction among and feedback between many parts. Any changes to such a system will cascade in ways that are difficult to predict; this is especially true when human actions are involved.

11   I started showing friends the Kaczynski quote from *The Age of Spiritual Machines;* I would hand them Kurzweil's book, let them read the quote, and then watch their reaction as they discovered who had written it. At around the same time, I found Hans Moravec's book *Robot: Mere Machine to Transcendent Mind.* Moravec is one of the leaders in robotics research, and was a founder of the world's largest robotics research program, at Carnegie Mellon University. *Robot* gave me more material to try out on my friends—material surprisingly supportive of Kaczynski's argument. For example:

> Biological species almost never survive encounters with superior competitors. Ten million years ago, South and North America were separated by a sunken Panama isthmus. South America, like Australia today, was populated by marsupial mammals, including pouched equivalents of rats, deers, and tigers. When the isthmus connecting North and South America rose, it took only a few thousand years for the northern placental species, with slightly more effective metabolisms and reproductive and nervous systems, to displace and eliminate almost all the southern marsupials.
>
> In a completely free marketplace, superior robots would surely affect humans as North American placentals affected South American marsupials (and as humans have affected countless species). Robotic industries would compete vigorously among themselves for matter, energy, and space, incidentally driving their price beyond human reach. Unable to afford the necessities of life, biological humans would be squeezed out of existence.
>
> There is probably some breathing room, because we do not live in a completely free marketplace. Government coerces nonmarket behavior, especially by collecting taxes. Judiciously applied, governmental coercion could support human populations in high style on the fruits of robot labor, perhaps for a long while.

12   A textbook dystopia—and Moravec is just getting wound up. He goes on to discuss how our main job in the 21st century will be "ensuring continued

cooperation from the robot industries" by passing laws decreeing that they be "nice,"[3] and to describe how seriously dangerous a human can be "once transformed into an unbounded superintelligent robot." Moravec's view is that the robots will eventually succeed us—that humans clearly face extinction.

13   I decided it was time to talk to my friend Danny Hillis. Danny became famous as the cofounder of Thinking Machines Corporation, which built a very powerful parallel supercomputer. Despite my current job title of Chief Scientist at Sun Microsystems, I am more a computer architect than a scientist, and I respect Danny's knowledge of the information and physical sciences more than that of any other single person I know. Danny is also a highly regarded futurist who thinks long-term: four years ago he started the Long Now Foundation, which is building a clock designed to last 10,000 years, in an attempt to draw attention to the pitifully short attention span of our society.

14   So I flew to Los Angeles for the express purpose of having dinner with Danny and his wife, Pati. I went through my now-familiar routine, trotting out the ideas and passages that I found so disturbing. Danny's answer—directed specifically at Kurzweil's scenario of humans merging with robots—came swiftly, and quite surprised me. He said, simply, that the changes would come gradually, and that we would get used to them.

15   But I guess I wasn't totally surprised. I had seen a quote from Danny in Kurzweil's book in which he said, "I'm as fond of my body as anyone, but if I can be 200 with a body of silicon, I'll take it." It seemed that he was at peace with this process and its attendant risks, while I was not.

16   While talking and thinking about Kurzweil, Kaczynski, and Moravec, I suddenly remembered a novel I had read almost 20 years ago—*The White Plague*, by Frank Herbert—in which a molecular biologist is driven insane by the senseless murder of his family. To seek revenge he constructs and disseminates a new and highly contagious plague that kills widely but selectively. (We're lucky Kaczynski was a mathematician, not a molecular biologist.) I was also reminded of the Borg of *Star Trek*, a hive of partly biological, partly robotic creatures with a strong destructive streak. Borg-like disasters are a staple of science fiction, so why hadn't I been more concerned about such robotic dystopias earlier? Why weren't other people more concerned about these nightmarish scenarios?

17   Part of the answer certainly lies in our attitude toward the new—in our bias toward instant familiarity and unquestioning acceptance. Accustomed to living with almost routine scientific breakthroughs, we have yet to come to terms with the fact that the most compelling 21st-century technologies—robotics, genetic engineering, and nanotechnology—pose a different threat than the technologies that have come before. Specifically, robots, engineered organisms, and nanobots share a dangerous amplifying factor: They can self-replicate. A bomb is blown up only once—but one bot can become many, and quickly get out of control.

18   Much of my work over the past 25 years has been on computer networking, where the sending and receiving of messages creates the opportunity for

out-of-control replication. But while replication in a computer or a computer network can be a nuisance, at worst it disables a machine or takes down a network or network service. Uncontrolled self-replication in these newer technologies runs a much greater risk: a risk of substantial damage in the physical world.

19   Each of these technologies also offers untold promise: the vision of near immortality that Kurzweil sees in his robot dreams drives us forward; genetic engineering may soon provide treatments, if not outright cures, for most diseases; and nanotechnology and nanomedicine can address yet more ills. Together they could significantly extend our average life span and improve the quality of our lives. Yet, with each of these technologies, a sequence of small, individually sensible advances leads to an accumulation of great power and, concomitantly, great danger.

20   What was different in the 20th century? Certainly, the technologies underlying the weapons of mass destruction (WMD)—nuclear, biological, and chemical (NBC)—were powerful, and the weapons an enormous threat. But building nuclear weapons required, at least for a time, access to both rare—indeed, effectively unavailable—raw materials and highly protected information; biological and chemical weapons programs also tended to require large-scale activities.

21   The 21st-century technologies—genetics, nanotechnology, and robotics (GNR)—are so powerful that they can spawn whole new classes of accidents and abuses. Most dangerously, for the first time, these accidents and abuses are widely within the reach of individuals or small groups. They will not require large facilities or rare raw materials. Knowledge alone will enable the use of them.

22   Thus we have the possibility not just of weapons of mass destruction but of knowledge-enabled mass destruction (KMD), this destructiveness hugely amplified by the power of self-replication.

23   I think it is no exaggeration to say we are on the cusp of the further perfection of extreme evil, an evil whose possibility spreads well beyond that which weapons of mass destruction bequeathed to the nation-states, on to a surprising and terrible empowerment of extreme individuals.

II

24 Nothing about the way I got involved with computers suggested to me that I was going to be facing these kinds of issues.

25   My life has been driven by a deep need to ask questions and find answers. When I was 3, I was already reading, so my father took me to the elementary school, where I sat on the principal's lap and read him a story. I started school early, later skipped a grade, and escaped into books—I was incredibly motivated to learn. I asked lots of questions, often driving adults to distraction.

26   As a teenager I was very interested in science and technology. I wanted to be a ham radio operator but didn't have the money to buy the equipment.

Ham radio was the Internet of its time: very addictive, and quite solitary. Money issues aside, my mother put her foot down—I was not to be a ham; I was antisocial enough already.

27   I may not have had many close friends, but I was awash in ideas. By high school, I had discovered the great science fiction writers. I remember especially Heinlein's *Have Spacesuit Will Travel* and Asimov's *I, Robot*, with its Three Laws of Robotics. I was enchanted by the descriptions of space travel, and wanted to have a telescope to look at the stars; since I had no money to buy or make one, I checked books on telescope-making out of the library and read about making them instead. I soared in my imagination.

28   Thursday nights my parents went bowling, and we kids stayed home alone. It was the night of Gene Roddenberry's original *Star Trek*, and the program made a big impression on me. I came to accept its notion that humans had a future in space, Western-style, with big heroes and adventures. Roddenberry's vision of the centuries to come was one with strong moral values, embodied in codes like the Prime Directive: to not interfere in the development of less technologically advanced civilizations. This had an incredible appeal to me; ethical humans, not robots, dominated this future, and I took Roddenberry's dream as part of my own.

29   I excelled in mathematics in high school, and when I went to the University of Michigan as an undergraduate engineering student I took the advanced curriculum of the mathematics majors. Solving math problems was an exciting challenge, but when I discovered computers I found something much more interesting: a machine into which you could put a program that attempted to solve a problem, after which the machine quickly checked the solution. The computer had a clear notion of correct and incorrect, true and false. Were my ideas correct? The machine could tell me. This was very seductive.

30   I was lucky enough to get a job programming early supercomputers and discovered the amazing power of large machines to numerically simulate advanced designs. When I went to graduate school at UC Berkeley in the mid-1970s, I started staying up late, often all night, inventing new worlds inside the machines. Solving problems. Writing the code that argued so strongly to be written.

31   In *The Agony and the Ecstasy*, Irving Stone's biographical novel of Michelangelo, Stone described vividly how Michelangelo released the statues from the stone, "breaking the marble spell," carving from the images in his mind.[4] In my most ecstatic moments, the software in the computer emerged in the same way. Once I had imagined it in my mind I felt that it was already there in the machine, waiting to be released. Staying up all night seemed a small price to pay to free it—to give the ideas concrete form.

32   After a few years at Berkeley I started to send out some of the software I had written—an instructional Pascal system, Unix utilities, and a text editor called vi (which is still, to my surprise, widely used more than 20 years later)—to others who had similar small PDP-11 and VAX minicomputers. These adventures in software eventually turned into the Berkeley version of the Unix

operating system, which became a personal "success disaster"—so many people wanted it that I never finished my PhD. Instead I got a job working for Darpa putting Berkeley Unix on the Internet and fixing it to be reliable and to run large research applications well. This was all great fun and very rewarding. And, frankly, I saw no robots here, or anywhere near.

33 Still, by the early 1980s, I was drowning. The Unix releases were very successful, and my little project of one soon had money and some staff, but the problem at Berkeley was always office space rather than money—there wasn't room for the help the project needed, so when the other founders of Sun Microsystems showed up I jumped at the chance to join them. At Sun, the long hours continued into the early days of workstations and personal computers, and I have enjoyed participating in the creation of advanced microprocessor technologies and Internet technologies such as Java and Jini.

34 From all this, I trust it is clear that I am not a Luddite. I have always, rather, had a strong belief in the value of the scientific search for truth and in the ability of great engineering to bring material progress. The Industrial Revolution has immeasurably improved everyone's life over the last couple hundred years, and I always expected my career to involve the building of worthwhile solutions to real problems, one problem at a time.

35 I have not been disappointed. My work has had more impact than I had ever hoped for and has been more widely used than I could have reasonably expected. I have spent the last 20 years still trying to figure out how to make computers as reliable as I want them to be (they are not nearly there yet) and how to make them simple to use (a goal that has met with even less relative success). Despite some progress, the problems that remain seem even more daunting.

36 But while I was aware of the moral dilemmas surrounding technology's consequences in fields like weapons research, I did not expect that I would confront such issues in my own field, or at least not so soon.

37 Perhaps it is always hard to see the bigger impact while you are in the vortex of a change. Failing to understand the consequences of our inventions while we are in the rapture of discovery and innovation seems to be a common fault of scientists and technologists; we have long been driven by the overarching desire to know that is the nature of science's quest, not stopping to notice that the progress to newer and more powerful technologies can take on a life of its own.

38 I have long realized that the big advances in information technology come not from the work of computer scientists, computer architects, or electrical engineers, but from that of physical scientists. The physicists Stephen Wolfram and Brosl Hasslacher introduced me, in the early 1980s, to chaos theory and nonlinear systems. In the 1990s, I learned about complex systems from conversations with Danny Hillis, the biologist Stuart Kauffman, the Nobel-laureate physicist Murray Gell-Mann, and others. Most recently, Hasslacher and the electrical engineer and device physicist Mark Reed have been giving me insight into the incredible possibilities of molecular electronics.

39   In my own work, as codesigner of three microprocessor architectures—SPARC, picoJava, and MAJC—and as the designer of several implementations thereof, I've been afforded a deep and firsthand acquaintance with Moore's law. For decades, Moore's law has correctly predicted the exponential rate of improvement of semiconductor technology. Until last year I believed that the rate of advances predicted by Moore's law might continue only until roughly 2010, when some physical limits would begin to be reached. It was not obvious to me that a new technology would arrive in time to keep performance advancing smoothly.

40   But because of the recent rapid and radical progress in molecular electronics—where individual atoms and molecules replace lithographically drawn transistors—and related nanoscale technologies, we should be able to meet or exceed the Moore's law rate of progress for another 30 years. By 2030, we are likely to be able to build machines, in quantity, a million times as powerful as the personal computers of today—sufficient to implement the dreams of Kurzwell and Moravec.

41   As this enormous computing power is combined with the manipulative advances of the physical sciences and the new, deep understandings in genetics, enormous transformative power is being unleashed. These combinations open up the opportunity to completely redesign the world, for better or worse: The replicating and evolving processes that have been confined to the natural world are about to become realms of human endeavor.

42   In designing software and microprocessors, I have never had the feeling that I was designing an intelligent machine. The software and hardware is so fragile and the capabilities of the machine to "think" so clearly absent that, even as a possibility, this has always seemed very far in the future.

43   But now, with the prospect of human-level computing power in about 30 years, a new idea suggests itself: that I may be working to create tools which will enable the construction of the technology that may replace our species. How do I feel about this? Very uncomfortable. Having struggled my entire career to build reliable software systems, it seems to me more than likely that this future will not work out as well as some people may imagine. My personal experience suggests we tend to overestimate our design abilities.

44   Given the incredible power of these new technologies, shouldn't we be asking how we can best coexist with them? And if our own extinction is a likely, or even possible, outcome of our technological development, shouldn't we proceed with great caution?

Notes

1. The passage Kurzweil quotes is from Kaczynski's "Unabomber Manifesto," which was published jointly, under duress, by *The New York Times* and *The Washington Post* to attempt to bring his campaign of terror to an end. I agree with David Gelernter, who said about their decision:

   "It was a tough call for the newspapers. To say yes would be giving in to terrorism, and for all they knew he was lying anyway. On the other hand, to say yes might stop the killing. There was also a chance that someone would read the tract and get a hunch about the author; and that is exactly what happened. The suspect's brother read it, and it rang a bell.

"I would have told them not to publish. I'm glad they didn't ask me. I guess."

(*Drawing Life: Surviving the Unabomber.* Free Press, 1997: 120.)

2. Garrett, Laurie. *The Coming Plague: Newly Emerging Diseases in a World Out of Balance.* Penguin, 1994: 47–52, 414, 419, 452.
3. Isaac Asimov described what became the most famous view of ethical rules for robot behavior in his book *I, Robot* in 1950, in his Three Laws of Robotics: 1. A robot may not injure a human being, or, through inaction, allow a human being to come to harm. 2. A robot must obey the orders given it by human beings, except where such orders would conflict with the First Law. 3. A robot must protect its own existence, as long as such protection does not conflict with the First or Second Law.
4. Michelangelo wrote a sonnet that begins:

> *Non ha l' ottimo artista alcun concetto*
> *Ch' un marmo solo in sè non circonscriva*
> *Col suo soverchio; e solo a quello arriva*
> *La man che ubbidisce all' intelleto.*

Stone translates this as:

> *The best of artists hath no thought to show*
> *which the rough stone in its superfluous shell*
> *doth not include; to break the marble spell*
> *is all the hand that serves the brain can do.*

Stone describes the process: "He was not working from his drawings or clay models; they had all been put away. He was carving from the images in his mind. His eyes and hands knew where every line, curve, mass must emerge, and at what depth in the heart of the stone to create the low relief."

(*The Agony and the Ecstasy.* Doubleday, 1961: 6, 144.) ■

Francis Fukuyama

Tale of Two Dystopias

Political economist Francis Fukuyama (born 1952) is the Bernard L. Schwartz Professor at Johns Hopkins University. While he has published numerous academic articles, he is perhaps best known as the author of The End of History and the Last Man *(1992), which argues that after the Cold War the citizens of the world basically agreed that liberal democracy is the ideology by which to live. Fukuyama has also authored* Trust: The Social Virtues and the Creation of Prosperity *(1995) and* Our Posthuman Future: Consequences of the Biotechnology Revolution *(2002), from which the excerpt below comes. More recently he edited* Blindside: How to Anticipate Forcing Events and Wild Cards in Global Politics *(2007). Fukuyama is concerned about the dangers and inequalities that can arise from the use of biotechnology to shape human nature. Fukuyama also currently serves on the Bush administration's President's Council on Bioethics.*

The threat to man does not come in the first instance from the potentially lethal machines and apparatus of technology. The actual threat has always afflicted man in his essence. The rule of enframing (*Gestell*) threatens man with the possibility that it could be denied to him to enter into a more original revealing and hence to experience the call of a more primal truth.

Martin Heidegger, *The Question Concerning Technology*[1]

I was born in 1952, right in the middle of the American baby boom. For any person growing up as I did in the middle decades of the twentieth century, the future and its terrifying possibilities were defined by two books, George Orwell's *1984* (first published in 1949) and Aldous Huxley's *Brave New World* (published in 1932).

2   The two books were far more prescient than anyone realized at the time, because they were centered on two different technologies that would in fact emerge and shape the world over the next two generations. The novel *1984* was about what we now call information technology: central to the success of the vast, totalitarian empire that had been set up over Oceania was a device called the telescreen, a wall-sized flat-panel display that could simultaneously send and receive images from each individual household to a hovering Big Brother. The telescreen was what permitted the vast centralization of social life under the Ministry of Truth and the Ministry of Love, for it allowed the government to banish privacy by monitoring every word and deed over a massive network of wires.

3   *Brave New World,* by contrast, was about the other big technological revolution about to take place, that of biotechnology. Bokanovskification, the hatching of people not in wombs but, as we now say, in vitro; the drug soma, which gave people instant happiness; the Feelies, in which sensation was simulated by implanted electrodes; and the modification of behavior through constant subliminal repetition and, when that didn't work, through the administration of various artificial hormones were what gave this book its particularly creepy ambiance.

4   With at least a half century separating us from the publication of these books, we can see that while the technological predictions they made were startlingly accurate, the political predictions of the first book, *1984,* were entirely wrong. The year 1984 came and went, with the United States still locked in a Cold War struggle with the Soviet Union. That year saw the introduction of a new model of the IBM personal computer and the beginning of what became the PC revolution. As Peter Huber has argued, the personal computer, linked to the Internet, was in fact the realization of

[1]Martin Heidegger, *Basic Writings* (New York: Harper and Row, 1957), p. 308.

Orwell's telescreen.² But instead of becoming an instrument of centralization and tyranny, it led to just the opposite: the democratization of access to information and the decentralization of politics. Instead of Big Brother watching everyone, people could use the PC and Internet to watch Big Brother, as governments everywhere were driven to publish more information on their own activities.

5   Just five years after 1984, in a series of dramatic events that would earlier have seemed like political science fiction, the Soviet Union and its empire collapsed, and the totalitarian threat that Orwell had so vividly evoked vanished. People were again quick to point out that these two events—the collapse of totalitarian empires and the emergence of the personal computer, as well as other forms of inexpensive information technology, from TVs and radios to faxes and e-mail—were not unrelated. Totalitarian rule depended on a regime's ability to maintain a monopoly over information, and once modern information technology made that impossible, the regime's power was undermined.

6   The political prescience of the other great dystopia, *Brave New World*, remains to be seen. Many of the technologies that Huxley envisioned, like in vitro fertilization, surrogate motherhood, psychotropic drugs, and genetic engineering for the manufacture of children, are already here or just over the horizon. But this revolution has only just begun; the daily avalanche of announcements of new breakthroughs in biomedical technology and achievements such as the completion of the Human Genome Project in the year 2000 portend much more serious changes to come.

7   Of the nightmares evoked by these two books, *Brave New World*'s always struck me as more subtle and more challenging. It is easy to see what's wrong with the world of *1984*: the protagonist, Winston Smith, is known to hate rats above all things, so Big Brother devises a cage in which rats can bite at Smith's face in order to get him to betray his lover. This is the world of classical tyranny, technologically empowered but not so different from what we have tragically seen and known in human history.

8   In *Brave New World*, by contrast, the evil is not so obvious because no one is hurt; indeed, this is a world in which everyone gets what they want. As one of the characters notes, "The Controllers realized that force was no good," and that people would have to be seduced rather than compelled to live in an orderly society. In this world, disease and social conflict have been abolished, there is no depression, madness, loneliness, or emotional distress, sex is good and readily available. There is even a government ministry to ensure that the length of time between the appearance of a desire and its satisfaction is kept to a minimum. No one takes religion seriously any longer, no one is introspective or has unrequited longings, the biological family has been abolished, no one reads Shakespeare. But no one (save John the Savage, the book's protagonist) misses these things, either, since they are happy and healthy.

---

²Peter Huber, *Orwell's Revenge: The 1984 Palimpsest* (New York: Free Press, 1994), pp. 222–228.

9   Since the novel's publication, there have probably been several million high school essays written in answer to the question, "What's wrong with this picture?" The answer given (on papers that get A's, at any rate) usually runs something like this: the people in *Brave New World* may be healthy and happy, but they have ceased to be *human beings*. They no longer struggle, aspire, love, feel pain, make difficult moral choices, have families, or do any of the things that we traditionally associate with being human. They no longer have the characteristics that give us human dignity. Indeed, there is no such thing as the human race any longer, since they have been bred by the Controllers into separate castes of Alphas, Betas, Epsilons, and Gammas who are as distant from each other as humans are from animals. Their world has become unnatural in the most profound sense imaginable, because *human nature* has been altered. In the words of bioethicist Leon Kass, "Unlike the man reduced by disease or slavery, the people dehumanized à la *Brave New World* are not miserable, don't know that they are dehumanized, and, what is worse, would not care if they knew. They are, indeed, happy slaves with a slavish happiness."[3]

10   But while this kind of answer is usually adequate to satisfy the typical high school English teacher, it does not (as Kass goes on to note) probe nearly deeply enough. For one can then ask, What is so important about being a human being in the traditional way that Huxley defines it? After all, what the human race is today is the product of an evolutionary process that has been going on for millions of years, one that with any luck will continue well into the future. There are no fixed human characteristics, except for a general capability to choose what we want to be, to modify ourselves in accordance with our desires. So who is to tell us that being human and having dignity means sticking with a set of emotional responses that are the accidental by-product of our evolutionary history? There is no such thing as a biological family, no such thing as human nature or a "normal" human being, and even if there were, why should that be a guide for what is right and just? Huxley is telling us, in effect, that we should continue to feel pain, be depressed or lonely, or suffer from debilitating disease, all because that is what human beings have done for most of their existence as a species. Certainly, no one ever got elected to Congress on such a platform. Instead of taking these characteristics and saying that they are the basis for "human dignity," why don't we simply accept our destiny as creatures who modify themselves?

11   Huxley suggests that one source for a definition of what it means to be a human being is religion. In *Brave New World*, religion has been abolished and Christianity is a distant memory. The Christian tradition maintains that man is created in God's image, which is the source of human dignity. To use

---

[3]Leon Kass, *Toward a More Natural Science: Biology and Human Affairs* (New York: Free Press, 1985), p. 35.

biotechnology to engage in what another Christian writer, C. S. Lewis, called the "abolition of man" is thus a violation of God's will. But I don't think that a careful reading of Huxley or Lewis leads to the conclusion that either writer believed religion to be the *only* grounds on which one could understand the meaning of being human. Both writers suggest that nature itself, and in particular human nature, has a special role in defining for us what is right and wrong, just and unjust, important and unimportant. So our final judgment on "what's wrong" with Huxley's brave new world stands or falls with our view of how important human nature is as a source of values.

12   The aim of my book is to argue that Huxley was right, that the most significant threat posed by contemporary biotechnology is the possibility that it will alter human nature and thereby move us into a "posthuman" stage of history. This is important, I will argue, because human nature exists, is a meaningful concept, and has provided a stable continuity to our experience as a species. It is, conjointly with religion, what defines our most basic values. Human nature shapes and constrains the possible kinds of political regimes, so a technology powerful enough to reshape what we are will have possibly malign consequences for liberal democracy and the nature of politics itself.

13   It may be that, as in the case of *1984*, we will eventually find biotechnology's consequences are completely and surprisingly benign, and that we were wrong to lose sleep over it. It may be that the technology will in the end prove much less powerful than it seems today, or that people will be moderate and careful in their application of it. But one of the reasons I am not quite so sanguine is that biotechnology, in contrast to many other scientific advances, mixes obvious benefits with subtle harms in one seamless package.

14   Nuclear weapons and nuclear energy were perceived as dangerous from the start, and therefore were subject to strict regulation from the moment the Manhattan Project created the first atomic bomb in 1945. Observers like Bill Joy have worried about nanotechnology—that is, molecular-scale self-replicating machines capable of reproducing out of control and destroying their creators.[4] But such threats are actually the easiest to deal with because they are so obvious. If you are likely to be killed by a machine you've created, you take measures to protect yourself. And so far we've had a reasonable record in keeping our machines under control.

15   There may be products of biotechnology that will be similarly obvious in the dangers they pose to mankind—for example, superbugs, new viruses, or genetically modified foods that produce toxic reactions. Like nuclear weapons or nanotechnology, these are in a way the easiest to deal with because once we have identified them as dangerous, we can treat them as a straightforward threat. The more typical threats raised by biotechnology, on the other hand, are those captured so well by Huxley, and are summed up in the title of

[4]Bill Joy, "Why the Future Doesn't Need Us," *Wired* 8 (2000): 238–246.

an article by novelist Tom Wolfe, "Sorry, but Your Soul Just Died."[5] Medical technology offers us in many cases a devil's bargain: longer life, but with reduced mental capacity; freedom from depression, together with freedom from creativity or spirit; therapies that blur the line between what we achieve on our own and what we achieve because of the levels of various chemicals in our brains.

16   Consider the following three scenarios, all of which are distinct possibilities that may unfold over the next generation or two.

17   The first has to do with new drugs. As a result of advances in neuropharmacology, psychologists discover that human personality is much more plastic than formerly believed. It is already the case that psychotropic drugs such as Prozac and Ritalin can affect traits like self-esteem and the ability to concentrate, but they tend to produce a host of unwanted side effects and hence are shunned except in cases of clear therapeutic need. But in the future, knowledge of genomics permits pharmaceutical companies to tailor drugs very specifically to the genetic profiles of individual patients and greatly minimize unintended side effects. Stolid people can become vivacious; introspective ones extroverted; you can adopt one personality on Wednesday and another for the weekend. There is no longer any excuse for anyone to be depressed or unhappy; even "normally" happy people can make themselves happier without worries of addiction, hangovers, or long-term brain damage.

18   In the second scenario, advances in stem cell research allow scientists to regenerate virtually any tissue in the body, such that life expectancies are pushed well above 100 years. If you need a new heart or liver, you just grow one inside the chest cavity of a pig or cow; brain damage from Alzheimer's and stroke can be reversed. The only problem is that there are many subtle and some not-so-subtle aspects of human aging that the biotech industry hasn't quite figured out how to fix: people grow mentally rigid and increasingly fixed in their views as they age, and try as they might, they can't make themselves sexually attractive to each other and continue to long for partners of reproductive age. Worst of all, they just refuse to get out of the way, not just of their children, but their grandchildren and great-grandchildren. On the other hand, so few people have children or any connection with traditional reproduction that it scarcely seems to matter.

19   In a third scenario, the wealthy routinely screen embryos before implantation so as to optimize the kind of children they have. You can increasingly tell the social background of a young person by his or her looks and intelligence; if someone doesn't live up to social expectations, he tends to blame bad genetic choices by his parents rather than himself. Human genes have been transferred to animals and even to plants, for research purposes and to produce new medical products; and animal genes have been added to certain embryos to increase their physical endurance or resistance to disease. Scientists have not dared to produce a full-scale chimera, half human and half ape,

[5]Tom Wolfe, "Sorry, but Your Soul Just Died," *Forbes ASAP*, December 2, 1996.

though they could; but young people begin to suspect that classmates who do much less well than they do are in fact genetically not fully human. Because, in fact, they aren't.

20   Sorry, but your soul just died . . .

21   Toward the very end of his life, Thomas Jefferson wrote, "The general spread of the light of science has already laid open to every view the palpable truth, that the mass of mankind has not been born with saddles on their backs, nor a favored few booted and spurred, ready to ride them legitimately, by the grace of God."[6] The political equality enshrined in the Declaration of Independence rests on the empirical fact of natural human equality. We vary greatly as individuals and by culture, but we share a common humanity that allows every human being to potentially communicate with and enter into a moral relationship with every other human being on the planet. The ultimate question raised by biotechnology is, What will happen to political rights once we are able to, in effect, breed some people with saddles on their backs, and others with boots and spurs?

A Straightforward Solution

22   What should we do in response to biotechnology that in the future will mix great potential benefits with threats that are either physical and overt or spiritual and subtle? The answer is obvious: *We should use the power of the state to regulate it.* And if this proves to be beyond the power of any individual nation-state to regulate, it needs to be regulated on an international basis. We need to start thinking concretely now about how to build institutions that can discriminate between good and bad uses of biotechnology, and effectively enforce these rules both nationally and internationally.

23   This obvious answer is not obvious to many of the participants in the current biotechnology debate. The discussion remains mired at a relatively abstract level about the ethics of procedures like cloning or stem cell research, and divided into one camp that would like to permit everything and another camp that would like to ban wide areas of research and practice. The broader debate is of course an important one, but events are moving so rapidly that we will soon need more practical guidance on how we can direct future developments so that the technology remains man's servant rather than his master. Since it seems very unlikely that we will either permit everything or ban research that is highly promising, we need to find a middle ground.

24   The creation of new regulatory institutions is not something that should be undertaken lightly, given the inefficiencies that surround all efforts at regulation. For the past three decades, there has been a commendable worldwide movement to deregulate large sectors of every nation's economy, from airlines to telecommunications, and more broadly to reduce the size and scope of government. The global economy that has emerged as a result is a far

[6]Letter to Roger C. Weightman, June 24, 1826, in *The Life and Selected Writings of Thomas Jefferson*, Thomas Jefferson (New York: Modern Library, 1944), pp. 729–730.

more efficient generator of wealth and technological innovation. Excessive regulation in the past has led many to become instinctively hostile to state intervention in any form, and it is this knee-jerk aversion to regulation that will be one of the chief obstacles to getting human biotechnology under political control.

25   But it is important to discriminate: what works for one sector of the economy will not work for another. Information technology, for example, produces many social benefits and relatively few harms and therefore has appropriately gotten by with a fairly minimal degree of government regulation. Nuclear materials and toxic waste, on the other hand, are subject to strict national and international controls because unregulated trade in them would clearly be dangerous.

26   One of the biggest problems in making the case for regulating human biotechnology is the common view that even if it were desirable to stop technological advance, it is impossible to do so. If the United States or any other single country tries to ban human cloning or germline genetic engineering or any other procedure, people who wanted to do these things would simply move to a more favorable jurisdiction where they were permitted. Globalization and international competition in biomedical research ensure that countries that hobble themselves by putting ethical constraints on their scientific communities or biotechnology industries will be punished.

27   The idea that it is impossible to stop or control the advance of technology is simply wrong. We in fact control all sorts of technologies and many types of scientific research: people are no more free to experiment in the development of new biological warfare agents than they are to experiment on human subjects without the latter's informed consent. The fact that there are some individuals or organizations that violate these rules, or that there are countries where the rules are either nonexistent or poorly enforced, is no excuse for not making the rules in the first place. People get away with robbery and murder, after all, which is not a reason to legalize theft and homicide.

28   We need at all costs to avoid a defeatist attitude with regard to technology that says that since we can't do anything to stop or shape developments we don't like, we shouldn't bother trying in the first place. Putting in place a regulatory system that would permit societies to control human biotechnology will not be easy: it will require legislators in countries around the world to step up to the plate and make difficult decisions on complex scientific issues. The shape and form of the institutions designed to implement new rules is a wide-open question; designing them to be minimally obstructive of positive developments while giving them effective enforcement capabilities is a significant challenge. Even more challenging will be the creation of common rules at an international level, the forging of a consensus among countries with different cultures and views on the underlying ethical questions. But political tasks of comparable complexity have been successfully undertaken in the past. ■

Ralph C. Merkle

Nanotechnology: Designs for the Future

Ubiquity is a Web-based publication of the Association for Computing Machinery focusing on a variety of issues related to the information technology industry. In 2000, Ubiquity interviewed Ralph C. Merkle, a former research scientist at Xerox Parc; advisor at the Foresight Institute; and at the time a nanotechnology theorist at Zyvex, a nanotechnology research and development company. Merkle's main research interests are nanotechnology (also called molecular manufacturing), cryptography, and cryonics. He served as executive editor of the journal Nanotechnology *for several years. In 1998, Merkle won the Feynman Prize in Nanotechnology for his theoretical work. As you will see, the interview excerpted below is partly in response to Bill Joy's "Why the Future Doesn't Need Us," the first selection in this chapter.*

UBIQUITY: Bill Joy's recent *Wired* article on the perils of today's advanced technologies—including nanotechnology—has certainly received a lot of attention, and we did a follow-up interview with him in *Ubiquity*. What are your thoughts on that subject?

2   RALPH C. MERKLE   Well, certainly the idea that nanotechnology would raise concerns is something that actually was a major impetus for the founding of the Foresight Institute back in 1986—and by 1989, Foresight had its first technical conference on nanotechnology, and in fact Bill Joy spoke at that meeting. So one of the things that's a bit surprising is that Bill's concerns about nanotechnology seem to be quite recent— just the last year or two—even though the understanding that this particular technology was going to be very powerful and would raise significant concerns has been around for at least a couple of decades.

3   UBIQUITY: Why don't you take a moment now to tell us about the Foresight Institute?

4   MERKLE: The Foresight Institute (www.foresight.org/guidelines/index.html) was created primarily to guide the development of nanotechnology, and it was founded in large part because, when you look at where the technology is going, you reach the conclusion that, though it has great potential for good, there are also some concerns which need to be addressed. We've been having a series of gatherings at Foresight now for some years where Senior Associates (people who have pledged to support the Foresight Institute) can get together informally and off the record and discuss the various issues.

5   UBIQUITY: What are the meetings like?

6   MERKLE: The most recent gathering had over 250 people—including Bill Joy, as a matter of fact—and one of the sessions was a discussion of the

Nanotechnology, a field named after the nanometer (one-billionth of a meter), uses incredibly small devices to advance areas like telecommunications. Some of these technologies have already been adapted by companies with practical and commercial success.

Foresight guidelines for safe development of nanotechnology. A year and a half ago we had a workshop where we discussed the guidelines and worked out an initial draft, which was discussed at the 1999 gathering at Foresight, and then further modified and updated and then discussed again at the most recent gathering.

7 UBIQUITY: What do you think would explain the sudden increase of concern about this?

8 MERKLE: Well, I can't really address the specifics of Bill Joy's situation. I do know that nanotechnology is an idea that most people simply didn't believe, even though the roots of it go back to a lecture by Richard Feynman in 1959 (www.zyvex.com/nanotech/feynman.html). That was a very famous talk in which he basically said the laws of physics should allow us to arrange things molecule by molecule and even atom by atom, and that at some point it was inevitable that we would develop a technology that would let us do this. I don't think that it was taken very seriously at that time, but as the years progressed it gradually began to be more accepted. If you think the technology is infeasible, you don't worry about what it might do and what its potential is. However, as you begin to internalize the fact that this technology is going to arrive and that we are going to have a very powerful manufacturing technology that will let us build a wide range of remarkable new products, then one of the things that arises is a concern that this new set of capabilities could create new problems, new concerns, and that these should be addressed.

9 UBIQUITY: But not the way Bill Joy is addressing them?

10 MERKLE: One of the things about Bill Joy's original article that concerned me is that he was calling for a relinquishment, as he put it, of research—and I think that's a *very* foolish strategy. If you look at the various strategies available for dealing with a new technology, sticking your head in the sand is not the most plausible strategy and in fact actually makes the situation more dangerous.

11 UBIQUITY: Why so?

12	MERKLE:	For at least three reasons. The first, of course, is that we need to have a collective understanding of the new technology in order to ensure that we develop it appropriately. The second reason is that the new technologies that we see coming will have major benefits, and will greatly alleviate human suffering. The third reason is that, if we attempt to block the development of new technology, if we collectively try and say, "These technologies are technologies that are not meant for humans to understand," and we try to back away from them, what we effectively have done is not to block the technologies, we have simply ensured that the most responsible parties will not develop them.
13	UBIQUITY:	So you think "relinquishment" is exactly the wrong strategy.
14	MERKLE:	Right. Those people who pay no attention to a call for relinquishment, and in particular those people who are least inclined to be concerned about safe development will, in fact, be the groups that eventually develop the technology. In other words, a relinquishment of the new technology, unless it is absolutely 100 percent effective, is not effective at all. If it's 99.99 percent effective, then you simply ensure that the .01 percent who pays no attention to such calls for relinquishment is the group that will develop it. And that actually creates a worse outcome than if the responsible players move forward and develop the technology with the best understanding that they have and the best efforts to ensure that the technology is developed in a safe and responsible fashion.
15	UBIQUITY:	Let's go back to the second reason and expand on that to the extent of enumerating what you consider are the most prominent hopes that it offers.
16	MERKLE:	Well, certainly what we see today is an entire planet, which has many limitations. I'm not quite sure how to express it, but certainly if you look at the human condition today, not everyone is well fed. Not everyone has access to good medical care. Not everyone has the basics—the physical basics that provide for a healthy and a happy life. And clearly, if you have a lower cost manufacturing technology, which can build a wide range of products less expensively, it can build, among other things, better medical products. Disease and ill health are caused largely by damage at the molecular and cellular level, yet today's surgical tools are too large to deal with that kind of problem. A molecular manufacturing technology will let us build molecular surgical tools, and those tools will, for the first time, let us directly address the problems at the very root level. So today we see a human population of over six billion people, many of whom have serious medical conditions, which either can't be treated or cannot be treated economically. In other words, we don't have the resources to effectively treat all the conditions that we see. If we can reduce the cost and improve the quality of medical technology through advances

in nanotechnology, then we can more widely address the medical conditions that are prevalent and reduce the level of human suffering. (See www.foresight.org/Nanomedicine for more information about medical applications.)

17 UBIQUITY: And besides the opportunities in medicine? What else?

18 MERKLE: On another level, food; the simple process of feeding the human population. Today because of technological limits there is a certain amount of food that we can produce per acre. If we were to have intensive greenhouse agriculture, which would be something we could do economically, if we could economically manufacture the appropriate computer controlled enclosures that would provide protection and would provide a very controlled environment for the growth of food we could have much higher production. It looks as though yields of over 10 times what we can currently grow per acre are feasible if you control, for example, the CO_2 concentration, the humidity, the temperature, all the various factors that plants depend on to grow rapidly. If we control those, if we make those optimal for the growth of various crops then we can grow more per acre. And furthermore, we can grow it less expensively because molecular manufacturing technology is inherently low cost, and therefore it will let us grow more food more easily.

19 UBIQUITY: What are the implications?

20 MERKLE: The first is that it makes food less expensive. The second is that many of the people in the world today who are starving are not starving because there is an inherent inability to produce food, they are starving because they are caught in the middle of political fights and blockades that have been used as political weapons. As a consequence, food is available but it cannot be shipped into an area and so the people in that area suffer the consequences. However, if you have a distributed manufacturing technology, one of the great advantages is that it should let us have a much lower cost infrastructure. In other words, today manufacturing takes place in very large facilities. If you want to build, for example, a computer chip, you need a giant semiconductor fabrication facility. But if you look at nature, nature can grow complex molecular machines using nothing more than a plant.

21 UBIQUITY: Example?

22 MERKLE: Well, a potato, for example, can grow quite easily on a very small plot of land. With molecular manufacturing, in a similar fashion, we'll be able to have distributed manufacturing, which will permit manufacturing at the site using technologies that are low cost and easily available once the core technology has been developed. And as a consequence, you would have people able to build low-cost greenhouse agriculture tools even if there were a blockade because the manufacturing facilities would be widely distributed, and

therefore they could avoid the blockade by simply making what they need inside the blockaded region using cheap raw materials and sunlight.

23 UBIQUITY: And if nanotechnology did so much for people's health and food production, what would it do, do you suppose, for their current economic institution? Would it transition to large-scale nanotechnology? Have unintended consequences in terms of disrupting the economy?

24 MERKLE: I think we would see changes in the economy. Previous technologies have made major changes. Old companies that have had major advantages in the past certainly find those advantages go away. Certainly as manufacturing becomes less expensive, then today's major manufacturing companies would find that they would be at a disadvantage in the future. Other companies that are producing intellectual products, software companies or companies that are not dealing with material objects—banks and financial institutions, for example—fundamentally are dealing with a flow of information so would be relatively less affected. I think you would see some major shifts in the economy in that manufacturing companies would find that what they were doing was either greatly changed or outright replaced. As in any technological revolution, there will be winners and losers. On balance, everyone will come out ahead, although there will be specific instances where particular companies will have major problems, and in fact, will simply not be able to cope with a new environment and presumably suffer the consequences.

25 UBIQUITY: What about the competition between different countries? Would, for example, the severely underdeveloped countries have an ability to do very rapid catch-up?

26 MERKLE: Yes. I think they would. Also, you have to remember that we are looking at a future where to a first approximation everyone is wealthy. Now, there are certain things that are inherently scarce. For example, there is only a certain amount of beachfront property in California. It is going to be scarce, it is going to be expensive, and only a small percentage of the population will be able to afford it. But if you look at other material possessions—housing or electronics—you find that the only limitation is our ability to manufacture them inexpensively. So the first approximation in this future that we're looking at is that everyone will be physically well off. They will have a great abundance in material goods, and as a consequence, I think that will soften and ease some of the conflicts that we see now. One of the issues facing us today is that there are countries where there is a serious lack of resources, the standards of living are very low, and as a consequence this creates a

fundamental unease and discomfort in entire populations. If you have a higher standard of living, at least that source of conflict will be greatly reduced. Now, as we all know, there are many potential sources of conflict in the world, but even easing some of them will be very helpful.

27 UBIQUITY: Give us an example of a product that would be improved using molecular manufacturing?

28 MERKLE: The answer that comes most readily to mind is diamonds. Diamond has a better strength-to-weight ratio than steel or aluminum. Its strength-to-weight ratio is more than 50 times that of steel or aluminum alloy. So, it's much stronger and much lighter. If we had a shatterproof variant of diamond, we would have a remarkably light and strong material from which to make all of the products in the world around us. In particular, aerospace products—airplanes or rockets—would benefit immensely from having lighter, stronger materials. So one of the things that we can say with confidence is that we will have much lighter, much stronger materials, and this will reduce the cost of air flight, and it will reduce the cost of rockets. It will let us go into space for literally orders of magnitude lower cost.

29 UBIQUITY: Has NASA shown any interest in this?

30 MERKLE: Needless to say, they are pursuing research in nanotechnology with the idea of having lighter, stronger materials as one of the significant objectives. There is a whole range of other capabilities, of course, that would be of interest in NASA. For example, lighter computers and lighter sensors would let you have more function in a given weight, which is very important if you are launching things into space, and you have to pay by the pound to put things there.

31 UBIQUITY: Are there any other areas that would be significantly affected by nanotechnology?

32 MERKLE: The other area is in advanced computer technology. The computer hardware revolution has been continuing with remarkable steadiness over the last few decades. If you extrapolate into the future you find that, in the coming decades, we'll have to build molecular computers to keep the computer hardware revolution on track. Nanotechnology will let us do that, and it will let us build computers that are incredibly powerful. We'll have more power in the volume of a sugar cube than exists in the entire world today.

33 UBIQUITY: Can you put any kind of timeframe on that?

34 MERKLE: We're talking about decades. We're not talking about years; we're not talking about a century. We're talking decades—and probably not many decades. ∎

Ursula Franklin

Beautiful, Functional, and Frugal

Ursula Franklin is a pacifist, feminist, member of the Society of Friends (the Quakers), and scientist. Though she was born in Germany, Franklin has spent much of her life in Canada, where she dedicates her time to public speaking about science, society, and technology as well as encouraging young people (especially girls, who are typically underrepresented in the sciences) to pursue further education and careers in science. In the speech excerpted below, printed in the Canadian journal Alternatives, *Franklin expands on the following thesis statement: "Every scientific finding contains knowledge of beauty, functionality, and frugality."*

I am very happy that I can speak at a science convocation because the practice of science, the daily work in the lab, has been the source of so much pleasure and fulfillment in my own life. Allow me, then, to speak about the common insights that have flown from the advances of science, both recent and traditional. These insights have come from all the diverse disciplines within the sciences, including all the disciplines from which you are graduating today. If we accept, be it only for this discussion, the simple definition that research in the sciences attempts to understand and illuminate the working of the natural world, from the structure of galaxies to interactions on an atomic level, then there are some amazingly general, overarching insights that the sciences can bring to us, in spite, or maybe because, of the great diversity of the various disciplines within the sciences.

2   Helped by modern imaging and communication techniques, scholars are able to share these insights with the larger community, and this is what emerges:

3   The natural world is incredibly beautiful, from the structure and arrangement of single molecules in an active cell, to the microstructure of crystalline surfaces or the new complex nanomaterials or the movement of the moons around the planets.

4   The natural world is incredibly functional. The more we learn about complexity, the greater is the marvel of functionality, whether it is the passage of molecules through a membrane, the ultra fast exchange of electrons in a chemical reaction triggered by light, or the formation of planetary materials over very long periods of time. The natural world, the great biosphere of which we are such a small part, functions, and it functions with delicate complexity.

5   The natural world is extremely frugal. Ongoing developments in thermodynamics, the great common yardstick of energy and change, have helped to illuminate just how frugal are the workings of the natural world, how effectively energy is utilized in the natural world, how symbiotically functions are intertwined.

6   As each piece of newly revealed knowledge about the natural world elaborates just how beautiful, how functional, and how frugal the planet is, it

becomes equally clear how many of our human and social structures and processes are not beautiful, functional or frugal. Indeed, often they tend to be ugly, dysfunctional and wasteful. Ironically, many of these enterprises and processes have been designed by drawing on the latest and best scientific findings. Frequently, but let me stress emphatically, by no means always, the scientific information is used to outsmart or outfox the natural world, to facilitate shortcuts or conduct end runs of the very processes studied. You will realize how often this approach has resulted in increased efficiencies in one social or economic activity while occasioning a great deal of waste in other areas.

7   By the same token, the cumbersome ugliness of many of the so-called economies of scale, not to mention the overall disregard of the dynamics of the biosphere in industrial and political planning, are frequently seen as the triumph of scientific management and control. Yet, while specific research results might have motivated particular designs or processes, the overarching insight of the study of the natural world brings counter evidence into the picture, evidence that should not be overlooked.

8   Every scientific finding contains knowledge of beauty, functionality and frugality. In fact, functionality, frugality and beauty may be existentially so profoundly interrelated that nothing but an optimization of these attributes will work in the long run as the design principle for human society. Why do I raise these issues with you, here, and at this moment in your lives?

9   In the first place, I would like to highlight for you the great common insight that science has brought to our knowledge and understanding of the natural world, because this is sometimes overlooked in the great rush to find profitable applications of specific research. And then, I would also like you to accept these thoughts for use in your work. As you apply and augment your own scientific knowledge, respect the trio of beauty, functionality and frugality, and check for their simultaneous presence in all you undertake. It would not surprise me if, within your lifetime, it will become common knowledge that the simultaneous presence of beauty, functionality and frugality are needed to secure and maintain a livable world. ■

Bill Gates

A Robot in Every Home

Since 1995, Bill Gates has been ranked by Forbes *magazine as the richest person in the world. Best known for his role with Microsoft, the company he cofounded with Paul Allen, Gates now serves as the primary stockholder for that corporation. He spends most of his time doing philanthropic work with the Gates Foundation, which he and his wife, Melinda, founded in 2000. In "A Robot in Every Home," which first appeared in the December 2006 issue of* Scientific American, *Gates waxes enthusiastic and optimistic about the prospect of bringing robotics into every American household—much as Microsoft did with personal computers.*

I magine being present at the birth of a new industry. It is an industry based on groundbreaking new technologies, wherein a handful of well-established corporations sell highly specialized devices for business use and a fast-growing number of start-up companies produce innovative toys, gadgets for hobbyists and other interesting niche products. But it is also a highly fragmented industry with few common standards or platforms. Projects are complex, progress is slow, and practical applications are relatively rare. In fact, for all the excitement and promise, no one can say with any certainty when—or even if—this industry will achieve critical mass. If it does, though, it may well change the world.

2   Of course, the paragraph above could be a description of the computer industry during the mid-1970s, around the time that Paul Allen and I launched Microsoft. Back then, big, expensive mainframe computers ran the back-office operations for major companies, governmental departments and other institutions. Researchers at leading universities and industrial laboratories were creating the basic building blocks that would make the information age possible. Intel had just introduced the 8080 microprocessor, and Atari was selling the popular electronic game Pong. At homegrown computer clubs, enthusiasts struggled to figure out exactly what this new technology was good for.

3   But what I really have in mind is something much more contemporary: the emergence of the robotics industry, which is developing in much the same way that the computer business did 30 years ago. Think of the manufacturing robots currently used on automobile assembly lines as the equivalent of yesterday's mainframes. The industry's niche products include robotic arms that perform surgery, surveillance robots deployed in Iraq and Afghanistan that dispose of roadside bombs, and domestic robots that vacuum the floor. Electronics companies have made robotic toys that can imitate people or dogs or dinosaurs, and hobbyists are anxious to get their hands on the latest version of the Lego robotics system.

4   Meanwhile some of the world's best minds are trying to solve the toughest problems of robotics, such as visual recognition, navigation and machine learning. And they are succeeding. At the 2004 Defense Advanced Research Projects Agency (DARPA) Grand Challenge, a competition to produce the first robotic vehicle capable of navigating autonomously over a rugged 142-mile course through the Mojave Desert, the top competitor managed to travel just 7.4 miles before breaking down. In 2005, though, five vehicles covered the complete distance, and the race's winner did it at an average speed of 19.1 miles an hour. (In another intriguing parallel between the robotics and computer industries, DARPA also funded the work that led to the creation of Arpanet, the precursor to the Internet.)

5   What is more, the challenges facing the robotics industry are similar to those we tackled in computing three decades ago. Robotics companies have no standard operating software that could allow popular application programs to run in a variety of devices. The standardization of robotic processors and other hardware is limited, and very little of the programming code used in one machine can be applied to another. Whenever somebody wants to build a new robot, they usually have to start from square one.

6   Despite these difficulties, when I talk to people involved in robotics—from university researchers to entrepreneurs, hobbyists and high school students—the level of excitement and expectation reminds me so much of that time when Paul Allen and I looked at the convergence of new technologies and dreamed of the day when a computer would be on every desk and in every home. And as I look at the trends that are now starting to converge, I can envision a future in which robotic devices will become a nearly ubiquitous part of our day-to-day lives. I believe that technologies such as distributed computing, voice and visual recognition, and wireless broadband connectivity will open the door to a new generation of autonomous devices that enable computers to perform tasks in the physical world on our behalf. We may be on the verge of a new era, when the PC will get up off the desktop and allow us to see, hear, touch and manipulate objects in places where we are not physically present.

From Science Fiction to Reality

7 The word "robot" was popularized in 1921 by Czech playwright Karel Capek, but people have envisioned creating robot-like devices for thousands of years. In Greek and Roman mythology, the gods of metalwork built mechanical servants made from gold. In the first century A.D., Heron of Alexandria—the great engineer credited with inventing the first steam engine—designed intriguing automatons, including one said to have the ability to talk. Leonardo da Vinci's 1495 sketch of a mechanical knight, which could sit up and move its arms and legs, is considered to be the first plan for a humanoid robot.

8   Over the past century, anthropomorphic machines have become familiar figures in popular culture through books such as Isaac Asimov's *I, Robot*, movies such as *Star Wars* and television shows such as *Star Trek*. The popularity of robots in fiction indicates that people are receptive to the idea that these machines will one day walk among us as helpers and even as companions. Nevertheless, although robots play a vital role in industries such as automobile manufacturing—where there is about one robot for every 10 workers—the fact is that we have a long way to go before real robots catch up with their science-fiction counterparts.

9   One reason for this gap is that it has been much harder than expected to enable computers and robots to sense their surrounding environment and to react quickly and accurately. It has proved extremely difficult to give robots the capabilities that humans take for granted—for example, the abilities to orient themselves with respect to the objects in a room, to respond to sounds

and interpret speech, and to grasp objects of varying sizes, textures and fragility. Even something as simple as telling the difference between an open door and a window can be devilishly tricky for a robot.

10   But researchers are starting to find the answers. One trend that has helped them is the increasing availability of tremendous amounts of computer power. One megahertz of processing power, which cost more than $7,000 in 1970, can now be purchased for just pennies. The price of a megabit of storage has seen a similar decline. The access to cheap computing power has permitted scientists to work on many of the hard problems that are fundamental to making robots practical. Today, for example, voice-recognition programs can identify words quite well, but a far greater challenge will be building machines that can understand what those words mean in context. As computing capacity continues to expand, robot designers will have the processing power they need to tackle issues of ever greater complexity.

11   Another barrier to the development of robots has been the high cost of hardware, such as sensors that enable a robot to determine the distance to an object as well as motors and servos that allow the robot to manipulate an object with both strength and delicacy. But prices are dropping fast. Laser range finders that are used in robotics to measure distance with precision cost about $10,000 a few years ago; today they can be purchased for about $2,000. And new, more accurate sensors based on ultrawideband radar are available for even less.

12   Now robot builders can also add Global Positioning System chips, video cameras, array microphones (which are better than conventional microphones at distinguishing a voice from background noise) and a host of additional sensors for a reasonable expense. The resulting enhancement of capabilities, combined with expanded processing power and storage, allows today's robots to do things such as vacuum a room or help to defuse a roadside bomb—tasks that would have been impossible for commercially produced machines just a few years ago.

A BASIC Approach

13   In February 2004 I visited a number of leading universities, including Carnegie Mellon University, the Massachusetts Institute of Technology, Harvard University, Cornell University and the University of Illinois, to talk about the powerful role that computers can play in solving some of society's most pressing problems. My goal was to help students understand how exciting and important computer science can be, and I hoped to encourage a few of them to think about careers in technology. At each university, after delivering my speech, I had the opportunity to get a firsthand look at some of the most interesting research projects in the school's computer science department. Almost without exception, I was shown at least one project that involved robotics.

14   At that time, my colleagues at Microsoft were also hearing from people in academia and at commercial robotics firms who wondered if our company was

doing any work in robotics that might help them with their own development efforts. We were not, so we decided to take a closer look. I asked Tandy Trower, a member of my strategic staff and a 25-year Microsoft veteran, to go on an extended fact-finding mission and to speak with people across the robotics community. What he found was universal enthusiasm for the potential of robotics, along with an industry-wide desire for tools that would make development easier. "Many see the robotics industry at a technological turning point where a move to PC architecture makes more and more sense," Tandy wrote in his report to me after his fact-finding mission. "As Red Whittaker, leader of [Carnegie Mellon's] entry in the DARPA Grand Challenge, recently indicated, the hardware capability is mostly there; now the issue is getting the software right."

15   Back in the early days of the personal computer, we realized that we needed an ingredient that would allow all of the pioneering work to achieve critical mass, to coalesce into a real industry capable of producing truly useful products on a commercial scale. What was needed, it turned out, was Microsoft BASIC. When we created this programming language in the 1970s, we provided the common foundation that enabled programs developed for one set of hardware to run on another. BASIC also made computer programming much easier, which brought more and more people into the industry. Although a great many individuals made essential contributions to the development of the personal computer, Microsoft BASIC was one of the key catalysts for the software and hardware innovations that made the PC revolution possible.

16   After reading Tandy's report, it seemed clear to me that before the robotics industry could make the same kind of quantum leap that the PC industry made 30 years ago, it, too, needed to find that missing ingredient. So I asked him to assemble a small team that would work with people in the robotics field to create a set of programming tools that would provide the essential plumbing so that anybody interested in robots with even the most basic understanding of computer programming could easily write robotic applications that would work with different kinds of hardware. The goal was to see if it was possible to provide the same kind of common, low-level foundation for integrating hardware and software into robot designs that Microsoft BASIC provided for computer programmers.

17   Tandy's robotics group has been able to draw on a number of advanced technologies developed by a team working under the direction of Craig Mundie, Microsoft's chief research and strategy officer. One such technology will help solve one of the most difficult problems facing robot designers: how to simultaneously handle all the data coming in from multiple sensors and send the appropriate commands to the robot's motors, a challenge known as concurrency. A conventional approach is to write a traditional, single-threaded program—a long loop that first reads all the data from the sensors, then processes this input and finally delivers output that determines the

robot's behavior, before starting the loop all over again. The shortcomings are obvious: if your robot has fresh sensor data indicating that the machine is at the edge of a precipice, but the program is still at the bottom of the loop calculating trajectory and telling the wheels to turn faster based on previous sensor input, there is a good chance the robot will fall down the stairs before it can process the new information.

18   Concurrency is a challenge that extends beyond robotics. Today as more and more applications are written for distributed networks of computers, programmers have struggled to figure out how to efficiently orchestrate code running on many different servers at the same time. And as computers with a single processor are replaced by machines with multiple processors and "multicore" processors—integrated circuits with two or more processors joined together for enhanced performance—software designers will need a new way to program desktop applications and operating systems. To fully exploit the power of processors working in parallel, the new software must deal with the problem of concurrency.

19   One approach to handling concurrency is to write multi-threaded programs that allow data to travel along many paths. But as any developer who has written multithreaded code can tell you, this is one of the hardest tasks in programming. The answer that Craig's team has devised to the concurrency problem is something called the concurrency and coordination runtime (CCR). The CCR is a library of functions—sequences of software code that perform specific tasks—that makes it easy to write multithreaded applications that can coordinate a number of simultaneous activities. Designed to help programmers take advantage of the power of multicore and multiprocessor systems, the CCR turns out to be ideal for robotics as well. By drawing on this library to write their programs, robot designers can dramatically reduce the chances that one of their creations will run into a wall because its software is too busy sending output to its wheels to read input from its sensors.

20   In addition to tackling the problem of concurrency, the work that Craig's team has done will also simplify the writing of distributed robotic applications through a technology called decentralized software services (DSS). DSS enables developers to create applications in which the services—the parts of the program that read a sensor, say, or control a motor—operate as separate processes that can be orchestrated in much the same way that text, images and information from several servers are aggregated on a Web page. Because DSS allows software components to run in isolation from one another, if an individual component of a robot fails, it can be shut down and restarted—or even replaced—without having to reboot the machine. Combined with broadband wireless technology, this architecture makes it easy to monitor and adjust a robot from a remote location using a Web browser.

21   What is more, a DSS application controlling a robotic device does not have to reside entirely on the robot itself but can be distributed across more than one computer. As a result, the robot can be a relatively inexpensive device

that delegates complex processing tasks to the high-performance hardware found on today's home PCs. I believe this advance will pave the way for an entirely new class of robots that are essentially mobile, wireless peripheral devices that tap into the power of desktop PCs to handle processing-intensive tasks such as visual recognition and navigation. And because these devices can be networked together, we can expect to see the emergence of groups of robots that can work in concert to achieve goals such as mapping the seafloor or planting crops.

22   These technologies are a key part of Microsoft Robotics Studio, a new software development kit built by Tandy's team. Microsoft Robotics Studio also includes tools that make it easier to create robotic applications using a wide range of programming languages. One example is a simulation tool that lets robot builders test their applications in a three-dimensional virtual environment before trying them out in the real world. Our goal for this release is to create an affordable, open platform that allows robot developers to readily integrate hardware and software into their designs.

Should We Call Them Robots?

23 How soon will robots become part of our day-to-day lives? According to the International Federation of Robotics, about two million personal robots were in use around the world in 2004, and another seven million will be installed by 2008. In South Korea the Ministry of Information and Communication hopes to put a robot in every home there by 2013. The Japanese Robot Association predicts that by 2025, the personal robot industry will be worth more than $50 billion a year worldwide, compared with about $5 billion today.

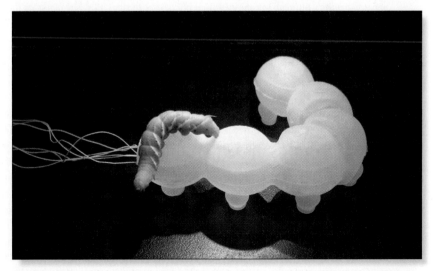

Squishy robots: How does this image affect your perception of what it means to be a robot?

24   As with the PC industry in the 1970s, it is impossible to predict exactly what applications will drive this new industry. It seems quite likely, however, that robots will play an important role in providing physical assistance and even companionship for the elderly. Robotic devices will probably help people with disabilities get around and extend the strength and endurance of soldiers, construction workers and medical professionals. Robots will maintain dangerous industrial machines, handle hazardous materials and monitor remote oil pipelines. They will enable health care workers to diagnose and treat patients who may be thousands of miles away, and they will be a central feature of security systems and search-and-rescue operations.

25   Although a few of the robots of tomorrow may resemble the anthropomorphic devices seen in *Star Wars*, most will look nothing like the humanoid C-3PO. In fact, as mobile peripheral devices become more and more common, it may be increasingly difficult to say exactly what a robot is. Because the new machines will be so specialized and ubiquitous—and look so little like the two-legged automatons of science fiction—we probably will not even call them robots. But as these devices become affordable to consumers, they could have just as profound an impact on the way we work, communicate, learn and entertain ourselves as the PC has had over the past 30 years. ■

Christine Soares

Attitude Screen

Christine Soares writes about a variety of biomedical issues ranging from flu pandemics to global warming's influence on the evolution of diseases to stem cells. She works as the regular biomedical journalist for Scientific American, *in whose August 2007 issue "Attitude Screen" appeared. In "Attitude Screen," Soares ponders whether U.S. citizens are prepared to contribute personal genetic information in exchange for reducing their susceptibility to serious diseases.*

A chance to peek into the future—at least one possible future—is always a tempting fantasy. But if it were offered in reality, would you take it? And if you didn't like what you saw, how hard would you try to change it? After almost 20 years spent reading, mapping and analyzing human DNA, researchers at the National Human Genome Research Institute (NHGRI) believe that personal genetic information is nearly ready for use by consumers in managing their health, so the institute is launching a large-scale study to gauge whether consumers are ready for the information.

2   The year-long Multiplex Initiative will ultimately involve thousands of subjects, who will be offered a personal genetic report card based on screening for gene variations associated with increased risk for major diseases. The investigators are interested in how many take up the offer, why, and how

participants respond to their results. The researchers also hope to gain insights into the best ways for health professionals to communicate information about genetic risk.

3   "Our major outcomes and measures are going to be . . . do they understand the tests, because this is hard stuff to package for the general public," explained senior investigator Lawrence Brody of the NHGRI's Genome Technology branch, when announcing the initiative in early May in Washington, D.C., "and whether or not they find the test useful, what are their attitudes about it?"

4   The investigators are recruiting among members of the Henry Ford Health System, a Detroit-area HMO, and will follow up with participants to see if learning their genotype prompts them to seek out wellness programs or change any behaviors.

5   As many as 10,000 potential participants between the ages of 25 and 40 will be receiving mailed invitations to be screened for versions of some 15 genes associated with higher risk for developing major conditions such as type 2 diabetes, coronary artery disease, osteoporosis, lung cancer, colorectal cancer, and melanoma.

6   By mid-June, about 70 people, or 20 percent of the recipients who responded to the first wave of invitations, had signed on to be tested, according to the lead investigator, Colleen M. McBride, chief of the NHGRI's Social and Behavioral Research branch. "That's about what we expected," she says. "These are young, healthy individuals. . . . They are the best target population for prevention, but it's hard to get on their radar screen." Her goal is to have 1,000 people tested over the coming year.

7   "I think the NHGRI study is very valuable," says Catherine Schaefer, the lead investigator of a larger Kaiser Permanente research project that is currently recruiting among the 3.5 million members of that California HMO. Schaefer is gathering DNA samples and other health information in the hope of discovering new gene variants that confer disease risk or protection. One of her group's challenges is explaining to potential participants the importance of understanding even small genetic influences on complex diseases and the ways they might suggest interventions. The influence of most known susceptibility variations "is really quite modest," she says. "It's very important to learn how people respond to this very complex genetic information." Indeed, the NHGRI's study was prompted in part by McBride's own doubts about whether personal genomics was ready for consumers.

8   In the past, genetic testing has been mostly limited to single-gene diseases, such as Huntington's or cystic fibrosis, where the grim association between genotype and eventual illness is clear and certain. Conditions such as diabetes, in contrast, might involve the activity of hundreds or thousands of genes in different aspects or stages of the disease, and diet or other environmental factors may also interact with those genes over a lifetime. The statistical association between a variant gene and increased risk of developing diabetes may therefore be clear, but it is far from the entire picture.

9   "For better or worse, we've convinced the public that genetics is very important and deterministic," Brody explained. "And now we have to back off of that a little bit."

10   All the conditions included in the Multiplex Initiative screening are preventable, so participants can decide for themselves whether the results are worth acting on. Current measures of future risk typically rely on symptoms that have already appeared, such as high blood pressure or spinal degeneration, noted NHGRI director Francis Collins during the announcement. Genetic testing, he said, "has the potential of moving the timetable back to an earlier point so that you can begin to practice prevention before you're already half in the grave." ■

Issue in Focus
STEM CELL RESEARCH

Many current debates surround the study and manipulation of life's basic codes: mapping human genes in the Human Genome Project, developing disease- and insect-resistant crops, altering genes to help grow larger poultry, and pursuing ways to clone animals or even human beings. In the tradition of many sci-fi thrillers, critics of these technologies worry about unforeseen consequences, and they often raise questions about the ethical implications of intervening in basic life processes. One area of genetic research that has received a great deal of attention lately is that of embryonic stem cell research. On the one hand, stem cell research seems to offer great potential for the treatment of debilitating diseases like Parkinson's and Alzheimer's; on the other hand, the research troubles many people because of its reliance on human embryos.

The debate over stem cell research has taken on a very public face through very public people: Michael J. Fox (who suffers from Parkinson's disease); Christopher Reeve (who suffered paralyzing, ultimately fatal spine damage in a horseback riding accident); Nancy Reagan (who cared for former president Ronald Reagan during his ten-year battle with Alzheimer's); Republican Senator Arlen Specter (who suffers from cancer); and, at the Democratic National Convention in 2004, the ex-president's son, Ron Reagan. All these people advocate stem cell research.

Still, there are many others who find stem cell research to be dangerous and/or unethical, and who find claims of potential miracle cures to be highly exaggerated (and sometimes motivated by the prospect of grant money). Some opponents fear that stem cell research, if approved, would lead to and encourage cloning or the use of aborted fetal tissue—or perhaps even to planned pregnancies and subsequent abortions designed to create the necessary stem cells. If opponents of stem cell research lack high-profile advocates like Fox and the Reagans, they do not lack in fervor and organization.

On both sides the arguments can become complex and emotional because they involve highly charged questions of science, ethics, and religion and because they connect with personal tragedies and human loss. In 2001, when President George W. Bush placed restrictions on funding for stem cell research, emotions were running particularly high. In a nationally televised address, Bush offered the following argument for this restriction: "Research on embryonic stem cells raises profound ethical questions

Christopher Reeve (1952–2004)

because extracting the stem cell destroys the embryo and thus destroys its potential for life." His policy of restricting research to already existing cell lines, he suggested, still allowed researchers "to explore the promise and potential of stem-cell research without crossing a fundamental moral line" (quoted in *The Lancet*, March 13, 2004). Bush's compromise did not hold for long, however. While many people appreciated his holding to that "fundamental moral line," others scoffed at the assertion that human embryos required for stem cell research hold the potential for human life. And the research community has complained that this restriction has hampered their efforts to cure injury and disease and has put them at a disadvantage relative to researchers in other countries.

The images and words that follow give you a glimpse of some of the arguments, visual and verbal, that recur in the debate over stem cell research. In addition to photos, cartoons, and excerpts, we include Ron Reagan's highly publicized speech at the 2004 Democratic National Convention and two responses to it—one by Steven Milloy, author of *Junk Science Judo* and employed by the conservative Cato Institute, and one by Richard M. Doerflinger, an advocate for prolife issues employed by the United States Conference of Catholic Bishops. Perhaps you too have personal, moral, religious, or occupational reasons to be concerned about this debate. If so, the words and images that follow can give you a start in understanding the key points in the argument over stem cell research—and perhaps encourage you to write your own essay on the subject.

Ron Reagan

Speech at the Democratic National Convention, July 27, 2004

G ood evening, ladies and gentlemen.

2   A few of you may be surprised to see someone with my last name showing up to speak at a Democratic Convention. Apparently some of you are not. Let me assure you, I am not here to make a political speech and the topic at hand should not—must not—have anything to do with partisanship.

3   I am here tonight to talk about the issue of research into what may be the greatest medical breakthrough in our or any lifetime: the use of embryonic stem cells—cells created using the material of our own bodies—to cure a wide range of fatal and debilitating illnesses: Parkinson's disease, multiple sclerosis, diabetes, lymphoma, spinal cord injuries, and much more.

4   Millions are afflicted. And every year, every day, tragedy is visited upon families across the country, around the world. Now, it may be within our power to put an end to this suffering. We only need to try.

5   Some of you already know what I'm talking about when I say embryonic stem cell research. Others of you are probably thinking, that's quite a mouthful. Maybe this is a good time to go for a tall cold one. Well, wait a minute, wait a minute.

6   Let me try and paint as simple a picture as I can while still doing justice to the science, the incredible science involved. Let's say that ten or so years from now you are diagnosed with Parkinson's disease. There is currently no cure, and drug therapy, with its attendant side-effects, can only temporarily relieve the symptoms.

7   Now, imagine going to a doctor who, instead of prescribing drugs, takes a few skin cells from your arm. The nucleus of one of your cells is placed into a donor egg whose own nucleus has been removed. A bit of chemical or electrical stimulation will encourage your cell's nucleus to begin dividing, creating new cells which will then be placed into a tissue culture. Those cells will generate embryonic stem cells containing only your DNA, thereby eliminating the risk of tissue rejection. These stem cells are then driven to become the very neural cells that are defective in Parkinson's patients. And finally, those cells—with your DNA— are injected into your brain where they will replace the faulty cells whose failure to produce adequate dopamine led to the Parkinson's disease in the first place.

8   In other words, you're cured.

9   And another thing, these embryonic stem cells, they could continue to replicate indefinitely and, theoretically, can be induced to recreate virtually any tissue in your body.

10   How'd you like to have your own personal biological repair kit standing by at the hospital? Sound like magic? Welcome to the future of medicine.

11   Now by the way, no fetal tissue is involved in this process. No fetuses are created, none destroyed. This all happens in the laboratory at the cellular level.

12   Now, there are those who would stand in the way of this remarkable future, who would deny the federal funding so crucial to basic research. They argue that interfering with the development of even the earliest stage embryo, even one that will never be implanted in a womb and will never develop into an actual fetus, is tantamount to murder.

13   A few of these folks, needless to say, are just grinding a political axe and they should be ashamed of themselves. But many are well-meaning and sincere. Their belief is just that, an article of faith, and they are entitled to it. But it does not follow that the theology of a few should be allowed to forestall the health and well-being of the many.   *fairness*   *logic/emotion*

14   And how can we affirm life if we abandon those whose own lives are so desperately at risk? It is a hallmark of human intelligence that we are able to make distinctions.

15   Yes, these cells could theoretically have the potential, under very different circumstances, to develop into human beings—that potential is where their magic lies. But they are not, in and of themselves, human beings. They have no fingers and toes, no brain or spinal cord. They have no thoughts, no fears. They feel no pain.

16   Surely we can distinguish between these undifferentiated cells multiplying in a tissue culture and a living, breathing person—a parent, a spouse, a child.

17   I know a child—well, she must be 13 now so I guess I'd better call her a young woman. She has fingers and toes. She has a mind. She has memories. She has hopes. She has juvenile diabetes. Like so many kids with this disease, she's adjusted amazingly well. The insulin pump she wears—she's decorated hers with rhinestones. She can handle her own catheter needle. She's learned to sleep through the blood drawings in the wee hours of the morning.

18   She's very brave. She is also quite bright and understands full well the progress of her disease and what that might ultimately mean: blindness, amputation, diabetic coma. Every day she fights to have a future.

19   What excuse will we offer this young woman should we fail her now? What might we tell her children? Or the millions of others who suffer? That when given an opportunity to help, we turned away? That facing political opposition, we lost our nerve? That even though we knew better, we did nothing?

20   And, should we fail, how will we feel if, a few years from now, a more enlightened generation should fulfill the promise of embryonic stem cell therapy? Imagine what they would say of us who lacked the will.

21   No, we owe this young woman and all those who suffer—we owe ourselves—better than that. We are better than that. We are a wiser people, a finer nation.

22   And for all of us in this fight, let me say: we will prevail. The tide of history is with us. Like all generations who have come before ours, we are motivated by a thirst for knowledge and compelled to see others in need as fellow angels on an often difficult path, deserving of our compassion.

23   In a few months, we will face a choice. Yes, between two candidates and two parties, but more than that. We have a chance to take a giant stride forward

THE RONALD REAGAN EULOGY WILL BE DELIVERED BY A LEADING OPPONENT OF STEM CELL RESEARCH.

The most widely syndicated political cartoonist in the world, Pat Oliphant creates what he calls "confrontational art" that offers powerful visual perspectives on the issues of the day. Oliphant began creating cartoons in 1952 and won a Pulitzer Prize in 1967.

for the good of all humanity. We can choose between the future and the past, between reason and ignorance, between true compassion and mere ideology.

24   This—this is our moment, and we must not falter.

25   Whatever else you do come November 2, I urge you, please, cast a vote for embryonic stem cell research.

26   Thank you for your time. ■

Steven Milloy

Ron Reagan Wrong on Stem Cells

July 16, 2004

Ron Reagan, the younger son of the late Republican president, announced this week that he would give a prime-time address in support of stem cell research at the Democratic National Convention in Boston later this month.

2   "Ron Reagan's courageous pleas for stem cell research add a powerful voice to the millions of Americans hoping for cures for their children, for their parents and for their grandparents," said a spokesman for John Kerry to the Associated Press.

3   Reagan told the *Philadelphia Inquirer* that the speech was intended "to educate people about stem cell research" rather than be critical of President George Bush.

But the Kerry campaign seems to want to scare people by having the son of the revered late President Ronald Reagan decry President Bush and his pro-life supporters as the major roadblocks to a host of supposedly just-around-the-corner miracle cures for cancer, Alzheimer's, diabetes and other dreaded diseases.

4   It will be a junk-science-fueled spectacle.

5   The controversy centers around the use of stem cells derived from destroyed human embryos. So-called "embryonic stem cells" give rise to all other cells and tissues in the human body and have been touted as possibly yielding treatments for a variety of diseases.

6   Moral concerns over the destruction of human embryos caused President Bush to limit taxpayer funding for embryonic stem cell research to stem cell lines already in existence. Researchers who were counting on taxpayer funding to conduct research on embryonic stem cells—and then rake in millions of dollars from naive investors—were enraged and began a campaign to pressure the President into opening the taxpayer spigots for embryonic stem cell research on the basis of a wide-eyed hope that cures are near at hand.

7   Though embryonic stem cell research advocates euphemistically refer to the current state of research as an "early stage," the unfortunate reality is that the goal of embryonic stem cell therapies is, at this point, more accurately described as a pipe dream. No researcher is anywhere close to significant progress in developing practical embryonic stem cell therapies.

8   Mouse embryonic stem cells were first grown in a laboratory in 1981. It took 20 years to make similar achievements with human embryonic stem cells—and merely growing stem cells is nowhere close to employing those cells in therapies. Embryonic stem cells must be directed to grow into specific cell types and that growth must be controlled—they can proliferate indefinitely in the lab. Uncontrolled stem cell growth may have tumor-forming potential. Because embryonic stem cells don't come from the patient being treated, there may also be problems associated with immune system rejection following transplantation of foreign stem cells.

9   The difficulty of embryonic stem cell research is underscored by the lack of progress in cancer research. Despite a 30-year, $40-billion "War on Cancer" launched by President Nixon, researchers continue to have great difficulty in controlling, let alone eradicating, the vast majority of cancer cell growth. Conceptually, controlled deployment of "good" stem cells should be vastly more complex than simply destroying "bad" cancer cells.

10   None of this is to say that embryonic stem cell research can't possibly lead to some improvements in biological understanding or future therapeutic treatments, but such speculative progress of who-knows-what value isn't in the foreseeable future. The only thing certain is that the cost of that research will be high. If embryonic stem cell research had real and imminent possibilities, private investors would be pouring capital into research hoping for real and imminent profits. Instead, venture capital firms are contributing to political efforts to get taxpayers to fund research.

11   A proposed ballot initiative in California known as Proposition 71 would provide $3 billion in taxpayer money for stem cell research. Supporters hope to

Actor Michael J. Fox, who was diagnosed in 1991 with Parkinson's Disease, spoke at the Bio International Convention in 2007. Fox appealed to scientists and investors to aggressively translate scientific research into creative treatments for debilitating diseases, including Parkinson's.

raise $20 million to get the initiative passed. What the venture capitalists seem to be hoping for is that taxpayer funding of stem cell research will increase the value of their stakes in biotech companies. The venture capitalists can then cash out at a hefty profit, leaving taxpayers holding the bag of fruitless research.

12   The spectacle of Ron Reagan at the Democratic Convention will be sad— the disgruntled son of the beloved former president misleading the public with naive hopes while being exploited for political gain by opponents of his father's party. That cynical strategy may get John Kerry a few more votes in November, but it's not going to produce any medical miracles anytime soon, if at all. ■

Richard M. Doerflinger

Don't Clone Ron Reagan's Agenda

July 28, 2004

Ron Reagan's speech at the Democratic convention last night was expected to urge expanded funding for stem cell research using so-called "spare" embryos—and to highlight these cells' potential for treating the Alzheimer's disease that took his father's life.

2   He did neither. He didn't even mention Alzheimer's, perhaps because even strong supporters of embryonic stem cell research say it is unlikely to be of use for that disease. (Reagan himself admitted this on a July 12 segment of MSNBC's *Hardball*.) And he didn't talk about current debates on funding research using existing embryos. Instead he endorsed the more radical agenda of human cloning—mass-producing one's own identical twins in the laboratory so they can be exploited as (in his words) "your own personal biological repair kit" when disease or injury strikes.

3   Politically this was, to say the least, a gamble. Americans may be tempted to make use of embryos left over from fertility clinics, but most polls show them to be against human cloning for any purpose. Other advanced nations—Canada, Australia, France, Germany, Norway—have banned the practice completely, and the United Nations may approve an international covenant against it this fall. Many groups and individuals who are "pro-choice" on abortion oppose research cloning, not least because it would require the mass exploitation of women to provide what Ron Reagan casually calls "donor eggs." And the potential "therapeutic" benefits of cloning are even more speculative than those of embryonic stem cell research—the worldwide effort even to obtain viable stem cells from cloned embryos has already killed hundreds of embryos and produced exactly one stem cell line, in South Korea.

4   But precisely for these reasons, Ron Reagan should be praised for his candor. The scientists and patient groups promoting embryonic stem cell research know that the current debate on funding is a mere transitional step. For years they have supported the mass manufacture of human embryos through cloning, as the logical and necessary goal of their agenda, but lately they have been coy about this as they fight for the more popular slogan of "stem cell research." With his speech Reagan has removed the mask, and allowed us to debate what is really at stake.

5   He claimed in his speech, of course, that what is at stake in this debate is the lives of millions of patients with devastating diseases. But by highlighting Parkinson's disease and juvenile diabetes as two diseases most clearly justifying the move to human cloning, he failed to do his homework. These are two of the diseases that pro-cloning scientists now admit will probably *not* be helped by research cloning.

6   Scottish cloning expert Ian Wilmut, for example, wrote in the *British Medical Journal* in February that producing genetically matched stem cells through cloning is probably quite unnecessary for treating any neurological disease. Recent findings suggest that the nervous system is "immune privileged," and will not generally reject stem cells from a human who is genetically different. He added that cloning is probably useless for auto-immune diseases like juvenile diabetes, where the body mistakenly rejects its own insulin-producing cells as though they were foreign. "In such cases," he wrote, "transfer of immunologically identical cells to a patient is expected to induce the same rejection."

7   Wilmut's observations cut the ground out from under Ron Reagan's simple-minded claim that cloning is needed to avoid tissue rejection. For some

diseases, genetically matched cells are unnecessary; for others, they are useless, because they only replicate the genetic profile that is part of the problem. (Ironically, for Alzheimer's both may be true—cloning may be unnecessary to avoid tissue rejection in the brain, and useless because the cloned cells would have the same genetic defect that may lead to Alzheimer's.) Reagan declared that this debate requires us to "choose between . . . reason and ignorance," but he did not realize which side has the monopoly on ignorance.

8   That ignorance poses an obstacle to real advances that are right before our eyes. Two weeks before Ron Reagan declared that a treatment for Parkinson's may arrive "ten or so years from now," using "the material of our own bodies," a Parkinson's patient and his doctor quietly appeared before Congress to point out that this has already been done. Dennis Turner was treated in 1999 by Dr. Michel Levesque of Cedars-Sinai Medical Center in Los Angeles, using his own adult neural stem cells. Dr. Levesque did not use the Rube Goldberg method of trying to turn those cells into a cloned embryo and then killing the embryo to get stem cells—he just grew Turner's own adult stem cells in the lab, and turned them directly into dopamine-producing cells. And with just one injection, on one side of Turner's brain, he produced an almost complete reversal of Parkinson's symptoms over four years.

9   Turner stopped shaking, could eat without difficulty, could put in his own contact lenses again, and resumed his avocation of big-game photography—on one occasion scrambling up a tree in Africa to escape a charging rhinoceros.

10   Amazingly, while this advance has been presented at national and international scientific conferences and featured on ABC-TV in Chicago, the scientific establishment supporting embryonic stem cell research has almost completely ignored it, and most news media have obediently imposed a virtual news blackout on it. That did not change even after the results were presented to the Senate Commerce Subcommittee on Science, Technology and Space this month. Pro-cloning Senators on the panel actually seemed angry at the witnesses, for trying to distract them from their fixation on destroying embryos.

11   Turner also testified that his symptoms have begun to return, especially arising from the side of his brain that was left untreated, and he would like to get a second treatment. For that he will have to wait Dr. Levesque has received insufficient appreciation and funding for his technique, and is still trying to put together the funds for broader clinical trials—as most Parkinson's foundations and NIH peer reviewers look into the starry distance of Ron Reagan's dreams about embryonic stem cells.

12   But hey, who cares about real Parkinson's patients when there's a Brave New World to sell? ■

From Reading to Writing

1. In his speech printed here, Ron Reagan made some large claims for embryonic stem cell research; the two respondents to Reagan's speech

raised many objections to his claims. Do your own research in order to find how much of what Reagan claims is likely to result from stem cell research. Then write a rebuttal either to Reagan's speech or to the responses to it by Milloy and Doerflinger (see Chapter 12 on writing rebuttals).

2. One of the major concerns of those who oppose stem cell research lies in the use of human embryo stem cells—and the source of those stem cells in aborted tissue or in therapeutic cloning. And one of the impediments to public discussion is the fact that highly technical scientific processes and techniques are involved—processes and techniques that laypeople imperfectly understand. Do some research to further clarify for yourself and your audience the processes for producing and harvesting stem cells. Then, after looking once again at Chapter 8 on definition arguments, write an essay defining *embryonic stem cells* or *stem cell research* in such a way that you either support or oppose stem cell research.

3. Many people have made arguments against the use of stem cell research by citing religious authorities and traditions. Research the stances of various religions on embryonic stem cell research to see if there is relatively universal concern, or whether there are some religions that support this research. Then write an essay in support or opposition that makes use of the information you find.

4. Select an organizational (political, activist, religious) policy on stem cell research. After summarizing the policy, examine it in light of aesthetic, practical, and ethical criteria, which are presented in Chapter 10.

5. One of the major methods for convincing people of the necessity of stem cell research is the use of personal examples—narratives—about people who might benefit from this technology. Beginning from your own informed beliefs about the use of embryonic stem cells, write a story that illustrates your position on this topic. If possible, draw from your personal experience with Parkinson's, childhood diabetes, or some other disease or condition that could be affected by stem cell research. (See Chapter 11 on narrative arguments.)

6. Do a rhetorical analysis of the arguments of Ron Reagan. How is his speech a product of the particular rhetorical situation that he found himself in—before the Democratic National Convention, and before a national television audience? How might he have presented his argument if he had appeared before Republicans? Do you agree with Reagan's assertion that his speech is not political?

7. Based on the guidelines in Chapter 13, write a proposal that defends or undermines the practice of stem cell research.

26

Privacy

How does a new bathroom design, like this colored glass structure in the middle of an apartment, reflect (or push for) new attitudes about privacy?

New Challenges to Personal Privacy

The Dog Poop Girl (as she came to be known) was riding the subway in Seoul, South Korea, one day when her dog decided to "take care of business." According to a *Washington Post* story written by Jonathan Krim on July 7, 2005, the woman (a university student) made no move to clean up the mess, so fellow passengers grew agitated. One of them recorded the scene on a cell phone camera and then posted photos on a Web site. Web surfers came upon the photos and began referring to her as Dog Poop Girl. One thing led to another, and soon her privacy was completely gone: people revealed her true name, began asking for and sharing more information about her, launched blogs commenting about her and her relatives, and generally crackled with gossip about her and her behavior. Ultimately she became the subject of sermons and online discussions, and her story made the national news. In humiliation, Dog Poop Girl withdrew from her university.

A second incident was reported by Felisa Cardona in the *Denver Post* on August 2, 2005. A computer security breach at the University of Colorado left 29,000 students and 7,000 faculty and staff vulnerable to identity theft. It seems that hackers attacked the university computers in order to gain access to the Buff One ID card used by many students and staff. Though no information seems to have been used due to this attack, 6,000 students had to be issued new cards in order to gain access to their dorms. More-

> "You have zero privacy now—get over it."
>
> —SCOTT MCNEALY, CEO OF SUN MICROSYSTEMS

over, after the incident, Colorado officials decided to stop using Social Security number identifications, and many other universities have done the same because they too have been targeted by identity thieves.

These two incidents illustrate some of the new challenges to personal privacy that have been raised in response to technology developments and concerns about security in the wake of September 11. There is no doubt that electronic technologies have given people a new degree of personal freedom: hand-held computers, cell phones, email, and Web shopping are now routine time-savers. But there is also no doubt that a price has been paid for that freedom: That price is the surveillance side of the Internet and other technologies. In the wake of September 11, other terrorist attacks, and the increased attention to security that has ensued, privacy issues have been an increasing concern in American life. Law enforcement officials seek access to information about potential conspiracies, and businesses increasingly gather information about people to individualize marketing campaigns, keep an eye out for good (and bad) credit risks, and customize customers.

A biometric measuring instrument at Busch Gardens helps staff make sure the same person uses the same ticket each day.

One emerging technology—biometrics—measures physical and behavioral data, such as fingerprints or keystroke patterns, in order to identify individual human beings. Biometric recognition provides a deeply personalized means of identification that enhances security, say its supporters, but a national biometric database also raises questions of privacy, say its detractors. What would it mean in terms of national security and surveillance to store citizens' inherently unique characteristics in a nationwide database?

And when is freedom too much freedom? If bloggers act as a posse, tracking down criminals and turning them over to law enforcement, is that appropriate action or vigilante action? What about efforts to replicate what was done to the Dog Poop Girl? Should laws prevent people from publicizing and branding people who seem undesirable? Should people who wish to share secrets—whether the secrets are true or not—have the anonymity and apparent protection afforded by the Internet? Must email users simply accept as a fact of life that they are bombarded by hundreds of unauthorized, unsolicited spam messages? And what are the limits of what government officials should be able to do to inspect the personal records of citizens?

Contemporary Arguments

Is it possible to have both security and freedom in the United States? What is the proper balance of the two? On the one hand, some people support a national ID card (like those already used, incidentally, in several European nations) or sign up for in-vehicle security systems such as OnStar (always on the watch!) as a safety feature. They root for police to pursue potential terrorists, wink when Internet service providers disclose customer records to government agents if they feel that a crime is being committed, and appreciate being notified that convicted felons have moved into the neighborhood. On the other hand, they also protest when police use wiretaps without explicit legal permission, worry about the ability of global positioning systems to snoop on people from satellites (especially by zeroing in on cell phones or implanted homing devices), and protest when roving surveillance cameras are mounted in stores and at street corners, in public parks and on school playgrounds. Everyone seems to be monitored or monitoring: Online data collectors record which Web sites people visit; airlines record data on people's travels; companies routinely perform background checks on potential employees; bus and train companies check passenger lists against records of "suspicious" characters; businesses seek to develop systems that can deliver customized marketing information to particular households and commuters; and supermarkets record purchases in order to fine-tune their stocking patterns. In the future, some say, we can look forward to smart cars, smart airports, smart TVs, smart credit cards, and smart homes—all designed to give us certain freedoms, if at the risk of losing our privacy.

The arguments in this chapter discuss questions related to privacy. David Brin's "Three Cheers for the Surveillance Society!" overviews the brave new world that is now developing (for better or for worse), and Ted Koppel meditates on the "miracles [that] microchip and satellite technologies offer"— as well as on the need to oversee how "companies share and exchange their harvest of private data." Randall Larsen proposes a national identification card to improve homeland security, and Jennifer Burk, in the wake of the Virginia Tech shootings

This artistic rendering of the all-seeing eye of surveillance cameras suggests that while such cameras may be designed to provide security, they also intrude on individuals' privacy without their knowledge.

of April, 2007 (when a mentally disturbed student killed 32 people), dramatizes the difficulties and dilemmas that university personnel face in balancing safety and privacy.

Because the emerging field of biometrics effectively illustrates the tensions between protection and privacy, we look in detail at this emerging technology in the Issue in Focus. The selections reproduced there describe the technologies (such as signature analysis, keystroke patterns, and vein biometric systems) and dramatize the excitement—and the fears—that accompany them. On one hand, biometric technologies hold out the promise of improved crime fighting and national security. On the other, such technologies encroach on individuals' privacy and may even open the door to DNA identify theft. What price are we willing to pay for privacy (or security)? At what point does it make sense to forfeit private information for protection and convenience?

David Brin

Three Cheers for the Surveillance Society!

David Brin (born 1950) provided "Three Cheers," a short version of a longer project he is working on, for the Web publication Salon.com. The article appeared on August 3, 2004, on his news and culture Web site founded in 1995. The author of several popular novels, including the Hugo Award–winning science fiction volumes Startide Rising *(1983) and* The Uplift War *(1987), Brin is also a scientist who writes and speaks about contemporary technological advancements. His 1985 novel* The Postman *was made into a popular film in 1997, and his nonfiction work* The Transparent Society *(1998) won the American Library Association's Freedom of Speech Award for its examination of privacy and security concerns.*

Ten centuries ago, at the previous millennium, a Viking lord commanded the rising tide to retreat. No deluded fool, King Canute aimed in this way to teach flatterers a lesson—that even sovereign rulers cannot halt inexorable change.

2   A thousand years later, we face tides of technology-driven transformation that seem bound only to accelerate. Waves of innovation may liberate human civilization, or disrupt it, more than anything since glass lenses and movable type. Critical decisions during the next few years—about research, investment, law and lifestyle—may determine what kind of civilization our children inherit. Especially problematic are many information-related technologies that loom on the near horizon—technologies that may foster tyranny, or else empower citizenship in a true global village.

3   Typically we are told, often and passionately, that Big Brother may abuse these new powers. Or else our privacy and rights will be violated by some other group. Perhaps a commercial, aristocratic, bureaucratic, intellectual, foreign, criminal or technological elite. (Pick your favorite bogeyman.)

4   Because one or more of these centers of power might use the new tools to see better, we're told that we should all be very afraid. Indeed, our only hope may be to squelch or fiercely control the onslaught of change. For the sake of safety and liberty, we are offered one prescription: We must limit the power of others to see.

5   Half a century ago, amid an era of despair, George Orwell created one of the most oppressive metaphors in literature with the telescreen system used to surveil and control the people in his novel *1984*. We have been raised to a high degree of sensitivity by Orwell's *self-preventing* prophecy, and others like it. Attuned to wariness, today's activists preach that any growth in the state's ability to see will take us down a path of no return, toward the endless hell of Big Brother.

6   But consider. The worst aspect of Orwell's telescreen—the trait guaranteeing tyranny—was not that agents of the state could use it to see. The one thing that despots truly need is to avoid accountability. In *1984*, this is achieved by keeping the telescreen aimed in just one direction! By preventing the people from looking back.

7   While a flood of new discoveries may seem daunting, they should not undermine the core values of a calm and knowledgeable citizenry. Quite the opposite: While privacy may have to be redefined, the new technologies of surveillance should and will be the primary countervailing force against tyranny.

8   In any event, none of those who denounce the new technologies have shown how it will be possible to stop this rising tide. Consider a few examples:

■   Radio frequency identification (RFID) technology will soon replace the simple, passive bar codes on packaged goods, substituting inexpensive chips that respond to microwave interrogation, making every box of toothpaste or razor blades part of a vast, automatic inventory accounting system. Wal-Mart announced in 2003 that it will require its top 100 suppliers to use RFID on all large cartons, for purposes of warehouse inventory keeping. But that is only the beginning. Inevitably as prices fall, RFID chips will be incorporated into most products and packaging.

■   Supermarket checkout will become a breeze, when you simply push your cart past a scanner and grab a printout receipt, with every purchase automatically debited from your account.

9   Does that sound simultaneously creepy and useful? Well, it goes much further. Under development are smart washers that will read the tags on clothing and adjust their cycles accordingly, and smart medicine cabinets that track tagged prescriptions, in order to warn which ones have expired or need refilling. Cars and desks and computers will adjust to your preferred settings as you approach. Paramedics may download your health status—including allergies and dangerous drug-conflicts—even if you are unconscious or unable to speak.

10   There's a downside. A wonderful 1960s paranoia satire, *The President's Analyst*, offered prophetic warning against implanted devices, inserted into people, that would allow them to be tracked by big business and government. But who needs implantation when your clothing and innocuous possessions will carry cheap tags of their own that can be associated with their owners? Already some schools—especially in Asia—are experimenting with RFID systems that will locate all students, at all times.

11   Oh, there will be fun to be had, for a while, in fooling these systems with minor acts of irreverent rebellion. Picture kids swapping clothes and possessions, furtively, in order to leave muddled trails. Still, such measures will not accomplish much over extended periods. Tracking on vast scales, national and worldwide, will emerge in rapid order. And if we try to stop it with legislation, the chief effect will only be to drive the surveillance into secret networks that are just as pervasive. Only they will operate at levels we cannot supervise, study, discuss or understand.

12   Wait, there's more. For example, a new Internet protocol (IPv6) will vastly expand available address space in the virtual world.

13   The present IP, offering 32-bit data labels, can now offer every living human a unique online address, limiting direct access to something like 10 billion Web pages or specific computers. In contrast, IPv6 will use 128 bits. This will allow the virtual tagging of every cubic centimeter of the earth's surface, from sea level to mountaintop, spreading a multidimensional data overlay across the planet. Every tagged or manmade object may participate, from your wristwatch to a nearby lamppost, vending machine or trash can—even most of the discarded contents of the trash can.

14   Every interest group will find some kind of opportunity in this new world. Want to protect forests? Each and every tree on earth might have a chip fired into its bark from the air, alerting a network if furtive loggers start transporting stolen hardwoods. Or the same method could track whoever steals your morning paper. Not long after this, teens and children will purchase rolls of ultra-cheap digital eyes and casually stick them onto walls. Millions of those "penny cams" will join in the fun, contributing to the vast IPv6 datasphere.

15   Oh, this new Internet protocol will offer many benefits—for example, embedded systems for data tracking and verification. In the short term, expanded powers of vision *may* embolden tyrants. But over the long run, these systems could help to empower citizens and enhance mutual trust.

16   In the mid-'90s, when I began writing *The Transparent Society*, it seemed dismaying to note that Great Britain had almost 150,000 CCD police cameras scanning public streets. Today, they number in the millions.

17   In the United States, a similar proliferation, though just as rapid, has been somewhat masked by a different national tradition—that of dispersed ownership. As pointed out by UC-San Diego researcher Mohan Trivedi, American constabularies have few cameras of their own. Instead, they rely on vast numbers of security monitors operated by small and large companies,

banks, markets and private individuals, who scan ever larger swaths of urban landscape. Nearly all of the footage that helped solve the Oklahoma City bombing and the D.C. sniper episode—as well as documenting the events of 9/11—came from unofficial sources.

18   This unique system can be both effective and inexpensive for state agencies, especially when the public is inclined to cooperate, as in searches for missing children. Still, there are many irksome drawbacks to officials who may want more pervasive and direct surveillance. For one thing, the present method relies upon high levels of mutual trust and goodwill between authorities and the owners of those cameras—whether they be convenience-store corporations or videocam-equipped private citizens. Moreover, while many crimes are solved with help from private cameras, more police are also held accountable for well-documented lapses in professional behavior.

19   This tattletale trend began with the infamous beating of Rodney King, more than a decade ago, and has continued at an accelerating pace. Among recently exposed events were those that aroused disgust (the tormenting of live birds in the Pilgrim's Pride slaughterhouse) and shook America's stature in the world (the prisoner abuse by jailers at Abu Ghraib prison in Iraq). Each time the lesson is the same one: that professionals should attend to their professionalism, or else the citizens and consumers who pay their wages will find out and—eventually—hold them accountable.

20   (Those wishing to promote the trend might look into Project Witness which supplies cameras to underdogs around the world.)

21   Will American authorities decide to abandon this quaint social bargain of shared access to sensors under dispersed ownership? As the price of electronic gear plummets, it will become easy and cheap for our professional protectors to purchase their own dedicated systems of surveillance, like those already operating in Britain, Singapore and elsewhere. Systems that "look down from above" (surveillance) without any irksome public involvement.

22   Or might authorities simply use our networks without asking? A decade ago, the U.S. government fought activist groups such as the Electronic Frontier Foundation, claiming a need to unlock commercial-level encryption codes at will, for the sake of law enforcement and national defense. Both sides won apparent victories. High-level commercial encryption became widely available. And the government came to realize that it doesn't matter. It never did.

23   Shall I go on?

24   Driven partly by security demands, a multitude of biometric technologies will identify individuals by scanning physical attributes, from fingerprints, iris patterns, faces and voices to brainwaves and possibly unique chemical signatures. Starting with those now entering and leaving the United States, whole classes of people will grow accustomed to routine identification in this way. Indeed, citizens may start to demand more extensive use of biometric identification, as a safety measure against identity theft. When your car recognizes your face, and all the stores can verify your fingerprint, what need will you have for keys or a credit card?

25   Naturally, this is yet another trend that has put privacy activists in a lather. They worry—with some justification—about civil liberties implications when the police or FBI might scan multitudes (say, at a sporting event) in search of fugitives or suspects. Automatic software agents will recognize individuals who pass through one camera view, then perform a smooth handoff to the next camera, and the next, planting a "tail" on dozens, hundreds, or tens of thousands of people at a time.

26   And yes, without a doubt this method could become a potent tool for some future Big Brother. So? Should that legitimate and plausible fear be addressed by reflexively blaming technology and seeking ways to restrict its use? Or by finding ways that technology may work for us, instead of against us?

27   Suppose you could ban or limit a particular identification technique. (Mind you, I've seen no evidence that it can be done.) The sheer number of different, overlapping biometric approaches will make that whole approach fruitless. In fact, human beings fizz and froth with unique traits that can be spotted at a glance, even with our old-fashioned senses. Our ancestors relied on this fact, building and correlating lists of people who merited trust or worry, from among the few thousands that they met in person. In a global village of 10 billion souls, machines will do the same thing for us by prosthetically amplifying vision and augmenting memory.

28   With so many identification methodologies working independently and in parallel, our children may find the word "anonymous" impossibly quaint, perhaps even incomprehensible. But that needn't mean an end to freedom— or even privacy. Although it will undoubtedly mean a redefinition of what we think privacy means.

29   But onward with our scan of panopticonic technologies. Beyond RFID, IPv6 and biometrics there are smart cards, smart highways, smart airports, smart automobiles, smart televisions, smart homes and so on.

30   The shared adjective may be premature. These systems will provide improved service long before anything like actual "artificial intelligence" comes online. Yet machinery needn't be strictly intelligent in order to transform our lives. Moreover, distributed "smart" units will also gather information, joining together in cross-correlating networks that recognize travelers, perform security checks, negotiate micro-transactions, detect criminal activity, warn of potential danger and anticipate desires. When these parts fully interlink, the emerging entity may not be self-aware, but it will certainly know the whereabouts of its myriad parts.

31   Location awareness will pervade the electronic world, thanks to ever more sophisticated radio transceivers, GPS chips, and government-backed emergency location initiatives like Enhanced-911 in the United States and Enhanced-112 in Europe. Cellphones, computers and cars will report position and unique identity in real time, with (or possibly without) owner consent. Lives will be saved, property recovered, and missing children found. But these benefits aren't the real reason that location awareness and reporting will spread to nearly every device. As described by science fiction author Vernor Vinge, it is going to happen

because the capability will cost next to nothing as an integrated part of wireless technology. In the future, you can assume that almost any electronic device will be trackable, though citizens still have time to debate who may do the tracking.

32   The flood of information has to go someplace. Already databases fill with information about private individuals, from tax and medical records to credit ratings: from travel habits and retail purchases to which movies they recently downloaded on their TiVo personal video recorder. Yahoo's HotJobs recently began selling "self" background checks, offering job seekers a chance to vet their own personal, financial and legal data—the same information that companies might use to judge them. (True, a dating service that already screens for felons, recently expanded its partnership with database provider Rapsheets to review public records and verify a user's single status.) Data aggregators like Acxiom Corp., of Arkansas, or ChoicePoint, of Georgia, go even further, listing your car loans, outstanding liens and judgments, any professional or pilot or gun licenses, credit checks, and real estate you might own—all of it gathered from legal and open sources.

33   On the plus side, you'll be able to find and counter those rumors and slanderous untruths that can slash from the dark. The ability of others to harm you with lies may decline drastically. On the other hand, it will be simple for almost anybody using these methods to appraise the background of anyone else, including all sorts of unpleasant things that are inconveniently true. In other words, the rest of us will be able to do what elites (define them as you wish, from government to aristocrats to criminal masterminds) already can.

34   Some perceive this trend as ultimately empowering, while others see it as inherently oppressive. For example, activist groups from the ACLU to the Electronic Privacy Information Center call for European-style legislation aiming to seal the data behind perfect firewalls into separate, isolated clusters that cannot cross-link or overlap. And in the short term, such efforts may prove beneficial. New database filters may help users find information they legitimately need while protecting personal privacy . . . for a while, buying us time to innovate for the long term.

35   But we mustn't fool ourselves. No firewall, program or machine has ever been perfect, or perfectly implemented by fallible human beings. Whether the law officially allows it or not, can any effort by mere mortals prevent data from leaking? (And just one brief leak can spill a giant database into public knowledge, forever.) Cross-correlation will swiftly draw conclusions that are far more significant than the mere sum of the parts, adding up to a profoundly detailed picture of every citizen, down to details of personal taste.

36   Here's a related tidbit from the *Washington Post*: Minnesota entrepreneur Larry Colson has developed Web Voter, a program that lets Republican activists in the state report their neighbors' political views into a central database that the Bush-Cheney campaign can use to send them targeted campaign literature. The Bush campaign has a similar program on its Web site. And here's Colson's response to anyone who feels a privacy qualm or two about this program: "[It's] not as if we're asking for Social Security number and make and model and

serial number of car. We're asking for party preference. . . . Party preference is not something that is such a personal piece of data."

37   That statement may be somewhat true in today's America. We tend to shrug over each other's harmless or opinionated eccentricities. But can that trait last very long when powerful groups scrutinize us, without being scrutinized back? In the long run, tolerance depends on the ability of any tolerated minority to enforce its right to be left alone. This is achieved assertively, not by hiding. And assertiveness is empowered by knowledge.

38   The picture so far may seem daunting enough. Only now add a flood of new sensors. We have already seen the swift and inexpensive transformation of mere cellphones into a much more general, portable, electronic tool by adding the capabilities of a digital camera, audio recorder and PDA. But have we fully grasped the implications, when any well-equipped pedestrian might swiftly transform into an ad hoc photojournalist—or peeping Tom—depending on opportunity or inclination?

39   On the near horizon are wearable multimedia devices, with displays that blend into your sunglasses, along with computational, data-storage and communications capabilities woven into the very clothes you wear. The term "augmented reality" will apply when these tools overlay your subjective view of the world with digitally supplied facts, directions or commentary. You will expect—and rely on—rapid answers to queries about any person or object in sight. In essence, this will be no different than querying your neuron-based memories about people in the village where you grew up. Only we had a million years to get used to tracking reputations that way. The new prosthetics that expand memory will prove awkard at first.

40   Today we worry about drivers who use cellphones at the wheel. Tomorrow will it be distracted pedestrians, muttering to no one as they walk? Will we grunt and babble while strolling along, like village idiots of yore?

41   Maybe not. Having detected nerve signals near the larynx that are preparatory to forming words, scientists at NASA Ames Research Center lately proposed *subvocal speech systems*—like those forecast in my 1989 novel *Earth*— that will accept commands without audible sounds. They would be potentially useful in spacesuits, noisy environments and to reduce the inevitable babble when we are all linked by wireless all the time.

42   Taking this trend in more general terms, *volition sensing* may pick up an even wider variety of cues, empowering you to converse, give commands, or participate in faraway events without speaking aloud or showing superficial signs.

43   Is this the pre-dawn of tech-mediated telepathy? It may be closer than you think. Advertising agencies are already funding research groups that use PET scans and fMRI to study the immediate reactions of test subjects to marketing techniques and images. "We are crossing the chasm," said Adam Koval, chief operating officer of Thought Sciences, a division of Bright House, an Atlanta advertising and consulting firm whose clients include Home Depot, Delta Airlines and Coca-Cola, "and bringing a new paradigm in analytic rigor

to the world of marketing and advertising." Those who decry such studies face a tough burden, since all of the test subjects are paid volunteers. But how about when these methods leave the laboratory and hit the street? It is eerie to imagine a future when sensitive devices might scan your very thoughts when you pass by. Clearly there must be limits, only how? Will you be better able to protect yourself if these technologies are banned (and thus driven underground) or *regulated*, with a free market that might offer us all pocket detectors, to catch scanners in the act?

44   Microsoft recently unveiled Sensecam, a camera disguisable as jewelry that automatically records scores of images per hour from the wearer's point of view, digitally documenting an ongoing daily photo-diary. Such "Boswell machinery" may go far beyond egomania. For example, what good will your wallet do to a mugger when images of the crime are automatically broadcast across the Web? Soon, cyber-witnessing of public events, business deals, crimes and accidents will be routine. In movie parlance, you will have to assume that everybody you meet is carrying a "wire."

45   Meanwhile, you can be sure that military technologies will continue spinning off civilian versions, as happened with infrared night vision. Take "sniffers" designed to warn of environmental or chemical dangers on the battlefield. Soon, cheap and plentiful sensors will find their way into neighborhood storm drains, onto lampposts, or even your home faucet, giving rapid warnings of local pollution. Neighborhood or activist groups that create detector networks will have autonomous access to data rivaling that of local governments. Of course, a better-informed citizenry is sure to be more effective...

46   ...and far more noisy.

47   The same spinoff effect has emerged from military development of inexpensive UAV battlefield reconnaissance drones. Some of the "toys" offered by Draganfly Innovations can cruise independently for more than an hour along a GPS-guided path, transmit 2.4 GHz digital video, then return automatically to the hobbyist owner. In other companies and laboratories, the aim is toward miniaturization, developing micro-flyers that can assist an infantry squad in an urban skirmish or carry eavesdropping equipment into the lair of a suspected terrorist. Again, civilian models are already starting to emerge. There may already be some in your neighborhood.

48   Cheap, innumerable eyes in the sky. One might envision dozens of potentially harmful uses ... hundreds of beneficial ones ... and millions of others in between ranging from irksome to innocuous ... all leading toward a fundamental change in the way each of us relates to the horizon that so cruelly constrained the imagination of our ancestors. Just as baby boomers grew accustomed to viewing faraway places through the magical—though professionally mediated—channel of network television, so the next generation will simply assume that there is always another independent way to glimpse real-time events, either far away or just above the streets where they live.

49   Should we push for yet another unenforceable law to guard our backyards against peeping Toms and their drone planes? Or perhaps we'd be better

off simply insisting that the companies that make the little robot spies give us the means to trace them back to their nosy pilots. In other words, looking back may be a more effective way to protect privacy.

50   One might aim for reciprocal transparency using new technology. For example, Swiss researcher Marc Langheinrich's personal digital assistant application detects nearby sensors and then lists what kind of information they're collecting. At a more radical and polemical level, there is the *sousveillance* movement, led by University of Toronto professor Steve Mann. Playing off "surveillance" (overlooking from above), Mann's coined term suggests that we should all get in the habit of looking from below, proving that we are sovereign and alert citizens down here, not helpless sheep. Mann contends that private individuals will be empowered to do this by new senses, dramatically augmented by wearable electronic devices.

51   We have skimmed over a wide range of new technologies, from RFID chips and stick-on penny cameras to new Internet address protocols and numerous means of biometric identification. From database mining and aggregation to sensors that detect chemical pollution or the volition to speak or act before your muscles get a chance to move. From omni-surveillance to universal localization. From eyes in the sky to those that may invade your personal space.

52   Note a common theme. Every device or function that's been described here serves to enhance some human sensory capability, from sight and hearing to memory. And while some may fret and fume, there is no historical precedent for a civilization refusing such prosthetics when they become available.

53   Such trends cannot be boiled down to a simple matter of good news or bad. While technologies of distributed vision may soon empower common folk in dramatic ways, giving a boost to participatory democracy by highly informed citizens, you will not hear that side of the message from most pundits, who habitually portray the very same technologies in a darker light, predicting that machines are about to destroy privacy, undermine values and ultimately enslave us.

54   In fact, the next century will be much too demanding for fixed perspectives. (Or rigid us-vs.-them ideologies.) Agility will be far more useful, plus a little healthy contrariness.

55   When in the company of reflexive pessimists—or knee-jerk optimists— the wise among us will be those saying . . . "Yes, but . . ."

56   Which way will the pendulum of good and bad news finally swing?

57   We are frequently told that there is a fundamental choice to be made in a tragic trade-off between safety and freedom. While agents of the state, like Attorney General John Ashcroft, demand new powers of surveillance— purportedly the better to protect us—champions of civil liberties such as the ACLU warn against surrendering traditional constraints upon what the government is allowed to see. For example, they decry provisions of the PATRIOT Act that open broader channels of inspection, detection, search and data collection, predicting that such steps take us on the road toward Big Brother.

58   While they are right to fear such an outcome, they could not be more wrong about the specifics. As I discuss in greater detail elsewhere, the very idea of a *trade-off* between security and freedom is one of the most insidious and dismal notions I have ever heard—a perfect example of a devil's dichotomy. We modern citizens are living proof that people can and should have both. Freedom and safety, in fact, work together, not in opposition. Furthermore, I refuse to let anybody tell me that I must choose between liberty for my children and their safety! I refuse, and so should you.

59   As we've seen throughout this article, and a myriad other possible examples, there is no way that we will ever succeed in limiting the power of the elites to see and know. If our freedom depends on blinding the mighty, then we haven't a prayer.

60   Fortunately, that isn't what really matters after all. Moreover, John Ashcroft clearly knows it. By far the most worrisome and dangerous parts of the PATRIOT Act are those that remove the tools of supervision, allowing agents of the state to act secretly, without checks or accountability. (Ironically, these are the very portions that the ACLU and other groups have most neglected.)

61   In comparison, a few controversial alterations of procedure for search warrants are pretty minor. After all, appropriate levels of surveillance may shift as society and technology experience changes in a new century. (The Founders never heard of a wiretap, for example.)

62   But our need to watch the watchers will only grow.

63   It is a monopoly of vision that we need to fear above all else. So long as most of the eyes are owned by the citizens themselves, there will remain a chance for us to keep arguing knowledgeably among ourselves, debating and bickering, as sovereign, educated citizens should.

64   It will not be a convenient or anonymous world. Privacy may have to be redefined much closer to home. There will be a lot of noise.

65   But we will not drown under a rising tide of overwhelming technology. Keeping our heads, we will remain free to guide our ships across these rising waters—to choose a destiny of our own. ■

Ted Koppel

Take My Privacy, Please!

You know Ted Koppel for his reporting and anchor role on the late-night (and long-running) news show Nightline *(from which he recently retired). However, Koppel also has served ABC News as a diplomatic correspondent, anchor, and bureau chief. As a diplomatic correspondent, he traveled with Henry Kissinger on most of his foreign missions during the Nixon administration. Koppel's awards include 37 Emmys and six Peabody Awards, and he is the coauthor, with Marvin Kalb, of* In the National Interest *(1977). Koppel's article reprinted here initially appeared on the op-ed page of* The New York Times *on June 13, 2005.*

T he Patriot Act—brilliant! Its critics would have preferred a less stirring title, perhaps something along the lines of the Enhanced Snooping, Library and Hospital Database Seizure Act. But then who, even right after 9/11, would have voted for that?

2   Precisely. He who names it and frames it, claims it. The Patriot Act, however, may turn out to be among the lesser threats to our individual and collective privacy.

3   There is no end to what we will endure, support, pay for and promote if only it makes our lives easier, promises to save us money, appears to enhance our security and comes to us in a warm, cuddly and altogether nonthreatening package. To wit: OnStar, the subscription vehicle tracking and assistance system. Part of its mission statement, as found on the OnStar Web site, is the creation of "safety, security and peace of mind for drivers and passengers with thoughtful wireless services that are always there, always ready." You've surely seen or heard their commercials, one of which goes like this:

4   ANNOUNCER: The following is an OnStar conversation. (Ring)
5   ONSTAR: OnStar emergency, this is Dwight.
6   DRIVER: (crying) Yes, yes??!
7   ONSTAR: Are there any injuries, ma'am?
8   DRIVER: My leg hurts, my arm hurts.
9   ONSTAR: O.K. I do understand. I will be contacting emergency services.
10 ANNOUNCER: If your airbags deploy, OnStar receives a signal and calls to check on you. (Ring)
11 EMERGENCY
    SERVICES: Police.
12 ONSTAR: This is Dwight with OnStar. I'd like to report a vehicle crash with airbag deployment on West 106th Street.
13 EMERGENCY
    SERVICES: We'll send police and E.M.S. out there.
14 DRIVER: (crying) I'm so scared!
15 ONSTAR: O.K., I'm here with you, ma'am; you needn't be scared.

16   Well, maybe just a little scared. Tell us again how Dwight knows just where the accident took place. Oh, right! It's those thoughtful wireless services that are always there. Always, as in any time a driver gets into an OnStar-equipped vehicle. OnStar insists that it would disclose the whereabouts of a subscriber's vehicle only after being presented with a criminal court order or after the vehicle has been reported stolen. That's certainly a relief. I wouldn't want to think that anyone but Dwight knows where I am whenever I'm traveling in my car.

17   Of course, E-ZPass and most other toll-collecting systems already know whenever a customer passes through one of their scanners. That's because of radio frequency identification technology. In return for the convenience of zipping through toll booths, you need to have in your car a wireless device.

This tag contains information about your account, permitting E-ZPass to deduct the necessary toll—and to note when your car whisked through that particular toll booth. They wouldn't share that information with anyone, either; that is, unless they had to.

18   The State Department plans to use radio frequency identification technology in all new American passports by the end of 2005. The department wants to be sure that we all move through immigration quickly and efficiently when we return from overseas. Privacy advocates have suggested that hackers could tap into the information stored on these tags, or that terrorists might be able to use them to pinpoint American tourists in a crowd. The State Department assures us that both concerns are unfounded, and that it will allow privacy advocates to review test results this summer.

19   Radio frequency identification technology has been used for about 15 years now to reunite lost pets with their owners. Applied Digital Solutions, for example, manufactures the VeriChip, a tiny, implantable device that holds a small amount of data. Animal shelters can scan the chip for the name and phone number of the lost pet's owner. The product is now referred to as the HomeAgain Microchip Identification System.

20   Useful? Sure. Indeed, it's not much of a leap to suggest that one day, the VeriChip might be routinely implanted under the skin of, let's say, an Alzheimer's patient. The Food and Drug Administration approved the VeriChip for use in people last October. An Applied Digital Solutions spokesman estimates that about 1,000 people have already had a VeriChip implanted, usually in the right triceps. At the moment, it doesn't carry much information, just an identification number that health care providers can use to tap into a patient's medical history. A Barcelona nightclub also uses it to admit customers with a qualifying code to enter a V.I.P. room where drinks are automatically put on their bill. Possible variations on the theme are staggering.

21   And how about all the information collected by popular devices like TiVo, the digital video recorder that enables you to watch and store an entire season's worth of favorite programs at your own convenience? It also lets you electronically mark the programs you favor, allowing TiVo to suggest similar programs for your viewing pleasure. In February, TiVo announced the most frequently played and replayed commercial moment during the Super Bowl (it involves a wardrobe malfunction, but believe me, you don't want to know), drawing on aggregated data from a sample of 10,000 anonymous TiVo households. No one is suggesting that TiVo tracks what each subscriber records and replays. But could they, if they needed to? That's unclear, although TiVo does have a privacy policy. "Your privacy," it says in part, "is very important to us. Due to factors beyond our control, however, we cannot fully ensure that your user information will not be disclosed to third parties."

22   Unexpected and unfortunate things happen, of course, even to the most reputable and best-run organizations. Only last February, the Bank of America Corporation notified federal investigators that it had lost computer backup tapes

containing personal information about 1.2 million federal government employees, including some senators. In April, LexisNexis unintentionally gave outsiders access to the personal files (addresses, Social Security numbers, drivers license information) of as many as 310,000 people. In May, Time Warner revealed that an outside storage company had misplaced data stored on computer backup tapes on 600,000 current and former

What connotations do you get from this image of identify theft? How do you think this image was put together?

employees. That same month, United Parcel Service picked up a box of computer tapes in New Jersey from CitiFinancial, the consumer finance subsidiary of Citigroup, that contained the names, addresses, Social Security numbers, account numbers, payment histories and other details on small personal loans made to an estimated 3.9 million customers. The box is still missing.

23   Whoops!

24   CitiFinancial correctly informed its own customers and, inevitably, the rest of the world about the security breach. Would they have done so entirely on their own? That is less clear. In July 2003, California started requiring companies to inform customers living in the state of any breach in security that compromises personally identifiable information. Six other states have passed similar legislation.

25   No such legislation exists on the federal stage, however—only discretionary guidelines for financial institutions about whether and how they should inform their customers with respect to breaches in the security of their personal information.

26   Both the House and Senate are now considering federal legislation similar to the California law. It's a start but not nearly enough. We need mandatory clarity and transparency, not just with regard to the services that these miracles of microchip and satellite technology offer but also the degree to which companies share and exchange their harvest of private data.

27   We cannot even begin to control the growing army of businesses and industries that monitor what we buy, what we watch on television, where we drive, the debts we pay or fail to pay, our marriages and divorces, our litigations, our health and tax records and all else that may or may not yet exist on some computer tape, if we don't fully understand everything we're signing up for when we avail ourselves of one of these services. ■

"It's part of the government's new emphasis on patient privacy, ma'am."

In 1992, John McPherson began working on *Close to Home*, a comic strip that takes up issues that hit "close to home," such as marriage, work, and health care. The strip appears in nearly 700 newspapers around the world. This one appeared in 2003.

Randall Larsen

Traveler's Card Might Just Pave the Way for a National ID Card

When my family members fly on an airliner, I would like to think America has a system to ensure that they are not seated next to someone on a terrorist watch list. But this is not the case. The Transportation Security Administration (TSA) does screen passengers against terrorist watch lists, but the system is horribly flawed. It's like putting three dead bolts on the front door and leaving the back door wide open.

2 What ID card do you show at an airport? Most passengers use their driver's licenses. How difficult is it to obtain a counterfeit driver's license? Not very. Seven of the nineteen 9/11 hijackers had Virginia driver's licenses, yet none lived there. America needs a better system for identification.

3 Many Americans worry about creating a national ID card. I have serious concerns, too. But we have reached a point where the lack of an ID card may be a greater threat than the creation of such a system.

4 Sen. Lamar Alexander, R-Tenn., recently changed his mind. Twenty years ago, as governor of Tennessee, he vetoed a bill requiring photos on driver's licenses. He saw it as a breach of privacy. Today, he is calling for national ID cards—with photos and biometrics.

5 Why the change?

6 The reason he and others have changed their minds is that the creation of national ID cards is something akin to medical procedures—they all have risks, but when the risk of inaction becomes greater than the risk of action, action becomes the better choice.

7 Today, 15 European democracies have national ID cards. The United Kingdom debated the issue for several years after 9/11 and has recently decided to move forward with such a system. Our debate should begin now, and it should begin with these four questions:

1. Does an organization and system exist that can ensure ID credentials are properly issued?
2. Does the technology exist to create IDs that cannot be altered or counterfeited?
3. Can we build an affordable system?
4. Does the public feel secure that such a system would protect privacy?

8 Today, the answers are: no, yes, yes, no. It is unlikely that the public will support a national identity system until we can obtain four yeses. Is this possible? Absolutely, but much work is needed.

9 The first question (ensuring credentials are properly issued) will be the most difficult to resolve. It will require that we first answer other questions, many involving immigration and illegal aliens. The last question (privacy) is the one that causes many to object, but technologies exist that can help alleviate those "Big Brother" fears. Even so, a national ID remains, for now, out of reach. But the country is taking incremental steps worth embracing.

10 A month ago, President Bush signed the Real ID Act to establish national standards for state-issued driver's licenses. The good news: It may be a step toward improving identification at airports. The bad news: It won't take effect until 2008, and that may be too late.

Scrutiny by Congress

11 Thursday, the House Committee on Homeland Security will hold a public hearing to examine options for travelers' IDs, including privately issued ones.

Frequent travelers could have the option to pay for such a card. They would be fingerprinted, retina-scanned and background-checked so that the TSA could speed them through security.

12   The card, similar to TSA's pilot program "Registered Traveler," would allow TSA to focus on other passengers who might actually have nefarious plans. This is a winning strategy for all homeland security programs—focus resources where the threat is highest.

13   A national identity card is what we ultimately need, but until then, we should consider privately issued travelers cards. They would be voluntary with limited costs to taxpayers and, most important, would assist TSA in ensuring safe travel for my family, and yours. ■

Jennifer Burk

Counselors Walk a Fine Line Weighing the Rights of Student and College

The article below, by Jennifer Burk, appeared in The Macon Telegraph *shortly after the April 2007 shootings at Virginia Tech, where gunman Seung-Hui Cho killed 32 people before committing suicide. Because many of his peers and professors had voiced concerns about Cho's emotional stability and mental health prior to his shooting spree, the Virginia Tech tragedy raised questions about the responsibilities and rights of educational communities to report troubled students and to protect unsuspecting citizens. In the article, Burk enters that conversation by discussing the difficulties of balancing student privacy with community security, particularly in the aftermath of the widely publicized shootings—the deadliest in modern U.S. history.*

In the nearly two weeks following a deadly shooting rampage at Virginia Tech in which the gunman had been deemed mentally ill, college mental health professionals have been looking at their own policies regarding how far they can go to help a student. "You have to assess every situation as you see it," said Mary Jane Phillips, director of counseling services at Georgia College & State University. The fact is that maybe only two or three students out of 10 who exhibit similar symptoms are a serious danger, Phillips said, and "predicting which two or three out of those 10 who might actually do that—we're not very good at that." In the Virginia Tech case, a faculty member had encouraged gunman Seung-Hui Cho to seek counseling, and a court had declared him mentally ill.

2   Mental health professionals always have had to walk a fine line between responsibility to a student and responsibility to the institution. Colleges are

allowed to breach privacy when there is a "clear and imminent danger" of harm to self or others, Phillips said, but despite guidelines to help determine if there's a danger, it's not always clear. "What's clear and imminent? Well, that's where it gets a little fuzzy," she said.

3   If a clear and imminent danger can't be documented, once students are 18, privacy laws prevent counselors from sharing medical information with anyone, including college administrators and even a student's parents. "A student may have [a] psychological disability that causes them to act 'strangely' in some people's eyes," Doug Pearson, vice president and dean of students at Mercer University, wrote in an e-mail to *The Telegraph*. "This in and of itself does not mean they are necessarily a threat to others. Universities have to temper any response to such complaints that all students have rights." Students with psychological disabilities are protected under the Americans With Disabilities Act, he said. Universities have the power to act only if a student's behavior "crosses the line" or becomes clearly disruptive, he said.

4   Today, more and more students are coming to college with psychological and psychiatric disorders, said Jerald Kay, chairman of the American Psychiatric Association committee on college mental health. Compared to 25 years ago, the number of students who have experienced depression has doubled and suicidal behavior has tripled, said Kay, who also is a professor at Wright State University in Dayton, Ohio. More students are seeking help as well, he said. But once they seek help, it's unclear how far a college can go in mandating treatment. National standards need to be put in place regarding treatment, he said.

5   George Washington University and the Massachusetts Institute of Technology have been sued for telling suicidal students they needed to leave campus, Kay said. "It's very hard to make people do anything in this world unless you can readily document that this person is a harm to himself or a harm to others," he said.

6   "At Macon State College, students are told upfront that they lose confidentiality if counselors find them to be a harm to themselves or someone else," said Ann Loyd, director of counseling and the career center. "We're here to help students help themselves and do that in a way of growth and understanding," Loyd said. "We do try every effort to get them assistance that they need." Jamie Thames, director of student counseling services at Wesleyan College, said she encourages students to contact their parents if they need help. However, in the event of a crisis, the college has the right to do so, she said.

7   Most experiences college counselors have are with suicidal risks, Thames said. Counselors can determine the strength of a threat by asking students if they have a plan, if they don't feel safe from themselves and if they have intent. "It's just a case-by-case basis," Thames said. ∎

Jeffrey Zaslow

The End of Youthful Indiscretions: Internet Makes Them Permanent Blots

Jeffrey Zaslow's social commentaries (entitled "Moving On") appeared first on August 12, 2004, in the business-oriented Wall Street Journal, *where he works as a staff writer. Zaslow is the author of* Tell Me All About It: A Personal Look at the Advice Business *(1989) and* Take It from Us: Advice from 262 Celebrities on Everything That Matters—To Them and to You *(1994). Zaslow also has worked as an advice columnist at the* Chicago Sun-Times—*he even replaced Ann Landers for a number of years.*

O nce upon a time, we all did things in public that quickly became simple private memories.

2   We appeared in grade-school choir concerts, scratching ourselves awkwardly or finding our noses with our fingers. As feisty teens, we wrote angry manifestos for college newspapers. As young adults, we kissed our sweethearts on busy street corners, thrilled by the private publicness of it all.

3   Those public moments were fleeting, and rarely had any bearing on the rest of our lives.

4   But young people today, who live in an age of reality TV and security concerns that led to the Patriot Act, likely won't have that luxury. While most adults have a Web presence that dates back no further than 1994, today's kids will enter adulthood with far more of their lives in plain view. This could impact their interactions with college-admissions officers, prospective employers, even love interests.

5   Those children's choir concerts that used to be relatively private affairs? They now air repeatedly on school-district cable outlets, allowing any channel surfer to focus on your child's familiarity with his nose.

6   If our teens write political screeds, their words can end up posted forever on Internet Web sites. Every time someone Googles them, their one-time activism will pop up—even if they no longer hold those beliefs.

7   As for stolen kisses: Several million surveillance cameras mounted in public locations now feed footage not just to the police, but also to thousands of community Web sites for all to see.

8   These days, nothing public is private anymore. New parents can now build customized Web sites through OurBabyNews.com, posting photos and details about their baby's young life. The Web sites cost as little as $14.95 a year, and just 10% of customers opt for password protection—the other 90% are open to anybody to peruse.

9   "Camp cams" provide online video and photos of kids' adventures at summer camp for their parents and others to examine. "Hopefully, 30 years from now, you can see images from the summer of 2004," says Ari Ackerman,

founder of Bunk1.com, which uploads photos and videos for 2,000 camps. Camp owners decide how secure to make the sites.

10   Meanwhile, teens create confessional Web logs—musings more suited for private diaries—and even after they mature, their adolescent ramblings remain accessible in cyberspace. Job recruiters will increasingly sift through "idiotic blogs" from applicants' teen years, predicts Alan Schlein, a Washington, D.C., consultant who helps businesses find information online. He advises: "Tell your kids to think of the Internet as a public stage that'll still be playing their show 20 years from now."

11   In the cacophony of online revelations, a yearning for privacy can seem quaint. People wonder: Why not expose yourself to the world?

12   I have a colleague who was invited back to his high school this year to receive a distinguished alumni award. If this had happened a decade ago, few people outside his hometown would know about his honor unless he chose to tell them. However, because details of his award appeared online, our company's employee-relations folks found out and posted the news (with his high-school photo) on our in-house Web site for thousands of employees to see. My colleague was embarrassed by the exposure; did people think he had orchestrated the attention?

13   I sympathized with him. In 1991, I wrote a column that happened to include a couple of inane puns. Months later, the International Save the Pun Foundation named me "Punster of the Year" at its annual dinner. I gave an acceptance speech, mustering up a few lame puns. Since then, when people search for my name online, my punster award pops up, making me seem like a pun fanatic. A public-relations woman recently tried to sweet-talk me into writing about her client; she said she always enjoys my puns. Oh, please!

14   It is true that the face we show the world via the Web often gives others a sense of our accomplishments and interests. But so much of it is out of context and incomplete. Incoming college freshmen today routinely Google their roommates-to-be. That makes it harder for students to reinvent themselves or polish rough edges.

15   Colleges might consider offering required courses on privacy rights and risks. Yes, it is helpful that birth, death, marriage, genealogy and residency records are just a few keystrokes away (anywho.com, anybirthday.com, searchsystems.net). But this ready access also makes it easier for identity thieves, salespeople and stalkers to find us. And it isn't always clear how we should use public records. At NationalAlertRegistry.com, we can learn how many sex offenders are in our neighborhoods, and get maps to their homes. But what do we do with these maps once we download them?

16   As we teach our kids about the decline of privacy, and the moral quandaries of the Internet, we must also be vigilant about protecting ourselves. That means combing the Internet to remove troublesome personal references. It also means being aware that a surveillance or cellphone camera may capture us in public, or that satellite photos of our homes can be purchased by anyone for $7 at PeopleData.com.

17   In this post-private world, it may be time to redefine ethical behavior. Millions of single people do online searches before dating someone. Deborah Pierce, executive director of Privacy Activism, an advocacy group, argues that it is more polite and ethical to ask for permission first: Do you mind if I Google you?

18   It is hard to picture people asking each other that question.

19   But talking about the issue might remind our kids they still have a right to privacy, and that they should afford a measure of privacy to others. ■

Issue in Focus
BIOMETRICS: MEASURING THE BODY FOR IDENTITY

The 1997 film *Gattica*, starring Ethan Hawke and Uma Thurman, features the supposedly futuristic plot of a "natural" man stealing genetic information to pose as an elite citizen—someone who was genetically engineered before birth. Using stolen biometric identifiers, Hawke's character poses as another person, but the film's final message just may be that the "natural" man still triumphs: spirit trumps technology. Another recent film, *Minority Report* (2002), starring Tom Cruise, also involves biometric technologies. Cruise's character takes someone else's retinas in order to clear his name of a crime he supposedly commits in the future. Like *Gattica*, *Minority Report* employs futuristic biometric technologies that today are not entirely feasible but are no longer beyond the realm of possibility. Indeed, both films characterize the possibilities—fascinating and frightening—of biometrics that no longer belong exclusively to the realm of science fiction.

Biometrics encompasses a variety of identification strategies. Biometric devices can record physical characteristics such as irises, retinas, fingerprints, hands, knuckles, palms, veins, faces, DNA, sweat, pores, lips, odors, and voices. In addition, biometric technologies can analyze human behavior patterns such as signatures, keyboard keystroke patterns, and gaits. Some of these technologies are more advanced and more feasible than others, but the goal of biometrics is to conclusively determine individual identity and thus remove the element of human error that comes with lost, stolen, hacked, copied, or shared passwords and tokens. Biometrics helps us bypass these pitfalls by securing data that belongs exclusively to one person—since that data is actually part of the person.

There are more everyday problems with biometrics than the movies *Gattica* and *Minority Report* suggest. For one thing, in large-scale uses of biometrics, there are likely to be portions of the population for whom some facets of the technology simply don't work, as well as small percentages of overlap that make identity difficult to determine. In addition to concerns about the cleanliness and safety of the machinery used to collect and measure biometric data, some detractors raise concerns about security and privacy: if biometric data is stolen, individuals can be permanently vulnerable because, unlike passwords and tokens, biometric information is difficult, if not impossible, to change. Furthermore, biometrics incites fears that individuals who protect valuable property with biometrics might be physically harmed or endangered if someone tries to steal the property. These concerns about biometrics extend beyond the cost and logistics to the ways in which we use, store, and manipulate our bodies for security's sake.

The reading selections in this section describe the range of types and uses of biometrics and argue about advantages and disadvantages that accompany this emerging technology. Because biometric recognition technologies effectively illustrate the tensions between protection and privacy, we include images and articles that dramatize the excitement and fear surrounding them.

The section opens with an article by Steven C. Bennett, a partner in a law firm who teaches a course in privacy law at Hunter College. He gives an even-handed discussion of the pros and cons of biometric technologies and goes on to argue that the biometrics industry should set standards that protect the privacy of individuals. Less even-handed is a page from the FBI Web site, which extols the benefits of these technologies. Then Paul Saffo, the Roy Amara Fellow at the Institute for the Future and a writer whose essays have appeared in *Fortune, The Harvard Business Review*, the *Los Angeles Times, Newsweek, The New York Times, The Washington Post*, and *Wired*, explains the not-so-science-fiction possibility of DNA identity theft and cautions against blind faith in biometrics.

The next selection is "Emerging Biometric Technologies" by Russ Ryan, who is vice president of information and communications at the National Biometric Security Project, a nonprofit organization that supports government and private efforts to implement biometric technology. Ryan gives an optimistic description of the latest additions to biometric recognition, but he concludes with a warning about the importance of balancing security with civil liberties. Ryan's article is followed by writer and photographer J. G. Domke, who concludes the section with an explanation of new technologies that may improve shoppers' experiences by gathering data about both stores and consumers. Once again, however, Domke asks us to consider the cost of forfeiting our personal information for the sake of protection and convenience. For a related writing activity on privacy and surveillance, see page 39.

As you read and analyze the texts and images, consider the desirability of biometrics—a technology that started as science fiction but has been studied and advanced by the U.S. military in efforts to secure the nation and catch terrorists. What about this technology captivates our imaginations in so many different ways? What balance are we willing to strike between personal privacy and national security, or even personal protection? How does biometrics alter our sense of ourselves as unique individuals—both in terms of what information we would share publicly and in terms of identity theft? These selections introduce you to a complex and significant technological advance, and they can prompt further thinking, reading, research, and writing as you enter this important contemporary argument about security and privacy.

Steven C. Bennett

Privacy Implications of Biometrics

Broadly speaking, biometrics is a term for any measurement of individuals used either to identify or authenticate their claimed identity. Fingerprints and wanted posters, for example, are well-established biometric methods used by law enforcement to track down, identify, and authenticate suspects. Modern information technology has added a number of new machine-based identification techniques, such as facial scanning and recognition, and improved the older techniques. These mechanical innovations offer a host of benefits, chiefly speed, efficiency, and vast analytical power. Several nations, including the United States and most of Europe, have begun to take advantage of the security benefits of these advances by issuing passports and other forms of identification encoded with biometric information. With such benefits, however, may come significant risks to the privacy and data security rights of consumers, workers, and citizens at large. The development of "best practices" in managing the use of biometrics is essential to strike an appropriate balance, ensuring proper use of these techniques and safeguards against abuse. If industry does not develop and follow such guidelines, more stringent regulations may be imposed.

2   A prime example of both the potential benefits and the threats of rapidly evolving biometric technology appears in the use of facial scanning technology at several recent NFL Superbowls. Before the 2001 Superbowl in Tampa, over 30 closed-circuit television cameras were installed to monitor the crowd and compare images of spectators to images of known criminals. Approximately 20 matches were made, several during the game. There was a widespread outcry, including dramatic media accounts labeling the game the "Snooper Bowl," disparaging the Orwellian overtones, after this use of biometrics became public knowledge. These complaints were muted at the New Orleans Superbowl in 2002, perhaps as a consequence of the September 11th attacks. Nonetheless, the use of facial recognition technology during the Superbowl has since been abandoned.

WHAT IS BIOMETRICS?

3   Essentially, biometrics is the use of human physical characteristics as identifiers. While any trait can be used, several specific types have proven to be most useful. The three most common genres of biometric identifiers are appearance, physiography, and bio-dynamics. Physical appearance is primarily judged through the use of photographs or other still images, but can also be validated

through written descriptions of an individual's height, weight, coloration, hair, and visible markings. Physiography, on the other hand, requires some form of measurement—such as fingerprints, dental measurements, optical scans of the retina or iris, hand geometry, or DNA testing. As opposed to these two static characteristics, bio-dynamics measures patterned active behavior—voice fluctuation, keystroke tendencies, manner of writing a signature, and habituated body signals such as gait.

4   To perform the task of identification or authentication, biometrics relies on the comparison of live data supplied—voluntarily or not—by the subject to a dataset or template containing pre-existing information. The prime difference between the objectives of identification and authentication lies in the scope of pre-existing information required for each task. Identification can assign a name or other value to a previously anonymous person by comparing the live data to a large number of samples, a "1:N search," to determine whether there is a match. Authentication, on the other hand, merely requires confirmation that individuals are who they claim to be. The comparison, then, is between the live data and previously supplied data from a single individual, or a "1:1 search." Both searches can either be positive or negative; they can ensure either that a person is already within the database and permitted access (positive) or, as in the Super-bowl example, that a person is not within a database and therefore permitted access (negative).

5   Basic forms of biometrics are all around us. The typical driver's license or state identification card, for example, contains a photograph and some form(s) of physical description (such as height and eye color). The license often also contains a sample signature from the individual; and the individual's address. All of these, in some ways, are forms of biometrics:

- The photograph may be compared to the individual carrying the license;
- The physical characteristics described on the license may also be compared to those of the individual;
- The individual may be asked for a signature sample, and that sample compared to the license sample;
- The individual may be asked to recall (unaided) his or her address, and that answer compared to the license information.

What Is Different About Machine Biometrics?

6   Biometrics standing alone are just characteristics; they neither protect nor threaten individual privacy. As the license example suggests, the use of biometrics has been accepted and commonplace for over 100 years. It is how biometric technologies are used that determines their effect on privacy. The rise of mechanical biometric technology, especially computers and computerized databases, and the consequent automation of the identification process have radically increased both the ability to identify individuals biometrically and the potential for abuse of biometrics. These changes extend to almost every aspect

of biometrics—data capture, analysis, communication, and storage—and must be understood before analyzing their implications for privacy and data security rights of individuals.

Data Capture

7 Technological advances now allow for involuntary or unknowing capture of biometric characteristics. The Superbowl provides an example—if the security firm had chosen to store the captured images rather than merely test and destroy them, it would have created the possibility for biometric identification of all who attended the game. Even when the submission of information is voluntary, many biometrics are very difficult for a human to gather unaided. For example, scanning the retina of the human eye requires light-producing and magnification devices, and meaningful analysis of the results requires imaging and comparison technology. These techniques, however, may offer highly individualized identification when used properly. Even biometric methods that can be performed competently by humans (such as fingerprint or hand shape identification) can be greatly improved through machine operation.

Data Analysis

8 Though Moore's law of increasing computer capacity is only observational, the exponential growth of computing power has allowed for ever more rapid identification searches, even as databases expand. Fingerprinting technology provides the perfect lens through which to view this growth. Originally, fingerprinting could only be used to authenticate the identity of criminals who had left their prints at a crime scene, noting any 1:1 matches. Gradually, a classification system (the Henry system) developed, which allowed for identification searches, but these searches required significant amounts of time to perform. By 1971, the FBI possessed over 200 million paper fingerprint files, including records on 30 million criminals, and J. Edgar Hoover had unsuccessfully promoted universal fingerprinting. The true technological shift, however, came in the 1990s, when new fingerprint scanners cut the time to identify prints from months to hours.

Data Communication

9 Many forms of biometrics were impossible to communicate until recently. Before the creation of reasonably high quality photographs and copies, accurate re-creation of most biometrics via transmission was impossible. The year 1924 witnessed the first transmission of fingerprints from Australia to Scotland Yard via telegraph. Since then, modern communication has dramatically enhanced the efficiency of biometrics. Just as computational analysis has followed the predictions of Moore's law, so too the field of communications has lived up to the even more aggressive predictions of the "Photon Law"—that bandwidth will more than double every year. As bandwidth increases, more biometrics can be transmitted, and data transfer is faster. This allows for linkage of varied biometric data sets, as well as non-biometric information.

Data Storage

10 Finally, the ability to reduce biometrics to electronic datasets of relatively small size has allowed for construction of large, searchable electronic databases. As a result of the falling costs of electronic data storage and the rising ability to transmit that data rapidly across long distances, technological shifts have allowed for creation of massive interlinked databases of biometric information. The FBI's Integrated Automated Fingerprint Identification System ("IAFIS") is the largest biometric database in the world, containing the fingerprints and related criminal history of over 47 million individuals. Remote electronic submissions for criminal inquiries can receive a response from IAFIS within two hours. The IAFIS data illustrate a final observational law of technology, Metcalfe's law, which states that the power of a network increases (exponentially, though this value is debated) as every node is added. Thus, the ability to integrate and store information from many different databases dramatically increases the value of biometric data.

THE VALUE OF MACHINE BIOMETRICS

11 The efficiency gained from mechanization of biometrics is clear. Fingerprint searches that a decade ago took three months to complete now can be completed in under two hours. Biometrics also has an intrinsic value in its ability to function as (potentially) the most effective security safeguard, restricting access to sensitive information or physical areas. To secure such access, authorization (or identity) must be validated. The rise in identity theft demonstrates the weakness of validating systems based purely on possession of particular information about the individual. These faults have caused many in business to turn to biometrics as a more secure method of identifying or authenticating individuals.

12 In response to digital hackers, many password systems now require frequent changes or the use of special symbols and non-repetitive character strings. These shifts, designed to protect security, tend instead to undermine it as users often write their passwords on a sticky note by their desks. Relying on access cards is equally problematic—such cards can be lost, stolen, or left right by the computer to which they provide access. A recent survey, moreover, found that 70 percent of Americans, in response to an unsolicited email or phone call, would share information such as an account number, or provide the answer to a security code question. A majority also indicated they would not want their accounts locked after three failed attempts to verify the identity of someone trying to gain access. More than two-thirds of respondents in this survey were open to using biometric technologies—they want technology that is as secure as it is convenient.

13 The weaknesses and security lapses in other validation mechanisms have increasingly caused industry innovators to turn to biometrics. Banco Azteca was created in 2001 by the massive Grupo Elektra, to target the previously untapped 70 percent of Mexico's population that did not use banks at all. One of the problems the new bank confronted in enrolling customers in underserved communities

was the lack of any form of secure identification papers, driver's licenses, or the like. In response, the bank turned to biometrics and fingerprint scans. Over seven million Banco Azteca customers have enrolled in the biometric identification program; more than 75 percent of the bank's business comes from customers who have dealt with a bank for the first time due to this program.

HOW CAN MACHINE BIOMETRICS THREATEN PRIVACY?

14   Although biometrics techniques may provide new opportunities for security, these techniques also present the potential for abuse. Biometric information is inherently linked to individuality and functions as a unique identifier in a way that would make its loss irreplaceable. The potentially unrestrained scope of data collecting, sharing, linking, and warehousing also may invite misuse. Finally, the potential for pervasive monitoring of movement and activities may chill discourse and protest.

15   Identity theft in a biometric world may be particularly problematic. When a check is lost or stolen, one immediately requests a stop payment order. When a credit card is taken, one calls the company to freeze the account and order a new card. What does one do when biometric information is stolen? Once biometric information is reduced to electronic data, that data can be captured or altered by hackers. Hackers can then reproduce the data in a way that convinces biometric scanners that they are authorized, and thereby gain access to supposedly secure information or locations. Essentially, biometrics are the equivalent of a PIN that is impossible to change. The theft of biometric information amounts to permanent identity theft, and thus may be extremely difficult to counteract.

16   Use of biometrics also risks the problem of data creep, in which information given voluntarily to one recipient for one purpose may be transferred, without permission or knowledge, to another recipient, linked with other data, or applied to a new purpose. The average American's personal information is now available in approximately 50 different commercial databases. Linkage of such information could permit discrimination based on physical characteristics that might otherwise remain unknown.

17   Followed to its logical extreme, moreover, the linkage of digital images into a single database with facial recognition technology would permit the tracking of everyone's movements. The possibility of such tracking, however remote, epitomizes the threat that widespread use of biometrics poses for personal privacy. If an organization or government can monitor movement and actions, it could discriminate against individuals based on their associations. As anonymous behavior becomes less possible, dissent may be suppressed.

What Form of Regulation Is Appropriate?

18   Individual autonomy is the cornerstone of the American legal and social structure. The free flow of information, however, is equally essential to a functioning democracy. The challenge of regulating biometrics lies in resolving the tension between the rights to privacy, free speech, and information security.

19   Americans generally disfavor broad government regulation of industry practices regarding personal information. Congress prefers to rely on industry self-regulation when possible. Nevertheless, the government will step in to regulate a market when the market clearly has failed to provide adequate safeguards. Notable examples of such government intervention include the Child Online Protection Act, the Graham-Leach-Bliley Act, and the Health Insurance Portability and Accountability Act. If the biometrics industry wishes to avoid potentially strict sector-specific government regulations, it must self-regulate, to harmonize the tensions between the fundamental benefits of biometrics while limiting the potential for abuse. In establishing such best practices, the industry must proceed from two basic principles: notice and security.

Notice

20 Individuals must know when data collection occurs. A notice requirement recognizes the importance of individual autonomy and enables people to choose whether to participate. Notice, however, means more than simply saying "surveillance cameras are in use," when police apply facial recognition software at the Superbowl. When any biometric system is used, there should ideally be an open statement of its scope, purpose, function, and application, including the system's potential uses. The evaluation of potential uses is beneficial because biometric systems rarely threatens abuse in themselves. The true threat to privacy comes from the mission creep permitted by latent capabilities. Biometric systems should be narrowly tailored to the job they are to perform. Participation, if at all possible, should be optional. Any change in scope once in use should have the same public disclosure, and participants should be given the option to unenroll from the system.

21   While enrolled within a system, participants should be able to access and correct their personal information contained within the system. Failure to provide for access and correction will increase error in the program and may violate privacy principles.

22   The final notice element of a good self-regulatory program is third-party oversight. Some independent oversight should be implemented to ensure conformity with "best practices," and to suggest other improvements. Periodic audits of the scope and operation of the system coupled with public disclosure of the results of the audits may provide particular deterrence against abuse.

Security

23 To ensure adequate security of biometric information requires both limits on construction of system capabilities as well as protections for data use. System operators should inform participants of the different security measures a biometric identification system will undertake.

24   Data collected should be protected by techniques such as encryption, data hashing, and the use of closed networks and secure facilities. Wireless transmissions of data, even when encrypted, should be avoided. To the extent possible, data should not be stored in a warehouse or database but

rather with the individual participant, by means of an encrypted smart card. If storage is necessary, the initial collection of biometric data should be used to generate templates of authorized people and not linked to any one individual.

Government Oversight

25   If the biometrics industry establishes adequate notice and security practices, it may avoid potentially more restrictive governmental regulations. Some system of enforcement of best practice principles may be necessary. The Federal Trade Commission's power to prosecute unfair, deceptive, or fraudulent business activities may help prevent violations of security procedures or unannounced expansions of a biometric system's purview. The FTC already leads in the data protection field, having developed its own set of information practice principles.

WHAT IS THE FUTURE OF BIOMETRICS?

26   A decade ago, Bill Gates forecast that biometrics would be among "the most important IT innovations of the next several years." Technological innovation has dramatically increased the breadth, depth, and speed with which disparate data sets can be connected and analyzed. Recent developments demonstrate the widespread growth and potential power of biometrics. Use of this technology will certainly continue to grow in the next decade. Taken on its own, biometrics is neither a friend nor a foe to privacy rights; their relationship depends on the manner in which the technology is used.

27   If the biometrics industry wishes to maintain its current flexibility and avoid overly stringent regulations, it must respond to the potential threats to privacy by formulating and adopting best practice principles, keeping in mind the essential need for notice and security. Such self-regulation in managing the use of biometrics will allow the market to strike an appropriate balance between the rights to privacy, free speech, and effective use of information technology. ■

Paul Saffo

A Trail of DNA and Data

If you're worried about privacy and identity theft, imagine this:

2   The scene: Somewhere in Washington. The date: April 3, 2020.

3   You sit steaming while the officer hops off his electric cycle and walks up to the car window. "You realize that you ran that red light again, don't you, Mr. Witherspoon?" It's no surprise that he knows your name; the intersection

camera scanned your license plate and your guilty face, and matched both in the DMV database. The cop had the full scoop before you rolled to a stop.

4   "I know, I know, but the sun was in my eyes," you plead as you fumble for your driver's license.

5   "Oh, don't bother with that," the officer replies, waving off the license while squinting at his hand-held scanner. Of course. Even though the old state licensing system had been revamped back in 2014 into a "secure" national program, the new licenses had been so compromised that the street price of a phony card in Tijuana had plummeted to five euros. In frustration, law enforcement was turning to pure biometrics.

6   "Could you lick this please?" the officer asks, passing you a nanofiber blotter. You comply and then slide the blotter into the palm-sized gizmo he is holding, which reads your DNA and runs a match against a national genomic database maintained by a consortium of drug companies and credit agencies. It also checks half a dozen metabolic fractions looking for everything from drugs and alcohol to lack of sleep.

7   The officer looks at the screen, and frowns, "Okay. I'll let you off with a warning, but you really need more sleep. I also see that your retinal implants are past warranty, and your car tells me that you are six months overdue on its navigation firmware upgrade. You really need to take care of both or next time it's a ticket."

8   This creepy scenario is all too plausible. The technologies described are already being developed for industrial and medical applications, and the steadily dropping cost and size of such systems will make them affordable and practical police tools well before 2020. The resulting intrusiveness would make today's system of search warrants and wiretaps quaint anachronisms.

9   Some people find this future alluring and believe that it holds out the promise of using sophisticated ID techniques to catch everyone from careless drivers to bomb-toting terrorists in a biometric dragnet. We have already seen places such as Truro, Mass., Baton Rouge, La. and Miami ask hundreds or thousands of citizens to submit to DNA mass-testing to catch killers. Biometric devices sensing for SARS symptoms are omnipresent in Asian airports. And the first prototypes of systems that test in real time for SARS, HIV and bird flu have been deployed abroad.

10   The ubiquitous collection and use of biometric information may be inevitable, but the notion that it can deliver reliable, theft-proof evidence of identity is pure science fiction. Consider that oldest of biometric identifiers—fingerprints. Long the exclusive domain of government databases and FBI agents who dust for prints at crime scenes, fingerprints are now being used by electronic print readers on everything from ATMs to laptops. Sticking your finger on a sensor beats having to remember a password or toting an easily lost smart card.

11   But be careful what you touch, because you are leaving your identity behind every time you take a drink. A Japanese cryptographer has demonstrated how, with a bit of gummi bear gelatin, some cyanoacrylic glue, a digital camera and a bit of digital fiddling, he can easily capture a print off a glass and confect an artificial finger that foils fingerprint readers with an 80 percent success rate. Frightening as this is, at least the stunt is far less grisly than the tale, perhaps aprocryphal, of some South African crooks who snipped the finger off an elderly retiree, rushed her still-warm digit down to a government ATM, stuck it on the print reader and collected the victim's pension payment. (Scanners there now gauge a finger's temperature, too.)

12   Today's biometric advances are the stuff of tomorrow's hackers and clever crooks, and anything that can be detected eventually will be counterfeited. Iris scanners are gaining in popularity in the corporate world, exploiting the fact that human iris patterns are apparently as unique as fingerprints. And unlike prints, iris images aren't left behind every time someone gets a latte at Starbucks. But hide something valuable enough behind a door protected by an iris scanner, and I guarantee that someone will figure out how to capture an iris image and transfer it to a contact lens good enough to fool the readers. And capturing your iris may not even require sticking a digital camera in your face—after all, verification requires that the representation of your iris exist as a cloud of binary bits of data somewhere in cyberspace, open to being hacked, copied, stolen and downloaded. The more complex the system, the greater the likelihood that there are flaws that crooks can exploit.

13   DNA is the gold standard of biometrics, but even DNA starts to look like fool's gold under close inspection. With a bit of discipline, one can keep a card safe or a PIN secret, but if your DNA becomes your identity, you are sharing your secret with the world every time you sneeze or touch something. The novelist Scott Turow has already written about a hapless sap framed for a murder by an angry spouse who spreads his DNA at the scene of a killing.

14   The potential for DNA identity theft is enough to make us all wear a gauze mask and keep our hands in our pockets. DNA can of course be easily copied—after all, its architecture is designed for duplication—but that is the least of its problems. Unlike a credit card number, DNA can't be retired and swapped for a new sequence if it falls into the hands of crooks or snoops. Once your DNA identity is stolen, you live with the consequences forever.

15   This hasn't stopped innovators from using DNA as an indicator of authenticity. The artist Thomas Kinkade signs his most valuable paintings with an ink containing a bit of his DNA. (He calls it a "forgery-proof DNA Matrix signature.") We don't know how much of Tom is really in his paintings, but perhaps it's enough for forgers to duplicate the ink, as well as the distinctive brush strokes.

16   The biggest problem with DNA is that it says so much more about us than an arbitrary serial number does. Give up your Social Security number and a stranger can inspect your credit rating. But surrender your DNA and a snoop can discover your innermost genetic secrets—your ancestry, genetic defects and predispositions to certain diseases. Of course we will have strong genetic privacy laws, but those laws will allow consumers to "voluntarily" surrender their information in the course of applying for work or pleading for health care. A genetic marketplace not unlike today's consumer information business will emerge, swarming with health insurers attempting to prune out risky individuals, drug companies seeking customers and employers managing potential worker injury liability.

17   Faced with this prospect, any sensible privacy maven would conclude that DNA is too dangerous to collect, much less use for a task as unimportant as turning on a laptop or working a cash machine. But society will not be able to resist its use. The pharmaceutical industry will need our DNA to concoct customized wonder drugs that will fix everything from high cholesterol to halitosis. And crime fighters will make giving DNA information part of our civic duty and national security. Once they start collecting, the temptation to use it for other purposes will be too great.

18   Moreover, snoops won't even need a bit of actual DNA to invade our privacy because it will be so much easier to access its digital representation on any number of databanks off in cyberspace. Our Mr. Witherspoon will get junk mail about obscure medical conditions that he's never heard of because some direct marketing firm "bot" will inspect his digital DNA and discover that he has a latent disease or condition that his doctor didn't notice at his annual checkup.

19   It is tempting to conclude that Americans will rise up in revolt, but experience suggests otherwise. Americans profess a concern for privacy, but they happily reveal their deepest financial and personal secrets for a free magazine subscription or cheesy electronic trinket. So they probably will eagerly surrender their biometric identities as well, trading fingerprint IDs for frequent shopper privileges at the local supermarket and genetic data to find out how to have the cholesterol count of a teenager.

20   Biometric identity systems are inevitable, but they are no silver bullet when it comes to identity protection. The solution to identity protection lies in the hard work of implementing system-wide and nationwide technical and policy changes. Without those changes, the deployment of biometric sensors will merely increase the opportunities for snoops and thieves—and escalate the cost to ordinary citizens.

21   It's time to fix the problems in our current systems and try to anticipate the unique challenges that will accompany the expanded use of biometrics. It's the only way to keep tomorrow's crooks from stealing your fingers and face and, with them, your entire identity. ■

FBI

Using Technology to Catch Criminals

Home | Site Map | FAQs

FEDERAL BUREAU OF INVESTIGATION

Celebrating a Century 1908-2008

SEARCH

Contact Us
- Your Local FBI Office
- Overseas Offices
- Submit a Crime Tip
- Report Internet Crime
- More Contacts

Learn About Us
- Quick Facts
- What We Investigate
- Natl. Security Branch
- Information Technology
- Fingerprints & Training
- Laboratory Services
- Reports & Publications
- History
- More About Us

Get Our News
- Press Room
- E-mail Updates ✉
- News Feeds 🔊

Be Crime Smart
- Wanted by the FBI
- More Protections

Use Our Resources
- For Law Enforcement
- For Communities
- For Researchers
- More Services

Visit Our Kids' Page

Apply for a Job

Headline Archives

USING TECHNOLOGY TO CATCH CRIMINALS
Fingerprint Database "Hits" Felons at the Border

12/27/05

A CBP officer takes a passenger's fingerprint scan to compare with the IAFIS database.

When U.S. Customs and Border Protection installed technology that can quickly check the fingerprints of illegal immigrants against the FBI's massive biometric database, its chief called the measure "absolutely critical."

"This technology helps...shed light on those with criminal backgrounds we could never have identified before," Commissioner Robert C. Bonner said in a press statement in October, a month after our Integrated Automated Fingerprint Identification System (IAFIS) became fully available in all 136 border patrol stations.

A very bright light, it turns out. Since last September, IAFIS has returned "hits" on 118,557 criminal subjects who were trying to enter this country illegally, according to Customs and Border Protection officials.

Many of the "hits"—a match of an individual's 10 fingerprints—led to arrests of dangerous criminal suspects, including:

- 460 individuals for homicide
- 155 for kidnapping
- 599 for sexual assault
- 970 for robbery
- 5,919 for assault
- 12,077 for drug-related charges

Border Patrol officials began using our biometric tool in the summer of 2001, connecting two of their facilities in San Diego to our Criminal Justice Information Services Division facility in Clarksburg, West Virginia. Congress sought the deployment to supplement the Border Patrol's 10-year-old biometric database called IDENT, which relies on matching an individual's index fingers, rather than the comprehensive 10-finger prints made by IAFIS.

With IAFIS in place, Border Patrol agents can simultaneously check IDENT's specialized databases and IAFIS's 49 million sets of prints.

The FBI's enthusiasm for biometric technologies is reflected on its Web site. The page shown here was posted on December 27, 2005.

Russ Ryan

Emerging merging Biometric Technologies

Biometric technologies measure and analyze human biological and behavioral characteristics. When used for identification and authentication, they compare a live biometric reading with the stored biometric templates of enrolled users to come up with a match. Some of the more common biometric technologies in use today are fingerprint recognition, facial recognition, hand geometry, iris recognition and speaker recognition. A number of other biometrics are just beginning to find their niche in identity assurance applications, and still others remain in the developmental stage. This article will examine a few technologies from both categories.

DYNAMIC SIGNATURE ANALYSIS

2 Signature recognition authentication, or dynamic signature analysis, authenticates identity by measuring and analyzing handwritten signatures. It does not rely on the physical appearance of the signature, but instead on the manner in which the signature is written. During enrollment, users sign their name multiple times on a pressure-sensitive writing tablet or PDA. This technology measures changes in pressure, position, and velocity of the pen during signing, as well as the overall size of the signature and the quantity and various directions of the strokes in the signature.

3 While it may be easy to duplicate the visual appearance of a signature, it is very difficult to duplicate the behavioral characteristics of the signer.

4 *Robustness.* Dynamic signature analysis devices have proved to be reasonably accurate and lend themselves to applications in which the signature is an accepted identifier. Some systems have difficulties with left-handed people and individuals whose signature changes substantially each time they write it.

5 *Applications.* Despite its user friendliness, long history, and lack of invasiveness, signature verification has not become a market leader. The biggest market application for this technology will most likely be in document verification and authorization.

KEYSTROKE DYNAMICS

6 Keystroke dynamics monitors keyboard inputs at thousands of times per second to identify a user by his or her habitual typing rhythm patterns. It examines dynamics such as speed, pressure, the time it takes a user to type particular words, "dwell time"—the amount of time a person holds down a particular key—and "flight time," the amount of time the user pauses between keys.

7 Keystroke verification techniques can be classified as either static or continuous. Static verification approaches analyze keystroke verification characteristics only at specific times—usually only when the user types the username and password—while continuous verification monitors the user's typing behavior throughout the interaction.

8 Keystroke dynamics is probably one of the easiest biometric technologies to implement and administer, because it is completely software-based; there is no need to install any new hardware. All that is needed is the existing computer and keyboard.

9 *Limitations.* Keystroke dynamics-based systems do not replace the username and password. Therefore, they do not eliminate the need to remember multiple passwords, decrease the administrative costs of resetting passwords, nor enhance convenience for the users. Rather, they enhance the security of existing username/password-based systems.

10 Keystroke dynamics-based systems are only used in one-to-one verification applications and cannot be used in one-to-many applications due to the limitations in the matching accuracy. Additionally, at the time of this writing, keystroke dynamics has not been fully tested in wide-scale deployments.

11 *Applications.* One potentially useful application is computer access, where this biometric could be used to continuously verify the computer user's identity. An ideal scenario: monitoring the keyboard interaction of users while they're accessing highly restricted documents or executing tasks in environments where they must be alert at all times (for example, air traffic control).

SKIN SPECTROSCOPY

12 Skin spectroscopy recognizes skin by its optical properties. The system uses a sensor to illuminate a small patch of skin with multiple wavelengths of visible and near-infrared light. The light is reflected back after being scattered in the skin and is then measured for each of the wavelengths. The system analyzes the reflectance variability of the various light frequencies as they pass through the skin. Because the optical signal is affected by chemical and other changes to the skin, skin spectroscopy also provides a sensitive and relatively easy way to confirm that a sample is living tissue.

13 *Limitations.* This type of system is best used for applications with moderate environmental conditions since having to require users to remove gloves could slow down the access control process to unacceptable levels.

14 *Applications.* This technology is ideally suited to layering in dual biometric systems, helping to build ultra high-performance systems that measure two or more independent biometric identifiers. Because skin spectroscopy-based systems require contact with skin, fingerprint sensors and hand/finger geometry systems are particularly compatible with it.

15 Some vendors' sensors can operate on nearly any portion of the skin, making them ideal for integration into consumer products in ways that easily and conveniently ensure security. Initial designs show system sensors to be small, fast, and durable. Their low cost and low power consumption, and the algorithm's processing efficiency and low memory requirements, make this technology promising for use in portable devices if it is perfected. Smart phones, PDAs, and other mobile products could provide general-purpose authentication capability for applications ranging from m-commerce to physical security.

VEIN PATTERN

16 Vein biometric systems (also called vascular pattern recognition systems) record subcutaneous infrared absorption patterns to produce distinctive identification templates. Veins and other subcutaneous features present large, robust, stable, and largely hidden patterns that can be conveniently imaged within the wrist, palm, and dorsal surfaces of the hand.

17 The user places his hand under an imager, which takes an image of the back of the hand. The main dorsal blood vessels have higher temperatures than the surrounding tissue, so they appear brighter in the image. The system carefully selects the region of interest of the hand and extracts the vein patterns. After it reduces the noise reduction, it separates the vein patterns from the background. Since blood vessels grow as people grow, only the shape and distribution of the veins is considered.

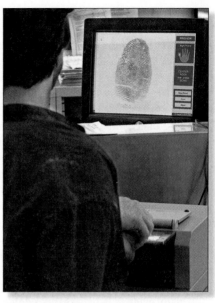

Biometrics offers new uses for fingerprints beyond identifying criminals.

18 *Limitations.* Obviously, extremely dirty hands cannot easily be identified using a vein pattern recognition system. Also, current systems use cameras that are not portable—or certainly less portable than other technologies.

19 *Applications.* The technology can be applied to small personal biometric systems and to generic biometric applications, including intelligent door handles and locks. Some businesses are using vein recognition technology for such applications as time and attendance (to prevent buddy punching), allowance and payment control, login and information protection, safe deposit box access, e-commerce, and membership management.

BODY SALINITY

20 This developmental system works by exploiting the natural level of salt in the human body. The system uses an electric field and salt's natural conductivity to measure a tiny electrical current that is passed through the body. (The electrical current is approximately one-billionth of an amp, which is less than the natural currents already present in the body.) Speeds equivalent to a 2,400-baud modem have been claimed, yielding a data transfer rate of up to 400,000 bits per second.

21 *Applications.* Applications for this kind of biometric technology could include authentication of data transfer devices carried on the body, such as watches, mobile phones, and pagers. Also, applications could include "waking up" household appliances or devices as one enters a room.

FACIAL THERMOGRAPHY

22 Facial thermography refers to the pattern of heat in the face caused by the flow of blood under the skin. IR cameras capture this heat to produce a thermal pattern. Because the vein patterns in a person's face are distinctive to each person, the IR thermal pattern they produce is also distinctive.

23 *Limitations.* While the underlying vein and tissue structure is stable, the dynamic nature of blood flow causes fluctuations and the appearance/disappearance of secondary patterns. Environmental conditions (such as ambient temperature) and the introduction of alcohol or drugs, for example, can alter the thermal signature of the face.

24 *Applications.* This technology is better suited to determine "liveness" of the subject (no thermal image indicates no life) than identification. Facial thermography, used in conjunction with other biometric technologies, could indicate a rested or fatigued person or determine physical condition, although this has never been demonstrated in any commercially available technology. One major technical advantage of this technology is that it does not use infrared illuminators but rather relies on the infrared emissions generated by the face itself. This capability is extremely useful in surveillance applications, especially when it is necessary to detect people in dark places or at night.

A DOUBLE-EDGED SWORD

25 The search for the perfect assurance of our identity or uniqueness may not yet be over. But the technology of biometrics has clearly established that such an objective is not only achievable, but in early practical form, ready and waiting for effective use.

26 The issue of how this technology impacts the treasured right of privacy and civil liberties is a valid concern. Any advance in automated human identification can be a double-edged sword; abused by those who dismiss the importance of the individual for the "greater good," yet also holding the potential as a tool for enhanced individuality and protection of identity when used properly. Achieving the proper balance is critical. ■

Voice Verification for Transactions

VoiceVerified's patent-pending Point Service Provider (PSP) platform uses voice verification to help businesses secure remote transactions, protect consumer data, and combat identity fraud. During the verification process, a user is prompted to repeat five random numeric digits to create a voice sample that is compared to a previously enrolled voiceprint to determine a match.

Somerset, Pa.-based Somerset Trust has purchased the PSP to secure wire transfers, and the bank envisions future usage across all banking services requiring multi-factor authentication. VoiceVerified is currently in discussions with several other financial institutions as banks seek to comply with the Federal Financial Institutions Examination Council's recent guidelines advocating multi-factor user authentication during electronic transactions.

J. G. Domke

Will Cash and Credit Cards Become Extinct in the Not-So-Distant Future?

It's going to happen. As identity theft rockets out of proportion, it's forcing changes to the old credit card with the magnetic strip, which "scammers" can quickly access the information from, enabling them to make thousands of counterfeit cards. To fight back, the frustrated merchant now must stop and check the customer's driver's license and look for the card's authorization number before closing the sale, which annoys many consumers who simply don't have time to wait.

2   Radio Frequency Identification (RFID) chip technology, developed for automating inventory and put into use this year by the world's largest retailer, Wal-Mart, has been seen as an efficient system for controlling inventory and replacing the bar code. But RFID may also help protect customer identity. The financial industry sees RFID as a way to stop counterfeit cards. Card issuers like American Express, JPMorgan Chase, Citibank, and others have begun marketing them heavily in several metropolitan areas. The advantage, they claim, is that chips hold "dynamic data," which changes with every use and can't be reproduced. The RFID card looks different. Users simply wave the card or a "fob" hanging on their keychain over a reader, and the embedded chip is quickly read.

THE FUTURE IS NOW

3   By the end of this year, Duane Reade drugstores in New York will be accepting the MasterCard Pay Pass card, which will have both a magnetic strip and a Radio Frequency ID chip. Duane Reade feels its customers will take advantage of this card, since it eliminates "fumbling for cash and coins, or signing receipts."

4   The "mobile wallet" introduced in Japan in 2005 gives handsets—formerly called cell phones—the functionality of debit cards, credit cards, and a personal identification device. It will also let the user immediately see her account balance and payment records, so she'll know whether she has enough money to buy the digital camera she just saw in the window.

5   The smart-card technology called i-mode FeliCa service is being developed by Sony and NTT DoCoMo, Inc., who are already boasting that 9,000 retailers in Japan will accept payments from MWallet cell phones.

6   The Associated Press reports that Coral Gable residents can use their cell phones by calling up an automatic answering system that will enable them to charge their credit card to an assigned parking meter (however, customers need to remember to call back to stop the charge).

7   Testing is now under way using biometric payment systems, or Automated Fingerprint Identification System (FPIS), an identification system already used by the government and law enforcement agencies.

8   Cogent Systems, the leading AFIS provider, says in a recent press release that it allows shoppers to quickly and securely pay for purchases or cash checks using a finger scan "linked to their identification information, financial accounts, and loyalty programs." This information has to already be in the system, so there needs to be a safe data bank where all the information is stored and there's a way to get to it quickly.

9   Earlier this year, Fujitsu Computer Products of America launched a new device that captures a person's palm vein pattern—without skin contact. Once captured, the device verifies the person's palm vein pattern against a preregistered pattern. According to the company, the system is extremely accurate and difficult to forge. Developed for such markets as financial/banking, health care, and government, systems are already in use in Asia.

10   The phone line is also going the way of the magnetic strip, as companies like Intel, Microsoft, IBM, and Cisco Systems encourage businesses to link their wireless devices to the Internet, promoting how authorizing a sale takes only a few seconds when using the World Wide Web.

11   With advancements in "retail-optimized technology," a waiter or waitress is now able to charge accounts immediately without having to leave the table and risk leaving a credit card unattended.

12   Pete Bartolik at VeriFone Inc., says they support Wi-Fi, but they feel the contactless smart cards are more robust and secure than RFID. Keeping up with technology, VeriFone has also introduced the Visual Payments suite, a new multimedia point-of-sale device that merges "full-motion video" to "engage the customer on a high level and optimize their time." VeriFone offers a range of solutions using such payment options as contactless/RFID cards, Smart Cards, prepaid gift and value cards, debit and credit cards, and more.

13   Technology is offering a lot of options to the retailer, says Bryant Dowden, managing director at Trilogy Payment Solutions, a merchant's service provider in Fort Worth, Texas. "Everyone has to work in tandem before it will work," he says. "If the bank issues an RFID device to card holders, the equipment to read it must be available, and retailers have to be set up to accept it."

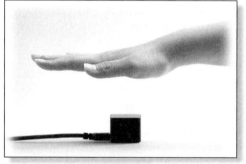

Fujitsu Computer Products of America recently launched its palm vein authentication device. The device captures a person's palm vein pattern and checks it against a preregistered palm vein pattern from that individual. The device offers users a high level of accuracy and security. It is already in use at some of Asia's leading financial institutions.

14   A white paper entitled "Transforming the Shopping Experience Through Technology," sponsored by Intel, Cap

Gemini, Cisco Systems, and Microsoft, claims that consumers are frustrated with flaws in traditional shopping methods, such as the difficulty in locating items and overly congested checkouts. This causes consumers "to punish retailers by shopping elsewhere." IT leaders feel that technology saves time and will make shopping easier, which will help build customer loyalty. Technology, they say, will improve the customer's experience and reverse the consumer trend toward spending less time in stores. They feel this will be accomplished by turning computers into "personalized shopping assistants" that offer easy access to product information and "make consumers more confident and prolific buyers."

15   Clarendon estimates that 12 million "point-of-service terminals" will be shipped by 2007, and the IHL Consulting Group reports that there should also be 192,000 self-checkout systems in operation in the United States by then.

16   Dynamic data from using the APIS, i-mode FeliCa, or RFID chips also gives retailers personal information about their customers (such as age or marital status) that enables them to immediately match customers to special promotions tailored to their lifestyles and interests.

17   In the coming year, technology that was once so expensive only Fortune 500 companies could afford to take advantage of it will become affordable for all retailers. Providing "real-time" information on the store's inventory levels, sales patterns, slow movers, and tracking historical sales trends, the technology will help companies make accurate sales projections and better serve their customers. ■

From Reading to Writing

1. Examine the outcries of biometrics critics and consider writing a rebuttal of one or more of their arguments. (Consult Chapter 12 on writing a rebuttal.)

2. In a causal argument (see Chapter 9), consider how the technological age in which we live exacerbates issues of privacy. Since computers can assemble information more rapidly and have a much greater capacity for accessing it, could it be that traditional laws concerning privacy should not be applied to computer technologies?

3. Evaluate biometrics according to its effects. Has the technology actually helped in the war on terrorism? Has it actually led to significant privacy violations? (See Chapter 10 for advice on evaluation.)

4. Consider popular portrayals of biometrics (like *Gattica* and *Minority Report*). Why is biometrics so fascinating within the realm of science fiction? What qualities of biometrics do these popular versions exaggerate, and why? What effect might these popular images have on viewers' opinions of real-life biometrics, and why?

5. Analyze the visual images associated with this issue, building on Chapter 6 of this text. What is the nature of the arguments made in these visuals? How do they work to persuade an audience?

6. Write a narrative argument (such as the ones described in Chapter 11) that contributes to the debate on biometrics. How does a single incident—drawn from the news, an interview, or your own experience—contribute to this conversation? Alternatively, write a short story portraying the issue with a science fiction or futuristic slant.

Regulating Substances, Regulating Bodies

Regulation is often about deciding where lines may be crossed—and where they should not be crossed. How would we decide which burgers or fries (if any) should be regulated?

Private Bodies, Public Controls

The U.S. prison population—now at 2.38 million, the Justice Department reported on December 5, 2007—has more than quadrupled since the early 1980s, which means that our nation now has the highest rate of incarceration in the world. Although only 4 percent of the world population is in the United States, the United States has a quarter of the entire world's prison population. A great many of those in prison are nonviolent drug offenders, usually small-timers who need help with their own addictions. In the late 1980s, in the face of a cocaine epidemic that was ravaging the nation's cities and claiming the lives of citizens as prominent as Boston Celtics draftee Len Bias, legislators and law enforcement agents cracked down by instituting mandatory minimum sentences. Because people who inform on others can often secure reduced sentences, small-time drug violators often get stiffer sentences than major dealers. According to *Newsweek*, 6 percent of inmates in state prisons in 1980 were there for drug violations; in 1996 the figure was 23 percent. In 1980, 25 percent of inmates in federal prisons were drug violators, while in 2005 the figure had risen to over 60 percent.

> An estimated 80–100 million Americans have tried marijuana.

Should we be so hard on drug dealers and abusers? Is the state and federal governments' "war on drugs" going so poorly that it should be abandoned? Many people think so. Critics call attention not only to the figures on incarceration but also to the other social costs associated with strict drug laws. For example, many addicts resist treatment because they fear punishment; instead, they commit crimes to support their bad habits. Widespread urine testing and seizures of drug-related property have threatened basic civil rights and undermined respect for police. Extensions of the drug war have led to conflicts with other nations where drugs are produced. Moreover, if drugs were considered a medical and social problem rather than a criminal one, citizens could be helped rather than sent to prison. Needle-exchange programs could help check the spread of AIDS by reducing the incidence of shared needles. Recognizing that illegal drugs often are no worse and no better than alcohol (legal since the disastrous 1920s experiment known as Prohibition), Californians voted to legalize marijuana use for cancer and AIDS patients. Many people, drawing from the experiences of other na-

> Of every one hundred people who have smoked marijuana, twenty-eight have tried cocaine—but only one uses cocaine weekly.

tions, are now calling for moves to decriminalize some kinds of drug use, or at least to reduce penalties and increase treatment. In other words, the war on drugs might be maintained—but without quite so much prison warehousing.

On the other hand, many people argue for a continuing hard line on drugs because of the damage that illegal drugs do. They point to the health risks and social costs—to early deaths, lost work days, and broken lives attributable to substance abuse. In the tradition of Carry Nation and other temperance warriors who successfully lobbied for prohibition of alcohol in the 1920s, they have evidence that drug use (especially cocaine use) has decreased during the years of the war on drugs, that marijuana may be a "gateway drug" to more dangerous substances (because marijuana smokers are far more likely to try other drugs, such as cocaine), and that the war on drugs is worth waging for all sorts of other reasons.

Advocates of a hard line on drugs sometimes take on not only drug kingpins but also others—alcohol producers, Big Tobacco, performance-enhancing drug users. For example, they promote stiff taxes

Reformer Carry Nation holding the weapons of her trade: a hatchet for destroying liquor containers and a copy of the Bible.

on cigarettes and alcohol on the grounds that making harmful substances expensive discourages use and pays for the social costs involved. And they are often proponents of testing athletes for the use of unfair and dangerous performance-enhancing substances, such as steroids (which promote muscle growth but have harmful side effects), synthetic forms of testosterone (for which 2006 Tour de France winner Floyd Landis tested positive, causing him to be stripped of his title), and creatine (a dietary supplement that many athletes feel helps their training). They point to the popularity of such substances among young people. They also work to combat binge drinking on campuses because they see it as a frightening epidemic that encourages date rape, promotes vandalism, and otherwise ruins or undermines the lives of countless college students.

Contemporary Arguments

Should certain substances be regulated—and, if so, which ones? Is substance abuse a victimless crime that we have to live with in order to preserve a free society? Is education the only proper approach to the problem? If not, what exactly should be done about various drugs, alcohol, tobacco, and other controversial and harmful practices and substances? Just how should we weigh the risks of drug and alcohol use against the social costs of overzealous law enforcement?

The essays in this section provide a number of perspectives on public control over private bodies, with a focus on drug use. Consider, for instance, the debate between Joseph Califano ("The Right Drug to Target: Cutting Marijuana Use") and Eric Schlosser ("Make Peace with Pot"). Each writer looks at the legalization and criminalization of marijuana from a different perspective and with a different ultimate proposal. Look carefully at the related "Issue in Focus" on the regulation of tobacco. Where exactly should lines be drawn between personal

When Barry Bonds hit his 756th Major League Baseball home run on August 7, 2007, he broke the all-time record held by Henry Aaron. Although Bonds has never failed an official steroid test, he has been implicated frequently in the taking of steroids, and his home run record is embroiled in controversy. Other prominent players also have been implicated.

e choose to do with our own bodies—and government inter- behalf of health and public safety? With that question in mind, you can ...examine the essays that follow in this chapter. All of the readings take up the theme of substances and bodies through the topics of (dis)ability, body weight and body image, body modification through tattoos and piercing, and a sorority that regulates members' bodies in unexpected ways.

Finally, consider how visuals can serve to regulate bodies indirectly, both through the ideals that are present and the concepts and values that are omitted. Photos, cartoons, and other visuals in this chapter suggest that our identifications with certain body types can influence our behaviors; that argument also applies to advertisements in magazines and on TV. These issues concerning written and visual arguments arise in the essays by Michael Bérubé (on disability rights as civil rights), Terrence Rafferty (on film and body image), Susan Llewelyn Leach (on anti-obesity movements), Mim Udovitch (on eating disorders), Pippa Wysong (on body modification), and Susan Kinzie (on an Islamic sorority).

Joseph A. Califano Jr.

The Right Drug to Target: Cutting Marijuana Use

Joseph A. Califano Jr. is president of the National Center on Addiction and Substance Abuse at Columbia University, a nonprofit research center dealing with all forms of drug abuse. From 1977 to 1979 he was the U.S. secretary of health, education, and welfare under President Carter. During his political service he led antismoking campaigns—after having quit smoking four packs a day in 1975. Califano is the author of Inside: A Public and Private Life *(2004)* and High Society: How Substance Abuse Ravages America and What to Do About It *(2007). His argument reprinted here appeared in the* Washington Post *on May 17, 2005.*

The increased potency of today's marijuana and the greater knowledge we have of the dangers of using marijuana justify the increased attention that law enforcement is giving to illegal possession of the drug. But the disappointing reality is that a nearly 30 percent increase in marijuana arrests does not translate into a comparable reduction in use of the drug. Something more is needed.

Rudolph Giuliani's success in slashing New York City's crime rate by, among other things, going after low-level street crimes such as smoking and selling small amounts of marijuana inspired many other mayors to follow suit. When President Bush announced in 2002 a goal of reducing illegal drug use by 10 percent in two years and 25 percent in five years, he knew he had to focus on cutting marijuana use. Eliminating all other illegal drug use combined would not even get him close to his highly touted objective.

3   From the standpoint of protecting children, teens and the public health, reducing marijuana use makes eminent sense. For even though marijuana use has leveled off or waned slightly over the past several years, the number of children and teenagers in treatment for marijuana dependence and abuse has jumped 142 percent since 1992, and the number of teen emergency room admissions in which marijuana is implicated is up almost 50 percent since 1999. Though alcohol remains by far the teen substance of choice, teens are three times likelier to be in treatment for marijuana than for alcohol (and six times likelier to be in treatment for marijuana than for all other illegal drugs combined).

4   As has been true of tobacco since the 1960s, we've learned a lot about the dangers of marijuana since the 1970s. The drug adversely affects short-term memory, the ability to concentrate, and motor skills. Recent studies indicate that it increases the likelihood of depression, schizophrenia, and other serious mental health problems. Nora Volkow, director of the National Institute on Drug Abuse, has repeatedly expressed concern about the adverse impact of marijuana on the brain, a matter of particular moment for youngsters whose brains are still in the development stage. Volkow has stated: "There is no question marijuana can be addictive; that argument is over. The most important thing right now is to understand the vulnerability of young, developing brains to these increased concentrations of cannabis."

5   The issue of marijuana use (and most illegal drug use) is all about kids. If we can get kids not to smoke marijuana before they reach age 21, they are virtually certain never to do so. So let's do more than trumpet the arrest rate. Let's focus on discouraging children and teens from getting involved with the drug in the first place.

6   This begins with understanding the importance of preventing kids from becoming cigarette smokers. Most kids who smoke cigarettes will not smoke marijuana, but a 2003 survey of 12- to 17-year-olds, conducted by the National Center on Addiction and Substance Abuse (CASA) at Columbia University, reveals that teens who smoke cigarettes are much likelier than non-smokers to try marijuana; they are also likelier to become regular marijuana users.

7   The next question is how to make public policies, including law enforcement approaches, more effective in discouraging marijuana use. Availability is the mother of use, so doing a far better job of reducing availability is high on the list. Beyond that—and recognizing that reducing demand is key to that goal— we should use the increased arrest rate as an opportunity to discourage use.

8   Years ago, while I was visiting Los Angeles, then-Mayor Dick Riordan told me that in his city kids were arrested an average of nine times for possession of marijuana before anything happened to them. I have since discovered that this situation is common in many American communities. Most kids do not even get a slap on the wrist the first few times they're nabbed for smoking a joint. As a result, we let them sink deeper and deeper into drug use, with its dangers to their physical, mental and emotional development and its risk of addiction.

9   I am not suggesting that we put kids in jail for smoking pot. But why not treat a teen arrested for marijuana use much the same way we treat a teen arrested for drunk driving? Why not require kids arrested for marijuana possession to attend classes to learn about the dangers of marijuana use and to develop some skills (and the will) to decline the next time they are offered the drug? The incentive to attend such classes would be the threat of the alternative; for the first couple of arrests, loss of a driver's license or a fine stiff enough to hurt; for continued use, a few nights in a local prison. Getting kids to attend sessions designed to discourage their marijuana use would give some practical meaning to increased law enforcement and would bring reductions in drug use more in line with increased arrest rates.

10   These steps will help, but the fact is that we cannot arrest our way out of the teen marijuana problem when (in a recent CASA survey) 40 percent of 12- to 17-year-olds report that they can buy the drug within a day, and 21 percent say they can buy it within an hour.

11   Parents are the first line of defense. Parents must understand that the drug available today is far more potent than what they might have smoked in the 1970s. For their children, smoking marijuana is not a harmless rite of passage but rather a dangerous game of Russian roulette. ∎

Eric Schlosser

Make Peace with Pot

Author of the best-selling book Fast Food Nation *(2001), which explains how the fast-food industry dominates everything from cattle farming to teenage jobs to scientific labs (see page 140), Eric Schlosser contributes frequently to* Atlantic Monthly *magazine. Having also published a book—*Reefer Madness *(2003)—about the criminalization of marijuana and the drug's importance to the economy, he continues to work at the juncture of economics, the legal system, and cultural norms. "Make Peace with Pot" appeared in the April 26, 2004, edition of the* New York Times. *Shortly after the essay was published, the United States Supreme Court ruled that the federal government can prosecute citizens who use marijuana for medicinal purposes, even in states where medical marijuana is allowed.*

Starting in the fall, pharmacies in British Columbia will sell marijuana for medicinal purposes, without a prescription, under a pilot project devised by Canada's national health service. The plan follows a 2002 report by a Canadian Senate committee that found there were "clear, though not definitive" benefits for using marijuana in the treatment of chronic pain, multiple sclerosis, epilepsy and other ailments. Both Prime Minister Paul Martin and Stephen Harper, leader of the opposition conservatives, support the decriminalization of marijuana.

2   Oddly, the strongest criticism of the Canadian proposal has come from patients already using medical marijuana who think the government, which charges about $110 an ounce, supplies lousy pot. "It is of incredibly poor quality," said one patient. Another said, "It tastes like lumber." A spokesman for Health Canada promised the agency would try to offer a better grade of product.

3   Needless to say, this is a far cry from the situation in the United States, where marijuana remains a Schedule 1 controlled substance, a drug that the government says has a high potential for abuse, no accepted medical uses, and no safe level of use.

4   Under federal law it is illegal to possess any amount of marijuana anywhere in the United States. Penalties for a first marijuana offense range from probation to life without parole. Although 11 states have decriminalized marijuana, most still have tough laws against the drug. In Louisiana, selling one ounce can lead to a 20-year prison sentence. In Washington State, supplying any amount of marijuana brings a recommended prison sentence of five years. *logic - emotions. Pretty harsh?*

5   About 700,000 people were arrested in the United States for violating marijuana laws in 2002 (the most recent year for which statistics are available)—more than were arrested for heroin or cocaine. Almost 90 percent of these marijuana arrests were for simple possession, a crime that in most cases is a misdemeanor. But even a misdemeanor conviction can easily lead to time in jail, the suspension of a driver's license, the loss of a job. And in many states possession of an ounce is a felony. Those convicted of a marijuana felony, even if they are disabled, can be prohibited from receiving federal welfare payments or food stamps. Convicted murderers and rapists, however, are still eligible for those benefits. *emotional comparison — also more logic to stun reader*

6   The Bush administration has escalated the war on marijuana, raiding clinics that offer medical marijuana and staging a nationwide roundup of manufacturers of drug paraphernalia. In November 2002 the Office of National Drug Control Policy circulated an "open letter to America's prosecutors" spelling out the administration's views. "Marijuana is addictive," the letter asserted. "Marijuana and violence are linked . . . no drug matches the threat posed by marijuana."

7   This tough new stand has generated little protest in Congress. Even though the war on marijuana was begun by President Ronald Reagan in 1982, it has always received strong bipartisan support. Some of the toughest drug war legislation has been backed by liberals, and the number of annual marijuana arrests more than doubled during the Clinton years. In fact, some of the strongest opposition to the arrest and imprisonment of marijuana users has come from conservatives like William F. Buckley, the economist Milton Friedman, and Gary Johnson, the former Republican governor of New Mexico.

8   This year the White House's national antidrug media campaign will spend $170 million, working closely with the nonprofit Partnership for a Drug-Free America. The idea of a "drug-free America" may seem appealing.

[handwritten margin notes: faulty analogy / what kind of pot are we really sitting at here?]

But it's hard to believe that anyone seriously hopes to achieve that goal in a nation where millions of children are routinely given Ritalin, antidepressants are prescribed to cure shyness, and the pharmaceutical industry aggressively promotes pills to help middle-aged men have sex.

9   Clearly, some recreational drugs are thought to be O.K. Thus it isn't surprising that the Partnership for a Drug-Free America originally received much of its financing from cigarette, alcohol and pharmaceutical companies like Hoffmann-La Roche, Philip Morris, R. J. Reynolds and Anheuser-Busch.

10   More than 16,000 Americans die every year after taking nonsteroidal anti-inflammatory drugs like aspirin and ibuprofen. No one in Congress, however, has called for an all-out war on Advil. Perhaps the most dangerous drug widely consumed in the United States is the one that I use three or four times a week: alcohol. It is literally poisonous; you can die after drinking too much. It is directly linked to about one-quarter of the suicides in the United States, almost half the violent crime and two-thirds of domestic abuse. And the level of alcohol use among the young far exceeds the use of marijuana. According to the Justice Department, American children aged 11 to 13 are four times more likely to drink alcohol than to smoke pot.

[handwritten margin note: eludes topic]

11   None of this should play down the seriousness of marijuana use. It is a powerful, mind-altering drug. It should not be smoked by young people, schizophrenics, pregnant women and people with heart conditions. But it is remarkably nontoxic. In more than 5,000 years of recorded use, there is no verified case of anybody dying of an overdose. Indeed, no fatal dose has ever been established. *[handwritten: Non sequitir]*

12   Over the past two decades billions of dollars have been spent fighting the war on marijuana, millions of Americans have been arrested and tens of thousands have been imprisoned. Has it been worth it? According to the government's National Household Survey on Drug Abuse, in 1982 about 54 percent of Americans between the ages of 18 and 25 had smoked marijuana. In 2002 the proportion was ... about 54 percent.

13   We seem to pay no attention to what other governments are doing. Spain, Italy, Portugal, the Netherlands and Belgium have decriminalized marijuana. This year Britain reduced the penalty for having small amounts. Legislation is pending in Canada to decriminalize possession of about half an ounce (the Bush administration is applying strong pressure on the Canadian government to block that bill). In Ohio, possession of up to three ounces has been decriminalized for years—and yet liberal marijuana laws have not transformed Ohio into a hippy-dippy paradise; conservative Republican governors have been running the state since 1991. *[handwritten margin note: transitions?]*

14   Here's an idea: people who smoke too much marijuana should be treated the same way as people who drink too much alcohol. They need help, not the threat of arrest, imprisonment and unemployment. *[handwritten margin note: over simplifying?]*

15   More important, denying a relatively safe, potentially useful medicine to patients is irrational and cruel. In 1972 a commission appointed by President

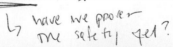

[handwritten: ↳ have we proven the safety yet?]

Richard Nixon concluded that marijuana should be decriminalized in the United States. The commission's aim was not to encourage the use of marijuana, but to "demythologize it." Although Nixon rejected the commission's findings, they remain no less valid today: "For the vast majority of recreational users," the 2002 Canadian Senate committee found, "cannabis use presents no harmful consequences for physical, psychological or social well-being in either the short or long term."

16   The current war on marijuana is a monumental waste of money and a source of pointless misery. America's drug warriors, much like its marijuana smokers, seem under the spell of a powerful intoxicant. They are not thinking clearly. ▪

seems contradictory to previous points

Issue in Focus
REGULATING TOBACCO

In 1998 the attorneys general in 46 states, 5 U.S. territories, and the District of Columbia reached a landmark agreement with America's preeminent tobacco companies concerning damages caused by smoking, as well as the marketing and promotion of tobacco products. According to the settlement, tobacco companies must pay more than $200 billion over 25 years to cover costs associated with smoking-related diseases, restrict their advertising and offer counter-ads, support smoking-cessation efforts, and take steps to discourage children from taking up smoking. Cigarette manufacturers cannot use cartoon characters in ads; cannot advertise in media that are especially accessible to children (e.g., shopping malls, buses, sports arenas, and video game arcades); cannot pay for product placements in movies and television shows; and cannot promote smoking through free merchandise such as caps, shirts, and backpacks.

In addition, as you have no doubt noticed, airlines no longer permit passengers to smoke; smoking is prohibited in many public places, such as schools and office buildings; and public places such as restaurants must accommodate nonsmokers. There is nearly universal agreement that cigarette smoking causes lung cancer, heart disease, emphysema, and other diseases, and warnings to that effect have appeared on cigarette packages and ads for decades. In 1964, when 70 million Americans smoked, the first Surgeon General's Report

The American Legacy Foundation, based in Washington, D.C., is dedicated to "building a world where young people reject tobacco and where anyone can quit," according to its Web site (www.americanlegacy.org). Among other things, the foundation places antismoking ads in the mass media. The one published here appeared in the *New Yorker* in September 2002.

on Smoking and Health launched what became a series of reports on the link between smoking and various diseases. Those reports promoted a new era of industry regulation and consumer lawsuits that have reduced the incidence of smoking in American life.

Since the agreement about the health hazards of smoking and the implementation of warnings and regulations, smoking among teenagers and adults has decreased modestly but perceptibly, and nonsmokers feel more comfortable away from distracting and dangerous secondhand smoke. Restrictions on smoking remain controversial, however. On the one hand, risks to public health caused by smoking seem to cry out for intervention. If the government inspects food,

The American Legacy Foundation, based in Washington, D.C., is dedicated to "building a world where young people reject tobacco and where anyone can quit," according to its Web site (www.americanlegacy.org). Among other things, the foundation places antismoking ads in the mass media. The one published here appeared in the *New Yorker* in September 2002.

insists on safe work environments, and requires drivers to wear seat belts, should it not regulate smoking as well? On the other hand, some consumer freedom advocates worry that restrictions on smoking (and other habits) violate Americans' right to personal choice. Should the government be interfering with the production, sale, and consumption of consumer products? In a free society, should the government educate citizens to adopt particular lifestyles and to avoid certain habits? Is it right for the government to require high taxes on consumer products that it deems dangerous? Where should that power begin and end? If smoking can be restricted, then why not place similar restrictions on beer and other alcoholic beverages, since the social costs associated with alcohol use are similarly high? And what about placing restrictions on certain kinds of foods, such as the burgers and fries sold in fast-food restaurants? What about products like SUVs, dietary supplements, and firearms?

On these pages you will find brief arguments that address questions like these. Tobacco companies continue to advertise their products widely, continue to face lawsuits because of ads they place in magazines popular with young people, continue to refine their practices—see, for example, the Philip Morris Web site at www.philipmorrisusa.com—and continue to generate opposition from organizations like the American Legacy Foundation. Here we reprint an ad from the American Legacy Foundation's "truth" campaign, a cartoon by Garry Trudeau that is critical of Big Tobacco (see the previous two pages), an argument by Douglas Bettcher and Chitra Subramaniam on behalf of the World Health Organization that restrictions on smoking should be spread worldwide—and a defense of the individual freedom to smoke by Walter E. Williams, a professor of economics best known for his conservative commentaries in popular publications such as *Reader's Digest,* the *Wall Street Journal,* and *Newsweek,* and through his syndicated weekly column "A Minority View." As you read, decide where you stand on the issue of whether or not to regulate tobacco (and other harmful consumer products). Where should the line be drawn between personal freedom and social responsibility?

Douglas Bettcher and Chitra Subramaniam

The Necessity of Global Tobacco Regulations

While multinational tobacco companies market high tar and nicotine cigarettes worldwide, in developing countries they advertise these products with techniques that are banned in their home countries.[1] Of the 8.4 million deaths that tobacco is expected to cause by 2020, 70% will occur in transitional countries.[2]

2   Global legislation must hold tobacco companies to the same standards of safety in developing markets that they are held to in their industrialized home markets. To create such global legislation, the World Health Organisation's (WHO's) 191 member states are currently negotiating a legally binding interna-

tional agreement, the Framework Convention on Tobacco Control (FCTC), which may include legally binding rules on tobacco smuggling, international standardization, disclosure of product contents, and package design and labeling.[3]

3   The ethical basis of the FCTC is the principle that a multinational corporation has a nondelegable duty to protect citizens from harm caused by its products. This includes the duty to ensure that all activities are conducted with the highest standards of safety and to provide all necessary information and warnings regarding the activity involved.[4] In addition, the "negative harm" principle of business ethics requires that, in their operations abroad, corporations have an obligation not to add to the suffering and deprivation of people.

4   Tobacco companies have argued that people should be allowed to consume products of their choice freely.[5] However, a recent World Bank report cites three ways in which the choice to buy tobacco products differs from the purchase of other consumer goods. First, many smokers are not aware of the high probability of disease and premature death their choice to smoke entails, and thus, their consent to be exposed to harm is uninformed. Children and teenagers in particular may not have the capacity to assess properly information on the health effects of smoking. Second, the highly addictive nature of nicotine, particularly as it is delivered in a manufactured cigarette, limits the tobacco user's freedom to choose not to smoke.[6] Third, smokers impose both direct and indirect costs on other non-consenting individuals. These failures to meet "free" market standards provide a rationale for demand-reduction interventions.[7]

5   Beyond this theoretical justification for action, there is also a practical one. Tobacco companies have shown themselves to be incapable of self-regulation.[8] Despite the fact that cigarette smoke contains some 4000 different constituents, 60 of which are known carcinogens,[9] there is evidence that tobacco companies have failed to perform inhouse smoking and health research, and that this failure was, in part, the result of tobacco company efforts to mislead the public about the health effects of smoking.[10]

6   The tobacco companies have deliberately increased the addictive potential of cigarettes through their well-documented strategy of manipulating nicotine levels. Furthermore, a WHO committee concluded that tobacco companies had conspired to undermine the agency's tobacco control programs around the world. The committee made 58 recommendations to protect against the subterfuge of the tobacco industry.[11]

7   During a global public hearing in October 2000, the WHO supported measures and policies to restrict youth access to tobacco. Recently, three major tobacco companies proposed weak voluntary global marketing standards, but such measures are known to have only limited impact on youth and adult consumption of tobacco.[12] At the same time, tobacco companies opposed comprehensive advertising bans and price increases, interventions that have had a measurable and sustained impact to decrease tobacco use.

8   Tobacco companies have an ethical responsibility to minimize the harm caused by their products in developing countries and to adhere to the same safety standards in developing countries that they use in their home countries.

9   They have proven themselves unwilling or unable to meet this responsibility voluntarily, and the cost of this failure is enormous. The kind of legally binding global regulation of dangerous practices that the FCTC could provide has become necessary.

Notes
1. Giddens, A. Globalization. Available at: news.bbc.co.uk/hi/english/static/events/reith_99/week1/week1/week1.htm. Accessed November 14, 2001.
2. Murray, C. L., and Lopez, A. D. Alternative projections of mortality and disability by cause 1990–2020: Global Burden of Disease Study. *Lancet,* 1997; 349:1498–1504.
3. Taylor, A. L., and Bettcher, D. W. WHO Framework Convention on Tobacco Control: A global "good" for public health. *Bull World Health Organ.* 2000; 78:920–929.
4. Finzen, B. A., and Walburn, R. B. *Union Carbide Corporation's Liability for the Bhopal Disaster. Multinational Enterprise Liability.* Westport, Conn: Quorum Books; 1990:145–150.
5. British American Tobacco. Answer to frequently asked question: "How can you justify being in the business of selling a product that is harmful to people's health?" Available at: http://www.bat.com. Accessed November 14, 2001.
6. Hurt, R. D., and Robertson, C. R. Prying open the tobacco industry's secrets about nicotine. *JAMA.* 1998; 280:1173–1181.
7. Jha, P., and Chaloupka, F. J., eds. *Curbing the Epidemic: Governments and the Economics of Tobacco Control.* Washington, DC: World Bank; 1999:3–4.
8. Richards, J. W., Tye, J. B., and Fischer, P. M. The tobacco industry's code of advertising in the United States: Myth and reality. *Tob Control.* 1996; 5:295–311.
9. Shopland, D. Machine Testing for constituent levels in cigarettes. Monograph: *Advancing Knowledge on Regulating Tobacco Products.* Paper presented at International Conference: Advancing Knowledge on Regulating Tobacco Products. Oslo, Norway, 9–11 February 2000.
10. Zeltner, T., Kessler, D., Martiny, A., and Randera, F. *Tobacco Company Strategies to Undermine Tobacco Control Activities at the World Health Organization.* Report of the Committee of Experts on Tobacco Industry Documents, July 2000:229–243.
11. Goldman, L. K., and Glantz, S. A. Evaluation of antismoking advertising campaigns. *JAMA.* 1998; 279:772–777.
12. Philip Morris' comments on the Framework Convention for Tobacco Control for the Public Hearings on the FCTC, October 12–13, 2000. Available at: http://www3.who.int/whosis/fctc/fctc.cfm. Accessed November 14, 2001. ■

Walter E. Williams

Nazi Tactics

Prior to the 1930s, Germany was Europe's most hospitable country for Jews. While Jews were only 1 percent of the population, they were one-fourth of Germany's law and medical students. In some German cities, Jews were the majority of doctors. While Jews were only 5 percent of the Berlin population in 1905, they paid 31 percent of all income taxes collected. For Germany as a whole, Jewish income was more than three times the national average. In his book, *Migration and Cultures,* Thomas Sowell adds that Jews were so highly integrated into German economic and social life that in nearly half of all Jewish marriages during the 1920s one of the spouses was gentile. During World War I, Jewish-American publications were investigated and prosecuted by the U.S. government for writing favorably about Germany, a nation at war with the United States.

2   Much of German history has been one of racial toleration. This is partially seen by their anti-slavery positions in Brazil and the United States. In the United States, Germans had a large hand in assisting runaway slaves by way of the "underground railroad." Germans also had an established reputation of getting along well with American Indians.

3   So why the story about pre-Nazi Germany? I think examining it raises an interesting question that few bother to answer; namely, if Germany was so hospitable to Jews, relative to other countries, how in the world did the Holocaust happen? There are several alternative explanations, such as Hitler's massive consolidation of government power. Then there's the fact that German culture places high values on regimentation and obedience to authority. An important part of the answer of how Germans came to accept Jewish persecution was a massive and successful Nazi Jewish-vilification program. Teaching Germans to think of Jews as inferiors and as responsible for the post–World War I economic devastation made it possible for Germans to accept the mistreatment of Jews.

4   You say, "Okay, you're right, but what's the relevance to us?" There are about 40 million Americans who smoke cigarettes. Prior to the 1980s, all efforts to curb tobacco use relied on arguments pertaining to the health risks borne by smokers. The only way to achieve today's level of sustained attack on smokers and tobacco companies was to create an argument that tobacco smoke harmed not only smokers but others as well. Thanks to a fraudulent Environmental Protection Agency study on secondhand smoke, "Respiratory Health Effects of Passive Smoking," we have today's tobacco regulations. This is despite devastating evidence that EPA's study made subjective judgments, failed to account for important factors that could bias the results, and relaxed a crucial scientific standard to achieve the result the researchers were looking for.

5   The "relaxed" scientific standard was the EPA's lowering of the confidence interval applied to its analysis from the more standard 95 percent to 90 percent— in effect, doubling the chance of error. A federal court in *Flue-Cured Tobacco Cooperative Stabilization Corporation v. EPA* added that the EPA "disregarded information and made findings based on selective information . . . ; deviated from its risk assessment guidelines; failed to disclose important [opposition] findings and reasoning; and left significant questions without answers."

6   As a result of both official and non-official fraudulent claims about the health effects, as well as the health-care costs, of smoking, there has been widely successful vilification of cigarette smokers and tobacco manufacturers. Lawmakers have little hesitance in imposing confiscatory tobacco taxes, in some jurisdictions of one to three dollars per pack. Zealous lawmakers and other public officials have attempted to ban smoking on streets and in parks. In at least a

couple of jurisdictions there have been attempts to outlaw smoking in one's own home or apartment under the flimflam reasoning that neighbors are injured by secondhand smoke. Americans don't mind at all seeing their fellow Americans huddled in the winter outside their workplaces in order to have a cigarette. In the state of Washington, a condemned prisoner was denied a last request for a cigarette. Last summer, California banned smoking in some of its prisons.

7   None of this could have happened during a much more civilized era in our country. Nazi-like vilification tactics had to be employed to convince decent Americans that smokers and tobacco companies deserved any harsh treatment.

ALL SHOULD BE CONCERNED

8   I'm by no means suggesting that smokers are headed off to concentration camps and gas chambers, although they might have been in Germany because Hitler was a rabid anti-cigarette zealot. Instead, I'm suggesting that the cigarette-smoker vilification campaign is something about which we all should be concerned, whether we smoke cigarettes or not. These people who want to control our lives are almost finished with smokers; but never in history has a tyrant arisen one day and then decided to tyrannize no more. The nation's tyrants have now turned their attention to the vilification of fast-food chains such as McDonald's, Burger King, Wendy's, and KFC, charging them with having created an addiction to fatty foods. Thus, the tyrants claim, fast-food chains have contributed to obesity-related problems and growing health-care costs. Like the anti-tobacco zealots, they call for regulation, compensation for injury, and taxes on foods they deem to be nonnutritious. In addition to fast-food chains, these tyrants have targeted soft drink and candy manufacturers. Chinese and Mexican restaurants are also in their sights because they have meal servings deemed to be too large.

9   In their campaign against fast-food chains, restaurants, and soda and candy manufacturers, the nation's food Nazis always refer to the anti-tobacco campaign as the model for their agenda. ■

From Reading to Writing

1. Analyze the arguments made by Douglas Bettcher and Chitra Subramaniam or Walter Williams. How is each argument a product of its audience and purpose? What sources of argument (ethical appeals, emotional appeals, logical appeals, and good reasons) do the authors choose, and why? (See Chapter 5 for information on rhetorical analysis.)

2. Compare the various photos and ads that appear on the preceding pages. What visual argument does each photo or ad make? How does it support its argument? (See Chapter 6 for information on analyzing visuals.)

3. Write an argument that makes its point by defining a key term related to the regulation of substances like tobacco. You might choose to change someone's attitude by redefining *freedom* or *government regulation* or

advertising in such a way that your definition supports your views on regulating substances like tobacco. (See Chapter 8 for more on writing definition arguments.)

4. Propose a certain policy concerning the regulation of tobacco or some other substance that is an issue in your community. For instance, should your campus permit fans to purchase beer at athletic events? What should be a proper policy on performance-enhancing drugs in college athletics? (See Chapter 13 for advice.)

5. Write a rebuttal of an article related to tobacco, alcohol, steroids, or obesity that you notice in your local newspaper. (See Chapter 12.) Consider whether you wish to show the weakness in the article, whether you wish to counter-argue, or both.

6. Write an essay that recounts a personal experience of yours that makes an argumentative point related to smoking. What exactly does your personal experience with tobacco lead you to believe? See Chapter 11 for advice on narrative arguments.

Malcolm Gladwell

Drugstore Athlete

Malcolm Gladwell has been writing for some time about fascinating cultural developments of one kind or another—why crime can drop suddenly, how a particular book becomes a best seller, the rise of hair coloring products for women and suicide rates in Micronesia, the fascination for Ritalin, or the spread of coffee. Gladwell is the author of two books: The Tipping Point *(2000) and* Blink: The Power of Thinking Without Thinking *(2005). Gladwell was a reporter, often on science, for the* Washington Post *from 1987 to 1996; since then his work has often appeared in the* New Yorker, *as did the following piece (September 10, 2001).*

1.

At the age of twelve, Christiane Knacke-Sommer was plucked from a small town in Saxony to train with the elite SC Dynamo swim club, in East Berlin. After two years of steady progress, she was given regular injections and daily doses of small baby-blue pills, which she was required to take in the presence of a trainer. Within weeks, her arms and shoulders began to thicken. She developed severe acne. Her pubic hair began to spread over her abdomen. Her libido soared out of control. Her voice turned gruff. And her performance in the pool began to improve dramatically, culminating in a bronze medal in the hundred-metre butterfly at the 1980 Moscow Olympics. But then the Wall fell and the truth emerged about those little blue pills. In a new book about the East German sports establishment, *Faust's Gold*, Steven Ungerleider recounts

Bill Amend's comic strip, *Foxtrot*, has run in newspapers since 1988. This strip appeared on March 16, 2005.

the moment in 1998 when Knacke-Sommer testified in Berlin at the trial of her former coaches and doctors:

2   "Did defendant Gläser or defendant Binus ever tell you that the blue pills were the anabolic steroid known as Oral-Turinabol?" the prosecutor asked. "They told us they were vitamin tablets," Christiane said, "just like they served all the girls with meals." "Did defendant Binus ever tell you the injection he gave was Depot-Turinabol?" "Never," Christiane said, staring at Binus until the slight, middle-aged man looked away. "He said the shots were another kind of vitamin." "He never said he was injecting you with the male hormone testosterone?" the prosecutor persisted. "Neither he nor Herr Gläser ever mentioned Oral-Turinabol or Depot-Turinabol," Christiane said firmly. "Did you take these drugs voluntarily?" the prosecutor asked in a kindly tone. "I was fifteen years old when the pills started," she replied, beginning to lose her composure. "The training motto at the pool was, "You eat the pills, or you die. It was forbidden to refuse."

3   As her testimony ended, Knacke-Sommer pointed at the two defendants and shouted, "They destroyed my body and my mind!" Then she rose and threw her Olympic medal to the floor.

4   Anabolic steroids have been used to enhance athletic performance since the early sixties, when an American physician gave the drugs to three weight lifters, who promptly jumped from mediocrity to world records. But no one ever took the use of illegal drugs quite so far as the East Germans. In a military hospital outside the former East Berlin, in 1991, investigators discovered a ten-volume archive meticulously detailing every national athletic achievement from the mid-sixties to the fall of the Berlin Wall, each entry annotated with the name of the drug and the dosage given to the athlete. An average teenage girl naturally produces somewhere around half a milligram of testosterone a day. The East German sports authorities routinely prescribed steroids to young adolescent girls in doses of up to thirty-five milligrams a day. As the investigation progressed, former female athletes, who still had masculinized physiques and voices, came forward with tales of deformed babies, inexplicable tumors, liver dysfunction, inter-

nal bleeding, and depression. German prosecutors handed down hundreds of indictments of former coaches, doctors, and sports officials, and won numerous convictions. It was the kind of spectacle that one would have thought would shock the sporting world. Yet it didn't. In a measure of how much the use of drugs in competitive sports has changed in the past quarter century, the trials caused barely a ripple.

5   Today, coaches no longer have to coerce athletes into taking drugs. Athletes take them willingly. The drugs themselves are used in smaller doses and in creative combinations, leaving few telltale physical signs, and drug testers concede that it is virtually impossible to catch all the cheaters, or even, at times, to do much more than guess when cheating is taking place. Among the athletes, meanwhile, there is growing uncertainty about what exactly is wrong with doping. When the cyclist Lance Armstrong asserted last year, after his second consecutive Tour de France victory, that he was drug-free, some doubters wondered whether he was lying, and others simply assumed he was, and wondered why he had to. The moral clarity of the East German scandal—with its coercive coaches, damaged athletes, and corrupted competitions—has given way to shades of gray. In today's climate, the most telling moment of the East German scandal was not Knacke-Sommer's outburst. It was when one of the system's former top officials, at the beginning of his trial, shrugged and quoted Brecht: "Competitive sport begins where healthy sport ends."

2.

6   Perhaps the best example of how murky the drug issue has become is the case of Ben Johnson, the Canadian sprinter who won the one hundred metres at the Seoul Olympics, in 1988. Johnson set a new world record, then failed a post-race drug test and was promptly stripped of his gold medal and suspended from international competition. No athlete of Johnson's calibre has ever been exposed so dramatically, but his disgrace was not quite the victory for clean competition that it appeared to be.

7   Johnson was part of a group of world-class sprinters based in Toronto in the nineteen-seventies and eighties and trained by a brilliant coach named Charlie Francis. Francis was driven and ambitious, eager to give his athletes the same opportunities as their competitors from the United States and Eastern Europe; and in 1979 he began discussing steroids with one of his prize sprinters, Angella Taylor. Francis felt that Taylor had the potential that year to run the two hundred metres in close to 22.90 seconds, a time that would put her within striking distance of the two best sprinters in the world, Evelyn Ashford, of the United States, and Marita Koch, of East Germany. But, seemingly out of nowhere, Ashford suddenly improved her two-hundred-metre time by six-tenths of a second. Then Koch ran what Francis calls, in his autobiography, *Speed Trap*, a "science fictional" 21.71. In the sprints, individual improvements are usually measured in hundredths of a second; athletes, once they have reached their early twenties, typically improve their performance in small, steady increments, as experieınce and strength increase. But these were quan-

tum leaps, and to Francis the explanation was obvious. "Angella wasn't losing ground because of a talent gap," he writes, "she was losing because of a drug gap, and it was widening by the day." (In the case of Koch, at least, he was right. In the East German archives, investigators found a letter from Koch to the director of research at VEB Jenapharm, an East German pharmaceutical house, in which she complained, "My drugs were not as potent as the ones that were given to my opponent Brbel Eckert, who kept beating me." In East Germany, Ungerleider writes, this particular complaint was known as "dope-envy.") Later, Francis says, he was confronted at a track meet by Brian Oldfield, then one of the world's best shot-putters:

8   "When are you going to start getting serious?" he demanded. "When are you going to tell your guys the facts of life?" I asked him how he could tell they weren't already using steroids. He replied that the muscle density just wasn't there. "Your guys will never be able to compete against the Americans—their careers will be over," he persisted.

9   Among world-class athletes, the lure of steroids is not that they magically transform performance—no drug can do that—but that they make it possible to train harder. An aging baseball star, for instance, may realize that what he needs to hit a lot more home runs is to double the intensity of his weight training. Ordinarily, this might actually hurt his performance. "When you're under that kind of physical stress," Charles Yesalis, an epidemiologist at Pennsylvania State University, says, "your body releases corticosteroids, and when your body starts making those hormones at inappropriate times it blocks testosterone. And instead of being anabolic—instead of building muscle—corticosteroids are catabolic. They break down muscle. That's clearly something an athlete doesn't want." Taking steroids counteracts the impact of corticosteroids and helps the body bounce back faster. If that home-run hitter was taking testosterone or an anabolic steroid, he'd have a better chance of handling the extra weight training.

10   It was this extra training that Francis and his sprinters felt they needed to reach the top. Angella Taylor was the first to start taking steroids. Ben Johnson followed in 1981, when he was twenty years old, beginning with a daily dose of five milligrams of the steroid Dianabol, in three-week on-and-off cycles. Over time, that protocol grew more complex. In 1984, Taylor visited a Los Angeles doctor, Robert Kerr, who was famous for his willingness to provide athletes with pharmacological assistance. He suggested that the Canadians use human growth hormone, the pituitary extract that promotes lean muscle and that had become, in Francis's words, "the rage in elite track circles." Kerr also recommended three additional substances, all of which were believed to promote the body's production of growth hormone: the amino acids arginine and ornithine and the dopamine precursor L-dopa. "I would later learn," Francis writes, "that one group of American women was using three times as much growth hormone as Kerr had suggested, in addition to 15 milligrams per day of Dianabol, another 15 milligrams of Anavar, large amounts of testosterone, and thyroxine, the synthetic thyroid hormone used by athletes to speed the metabolism and

keep people lean." But the Canadians stuck to their initial regimen, making only a few changes: Vitamin B$_{12}$, a non-steroidal muscle builder called inosine, and occasional shots of testosterone were added; Dianabol was dropped in favor of a newer steroid called Furazabol; and L-dopa, which turned out to cause stiffness, was replaced with the blood-pressure drug Dixarit.

11   Going into the Seoul Olympics, then, Johnson was a walking pharmacy. But—and this is the great irony of his case—none of the drugs that were part of his formal pharmaceutical protocol resulted in his failed drug test. He had already reaped the benefit of the steroids in intense workouts leading up to the games, and had stopped Furazabol and testosterone long enough in advance that all traces of both supplements should have disappeared from his system by the time of his race—a process he sped up by taking the diuretic Moduret. Human growth hormone wasn't—and still isn't—detectable by a drug test, and arginine, ornithine, and Dixarit were legal. Johnson should have been clean. The most striking (and unintentionally hilarious) moment in *Speed Trap* comes when Francis describes his bewilderment at being informed that his star runner had failed a drug test—for the anabolic steroid stanozolol. "I was floored," Francis writes:

> To my knowledge, Ben had never injected stanozolol. He occasionally used Winstrol, an oral version of the drug, but for no more than a few days at a time, since it tended to make him stiff. He'd always discontinued the tablets at least six weeks before a meet, well beyond the accepted "clearance time."... After seven years of using steroids, Ben knew what he was doing. It was inconceivable to me that he might take stanozolol on his own and jeopardize the most important race of his life.

12   Francis suggests that Johnson's urine sample might have been deliberately contaminated by a rival, a charge that is less preposterous than it sounds. Documents from the East German archive show, for example, that in international competitions security was so lax that urine samples were sometimes switched, stolen from a "clean" athlete, or simply "borrowed" from a noncompetitor. "The pure urine would either be infused by a catheter into the competitor's bladder (a rather painful procedure) or be held in condoms until it was time to give a specimen to the drug control lab," Ungerleider writes. (The top East German sports official Manfred Höppner was once in charge of urine samples at an international weight-lifting competition. When he realized that several of his weight lifters would not pass the test, he broke open the seal of their specimens, poured out the contents, and, Ungerleider notes, "took a nice long leak of pure urine into them.") It is also possible that Johnson's test was simply botched. Two years later, in 1990, track and field's governing body claimed that Butch Reynolds, the world's four-hundred-metre record holder, had tested positive for the steroid nandrolone, and suspended him for two years. It did so despite the fact that half of his urine-sample data had been misplaced, that the testing equipment had failed during analysis of the other half of his sample, and that the lab technician who did the test identified

Sample H6 as positive—and Reynolds's sample was numbered H5. Reynolds lost the prime years of his career.

13   We may never know what really happened with Johnson's assay, and perhaps it doesn't much matter. He was a doper. But clearly this was something less than a victory for drug enforcement. Here was a man using human growth hormone, Dixarit, inosine, testosterone, and Furazabol, and the only substance that the testers could find in him was stanozolol—which may have been the only illegal drug that he hadn't used. Nor is it encouraging that Johnson was the only prominent athlete caught for drug use in Seoul. It is hard to believe, for instance, that the sprinter Florence Griffith Joyner, the star of the Seoul games, was clean. Before 1988, her best times in the hundred metres and the two hundred metres were, respectively, 10.96 and 21.96. In 1988, a suddenly huskier FloJo ran 10.49 and 21.34, times that no runner since has even come close to equalling. In other words, at the age of twenty-eight—when most athletes are beginning their decline—Griffith Joyner transformed herself in one season from a career-long better-than-average sprinter to the fastest female sprinter in history. Of course, FloJo never failed a drug test. But what does that prove? FloJo went on to make a fortune as a corporate spokeswoman. Johnson's suspension cost him an estimated $25 million in lost endorsements. The real lesson of the Seoul Olympics may simply have been that Johnson was a very unlucky man.

3.

14   The basic problem with drug testing is that testers are always one step behind athletes. It can take years for sports authorities to figure out what drugs athletes are using, and even longer to devise effective means of detecting them. Anabolic steroids weren't banned by the international Olympic Committee until 1975, almost a decade after the East Germans started using them. In 1996, at the Atlanta Olympics, five athletes tested positive for what we now know to be the drug Bromantan, but they weren't suspended, because no one knew at the time what Bromantan was. (It turned out to be a Russian-made psychostimulant.) Human growth hormone, meanwhile, has been around for twenty years, and testers still haven't figured out how to detect it.

15   Perhaps the best example of the difficulties of drug testing is testosterone. It has been used by athletes to enhance performance since the fifties, and the International Olympic Committee announced that it would crack down on testosterone supplements in the early eighties. This didn't mean that the I.O.C. was going to test for testosterone directly, though, because the testosterone that athletes were getting from a needle or a pill was largely indistinguishable from the testosterone they produce naturally. What was proposed, instead, was to compare the level of testosterone in urine with the level of another hormone, epitestosterone, to determine what's called the T/E ratio. For most people, under normal circumstances, that ratio is 1:1, and so the theory was that if testers found a lot more testosterone than epitestosterone it would be a sign that the athlete was cheating. Since a small number of people

have naturally high levels of testosterone, the I.O.C. avoided the risk of falsely accusing anyone by setting the legal limit at 6:1.

16   Did this stop testosterone use? Not at all. Through much of the eighties and nineties, most sports organizations conducted their drug testing only at major competitions. Athletes taking testosterone would simply do what Johnson did, and taper off their use in the days or weeks prior to those events. So sports authorities began randomly showing up at athletes' houses or training sites and demanding urine samples. To this, dopers responded by taking extra doses of epitestosterone with their testosterone, so their T/E would remain in balance. Testers, in turn, began treating elevated epitestosterone levels as suspicious, too. But that still left athletes with the claim that they were among the few with naturally elevated testosterone. Testers, then, were forced to take multiple urine samples, measuring an athlete's T/E ratio over several weeks. Someone with a naturally elevated T/E ratio will have fairly consistent ratios from week to week. Someone who is doping will have telltale spikes—times immediately after taking shots or pills when the level of the hormone in his blood soars. Did all these precautions mean that cheating stopped? Of course not. Athletes have now switched from injection to transdermal testosterone patches, which administer a continuous low-level dose of the hormone, smoothing over the old, incriminating spikes. The patch has another advantage; once you take it off, your testosterone level will drop rapidly, returning to normal, depending on the dose and the person, in as little as an hour. "It's the peaks that get you caught," says Don Catlin, who runs the U.C.L.A. Olympic Analytical Laboratory. "If you took a pill this morning and an unannounced test comes this afternoon, you'd better have a bottle of epitestosterone handy. But, if you are on the patch and you know your own pharmacokinetics, all you have to do is pull it off." In other words, if you know how long it takes for you to get back under the legal limit and successfully stall the test for that period, you can probably pass the test. And if you don't want to take that chance, you can just keep your testosterone below 6:1, which, by the way, still provides a whopping performance benefit. "The bottom line is that only careless and stupid people ever get caught in drug tests," Charles Yesalis says. "The elite athletes can hire top medical and scientific people to make sure nothing bad happens, and you can't catch them."

4.

17 But here is where the doping issue starts to get complicated, for there's a case to be made that what looks like failure really isn't—that regulating aggressive doping, the way the 6:1 standard does, is a better idea than trying to prohibit drug use. Take the example of erythropoietin, or EPO. EPO is a hormone released by your kidneys that stimulates the production of red blood cells, the body's oxygen carriers. A man-made version of the hormone is given to those with suppressed red-blood-cell counts, like patients undergoing kidney dialysis or chemotherapy. But over the past decade it has also become the drug of choice for endurance athletes, because its ability to increase the amount of

oxygen that the blood can carry to the muscles has the effect of postponing fatigue. "The studies that have attempted to estimate EPO's importance say it's worth about a three-, four-, or five-per-cent advantage, which is huge," Catlin says. EPO also has the advantage of being a copy of a naturally occurring substance, so it's very hard to tell if someone has been injecting it. (A cynic would say that this had something to do with the spate of remarkable times in endurance races during that period.)

18 So how should we test for EPO? One approach, which was used in the late nineties by the International Cycling Union, is a test much like the T/E ratio for testosterone. The percentage of your total blood volume which is taken up by red blood cells is known as your hematocrit. The average adult male has a hematocrit of between thirty-eight and forty-four per cent. Since 1995, the cycling authorities have declared that any rider who had a hematocrit above fifty per cent would be suspended—a deliberately generous standard (like the T/E ratio) meant to avoid falsely accusing someone with a naturally high hematocrit. The hematocrit rule also had the benefit of protecting athletes' health. If you take too much EPO, the profusion of red blood cells makes the blood sluggish and heavy, placing enormous stress on the heart. In the late eighties, at least fifteen professional cyclists died from suspected EPO overdoses. A fifty-per-cent hematocrit limit is below the point at which EPO becomes dangerous.

19 But, like the T/E standard, the hematocrit standard had a perverse effect: it set the legal limit so high that it actually encouraged cyclists to titrate their drug use up to the legal limit. After all, if you are riding for three weeks through the mountains of France and Spain, there's a big difference between a hematocrit of forty-four per cent and one of 49.9 per cent. This is why Lance Armstrong faced so many hostile questions about EPO from the European press—and why eyebrows were raised at his five-year relationship with an Italian doctor who was thought to be an expert on performance enhancing drugs. If Armstrong had, say, a hematocrit of forty-four per cent, the thinking went, why wouldn't he have raised it to 49.9, particularly since the rules (at least, in 2000) implicitly allowed him to do so. And, if he didn't, how on earth did he win?

20 The problems with hematocrit testing have inspired a second strategy, which was used on a limited basis at the Sydney Olympics and this summer's World Track and Field Championships. This test measures a number of physiological markers of EPO use, including the presence of reticulocytes, which are the immature red blood cells produced in large numbers by EPO injections. If you have a lot more reticulocytes than normal, then there's a good chance you've used EPO recently. The blood work is followed by a confirmatory urinalysis. The test has its weaknesses. It's really only useful in picking up EPO used in the previous week or so, whereas the benefits of taking the substance persist for a month. But there's no question that, if random EPO testing were done aggressively in the weeks leading to a major competition, it would substantially reduce cheating.

21   On paper, this second strategy sounds like a better system. But there's a perverse effect here as well. By discouraging EPO use, the test is simply pushing savvy athletes toward synthetic compounds called hemoglobin-based oxygen carriers, which serve much the same purpose as EPO but for which there is no test at the moment. "I recently read off a list of these new blood-oxygen expanders to a group of toxicologists, and none had heard of any of them," Yesalis says. "That's how fast things are moving." The attempt to prevent EPO use actually promotes inequity: it gives an enormous advantage to those athletes with the means to keep up with the next wave of pharmacology. By contrast, the hematocrit limit, though more permissive, creates a kind of pharmaceutical parity. The same is true of the T/E limit. At the 1986 world swimming championships, the East German Kristin Otto set a world record in the hundred-metre freestyle, with an extraordinary display of power in the final leg of the race. According to East German records, on the day of her race Otto had a T/E ratio of 18:1. Testing can prevent that kind of aggressive doping; it can insure no one goes above 6:1. That is a less than perfect outcome, of course, but international sports is not a perfect world. It is a place where Ben Johnson is disgraced and FloJo runs free, where Butch Reynolds is barred for two years and East German coaches pee into cups—and where athletes without access to the cutting edge of medicine are condemned to second place. Since drug testers cannot protect the purity of sport, the very least they can do is to make sure that no athlete can cheat more than any other.

5.

22   The first man to break the four-minute mile was the Englishman Roger Bannister, on a windswept cinder track at Oxford, nearly fifty years ago. Bannister is in his early seventies now, and one day last summer he returned to the site of his historic race along with the current world-record holder in the mile, Morocco's Hicham El Guerrouj. The two men chatted and compared notes and posed for photographs. "I feel as if I am looking at my mirror image," Bannister said, indicating El Guerrouj's similarly tall, high-waisted frame. It was a polite gesture, an attempt to suggest that he and El Guerrouj were part of the same athletic lineage. But, as both men surely knew, nothing could be further from the truth.

23   Bannister was a medical student when he broke the four-minute mile in 1954. He did not have time to train every day, and when he did he squeezed in his running on his hour-long midday break at the hospital. He had no coach or trainer or entourage, only a group of running partners who called themselves "the Paddington lunch time club." In a typical workout, they might run ten consecutive quarter miles—ten laps—with perhaps two minutes of recovery between each repetition, then gobble down lunch and hurry back to work. Today, that training session would be considered barely adequate for a high-school miler. A month or so before his historic mile, Bannister took a few days off to go hiking in Scotland. Five days before he broke the four-minute barrier, he stopped running entirely, in order to rest. The day before

the race, he slipped and fell on his hip while working in the hospital. Then he ran the most famous race in the history of track and field. Bannister was what runners admiringly call an "animal," a natural.

24   El Guerrouj, by contrast, trains five hours a day, in two two-and-a-half-hour sessions. He probably has a team of half a dozen people working with him; at the very least, a masseur, a doctor, a coach, an agent, and a nutritionist. He is not in medical school. He does not go hiking in rocky terrain before major track meets. When Bannister told him, last summer, how he had prepared for his four-minute mile, El Guerrouj was stunned. "For me, a rest day is perhaps when I train in the morning and spend the afternoon at the cinema," he said. El Guerrouj certainly has more than his share of natural ability, but his achievements are a reflection of much more than that: of the fact that he is better coached and better prepared than his opponents, that he trains harder and more intelligently, that he has found a way to stay injury free, and that he can recover so quickly from one day of five-hour workouts that he can follow it, the next day, with another five-hour workout.

25   Of these two paradigms, we have always been much more comfortable with the first: we want the relation between talent and achievement to be transparent, and we worry about the way ability is now so aggressively managed and augmented. Steroids bother us because they violate the honesty of effort: they permit an athlete to train too hard, beyond what seems reasonable. EPO fails the same test. For years, athletes underwent high-altitude training sessions, which had the same effect as EPO—promoting the manufacture of additional red blood cells. This was considered acceptable, while EPO is not, because we like to distinguish between those advantages which are natural or earned and those which come out of a vial.

26   Even as we assert this distinction on the playing field, though, we defy it in our own lives. We have come to prefer a world where the distractable take Ritalin, the depressed take Prozac, and the unattractive get cosmetic surgery to a world ruled, arbitrarily, by those fortunate few who were born focused, happy, and beautiful. Cosmetic surgery is not "earned" beauty, but then natural beauty isn't earned, either. One of the principal contributions of the late twentieth century was the moral deregulation of social competition—the insistence that advantages derived from artificial and extraordinary intervention are no less legitimate than the advantages of nature. All that athletes want, for better or worse, is the chance to play by those same rules. ■

Michael Bérubé

Citizenship and Disability

Michael Bérubé teaches literature and disability studies at Penn State University. Included in David Horowitz's book The Professors: The 101 Most Dangerous Academics in America, *Bérubé nevertheless remains passionately engaged with issues such as academic freedom, student and faculty rights and responsibilities, disabilities, and sports. In addition to his political blogging and service for the American Association of University Professors, Bérubé publishes prolifically in the* New York Times, *the* Washington Post, *the* Chronicle of Higher Education, Dissent, *the* Nation, *and the* New Yorker. *His book* Life As We Know It: A Father, a Family, and an Exceptional Child *was acclaimed when it appeared in 1996. More recently he has published* What's Liberal about the Liberal Arts?

I n the six years since I published a book about my son Jamie, *Life As We Know It*, a great deal has changed in Jamie's life—starting with his realization that there is a book about him. When I completed the book Jamie was only four, and had not yet entered the public K–12 system. But I did not stop serving as Jamie's recorder and public representative when I finished that book: I still represent him all the time, to school officials, camp counselors, babysitters and friends, to academic audiences, and to Down Syndrome Associations. I take it as one of my tasks to watch for important things he's never done before, as a way of charting and understanding the irreplaceable and irreducible little person he is, especially as he gets less and less little, and more and more capable of representing himself.

2 Jamie is now in his sixth year of school, having entered kindergarten in 1997–1998. In the intervening years he has not continued to perform at grade level (he is repeating fourth grade, at age eleven), and he has occasionally presented his schoolmates with some eccentric behavior. On the other hand, he has learned to read, to do two- and three-digit addition and subtraction, to multiply two-digit numbers, and most recently to do division by single numbers, with and without remainders. My wife, Janet, and I did not teach him these things, but the minute it became clear that he could do them in school, we picked up the ball and ran with it. We've tried to make every available use of his startlingly prodigious memory, and we've learned that when he tells us that such and such bird is not a parrot but is instead a scarlet macaw, he's usually right. He has some idiosyncrasies that do not serve him well in school or in testing situations: at one point he memorized the numbers on the wrong side of his flash cards, the serial numbers that indicate each card's place in the deck. He likes to pretend that he does not know left from right, referring instead (with perverse delight) to his "left foot" and his "other foot." He is a stubborn ignatz, as people find whenever they try to get him to do something he has no interest in, or whenever his teachers or aides try to make him move from one task to another. For a while he tried to put off unpleasant tasks by telling his teachers or therapists, "Let's do that tomorrow"; before long he realized that this didn't work, and began saying instead, "We did that yesterday"— a ruse with which he has had some success.

3 His conversational skills are steadily improving, but unless you're talking to him about one of the movies he's seen or one of the routines he's developed at school or at home, you'll find that his sense of the world is sometimes unintelligible, sometimes merely a bit awry. He recently received an invitation to a classmate's birthday party (his third such invitation since we

moved to central Pennsylvania sixteen months ago: we count and cherish each one), and Janet asked him what the birthday boy looked like: "he's a small boy," said Jamie, holding his hand around his shoulder level.

4   "What color is his hair?" she asked.

5   "Black," Jamie replied.

6   "What color are his eyes?"

7   "Blue."

8   "Does he wear glasses?" (Jamie has worn glasses for about five years.)

9   "No," Jamie said, "just eyes."

10   But then, Janet and I did not expect him to be able to describe his classmates at all. Nor did we expect him to be so talented a mimic; he can imitate both of us, just as he can imitate break dancers and gymnasts and snakes and lemurs. We did not expect him to be able to do multiplication or division; we did not expect him to open books and ask us to "read and tell all the things"; we did not expect him to be able to ask us "why" questions, as when he asked me why I could not leave him alone in a hotel room while I went to park the car. We did not expect him to win a spelling award in second grade for maintaining an average above 90 on his spelling tests for the year. We did not expect him to be designated by his classmates in third grade as the kid with the best sense of humor.

11   Over eleven years, then, we've come to expect that Jamie will defeat or exceed our expectations when we least expect him to. And from this I draw two points. One, he's a child. Two, and this is a somewhat more elaborate conclusion, although it can be derived from point one: it might be a good idea for all of us to treat other humans as if we do not know their potential, as if they just might in fact surprise us, as if they might defeat or exceed our expectations. It might be a good idea for us to check the history of the past two centuries whenever we think we know what "normal" human standards of behavior and achievement might be. And it might be a very good idea for us to expand the possibilities of democracy precisely because democracy offers us unfinished and infinitely revisable forms of political organization that stand the best chance, in the long run, of responding adequately to the human rights of the unpredictable creatures we humans are. That might be one way of recognizing and respecting something you might want to call our human dignity.

12   Jamie is, of course, one reason why I am drawn to the question of disability rights and their relation to democracy: every morning I take him to school, I know how very fortunate he is to be living under a social dispensation that entitles him to a public education alongside his nondisabled peers. But beyond my immediate interest in forwarding Jamie's interests, I want to argue that disability issues are—or should be—central to theories of social justice in a much broader sense. Nancy Fraser's account of the "politics of recognition" and the "politics of redistribution" (*Adding Insult to Injury: Social Justice and the Politics of Recognition*), for example, offers a theory that tries to accommodate what were the two major strands of American progressive-left thought in the 1990s, multiculturalism and democratic socialism (in all their varieties)—or what Richard Rorty, in *Achieving Our Country*, termed the

"cultural left" and the "reformist left," the former concerned primarily with combating social stigma and the latter concerned primarily with combating greed. Fraser has shown convincingly that the politics of recognition and re-distribution offer a productive way to think about feminism: cultural politics with regard to body images or sexual harassment, for example, are not to be understood as distractions from "real" politics that address comparative worth or the minimum wage. Rather, recognition politics have consequences for the redistribution of social goods and resources even though they cannot be re-duced to their redistributive effects. And since many left intellectuals in the 1990s were all too willing to think of politics as a zero-sum game in which any attention paid to multiculturalism had to come at the expense of democratic socialism and vice versa, Fraser's work seems to offer a way for the left to cham-pion a progressive tax code and an end to racial profiling at the same time.

13   It is striking, nonetheless, that so few leftists have understood disability in these terms. Disability is not the only area of social life in which the politics of recognition are inseparable from the politics of redistribution; other mat-ters central to citizenship, such as immigration, reproductive rights, and crim-inal justice, are every bit as complex. Nonetheless, our society's representations of disability are intricately tied to, and sometimes the very basis for, our public policies for "administering" disability. And when we contemplate, in these terms, the history of people with cognitive and developmental disabilities, we find a history in which "representation" takes on a double valence: first, in that people who were deemed incapable of representing themselves were therefore represented by a socio-medical apparatus that defined—or, in a social-constructionist sense, created—the category of "feeblemindedness"; and second, in the sense that the visual and rhetorical representations of "feeble-minded" persons then set the terms for public policy. One cannot plausibly narrate a comprehensive history of ideas and practices of national citizenship in the post–Civil War United States without examining public policy regarding disability, especially mental disability, all the more especially when mental disability was then mapped onto certain immigrant populations who scored poorly on intelligence tests and were thereby pseudo-scientifically linked to criminality. And what of reproductive rights? By 1927, the spurious but power-ful linkages among disability, immigration, poverty, and criminality provided the Supreme Court with sufficient justification for declaring involuntary ster-ilization legal under the Constitution.

14   There is an obvious reason why disability rights are so rarely thought of in terms of civil rights: disability was not covered in the Civil Rights Act of 1964. And as Anita Silvers points out, over the next twenty-five years, groups covered by civil rights law sometimes saw disability rights as a dilution of civil rights, on the grounds that people with disabilities were constitutively incom-petent, whereas women and minorities faced discrimination merely on the basis of social prejudice. Silvers writes, "[t]o make disability a category that activates a heightened legal shield against exclusion, it was objected, would alter the purpose of legal protection for civil rights by transforming the goal

from protecting opportunity for socially exploited people to providing assistance for naturally unfit people." The passage of the Americans with Disabilities Act (ADA) in 1990 did add disability to the list of stigmatized identities covered by antidiscrimination law, but thus far the ADA has been interpreted so narrowly, and by such a business-friendly judiciary, that employers have won over 95 percent of the suits brought under the act.

15   Perhaps if plaintiffs with disabilities had won a greater number of cases over the past thirteen years, the conservative backlash against the ADA—currently confined to a few cranks complaining about handicapped parking spaces and a wheelchair ramp at a Florida nude beach—would be sufficiently strong as to spark a movement to repeal the law altogether. But then again, perhaps if the law were read more broadly, more Americans would realize their potential stake in it. In 1999, for instance, the Supreme Court ruled on three lower-court cases in which people with "easily correctable" disabilities—high blood pressure, nearsightedness—were denied employment. In three identical 7-2 decisions, the Court found that the plaintiffs had no basis for a suit under the ADA precisely *because* their disabilities were easily correctable. As disability activists and legal analysts quickly pointed out, this decision left these plaintiffs in the ridiculous situation of being too disabled to be hired but somehow not disabled enough to be covered by the ADA; or, to put this another way, plaintiffs' "easily correctable" disabilities were not so easily correctable as to allow them access to employment. One case involved twin sisters who were denied the opportunity to test as pilots for United Airlines on the grounds that their eyesight did not meet United's minimum vision requirement (uncorrected visual acuity of 20/100 or better without glasses or contacts) even though each sister had 20/20 vision with corrective lenses (*Sutton v. United Airlines, Inc.*); another involved a driver/mechanic with high blood pressure (*Murphy v. United Parcel Service*); the third involved a truck driver with monocular vision (20/200 in one eye) who in 1992 had received a Department of Transportation waiver of the requirement that truck drivers have distant visual acuity of 20/40 in each eye as well as distant binocular acuity of 20/40 (*Albertson's, Inc. v. Kirkingburg*). Because, as Silvers argues, "litigation under the ADA commonly turns on questions of classification rather than access," all three plaintiffs were determined to have no standing under the law. The question of whether any of them was justly denied employment was simply not addressed by the Court. Indeed, in writing her opinion for the majority, Justice Sandra Day O'Connor explicitly refused to consider the wider question of "access," noting that 160 million Americans would be covered by the ADA if it were construed to include people with "easily correctible" disabilities (under a "health conditions approach"), and since Congress had cited the number 43 million in enacting the law, Congress clearly could not have intended the law to be applied more widely. "Had Congress intended to include all persons with corrected physical limitations among those covered by the Act, it undoubtedly would have cited a much higher number of disabled persons in the findings," wrote O'Connor. "That it did not is evidence that the ADA's coverage is restricted to only those whose impairments are not mitigated by corrective measures."

16   It is possible to object that O'Connor's decision was excessively literal-ist, and that the potential number of Americans covered by the ADA is, in any case, quite irrelevant to the question of whether a woman can fly a plane when she's got her glasses on. But I've since come to believe that the literalism of the decision is an indirect acknowledgment of how broad the issues at stake here really are. If the ADA were understood as a broad civil rights law, and if it were understood as a law that potentially pertains to the entire population of the country, then maybe disability law would be understood not as a fringe addition to civil rights law but as its very fulfillment.

17   Rights can be created, reinterpreted, extended, and revoked. The pas-sage of the ADA should therefore be seen as an extension of the promise of democracy, but only as a promise: any realization of the potential of the law depends on its continual reinterpretation. For the meaning of the word, just as Wittgenstein wanted us to believe (in order that we might be undeceived about how our words work), lies in its use in the language. Similarly, the In-dividuals with Disabilities Education Act of 1975 (originally the Education for All Handicapped Children Act) was not some kind of breakthrough discovery whereby children with disabilities were found to be rights-bearing citizens of the United States after all, and who knew that we'd had it all wrong for 199 years? On the contrary, the IDEA invented a new right for children with disabilities, the right to a "free and appropriate public education in the least restrictive environment." And yet the IDEA did not wish that right into being overnight; the key terms "appropriate" and "least restrictive" had to be inter-preted time and again, over the course of fifteen years, before they were understood to authorize "full inclusion" of children with disabilities in "reg-ular" classrooms. Nothing about the law is set in stone. The only philosophi-cal "foundation" underlying the IDEA and its various realizations is our own collective political will, a will that is tested and tested again every time the Act comes up for reauthorization. Jamie Bérubé currently has a right to an inclusive public education, but that right is neither intrinsic nor innate. Rather, Jamie's rights were invented, and implemented slowly and with great difficulty. The recognition of his human dignity, enshrined in those rights, was invented. And by the same token, those rights, and that recognition, can be taken away. While I live, I promise myself that I will not let that happen, but I live with the knowledge that it may: to live any other way, to live as if Jamie's rights were somehow intrinsic, would be irresponsible.

18   Of course, many of us would prefer to believe that our children have intrinsic human rights and human dignity no matter what; irrespective of any form of human social organization; regardless of whether they were born in twentieth-century Illinois or second-century Rome or seventh-century central Asia. But this is just a parent's—or a philosophical foundationalist's—wishful thinking. For what would it mean for Jamie to "possess" rights that no one on earth recognized? A fat lot of good it would do him. My argument may sound either monstrous or all too obvious: if, in fact, no one on earth recognized Jamie's human dignity, then there would in fact be no human perspective

from which he would be understood to possess "intrinsic" human dignity. And then he wouldn't have it, and so much the worse for the human race.

19   In one respect, the promise of the IDEA, like the promise of the ADA, is clear: greater inclusion of people with disabilities in the social worlds of school and work. But in another sense the promise is unspecifiable; its content is something we actually cannot know in advance. For the IDEA does not merely guarantee all children with disabilities a free appropriate public education in the least restrictive environment. Even more than this, it grants the right to education in order that persons with disabilities might make the greatest possible use of their other rights—the ones having to do with voting, or employment discrimination, or with life, liberty, and the pursuit of happiness.

20   IDEA is thus designed to enhance the capabilities of all American children with disabilities regardless of their actual abilities—and this is why it is so profound a democratic idea. Here again I'm drawing on Nancy Fraser, whose theory of democracy involves the idea of "participatory parity," and the imperative that a democratic state should actively foster the abilities of its citizens to participate in the life of the polity as equals. Fraser's work to date has not addressed disability, but as I noted above, it should be easy to see how disability is relevant to Fraser's account of the politics of recognition and the politics of redistribution. This time, however, I want to press the point a bit harder. Fraser writes as if the promise of democracy entails the promise to enhance participatory parity among citizens, which it does, and she writes as if we knew what "participatory parity" itself means, which we don't. (This is why the promise of disability rights is unspecifiable.)

21   Let me explain. First, the idea of participatory parity does double duty in Fraser's work, in the sense that it names both the state we would like to achieve and the device by which we can gauge whether we're getting there. For in order to maintain a meaningful democracy in which all citizens participate as legal and moral equals, the state needs to judge whether its policies enhance equal participation in democratic processes. Yet at the same time, the state needs to enhance equal participation among its citizens simply in order to determine what its democratic processes will be. This is not a meta-theoretical quibble. On the contrary, the point is central to the practical workings of any democratic polity. One of the tasks required of democrats is precisely this: to extend the promise of democracy to previously excluded individuals and groups some of whom might have a substantially different understanding of "participatory parity" than that held by previously dominant groups and individuals.

22   Could anything make this clearer than the politics of disability? Imagine a building in which political philosophers are debating, in the wake of the attacks of September 11, 2001, the value and the purpose of participatory parity over against forms of authoritarianism or theocracy. Now imagine that this building has no access ramps, no Braille or large-print publications, no American Sign Language interpreters, no elevators, no special-needs paraprofessionals, no in-class aides. Contradictory as such a state of affairs may sound, it's a reasonably accurate picture of what contemporary debate over the meaning of

democracy actually looks like. How can we remedy this? Only when we have fostered equal participation in debates over the ends and means of democracy can we have a truly participatory debate over what "participatory parity" itself means. That debate will be interminable in principle, since our understandings of democracy and parity are infinitely revisable, but lest we think of deliberative democracy as a forensic society dedicated to empyreal reaches of abstraction, we should remember that debates over the meaning of participatory parity set the terms for more specific debates about the varieties of human embodiment. These include debates about prenatal screening, genetic discrimination, stem-cell research, euthanasia, and, with regard to physical access, ramps, curb cuts, kneeling buses, and buildings employing what is now known as universal design.

Barry Blitt's art has appeared in many publications, including the *New York Times, Entertainment Weekly,* the *Chicago Tribune,* and the *New Yorker,* which published this art on its March 26, 2007, cover. Blitt comments on the inaccessibility of many spaces for individuals with physical disabilities—in this case, a soldier who has returned wounded from the war in Iraq.

23   Leftists and liberals, particularly those associated with university humanities departments, are commonly charged with being moral relativists, unable or unwilling to say (even after September 11) why one society might be "better" than another. So let me be especially clear on this final point. I think there's a very good reason to extend the franchise, to widen the conversation, to democratize our debates, and to make disability central to our theories of egalitarian social justice. The reason is this: a capacious and supple sense of what it is to be human is better than a narrow and partial sense of what it is to be human, and the more participants we as a society can incorporate into the deliberation of what it means to be human, the greater the chances that that deliberation will in fact be transformative in such a way as to enhance our collective capacities to recognize each other as humans entitled to human dignity. As Jamie reminds me daily, both deliberately and unwittingly, most Americans had no idea what people with Down syndrome could achieve until we'd passed and implemented and interpreted and reinterpreted a law entitling them all to a free appropriate public education in the least restrictive environment. I can say all this without appealing to any innate justification for human dignity and human rights, and I can also say this: Without a sufficient theoretical and practical account of disability, we can have no account of democracy worthy of the name.

24   Perhaps some of our fellow citizens with developmental disabilities would not put the argument quite this way; even though Jamie has led me to think this way, he doesn't talk the way I do. But those of us who do participate in political debates, whether about school funding in a specific district or about the theory and practice of democracy at its most abstract, have the obligation to enhance the abilities of our children and our fellow citizens with disabilities to participate in the life of the United States as political and moral equals with their nondisabled peers—both for their own good, and for the good of democracy, which is to say, for the good of all of us. ■

Terrence Rafferty

Kate Winslet, Please Save Us!

Brooklyn native Terrence Rafferty is a film critic whose articles have appeared in the Atlantic, *the* Village Voice, Film Quarterly, *the* New York Times, *and many other publications. He also has been the "critic-at-large" for* GQ *(short for* Gentleman's Quarterly*), a fashion and culture magazine geared to young professional men. GQ carried the following argument in May 2001. Do you think the argument would have been constructed differently if it had been published elsewhere?*

When I go to the movies these days, I sometimes find myself gripped by a very peculiar sort of nostalgia: I miss flesh. I see skin, I see bones, I see many rocklike outcroppings of muscle, but I rarely see, in the

angular bodies up there on the screen—
either the hard, sculpted ones or the brittle,
anorexic ones—anything *extra*, not even a
hint of the soft layer of fatty tissue that was
once an essential component of the movies'
romantic fantasy, the cushion that made
encounters between the sexes seem like
pleasant, sensual experiences rather than
teeth-rattling head-on collisions. The sleek
form-follows-function physiques of today's
film stars suggest a world in which power
and brutal efficiency are all that matter, in
the bedroom no less than in the pitiless, sun-
seared arena of *Gladiator*. This may well be an
accurate reflection of our anxious time, but
it's also mighty depressing. When I come out
of the multiplex now, I often feel like the

Kate Moss, waiflike

archetypal ninety-eight-pound weakling in the old Charles Atlas ads—like big bul-
lies have been kicking sand in my face for two hours. And that's just the women.

2   This is a touchy area, I realize. Where body type is concerned, an amazingly high percentage of social and cultural commentary is fueled by simple
envy, resentment of the young and the buff. A few years ago, when Calvin Klein
ads featuring the stunning, waiflike Kate Moss appeared on the sides of New
York City buses, they were routinely defaced with bitter-sounding graffiti—
FEED ME was the most popular—which was, you had to suspect, largely the
product of women who were enraged by her distinctive beauty. (Men, to my
knowledge, had few complaints about having to see Moss in her underwear
whiz past them on Madison Avenue.) Protesters insisted that images such as
those in the Klein ads promote eating disorders in impressionable teenage girls.
Maybe that's so—I don't have the statistics—but the sheer violence of the attacks on Moss, along with the fact that they seemed to be directed more at the
model herself than at the marketing wizards who exploited her, strongly suggested another, less virtuous agenda. The taste of sour grapes was unmistakable.

3   I happened to think Moss looked great—small, but well-proportioned,
and mercifully lacking the ropy musculature that had begun to creep into
pop-culture images of femininity, in the cunning guise of "empowerment."
The Bionic Woman could only dream of the bulging biceps sported by Linda
Hamilton in *Terminator 2: Judgment Day* (1991); and Ginger Rogers, even when
she was struggling to match steps with Astaire, never had the calf muscles of
the mighty Madonna. (Nor would she have wanted them: She was a dancer
and not, like Mrs. Ritchie or any of her brood of MTV chicks, a kinky aerobics
instructor.) It's understandable, I suppose, that women might have felt the

impulse to bulk up during the might-makes-right regimes of Ronald Reagan and George Herbert Walker Bush, when the rippling behemoths of machismo, Arnold and Sly, ruled the screen; in that context, working on one's abs and pecs could be considered a prudent strategy of self-defense. But the arms buildup in the Cold War between the sexes was not a pretty sight. Applied to sex, the doctrine of Mutually Assured Destruction is kind of a bummer. The wages of sinew is the death of romance.

4   At least that's how it looks to people of my generation, whose formative years were the '60s, and to many of Moss's generation (the one commonly designated "X"), who in their youth embraced, for a while, the antipower aesthetic of grunge. What we oversaturated pop-culture consumers consider attractive— i.e., what's sexy in the opposite gender and worth aspiring to in one's own— usually develops in adolescence, as the relevant body parts do, and doesn't change much thereafter. For men older than I am, the perfect woman might have been Sophia Loren or Elizabeth Taylor or Marilyn Monroe or Rita Hayworth or the wartime pinup Betty Grable or (reaching back to the hugely eroticized flapper era) the original It girl, Clara Bow. And for them, the image of the ideal masculine self might have been Cary Grant or Clark Gable or Henry Fonda or Gary Cooper or even, for the less physically prepossessing— OK, shorter—guys, Cagney or Bogart or Tracy. By the time the '60s rocked and rolled into history, some subtle transformations had occurred, primarily in female sexual iconography. While the male stars of that decade remained more or less within the range of body types of their predecessors—Steve McQueen and Sean Connery might have looked a bit more athletic than the old norms demanded, but they wouldn't qualify as hard-bodies by today's standards—the shape of desirability in women distinctly altered, to something less voluptuous and more elongated. The fashions of the era tended to shift the erotic focus southward, from the breasts and the hips down to the legs, which, in a miniskirt, did rather overwhelm all other possible indicators of a woman's sexual allure. Although smaller-chested, leaner-hipped women, such as Julie Christie, stole some thunder from the conspicuously curvaceous, a certain amount of flesh was still required. Minis didn't flatter skinny legs any more than they did chubby ones.

5   So there was, to the avid eyes of teenage boys like me, a fine balance struck in the body aesthetic of the '60s, between, so to speak, length and width, Giacometti and Rubens. And muscles weren't part of the equation. He-men such as Steve Reeves—whose 1959 *Hercules,* a cheap Italian import initiated a spate of "sword and sandal" epics—seemed, to both sexes, ridiculous, vain rather than truly manly. (It's worth noting that in those days it was widely perceived that the primary market for body-building magazines was gay men.) And women? Forget it. The epitome of the muscular gal was the Russian or East German Olympic athlete, an Olga or a Helga, whose gender identity was frequently, and often justly, a matter of some dispute. There's an echo of that attitude in Ridley Scott's 1997 *G.I. Jane,* in which a feminist senator played by Anne Bancroft, trying to select a candidate for the first woman to undergo

Navy SEAL training, summarily dismisses several of the beefier applicants on the grounds of ambiguous sexuality. She settles on Demi Moore, who is slender and pretty and, on the evidence of a spectacularly obvious boob job, unquestionably straight.

6   But bodies like Moore's puzzle me. What, exactly, is the empowering element here—the iron she's pumped or the silicone that's been pumped into her chest? My number one teenage crush, Diana Rigg, didn't need either in order to be wholly convincing as kick-ass secret agent Emma Peel in the TV series *The Avengers.* Paired with a dapper male partner, John Steed (played by Patrick Macnee), Mrs. Peel was not only fully empowered but was also by far the more physically active of the two. In her mod pantsuits and go-go boots, she did most of the actual fighting in the kung fu-ish battles that climaxed virtually every episode, while Steed, perhaps mindful of potential damage to his impeccably cut Pierre Cardin suits, generally limited his martial activity to an occasional deft thrust with the umbrella.

7   Maybe if I'd come of age with visions of Madonna dancing in my head, I might find GI Demi devastatingly sexy rather than grotesque, but, objectively, I think the idea that women's power depends on either sculpted muscles or gigantic, orblike breasts (much less both) smacks of desperation. Mrs. Peel wielded her power so coolly, so confidently, and clearly never felt the need to enhance it by strenuous training or expensive medical procedures. Comfort in one's own skin is always appealing, which is probably why, in this sweating, striving, aggressively self-improving era, I find bodies as diverse as Kate Moss's and Kate Winslet's mighty attractive. It's not the body type per se—neither the frail Kate nor the ampler one precisely conforms to my Riggian ideal—but a woman's attitude toward her body that makes her sexy.

8   What's unnerving about today's pop-culture images of women is how extreme they are—and how much emphasis they place on the *effort* required to correct nature, to retard the aging process, to be all that you can be (and not, God forbid, simply what you are). The ethic of progress through hard work and technology is deeply ingrained in our society, as is the democratic notion that everyone should be whatever he or she wants to be— a noble idea that gets a tad problematic when what everyone wants to be is a star. And every star wants to be a bigger star. As a result, we're seeing, in the movies and on television and in the pages of fashion magazines, increasingly bizarre manifestations of our paradoxical

Kate Winslet from *Titanic* days

collective need to feel unique and, more, admired. Being really fat, for example, can confer on a person a certain distinction, but not the kind most of us
yearn for. (In the old days, for men, a degree of heft often indicated prosperity;
the movies embodied their image of financial success in portly figures such as
Eugene Pallette and Edward Arnold. No more.) To stand out on the runway
these days, a model has to be significantly gaunter—and younger—than even
the FEED ME–era Moss. And to make her mark on the screen, an actress has
several equally grueling options: starve herself skeletal, go to the gym and get
muscular, or—sometimes in perverse combination with one of the previous—
have her breasts inflated surgically. In each case, the result is a wild exaggeration of what would be, in moderation, a desirable quality: slimness, fitness or
voluptuousness. When I look at women in the movies now, I often feel as if I
were gazing not at real people but at cartoon characters—Olive Oyl, Popeye (in
drag) and Jessica Rabbit.

9   Of course, there are exceptions: the spectacular Winslet; the cherubic
and blissfully unself-conscious Drew Barrymore; the graceful, athletic Asian
stars Michelle Yeoh and Maggie Cheung; and (no epithet necessary) Julia
Roberts. But too many of the screen's great beauties have been developing a
lean and hungry look in recent years. They've felt the burn, and something
more than body fat appears to have been eliminated—a certain amount of joy
seems to have melted away at the same time. Clearly, we live in extraordinarily
ruthless and competitive times; and popular culture is bound to reflect that
condition, but I can't think of another age in which the competitive anxieties
of the performers themselves were so mercilessly exposed to the public's view.
When tough, chunky guys like Cagney squared off against one another in a
boxing ring or on the mean streets of New York or Chicago, you sensed that
the survival of an entire community of immigrants was at stake; you could see
it in every movement of their squat brawler's bodies. And when the Depression was over, those fierce small men just about vanished from the movies,
giving way to their larger, better-nourished children, who left the field, in
turn, to generations who would be conscious of their bodies without having
nearly as much use for them as their ancestors had had. What's at stake for today's action heroes and heroines, all pumped up with no place to go except to
the "explosive" climax of a fanciful plot? The steroidal action pictures of the
'80s and '90s created a race of pointless Supermen. Everyone in the audience
was in on the joke: Bruce Willis and Tom Cruise and Nicolas Cage and Keanu
Reeves didn't bulk up to save the world or any recognizable part of it; they did
it because starring in an action franchise was, and remains, a surefire means
of moving up the Hollywood ladder.

10   As the historian Lynne Luciano points out in her useful new book,
Looking Good: Male Body Image in America, in a white-collar, service economy
all most of us do with our bodies is compare them with everybody else's. We
look, we admire, we envy, we check the mirror, we get dissatisfied, we go back
to the old drawing board (the gym, the plastic surgeon, Jenny Craig, whatever).

And this strikes many as perfectly reasonable and natural: You have to keep an edge, and you have to *work* on it. Constant vigilance is required for both men and women, and folks are starting to look a little haggard. This applies even to the beautiful people of the silver screen. We can see the strain as they try to hang on to their precarious positions, like Tom Cruise at the beginning of *M.I.2*. And who, aside from the stars themselves, their families and their agents, could possibly care?

11   I haven't used the word *narcissism* yet, and it's long overdue. The unseemly vanity once ascribed to poor Steve Reeves has become the norm in Hollywood, which, kind of hilariously, apparently believes that we're so vain we probably think their movies are about us. I can't come up with another explanation for berserk pictures like David Fincher's *Fight Club* (1999), in which Edward Norton, as a harried white collar Everyman, takes as his guru and alter ego an alarmingly buff *Übermensch* played by Brad Pitt. If the weak box-office returns are any indication, *Fight Club* did not strike the deep chord in the hearts of American men that its makers evidently thought it would, and, to add insult to injury, the picture didn't even provoke the "controversy" that might have validated the artists' sense of their own fearlessness and edginess. The whole spectacle was simply self-important and silly—as silly as *Hercules* and, because no one involved seemed to recognize it, then some.

12   It's time to stop the madness. Sure, we viewers are stressed-out and perhaps slightly self-absorbed, but more of us than Hollywood thinks have some perspective on the absurdities of our lives and the inanities of our culture. Fewer of us than the studios imagine actually believe that a diet or a set of weights or silicone implants will change our lives, even if every movie star worth his or her (pardon the expression) salt apparently does believe it. That's their business, and, as we know—though Hollywood has obviously forgotten—there's *no* business like show business. The feral, predatory creatures prowling across the screen for our amusement are in a world of their own. And although they carry themselves as if they were wolves, magnificent in their power, they're really just coyotes, roaming the hills restlessly for scraps and deluding themselves even more doggedly than Chuck Jones's indefatigable Wile E. At least he knew what he was.

13   In a sense, body image represents the final frontier of postmodernism, the only area as yet untouched by our culture's pervasive irony. It would be useful, I think, for moviemakers to drop the pretense that entertainment is a life-and-death struggle, which only the strong survive. The stars of earlier eras, with their variety of unapologetically eccentric physiques, understood it was all a lovely con, a game played for pleasure: That's what those discreet little layers of flesh ultimately meant. But what would it take, I wonder, to make today's hard-bodies lighten up and laugh at their own desperate exertions or, failing that, merely stop gazing out at us cowed viewers as if they were dying to beat the crap out of us? I don't know, but I suspect that cranky magazine columns won't do the job. A higher power will have to be invoked. Mrs. Peel, you're needed. ■

Susan Llewelyn Leach

Those Extra Pounds—Are They Government's Business?

Susan Llewelyn Leach often writes about privacy issues and regulation concerns, including articles on identification cards, photograph usage and control, and food regulation. Obesity and food are the topic of the article below, which appeared in the April 28, 2004, edition of the Christian Science Monitor. *The* Monitor *is a church-founded newspaper, but it has an international scope and readership; for good reason it claims to have maintained a valuable independence since its founding in 1908.*

A s America's waistline expands and the anti-obesity movement gains momentum, what you eat may soon slip out of the private domain and into the public. Nobody will be regimenting your diet, but the government may start offering more pointed advice and regulating what goes into preprepared foods, among other things. Proposals include a tax on high-fat, low-nutrition food; better school meals; and nutrition labels on restaurant menus.

2   Having the government in your kitchen wouldn't be the first time private habits have come under outside scrutiny. Tobacco, alcohol, and drugs have all gone that route at various points in U.S. history. But where did personal responsibility fall off the bandwagon?

3   The shift of private behavior to public oversight, with new legislation to enforce it, happens in a quantifiable way, says Rogan Kersh, political scientist at Syracuse University's Maxwell School, who is writing a book on the politics of obesity.

4   The first and most significant of several triggers, he explains, is social disapproval. For instance, "it used to be sexy and desirable to smoke.... [Now] you're committing some grave moral wrong."

5   As disapproval gains momentum, he says, "public health crusades start to build around these behaviors": Sometimes the science is accurate (the medical establishment is unanimous on the evils of smoking); sometimes the science is a mixed bag (some studies suggest that alcohol isn't as dangerous as the Prohibitionists claimed); and sometimes the science is completely spurious (Victorian physicians warned that too much sex would maim, blind, or kill).

6   Despite almost two thirds of Americans being overweight, the U.S. is paradoxically one of the most antifat biased countries in the world. And that bias has only intensified in recent decades. Only a couple of brief periods in the 20th century showed a return to the acceptance of corpulence, Professor Kersh says, and both were after the world wars when Americans had undergone deprivation.

7   With social disapproval already widespread, medical science is reinforcing that view. Numerous studies and articles, some more alarmist that others, point to the health consequences of being heavy.

8   The message is no longer that being overweight is not good for you. It's now, "you're killing yourself through your obesity and the government must help you" to change, Kersh says.

9   That sort of shift in reasoning, reframing the problem in terms of a toxic food environment rather than weak will and failing personal responsibility, is key to the government stepping in. The individual is no longer blamed for not pushing back from the table. It's now a social problem.

10   What has helped accelerate that redefinition is the medical bill for dealing with weight-related illnesses, which reached $117 billion last year, according to the U.S. surgeon general, and may soon surpass the toll on healthcare taken by smoking. "When something becomes an economic problem in this country, government tends to act in a more urgent way than if it's a different kind of problem like constitutional rights."

11   "The point is, even though I'm not obese I'm paying for people who are. This really burns Americans and they want their policymakers to act in response," Kersh says. Already, more than 140 anti-obesity laws have been introduced in state legislatures this year.

12   But Sandle Sabo-Russo disputes the health-bill figure. "If a person is large-sized and goes to the doctor for something that has nothing to do with their size, it's often trumped up to be obesity related," says Ms. Sabo-Russo, a member of the board of NAAFA, the National Association to Advance Fat Acceptance and the largest obesity-rights organization in the U.S. "I don't trust what we're getting on that information."

13   She also points out the complexity of the issue. Being obese, or overweight, she says, is not always about food. "There are as many reasons as to how or why people are fat as there are fat people."

14   As for studies on obesity and its consequences, she questions their accuracy because many come from sources with a vested interest. "The first thing we try to look at when a new study comes out is who funded it. If it's funded by Weight Watchers International [for example], I'm not sure I'm going to believe what it says."

15   As societal pressure builds, and government reluctantly eyes new legislation, the courts are already grappling with obesity issues. More and more class-action lawsuits are taking aim at the food industry. And of the 10 major cases filed so far, mostly consumer protection suits, five have had some success. McDonald's, for example, had to fork over $12 million for not disclosing that its fries were cooked in beef fat. Pirates Booty paid $4 million over a cheese snack that misstated the amount of fat it contained.

16   Even though no personal-injury suits have yet won in court, a case brought against McDonald's elicited an unusual response from the judge. A man who sued the fast-food chain when he gained large amounts of

weight lost his case twice. But the judge spelled out what the plaintiff could have done to make the case stronger and suggested ways obesity cases could be argued.

17 "With judges doing that, trial lawyers are catching on and it's only a matter of time before they strike," says Kersh. The class-action suit, Kersh adds, has its roots in social movements that once took to the streets to demand change. Now large numbers of people can gather together through the courts.

18 Another historical pattern Kersh has identified in this gradual shift away from personal responsibility is the self-help movement. Twelve-step programs which usually spring up in response to medical warnings—Alcoholics Anonymous, Nicotine Anonymous, Overeaters Anonymous and so on—encourage Americans to live healthier lives. When that encouragement doesn't bear fruit fast enough, the users (in this case, the fat) tend to get "demonized" and so do the producers—the food and restaurant industries, who throw temptation the public's way.

19 The government has responded to public concern by telling people to exercise more and eat less—noncontroversial advice, as critics have noted, which won't rock the boat with the food lobby.

20 With the demonization of big tobacco fresh in memory, however, McDonald's and others are trying to minimize their liability by cutting portion sizes, ending supersizing, eliminating school marketing, and offering more salads. The fast-food industry is still big on individual choice, and even NAAFA's Sabo-Russo doesn't want the government legislating menus.

21 The danger of this growing push to trim the fat, Kersh says, is that it takes such a head of steam to change laws that the momentum often carries action beyond what's necessary. He cites Prohibition's 15-year fiasco and the zero-tolerance drug sentencing of the 1980s that is now being rolled back.

22 "Demonization makes very powerful politics, but it makes miserable public policy. You get these all out prohibitions, zero-tolerance policies which in practice are unrealistic and quite unjust," he says. ■

Mim Udovitch

A Secret Society of the Starving

Mim Udovitch's journalistic work on popular culture and the arts has appeared in publications such as Rolling Stone, Entertainment Weekly, *and the* New York Times. *In "A Secret Society of the Starving," which was published in the September 8, 2002, edition of the* New York Times Magazine, *Udovitch exposes the trend of young people (mostly female) using pro-eating disorder sites to encourage unhealthy behaviors. On these sites, says Udovitch, girls are viewed not as passive receptacles for images—like the ubiquitous pictures of ultrathin supermodels—but as active and aggressive participants in a disturbing cycle of unhealthy patterns and body perceptions.*

Claire is 18. She is a pretty teenager, with long strawberry-blond hair, and she is almost abnormally self-possessed for a girl from a small town who has suddenly been descended upon by a big-city reporter who is there to talk to her, in secret, about her secret life. She is sitting on the track that runs around the field of her high school's football stadium, wearing running shorts and a T-shirt and shivering a little because even though we are in Florida—in the kind of town where, according to Claire, during "season" when you see yet another car with New York plates, you just feel like running it down—there's an evening chill.

Photograph by Jocelyn Lee

2   Claire's is also the kind of town where how the local high school does in sports matters. Claire herself plays two sports. Practice and team fund-raisers are a regular part of her life, along with the typical small-town-Florida teenage occupations—going to "some hick party," hanging out with friends in the parking lot of the Taco Bell, bowling, going to the beach.

3   Another regular part of her life, also a common teenage occupation, is anorexia—refusal to eat enough to maintain a minimally healthy weight. So she is possibly shivering because she hasn't consumed enough calories for her body to keep itself warm. Claire first got into eating disorders when she was 14 or 15 and a bulimic friend introduced her to them. But she was already kind of on the lookout for something: "I was gonna do it on my own, basically. Just because, like, exercise can only take you so far, you know? And I don't know, I just started to wonder if there was another way. Because they made it seem like, 'You do drugs, you die; be anorexic and you're gonna die in a year.' I knew that they kind of overplayed it and tried to frighten you away. So I always thought it can't be *that* bad for you."

4   Bulimia—binge eating followed by purging through vomiting or laxatives—didn't suit her, however, so after a little while she moved onto anorexia. But she is not, by her own lights, anorexic. And her name isn't Claire. She is, in her terms, "an ana" or "pro-ana" (shortened from pro-anorexia), and Claire is a variation of Clairegirl, the name she uses on the Web sites that are the fulcrum of the pro-ana community, which also includes people who are pro-mia (for bulimia) or simply pro-E.D., for eating disorder.

5   About one in 200 American women suffers from anorexia; two or three in 100 suffer from bulimia. Arguably, these disorders have the highest fatality

rates of any mental illness, through suicide as well as the obvious health problems. But because they are not threatening to the passer-by, as psychotic disorders are, or likely to render people unemployable or criminal, as alcoholism and addiction are, and perhaps also because they are disorders that primarily afflict girls and women, they are not a proportionately imperative social priority.

6   They have been, however, topics of almost prurient media fascination for more than 20 years—regularly the subject of articles in magazines that have a sizable young female readership. In these forums, eating disorders are generally depicted as fundamentally body-image disorders, very extreme versions of the non-eating-disordered woman's desire to be thin, which just happen, rivetingly, to carry the risk of the ultimate consequence. "So many women who don't have the disorder say to me: 'Well, what's the big deal? It's like a diet gone bad,'" says Ellen Davis, the clinical director of the Renfrew Center of Philadelphia, an eating-disorder treatment facility. "And it is so different from that. Women with the vulnerability, they really fall into an abyss, and they can't get out. And it's not about, 'O.K., I want to lose the 10 pounds and go on with my life.' It's, 'This has consumed my entire existence.'"

7   And now there's pro-ana, in many ways an almost too lucid clarification of what it really feels like to be eating disordered. "Pain of mind is worse than pain of body" reads the legend on one Web site's live-journal page, above a picture of the Web mistress's arm, so heavily scored with what look like razor cuts that there is more open wound than flesh. "I'm already disturbed," reads the home page of another. "Please don't come in." The wish to conform to a certain external ideal for the external ideal's sake is certainly a component of anorexia and bulimia. But as they are experienced by the people who suffer from them, it is just that: a component, a stepping-off point into the abyss.

8   As the girls (and in smaller numbers, boys) who frequent the pro-E.D. sites know, being an ana is a state of mind—part addiction, part obsession and part seesawing sense of self-worth, not necessarily correlating to what you actually weigh. "Body image is a major deal, but it's about not being good enough," says Jill M. Pollack, the executive director of the Center for the Study of Anorexia and Bulimia, "and they're trying to fix everything from the outside." Clairegirl, like many of the girls who include their stats—height, weight and goal weight—when posting on such sites, would not receive a diagnosis of anorexia, because she is not 15 percent under normal weight for her height and age.

9   But she does have self-devised rules and restrictions regarding eating, which, if she does not meet them, make her feel that she has erred—"I kind of believe it is a virtue, almost," she says of pro-ana. "Like if you do wrong and you eat, then you sin." If she does not meet her goals, it makes her dislike herself, makes her feel anxiety and a sense of danger. If she does meet them, she feels "clean." She has a goal weight, lower than the weight she is now. She plays sports for two hours a day after school and tries to exercise at least another hour after she gets home. She also has a touch of obsessive-compulsive disor-

der regarding non-food-related things—cleaning, laundry, the numeral three. ("Both anorexia and bulimia are highly O.C.D.," says Pollack. *"Highly."*)

10   And she does spend between one and three hours a day online, in the world of pro-ana. Asked what she likes best about the sites, Claire says: "Just really, like at the end of the day, it would be really nice if you could share with the whole world how you felt, you know? Because truthfully, you just don't feel comfortable, you can't tell the truth. Then, like, if I don't eat lunch or something, people will get on my case about it, and I can't just come out and tell them I don't eat, or something like that. But at the end of the day, I can go online and talk to them there, and they know exactly what I'm going through and how I feel. And I don't have to worry about them judging me for how I feel."

11   Pro-ana, the basic premise of which is that an eating disorder is not a disorder but a lifestyle choice, is very much an ideology of the early 21st century, one that could not exist absent the anonymity and accessibility of the Internet, without which the only place large numbers of anorexics and bulimics would find themselves together would be at in-patient treatment. "Primarily, the sites reinforce the secretiveness and the 'specialness' of the disorder," Davis says. "When young women get into the grips of this disease, their thoughts become very distorted, and part of it is they believe they're unique and special. The sites are a way for them to connect with other girls and to basically talk about how special they are. And they become very isolated. Women with eating disorders really thrive in a lot of ways on being very disconnected. At the same time, of course, they have a yearning to be connected."

12   Perfectionism, attention to detail and a sense of superiority combine to make the pro-ana sites the most meticulous and clinically fluent self-representations of a mental disorder you could hope to find, almost checklists of diagnostic criteria expressed in poignantly human terms. Starving yourself, just on the basis of its sheer difficulty, is a high-dedication ailment—to choose to be an ana, if choice it is, is to choose a way of life, a hobby and a credo. And on the Web, which is both very public and completely faceless, the aspects of the disorder that are about attention-getting and secret-keeping are a resolved paradox. "I kind of want people to understand," Clairegirl says, "but I also like having this little hidden thing that only I know about, like—this little secret that's all yours."

13   Pro-ana has its roots in various newsgroups and lists deep inside various Internet service providers. Now there are numerous well-known-to-those-who-know sites, plus who knows how many dozens more that are just the lone teenager's Web page, with names that put them beyond the scope of search engines. And based on the two-week sign-up of 973 members to a recent message-board adjunct to one of the older and more established sites, the pro-ana community probably numbers in the thousands, with girls using names like Wannabeboney, Neverthinenuf, DiETpEpSi UhHuh! and Afraidtolookinthemirror posting things like: "I can't take it anymore! I'm fasting! I'm going out, getting all diet soda, sugar-free gum, sugar-free candy and having myself a 14-day fast. Then we'll see who is the skinny girl in the family!"

14 That ana and mia are childlike nicknames, names that might be the names of friends (one Web site that is now defunct was even called, with girlish fondness, "My Friend Ana"), is indicative. The pro-ana community is largely made up of girls or young women, most of whom are between the ages of 13 and 25. And it is a close community, close in the manner of close friendships of girls and young women. The members of a few sites send each other bracelets, like friendship bracelets, as symbols of solidarity and support. And like any ideology subscribed to by many individuals, pro-ana is not a monolithic system of belief.

15 At its most militant, the ideology is something along the lines of, as the opening page of one site puts it: "Volitional, proactive anorexia is not a disease or a disorder.... There are no VICTIMS here. It is a lifestyle that begins and ends with a particular faculty human beings seem in drastically short supply of today: the will.... Contrary to popular misconception, anorectics possess the most iron-cored, indomitable wills of all. Our way is not that of the weak. ...If we ever *completely* tapped that potential in our midst... we could change the world. Completely. Maybe we could even rule it."

16 Mostly, though, the philosophical underpinnings of pro-ana thought are not quite so Nietzschean. The "Thin Commandments" on one site, which appear under a picture of Bugs Bunny smiling his toothy open-mouthed smile, leaning against a mailbox and holding a carrot with one bite taken out of it, include: "If thou aren't thin, thou aren't attractive"; "Being thin is more important than being healthy"; "Thou shall not eat without feeling guilty"; "Thou shall not eat fattening food without punishing thyself afterward"; and "Being thin and not eating are signs of true willpower and success."

17 The "Ana Creed" from the same site begins: "I believe in Control, the only force mighty enough to bring order into the chaos that is my world. I believe that I am the most vile, worthless and useless person ever to have existed on this planet."

18 In fact, to those truly "in the disorder"—a phrase one anonymous ana used to describe it, just as an anonymous alcoholic might describe being in A.A. as being "in the rooms"—pro-ana is something of a misnomer. It suggests the promotion of something, rather than its defense, for reasons either sad or militant. That it is generally understood otherwise and even exploited ("Anorexia: Not just for suicidal teenage white girls anymore" read the home page of Anorexic Nation, now a disabled site, the real purpose of which was to push diet drugs) is a source of both resentment and secret satisfaction to the true pro-ana community. Its adherents might be vile and worthless, but they are the elite.

19 The usual elements of most sites are pretty much the same, although the presentation is variable enough to suggest Web mistresses ranging from young women with a fair amount of programming know-how and editorial judgment to angry little girls who want to assert their right to protect an unhealthy behavior in the face of parental opposition and who happen to know a little HTML. But there are usually "tips" and "techniques"—on the

face of it, the scariest aspect of pro-ana, but in reality, pretty much the same things that both dieters and anorexics have been figuring out on their own for decades. There are "thinspirational" quotes—"You can never be too rich or too thin"; "Hunger hurts but starving works"; "Nothing tastes as good as thin feels"; "The thinner, the winner!" There are "thinspirational" photo galleries, usually pretty much the same group of very thin models, actresses and singers—Jodie Kidd, Kate Moss, Calista Flockhart, Fiona Apple. And at pro-ana's saddest extreme, balancing the militance on the scales of the double-digit goal weight, there are warnings of such severity that they might as well be the beginning of the third canto of Dante's "Inferno": "I am the way into the city of woe. I am the way to a forsaken people. I am the way into eternal sorrow." The pro-ana version of which, from one site, is:

> PLEASE NOTE: anorexia is NOT a diet. Bulimia is NOT a weight-loss plan. These are dangerous, potentially life-threatening DISORDERS that you cannot choose, catch or learn. If you do not already have an eating disorder, that's wonderful! If you're looking for a new diet, if you want to drop a few pounds to be slimmer or more popular or whatever, if you're generally content with yourself and just want to look a bit better in a bikini, GO AWAY. Find a Weight Watchers meeting. Better yet, eat moderate portions of healthy food and go for a walk.
>
> However.
>
> If you are half as emotionally scarred as I am, if you look in the mirror and truly loathe what you see, if your relationships with food and your body are already beyond "normal" parameters no matter what you weigh, then come inside. If you're already too far into this to quit, come in and have a look around. I won't tell you to give up what I need to keep hold of myself.

20   Most of the pro-ana sites also explicitly discourage people under 18 from entering, partly for moral and partly for self-interested reasons. Under pressure from the National Eating Disorders Association, a number of servers shut down the pro-ana sites they were hosting last fall. But obviously, pretty much anyone who wanted to find her way to these sites and into them could do so, irrespective of age. And could find there, as Clairegirl did, a kind of perverse support group, a place where a group of for the most part very unhappy and in some part very angry girls and women come together to support each other in sickness rather than in health.

21   Then there's Chaos—also her Web name—who like her friend Futurebird (ditto) runs an established and well-respected pro-E.D. site. Chaos, whom I met in Manhattan although that's not where she lives, is a very smart, very winning, very attractive 23-year-old who has been either bulimic or anorexic since she was 10. Recently she's been bingeing and purging somewhere between 4 and 10 times a week. But when not bingeing, she also practices "restricting"—she doesn't eat in front of people, or in public, or food that isn't sealed, or food that she hasn't prepared herself, or food that isn't one of

her "safe" foods, which since they are a certain kind of candy and a certain kind of sugar-free gum, is practically all food. ("You're catching on quickly," she says, laughing, when this is remarked on.) Also recently, she has been having trouble making herself throw up. "I think my body's just not wanting to do it right now," she says. "You have the toothbrush trick, and usually I can just hit my stomach in the right spot, or my fingernails will gag me in the right spot. It just depends on what I've eaten. And if that doesn't work, laxis always do."

22   Chaos, like Clairegirl, is obsessive-compulsive about a certain number (which it would freak her out to see printed), and when she takes laxatives she either has to take that number of them, which is no longer enough to work, or that number plus 10, or that number plus 20, and so forth. The most she has ever taken is that number plus 60, and the total number she takes depends on the total number of calories she has consumed.

23   While it hardly needs to be pointed out that starving yourself is not good for you, bulimia is in its own inexorable if less direct way also a deadly disorder. Because of the severity of Chaos's bulimia, its long-standing nature and the other things she does—taking ephedra or Xenadrine, two forms of, as she says, "legal speed," available at any health food or vitamin store; exercising in excess; fasting—she stands a very real chance of dying any time.

24   As it is, she has been to the emergency room more than half a dozen times with "heart things." It would freak her out to see the details of her heart things in print. But the kinds of heart things a severe bulimic might experience range from palpitations to cardiac arrest. And although Chaos hasn't had her kidney function tested in the recent past, it probably isn't great. Her spleen might also be near the point of rupturing.

25   Chaos is by no means a young woman with nothing going for her. She has a full-time job and is a full-time college student, a double major. She can play a musical instrument and take good photographs. She writes beautifully, well enough to have won competitions.

26   But despite her many positive attributes, Chaos punishes herself physically on a regular basis, not only through bulimia but also through cutting—hers is the live-journal page with the picture of the sliced-up arm. To be beheld is, to Chaos, so painful that after meeting me in person, she was still vomiting and crying with fear over the possible consequences of cooperating with this story a week later. "Some days," she says of her bulimia, "it's all I have."

27   One thing that she does not have is health insurance, so her treatment options are both limited and inadequate. So with everything she has going for her, with all her real-world dreams and aspirations, the palpitating heart of her emotional life is in the pro-E.D. community. As another girl I spoke with described herself as telling her doctors: "Show me a coping mechanism that works as well as this and I'll trade my eating disorder for it in a minute."

28   And while in some moods Chaos says she would do anything to be free of her eating disorders, in others she has more excuses not to be than the mere lack of health insurance: she has a job, she is in school, she doesn't deserve help. And what she has, on all days, is her Web site, a place where people who have only their eating disorders can congregate, along with the people who *aspire* to having eating disorders—who for unknowable reasons of neurochemistry and personal experience identify with the self-lacerating worlds of anorexia and bulimia.

29   Futurebird, whom I also met in Manhattan, says that she has noticed a trend, repeating itself in new member after new member, of people who don't think they're anorexic *enough* to get treatment. And it's true, very much a function of the Internet—its accessibility, its anonymity—that the pro-ana sites seem to have amplified an almost-diagnostic category: the subclinical eating disorder, for the girl who's anorexic on the inside, the girl who hates herself so much that she forms a virtual attachment to a highly traumatized body of women, in a place where through posts and the adoption of certain behaviors, she can make her internal state external.

30   Futurebird and Chaos are sitting in a little plaza just to the south of Washington Square Park, with the sun behind them. Futurebird is a small African-American woman. As she notes, and as she has experienced when being taken to the hospital, it is a big help being African-American if you don't want people to think you have anorexia, which is generally and inaccurately considered to be solely an affliction of the white middle class. Futurebird has had an eating disorder since she was in junior high school and is now, at 22, looking for a way to become what you might call a maintenance anorexic—eating a little bit more healthily, restricting to foods like fruits and whole-grain cereal and compensating for the extra calories with excessive exercising.

31   Like Chaos, she is opposed, in principle, to eating disorders in general and says that she hates anorexia with a blind and burning hatred. Although she also says she thinks she's fat, which she so emphatically is not that in the interest of not sounding illogical and irrational, she almost immediately amends this to: she's not as thin as she'd like to be.

32   Both she and Chaos would vigorously dispute the assertion that the sites can *give* anyone an eating disorder. You certainly can't give anyone without the vulnerability to it an eating disorder. But many adolescent girls teeter on the edge of vulnerability. And the sites certainly might give those girls the suggestion to... hey, what the hell, give it a try.

33   "What I'd like people to understand," Futurebird says, "is that it is very difficult for people who have an eating disorder to ask for help. What a lot of people are able to do is to say, well, I can't go to a recovery site and ask for help. I can't go to a doctor or a friend and ask for help. I can't tell anyone. But I can go to this site because it's going to quote-unquote make me worse. And instead what I hope they find is people who share their experience and that

they're able to just simply talk. And I've actually tested this. I've posted the same thing that I've posted on my site on some recovery sites, and I've read the reactions, and in a lot of ways it's more helpful."

34   In what ways?

35   "The main difference is that if you post—if someone's feeling really bad, like, I'm so fat, et cetera, on a recovery site, they'll say, that's not recovery talk. You have to speak recovery-speak."

36   "Fat is not a feeling," Chaos says, in tones that indicate she is echoing a recovery truism.

37   "And they'll use this language of recovery," Futurebird continues. "Which does work at some point in the negative thinking patterns that you have. But one tiny thing that I wish they would do is validate that the feeling does exist. To say, yes, I understand that you might feel that way. And you get not as much of that. A lot of times people just need to know that they aren't reacting in a completely crazy way."

38   The problem is that by and large, the people posting on these sites are reacting in a completely crazy way. There are many, many more discussions answering questions like, "What do you guys do about starvation headaches?" than there are questions like, "I am feeling really down; can you help me?" And in no case, in answering the former question, does anyone say, "Um... stop starving yourself." A site like Futurebird's, or like the message board of Chaos's, are designed with the best intentions. But as everybody knows, that is what the way into the city of woe, the way to a forsaken people and the way into eternal sorrow are paved with.

39   What Clairegirl, sitting shivering on the running track, would say today is that when she reaches her current goal weight, she will stay there. But she can't ever really see herself giving ana up altogether. "I don't think I could ever stop, like, wanting to not eat. Like, I could keep myself from eating below 300 calories a day. But I could never see myself eating more than 1,000," she says, wrapping her arms around her knees. "I consider myself to be one of the extreme dieters. Like, I could never want to be—I mean, it would be so awesome to be able to say a double-digit number as your weight, but it would look sick, you know?" (Clairegirl is 5 feet 7 inches.)

40   And what about the people on the pro-ana sites who are not so happy, who describe the disorder as a living hell, who are in very bad shape? "Those girls have been going at it a lot longer than me. But you can't ever really say that ana isn't a form of self-hatred, even though I try to say that. If I was truthfully happy with myself, then I would allow myself to eat. But I don't. And it's kind of like a strive for perfection, and for making myself better. So I can't honestly say there's no...."

41   She trails off, and gazes up, as if the answer were written in the night sky, waiting to be decoded. "Like, you can't say that every ana loves herself and that she doesn't think anything is wrong with her at all," she says. "Or else she wouldn't be ana in the first place." ■

Consumer Freedom

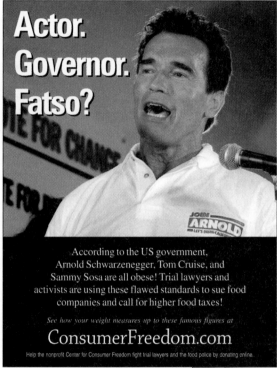

Actor.
Governor.
Fatso?

According to the US government,
Arnold Schwarzenegger, Tom Cruise, and
Sammy Sosa are all obese! Trial lawyers and
activists are using these flawed standards to sue food
companies and call for higher food taxes!

See how your weight measures up to these famous figures at

ConsumerFreedom.com

Help the nonprofit Center for Consumer Freedom fight trial lawyers and the food police by donating online.

**Did you hear
the one about the
fat guy suing the
restaurants?**

It's no joke.
He claims the food was too cheap so he ate too much!

*Learn more about the erosion of
personal responsibility and common sense. Go to:*

ConsumerFreedom.com

The two visual arguments on this
page, produced by an organization
called Consumer Freedom, ridicule
the idea that American corporations
might be responsible for obesity. ■

Pippa Wysong

Modified

Pippa Wysong is a Canadian journalist who specializes in medical and science writing, especially for children. Her "Ask Pippa" column, which has run in the Toronto Star *since 1988, answers kids' questions about scientific and medical matters. In "Modified," Wysong presents the potential dangers of piercings and tattoos and offers medical advice for those who simply cannot resist these increasingly popular forms of physical expression. Published in the March 2006 edition of* Current Health 2, *"Modified" comprises part of the* Weekly Reader *series of magazines for middle and high school classrooms.*

Alexis Valentine was only 18 months old when her ears were first pierced, a common practice in her Italian family. Now the 16-year-old from West Chester, Pa., has three earrings in each ear plus a belly button ring, and she is likely to have more piercings in her future. Maybe even a tattoo or two.

2   These days, piercings often go well beyond earlobes. Belly buttons, tongues, ear cartilage, eyebrows, nipples, lips, and even genitals are targets for metallic barbells, delicate chains, and stud jewelry. Tattoos run the gamut of images, from a discreet star to Celtic-inspired bracelets around an arm to huge artistic undertakings with the body as a canvas.

3   Body art (also called body modification) used to be just for Goths, bikers, and certain cultures both ancient and modern. Today, piercings and tattoos (including decals, henna, or permanent ink) are common. An estimated 23 percent of teens have piercings, about 8 percent have tattoos, and another 21 percent want tattoos. It's all part of the effort to be cool or to do something that looks a little different.

Teens Tell All

4 At age 12, Alexis opted for second holes in her ear lobes, and at 13 she had the third ones put in. When she turned 15, she got her belly button pierced. Does she want more? You bet. "I want to get my tongue pierced," she says. But her mom put a hold on that, as well as the flower tattoo Alexis would like on her back. In most states, minors need a parent's permission to get a tattoo or a piercing. In some states, it is illegal for minors to get these procedures at all. (The Association of Professional Piercers notes that many regulations exclude piercing done with piercing guns, frequently used at mall kiosks to insert ear-lobe earrings.) Alexis's classmate Jessica Adamiak, 15, has pierced ears but is waiting for her parents' OK to get her nose pierced. "My dad keeps saying he wants me to wait until I'm 30. Can you believe that?" she asks.

Problems With Piercings

5   Though they may seem a cool means of self-expression, piercings also come with potential dangers, cautions Dr. Lynn McKinley-Grant, a dermatologist from Chevy Chase, Md. Some problems include

- chipped or cracked teeth caused by chomping on a tongue stud;
- allergic reactions to metals used in jewelry—a severe allergy can even lead to death;
- choking if a tongue ring becomes loose;
- infection, which can cause swelling, pain, and oozing pus, and require a trip to the hospital.

6   Tongue infections are among the worst to treat, especially when the tongue is so swollen that the stud has to be surgically removed, McKinley-Grant says. The biggest risks for infections are new piercings or trauma to the newly pierced area, such as scratches or bruises. Infections can happen if piercing equipment is not properly sterilized or if a piercing is not cared for properly before it has healed.

7   Alexis is familiar with the risks after seeing what her older sister Amanda went through. Amanda, 20, has piercings in her earlobe, ear cartilage, nose, and lip. She also has a tattoo she designed herself. Amanda's first problem was a keloid, a big reddish-brown bump that grew at a piercing site on her ear cartilage. Keloids happen when too much scar tissue forms, and they can be quite unsightly. Amanda had to have plastic surgery to remove it.

8   Problems are common in cartilage, according to McKinley-Grant. "It has little blood flow and does not heal as easily as the earlobes," she says. Other big risks from piercings include infection with human immunodeficiency virus (HIV) or hepatitis from reused or unsterilized needles.

9   Amanda also had problems with a piercing in the flesh between her thumb and forefinger. A severe infection landed her in the emergency room to have the stud removed. But Amanda's problems don't faze Alexis, who plans to get more piercings. Alexis's mom, though cool with the idea of piercing (she has two earrings in each ear herself), is keeping a watchful eye.

Thinking Before Inking

10   Then there is the allure of tattoos. Although many teens go for temporary ones from decals or henna, others pick the permanent type. It's important to remember that ink tattoos don't go away, says Barbara Freyenberger, a nurse-practitioner at the Children's Hospital of Iowa. In fact, it's tough to get rid of tattoos if you don't like the pattern anymore or the artwork isn't what you expected. One study showed that close to 4 percent of college students with tattoos had them removed. As people age, tattoo removal is more common.

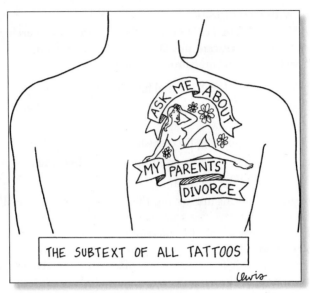

Eric Lewis's cartoon, published in the October 30, 2000, issue of the *New Yorker*, pokes fun at tattooing.

11   Over several visits, a dermatologist zaps unwanted tattoos with special medical lasers—a different laser for each color, and each color requires a separate trip. Tattoo removal generally means about $500 to $1,000 per treatment. (And health insurance usually doesn't cover it!) Removal can leave a slight scar and some skin discoloration. "It can take a minimum of eight treatments to completely remove a tattoo," says McKinley-Grant. Some parts of the body scar more than others from the procedure, the worst being the back, chest, and upper arms.

12   Another hidden danger of tattoos is a lack of regulation in the pigments used in ink. They can vary in quality, and some colors might contain lead, which can cause brain and nerve damage. Some people have allergic reactions to hennas or ink ingredients and can develop a rash or other health problems from the chemicals. In addition, tattoo needles—like piercing instruments—can pass on infections from other clients.

13   If you decide to get a tattoo, take your time thinking about it, Freyenberger advises. Get it done by a professional in a clean, sanitary environment. Make sure the tattoo artist uses new needles fresh out of the package and that the needles are dipped in fresh (not used) ink pots.

Before Seeking the Needle

14 Though tattoos and piercings may look cool, you should seriously mull over the health risks. And consider whether you'll still want the tattoo or piercing when you're in your 20s or 30s—or older. If you decide to go ahead, check the

age-limit laws in your state, get your parents' permission, research the medical implications, and find a safe, clean site.

Safety Tips for Piercings and Tattoos

15 ■ Go only to a professional, licensed piercer or tattooist.

■ Ask about cleanliness and infection control; if you don't feel safe or get satisfactory answers, leave.

■ Only patronize shops that use an autoclave, a device that sterilizes equipment between customers.

■ Make sure the tattooist or piercer uses new needles out of fresh, new packages, and that he or she disposes of needles in a special biohazard container after use.

■ Only use a tattooist who throws out leftover ink, instead of pouring it back into the bottle.

■ For new piercings, wear only noncorrosive metals (stainless steel, 14-karat gold) until the wound has healed.

■ Keep the tattoo or piercing clean: don't mess with it until the wounds are healed.

■ Remember: Waiting is always an option. If you do decide to get a body piercing or tattoo, consider selecting a discreet place for it on your body. You may not like it later—and if you have it removed, there will be scarring.

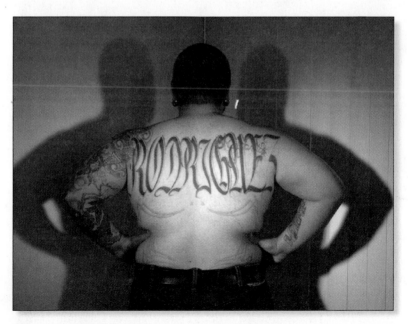

Can you imagine removing a tattoo as large as this one?

Mothers Against Drunk Driving

MADD—Mothers Against Drunk Driving—is one of the most respected nonprofit organizations in the United States. For the past 25 years MADD has championed the rights of victims of drunk driving and has promoted public awareness of the consequences of drunk driving. The ad on this page is one of many that were displayed on the MADD Web site (www.madd.org) in the summer of 2005. ■

Susan Kinzie

A Rare Kind of Rush: A Sorority Based on Islamic Principles

Susan Kinzie, a journalist for the Washington Post, *writes about a vast array of issues related to academic life, from the pressures facing current college presidents and student philanthropic efforts to the advantages and disadvantages of living in college towns. In "A Rare Kind of Rush," published on May 8, 2006, Kinzie takes a fresh perspective on Greek life by reporting on the start-up of an Islamic sorority. While there are many identity-group-based Greek organizations, Kinzie asserts that a sorority following Islamic ideals is unique because it adheres to Muslim rules for women: no alcohol and no socializing with men.*

Greek letters gleamed from a satin banner hanging at the front of the room, sequins flashed on little purses, and one woman holding a gold brochure blushed crimson, trying to explain why she liked the idea of this new group. Another widened dark eyes lined with kohl, watching everyone closely. Anwar smiled and said, with a little gush, "I am such a sorority type of girl."

2   And—long before the first Gamma Gamma Chi rush in Maryland was over—a student had politely interrupted to ask if they could break for maghrib, a sunset prayer. The women, draped in dark scarves, knelt to praise Allah in a hallway at the University of Maryland Baltimore County.

3   Forget everything you thought you knew about Greek life. These women came curious about a new kind of sorority, one that could change stereotypes of Muslim women, one based on Islamic beliefs: no drinking, no socializing with men. Like Anwar, a freshman at Johns Hopkins University, most of the students had never seriously considered going Greek. They've heard the stereotypes, such as keg parties with fraternity guys and, well, that's plenty right there. So they came to this new kind of rush, some covered head to toe in dark abayas, some with scarves pinned carefully around their heads and strappy four-inch heels, some with hair loose and jeans tight. Like so many Americans, most of these women don't fit into any easy cultural niche; they've been blending and balancing all their lives. And some wondered aloud whether this most American of college traditions might be too tricky to pull off. "I'm curious to see how that will be, that balance," Anwar said.

4   Greek life has changed dramatically from the days when wealthy, young white men drank gin and tonics on the verandas of fraternity houses. As the mix of students at colleges gets ever more varied, so do their campus groups. At schools across the country, there are Hispanic, Jewish, Indian, and lesbian sororities—and multicultural ones, sometimes formed in reaction to the others.

"There are a lot of ways to be Greek," said Ron Binder, president of the Association of Fraternity Advisors, who said he's seen an explosion of culturally-based groups in recent years and expects that growth to continue.

5   There isn't, apparently, any other Islamic sorority or fraternity in the United States. The idea for Gamma Gamma Chi started with Althia Collins, an educational consultant in Alexandria, and her daughter Imani Abdul-Haqq, who wanted to pledge a sorority in North Carolina. When Abdul-Haqq walked in with her hijab, Collins said, "everyone looked at her like she had three heads." Collins and her daughter, who became Muslim several years ago, thought sororities' emphasis on volunteering and leadership would make Muslim women more visible and help dispel stereotypes. And Collins, who was in a sorority in college, said she thinks the bonds are stronger and longer lasting than those formed in a club or dorm. So they dreamed up Gamma Gamma Chi, choosing letters, colors and such symbols as a waterlily, for its ability to flourish in difficult surroundings.

6   The first chapter recently started in Atlanta. Applications are coming in from Rutgers in New Jersey, and in the Washington area, there is interest from women out of college. And if enough students want to participate, the next chapter could soon be in Maryland, most likely starting as a regional group with members from several schools.

7   Not everyone likes the idea. Some places Collins has gone, hung up the green-and-purple banner, set out plates of grapes and cookies, explained the sorority—just like she did at UMBC—and no one has asked to join. The national Muslim Student Association welcomes the effort, but some members of campus chapters disapprove. "Sororities are played out to be very exclusive," said Haleema Yahya, a senior at UMBC, explaining why she thinks Gamma Gamma Chi would be controversial. Some people are skeptical just because the idea is new, said Misu Tasnim, a junior at Johns Hopkins. Some worry that the sorority sisters would splinter off the main Muslim student group. "And also because 'sorority' denotes drinking and dating and stuff," Tasnim said, "people are not sure how it will play into the Muslim ideals." Or traditions. In the Muslim Student Association, "the guys have more say than the girls do, just because that's how it is," said Narmin Anwar, Tasmim Anwar's sister, who introduced the sorority idea. "This would be more for the girls, to have more of a leadership role."

8   Tasmim Anwar came in a little late the night of the meeting, her long, wavy hair uncovered and an "I {heart} me" T-shirt on. She wasn't sure what to expect. It might be too strict, she thought, and a friend agreed, remembering how intimidated she had felt walking into a Muslim student group meeting not wearing hijab on her head. Collins told the students that they wouldn't preach but would support one another in a society that often misunderstands them. She suggested activities such as practicing public speaking and helping one another memorize the 99 names of Allah.

9   Like most Greek organizations, Gamma Gamma Chi wouldn't turn people away just because they're different—it would be open to non-Muslims as well—and it would have social events for women. But no drinking, clubbing, or hooking up. Lujain Said, whose tiny hands and big eyes peeked out from her enveloping black abaya, never considered Greek life until friends mentioned Gamma Gamma Chi. "I thought it was a great idea," she said, "to unite more Muslim women and get rid of some Muslim stereotypes." Yahya said, "We should step up into the light."

In early 2007 over half the members of DePauw University's Delta Zeta sorority house were asked to leave. A scandal arose over whether the women were asked to leave because of their perceived weight or unattractiveness. The photo above includes women who were asked to leave Delta Zeta, as well as others who left the sorority in protest over the expulsions.

10   For the sunset prayer, they moved into a hall of the UMBC commons building and lined up facing Mecca. An ethereal voice rose and fell in Arabic, and the rows of kneeling women rose and fell, dropping softly forward to the carpeted floor. A couple of male students in cargo shorts passed nearby, staring. After the prayer, the women went back in the room and gathered around the table of hors d'oeuvres, meeting one another or catching up, just like any sorority rush. It reminded Tasmim Anwar of the stories she'd heard at Johns Hopkins. "My friends would go to rush events, stay up all night talking to each other, wear high heels," she said, half wistful, half laughing at herself. "That sounds like so much fun." But then again, she said, sororities "have that reputation, which you hear right away." She thought she'd have to keep explaining, over and over, why she couldn't do this, why she wouldn't do that.

11   Because she's not strict enough to wear hijab, her friends are often surprised to find out she's so religious. "They're like, 'Muslim people are cool!'" she said. "Yeah, we are. We have fun, too! They think Muslim people are locked in their houses." Anwar came hoping to find something new, a middle ground between the stereotypes of Muslims and sorority girls. It didn't sound awful, as she thought it might, a weird kind of Sunday school thing. It sounded fun. Since then she's been telling her friends how cool Gamma Gamma Chi would be—already talking them up, maybe, for next year's rush. ■

28

New Media

Will the real character please stand up? A woman with her pets is on the left—and her avatar and online household is on the right. How do online identities reflect the the actual persons who construct them? Is the online identity actually any less real than the usual public person?

Personal Space in Cyberspace

On October 15, 2004, less than three weeks before the presidential elections, popular Comedy Central comedian Jon Stewart, a guest on CNN's political talk show *Crossfire,* got into a celebrated donnybrook with news commentator Tucker Carlson. Stewart, whose hilarious political satire in the form of a mock TV news show sends many Americans to bed with smiles on their faces (he has taken particular delight in lampooning the foibles of the Bush administration), took the opportunity of his appearance on *Crossfire* to challenge Carlson about the abysmal level of political commentary in the nation's media. At one point Stewart charged that *Crossfire* and shows like it—he was no doubt thinking of Bill O'Reilly and Rush Limbaugh, "Hardball" and "Hannity and Colmes," "The Capital Gang" and "The Beltway Boys"—are "bad, very bad," for America because they oversimplify and polarize discussion. "It's hurting America," said Stewart. "Stop, stop, stop, stop, stop hurting America." When Carlson protested that *Crossfire* presents intelligent debate from the political left and right, Stewart was outraged: "[Saying *Crossfire* is a debate show is] like saying pro wrestling is a show about athletic competition. You're doing theater when you should be doing debate. . . . What you do is not honest. What you do is partisan hackery . . . just knee-jerk reactionary talk."

While Stewart was taking his frustrations out on *Crossfire,* he was surely also thinking of much more. In the past decade many Americans have been increasingly concerned about certain trends in the popular media: the development of partisan (rather than "fair and balanced") news coverage; the concentration of news outlets and newspapers into the hands of a few powerful corporations; the impact of sensationalistic and one-sided talk radio and talk TV shows; the effects of the Internet on the political and cultural process; the dubious morality depicted on "reality TV"; and the effects of persistent advertising, violence, graphic sexuality, and cultural stereotyping that are associated with films, magazines, and television programs. Jerry Springer, a former TV news commentator transformed into the host of a trash "reality" show that has concentrated fantastic wealth in his hands, embodies all of the concerns. Is it any wonder, then, that Springer is often mentioned in Ohio as a viable political candidate?

Developments in new media—like Wikipedia, avatars, and Internet social networking sites—are making information and recreation more widely available, but the simplicity of posting anything on the Internet results in an overwhelming volume of material, a good deal of which is dubious in content. Between the partisanship (both obvious and subtle) of more traditional media and the unfettered democracy and questionable credibility of new media, many Americans are left wondering where to turn for reliable news sources. Many, in fact, turn to self-expression—a sort of personal space in cyberspace that may or may not reflect reality. The writers of the selections in this chapter tease out the tensions between freedom and censorship, public and private, in both old and new media.

Contemporary Arguments

This chapter opens with four pieces that explore the delicate balance between freedom and restriction on the Internet, as well as the potential consequences of swinging too far in one direction. In "Is Google's Data Grinder Dangerous?," Andrew Keen accuses Google of nefariously plotting for world domination and suggests that the Internet is not (and never will be) the utopian, free intellectual space that John Perry Barlow describes in "A Declaration of the Independence of Cyberspace." Similarly, John Seigenthaler describes a less-than-utopian experience of being the subject of a false Wikipedia biography and the obstacles to finding the identity of the writer. Walt Handelsman's "Information Superhighway" cartoon follows the Internet thread as well; his humorous roadway image shows a strikingly real portrait of priorities on the Internet. All these pieces come together under the broad topic of media and its uses. What is the Internet's purpose? Who should control it? Whose opinions should it publish and validate? And, finally, what are the hidden effects, sacrifices, and benefits when people (and small non-profit organizations) develop a significant Internet presence?

For many people worldwide, such questions take a backseat to the daily influence of the media in their lives. The balance of the selections in this chapter take up the issue of the Internet, identities, and the burgeoning trend of developing alter egos—and richly detailed alternative worlds—online. In "Where the Avatars Roam," Michael Gerson looks at cyberspace role-playing from a moral perspective: what happens to morality and freedom when we spend so much time in alternative realities where any choice is possible—even criminal or socially undesirable choices? Jessica Bennett and Malcolm Beith examine Second Life, a popular site for online living and a powerful and rapidly growing means of self-expression. In a debate, Joe Duffy and Andrew Keen weigh the advantages and disadvantages of the open environment of the Internet, where "everyone's an expert" and where questions of aesthetics and design quality are no longer left just to professionals. Meanwhile, in "Putting on Lip Gloss, and a Show, for YouTube Viewers," Marcelle Fischler argues that YouTube users and viewers create the demand for everyday design. She points out that not only do Internet users like to produce personal videos for online consumption, but that others enjoy viewing these sometimes edifying and sometimes profitable videos. danah boyd's article takes up questions of privacy and argues that the online community Facebook has some significant privacy problems.

Together, these articles tackle the tricky terrain of the private and the public in cyberspace. What kinds of personal expression are meant for public consumption? Should we differentiate between amateur and professional participation online, particularly if amateur expression is so common and so popular? Finally, just what is (and what should be) the purpose of new media—dissemination of information, recreation, commerce, or something else?

The chapter concludes with recreation in Stephen Williams's "Getting Off the Couch." As he discusses the possibility that Nintendo's Wii game system actually can provide some exercise for participants, he counters concerns that rampant child obesity is the result of all video games. Can other new technologies encourage people to be more active? Does Wii promote new purposes for video games? More broadly speaking, to what purposes can we put new media, and how will these technological shifts influence our lives and cultures?

Andrew Keen

Is Google's Data Grinder Dangerous?

In The Cult of the Amateur: How Today's Internet Is Killing Our Culture *(2007), Andrew Keen argues that the slew of amateur writing on the Internet—by anyone, about anything—doesn't contribute to knowledge or information, but rather bogs us down with uninformed opinions. Keen's view of the Internet is also evident in the article printed below. First published on July 12, 2007, in the* Los Angeles Times, *"Is Google's Data Grinder Dangerous?" puts a nefarious spin on the most popular Internet search engine—and its seeming quest to know all our private information so it can dominate the world (or at least make billions in advertising).*

W hat does Google want? Having successfully become our personal librarian, Google now wants to be our personal oracle. It wants to learn all about us, know us better than we know ourselves, to transform itself from a search engine into a psychoanalyst's couch or a priest's confessional. Google's search engine is the best place to learn what Google wants. Type "Eric Schmidt London May 22" into Google, and you can read about a May interview the Google chief executive gave to journalists in London. Here is how he described what he hoped the search engine would look like in five years: "The goal is to enable Google users to be able to ask the question such as 'What shall I do tomorrow?' And 'What job shall I take?'"

2   Schmidt's goal is not inconsiderable: By 2012, he wants Google to be able to tell all of us what we want. This technology, what Google co-founder Larry Page calls the "perfect search engine," might not only replace our shrinks but also all those marketing professionals whose livelihoods are based on predicting—or guessing—consumer desires. Schmidt acknowledges that Google is still far from this goal. As he told the London journalists: "We cannot even answer the most basic questions because we don't know enough about you. That is the most important aspect of Google's expansion."

3   So where is Google expanding? How is it planning to know more about us? Many—if not most—users don't read the user agreement and thus aren't aware that Google already stores every query we type in. The next stage is a personalized Web service called iGoogle. Schmidt, who perhaps not coincidentally sits on the board of Apple, regards its success as the key to knowing us better than we know ourselves.

4   iGoogle is growing into a tightly-knit suite of services—personalized homepage, search engine, blog, e-mail system, mini-program gadgets, Web-browsing history, etc.—that together will create the world's most intimate information database. On iGoogle, we all get to aggregate our lives, consciously or not, so artificially intelligent software can sort out our desires. It will piece together our recent blog posts, where we've been online, our e-commerce history and cultural interests. It will amass so much information about each of us that eventually it will be able to logically determine what we want to do tomorrow and what job we want.

5   The real question, of course, is whether what Google wants is what we want too. Do we really want Google digesting so much intimate data about us? Could iGoogle actually be a remix of "1984's" Room 101—that Orwellian dystopia in which our most secret desires and most repressed fears are revealed? Any comparison with 20th century, top-down totalitarianism is, perhaps, a little fanciful. After all, nobody can force us to use iGoogle. And—in contrast to Yahoo and Microsoft (which have no limits on how long they hang on to our personal data)—Google has committed to retaining data for only 18 months. Still, if iGoogle turns out to be half as wise about each of us as Schmidt predicts, then this artificial intelligence will challenge traditional privacy rights

as well as provide us with an excuse to deny responsibility for our own actions. What happens, for example, when the government demands access to our iGoogle records? And will we be able to sue iGoogle if it advises us to make an unwise career decision?

6   Schmidt, I suspect, would like us to imagine Google as a public service, thereby affirming the company's "do no evil" credo. But Google is not our friend. Schmidt's iGoogle vision of the future is not altruistic, and his company is not a nonprofit group dedicated to the realization of human self-understanding. Worth more than $150 billion on the public market, Google is by far the dominant Internet advertising outlet—according to Nielsen ratings, it reaches about 70% of the global Internet audience. Just in the first quarter of 2007, Google's revenue from its online properties was up 76% from the previous year. Personal data are Google's most valuable currency, its crown jewels. The more Google knows our desires, the more targeted advertising it can serve up to us and the more revenue it can extract from these advertisers.

7   What does Google really want? Google wants to dominate. Its proposed $3.1-billion acquisition of DoubleClick threatens to make the company utterly dominant in the online advertising business. The $1.65-billion acquisition of YouTube last year made it by far the dominant player in the online video market. And, with a personalized service like iGoogle, the company is seeking to become the algorithmic monopolist of our online behavior. So when Eric Schmidt says Google wants to know us better than we know ourselves, he is talking to his shareholders rather than us. As a Silicon Valley old-timer, trust me on this one. I know Google better than it knows itself. ∎

John Perry Barlow

A Declaration of the Independence of Cyberspace

After seventeen years as a Wyoming rancher who, on the side, wrote songs for the Grateful Dead, John Perry Barlow (born 1947) in the late 1980s began writing about computer-mediated communications. He served on the board of directors of WELL (the Whole Earth Lectronic Link), posts regularly on the WELL Web site, and is a cofounder of the Electronic Frontier Foundation, which advocates keeping government regulations out of the Internet. Since May 1998, he has been a fellow at Harvard Law School's Berkman Center for Internet and Society.

Governments of the Industrial World, you weary giants of flesh and steel, I come from Cyberspace, the new home of Mind. On behalf of the future, I ask you of the past to leave us alone. You are not welcome among us. You have no sovereignty where we gather.

John Seigenthaler

A False Wikipedia "Biography"

John Seigenthaler, now retired, is a distinguished journalist who founded the Freedom Forum First Amendment Center at Vanderbilt University—so he is anything but a censor at heart. Nevertheless, in the following essay (published in November 2005 in USA Today, a newpaper he helped launch) he expresses grave reservations about Wikipedia as he recounts a personal experience. The article printed below generated serious discussion about the reliability, credibility, and ethics of Wikipedia, which changed some of its policies subsequently. You can read more about the episode by going to en.wikipedia.org/wiki/Seigenthaler_controversy. For a writing activity on Wikipedia, see page 195.

> "John Seigenthaler Sr. was the assistant to Attorney General Robert Kennedy in the early 1960's. For a brief time, he was thought to have been directly involved in the Kennedy assassinations of both John, and his brother, Bobby. Nothing was ever proven." —*Wikipedia*

T his is a highly personal story about Internet character assassination. It could be your story. I have no idea whose sick mind conceived the false, malicious "biography" that appeared under my name for 132 days on Wikipedia, the popular, online, free encyclopedia whose authors are unknown and virtually untraceable. There was more:

2   We have no elected government, nor are we likely to have one, so I address you with no greater authority than that with which liberty itself always speaks. I declare the global social space we are building to be naturally independent of the tyrannies you seek to impose on us. You have no moral right to rule us nor do you possess any methods of enforcement we have true reason to fear.

3   Governments derive their just powers from the consent of the governed. You have neither solicited nor received ours. We did not invite you. You do not know us, nor do you know our world. Cyberspace does not lie within your borders. Do not think that you can build it, as though it were a public construction project. You cannot. It is an act of nature and it grows itself through our collective actions.

4   You have not engaged in our great and gathering conversation, nor did you create the wealth of our marketplaces. You do not know our culture, our ethics, or the unwritten codes that already provide our society more order than could be obtained by any of your impositions.

2   "John Seigenthaler moved to the Soviet Union in 1971, and returned to the United States in 1984," Wikipedia said. "He started one of the country's largest public relations firms shortly thereafter."

3   At age 78, I thought I was beyond surprise or hurt at anything negative said about me. I was wrong. One sentence in the biography was true. I was Robert Kennedy's administrative assistant in the early 1960s. I also was his pallbearer. It was mind-boggling when my son, John Seigenthaler, journalist with NBC News, phoned later to say he found the same scurrilous text on Reference.com and Answers.com.

4   I had heard for weeks from teachers, journalists and historians about "the wonderful world of Wikipedia," where millions of people worldwide visit daily for quick reference "facts," composed and posted by people with no special expertise or knowledge—and sometimes by people with malice.

5   At my request, executives of the three websites now have removed the false content about me. But they don't know, and can't find out, who wrote the toxic sentences.

5   You claim there are problems among us that you need to solve. You use this claim as an excuse to invade our precincts. Many of these problems don't exist. Where there are real conflicts, where there are wrongs, we will identify them and address them by our means. We are forming our own Social Contract. This governance will arise according to the conditions of our world, not yours. Our world is different.

6   Cyberspace consists of transactions, relationships, and thought itself, arrayed like a standing wave in the web of our communications. Ours is a world that is both everywhere and nowhere, but it is not where bodies live.

7   We are creating a world that all may enter without privilege or prejudice accorded by race, economic power, military force, or station of birth.

8   We are creating a world where anyone, anywhere may express his or her beliefs, no matter how singular, without fear of being coerced into silence or conformity.

9   Your legal concepts of property, expression, identity, movement, and context do not apply to us. They are based on matter. There is no matter here.

10   Our identities have no bodies, so, unlike you, we cannot obtain order by physical coercion. We believe that, from ethics, enlightened self-interest, and the commonweal, our governance will emerge. Our identities may be distributed across many of your jurisdictions. The only law that all our constituent cultures would generally recognize is the Golden Rule. We hope we will be able to build our particular solutions on that basis. But we cannot accept the solutions you are attempting to impose.

11   In the United States, you have today created a law, the Telecommunications Reform Act, which repudiates your own Constitution and insults the dreams of Jefferson, Washington, Mill, Madison, deToqueville, and Brandeis. These dreams must now be born anew in us.

Anonymous Author

6   I phoned Jimmy Wales, Wikipedia's founder and asked, "Do you . . . have any way to know who wrote that?"

"No, we don't," he said. Representatives of the other two websites said their computers are programmed to copy data verbatim from Wikipedia, never checking whether it is false or factual. Naturally, I want to unmask my "biographer." And, I am interested in letting many people know that Wikipedia is a flawed and irresponsible research tool.

7   But searching cyberspace for the identity of people who post spurious information can be frustrating. I found on Wikipedia the registered IP (Internet Protocol) number of my "biographer"—65-81-97-208. I traced it to a customer of BellSouth Internet. That company advertises a phone number to report "Abuse Issues." An electronic voice said all complaints must be e-mailed. My two e-mails were answered by identical form letters, advising me that the company would conduct an investigation but might not tell me the results. It was signed "Abuse Team."

12   You are terrified of your own children, since they are natives in a world where you will always be immigrants. Because you fear them, you entrust your bureaucracies with the parental responsibilities you are too cowardly to confront yourselves. In our world, all the sentiments and expressions of humanity, from the debasing to the angelic, are parts of a seamless whole, the global conversation of bits. We cannot separate the air that chokes from the air upon which wings beat.

13   In China, Germany, France, Russia, Singapore, Italy, and the United States, you are trying to ward off the virus of liberty by erecting guard posts at the frontiers of Cyberspace. These may keep out the contagion for a small time, but they will not work in a world that will soon be blanketed in bit-bearing media.

14   Your increasingly obsolete information industries would perpetuate themselves by proposing laws, in America and elsewhere, that claim to own speech itself throughout the world. These laws would declare ideas to be another industrial product, no more noble than pig iron. In our world, whatever the human mind may create can be reproduced and distributed infinitely at no cost. The global conveyance of thought no longer requires your factories to accomplish.

15   These increasingly hostile and colonial measures place us in the same position as those previous lovers of freedom and self-determination who had to reject the authorities of distant, uninformed powers. We must declare our virtual selves immune to your sovereignty, even as we continue to consent to your rule over our bodies. We will spread ourselves across the Planet so that no one can arrest our thoughts.

16   We will create a civilization of the Mind in Cyberspace. May it be more humane and fair than the world your governments have made before. ■

8   Wales, Wikipedia's founder, told me that BellSouth would not be help-ful. "We have trouble with people posting abusive things over and over and over," he said. "We block their IP numbers, and they sneak in another way. So we contact the service providers, and they are not very responsive."

9   After three weeks, hearing nothing further about the Abuse Team inves-tigation, I phoned BellSouth's Atlanta corporate headquarters, which led to conversations between my lawyer and BellSouth's counsel. My only remote chance of getting the name, I learned, was to file a "John or Jane Doe" lawsuit against my "biographer." Major communications Internet companies are bound by federal privacy laws that protect the identity of their customers, even those who defame online. Only if a lawsuit resulted in a court subpoena would BellSouth give up the name.

Little Legal Recourse

10   Federal law also protects online corporations—BellSouth, AOL, MCI, Wikipedia, etc.—from libel lawsuits. Section 230 of the Communications Decency Act, passed in 1996, specifically states that "no provider or user of an interactive computer service shall be treated as the publisher or speaker." That legalese means that, unlike print and broadcast companies, online service providers cannot be sued for disseminating defamatory attacks on citizens posted by others. Recent low-profile court decisions document that Congress effectively has barred defamation in cyberspace. Wikipedia's website acknowledges that it is not responsible for inaccurate information, but Wales, in a recent C-Span in-terview with Brian Lamb, insisted that his website is accountable and that his community of thousands of volunteer editors (he said he has only one paid employee) corrects mistakes within minutes.

11   My experience refutes that. My "biography" was posted May 26. On May 29, one of Wales' volunteers "edited" it only by correcting the misspelling of the word "early." For four months, Wikipedia depicted me as a suspected assassin before Wales erased it from his website's history Oct. 5. The falsehoods re-mained on Answers.com and Reference.com for three more weeks. In the C-Span interview, Wales said Wikipedia has "millions" of daily global visitors and is one of the world's busiest websites. His volunteer community runs the Wikipedia operation, he said. He funds his website through a non-profit foundation and estimated a 2006 budget of "about a million dollars."

12   And so we live in a universe of new media with phenomenal opportuni-ties for worldwide communications and research—but populated by volun-teer vandals with poison-pen intellects. Congress has enabled them and protects them.

13   When I was a child, my mother lectured me on the evils of "gossip." She held a feather pillow and said, "If I tear this open, the feathers will fly to the four winds, and I could never get them back in the pillow. That's how it is when you spread mean things about people." For me, that pillow is a metaphor for Wikipedia. ■

Michael Gerson

Where the Avatars Roam

Michael Gerson, who once worked as a policy analyst and speechwriter under President George W. Bush, is currently writing a book about the future of conservative politics. His areas of expertise span democracy and human rights, health and diseases, and religion and politics. Gerson's job with the Council on Foreign Relations (a nonpartisan group providing information and analysis at www.cfr.org) often has him writing about politics, but in "Where the Avatars Roam," Gerson tackles a slightly different form of his political subjects. In alternative realities constructed online, he asks, what happens to human freedom and human choices?

I am not usually found at bars during the day, though the state of the Republican Party would justify it. But here I was at a bar talking to this fox—I mean an actual fox, with fluffy tail and whiskers. It turns out that, in the online world of Second Life, many people prefer to take the shape of anthropomorphic animals called "furries," and this one is in a virtual bar talking about her frustrating job at a New York publishing house. But for all I know, she could be a man in outback Montana with a computer, a satellite dish and a vivid imagination.

2   For a columnist, this is called "research." For millions of Americans, it is an addictive form of entertainment called MMORPGs—massively multi-player online role-playing games. In this entirely new form of social interaction, people create computer-generated bodies called avatars and mingle with other players in 3-D fantasy worlds.

3   Some of these worlds parallel a form of literature that J.R.R. Tolkien called "sub-creation"—the Godlike construction of a complex, alternative reality, sometimes with its own mythology and languages. I subscribe along with my two sons (an elf and a dwarf) to The Lord of the Rings Online, based on Tolkien's epic novels, which sends its participants on a series of heroic quests. I'm told that World of Warcraft, which has more than 8 million subscribers, takes a similar approach. Some of the appeal of these games is the controlled release of aggression—cheerful orc killing. But they also represent a conservative longing for medieval ideals of chivalry—for a recovery of honor and adventure in an age dominated by choice and consumption.

4   Second Life, however, is a different animal. Instead of showing the guiding hand of an author, this universe is created by the choices of its participants, or "residents." They can build, buy, trade and talk in a world entirely without rules or laws; a pure market where choice and consumption are the highest values. Online entrepreneurs make real money selling virtual clothing, cars and "skins"—the photorealistic faces and bodies of

If you were to create an avatar, would you want to look like yourself or someone or something else? Why?

avatars. Companies such as Dell, IBM and Toyota market aggressively within Second Life.

5   The site has gotten some recent attention for its moral lapses. A few of its residents have a disturbing preference for "age play"—fantasy sex with underage avatars—which has attracted the attention of prosecutors in several countries.

6   But Second Life is more consequential than its moral failures. It is, in fact, a large-scale experiment in libertarianism. Its residents can do and be anything they wish. There are no binding forms of community, no responsibilities that aren't freely chosen and no lasting consequences of human actions. In Second Life, there is no human nature at all, just human choices.

7   And what do people choose? Well, there is some good live music, philanthropic fundraising, even a few virtual churches and synagogues. But the main result is the breakdown of inhibition. Second Life, as you'd expect, is highly sexualized in ways that have little to do with respect or romance. There are frequent outbreaks of terrorism, committed by online anarchists who interrupt events, assassinate speakers (who quickly reboot from the dead) and vandalize buildings. There are strip malls everywhere, pushing a relentless consumerism. And there seems to be an inordinate number of vampires, generally not a sign of community health.

8   Libertarians hold to a theory of "spontaneous order"—that society should be the product of uncoordinated human choices instead of human design. Well, Second Life has plenty of spontaneity, and not much genuine order. This experiment suggests that a world that is only a market is not a utopia. It more closely resembles a seedy, derelict carnival—the triumph of amusement and distraction over meaning and purpose.

9   Columnists, like frontier trackers, are expected to determine cultural directions from faint scents in the wind. So maybe there is a reason that *The Lord of the Rings* is ultimately more interesting than Second Life. Only in a created world, filled with moral rules, social obligations and heroic quests, do our free choices seem to matter. And even fictional honor fills a need deeper than consumption.

10 G.K. Chesterton wrote that when people are "really wild with freedom and invention" they create institutions, such as marriages and constitutions; but "when men are weary they fall into anarchy." In that anarchy, life tends to be nasty, brutish, short—and furry. ■

Jessica Bennett and Malcolm Beith

Alternate Universe

Jessica Bennett and Malcolm Beith work for Newsweek, *Bennett as a reporter and Beith as a general editor. In the July 30, 2007* Newsweek *article reprinted below, Bennett and Beith explore the virtual world of Second Life, a Web site on which users create their own alternative realities. Started in San Francisco in 1998, Second Life grew from 1.5 million to 8 million users between 2006 and 2007. According to Dutch researchers, more than half of Second Life's users spend 18 hours a week in this virtual world, and one-third of users spend more than 30 hours a week. On an average day, Second Lifers spend more than one million dollars outfitting their online lives and avatars.*

It's 1 a.m., and the "Dublin" nightclub is packed. Women in trendy ball gowns and men in miniskirts dance to Bon Jovi. Simon Stevens spins his wheelchair across the room, then leaps up and starts dancing, a move he can execute only here in Second Life, a 3-D virtual world that Stevens roams on his PC screen, using an avatar—a graphic rendering of himself, liberated from his cerebral palsy. "I flourish in Second Life," says the 33-year-old, who heads a disability-consulting firm called Enable Enterprises, out of his home in England. "It's no game—it's a serious tool."

2   Rhonda Lillie and Paul Hawkins live thousands of miles apart—she in California, he in Wales—and until this week, had never met face to face. But they've been dating for more than two years—in Second Life. The detachment of meeting through their avatars allowed them to open up to one another in a way they might never have done in the real world. "We felt like we could go in and really be ourselves," Lillie says.

3   Anshe Chung is a virtual land baroness with a real-life fortune. The woman behind the Anshe avatar is Ailin Graef, a former language teacher living near Frankfurt, Germany. Three years ago she started buying and developing virtual land in Second Life to see whether its virtual economy could sustain a real life. Turns out it can: Chung became Second Life's first millionaire in 2006. Her business, Anshe Chung Studios, with a staff of 60, buys virtual property and builds homes or other structures that it rents or sells to other denizens of Second Life.

4   When San Francisco software developer Philip Rosedale dreamed up the idea for Second Life in 1998, he never imagined that it might have such an impact on the world at large. Just as Google sexed up the way we search, and Instant Messaging altered the way we interact, Second Life is fast becoming the next red-hot tool on the Internet.

5   The numbers tell the story. Rosedale launched Second Life in 2001, but it got off to a slow start, reaching only 1.5 million registered users in 2006. In the past year, membership has soared to more than 8 million users—2 million having signed on in the last two months alone. This hypergrowth, driven mainly by word of mouth, is now attracting competitors. South Korea's Cyworld started out as a social-networking site, but has evolved into a two-dimensional equivalent of Second Life, claiming 20 million registered users from Asia to Latin America. Richard Branson's Virgin recently announced plans to create its own 3-D community called A World of My Own. By 2011, four of every five people who use the Internet will actively participate in Second Life or some similar medium, according to Gartner Research, which recently did a study looking at the investment potential of virtual worlds. If Gartner is to be believed (and it is

one of the most respected research firms in the field) this means 1.6 billion—out of a total 2 billion Internet users—will have found new lives online.

6   The power of Second Life lies in its utility for the gamut of human activities. It's a potent medium for socializing—it provides people with a way to express, explore and experiment with identity, vent their frustrations, reveal alter egos. The likes of MySpace and Facebook have already created online communities, but they lack the three-dimensional potential for interaction that Second Life provides. The people who are coming to this online universe aren't just socializing, however. They're also doing business, collaborating on research, teaching courses, dating and even having sex. More than 45 multinational companies, including the likes of American Apparel, IBM, General Motors and Dell are beginning to use the medium for customer service, sales and marketing. Many people are coupling the Second Life chat technology with Skype, the popular audio Internet software, so they can talk out loud while interacting inside the virtual world. Or they use live streaming video to talk and see each other in real life (sitting in front of a computer screen), as well as through their avatars inside Second Life. "The unique thing about Second Life is that it's immersive," says Michael Rowe, head of IBM's digital convergence team. "There's a huge opportunity here, just as in the early days of the Internet."

7   The medium sucks people in. A recent Dutch study found that 57 percent of Second Lifers spend more than 18 hours a week there, and 33 percent spend more than 30 hours a week. On a typical day, customers spend $1 million buying virtual clothes, cars, houses and other goods for their avatars, and total sales within this virtual economy are now growing at an annual rate of 10 percent. As a result, the money flowing through Second Life has attracted the attention of the U.S. tax authorities, who are currently investigating profits made in online businesses. And as it has evolved, those with ill intentions have apparently discovered Second Life, too. FBI agents are investigating possible gambling operations, and the German TV news program "Report Mainz" recently revealed allegations of child abuse in the virtual world. (Adults were purportedly using their avatars to have sex with the avatars of minors; they were expelled.)

8   Back in 1998, Rosedale simply hoped to create a vivid three-dimensional landscape in which graphic designers could create likenesses of their real-world ambitions—houses, cars, forests, anything one might find in a virtual game like EverQuest or World of Warcraft. Except Rosedale's creation wouldn't be a game: Second Life had no rules, no levels, no dragons to slay. It was open-ended, a digital landscape without regulations (much like the Internet in its early days). It was created on software that operates across multiple servers—a grid system that could easily grow to accommodate a large, far-flung community. A user in Germany could easily partner with a peer in Mexico to form their own mini-community inside Second Life, based on common interests—architectural designs, whatever. "It's basically Tom Friedman's flat world," says Philip Evans, an economist at Boston Consulting Group who studies the industry. "It's the globalization of the virtual world."

9   At first, it was a world with no rules. Rosedale's company, Linden Lab, over-
saw the allotments of server space, which translates into virtual real estate, but
imposed no controls over what went on inside the Garden of Eden it had created. A user's representation in Second Life—his avatar—would be bound by no
social constraints. And anything could be built, as long as you could write good
enough code. The first pioneers—graphic designers, for the most part—simply
set up display spaces for their technological projects. Then small communities
with common ideas and visions—much like an artistic community, say, in the
real world—sprang up. Since then, cities have grown, with urban amenities from
stores to clubs. Upon arrival, users are given the PC commands that enable them
to move around (walk, run, fly), dress their avatar and communicate with others.

10   Newcomers agree to a list of several do's and don'ts, but within the communities they form, residents can impose their own codes of conduct. That
laissez-faire attitude seems unsustainable—as Second Life expands, eventually Linden Lab will have to figure out a way to deal with the darker elements.
In one of the first troublesome incidents, residents reported last year that
"gangs" were forcing avatars out of public spaces. Rosedale declined to inter-
vene, saying his hope was that residents would organize to police their own
communities. They are currently doing so successfully, with rare exceptions
like the recent alleged child-abuse incident.

11   For the moment, the social freedom is one of Second Life's big draws.
One can teleport to a nightclub like Dublin, find a pristine beach on which to
relax, or start looking for business opportunities right away. Crowded urban
streets are lined with clothing stores, car lots, supermarkets, and nightclubs.
Real estate is the hot moneymaking market, with "islands"—private invitation-
only plots of Second Life land—selling for as much as $1,650.

12   Real-world entrepreneurs and businesses sense the opportunity. With its
large, densely settled population, which allows for division of labor, and citizens universally armed with ownership rights and the tools to produce just
about anything, Second Life is in some ways the ideal free market. Consider
40-year-old Peter Lokke. Toiling away as a department manager at a Pathmark
supermarket, the New York native had dreamed of opening his own design
business, but "never pushed myself to get into it professionally." Two and a half
years ago, a friend urged him to chase his goals in Second Life. So Lokke paid
$230 to Linden Lab to buy a 375-square-meter plot of Second Life land, and
opened up his own clothing shop.

13   Today his avatar—a woman, incidentally—earns nearly $300 a day selling
clothing he designs for users to drag and drop onto their avatars—twice what
Lokke earned at the supermarket. As for the clothes, he can make "infinite
copies of anything." Once he's designed a T shirt, he can make millions of replicas at no additional cost. "My supply is limitless," he says. "There's no bottom
line. The costs are only what I pay Linden Lab."

14   Linden Lab's "no control" policy allows for any income made inside
Second Life (the virtual world's currency is the Linden dollar) to be cashed out
through the company into U.S. dollars—even deposited directly into your check-

ing account (at an exchange that has remained fairly stable at about 270 Linden dollars per U.S. dollar). A product created in Second Life can also be sold outside it—on eBay, for example, a private island was recently listed for $1,395.

15 And unlike, say, Sony, which owns the rights to anything created in EverQuest, Linden Lab has relinquished all intellectual-property rights to creations in its world, spurring entrepreneurship. Roughly 90 percent of Second Life's content is created by the users themselves—Linden Lab built the basic architecture, like "Orientation Island," where users first create their avatar and learn about Second Life. Indeed, the barriers to entry and to commerce are so low, it is hard to imagine a more ideal business environment for entrepreneurs, which may prove to be the biggest driver of Second Life's growth. Lokke is so hooked, he says, "I'd rather panhandle on the street than leave Second Life."

16 A kind of alternate global economy is emerging in Second Life. Linden Lab keeps information on transactions within the virtual world to itself, but economists who study it closely forecast that by the end of the year users will have spent 125 billion Linden dollars in Second Life (about $460 million). About 5 billion Linden dollars were changed (through the official currency exchange, the LindeX) into $19 million in 2006. So far this year, they've converted $37 million, much of it earned in virtual-world transactions.

17 The multinational companies are using Second Life in a different way: some are holding staff meetings where avatars representing employees can discuss ideas via instant message, e-mail or Skype, in a souped-up virtual office. Others are using it to connect to customers. For instance, IBM is working with clients like Sears and Circuit City to enhance the shopping experience: adviser avatars can walk customers through models of, say, televisions, and actually show them how the product might fit in the living room. The 3-D, real-time experience also allows multiple customers, who might not be together in the real world, to communicate while shopping. A husband and wife on separate business trips can pick out a new couch "together," discussing the dimensions, color and material in real time. "Second Life allows you to strike up a natural conversation that you can't do on a two-dimensional Web site," says IBM's Rowe.

18 With face-to-face interaction on the decline in offices—where it's easier to e-mail or videoconference than schedule a live meeting—and companies increasingly use the Web for everything from distribution to customer service, a virtual world offers the potential to form relationships that are far more personal than online forms or e-mail. Nissan, for instance, lets customers talk to salespeople and even "test-drive" its new Sentra on a virtual driving track in Second Life. The Dutch bank ABN AMRO has financial advisers available as avatars.

19 That communication potential also makes Second Life attractive as an educational and research tool. Architecture professor Terry Beaubois began teaching a Montana State University course in Second Life two years ago, remotely from his California home. Now at MSU full time, he meets with classes each week out of "University Island," a mock campus that his students designed and built, with classrooms, workshops and an oceanside gallery where they display their work. Rather than using paper sketches and cardboard models, they build

interactive replicas of real buildings and neighborhood-development projects, adhering to proper structure, gravity and physics. The texture of these structures, though certainly animated, is detailed to the point where even a reporter can find herself lost in the arches and hallways of a virtual workshop.

20   The idea has caught on. Although Beaubois's colleagues questioned his decision to teach through what they called a "computer game," he's now head of MSU's Creative Research Lab and has the backing of the university's president (who has an avatar of his own). And more than 250 universities, including Harvard and MIT, now operate distance-learning programs in Second Life. Students meet in virtual classrooms to discuss history and political science. Teachers give virtual presentations, and lead virtual field trips. Guest lecturers visit from all over the world.

21   At the University of California, Davis, psychiatrist Peter Yellowlees has set up virtual simulations to show students what happens in a schizophrenic episode. Students can walk through a replica of his psychiatric ward, analyzing terrifying voices and eerie laughs, and can even see simulated schizophrenic hallucinations. Many students find the images disturbing, but Second Life helps them comprehend the "lived experience" of patients who "constantly complain" that doctors don't understand them, says Yellowlees.

22   True to the unofficial Second Life mantra—by the people, for the people—patients themselves are utilizing that clinical potential, too. "Brigadoon," for instance, is a Second Life island inhabited by a group of adults who suffer from Asperger's syndrome, a form of autism characterized by awkward, eccentric and obsessive behavior. Asperger's patients have trouble interacting socially and don't perceive things that should come naturally—how to introduce themselves or strike up a conversation, for instance. But in Second Life, these patients are learning to interact in ways that would be terrifying for them in real life. One sufferer has re-created a favorite restaurant, where the group regularly meets. Gradually, they are leaving their private island to venture into the rest of Second Life, integrating into the larger community. "The one thing that really amazes me about Second Life is the way it empowers people," says John Lester, the former Harvard Medical School researcher who set up the group (and now works for Linden Lab). "It frees them from the role of the biological device."

23   Not everyone is convinced that Second Life is a good thing. Some critics are uneasy with the idea of people's getting more and more of their social activity online. "No matter how you beef it up with little icons or fancy colors, [virtual worlds] don't have the nuance of face-to-face interaction," says Oxford University's Susan Greenfield, who heads the U.K.'s Institute for the Future of the Mind. It all depends, of course, on whether you see Second Life's taking the place of ordinary social interaction or supplementing it, or as just another kind of diversion—like "the 21st-century version of the novel," says Greenfield.

24   For diehard inhabitants, Second Life is a novel they won't put down soon. Elizabeth Ward, who suffers from reflex sympathetic dystrophy—a severe and chronic pain disorder that now keeps her at home—says "the interaction goes one step further than anything that could be achieved online." Ward, who lives with her husband, a software engineer, in Rhode Island, says her disability can

A home podcasting studio in Vancouver, British Columbia. Home podcasts can be set up for very little money. Is this ease of broadcasting always a good thing? What does this image tell you about this pair's broadcast?

make life "frustrating and lonely," but Second Life "has opened up another world." It's allowed her to continue working, to meet people, to visit her son, who lives in Nevada, and her best friend in India. She's gone sky diving, ice-skating—even played an eight-piece violin concerto with a group of mermaids under the sea. "I told my husband when I first started, 'I felt joy as I did when I was little, play-ing with paper dolls'," Ward explains. "But now the paper dolls are virtual and can interact with real people." Whether you think it's a pale imitation of reality or a vivid world of the mind, it's captivating the globe. ■

Marcelle S. Fischler

Putting on Lip Gloss, and a Show, for YouTube Viewers

Marcelle Fischler writes "The Long Island Journal" every week for the New York Times, in which she has published more than 400 articles. Fischler typically writes about popular culture, especially television and Internet trends. In this article about YouTube, Fischler illustrates the popularity of this Internet video site as well as the entrepreneurial possibilities for those brave souls who bare their "selves" on video for all the world to see.

Many women slap on their makeup in front of the mirror before they dash out the door: a quick coat of foundation, a dusting of blush, a brush of eye shadow, a twirl of the mascara wand and a quick smear of lip gloss. The beauty ritual hardly varies, and audiences generally aren't invited. Amy Powell applies her makeup in front of her computer, a Mac she named Ruby, with a built-in camera recording every brushstroke and dab. Then Ms. Powell, 19, from Myrtle Beach, S.C., uploads the video to YouTube for the world to see. "I have a real passion for makeup and the art of it," said Ms. Powell, who has made 39 video tutorials of her makeup techniques, including the application of party makeup, creating a smoky eye look and making lips shine. She posts her cosmetics clips on YouTube under the

Joe Duffy and Andrew Keen

Can Anyone Be a Designer?

Joe Duffy is the founder of Duffy & Partners, a branding and design consulting agency, and Andrew Keen is a writer who laments the current trend whereby nonprofessionals (on the Internet and elsewhere) pretend to be experts. (See the headnote on page 576 for a description of Keen's work.) In the following conversation, Duffy and Keen debate the merits of anyone being able to be a designer, creating everything from clothes to cars to couches. Whereas Duffy sees the rise of the everyday designer as a signal of the importance of aesthetics and a way to educate the public, Keen wants average folks to stay out of the way of the professionals. As you read their debate, consider what it means to be a designer. What role does design play in your life? What criteria should be used to evaluate good design and competent designers?

RESOLVED: Anyone can be a designer—and should be.

2 DUFFY: Design decisions are made by most everyone every day. What should I wear today? What kind of car should I buy? What color? Which options? What about the new sofa for the family room? Access to information and a myriad of choices allow people to quite literally design their lives. This is a good thing. As Americans act more like designers, they achieve a better understanding of design's importance in their lives.

3 KEEN: My 4½-year-old daughter thinks she's a clothes designer. She comes down to breakfast in deep purple and electric orange T-shirts, odd shoes, even odder headwear. Can dreadful aesthetics be cute? Only to a parent. The consequence of your design democracy is an ugly spectacle of deep purples and electric oranges. It's a culture of me-me-me: my hideously personalized car, my hideously personalized sofa, my hideously personalized house. If we care about maintaining an aesthetic of public space, design should be left to professionals. Let people pour their uniqueness inwardly—but don't let them clutter up the physical world.

name Amy04 and has 3,895 people who have signed up to be alerted whenever she uploads new videos.

2   In a show-it-all-off age where reality television programs about makeovers are ubiquitous and Web sites like YouTube have made nearly every activity worth sharing, grooming and primping routines are no longer kept behind bathroom doors. Ms. Powell, a sophomore at the College of Charleston, is among the hundreds of video bloggers—from stay-at-home mothers and television hopefuls to professional makeup artists and Ford models—putting what they do in front of

4	DUFFY:	Perhaps if your daughter develops in her experience of personal design, she won't turn into my son's (he's also a designer) worst nightmare of a client: someone who knows what he wants without any appreciation for how to get there. We'll make design part of everyday life and therefore more important in our culture if the public gets involved.
5	KEEN:	"Make design part of everyday life" sounds so Utopian, so open to ridicule, so Ministry of Truth-ish. It's the equivalent of saying we want to make creativity or spirituality or meaning central to existence.
6	DUFFY:	Well, Andrew, it's already happening. Target is bringing much better-designed, affordable products to the masses and succeeding in the marketplace by doing so. Does that sound at all Utopian?
7	KEEN:	Bringing better-designed products to the "masses" is not the same as turning the masses into designers. I'm all in favor of better-designed products at Target. I just don't want the Target customer designing her own products.
8	DUFFY:	The broader the participation in design, the more enthusiasm and demand for great design.
9	KEEN:	But design is neither important nor interesting for most consumers. Just as I don't want to know about engine physics when I drive a car, I don't want to be bothered by aesthetics when I wear my shoes or sit in my new loft.
10	DUFFY:	Sounds like you've resigned yourself to a pretty boring existence. And yes, I know many feel the same way you do. But I'm confident that the next generation will be much better at designing their lives.
11	KEEN:	I am afraid you are right. As technology democratizes cultural life, kids will be more and more seduced by easy-to-use design interfaces. They will grow up thinking of themselves as talented designers and go on to personalize their houses and even, given advances in cell research, their own children. ■

the vanity mirror on YouTube. They give lessons about mundane and usually private routines—applying mascara and eyeliner, putting on fake eyelashes, plucking eyebrows, blow drying hair or brushing one's cleavage with bronzer to make it look deeper.

3   In the last six months, said Julie Supan, a spokeswoman for YouTube, there has been a "huge shift towards being more than entertainment and focusing on how-tos. It is about people offering people expert advice and influencing and sharing their own ideas relating to style," she said. Jennifer Nielsen, another YouTube official, said it is impossible to say how many videos related to beauty are on the site, but she estimates there are thousands.

4   Elessa Vavon, 26, of San Diego, has posted 35 self-help beauty videos on YouTube since January. Ms. Vavon, who is known on YouTube as Pursebuzz, filmed a four-minute video about styling her highlighted long hair in curly pigtails, a six-minute tutorial on applying purple eye shadow using one brush, a short lesson in using liner and shimmery gloss to puff up her pout and a three-minute video, with subtitles, about sticking fake eyelashes on her dolled-up eyes. "I love computers and I love my makeup and helping others," said Ms. Vavon, who works weekdays at a real estate company.

5   She recently gave up weekend work doing freelance makeup applications to concentrate on the videos, a related beauty blog and a Web site, *pursebuzz.com*, hoping to build the material into a business. To make the videos, Ms. Vavon plops down in her bedroom and jabbers as she puts on eye makeup or lines her lips in front of a camera on a tripod. What shows up on YouTube is hardly edited.

6   Based on feedback from the more than 55,000 times her videos have been played, Ms. Vavon said high school girls, who often ask her questions about self-esteem or how to feel pretty, compose most of her audience. "It's really not just makeup at a surface level," she said.

7   Victoria Pitts-Taylor, an associate professor of sociology at Queens College and City University of New York Graduate Center who studies beauty culture, said that beauty work is no longer seen as "private, something we do behind closed doors." And, she said, "YouTube is an obvious place for formerly private acts to be made public."

8   Ford Models also sees the how-to beauty platform as a way to promote itself. The agency is using YouTube as a way to interact with consumers who care about fashion, beauty and style, and to subtly build the brand by posting more than 1,000 short video clips by its models and stylists since January, according to John Caplan, chief executive officer of Ford Models. The short beauty secrets range from the model Ariel Meredith's video tip about using a toothbrush to exfoliate lips before applying lip gloss to the plus-size model Tierney Smith's suggestion to use nonstick cooking spray to help nails sparkle and dry. "There is this insatiable demand out there for people to learn how to do what the people who know do," Mr. Caplan said. "With YouTube we are providing them a way to get the information and get it in an entertaining way and interact with us."

9   And some individuals see beauty videos as their own marketing opportunity, starring themselves—people like Madeline Merced, 22, who a year ago

made a television pilot, "How-To With Madeline," focusing on beauty hints that don't cost a lot. "I always wanted a show more catered to me," said Ms. Merced, who works as a bank teller and is a part-time student at a technical college in Madison, Wis. But when the show didn't succeed with a cable company, she posted it on YouTube under the channel WyethDigital and as a video podcast on iTunes. Now she is up to 30 videos and is working with a professional videographer, Eric Wyeth, 37. In her "53 Beauty Tips From Around the World" video, she suggests making a facial mask with a grated almond and vanilla yogurt exfoliant. "Don't eat it all," she said, advising viewers to slather it on their faces instead. "It moisturizes your skin." Her videos were recently picked up by TasteTV, a video-on-demand channel. Ms. Merced is hoping to move soon from her mother's living room and kitchen to a professional set.

10   Jessica Johansen, a 23-year-old wedding florist from Salt Lake City, makes do with her amateur setting. Late one night while her husband was at work, she propped a camera onto her ironing board and taped herself drying her curly hair, using a "curly wet set" method that made it less frizzy. Then she uploaded her four-part series on hair improvement. "I like to introduce people to their curly hair," Ms. Johansen said. "I had really frizzy hair for years and just thought that was my curse." Ms. Johansen said she didn't mind capturing every scrunch and twist of her wet hair on video, but was "slightly self-conscious" about filming in her bathroom. "I definitely made sure I cleaned well and wiped all the toothpaste off in there," Ms. Johansen said.

11   To the surprise of Ms. Powell, the college sophomore, thousands of viewers responded to her friendly approach to makeup and asked for more. (Her mother, though, until recently had no clue Ms. Powell was filming her mascara skills behind her closed bedroom door.) "I never claimed to be, like, this great artist," Ms. Powell said. "If I can spread what I know or what I think, that is a big thing for me." Ms. Powell said the feedback from professional artists greatly improved her techniques. And she could soon become more skillful if she lands a job at a MAC makeup counter at a nearby department store. "I would like to be trained by them," Ms. Powell said. ■

danah boyd

Facebook's "Privacy Trainwreck": Exposure, Invasion, and Drama

A doctoral candidate at UC Berkeley's School of Information, danah boyd is one of the nation's most respected experts on social networking sites like Facebook, Friendster, and MySpace. Boyd's work has appeared in such publications as the New York Times, USA Today, and Newsweek, as well as on such broadcast programs as National Public Radio and The O'Reilly Factor. Her research focuses on how people—especially young people—use online spaces to negotiate cultural norms and relationships.

On 5 September 2006, Facebook—a social network site primarily used by college students at the time—launched a feature called "News Feeds." Upon logging in, users faced a start page that listed every act undertaken by their Friends[1] within the system—who beFriended who, who commented on whose Wall[2], who altered their relationship status to "single," who joined what group, etc. None of the information displayed through this feature was previously private per say, but by aggregating this information and displaying it in reverse chronological order, News Feeds made the material far more accessible and visible. An individual did not need to remember whether or not someone indicated that they were "single" or "in a relationship"—the moment this bit flips, a state change is propagated to everyone's News Feed. At launch, this aggregated display outraged Facebook users (Schmidt 2006). Users formed groups like "Students Against Facebook News Feeds"[3] to protest the feature; over 700,000 people joined the group to express their frustration and confusion.

2   Less than 24 hours after the launch, Facebook's founder Mark Zuckerberg responded with a blog entry entitled "Calm down. Breathe. We hear you." (Zuckerberg 2006). This did not satiate participants' concerns and on 8 September, Zuckerberg returned to the blog with an apology and a peace offering in the form of new privacy options. He invited users to join him live on the "Free Flow of Information on the Internet"[4] group so that he could explain the motivation behind News Feeds. While hundreds of messages whizzed by, making it hard to follow any particular thread, Zuckerberg explained that News Feeds help people keep tabs on their friends—and only their friends. He continued on to argue that all of this information is already public anyhow.

3   It is true that all of the information made visible by the News Feeds was previously available to any user who took the time to look. That argument, while understandable, fails to capture how the feature alters the social dynamic of Facebook.

4   The tech world has a tendency to view the concept of "private" as a single bit that is either 0 or 1. Data is either exposed or not. When companies make a decision to make data visible in a more "efficient" manner, it is often startling, prompting users to speak of a disruption of "privacy." This is not new. In 1995, Deja introduced a tool that allowed anyone to search Usenet, an early Internet distributed newsgroup system, similar to contemporary bulletin boards. Prior to Deja, those interested in motorcycles were likely to be found hanging around rec.motorcycle while those who did not share this interest stayed out. The regular posters framed the norms of each newsgroup. When search was introduced,

[1] The term "Friends" is used in social network sites to indicate a consensual connection between two users. Not all connections represent a relationship that sociologists would recognize as friendship. For a deeper understanding of this feature, see (boyd 2006).
[2] The "Wall" is a space on an individual's profile where their Friends can leave messages that are viewable to anyone who has access to that profile.
[3] http://berkeley.facebook.com/group.php?gid=2208288769
[4] http://berkeley.facebook.com/group.php?gid=2208601394

Facebook founder Mark Zuckerberg. When users choose to put personal information on a social networking site, is the information still "private"? Who's responsible for an individual's privacy—does it rest with the user or with the site?

it became much easier to stumble on a newsgroup and even easier to read messages completely out of context. Tracking who participated in what group no longer required an individual to participate in all of the same groups. While the walls that separated newsgroups were always porous—anyone could come or go—they completely collapsed when search came along. Deja disrupted the delicate social dynamics in many Usenet groups; to regain some sense of control and "privacy," many groups shifted to mailing lists. Little did they know that, a few years later, Yahoo! would purchase two of the most popular free mailing list services and make them searchable as well.

5   Like Facebook, Deja did not make anything public that was not already public, but search disrupted the social dynamics. The reason for this is that privacy is not simply about the state of an inanimate object or set of bytes; it is about the sense of vulnerability that an individual experiences when negotiating data. Both Usenet and Facebook users felt exposed and/or invaded by the architectural shifts without having a good way of articulating why the feature made them feel "icky."

6   In this essay, I want to examine how technology that makes social information more easily accessible can rupture people's sense of public and private by altering the previously understood social norms. Offline, people are accustomed to having architecturally defined boundaries. Physical features like walls and limited audio range help people have a sense of just how public their actions are. The digital world has different properties and these can be easily altered through the development of new technologies, radically altering

the assumptions that people have when they interact online. As a result of new technological developments, social convergence is becoming the norm online, but people are still uncomfortable with the changes. What follows is a discussion of people's discomfort from two angles: exposure and invasion.

Exposure

7   Imagine that you are screaming to be heard in a loud environment when suddenly the music stops and everyone hears the end of your sentence. Most likely, they will turn to stare at you and you will turn beet red (unless exposure does not bother you).

8   When the music was still chirping away, you were speaking loudly in a room full of people. You felt (and were) protected by the acoustics and you made a judgment about how loud you should speak based on your understanding of the architecture of the environment. Sure, if someone came closer, they could've overheard you. But you didn't care because 1) you would've seen the person; 2) it's not abnormal to be overheard; and 3) what you were saying wouldn't really matter to them anyhow, right? Most people couldn't hear you even if they were visually proximate. This is security through obscurity.

9   When the music disappeared, the acoustics of the room changed. Suddenly, your voice carried much further than it had previously. Even if there was nothing embarrassing about the content of what you said, you're still startled by the change. Not only did you make a social faux pas, but you also lost control over the situation. The color of your face is a direct result of being unexpectedly exposed.

10   On Facebook, people were wandering around accepting others as friends, commenting on others' pages, checking out what others' posted, and otherwise participating in the networked environment. If you're a stalker or an anthropologist, you may have noticed that Bob accepted GirlfriendSally's Friend request after Justine's. You may have noticed that Ann wrote on Heather's page but not on Katherine's and you might have wondered why. You may also have caught that QuarterbackTed quietly accepted NerdGilbert's friend request. But even you might not have realized that your officemate joined the "If this group reaches 100,000 my girlfriend will have a threesome" group, simply because you didn't think to look.

11   Now, imagine that everyone involved notices all of this because it is displayed when they login. Sally's pissed at Bob; Katherine feels rejected; QuarterbackTed panics and deletes his friendship. And you feel awkward the next time you talk to your officemate. By aggregating all of this information and projecting it to everyone's News Feed, Facebook made what was previously obscure difficult to miss (and even harder to forget). That data was all there before but it was not efficiently accessible, it was not aggregated. The acoustics changed and the social faux pas was suddenly very visible. Without having privacy features[5],

---

[5]On 8 September 2006, after user outrage, Facebook provided privacy features that allowed users to control what would be announced to their Friends.

participants had to reconsider each change that they made because they knew it would be broadcast to all of their Friends. Participants had to shift their default expectation that each action would most likely be unnoticed to an expectation that every move would be announced.

12   In the late 1990s, researchers at AT&T placed a robot called Cobot into LambdaMOO to analyze the social dynamics (Isbell, et al. 2000). Cobot quietly collected data for well-intentioned researchers. The researcher's rationalized that everything that Cobot collected was public and visible to anyone present anyhow. Still, LambdaMOO users felt uncomfortable about the bot's silent presence and asked that it give something back. The researchers thought that this was fair and reprogrammed Cobot to answer questions about its observations. Unfortunately for both the researchers and the community, Cobot's answers disrupted the sense of community as people began evaluating others based on quantitative questions.

User:	"Who do I talk to the most?"
Cobot:	"Peter."
User:	"Who does Peter talk to the most?"
Cobot:	"Dan."
User (to self):	WHAT!?!? Why does Peter talk to Dan more than me? *$%& him, I'm not talking to Peter anymore. . . .

13   Just as with Facebook, all of the data with Cobot was "public." While most people do not think of their relationships in terms of quantity, Cobot counted and provided this information. Such information allows users to rate and rank connections, and their interpretation of quantity as quality highlights how people can problematically interpret social information.

14   With Facebook, participants have to consider how others might interpret their actions, knowing that any action will be broadcast to everyone that they consented to digital Friendship. For many, it's hard to even remember who they listed as Friends, let alone assess the different ways in which they may interpret information. Without being able to see their Friends' reactions, they aren't even aware of when their posts have been misinterpreted.

15   Users also have good reasons for not broadcasting their participation in certain Facebook groups. When the feature first launched, a group of queer students were uncertain about whether or not they could leave the "Queer This!" group. While they did not see themselves as closeted, discussing their sexual identity with everyone they knew was not something that they desired to do. Leaving the group would mean that previous affiliation was assumed and yet, what did it mean that they were leaving?

16   When the privacy features were launched, many exposure concerns were satiated. The queer students (and my officemate) could announce some things, but not announce when they joined or left groups. Others could turn off the ability to indicate when they beFriended people within the system. At the same time, the noticeable lack of this data can make someone suspicious—

what is it that they have to hide? An opt-out dynamic means that users have to consciously choose what it is that they wish to hide and then remember their choices as they are navigating the system. When the default is hyperpublic, individuals are not simply able to choose what they wish to expose—they have to choose what they wish to hide.

Invasion

17 I detest RSS feed readers—they play into my desire to read everything that everyone's ever written. I desperately want to see the cool things people I know posted over the weekend. And I want to follow all of the links that they saved and suggested that I read. But I can't. I simply don't have enough time in the day to follow every blog, Flickr, and del.icio.us of everyone I know. Feed readers make me feel guilty for being unable to deal with social information overload; as a result, I feel invaded by data. Unable to manage, I go cold turkey and read nothing.

18 My failure to cope is not simply a personal issue. Human cognition has a limitation to how much social information it can handle. In his work on social upkeep, evolutionary biologist Robin Dunbar found that humans gossip (as in they share personal information) for the same reason monkeys groom—to keep tabs on the social world around them (Dunbar 1996). There are a maximum number of monkeys that other monkeys can groom and there are a maximum number of people that humans can actively keep tabs on (Dunbar 1992).

19 Social network sites like Facebook imply that people can maintain infinite numbers of friends provided they have digital management tools. While having hundreds of Friends on social network sites is not uncommon, users are not actually keeping up with the lives of all of those people. These digital Friends are not necessarily close friends and friendship management tools are not good enough for building and maintaining close ties.

20 While Facebook assumes that all Friends are friends, participants have varied reasons for maintaining Friendship ties on the site that have nothing to do with daily upkeep (boyd 2006). For example, some users treat the Friends list as an address book. They may not wish to keep in contact with the girl that they knew from freshman psych, but having that connection may come in handy down the road. Yet, there is a difference between the ever-growing addressbook and the list of people that individuals pay attention to on a daily basis.

21 News Feeds do not distinguish between these—all Friends are treated equally and updates come from all Friends, not just those that an individual deems to be close friends. To complicate matters, when data is there, people want to pay attention, even if it doesn't help them. People relish personal information because it is the currency of social hierarchy and connectivity. Cognitive addiction to social information is great for Facebook because News Feeds make Facebook sticky. But is it good for people?

22 At a base level, most people have a voyeuristic streak and want to keep up with the details of other interesting people just because they can. Biologi-

cal programming makes us believe that individuals who are sharing personal details are indicating trust. In an unmediated society, social currency is a means to building a relationship. People reciprocally tell each other about their family, thoughts, and desires. Friendships are built on mutual knowledge of each other's lives and the lives of those they know. Social and emotional support is one of the outcomes of such friendships.

23   In June 2006, a group of sociologists argued that Americans have fewer friends now than they did 20 years ago (McPherson, et al. 2006). This made me wonder might social media be detrimental to friendship maintenance. If social information is easily available, it seems natural that people would tune in. Yet, if social information is the human equivalent of grooming, what happens when a computer provides that information asynchronously without demanding reciprocity?

24   This conundrum predates the Internet. Over the last century, celebrity gossip rags have made it much easier to obsessively follow the details of celebrities' lives, or at least those published for enquiring minds that want to know. Just because I can follow every detail of Angelina Jolie's life does not mean that she knows that I exist. Furthermore, she has absolutely no reason to respond to me when I ask for her support.

25   Strangers and celebrities are one thing, but what about acquaintances and other weak ties? Studies of e-mail have shown that the Internet helps people maintain both strong and weak ties by making ongoing communication easy (Boase and Wellman 2006). Does the same argument hold when it comes to social media that allows people to follow in lieu of reciprocal communication? My hunch is that the stream of social information gives people a fake sense of intimacy with others that they don't really know that well. If this is true, it could be emotionally devastating.

26   At a conference for women bloggers, I moderated a panel on "Sensitive Topics" and one concern that the panelists raised was that it has been quite difficult to handle the strangers who contact them seeking help. While these requestees felt a connection to the blogger through extended periods of following their output, the bloggers knew nothing about them. This inequality in perceived connection upset both parties. The requestee felt dissed, but the bloggers were also distraught. Most wanted to help because they hated seeing someone in pain, but as their blogs grew in popularity, they were unable to handle the quantity of requests for support. Most went from trying to help everyone to not responding to anyone.

27   Unlike these bloggers, most connections on Facebook are at least weak ties, but power differences still exist. Unreciprocated romantic crushes highlight this dynamic as the crusher follows the crushed intensely without the reverse being true. Through the regular updates, the crusher develops a feeling that she knows her crush, but her crush is barely aware of her presence.

28   Facebook gives the "gift" of infinite social information, but this can feel too much like the One Ring—precious upfront, but destructive long-term.

The Costs of Social Convergence

29   Mark Zuckerberg has repeatedly stated that his goal is to help people share information more efficiently. By aggregating social information and broadcasting it, News Feeds takes what people can access and places it at the forefront of their attention. Zuckerberg claims that no privacy was compromised in the process and, from a zeros and ones perspective, this is true. Yet, privacy is not simply about zeros and ones, it is about how people experience their relationship with others and with information. Privacy is a sense of control over information, the context where sharing takes place, and the audience who can gain access.

30   Information is not private because no one knows it; it is private because the knowing is limited and controlled. In most scenarios, the limitations are often more social than structural. Secrets are considered the most private of social information because keeping knowledge private is far more difficult than spreading it. There is immense gray area between secrets and information intended to be broadcast as publicly as possible. By and large, people treated Facebook as being in that gray zone. Participants were not likely to post secrets, but they often posted information that was only relevant in certain contexts. The assumption was that if you were visiting someone's page, you could access information in context. When snippets and actions were broadcast to the News Feed, they were taken out of context and made far more visible than seemed reasonable. In other words, with News Feeds, Facebook obliterated the gray zone.

31   In an era of convergence culture, it is easy to celebrate the shifts brought forth by media and technological convergence: participatory culture, user-generated content, connected communities of interest, destruction of the media industry hegemony, fluidity across platforms, etc. Media and technological convergence are introducing new practices and opportunities. Yet, as a direct result of these structural changes, another form of convergence is emerging: social convergence.

32   Social convergence occurs when disparate social contexts are collapsed into one. Even in public settings, people are accustomed to maintaining discrete social contexts separated by space. How one behaves is typically dependent on the norms in a given social context. How one behaves in a pub differs from how one behaves in a family park, even though both are ostensibly public. Social convergence requires people to handle disparate audiences simultaneously without a social script. While social convergence allows information to be spread more efficiently, this is not always what people desire. As with other forms of convergence, control is lost with social convergence. Can we celebrate people's inability to control private information in the same breath as we celebrate mainstream media's inability to control what information is broadcast to us?

33   Privacy is not an inalienable right—it is a privilege that must be protected socially and structurally in order to exist. The question remains as to whether or not privacy is something that society wishes to support.

34   When Facebook launched News Feeds, they altered the architecture of information flow. This was their goal and with a few tweaks, they were able to convince their users that the advantages of News Feeds outweighed security

through obscurity. Users quickly adjusted to the new architecture; they began taking actions solely so that they could be broadcast across to Friends' News Feed. While search took a toll on Usenet and Cobot crippled the social solidarity of LambdaMOO, Facebook continues to grow with no sign of slowing down. Young users, in particular, are adjusting to a digital landscape where limited scope broadcast is expected, if not desired.

35   Many questions still remain. What's next? How will future shifts alter social interactions? How will we adjust to social convergence? What will the costs of such adjustment be? Social convergence is most likely here to stay, but are we prepared for what this might mean?

Bibliography

Boase, Jeffrey and Barry Wellman. (2006) 'Personal Relationships: On and Off the Internet', The Cambridge Handbook of Personal Relationships (eds. Anita L. Vangelisti and Daniel Perlman). London: Cambridge University Press.

boyd, danah. (2006) 'Friends, Friendsters, and Top 8: Writing community into being on social network sites', First Monday 11(12), December.

Dunbar, Robin. (1992) 'Neocortex size as a constraint on group size in primates', Journal of Human Evolution 22: 469–493.

Dunbar, Robin. (1996) Gossip, Grooming and the Evolution of Language. London: Faber and Faber.

Isbell, Charles, Michael Kearns, Dave Kormann, Satinder Singh, and Peter Stone. (2000) 'Cobot in LambdaMOO: A Social Statistics Agent', Seventeenth National Conference on Artificial Intelligence (AAAI-00). Austin, Texas.

MySpace executives Adam Bain, left, and Arnie Gullov-Singh are helping to lead the company's effort to mine profile pages for ad purposes. The social networking companies see those pages, filled with personal information and preferences, as a potential gold mine for advertisers who want to customize the ads that pop up on users' screens. But do MySpace users want customized ads, or do they see the companies' efforts as intrusions into their privacy? What do you think?

McPherson, Miller, Lynn Smith-Lovin, and Matthew E. Brashears. (2006) 'Social Isolation in America: Changes in Core Discussion Networks over Two Decades', American Sociological Review, June.

Schmidt, Tracy Samantha. (2006) 'Inside the Backlash Against Facebook', Time.com, September 6. http://www.time.com/time/nation/article/0,8599,1532225,00.html

Zuckerberg, Mark. (2006) 'Calm down. Breathe. We hear you.', Facebook Blog, September 5. http://blog.facebook.com/blog.php?post=2208197130 ∎

Stephen Williams

Getting Off the Couch

Conceived in 2001 and officially launched in 2006, Nintendo's Wii outsold its competitors, Xbox 360, and Playstation, in the first six months of 2007. Nintendo touts its interactive system as "a new way to play." In the article below, Stephen Williams, a journalist for Newsday, *showcases the aerobic benefits of using the system and its popularity with gamers new and old.*

The sports games that come packaged with the Nintendo Wii video console are rather innocuous—there are no aliens to fry, no circuitous, rain-slicked racetracks to maneuver on, no virtual Shaq or Kobe to beat to the basket. But playing the "Wii Sports" version of bowling for a half hour raises Mickey DeLorenzo's blood pressure, hikes his heart rate, and leaves him sweaty and exhausted.

Wii exercise: perhaps you can get a real workout playing video games.

2   It's not exactly Pong.

3   The $250 Wii, which arrived in stores in November, at about the same time as Sony's much-heralded PlayStation 3, came with a novel bit of technology that separated it from the rest of the pack: motion-sensitive play that requires gamers to act out their character's on-screen movements in real time, wielding the Wii's remote controller like a sword, swinging it like a tennis racket or . . . well, rolling it like a bowling ball.

4   From the start, video-game addicts realized there were more benefits to these actions than simply making you hungry for more chips: Game play beefed up the biceps, flattened abs, improved cardio fitness. And, in some cases, doubled as a diet aid. "I just love the idea of this, and I never really liked video games. I can't even play Super Mario," admitted Rebecca Longo, a 26-year-old intensive-care nurse at New York Presbyterian Hospital-Cornell in Manhattan. Longo's game is kickboxing, played before a big-screen flat-panel TV in the Irving Place flat she shares with her husband, Kevin.

5   Why go to the gym?

6   "Playing kickboxing on Wii is like an aerobic workout for 15 or 20 minutes," she said. "It's so nice to do this at home, without having to go to a gym. There's a terrific potential here if they make new programs."

7   For DeLorenzo, 26, who lives in Philadelphia, the Wii payoff went beyond burning a few calories: He lost nine pounds in six weeks. DeLorenzo got hold of a Wii before it was officially released, to review it for an online publication. "While I was writing, I got this idea and dubbed it the Wii Sports Experiment, and that's how it was born." For six weeks, from December through mid-January, DeLorenzo maintained a strict program, 30 minutes a day at home with Wii and the sports games. "After 12 minutes, I was sweating, after 30 minutes I was sweating and tired," he said. He used all the games on the program—tennis, bowling ("If you play fairly quickly, step twice and roll, it's a good warmup and cooldown"), boxing and baseball—but skipped the golf. At the end of his self-appointed time, DeLorenzo had lost poundage. "I didn't change my diet, didn't do any additional exercise and, don't forget, I had to get through the fattening holiday season, too," he said. Of course, DeLorenzo charted his progress online (wiinintendo.net) and attracted a national following. He's since dispensed advice to dozens of people who have e-mailed him for encouragement. "I get letters from families saying they're all having Wii nights," he said. "Even my fiancee, a complete non-gamer, plays Wii Sport on a daily basis."

8   The buzz about Wii has created a whole culture of un-couch potatoes. In Los Angeles, parent Linda Perry has become an aggressive Wii advocate and helped attract a crowd to a "come out and play" night for Wii Sports at the posh Chateau Marmont. And more than a thousand fitness addicts have signed up for an informal Wii exercise group on a Web-based exercise site called Traineo.com, where they discuss the benefits of the game.

9   DeLorenzo says he's heard Nintendo is preparing to market a game similar to "DDR"—the high-flying Dance Dance Revolution game currently offered for Sony's PlayStation 2—as well as a "health pack. Not many details, except that

it will include yoga and Pilates." That information couldn't be confirmed by Nintendo spokesman Dan Mazie in New York, however.

10   Nintendo estimates it will ship 6 million Wii consoles to retailers worldwide by the end of this month. Nintendo itself has low-keyed the exercise benefits of Wii, focusing instead on game-play. Meanwhile, some Wii fans have complained about soreness or stiffness caused by playing the games. (In some instances, Wii-ers bowling or smashing tennis balls have reportedly let go of the controller in a moment of passion, flinging it at the TV screen or at another "bowler.")

11   Some medical experts have voiced concern that the interactive physical exertion required for Wii Sports may cause repetitive stress injuries or other types of discomfort. Dr. Mark Klion, a sports physician and orthopedic surgeon at Mount Sinai School of Medicine in Manhattan, recommends that Wii newbies start with short workouts and build up. He warns that for a person not used to physical exercise, a full-throttle Wii workout "is enough to cause injury to the soft tissues, whether it's the muscles, tendons or ligaments. I can't imagine people suffered these injuries from playing too much Pac-Man."

12   On the other hand, David Young, a Nintendo consumer service supervisor, told the Los Angeles Times that Wii Sports has proved a boon for people who can't exercise in conventional ways. He cited cases of a young girl with cerebral palsy playing the games from a wheelchair, a 44-year-old man with degenerative disc problems who can bowl and golf with Wii, and a teenage boy who uses the device to rehabilitate his right arm, which was impaired by a stroke.

These five games let you look, jab, slice . . .

13   Wii Sports was bundled into Nintendo's long-awaited game console system when it was launched in November, a collection of five simple-to-learn sports simulations designed to demonstrate the motion-sensing capabilities of the Wii Remote to new players. The five games are:

- Baseball—A three-inning game, where one player bats, another pitches. Batters grip and swing the controller like a bat, trying to time their swings correctly. Pitchers use the remote's buttons to choose screwball, curveball, splitter or fastball.
- Boxing—The controller is used to jab and punch; moving it side to side or back ah causes the fighter to lean, weave and duck.
- Golf—The faster the swing, the longer the ball will travel. Swing too fast, and the ball will slice or hook. Putting requires a delicate touch.
- Tennis—Forehands and backhands are controlled by flicking the remote. Body English can put some topspin on the ball. Takes some practice to get it right.
- Bowling—The controller becomes an extension of the arm, as one swings it backward then forward to release the ball. Awkward motions can hook the ball into the gutter or even into the neighboring lane. How embarrassing. ■

A Guide to Avoiding Plagiarism

Plagiarism is using someone else's work—words, ideas, or illustrations, published or unpublished—without giving the creator of that work proper credit. Plagiarism is a serious breach of scholarly ethics and can have severe consequences. Students risk a failing grade or disciplinary action ranging from suspension to expulsion. A record of such action can adversely affect professional opportunities in the future as well as graduate school admission.

This appendix presents an overview of how to avoid plagiarism. Additional and more detailed coverage of all aspects of writing from sources—conducting research, using and evaluating sources, avoiding plagiarism, and documenting sources in MLA and APA styles—can be found in Chapters 16–21.

Documentation: The Key to Avoiding Unintentional Plagiarism

It can be difficult to tell when you have unintentionally plagiarized something. The legal doctrine of **fair use** allows writers to use a limited amount of another's work in their own papers and books. However, to make sure that they are not plagiarizing that work, writers need to take care to credit the source accurately and clearly for *every* use. **Documentation** is the method writers employ to give credit to the creators of material they use. It involves providing essential information about the source of the material, which enables readers to find the material for themselves. It requires two elements: (1) a list of sources used in the paper and (2) citations in the text to items in that list. To use documentation and avoid unintentionally plagiarizing from a source, you need to know how to:

- Identify sources and information that need to be documented.
- Document sources in a list of works cited or list of references.
- Use material gathered from sources: in summary, paraphrase, and quotation.

- Create in-text references.
- Use correct grammar and punctuation to blend quotations into a paper.

Identifying Sources and Information That Must be Documented

Whenever you use information from **outside sources,** you need to identify the source of that material. Major outside sources include books, newspapers, magazines, government sources, radio and television programs, material from electronic databases, correspondence, films, plays, interviews, speeches, and information from Web sites. Virtually all the information you find in outside sources requires documentation. The one exception to this guideline is that you do not have to document common knowledge. **Common knowledge** is widely known information about current events, famous people, geographical facts, or familiar history. However, when in doubt, the safest strategy is to provide documentation. For more on what you do and do not have to document, see pages 271–272.

Documenting Sources in a List of Works Cited or List of References

You need to choose the documentation style that is dominant in your field or required by your instructor. Take care to use only one documentation style in any one paper and to follow its documentation formats consistently. The most widely used style manuals are the *MLA Handbook for Writers of Research Papers,* published by the Modern Language Association (MLA) and often used in the fields of English language and literature; the *Publication Manual of the American Psychological Association* (APA), favored in the social sciences; and *The Chicago Manual of Style,* published by the University of Chicago Press (CMS) and preferred in other humanities and sometimes business. Other, more specialized style manuals are used in various fields. Certain information is included in citation formats in all styles:

- Author or other creative individual or entity
- Source of the work
- Relevant identifying numbers or letters
- Title of the work
- Publisher or distributor
- Relevant dates

For detailed coverage of MLA style and sample works-cited entries, see Chapter 20 (pages 280–296). For detailed coverage of APA style, see Chapter 21 (pages 304–312).

Using Material Gathered From Sources: Summary, Paraphrase, and Quotation

You can integrate borrowed material into your paper in three ways—by summarizing, paraphrasing, and quoting. A quotation, paraphrase, or summary must be used in a manner that accurately conveys the meaning of the source. For detailed coverage of these topics, see pages 273–276.

A **summary** is a brief restatement in your own words of the source's main ideas. Summary is used to convey the general meaning of the ideas in a source without giving specific details or examples that may appear in the original. A summary is always much shorter than the work it treats. Take care to give the essential information as clearly and succinctly as possible in your own language.

Rules to Remember

- Write the summary using your own words.
- Indicate clearly where the summary begins and ends.
- Make sure your summary is an accurate restatement of the source's main ideas.
- Check that the summary is clearly separated from your own contribution.
- Use attribution and parenthetical reference to tell the reader where the material came from.

A **paraphrase** is a restatement, in your own words and using your own sentence structure, of specific ideas or information from a source. The chief purpose of a paraphrase is *to maintain your own writing style* throughout your paper. A paraphrase can be about as long as the original passage.

Rules to Remember

- Use your own words and sentence structure. Do not duplicate the source's words, phrases, or sentence structure.
- Use quotation marks within your paraphrase to indicate words and phrases you do quote.
- Make sure your readers know where the paraphrase begins and ends.
- Check that your paraphrase is an accurate and objective restatement of the source's specific ideas.
- Immediately follow your paraphrase with a parenthetical reference indicating the source.

A **quotation** reproduces an actual part of a source, word for word, to support a statement or idea, to provide an example, to advance an argument, or to add interest or color to a discussion. The length of a quotation can range from a word or a phrase to several paragraphs. In general, quote the least amount possible that gets your point across to the reader.

Rules to Remember

- Copy the words from your source to your paper exactly as they appear in the original. Do not alter the spelling, capitalization, or punctuation of the original. If a quotation contains an obvious error, you may insert [sic], which is Latin for "so" or "thus," to show that the error is in the original.
- Enclose short quotations (four or fewer lines of text) in quotation marks, and set off longer quotations as block quotations.
- Immediately follow each quotation with a parenthetical reference that gives the specific source information required.

Creating In-Text Citations

In-text citations need to supply enough information to enable a reader to find the correct source in the works-cited or references list. To cite a source properly in the text of your paper, you generally need to provide some or all of the following information for each use of the source:

- Name of the person or organization that authored the source.
- Title of the source (if there is more than one source by the same author or if no author is given).
- Page, paragraph, or line number, if the source has one.

These items can appear as an attribution in the text ("According to Smith . . .") or in a parenthetical reference placed directly after the summary, paraphrase, or quotation.

For detailed coverage and examples of MLA style, see Chapter 20 (pages 280–296). For detailed coverage of APA style, see Chapter 21 (pages 304–312).

Using Correct Grammar and Punctuation to Blend Quotations into a Paper

Quotations must blend seamlessly into the writer's original sentence, with the proper punctuation, so that the resulting sentence is neither ungrammatical nor awkward.

Using a Full-Sentence Quotation of Fewer Than Four Lines

A quotation of one or more complete sentences can be enclosed in double quotation marks and introduced with a verb, usually in the present tense and followed by a comma. Omit a period at the close of a quoted sentence, but keep any question mark or exclamation mark. Insert the parenthetical reference, then a period.

> One commentator asks, "What accounts for the government's ineptitude in safeguarding our privacy rights?" (Spinello 9).

> "The test had originally been scheduled for 4:00 A.M. on July 16," Jennet Conant writes, "when most of the surrounding population would be sound asleep" (304–05).

Introducing a Quotation with a Full Sentence

Use a colon after a full sentence that introduces a quotation.

> Spinello asks an important question: "What accounts for the government's ineptitude in safeguarding our privacy rights?" (9).

Introducing a Quotation with "That"

A single complete sentence can be introduced with a *that* construction.

> Chernow suggests that "the creation of New York's first bank was a formative moment in the city's rise as a world financial center" (199–200).

Quoting Part of a Sentence

Make sure that quoted material blends grammatically into the new sentence.

> McNichol and Lav assert that during that period, state governments were helped by "an array of fiscal gimmicks" (87).

Using a Quotation That Contains Another Quotation

Replace the internal double quotation marks with single quotation marks.

> Lowell was "famous as a 'confessional' writer, but he scorned the term," according to Bidart (vii).

Adding Information to a Quotation

Any addition for clarity or any change for grammatical reasons should be placed in square brackets.

> Describing how the weather would affect the testing of the first atom bomb, Jennet Conant says, "The test had originally been scheduled for 4:00 A.M. on July 16, [1945,] when most of the surrounding population would be sound asleep" (304–05).

Omitting Information from Source Sentences

Indicate an omission with ellipsis marks (three spaced dots).

> Describing how the weather would affect the testing of the first atom bomb, Jennet Conant says, "The test had originally been scheduled for 4:00 A.M. on July 16, when . . . there would be the least number of witnesses" (304–05).

Using a Quotation of More Than Four Lines

Begin a long quotation on a new line and set off the quotation by indenting it one inch from the left margin and double spacing it throughout. Do not enclose it in quotation marks. Put the parenthetical reference after the period at the end of the quotation.

> Human Rights Watch recently documented the repression of women's rights in Libya:
>
>> The government of Libya is arbitrarily detaining women and girls in "social rehabilitation" facilities, . . . locking them up indefinitely without due process. Portrayed as "protective" homes for wayward women and girls, . . . these facilities are de facto prisons . . . [where] the government routinely violates women's and girls' human rights, including those to due process, liberty, freedom of movement, personal dignity, and privacy. (114)

Is It Plagiarism? Test Yourself On In-Text Citations

Read the excerpt below. Can you spot the plagiarism in the examples that follow it?

Original source

To begin with, language is a system of communication. I make this rather obvious point because to some people nowadays it isn't obvious: they see language as above all a means of "self-expression." Of course, language is one way that we express our personal feelings and thoughts—but so, if it comes to that, are dancing, cooking and making music. Language does much more: it enables us to convey to others what we think, feel and want. Language-as-communication is the prime means of organizing the cooperative activities that enable us to accomplish as groups things we could not possibly do as individuals. Some other species also engage in cooperative activities, but these are either quite simple (as among baboons and wolves) or exceedingly stereo-typed (as among bees, ants and termites). Not surprisingly, the communica-tive systems used by these animals are also simple or stereotypes. Language, our uniquely flexible and intricate system of communication, makes possible our equally flexible and intricate ways of coping with the world around us: in a very real sense, it is what makes us human.

—Robert Claiborne. *Our Marvelous Native Tongue: The Life and Times of the English Language.* New York: New York Times, 1983.

Works-cited entry

Claiborne, Robert. *Our Marvelous Native Tongue: The Life and Times of the English Language.* New York: New York Times, 1983. Print.

Plagiarism Example 1

One commentator makes a distinction between language used as a **means of self-expression** and **language-as-communication.** It is the latter that distinguishes human interaction from that of other species and allows humans to work cooperatively on complex tasks (8).

What's wrong?

The source's name is not given, and there are no quotation marks around words taken directly from the source (in **boldface** in the example).

Plagiarism Example 2

Claiborne notes that language "is the prime means of organizing the cooperative activities." Without language, we would, consequently, not have civilization.

What's wrong?

The page number of the source is missing. A parenthetical reference should immediately follow the material being quoted, paraphrased, or summarized. You may omit a parenthetical reference only if the information that you have included in your attribution is sufficient to identify the source in your works-cited list and no page number is needed.

Plagiarism Example 3

> Other animals also **engage in cooperative activities.** However, these actions are not very complex. Rather they are either the very **simple** activities of, for example, **baboons and wolves** or the **stereotyped** activities of animals such as **bees, ants and termites** (Claiborne 8).

What's wrong?

A paraphrase should capture a specific idea from a source but must not duplicate the writer's phrases and words (in **boldface** in the example). In the example, the wording and sentence structure follow the source too closely.

Avoiding Plagiarism: Note-Taking Tips

The most effective way to avoid unintentional plagiarism is to follow a systematic method of note taking and writing.

- **Keep copies of your documentation information.** For all sources that you use, keep photocopies of the title and copyright pages and the pages with quotations you need. Highlight the relevant citation information in color. Keep these materials until you've completed your paper.

- **Quotation or paraphrase?** Assume that all the material in your notes is direct quotation unless you indicated otherwise. Double-check any paraphrase for quoted phrases, and insert the necessary quotation marks.

- **Create the list of works cited or references *first*.** Before you start writing your paper, your list is a **working bibliography,** a list of possible sources to which you add source entries as you discover them. As you finalize your list, you can delete the items you decided not to use in your paper.

Linda Stern
Publishing School of Continuing and Professional Studies
New York University

Glossary

A

abstract A summary of an article or book

aesthetic criteria Evaluative criteria based on perceptions of beauty and good taste

analogy An extended comparison of one situation or item to another

APA American Psychological Association

APA documentation Documentation style commonly used in social-science and education disciplines

argument A claim supported by at least one reason

assumption An unstated belief or knowledge that connects a claim with evidence

audience Real or assumed individuals or groups to whom a verbal or written communication is directed

B

bandwagon appeal A fallacy of argument based on the assumption that something is true or correct because "everyone" believes it to be so

bar chart Visual depiction of data created by the use of horizontal or vertical bars that comparatively represent rates or frequencies

because clause A statement that begins with the word *because* and provides a supporting reason for a claim

begging the question A fallacy of argument that uses the claim as evidence for its own validity

bias A personal belief that may skew one's perspective or presentation of information

bibliography List of books and articles about a specific subject

blog A Web-based journal or diary featuring regular entries about a particular subject or daily experiences (also known as a Web log)

brainstorming A method of finding ideas by writing a list of questions or statements about a subject

C

causal argument An argument that seeks to identify the reasons behind a certain event or phenomenon

claim A declaration or assertion made about any given topic

claim of comparison A claim that argues something is like or not like something else

common factor method A method used by scientists to identify a recurring factor present in a given cause–effect relationship

consequence The cause–effect result of a given action

context The combination of author, subject, and audience and the broader social, cultural, and economic influences surrounding a text

contextual analysis A type of rhetorical analysis that focuses on the author, the audience, the time, and the circumstances of an argument

counterargument An argument offering an opposing point of view with the goal of demonstrating that it is the stronger of two or more arguments

criteria Standards used to establish a definition or an evaluation

critical reading A process of reading that surpasses an initial understanding or impression of basic content and proceeds with the goal of answering specific questions or examining particular elements

cropping In photography, the process of deleting unwanted parts of an image

cultural assumptions Widely held beliefs that are considered common sense in a particular culture

D

database Large collection of digital information organized for efficient search and retrieval

debate A contest or game in which two or more individuals attempt to use arguments to persuade others to support their opinion

definition argument An argument made by specifying that something does or does not possess certain criteria

diction The choice and use of words in writing and speech

E

either–or A fallacy of argument that presents only two choices in a complex situation

emotional appeal An argumentation strategy that attempts to persuade by stirring the emotions of the audience

empirical research Research that collects data from observation or experiment

ethos An appeal to the audience based on the character and trustworthiness of the speaker or writer

evaluation argument An argument that judges something based on ethical, aesthetic, and/or practical criteria

evaluation of sources The assessment of the relevance and reliability of sources used in supporting claims

evidence Data, examples, or statistics used to support a claim

experimental research Research based on obtaining data under controlled conditions, usually by isolating one variable while holding other variables constant

F

fallacy of argument Failure to provide adequate evidence to support a claim. See *bandwagon appeal, begging the question, false analogy, hasty generalization, name calling, non sequitur, oversimplification, polarization, post hoc fallacy, rationalization, slippery slope, straw man*

false analogy A fallacy of argument that compares two unlike things as if they were similar

feasibility The ability of a proposed solution to be implemented

figurative language The symbolic transference of meaning from one word or phrase to another, such as with the use of metaphor, synecdoche, and metonymy

firsthand evidence Evidence such as interviews, observations, and surveys collected by the writer

font The specific size and weight of a typeface

freewriting A method of finding ideas by writing as fast as possible about a subject for a set length of time

G

generalization A conclusion drawn from knowledge based on past occurrences of the phenomenon in question

good reason A reason that an audience accepts as valid

H

hasty generalization A fallacy of argument resulting from making broad claims based on a few occurrences

HTML (HyperText Markup Language) Display language used for creating Web pages

hypertext Document that allows you to connect to other pages or documents by clicking on links (the Web can be thought of as one huge hypertext)

I

idea map A brainstorming tool that visually depicts connections among different aspects of an issue

image editor Software that allows you to create and manipulate images

intellectual property Any property produced by the intellect, including copyrights for literary, musical, photographic, and cinematic works; patents for inventions and industrial processes; and trademarks

J

JPEG (Joint Photographic Experts Group) The preferred Web format for photographs

journal A general category of publications that includes popular, trade, and scholarly periodicals

K

keyword search A Web-based search that uses a robot and indexer to produce results based on a chosen word or words

L

line graph A visual presentation of data represented by a continuous line or lines plotted at specific intervals

logos An appeal to the audience based on reasoning and evidence

M

metaphor A figure of speech using a word or phrase that commonly designates one thing to represent another, thus making a comparison

metonymy A type of figurative language that uses one object to represent another that embodies its defining quality

MLA Modern Language Association

MLA documentation Documentation style commonly used in humanities and fine-arts disciplines

N

name calling A fallacy of argument resulting from the use of undefined, and therefore meaningless, names

narrative arguments A form of argument based on telling stories that suggest the writer's position rather than explicitly making claims

non sequitur A fallacy of argument resulting from connecting two or more unrelated ideas

O

oversimplification A fallacy in argument caused by neglecting to account for the complexity of a subject

P

pathos An appeal based on the audience's emotions or deeply held values

periodical A journal, magazine, or newspaper published at standard intervals, usually daily, weekly, monthly, or quarterly

periodical index Paper or electronic resource that catalogs the contents of journals, magazines, and newspapers

pie chart A circular chart resembling a pie that illustrates percentages of the whole through the use of delineated wedge shapes

plagiarism The improper use of the unauthorized and unattributed words or ideas of another author

podcast Digital media files available on the Internet for playback on a portable media player, such as an iPod

polarization A fallacy of argument based on exaggerating the characteristics of opposing groups to highlight division and extremism

popular journal A magazine aimed at the general public; usually includes illustrations, short articles, and advertisements

position argument A general kind of argument in which a claim is made for an idea or way of thinking about a subject

post hoc fallacy A fallacy of argument based on the assumption that events that follow each other have a causal relationship

practical criteria Evaluative criteria based on usefulness or likely results

primary research Information collected directly by the writer through observations, interviews, surveys, and experiments

process of elimination method A means of finding a cause by systematically ruling out all other possible causes

proposal argument An argument that either advocates or opposes a specific course of action

R

rationalization A fallacy of argument based on using weak explanations to avoid dealing with the actual causes

reason In an argument, the justification for a claim

rebuttal argument An argument that challenges or rejects the claims of another argument

reference librarian Library staff member who is familiar with information resources and who can show you how to use them (you can find a reference librarian at the reference desk in your library)

refutation A rebuttal argument that points out the flaws in an opposing argument

rhetorical analysis Careful study of a written argument or other types of persuasion aimed at understanding how the components work or fail to work

rhetorical situation Factors present at the time of writing or speaking, including the writer or speaker, the audience, the purpose of communicating, and the context

S

sans serif type A style of type recognized by blunt ends and a consistency in thickness

scholarly journals Journals containing articles written by experts in a particular field; also called peer-reviewed or academic journals

secondary research Information obtained from existing knowledge, such as research in the library

secondhand evidence Evidence from the work of others found in the library, on the Web, and elsewhere

serif type A style of type developed to resemble the strokes of an ink pen and recognized by wedge-shaped ends on letter forms

single difference method A method of finding a cause for differing phenomena in very similar situations by identifying the one element that varies

slippery slope A fallacy of argument based on the assumption that if a first step is taken, additional steps will inevitably follow

straw man A fallacy of argument based on the use of the diversionary tactic of setting up the opposing position in such a manner that it can be easily rejected

sufficiency The adequacy of evidence supporting a claim

synecdoche A type of figurative language in which a part is used to represent the whole

T

textual analysis A type of rhetorical analysis that focuses exclusively on the text itself

thesis One or more sentences that state the main idea of an argument

typeface A style of type, such as serif, sans serif, or decorative

U

URL (Universal Resource Locator) An address on the Web

V

visual argument A type of persuasion using images, graphics, or objects

voice In writing, the distinctive style of a writer that provides a sense of the writer as a person

W

Web directory A subject guide to Web pages grouped by topic and subtopic

Web editors Programs that allow you to compose Web pages

wiki A Web-based application designed to let multiple authors write, edit, and review content, such as Wikipedia

working thesis A preliminary statement of the main claim of an argument, subject to revision

Credits

Image Credits

Text Credits

Thomas Bailey Aldrich, "The Unguarded Gates," 1895.

Ryan T. Anderson, "Struggling Alone," *First Things*, 170 (February 2007). Reprinted by permission.

John Perry Barlow, "A Declaration of the Independence of Cyberspace." Reprinted with permission of the author.

Jessica Bennett and Malcolm Beith, "Alternate Universe." From *Newsweek*, July 30, 2007. Copyright © 2007 *Newsweek*, Inc. All rights reserved. Used by permission and protected by the Copyright Laws of the United States. The printing, copying, redistribution, or retransmission of the Material without express written permission is prohibited.

Steven C. Bennett, "Privacy Implications of Biometrics," *Practical Lawyer*, June 1, 2007. Reprinted by permission of the author.

Wendell Berry, "Manifesto: The Mad Farmer Liberation Front" from *Collected Poems: 1957–1982* by Wendell Berry. Copyright © 1985 by Wendell Berry. Reprinted by permission of North Point Press, a division of Farrar, Straus and Giroux, LLC.

Michael Bérubé, "Citizenship and Disability," *Dissent*, April 1, 2003. Reprinted by permission of the author.

Douglas Bettcher and Chitra Subramaniam, "The Necessity of Global Tobacco Regulation," *JAMA*, December 5, 2001; 286: 2737. Reprinted by permission of the American Medical Association.

danah boyd, Reproduced with permission from Danah Boyd, "Facebook's Privacy Trainwreck: Exposure, Invasion and Social Convergence," *Convergence Journal*, Volume 14, Issue 1, 2008, Copyright © SAGE Publications 2008, by permission of Sage Publications Ltd.

David Brin, "Three Cheers for the Surveillance Society." This article first appeared in *Salon.com*, August 3, 2004, at www.Salon.com. An online version remains in the Salon archives. Reprinted with permission.

Robert Bullard, "Environmental Justice Professor Robert Bullard On How Race Affected the Federal Government's Response to Katrina," www.democracynow.org/article.pl?sid=05/10/24/1414234, October 24, 2005. Reprinted by permission of the author.

Randall J. Larsen, "Traveler's Card Might Just Pave the Way for a National ID Card," *USA Today* Op-Ed, June 8, 2005. Reprinted by permission of the author.

Emma Lazarus, "The New Colossus," 1883.

Susan Llewelyn Leach, "Those Extra Pounds—Are They Government's Business?" *Christian Science Monitor,* April 28, 2004. Copyright © 2004 by Christian Science Publishing Society. Reproduced with permission of Christian Science Publishing Society in the format textbook via Copyright Clearance Center.

Aldo Leopold, from "The Land Ethic," *Sand County Almanac.* New York: Oxford University Press, 1949.

Michelle Malkin, "Beware of Illegal Aliens Seeking Hazmat Licenses," *Human Events,* December 18, 2006. By permission of Michelle Malkin and Creators Syndicate, Inc.

Emily Martin and Katie Schwartzmann, opinion essay: "Bad for Both Boys and Girls," *USA TODAY,* August 17, 2006. Reprinted by permission.

Scott McCloud, pages 2–9 from *Understanding Comics* by Scott McCloud. Copyright © 1993, 1994 by Scott McCloud. Reprinted by permission of HarperCollins Publishers.

Ralph C. Merkle, "Nanotechnology: Designs for the Future," a conversation with *Ubiquity Magazine,* June 27, 2000. www.acm.org/ubiquity/interviews/r_merkle_1.html. © 2000 Association for Computing Machinery, Inc. Reprinted by permission.

Steven Milloy, "Ron Reagan Wrong on Stem Cells," as found at www.foxnews.com, July 16, 2004. Reprinted by permission of Steven Milloy.

N. Scott Momaday, "The Way to Rainy Mountain" from *The Way to Rainy Mountain.* Copyright © 1969. Reprinted by permission of the University of New Mexico Press.

Mae M. Ngai, "No Human Being is Illegal," *Women's Studies Quarterly,* 34.3/4 (2006). Reprinted by permission.

"Dulce et Decorum Est" by Wilfred Owen, 1921.

Participant Productions, "What Is Global Warming?" and "The Ten Things to Do to Stop Global Warming" from www.climatecrisis.net.

Annie Murphy Paul, "The Real Marriage Penalty," The New York Times Magazine, November 19, 2006. Copyright © 2006 by Annie Murphy Paul. Reprinted by permission.

Anna Quindlen, from *Thinking Out Loud,* copyright © 1993 by Anna Quindlen. Used by permission of Random House, Inc.

Terence Rafferty, "Kate Winslet, Please Save Us." Copyright © 2001 Condé Nast Publications. All rights reserved. Originally published in *GQ.* Reprinted by permission.

"Why Should I Be Nice to You? Coffee Shops and the Politics of Good Service," by Emily Raine, from *Bad Subjects,* issue 74, December 2005. Reprinted by permission of the author.

Ron Reagan, speech on the topic of Stem Cell Research given at the Democratic National Convention, July 27, 2004. Reprinted by permission of Ron Reagan.

Gregory Rodriguez, "Illegal Immigrants — They're Money," *Los Angeles Times,* March 4, 2007. Copyright © 2007 by Los Angeles Times. Reprinted with permission.

Elisabeth Rosenthal, "Can Polyester Save the World?" *New York Times,* January 25, 2007. Copyright © 2007 by The New York Times Co. Reprinted with permission. *New York Times,* "How Green is Your T-Shirt?" January

25, 2007. Copyright © 2007 by The New York Times Co. Reprinted with permission.

Russ Ryan, Reprinted with permission, "Emerging Biometric Technologies," *Security Technology & Design,* August 1, 2006. Copyright © 2007 Cygnus Business Media.

Paul Saffo, "A Trail of DNA and Data" as appeared in *The Washington Post,* April 3, 2005. Reprinted by permission of the author.

Eric Schlosser, "Make Peace with Pot," *The New York Times* Op Ed, April 26, 2004. Copyright © 2004 by *The New York Times.* Reprinted by permission.

John Seigenthaler, "A False Wikipedia 'Biography,'" *USA Today,* November 30, 2005, p. 11A. Reprinted

Leslie Marmon Silko, "The Border Patrol State." First published in *The Nation,* October 17, 1994. Copyright © 1994 by Leslie Marmon Silko, reprinted with permission of The Wylie Agency.

Christine Soares, "Attitude Screen," *Scientific American,* August 1, 2007. Reprinted with permission. Copyright © 2007 by Scientific American, Inc. All rights reserved.

"Crossing the Line" by Dan Stein, from the *Los Angeles Business Journal,* 2/26/07. Reprinted by permission of the author.

Andrew Sullivan, "The End of Gay Culture." First published in *The New Republic,* October 24, 2005. Copyright © 2005 by Andrew Sullivan. Reprinted with permission of The Wylie Agency, Inc.

Mim Udovitch, "A Secret Society of the Starving," *New York Times Magazine,* September 8, 2002. Reprinted by permission of the author.

Carmen Vasquez, "Appearances." From *Homophobia* by Warren J. Blumenfeld. Copyright © 1992 by Warren J. Blumenfeld. Reprinted by permission of Beacon Press, Boston.

Alex Williams, "Buying Into The Green Movement," *New York Times,* July 1, 2007. Copyright © 2007 by The New York Times Co. Reprinted with permission.

Stephen Williams, "Getting Off the Couch," *Newsday,* March 13, 2007. Copyright © 2007, Los Angeles Times. Reprinted with permission.

Walter Williams, "Nazi Tactics," *Ideas on Liberty,* January 2003. Reprinted with permission from Foundation for Economic Education. All rights reserved.

Edward O. Wilson, reprinted by permission of the publisher from "The Conservation Ethic" in *Biophelia: The Human Bond with Other Species* by Edward O. Wilson, pp. 119–123. Cambridge, Mass: Harvard University Press. Copyright © 1984 by the President and Fellows of Harvard College.

Pippa Wysong, "Modified," *Current Health 2,* March 1, 2006. Special permission granted by Weekly Reader, published and copyrighted by Weekly Reader corporation. All rights reserved.

Yahoo! Screen shot, "Issues and Causes in the Yahoo! Directory." Reproduced with permission of Yahoo! Inc. Copyright © 2007 by Yahoo! Inc. YAHOO! and the YA-HOO! logo are trademarks of Yahoo! Inc.

Jeffrey Zaslow, "The End of Youthful Indiscretions: Internet Makes Them Permanent Blots" from "Moving On" in *The Wall Street Journal,* Eastern Edition, August 12, 2004. Copyright © 2004 by Dow Jones & Company, Inc. Reproduced with permission of Dow.

Jones & Company, Inc. in the format textbook via Copyright Clearance Center.

Index

A

Academic OneFile, 257, 258
Academic Search Complete, 257, 258
Academic Search Premier, 257, 258
Active reading, 22
Advertisements, analysis of, 92–93
Aesthetic criteria, evaluation, 158
Aldrich, Thomas Bailey, 410
  as author of "The Unguarded Gates," 410
"Alternate Universe" (Bennett and
    Beith), 585–591
Alternative fuel, 159
Amend, Bill, "What's This . . ."
    (cartoon), 532
"American Legacy Foundation,
    "Antismoking Ad," 524
American Psychological Association
    (APA) format, 264, 265, 269,
    304–312
  book citations, 309–310
  documenting in, 304–312
  elements of, 304–307
  in-text citations, 307–307
Analogy, 48
Analysis
  of advertising media, 92–93
  of charts, 94–96
  of context, 97–98
  of tables, 94–96
  of textual evidence, 98–100
  of visual evidence, 92–94
Anderson, Ryan T., 354, 365–367, 369
  as author of "Struggling Alone,"
    365–367
Appeals, rhetorical, 17–18
"Appearances" (Vazquez), 356–362
Arguments
  causal. see Causal arguments
  compare and contrast, 45, 48–49
  from consequence, 46, 49
  construction of, 110
  definition, 33. see Definition
    arguments
  from definition, 44–45
  designing. see Designing arguments
  drafting and revising, 52
  evaluation. see Evaluation arguments
  finding, 30–52
  goals of, 16
  narrative. see Narrative arguments
  organization of, 57–58
  presenting. see Presenting arguments
  proposal. see Proposal arguments
  reading, 22
  rebuttal. see Rebuttal arguments
  success of, 12–16
  usefulness of, 9–12, 9–12
  from value, 45, 47
  visual, 90–109
  written. see Written arguments
ArticleFirst, 258
"Attitude Screen" (Soares), 460–462
Attitudes, 56
Audience, 12, 63, 238–239

B

Barlow, John Perry, 575, 578
  as author of "A Declaration of
    the Independence of
    Cyberspace," 578
"Bad for Both Boys and Girls" (Martin
    and Schwartzmann), 383–384
"Beautiful, Functional, and Frugal"
    (Franklin), 452–453
Because clause, 31, 47
Belief, statements of, 34
Bennett, Jessica and Malcolm Beith,
    576, 585–591
  as authors of "Alternate Universe,"
    585–591

Bennett, Steven C., 496–502
  as author of "Privacy Implications
    of Biometrics," 495, 496–502
Berry, Wendell, 317, 331–333
  as author of "Manifesto: Mad Farmer
    Liberation Front," 331–333
Bérubé, Michael, 518, 540–548
  as author of "Citizenship and
    Disability," 540–548
Bettcher, Douglas and Chitra
    Subramaniam, 526–528, 530
  as authors of "The Necessity of Global
    Tobacco Regulations," 526–528
"Beware of Illegal Aliens Seeking
    Hazmat Licenses" (Malkin),
    411–413
Blogs, 24, 261, 269, 294
Blogsearch.google.com, 24
Body language, during presentations, 243
Books, as sources, 256
  APA citations, 309–310
  MLA citations, 287–290
"Border Patrol State, The" (Silko),
    182–187
  analysis of, 71–79
boyd, danah, 576, 595–604
  as author of "Facebook's 'Privacy
    Trainwreck': Exposure, Invasion,
    and Drama," 595–604
Brainstorming, 38, 40
Brin, David, 474, 475–484
  as author of "Three Cheers for the
    Surveillance Society!," 475–484
Browsing, for research, 248–249
Bullard, Robert, 328–331
  as author of "How Race Affected the
    Federal Government's Response to
    Katrina," 328–331
Burk, Jennifer, 474, 490–491
  as author of "Counselors Walk a Fine
    Line Weighing the Rights of
    Student and College," 490–491
"Burning at the Stake" (Jenkins),
    343–345

Butalia, Urvashi, 404, 419–421
  as author of "Living the Dream,"
    415–421
"Buying into the Green Movement"
    (Williams), 345–349

C
Califano, Joseph A., Jr., 517, 518–520
  as author of "The Right Drug to
    Target: Cutting Marijuana
    Use," 518–520
"Can Anyone Be a Designer?" (Duffy
    and Keen), 592–595
Canons of rhetoric, 70–71
Carlsen, Laura, 404, 422–423
  as author of "Wal-Mart vs.
    Pyramids," 422–423
Carson, Rachel
  as author of *Silent Spring*, 9–16
  as author of "The Obligation to
    Endure," 19
Casual arguments
  identifying causes of, 138–139,
    141–142
Causal arguments, 49, 136–155
  building, 141–144
  statistics in, 144
  steps to writing, 153–155
  three forms of, 137–138
Cause and effect, 112
Charts and graphs
  analysis of, 94–97
  creating, 234–235
  for presentations, 240–242
Chicago Tribune Editorial, 349–350
  and "Fast Clothes vs. Green Clothes,"
    349–350
"Citizenship and Disability" (Bérubé),
    540–548
Claims, 31, 33
  of comparison, 48
  of contrast, 48
  finding, 40–42
  making, 31

"Coal in a Nice Shade of Green"
(Homer-Dixon and Friedmann),
215–217
Columbia Encyclopedia, 249
"Coming Out in the Line of Fire"
(Haeringer), 380–383
Common factor method, 139, 141
Compare and contrast, 45, 48–49
Completeness, 63
Concomitant variation, 139, 142
Consequence, arguing from, 46
Constitutional rights, 132
Consumer Freedom, "Obesity Ad," 565
Contextual analysis, 70, 71, 75–79
Contrast and compare, 45, 48–49
Conversation, arguments in, 30–31
"Conversation Ethic, The" (Wilson),
318–320
"Counselors Walk a Fine Line Weighing
the Rights of Student and
College" (Burk) 490–491
Counterarguments, 193, 194
Critical reading, 22
annotating, 25–26
questions for, 23
"Crossing the Line" (Stein), 200–202

D
Data collection, for research, 249–252
Database sources, 257
APA citations, 311
evaluating, 266
MLA citations, 293
Davies, Matt, "We're Here To Defend
A Sacred Institution . . ."
(cartoon), 370
Deardorff, Darla K., 405, 423–426
as author of "In Search of Intercultural
Competence," 423–426
"A Declaration of the Independence of
Cyberspace" (Barlow), 578
Decorum (appropriateness), 71
"Defense of Marriage Act" (House of
Representatives), 371–372

Definition
from example, 115–116
formal, 115
operational, 115
types of, 114–116
Definition argument, 33, 113,
113–136, 113–136
building, 118–121
sample, student, 129–133
steps to writing, 134–136
understanding, 113–114
Demography (journal), 145
Designing arguments, 229–237
Designing pages
for print, 235–236
for the web, 236–237
Discussion groups, online, 260–261
Dispostio (arrangement), 70
Diversity, 111
Documentation, of resources, 271–274
formatting. *see* American
Psychological Association
(APA) format; Modern Language
Association
(MLA) format
Doerflinger, Richard M., 463,
468–470, 471
as author of "Don't Clone Ron
Reagan's Agenda," 468–470
Dogpile, 260
Domke, J.G., 495, 511–513
as author of "Will Cash and Credit
Cards Become Extinct in the
Not-So-Distant Future?," 511–513
"Don't Clone Ron Reagan's Agenda"
(Doerflinger), 468–470
Draft evaluation, 60
"Drugstore Athlete" (Gladwell), 531–540
Duffy, Joe, and Andrew Keen, 576,
592–595
as authors of "Can Anyone Be a
Designer?," 592–595
"Dulce et Decorum Est" (Owen), 198–199
Dyson, Eric Michael, 162–168

E

EBSCOhost Research Databases, 258
Editing
  for style, 64
Elocutio (style), 70
Email communication, citing, 294–295
"Emerging merging Biometric
    Technologies" (Ryan), 507–510
Emotional fallacies, 28
"End of Gay Culture, The" (Sullivan),
    384–396
"End of Youthful Indiscretions: Internet
    Makes Them Permanent Blots,
    The" (Zaslow), 492–494
Environment, arguments on, 315–352
Epstein, Helen, 403, 413–415
  as author of "Immigration Maze,"
    413–415
Ethical criteria, evaluation, 158
Ethos, 18, 73–74
Evaluation, 112
  checklist, 61–62
  of database sources, 266
  of draft, 60
  of print sources, 263–264
  of Web sources, 266–269
Evaluation arguments, 33, 156–176
  building, 160–161
  evaluation criteria, 157–158
  sample, student, 169–173
  steps to writing, 174–176
"Evan's Two Moms" (Quindlen), 373–374
Evidence, 33

F

"Facebook's 'Privacy Trainwreck':
    Exposure, Invasion, and Drama"
    (Boyd), 595–604
Factiva, 258
Faith, statements of, 34
Fallacies
  of emotion, 28
  of logic, 26
"A False Wikipedia 'Biography'"
    (Seigenthaler), 579–582

"Fast Clothes vs. Green Clothes"
    (Chicago Tribune Editorial),
    349–350
Fast Food Nation (Schlosser), 140
Federal Bureau of Investigation, "Using
    Technology to Catch Criminals
    Web site," 506
Field research, 249, 250–251
Film resources, documentation
  APA citations, 312
  MLA citations, 295
First Amendment, 129, 131
FirstSearch, 258
Fischler, Marcelle S., 576, 591–592
  as author of "Putting on Lip Gloss,
    and a Show, for YouTube Viewers,"
    591–592
Focus, 63
Formal definitions, 115
Formal outline, 57
Franklin, Ursula, 429, 452–453
  as author of "Beautiful, Functional,
    and Frugal," 452–453
Free speech, 132
Freewriting, 38
Friedmann, S. Julio, "Coal is a Nice
    Shade of Green," 215–217
"From *In Search of Intercultural Compe-
    tence*" (Deardorff), 426–426
Froogle, 260
Fukuyama, Francis, 429, 438–445
  as author of "A Tale of Two Dystopias,"
    438–445

G

Gangsta rap, 162–168
Gates, Bill, 429, 453–460
  as author of "A Robot in Every
    Home," 453–460
Geis, Sonya, 355, 368, 374–376
  as author of "A New Tactic in Fighting
    Marriage Initiatives," 374–376
Gerson, Michael, 575, 583–585
  as author of "Where the Avatars
    Roam," 583–585

"Getting Off the Couch" (Williams), 604–606

Gilb, Dagoberto, "My Landlady's Yard," 187–189

Gitlin, Todd, 404, 415–419
    as author of "Under the Sign of Mickey Mouse & Co.," 415–419

Gladwell, Malcolm, 531–540
    as author of "Drugstore Athlete," 531–540

Globalization, arguments on, 400–426

Global warming, 142–144

Goals, of arguments, 16

Good reason, 33
    into action, 109–113
    evidence to support, 50–51
    finding a, 44–50

Google, 260

Google Blog Search, 261

Google Scholar, 258, 260

Gomes, Peter J., 354, 362–365
    as author of "Homophobic? Read Your Bible," 362–365

Gore, Al, 317, 334–337, 338, 339, 341–342, 348, 352
    as author of "What Is Global Warming?," 335–337
    "Ten Things to Do to Help Stop Global Warming," 338

Graphics, 230–231
    creating tables, charts and graphs, 234–235

Graphs
    analysis of, 94–97
    creating, 234–235

H

Hackbarth, Alexa, 355, 396–399
    as author of "Vanity, Thy Name Is Metrosexual," 396–399

Haeringer, Marc, 380–383
    as author of "Coming Out in the Line of Fire," 380–383

Handelsman, Walt, "Information Superhighway" (cartoon), 583

"A Hanging" (Orwell), 181

Homer-Dixon, Thomas, "Coal in a Nice Shade of Green," 215–217

"Homophobic? Read Your Bible" (Gomes), 362–365

Horner, Christopher C., 339–342
    as author of "Top Ten 'Global-Warming' Myths," 339–342

House of Representatives, 370, 371–372
    and "The Defense of Marriage Act," 371–372

"How 'Green' Is Your T-Shirt?" (Rosenthal), 350–351

"How Race Affected the Federal Government's Response to Katrina" (Bullard), 328–331

I

IceRocket, 261

Idea map, 40

"Illegal Immigrants—They're Money" (Rodriguez), 202–204

Images
    formatting, 231–233

"Immigration Maze" (Epstein), 413–415

InfoTrac OneFile, 257, 258

Internet, 24
    discussion groups, 260–261
    documenting resources, 272–273
    research, 195, 259–262, 266–269
    Web page design, 236–237

Interviews, research, 250–251

Introduction, 63

Inventio (invention), 70

"Is Google's Data Grinder Dangerous?" (Keen), 576–578

J

Jasper, William F., 377–379
    as author of "Subversion Through Perversion," 377–379

Jenkins, Philip, 335, 343–345
    as author of "Burning at the Stake," 343–345

Jordan, Barbara, "Statement on the Articles of Impeachment," 80–83

Journal articles
  APA citations, 310–311
  MLA citations, 291
  as sources, 256–257
Journals, scholarly vs. popular, 257, 259
Joy, Bill, 427, 429–438, 442, 446–447
  as author of "Why the Future
    Doesn't Need Us," 429–438
JSTOR, 258

K

"Kate Winslet, Please Save Us!"
  (Rafferty), 548–553
Keen, Andrew, 575, 576–578, 592–593
  as author of "Is Google's Data
    Grinder Dangerous?," 576–578
Keyword search engines, 259
Keyword searches, 255–256, 259
King, Martin Luther, Jr., "Letter From
  Birmingham Jail," 118–121
Kinzie, Susan, 518, 571–573
  as author of "A Rare Kind of Rush:
    A Sorority Based on Islamic
    Principles," 571–573
Koppel, Ted, 474, 484–487
  as author of "Take My Privacy,
    Please!," 484–487

L

"Land Ethic, The" (Leopold), 320–323
Lange, Dorothea, 91–92
Larsen, Randall, 474, 488–490
  as author of "Traveler's Card Might
    Just Pave the Way for a National
    ID Card," 488–490
Lazarus, Emma, 401, 408–410
  as author of "The New Colossus,"
    408–410
Leach, Susan Llewelyn, 518, 554–556
  as author of "Those Extra Pounds—
    Are They Government's
    Business?," 554–556
Leopold, Aldo, 319, 320–323
  as author of "The Land Ethic,"
    320–323

"Letter from Birmingham Jail," 118–121
Lewis, Eric, "The Subtext of All Tattoos"
  (cartoon), 568
LexisNexis Academic, 257
Library of Congress, 256
Limitations, 33
"Living the Dream" (Butalia), 415–421
Logical fallacies, 26
  begging the question, 27
  either-or, 27
  false analogies, 27
  hasty generalization, 27
  non sequitur, 27
  oversimplification, 27
  post hoc, 27
  rationalization, 27
  slippery slope, 27
Logos, 18, 72

M

"Make Peace with Pot" (Schlosser),
  520–523
Main idea, 62
Malkin, Michelle, 403, 411–413
  as author of "Beware of Illegal Aliens
    Seeking Hazmat Licenses,"
    411–413
"Manifesto: The Mad Farmer Liberation
  Front," 331–333
Martin, Emily and Katie Schwartzmann,
  383–384
  as authors of "Bad for Both Boys and
    Girls," 383–384
MasterFILE Premier, 257, 258
McCloud, Scott, "Setting the Record
  Straight," 121–128
McCoy, Glenn, "And Looking At Our . . ."
  (cartoon), 341
McPherson, John, "It's Part of the
  Government's New Emphasis . . ."
  (cartoon), 488
Memoria, 70
Merkle, Ralph C., 429, 446–451
  as author of "Nanotechnology:
    Designs for the Future," 446–451

Metacrawler, 260

Metasearch agents, 260

Method

common factor, 141

process of elimination, 142

single difference, 141

Mill, John Stuart, 151

Miller, Wiley, "What's the Worst That Can Happen . . ." (cartoon), 414

Milloy, Steven, 463, 466–468, 471

as author of "Ron Reagan Wrong on Stem Cells," 466–468

Modern Language Association (MLA) format, 264, 265, 269

book citations, 287–290

documenting in, 280–303

elements of, 280–284

in-text citations, 284–287

sample paper, 297–303

"Modified" (Wysong), 566–569

Momaday, N. Scott, 317, 323–327

as author of "The Way to Rainy Mountain," 323–327

Mothers Against Drunk Driving, "Anti-Drinking and Driving Ad," 570

Music

and narrative arguments, 179

rap, 162–168

"My Landlady's Yard" (Gilb), 187–189

N

"Nanotechnology, Designs for the Future" (Merkle), 446–451

Narrative arguments, 33, 177–191

building, 181–182

kinds of, 179, 181

steps to writing, 190–191

"Nazi Tactics" (Williams), 528–530

"Necessity of Global Tobacco Regulations, The" (Bettcher and Subramaniam), 526–528

"New Colossus, The" (Lazarus), 408–410

New Media, arguments on, 574–606

"A New Tactic in Fighting Marriage Initiatives" (Geis), 374–376

Ngai, Mae M., 403, 406–408

as author of "No Human Being Is Illegal," 400–408

"No Human Being Is Illegal" (Ngai), 400–408

Nonverbal communication, 242–243

O

Objections, countering, 33, 46, 49–50

"Obligation to Endure, The" (Carson), 19–21

Observation research, 252

Oliphant, Pat, "The Ronald Reagan Eulogy Will Be Delivered . . ." (cartoon), 466

Online sources, 259–262

APA citations, 269, 272–273, 311–312

evaluating, 266–269

MLA citations, 272–273, 293–295

Operational definitions, 115

Opposing views, 33

Organization, 63

Orwell, George, "A Hanging," 181

Owen, Wilfred, "Dulce et Decorum Est," 198–199

P

Paraphrasing, 275–276

Parody, 117, 200

Pathos, 18, 73

Paul, Annie Murphy, "The Real Marriage Penalty," 144–146

Payne, Henry, "The Bad News Is . . ." (cartoon), 401

Periodicals

APA citations, 310–311

MLA citations, 291–293

scholarly vs. popular, 257, 259

as sources, 256–257

Photographs

analysis of, 93–94

editing, 232–233

taking, 231

Pie charts
  creating, 235
  for presentations, 242–243
Plagiarism, 271–276
Podcasts, 261, 269
Position
counter objections to, 46, 49–50
Position arguments, 16
Powerpoint presentations, 240–242
Practical criteria, evaluation, 157–158
Presenting arguments, 238–244
  conclusion, 240
  delivery, 242–244
  introduction, 239–240
  nonverbal communication, 243
  organizing, 239–240
  support for, 239
  visuals, using, 240–242
Primary research, 249
Privacy, arguments about, 472–514
"Privacy Implications of Biometrics"
    (Bennett), 496–502
Process of elimination method,
    139, 142
Pronuntiatio, 70
Proofreading, 65
Proposal arguments, 16, 17, 49, 112,
    209–225
  building, 213–214
  components of, 211, 213
  sample, student, 218–221
  steps to writing, 222–225
Pubmed, 260
PubSub, 261
Purpose, 11, 62
"Putting on Lip Gloss, and a Show, for
    YouTube Viewers" (Fischler),
    591–592

Q

Quindlen, Anna, 355, 368, 373–374
  as author of "Evan's Two Moms,"
    373–374
Quotations, documenting, 273–278

R

Rafferty, Terrence, 518, 548–553
  as author of "Kate Winslet, Please
    Save Us!," 548–553
Raine, Emily, "Why Should I Be Nice
    to You? Coffee Shops and the
    Politics of Good Service,"
    147–152
"A Rare Kind of Rush: A Sorority
    Based on Islamic Principles"
    (Kinzie), 571–573
Readers
  attitudes toward subject, 56–57
  attitudes toward you, 56
  consideration of, 54, 229
  knowledge of, 54
Reading
  first, 62–63
  second, 63
  third, 63–64
Reagan, Ron, 429, 462–463, 464–466,
    466–470, 470–471
  as author of "Speech at the Democratic
    National Convention, July 27,
    2004," 464–466
"Real Marriage Penalty, The" (Paul),
    144–146
Reason, 31
Rebuttal arguments, 33, 192–208
  building, 199–200
  counterargument, 193, 194, 198–199
  refutation, 193, 194, 196–198
  steps to writing, 205–208
Refutation arguments, 193, 194, 196–198
Regulating Substances and Bodies,
    arguments on, 515–573
Relevance, 51
Research
  browsing, 248–249
  data collection methods, 249–252
  field, 249, 250–251
  interviews, 250–251
  observation, 252
  planning, 247–253

Research (continued)
primary, 249
secondary, 249
sources. *see* Sources
strategies for, 248
Research paper, writing, 270–279
documentation, 271–274
Researchable question, 249
Respond, to writing of others, 60–61
Rhetoric
canons of, 70–71
definition, 18
Rhetorical analysis
building, 69–70
definition, 69
sample, student, 84–86
steps to writing, 87–89
writing, 75
Rhetorical appeals, 17–18
Rhetorical situation, 75
"Right Drug to Target: Cutting
Marijuana Use, The" (Califano),
518–520
"A Robot in Every Home" (Gates),
453–460
Rodriquez, Gregory, "Illegal Immigrants—
They're Money," 202–204
"Ron Reagan Wrong on Stem Cells"
(Milloy), 466–468
Rosenthal, Elisabeth, 350–351
as author of "How 'Green' Is Your
T-Shirt?," 350–351
Ryan, Russ, 495, 507–510
as author of "Emerging merging
Biometric Technologies," 507–510

S
Saffo, Paul, 495, 502–505
as author of "A Trail of DNA and
Data," 502–505
Schlosser, Eric, 140, 517, 520–523
as author of "Make Peace with Pot,"
520–523
Science and Ethics, arguments on,
427–471

Search engines, 259–260
Searches
advanced, 260
Secondary research, 249
"A Secret Society of the Starving"
(Udovitch), 556–564
Seigenthaler, John, 575, 579–582
as author of "A False Wikipedia
'Biography,'" 579–582
"Setting the Record Straight"
(McCloud), 121–128
Sexual Difference, arguments on,
353–399
Silent Spring (Carson), 9–16
tactics of, 13
Silko, Leslie Marmon, "The Border
Patrol State," 182–187
analysis of, 71–79
Single difference method, 139, 141
Soares, Christine, 429, 460–462
as author of "Attitude Screen," 460–462
Sound media resources, documentation
APA citations, 312
MLA citations, 295
Sources, 63
agreement and disagreement with,
42–44
books as, 256
citing, 264–265, 269
evaluating, 263–269
finding, 254–262
finding visual, 261–262
finding with keywords, 255–256, 257
journal articles as, 257–259
Web as, 259–262
"Speech at the Democratic National
Convention, July 27, 2004"
(Reagan), 464–466
"Statement on the Articles of
Impeachment" (Jordan), 80–83
Statements of fact, 34
Statistics, in causal arguments, 144
Stein, Dan, "Crossing the Line," 200–202
Streaming video, 261

"Struggling Alone" (Anderson), 365–367
Style, 63
"Subversion Through Perversion"
    (Jasper), 377–379
Sufficiency, 51
Sullivan, Andrew, 355, 384–396
    as author of "The End of Gay
        Culture," 384–396
Summarizing, 274–275
Survey research, 251–252

T
Tables, creating, 234
Tables, charts and graphs
    analysis of, 93–97
"Take My Privacy, Please!" (Koppel),
    484–487
"Tale of Two Dystopias" (Fukuyama),
    438–445
Taste, personal, 34
Technorati.com, 24, 261
Television resources, documentation
    APA citations, 312
    MLA citations, 296
Textual analysis, 70, 71–75
Thesis, 52, 63
    evaluation of, 53
    focusing of, 52–53
    revised, 53
    sample, 53
    state and evaluate, 52
    working, 252–253
Thomasnet, 260
"Those Extra Pounds—Are they
    Government's Business?"
    (Leach), 554–556
"Three Cheers for the Surveillance
    Society!" (Brin), 475–484
Tone, 64
"Top Ten 'Global-Warming' Myths"
    (Horner), 339–342
Topic, choosing, 33, 34–35, 36–37, 238
"Traveler's Card Might Just Pave the Way
    for a National ID Card" (Larsen),
    488–490

"A Trial of DNA and Data" (Saffo),
    502–505
Trudeau, Garry, "Doonesbury: The Sin
    Lobby Gins Up. . ." (cartoon), 525

U
Udovitch, Mim, 518, 556–564
    as author of "A Secret Society of the
        Starving," 556–564
"Unguarded Gates, The" (Aldrich), 410
"Under the Sign of Mickey Mouse
    & Co." (Gitlin), 415–419

V
"Vanity, Thy Name Is Metrosexual"
    (Hackbarth), 396–399
Vazquez, Carmen, 354, 356–362
    as author of "Appearances," 356–362
Virginia Tech, 182
Visual analysis
    of advertising media, 92–93
    building, 96–97
    of context, 97–98
    sample, student, 101–103
    of tables, charts and graphs, 94–97
    of textual elements, 98–100
    writing of, 100
Visual arguments, 90–106
    definition, 90
Visual persuasion, 92–93
Visuals
    incorporating, 278–279
    sources for, 261–262

W
"Wal-Mart vs. Pyramids" (Carlsen),
    422–423
"Way to Rainy Mountain, The"
    (Momaday), 323–327
Web directories, 259–260
Web logs, 24, 261, 269, 294
Web page design, 236–237
Web sources, 259–262
    APA citation, 269
    APA citations, 272–273, 311–312

Web sources (continued)
evaluating, 266–269
MLA citations, 269, 272–273, 293–295
WebCrawler, 260
WebMD, 260
"What Is Global Warming?" (Gore),
335–337
"Where the Avatars Roam" (Gerson),
583–585
"Why the Future Doesn't Need Us"
(Joy), 429–438
"Why Should I Be Nice to You? Coffee
Shops and the Politics of Good
Service" (Raine), 147–152
Wikipedia, 261, 269
"Will Cash and Credits Cards Become
Extinct in the Not-So-Distant
Future?" (Domke), 511–513
Williams, Alex, 345–349
as author of "Buying into the Green
Movement," 345–349
Williams, Stephen, 576, 604–606
as author of "Getting Off the Couch,"
604–606

Williams, Walter E., 526, 528–530
as author of "Nazi Tactics,"
528–530
Wilson, Edward O., 318–320
as author of "The Conversation
Ethic," 317, 318–320
Working outline, 57–58
Working thesis, 52, 252–253
Written arguments
analyzing, 69–89
Wysong, Pippa, 518, 566–569
as author of "Modified," 566–569

Y
Yahoo, 260

Z
Zaslow, Jeffrey, 492–494
as author of "The End of Youthful
Indiscretions: Internet Makes
Them Permanent Blots,"
492–494